OLD TESTAMENT VII

PSALMS 1-50

EDITED BY

CRAIG A. BLAISING
AND CARMEN S. HARDIN

GENERAL EDITOR

THOMAS C. ODEN

IVP Academic

An imprint of InterVarsity Press
Downers Grove, Illinois

InterVarsity Press
P.O. Box 1400, Downers Grove, IL 60515-1426
ivpress.com
email@ivpress.com

InterVarsity Press® is the book-publishing division of InterVarsity Christian Fellowship/USA®, a movement of students and faculty active on campus at hundreds of universities, colleges, and schools of nursing in the United States of America, and a member movement of the International Fellowship of Evangelical Students. For information about local and regional activities, visit intervarsity.org.

Scripture quotations, unless otherwise noted, are from the Revised Standard Version of the Bible, copyright 1946, 1952, 1971 by the Division of Christian Education of the National Council of the Churches of Christ in the U.S.A., and are used by permission.

Selected excerpts from The Works of Saint Augustine: A Translation for the 21st Century, edited by John E. Rotelle, ©1990-. Used by permission of the Augustinian Heritage Institute.

Selected excerpts from John Chrysostom, Commentary on the Psalms, vol. 1, translated by Robert Charles Hill, ©1998. Used with permission of Holy Cross Orthodox Press, Brookline, Massachusetts.

Selected excerpts from Ambrose, Commentary on Twelve Psalms, translated by Íde M. Ní Riain, ©2000. Used by permission of Halcyon Press.

Selected excerpts from Athanasius, The Resurrection Letters, paraphrased and introduced by Jack N. Sparks, ©1979. Used by permission of Thomas Nelson, Inc., Nashville, Tennessee.

Selected excerpts from Fathers of the Church: A New Translation, ©1947-, used by permission of The Catholic University of America Press, Washington, D.C. Full bibliographic information on volumes of Fathers of the Church may be found in the Bibliography of Works in English Translation.

Selected excerpts from The Syriac Fathers on Prayer and the Spiritual Life, translated by Sebastian Brock, Cistercian Studies 101, ©1987; Bede the Venerable, Homilies on the Gospels, translated by Lawrence T. Martin and David Hurst, Cistercian Studies 110 and 111, ©1991; Pachomian Koinonia: The Lives, Rules, and Other Writings of Saint Pachomius, vol. 3, translated by Armand Veilleux, Cistercian Studies 46, ©1982. Used by permission of Cistercian Publications, Kalamazoo, Michigan. All rights reserved.

Selected excerpts from Evagrius of Pontus: The Greek Ascetic Corpus, translated by Robert E. Sinkewicz, Oxford Early Christian Studies, ©2003; Gregory of Nyssa's Treatise on the Inscriptions of the Psalms, translated by Ronald E. Heine, Oxford Early Christian Studies, ©1995. Used by permission of Oxford University Press, Inc.

Selected excerpts from Diodore of Tarsus, Commentary on Psalms 1-51, translated by Robert C. Hill, Writings from the Greco-Roman World 9, ©2005; Theodore of Mopsuestia, Commentary on the Psalms 1-81, translated by Robert C. Hill, Writings from the Greco-Roman World 5, ©2006. Used by permission of the Society of Biblical Literature, Atlanta, Georgia.

Selected excerpts from John Cassian, The Conferences, translated and annotated by Boniface Ramsey, Ancient Christian Writers 57, ©1997; Cassiodorus, Explanation of the Psalms, translated by P. G. Walsh, Ancient Christian Writers 51, 52 and 53, ©1990, 1991; Origen, An Exhortation to Martyrdom, Prayer and Selected Writings, translated by Rowan A. Greer, The Classics of Western Spirituality, ©1979; Pseudo-Dionysius, The Complete Works, translated by Colm Luibheid, The Classics of Western Spirituality, ©1987. Reprinted by permission of Paulist Press, Inc. <www.paulistpress.com>.

Selected excerpts from Athanasius of Alexandria, "On the Interpretation of the Psalms." In Early Christian Spirituality, translated by Pamela Bright, Sources of Early Christian Thought, ©1986. Used by permission of Fortress Press.

Selected excerpts from Augustine: Earlier Writings, translated by John H. S. Burleigh, The Library of Christian Classics 6, ©1953; Augustine: Later Works, edited and translated by John Burnaby, The Library of Christian Classics 8, ©1955; Christology of the Later Fathers, translated by Archibald Robertson and edited by Edward Rochie Hardy, The Library of Christian Classics 3, ©1954; Confessions and Enchiridion, translated by Albert C. Outler, The Library of Christian Classics 7, ©1955; Cyril of Jerusalem and Nemesius of Emesa, translated by William Telfer, The Library of Christian Classics 4, ©1955; Early Christian Fathers, translated by Cyril C. Richardson, The Library of Christian Classics 1, ©1953; Early Latin Theology, translated by S. L. Greenslade, The Library of Christian Classics 5, ©1956; Western Asceticism, edited and translated by Owen Chadwick, The Library of Christian Classics 12, ©1958. Used by permission of SCM and Westminster John Knox Presses, London, England, and Louisville, Kentucky.

Every effort has been made to trace and contact copyright holders for additional materials quoted in this book. The authors will be pleased to rectify any omissions in future editions if notified by copyright holders.

Cover design: David Fassett
Images: silver texture background: © Katsumi Murouchi / Getty Images
     stained glass cathedral window: © elzauer / Getty Images
     gold texture: © Katsumi Murouchi / Getty Images
     abstract marble pattern: © NK08gerd / iStock / Getty Images Plus

ISBN 978-0-8308-4342-8 (paperback)
ISBN 978-0-8308-1477-0 (hardcover)
ISBN 978-0-8308-9732-2 (digital)

Printed in the United States of America ∞

InterVarsity Press is committed to ecological stewardship and to the conservation of natural resources in all our operations. This book was printed using sustainably sourced paper.

Library of Congress Cataloging-in-Publication Data
A catalog record for this book is available from the Library of Congress.

P 32 31 30 29 28 27 26 25 24 23 22 21 20 19 18 17 16 15 14 13 12 11 10 9 8 7 6 5 4 3 2 1

Y 47 46 45 44 43 42 41 40 39 38 37 36 35 34 33 32 31 30 29 28 27 26 25 24 23 22 21 20 19

Contents

Introduction to Psalms 1-50 • • • • • • *xvii*

Commentary on Psalms 1-50 • • • • • • *1*

Appendix: Early Christian Writers
and the Documents Cited • • • • • *393*

Bibliography of Works in
Original Languages • • • • • *401*

Bibliography of Works in
English Translation • • • • • *411*

Subject Index • • • • • *423*

ANCIENT CHRISTIAN COMMENTARY
PROJECT RESEARCH TEAM

GENERAL EDITOR
Thomas C. Oden

ASSOCIATE EDITOR
Christopher A. Hall

OPERATIONS MANAGER AND
TRANSLATIONS PROJECT COORDINATOR
Joel Elowsky

RESEARCH AND ACQUISITIONS DIRECTOR
Michael Glerup

EDITORIAL SERVICES DIRECTOR
Jill Burnett Comings

ORIGINAL LANGUAGE VERSION DIRECTOR
Konstantin Gavrilkin

GRADUATE RESEARCH ASSISTANTS
Jennifer Barry-Lenger
Kathleen Gallagher Elkins
Stephen Finlan
Melissa M. Hartley
Shanell T. Smith

ADMINISTRATIVE ASSISTANT
Judy Cincotta

INTRODUCTION TO
PSALMS 1-50

This is the first of two ACCS volumes on the Psalms. Only two other Old Testament books have been allotted more than one volume in the series. In each case, the expanded treatment is due to the popularity of the biblical book in early Christian exposition and the amount of extant patristic literature addressing it.

When it comes to the Psalms, we are dealing with one of the most beloved and widely used portions of the Bible. Already the Psalms were the most frequently cited Scripture in the New Testament. Early Christian writers drew on the Psalms for apologetic, doctrinal and pastoral purposes. Aside from the many homilies, commentaries and expositional notes left to us, patristic literature generally is filled with allusions, citations, illustrations and applications drawn from the Psalms. It is from this literary wealth that these volumes of patristic citations on the Psalms are taken, with this first volume drawing on more than 160 different works from more than 65 different authors.

These works represent the whole range of patristic literary genre, as can be seen in the bibliography at the end of this volume. However, of primary interest is the group of commentaries and homilies specifically dedicated to the Psalms. The texts of some of these works have come down to us fairly well preserved and are available in modern critical editions. Others, however, must be reconstructed from fragmentary evidence in the late patristic and early medieval catenae, or chains—collections of patristic citations arranged in commentary fashion on the biblical text. (These ACCS volumes are modern catenae.)

In this introduction, we will survey the primary commentaries and homilies on the Psalms from which selections have been made for this volume. Marie-Josèphe Rondeau, in *Les Commentaires Patristiques du Psautier (IIIe-Ve Siècles)*, provides a survey of the state of these texts and the text-critical conditions taken into account in our selections. The survey offered here follows and summarizes Rondeau, although at various points we have differed from her, as more recent studies have led to different conclusions.[1]

Generally speaking, the text-critical situation differs significantly between Greek and Latin authors. For Latin authors, we mostly have texts that have been transmitted directly and are available in modern critical editions. By contrast, many of the Greek patristic commentaries are no longer extant as complete works. However, fragments do exist and are scattered among the

---

[1]Marie-Josèphe Rondeau, *Les commentaires patristiques du Psautier (IIIe-Ve siècles)*, vol.1, *Les travaux des pères grecs et latins sur le Psautier: Recherches et bilan*, Orientalia Christiana Analecta 219 (Rome: Pontificum Institutum Studiorum Orientalium, 1982).

catenae. Nevertheless, it is not always easy to identify these fragments properly. Some citations are wrongly attributed, some may be attributed to more than one author, and some are without attribution, appearing anonymously. Attributions may also vary from chain to chain, with a particular citation listed under a particular name in one chain but appearing under another name or as anonymous in another chain. Furthermore, these catenae have their own history, some going back to whole complete manuscripts but many having been composed from preceding catenae, the history of which we may or may not be able to trace.[2]

From the sixteenth century to the present, efforts have been undertaken to reconstruct from extant chains some of these ancient texts, or at least what is left of them. Some of the homilies and commentaries on the Psalms published in Migne's *Patrologia Graeca* or in Pitra's *Analecta Sacra* are composite texts drawn from chains on the basis of text-critical methods of an earlier era. However, study has continued on the chains and the textual remains within them, just as advances have been made in textual criticism. The identification of the Palestinian chains by Robert Devreesse and subsequent study, especially by Marcel Richard, Marguerite Harl and Ekkehard Mühlenberg, has led to a more accurate appraisal of these texts.[3] The Palestinian chains appear to date as early as the sixth century. They are primary chains in that they made use of direct sources rather than other chains. Consequently, the Palestinian chains have been used to help authenticate textual remains throughout the various chain fragments. We are particularly indebted to Devreesse and Mühlenberg for identifying portions in the Migne and Pitra texts that can be verified by means of the Palestinian chains. Although more work needs to be done, we have been fairly confident in the use of Devreesse and Mühlenberg as guides for making selections from Migne and Pitra for this volume. The situation for individual patristic commentators may consequently be described as follows.

Greek Authors

Hippolytus. The earliest person in the history of the church known to have written a commentary and/or a series of homilies on the Psalms is Hippolytus of Rome, writing around 200.[4] What remains are only fragments of his work: a homily on Psalms 1–2 (preserved in the chains), some fragments of either homilies or a commentary from Psalms 2, 22 [23] and 23 [24] (preserved in the *Eranistes* of Theodoret) and some fragments dealing with the titles of Psalms 5, 6, 8, 9, 15

---

[2]Gilles Dorival, "Aperçu sur l'Histoire des Caînes Exégétiques Grecques sur le Psautier (Ve-XIVe Siècles)," *Studia Patristica* 15 [TU 128] (1984), 146-69; idem, *Les Chaînes Exégétiques Grecques sur les Psaumes; Contribution à l'Etude d'une Forme Littéraire,* vol. 1 (Louvain: Peeters, 1986), 1-33.

[3]Robert Devreesse, *Chaînes Exégétiques Grecques,* in *Dictionnaire de la Bible; Supplément,* vol. 1 (Paris: Letouzey et Ane, 1928), 1084-1140; idem, *Les Anciens Commentateurs Grecs des Psaumes,* Studi e Testi 264 (Vatican City: Bibioteca Apostolica Vaticana, 1970); Marcel Richard, "Les Premières Chaînes sur le Psautier," *Bulletin de l'Institut de Recherche et d'Histoire des Textes* 5 (1956): 88-93; Marguerite Harl, *La Chaîne Palestinienne sur le Psaume 118,* SC 189, 190 (Paris: Éditions du Cerf, 1972); Ekkehard Mühlenberg, *Psalmenkommentare aus der Katenenüberlieferung,* vol. 1 (Berlin: Walter de Gruyter, 1975).

[4]There have been ongoing debates as to whether there may have been another author with the same or a similar name. See Rondeau, *Les Commentaires Patristiques,* 28-32. The situation is also summarized by Ronald E. Heine, "Hippolytus, Ps.-Hippolytus and the Early Canons," in *The Cambridge History of Early Christian Literature,* ed. Frances Young, Lewis Ayres and Andrew Louth (Cambridge: Cambridge University Press, 2004), 142-43.

[16], 31 [32] and 44 [45].[5] The latter are not generally considered authentic, and the question is still open as to whether the Theodoret fragments belong to the same composition as the homily or represent yet another work, possibly a commentary. A critical assessment of the text has been published by Nautin, although his views on authorship have been superseded by later studies.[6]

Origen. Eusebius tells us in his *Ecclesiastical History* 6.24.2 that Origen composed a commentary in Alexandria on Psalms 1–25. This was most likely between 222 and 225.[7] A second commentary, either completing the first work or starting afresh, was composed in Caesarea between 245 and 249.[8] Origen also delivered a series of homilies on the Psalms, most likely between 239 and 242,[9] and may have also composed, at some point, a set of notes, or *scholia*, on the Psalms.[10] Only a small portion of this material is available to us today in the form of citations in the extant catenae. We also have from Rufinus a fairly literal translation into Latin of a set of four homilies by Origen on Psalms 36 [37], 37 [38] and 38 [39].

The selections made in this volume have relied on Devreesse and Mühlenberg to identify the more reliable Origen material in the Migne (PG 12, 17, 23) and Pitra (AnSac 2, 3) collections.[11] Of course, selections have also been made from the homilies preserved by Rufinus (PG 12). The English translations are original to this volume.

Finally, it must be noted that Vittorio Peri has convinced many scholars that Jerome's *Tractatus 59 in Psalmos* is a translation of an edited version of Origen's homilies.[12] The translation, however, is not literal. Jerome has imposed his own style on the work and added some of his own comments to it. This poses a dilemma for citing this material. We have made the choice in this volume to cite these selections as from Jerome. Readers should be advised, however, that this material is an edited translation of Origen's work. More will be said about this when we come to Jerome below.

Of course, as is the case with most other authors, in addition to the selections from Origen's works on the Psalms, we have included selections from Origen's other works in which he offers comments on particular passages within the Psalms. Needless to say, Origen's influence on

---

[5]The reader should note the use of brackets to identify psalm numbers in the Hebrew and English texts. Patristic commentaries follow the Greek Septuagint numbering, which differs from the Hebrew and English numbering beginning at Psalm 10. In the Septuagint, Psalm 9 includes both of what are Psalms 9 and 10 in the Hebrew and English versions of the Psalter. Consequently, beginning at Psalm 10, the Hebrew and English numbering will always be one number higher than the Greek. Most translations of patristic commentaries keep the numbering as it appears in the critical texts. Therefore, in this ACCS volume, when referring to patristic works on the Psalter, we will give the number as it appears in the critical texts, which will be the number according to the Greek Septuagint, and then give, for the reader's benefit, the psalm number in the Hebrew and English texts to which it corresponds.

[6]Pierre Nautin, *Le Dossier d'Hippolyte et de Méliton dans les Florilèges Dogmatiques et Chez les Historiens Modernes* (Paris: Éditions du Cerf, 1953).

[7]Pierre Nautin, *Origène: Sa Vie et son Oeuvre* (Paris: Beauchesne, 1977), 368-71.

[8]Ibid., 380-84.

[9]Ibid., 53.

[10]Rondeau believes that a set of citations in the chain Vindobonensis Theologicus Graecus 8 may be remains of this *scholia*; *Les Commentaires Patristiques*, 61-62. Jerome also speaks of *excerpta*, but it is difficult to know for sure what he meant by this. See ibid., 46-51.

[11]See Devreesse, *Les Anciens Commentateurs Grecs*, 1-88. Because of its arrangement, one needs to consult the entirety of pp. 133-203 in Mühlenberg for each patristic author to whom it applies.

[12]Vittorio Peri, *Omelie origeniane sui Salmi: Contributo all'identificazione del testo latino* (Vatican City: Biblioteca Apostolica Vaticana, 1980).

those who followed him was immense. Many of those who are quoted in this volume reflect in some way or another thoughts that go back to or were inspired by Origen.

Eusebius of Caesarea. Eusebius composed a commentary on the whole Psalter between 325 and 330. However, except for his remarks on Psalm 37 [38], preserved among the works of Basil, the portion dealing with Psalms 1–50 is extant only in the chains. The Palestinian chain in particular has many citations from Eusebius's commentary. Consequently, we have again used in this work the critical guidance of Devreesse and Mühlenberg to identify the material in Migne (PG 23, 24, 30) and Pitra (AnSac 3) from which selections have been made.[13] These selections are appearing in English translation for the first time in this volume. Of course, selections have been made from other works of Eusebius as well. Readers will want to note especially the selections from Eusebius's extended comments on Psalm 22 taken from his *Demonstration of Apostolic Preaching*.

Athanasius. Interspersed among the catenae citations are commentary fragments attributed to Athanasius of Alexandria. A collection of these fragments was published in Migne (PG 27) as Athanasius's *Exposition of the Psalms*. Rondeau, however, notes that the text contains interpolations from various authors, she herself having demonstrated the dependence of the material on Eusebius.[14] Although many scholars have argued for Athanasian authorship, the judgment of Gilles Dorival has succeeded in convincing most today that the work is not genuine.[15] Nevertheless, because it exercised a notable presence in the history of the interpretation of the Psalms, we thought it appropriate to include some selections from this material, although under the label of Pseudo-Athanasius. The selections have been taken from Robert Thomson's critical translation of the Syriac short version of the *Exposition*.[16] Readers will note the concise, summary nature that typifies these comments.

We do, however, have an authentic work of Athanasius on the interpretation of the Psalms that is unique among the patristic works on the Psalms and that has been both influential and inspirational in the history of Christian thought down to the present day. This is the *Letter to Marcellinus on the Interpretation of the Psalms*. The text is well attested, appearing in the significant fifth-century biblical codex Alexandrinus, where it apparently functioned as a guide for reading the Psalms published in that codex.[17]

As the title indicates, the work is written in the form of a letter in response to Marcellinus's desire to understand the inner meanings of the Psalms. Written probably in the latter period of Athanasius's life and ministry (perhaps between 360 and 363), the letter purports to give the insights of "an old man deeply versed in his studies." He explains how the teachings of the Psalms are thoroughly integrated with the rest of Scripture, reflecting and being reflected in all

---

[13]Devreesse, *Les Anciens Commentateurs Grecs*, 89-146.

[14]Rondeau, *Les Commentaires Patristiques*, 80-87; idem, "Une Nouvelle Prevue de l'Influence Littéraire d'Eusèbe de Césarée sur Athanase: L'Interprétation des Psaumes," *Revue des Sciences Religieuses* 56 (1968): 385-434.

[15]Gilles Dorival, "Athanase ou Pseudo-Athanase?" *Rivista di Storia e Letteratura Religiosa* 16 (1980): 80-89.

[16]R. W. Thomson, *Athanasiana Syriaca*, pt. 4, *Expositio in Psalmos*, CSCO 386-87 (Louvain: Secrétariat du Corpus, 1977).

[17]Everett Ferguson, "Athanasius' 'Epistola ad Marcellinum in Interpretationem Psalmorum,'" *Studia Patristica* 16 (1985): 295-96.

parts of the canon. Especially important is the way the teachings of the prophets are manifested in the Psalms' depictions of Christ. However, the most striking feature of the letter is its teaching on the devotional use of the Psalter for the life of the soul. Here, the work proceeds psalm by psalm, giving a formulaic interpretation/exhortation in the form, "if you [find yourself in a given situation], say the words in [a given psalm]."[18] The "situation" here may be relational (to God or to human beings), emotional (from joy to distress), liturgical (the seasons of worship) or doctrinal (for learning or meditating on doctrinal truths), but in each case, the citing, singing or praying of the words of the psalm is an exercise in the spiritual life of the soul directly connected to the theme of each psalm. The comprehensive scope of these comments—covering the entire Psalter—along with their practical devotional nature and conciseness of expression has led us to position these selections, one for each psalm, uniquely at the beginning of each commentary section. This is a special feature of this ACCS volume that is fitting to this unique contribution from Athanasius. The translation used in the selections is that of Pamela Bright in the Fortress Press series, Sources of Early Christian Thought.

Basil of Caesarea. The homilies of Basil on the Psalms come down to us by direct tradition and are well attested in the Palestinian chain. There are ten authentic homilies that fall within the range of this ACCS volume: homilies on Psalms 1, 7, 14 [15], 28 [29], 29 [30], 32 [33], 33 [34], 44 [45], 45 [46] and 48 [49]. An English translation has been published by Agnes Clare Way in the Fathers of the Church series. The homilies were composed and delivered during Basil's episcopate (370-378) and are illustrations of his rhetorical and pastoral skill. As an example of such, readers should note especially the selection on Psalm 15, addressing the sin of usury.

Gregory of Nyssa. We have from Gregory a treatise, *On the Inscriptions of the Psalms*, which deals not only with psalm titles per se but more generally with the interpretation of the Psalter. Gregory was ordained bishop of Nyssa by his brother, Basil, in 372. Four years later, he was sent into exile and during that time (most likely between 376 and 378) composed the present work. The primary purpose of the treatise is to show how the Psalter leads one upward through the stages of spiritual progress. Readers should note, for example, Gregory's explanation of blessedness in the selection in Psalm 1. The critical edition of the text can be found in the Brill edition of Gregory's works. Ronald Heine has published an English translation that has been drawn on for selections in this volume.

Didymus the Blind. Fragments of Didymus the Blind's commentary on the whole Psalter come down to us in the Palestinian chains and have been recovered by means of the work of Mühlenberg. The Didymus selections for this work have mainly come from this material and are provided here in English in new translations. There is, however, another commentary that was apparently authored by Didymus, of which fragments pertaining to Psalms 20–44 were discovered in papyri in Tura in 1941. These have been published in five volumes by Michael Gronewald, Louis Doutreleau and others along with a German translation. The two commentaries, written

---

[18]Ibid., 298.

between 367 and 387, differ in style, with the first offering brief, succinct, almost aphoristic comments and the latter giving a more extended exposition. As noted by Rondeau, Didymus's interest is not in contextual interpretation, as that would be understood today, but rather provides insight into the structure of the soul and its moral operations. The selections chosen in this volume give ample evidence of his approach.

Evagrius of Pontus. The aphoristic style of Didymus's brief commentary is characteristic of Evagrius throughout his writings. Selections have been taken from several of Evagrius's works, making use of the recent translations published by Robert Sinkewicz.[19] However, following the work of von Balthasar, Rondeau and Mühlenberg, we are able to identify fragments of Evagrius's notes, or *scholia*, on the Psalms.[20] The notes were composed in the latter part of the fourth century, and fragments have been preserved in the catenae under the name of Origen or marked as anonymous. The index of Mühlenberg in particular may be used as a guide for separating authentic Evagrian material from the Origen compilation published by Pitra and in Migne. The selections made from this material are provided in English translation for the first time in this volume. As such, the present volume allows readers to compare the style evidenced in these selections from his notes on the Psalms with those taken from other Evagrian works.

Diodore of Tarsus. At the beginning of the twentieth century, Louis Mariès identified a previously unedited commentary on the psalms as the work of Diodore of Tarsus.[21] The attribution has been verified by others, and the work has been published in a critical edition by J.-M. Oliver in CCSG 6. Recently, an English translation by the late Robert Hill was published, making the work more widely accessible. This work provides a clear study of Antiochene exegesis and allows for the tracing of influence in the later works of Chrysostom, Theodore of Mopsuestia and Theodoret of Cyr (or Cyrrhus). For a comparison of Antiochene and Alexandrian views, readers should note the contrasting interpretations of the *diapsalma (selah)* in Psalm 3:2 given by Diodore and Gregory of Nyssa.

John Chrysostom. Unlike many of the other Greek authors, the text of Chrysostom's work on the Psalms has come to us directly. That work consists of what may have been homilies or lectures (given most likely between 390 and 398), although some have considered it a "work of leisure." The most recent critical text for this work is that published in Migne (PG 55). Again, an English translation with introduction by Robert Hill has been published, and it is from his work that selections have mostly been taken. In addition, some selections have been taken from other works of Chrysostom, but these are limited, since, as is the case with Augustine, the sheer volume of Chrysostom's output could easily warrant a volume of selections dedicated to him alone.

---

[19]Robert E. Sinkewicz, *Evagrius of Pontus: The Greek Ascetic Corpus*, Oxford Early Christian Studies (Oxford: Oxford University Press, 2003).

[20]Hans Urs von Balthasar, "Die Hiera des Evagrius," *Zeitschrift für Katholische Theologie* 63 (1939): 86-106; Marie-Josèphe Rondeau, "Le Commentaire sur les Psaumes d'Evagre le Pontique," *Orientalia Christiana Periodica* 26 (1960): 307-48.

[21]Louis Mariès, "Aurions-nous le Commentaire sur les Psaumes de Diodore de Tarse?" *Revue de Philologie* 35 (1911): 56-70. Mariés followed this with a number of publications. Note especially his article, "Études Preliminaires à l'Édition de Diodore de Tarse 'Sur les Psaumes,'" *Revue des Sciences Religieuses* 22 (1932): 385-408, 513-40.

Asterius the Homilist. Thanks to the work of Marcel Richard and Eiliv Skard, the extant remains of a collection of homilies on the Psalms by an author named Asterius have been identified.[22] These include some homilies that had previously been attributed to Chrysostom, which no doubt helped to preserve them since the Asterius material, from the time of Jerome, has traditionally been identified as being the work of an Arian. Richard and Skard identified the author as Asterius the Sophist, who played a role in the early Arian controversy. Rondeau also affirmed this identification.[23] However, Wolfram Kinzig has effectively refuted this position as well as an earlier proposal by Jean-Baptiste Cotelier designating the author as Asterius of Amaseia. Kinzig concluded that the author was not an Arian but a Nicene.[24] However, after reviewing all known Asterii, Kinzig initially relegated the homilies to an "Asterius Ignotus."[25] Later, he proposed the more fitting title of Asterius the Homilist, in recognition of the skillful rhetorical and expositional style exhibited in these late fourth- or early fifth-century homilies.[26] The selections given here are new translations. As an example of the homiletical style of this author, readers may want to see especially the selections on Psalm 14.

Theodore of Mopsuestia. One of the early accomplishments of Robert Devreesse's work on the catenae was a retrieval of the authentic fragments of Theodore of Mopsuestia's Commentary on the Psalms, covering Psalms 1–81.[27] Beyond Psalm 81, the attribution to Theodore in the catenae cannot be established with certainty. Devreesse's work has recently been republished with a facing English translation by Robert Hill.[28] The commentary is thought to be an early work by Theodore, most likely before his ordination in 392 (Rondeau dates the commentary between 370 and 380) and offers a study in the developing Antiochene tradition.

Theodoret of Cyr. Our subject—the exposition of the Psalms—offers a unique opportunity to study the development of the Antiochene tradition of biblical interpretation. English readers owe a debt of gratitude to Robert Hill, who once again has provided an excellent translation of yet another Antiochene commentary. Theodoret's commentary, unlike that of Theodore, came later in his career, being completed between 441 and 448, when, as Hill has noted, "he had completed two decades as bishop of Cyrus." Readers will be interested not only in similarities

---

[22]Marcel Richard, "Les Homélies d'Astérius sur les Psaumes 4-7," *Revue Biblique* 44 (1935): 548-58; Eiliv Skard, "Asterios von Amaseia und Asterios der Sophist," *Symbolae Osloenses* 20 (1940): 86-132; Marcel Richard, "Une Ancienne Collection d'Homélies Grecques sur les Psaumes 1-15," *Symbolae Osloenses* 25 (1947): 54-73; Eiliv Skard, "Bemerkungen zu den Aesterios-Texten," *Symbolae Osloenses* 27 (1949): 54-69; Marcel Richard, "Le Recueil d'Homélies d'Astérius le Sophiste," *Symbolae Osloenses* 29 (1952): 24-33; idem, "Deux Homélies Inédites du Sophiste Astérius," *Symbolae Osloenses* 29 (1952): 93-98; Marcel Richard, ed., *Asterii Sophistae Commentariorum in Psalmos quae Supersunt Accedunt Aliquot Homiliae Anonymae* (Oslo: A. W. Brogger, 1956); Eiliv Skard, "Zu Asterios," *Symbolae Osloenses* 34 (1958): 58-66.

[23]Rondeau, *Les Commentaires Patristiques*, 78-79.

[24]Wolfram Kinzig, *In Search of Asterius: Studies on the Authorship of the Psalms* (Göttingen: Vandenhoeck & Ruprecht, 1990).

[25]Ibid., 231.

[26]Wolfram Kinzig, "Asterius the Homilist," in *Dictionary of Early Christian Literature*, ed. Siegmar Döpp and Wilhelm Geerlings, trans. Matthew O'Connell (New York: Crossroad, 2000), 53-54.

[27]Robert Devreesse, *Le Commentaire de Théodore de Mopsueste sur les Psaumes (I-LXXX)*, Studi e Testi 93 (Vatican City: Biblioteca Apostolica Vaticana, 1948).

[28]Theodore of Mopsuestia, *Commentary on Psalms 1-81*, trans. with an introduction by Robert C. Hill, Writings from the Greco-Roman World 5 (Atlanta: Society of Biblical Literature, 2006).

between Antiochene exegetes but also the differences among them, when, for example, Theodoret takes what might be called an Alexandrian position over against Diodore or Theodore. Theodoret's commentary is notable for its brief, concise comments focusing on the language, imagery and historical facts in the text while also drawing moral and theological observations.

Cyril of Alexandria. As Rondeau has noted, the evidence suggests that Cyril produced a scholarly theological commentary on the Psalms. However, it has come down to us in bits and pieces mixed with material from many other authors. This is certainly the case with the edition produced by Mai and published in Migne (PG 69). Efforts to identify a reliable text were undertaken by Giovanni Mercati, working with two Bodleian manuscripts, and by Devreesse and Mühlenberg, working with the Palestinian chains.[29] The portions taken for the present work have, once again, followed the latter in making selections out of the material in Migne. However, readers will note selections from other works by Cyril that more clearly typify his theological reflection. An excellent example of the latter may be found in Cyril's comments on Psalm 22:1.

Hesychius of Jerusalem. We have from Hesychius the remains of three different works on the Psalms. The Large Commentary on the Psalms is preserved in Migne (PG 93) and has been evaluated textually by Devereese.[30] Using Devreesse as a guide, selections for the present volume have been mostly taken from the Large Commentary and are presented in English translation for the first time.[31] We also have a smaller commentary edited by V. Jagić and a work commenting on the titles of the psalms preserved in Migne (among the works of Athanasius, PG 27).[32] As Rondeau has noted, these smaller works consist of a collection of glosses, the latter interpreting the psalm titles allegorically and the former drawing connections between the psalms and the life of Christ.

Latin Authors

Hilary of Poitiers. The treatises of Hilary on the Psalms were well known among other Latin commentators, including Jerome, Augustine and Cassiodorus. However, they apparently did not cover all of the psalms, and the text that has come down to us includes only five within the range of this volume (Ps 1–2, 9, 13 [14], 14 [15]). Jerome charged that Hilary merely translated Origen into Latin. Rondeau has noted that what we have been able to recover from Origen discounts the charge of mere translation, but it does indicate that Hilary was familiar with Origen and freely used his work in his own composition.

Ambrose of Milan. There is extant from Ambrose a commentary on twelve Psalms. Eleven of the psalms fall within our range, covering Psalms 1, 35 [36]–40 [41], 43 [44], 45 [46], 47 [48] and 48 [49] (the twelfth is on Ps 61 [62]). In addition, a separate work gives a lengthy exposition of Psalm 118 [119]. Most likely, these were sermons; some clearly were. The influence of

---

[29]Giovanni Mercati, *Osservazioni a Proemi del Salterio di Origene, Ippolito, Eusebio, Cirillo Alessandrino e Altri, con Frammenti Inediti*, Studi e Testi 142 (Vatican City: Biblioteca Apostolica Vaticana, 1948), 133-39; Devreesse, *Les Anciens Commentateurs Grecs*, 224-38.

[30]Robert Devreesse, "La Chaine sur les Psaumes de Daniele Barbaro," *Revue Biblique* 33 (1924): 65-81; 498-521.

[31]Devreesse, *Les Anciens Commentateurs Grecs*, 250-53.

[32]V. Jagić, *Supplementum Psalterii Bononiensis: Incerti Auctoris Explanatio Psalmorum Graeca* (Vienna: A. Holzhausen, 1917).

Origen, Eusebius, Basil and Didymus can be seen in Ambrose's work, but this does not discount the contribution of his own thought or the rhetorical skill evident in his composition. In making selections for this work, we were able to make use of the recent English translation by Íde M. Ní Riain. In addition to the commentary, selections have also been taken from a number of other works by Ambrose in which comments have been made on passages within the first 50 psalms.

Jerome. From the pen of Jerome we have the *Commentariola*, the Brief Commentary on the Psalms offering brief comments and insights. Jerome tells us that he composed the *Commentariola* as a supplement to the *Enchiridion* of Origen. Selections have been taken from the *Commentariola* for the present work and are presented in fresh English translations.

In addition to the *Commentariola*, we have two collections designated as treatises on the Psalms, both published in CCSL 78, the second comprising some treatises from the first and adding others as well. Within the purview of this ACCS volume, only seven treatises from these two works concern us (on Ps 1, 5, 7, 9, 10 [11], 14 [15], 15 [16]). Recently, strong evidence has been put forward by Peri that this work is a translation of Origen's homilies on the Psalms.[33] Rondeau, in reviewing the arguments, has agreed with this conclusion, although noting that Jerome has inserted some of his own comments, imposed his own style somewhat on the text and included some references from his historical setting. We think that while it is probably best to regard this work as a translation of Origen, it is not as pure as what the modern reader might expect by the designation "translation." Of course, it could be argued that designating Jerome as the author also falls short of what the modern reader would expect by the attribution of authorship. Nevertheless, we have chosen to attribute selections made from these treatises to Jerome while alerting readers in this introduction to the fact that this material comes mostly from the pen of Origen with slight adaptation by Jerome.

Augustine. Augustine's *Expositions of the Psalms* has come down to us directly in an abundance of manuscripts. The work is massive and took more than thirty years for him to complete. It is a collection of works on the Psalms—homilies, notes, commentary—composed not in canonical order but singularly or in various compositional groups in an occasional fashion, put in order by Augustine when the task was completed. Influences from earlier and contemporary commentators have been detected, but the personality of Augustine dominates the composition with a profound originality that has greatly influenced succeeding generations. It is believed that Luther was reading Augustine's expositions of Psalms 31 and 32 when he came to understand justification by faith. Readers may want to consider the selections on Psalm 31:2 and Psalm 32:1 in this light.[34]

For our selections, we have used the new translation by Maria Boulding in the Works of Saint Augustine series by New City Press. Of course, selections have been made of other works by Augustine, but they are only a small sample of what could have been chosen. As Michael Fiedro-

---

[33]See n. 11 above.

[34]Note especially Uuras Saarnivaara, *Luther Discovers the Gospel: New Light upon Luther's Way from Medieval Catholicism to Evangelical Faith*, reprint ed. (St. Louis: Concordia, 2005), 60, 64, 66, 92-126.

wicz has pointed out in the introduction to the *WSA* edition, "in Augustine's whole output more than ten thousand citations of the psalms can be detected, making his work seem like one vast exposition of the psalms."[35] Or, in Rondeau's more graphic description, "Augustin était imprégné du Psautier."[36] As a result, we could have filled the entire volume, and more than one volume, with selections from Augustine alone. However, we hope that those that have been chosen will be an encouragement to avail oneself of the full texts of the *Expositions of the Psalms* and other writings of Augustine.

Arnobius the Younger. Writing around 460 from Rome, Arnobius the Younger composed a commentary on the entire Psalter. A critical text is available in CCSL 25. Selections made for this volume appear in English translation for the first time. The younger Arnobius has sometimes been classified as a semi-Pelagian because of his opposition to the Augustinian doctrine of predestination. The commentary focuses on Christ and the church as the key to interpreting the Psalms, demonstrating perhaps a Tychonian hermeneutical influence that is but one indication, as Rondeau has noted, of his African origin.

Cassiodorus. The commentary of Cassiodorus, written in the late 540s or early 550s, is one of the most accessible works on the Psalms that is available to us. The textual tradition is sound, and we have an excellent critical edition in CCSL 97-98. In addition, an excellent English translation by P. G. Walsh has appeared in the Ancient Christian Writers series. There are certain features of Cassiodorus's style that are difficult to show in a book of selections—matters that have to do with the systematic arrangement of his commentary, involving an introduction and conclusion to his comments on each psalm. Cassiodorus frequently offers word studies of terms in the Greek or Latin text, some examples of which can be seen in our selections. He also incorporates rhetorical observations in his work, classifying figures of speech and making observations on rhetorical patterns in the text. Sometimes he makes references to sources he has consulted, especially Augustine. Overall, his work shows a careful balance between literary, theological and pastoral concerns.

In addition to these Greek and Latin commentaries, homilies and notes on the Psalms, selections have been taken from a wide variety of patristic writings. The sampling is only a small indication of the impact of the Psalms on the mind of the church, whether that mind is engaged in teaching, worship, expressing faith or seeking to live according to the pattern and instruction of Christ. We hope that this volume will be informative not only about the thoughts and perspectives of early Christian writers but also in providing insight into the meaning and use of the Psalms, which was the purpose and intent of these writers' efforts. Ultimately, their goal was to know Christ, and if through the reflective and devotional use of this commentary readers come to or grow in that knowledge, then their work and ours will have been accomplished.

This ACCS volume on Psalms 1-50 has been a much larger task than it originally appeared.

---

[35]Michael Fiedrowicz, "Introduction," in *Expositions of the Psalms 1-32*, Works of Saint Augustine 3.15 (New York: New City Press, 2000), 13.

[36]Rondeau, *Les Commentaires Patristiques*, 174-75. Lit., "Augustine was impregnated with the Psalter."

The work could not have been completed except for the help that many people have provided along the way. I first of all would like to thank my coeditor, Carmen Hardin, who oversaw the translation work, providing the many translations of previously untranslated material. Also, thanks go to Stefana Laing and Vladimir Kharlamov, who assisted early in the project. The work involved a great deal of typing and word processing in which we were assisted by Norita Drake, Holly Groza and Steven James. Steven James has also helped immeasurably with preparations of the final draft. I am also grateful to the administration and trustees of Southern Baptist Theological Seminary who provided a sabbatical in 2000-2001 for work on the project, and to my president, Paige Patterson, of Southwestern Baptist Theological Seminary, where I now serve, for his encouragement to complete the work despite a very busy administrative schedule. Finally, much thanks goes to Tom Oden, who at the beginning invited me to do this project, and to Joel Elowsky and the project office team for their patience and continual help to me and my coeditor throughout the entire work.

Craig A. Blaising
Fort Worth, Texas

Publisher's Note to the Second Printing

Shortly after the appearance of the first printing of *Psalms 1-50*, it came to our attention that we had made a significant error in the proofing process that should not be attributed to the volume editor, to whom we duly apologize. It was the volume editor's intent to provide standard original-language identifications of sources supplemented by English-language numbering of the Psalms, such as that found on page 91 for Evagrius of Pontus's "Notes on the Psalms 9[10].28-29," where "9" represents the standard psalm designation in the Septuagint and "10" represents the standard numbering of the psalm in English-language versions (see his note 5 above). Readers will note that for citations of Evagrius's *Notes on the Psalms* and Jerome's *Homilies on Psalms* this method has been retained. Regrettably, the other source identifications were conformed at an earlier stage in the production process to the English-language numbering of the Psalms, leaving them out of sync with original-language sources. No one familiar with the Septuagint or standard patristic sources should have any difficulty in locating the sources; nonetheless, Inter-Varsity Press regrets the error.

PSALMS 1-50

1:1-6 THE BLESSED AND THE WICKED

> If you wish to declare someone blessed, you learn how to do so
> and whom to call upon and the words to say in Psalm 1.
>
> ATHANASIUS *ON THE INTERPRETATION OF THE PSALMS* 15 [OIP 66]

¹*Blessed is the man*
who walks not in the counsel of the wicked,
nor stands in the way of sinners,
nor sits in the seat of scoffers;
²*but his delight is in the law of the* LORD,
and on his law he meditates day and
night.
³*He is like a tree*
planted by streams of water,
that yields its fruit in its season,
and its leaf does not wither.

In all that he does, he prospers.

⁴*The wicked are not so,*
but are like chaff which the wind drives
away.
⁵*Therefore the wicked will not stand in the*
judgment,
nor sinners in the congregation of the
righteous;
⁶*for the* LORD *knows the way of the righteous,*
but the way of the wicked will perish.

OVERVIEW: The first psalm is foundational to understanding the whole book of Psalms (BASIL). It presents the crown of blessedness that will be bestowed on the one who wins the prize in Christ (AMBROSE), a blessedness that is none other than a participation in true being (GREGORY OF NYSSA), true goodness, which is God (BASIL).

The blessed man in this psalm is first of all Christ (AUGUSTINE), from whom blessedness comes (EUSEBIUS). We extend its meaning to refer also to those who are saved by Christ (JEROME), who conform themselves to Christ (HILARY OF POITIERS), whether men or women (BASIL). The soul of the one who is blessed does not experience the threefold inner movement of sin (BASIL, JEROME), a deepening corruption

(EUSEBIUS) that then influences others (JEROME), a pattern that replicates the fall of Adam in the individual soul (CASSIODORUS). Such are given over to vain musings (ORIGEN) because they reject God (HILARY OF POITIERS), following the devil (DIDYMUS) and their own natural instincts (HILARY OF POITIERS). The end result is a lasting persistence in evil (BASIL), complicity with worldly powers (CLEMENT OF ALEXANDRIA) and the persistent contagion of worldly business (HILARY OF POITIERS).

The one who is blessed delights in the law, expressing wholehearted obedience (JEROME), motivated not by fear but arising out of the will (HILARY OF POITIERS). By continued meditation on the Word of God, the will is grafted onto God (SAHDONA), and in this way, a person is formed by the Word (THEODORE OF MOPSUESTIA). As meditation leads to action (ORIGEN, HILARY OF POITIERS), what was destroyed by Adam is rebuilt (ARNOBIUS THE YOUNGER). The believer is blessed in knowledge (ORIGEN) illumined by the radiance of God (ATHANASIUS). Consequently, meditation on the Word should be preferred over other pursuits (CAESARIUS). On a practical note, a quiet time, such as evening affords, is most advantageous for meditation on the Word (NICETAS), and meditation is often assisted by conversation and writing (AUGUSTINE).

The one who is blessed is like a tree of life and wisdom (HILARY OF POITIERS), which is to say, he or she is like Christ (JEROME), stable in a flood of temporality (AUGUSTINE), bearing fruit by divine enablement (THEODORET). The leaves and fruit are the words and the meaning of Scripture (DIDYMUS, JEROME). The fruit can also be interpreted as faith and works (JOHN OF DAMASCUS), or wisdom (METHODIUS OF OLYMPUS) in the life of a Christian or as the churches that Christ has caused to spring up in the world (AUGUSTINE). It can also be understood as immortality (HILARY OF POITIERS), the glorious resurrection (CAESARIUS) of the believer.

The wicked, however, will be like dust (HILARY OF POITIERS), insubstantial (JEROME), driven by every temptation (CHRYSOSTOM). At the resurrection, they have no standing among the righteous (JEROME); rather, they rise to punishment (CYRIL OF JERUSALEM), being turned back to Sheol (APHRAHAT). Wickedness, consequently, will vanish (JEROME) as the wicked pass from God's favorable knowledge (ORIGEN, AUGUSTINE).

1:1a Blessed Is the Man

FOUNDATIONAL FOR THE BOOK OF PSALMS.
BASIL THE GREAT: Like the foundation in a house, the keel in a ship and the heart in a body, so is [Psalm 1 as a] brief introduction to the whole structure of the Psalms. For when David intended to propose in the course of his speech to the combatants of true religion many painful tasks involving unmeasured sweats and toils, he showed first the happy end, that in the hope of the blessings reserved for us we might endure without grief the sufferings of this life. HOMILIES ON THE PSALMS 10.3 (Ps 1).[1]

THE CROWN TO BE CONFERRED.
AMBROSE: What a delightfully apt beginning! Those who wish for a grand display and a great celebration to add glory to the games generally promise a prize. They make much of the honor of the crown to be conferred. All this is to make the contestants more eager to take part and to strain every nerve in order to win. This is what our Lord Jesus does. He promises us the glory of a heavenly kingdom, the sweetness of everlasting rest, the happiness of eternal life. COMMENTARY ON TWELVE PSALMS 1.13.[2]

PARTICIPATION IN TRUE BEING.
GREGORY OF NYSSA: The goal of the virtuous life is blessedness. . . . This is the summation and object of everything conceived in relation to the good. What is truly and properly contemplated and apprehended in this sublime concept, then, would reasonably be called the divine nature. For so the great Paul designated God when he put "blessed" before all the other words about God in one of his letters. He wrote in the following words, "The blessed and only ruler, the King of kings and Lord of lords, who alone has immortality and who dwells in unapproachable light, whom no human being has seen or can see. To him be honor and rule forever."[3] All these sublime concepts about the divine would, then, in my opinion, constitute a definition of blessedness. For if someone were asked what beatitude is, he would give a properly pious answer if he followed Paul's statement and said that the nature that transcends everything is first and properly called blessed. Among humans, however, that beatitude, which is the nature of the one participated

---

[1]FC 46:154. [2]ACTP 7. [3]1 Tim 6:15-16.

in, occurs to a certain extent and is specified by participation in true being. Likeness to God, therefore, is a definition of human blessedness. On the Inscriptions of the Psalms 1.1.5-6.[4]

True Goodness. Basil the Great: What is truly good is principally and primarily the most blessed. And that is God. . . . For truly blessed is Goodness itself toward which all things look, which all things desire, an unchangeable nature, lordly dignity, calm existence; a happy way of life, in which there is no alteration, which no change touches; a flowing fount, abundant grace, inexhaustible treasure. But stupid and worldly people, ignorant of the nature of good itself, frequently bless things worth nothing, riches, health, renown; not one of which is in its nature good, not only because they easily change to the opposite but also because they are unable to make their possessors good. What person is just because of his possessions? What person is self-controlled because of his health? On the contrary, in fact, each of these possessions frequently becomes the servant of sin for those who use them badly. Blessed is the one, then, who possesses that which is esteemed of the greatest value, who shares in the goods that cannot be taken away. How shall we recognize that person? "He who has not walked in the council of the ungodly." Homilies on Psalms 10.3 (Ps 1).[5]

1:1b *Is the Man Who Does Not Walk, Stand or Sit*

Christ the Blessed Man. Augustine: This statement should be understood as referring to our Lord Jesus Christ, that is, the Lord-man . . . "who has not gone astray" . . . as did the earthly man who conspired with his wife, already beguiled by the serpent, to disregard God's commandments. . . . Christ most certainly came in the way of sinners by being born as sinners are, but he did not stand in it, for worldly allurement did not hold him. Expositions of the Psalms 1.1.[6]

Blessedness Comes from Christ. Eusebius of Caesarea: Our Savior, who made many blessed, offers happiness in abundance. He is the first of them who rightly are called blessed. The first psalm, therefore, must refer to him inasmuch as he is the husband of his bride the church. Which, it seems, the Hebrew word for "man" indicates when it is written with the article added. Commentary on the Psalms 1.1.[7]

The One Saved by Christ. Jerome: We understand this person as one who is claimed and saved by our Savior . . . one and the same the Son of God and the Son of man, who before the ages always was the Word. Brief Commentary on Psalms 1.[8]

Conformity to the Incarnate Christ. Hilary of Poitiers: The one who is here extolled as happy by the prophet is the person who strives to conform himself to that body that the Lord assumed and in which he was born as human, by zeal for justice and perfect fulfillment of all righteousness. Homily on Psalm 1.4.[9]

Women Included. Basil the Great: Why, you say, does the prophet single out only man and proclaim him happy? Does he not exclude women from happiness? By no means. For the virtue of man and woman is the same, since creation is equally honored in both; therefore, there is the same reward for both. Listen to Genesis: "God created humankind," it says, "In the image of God he created him. Male and female he created them."[10] They whose nature is alike have the same reward. Homilies on the Psalms 10.3 (Ps 1).[11]

An Inner Movement of the Soul. Basil the Great: He put before us three acts that must be guarded against. . . . In accordance with the nature of things, he set up this order by his words. First, we take counsel with ourselves;

---

[4]GNTIP 84. [5]FC 46:155. [6]WSA 3 15:67. [7]PG 23:76. [8]CCL 72:180. [9]NPNF 2 9:237*. [10]Gen 1:27. [11]FC 46:155-56.

next, we strengthen our resolution; then, we continue unchanged in what has been determined. HOMILIES ON THE PSALMS 10.4 (Ps 1).[12]

WAYS OF COMMITTING SIN. JEROME: Scripture describes the three usual ways of committing sin: we entertain sinful thoughts; we commit sin in act; or we teach what is sinful. First, we entertain a sinful thought; then, after we have reflected on it, we convert that thought into action. When we commit sin, moreover, we multiply sin by teaching others to do what we have done. HOMILY ON PSALM 1.[13]

A DEEPENING CORRUPTION. EUSEBIUS OF CAESAREA: The first are the people who are saturated with well-known false reasoning, wicked people who grasp nothing firmly and with stability; they are swayed through their own will with no testing of their oppressive thought. The second are people who time after time fall into sin after the understanding of truth. The third group includes morally corrupt people who labor in no measure of grief, but they will thoroughly fill others with corrupt doctrine, either by their thinking, or by their behavior or by both. These are people who are grounded in evil, while the second group continues in sin and the first walks the way of error. The one who is called blessed is freed and delivered from all of these. COMMENTARY ON PSALMS 1.1.[14]

A PATTERNED CONDEMNATION. CASSIODORUS: The order of phrases must also be studied as a patterned condemnation of Adam; he departed when he forsook the Lord's command, stood when he took delight in sin, that is, when as lord of paradise he was gulled into believing that he would obtain knowledge of good and evil, and he sat in the chair of pestilence when he left to posterity the precedents of wicked teaching. EXPLANATION OF THE PSALMS 1.1.[15]

VAIN AND UNSUBSTANTIATED MUSINGS. ORIGEN: Generally there are three types: the first type is the one who does not acknowledge the truth at all, but, as chance has it, when he hands himself over to the vain and unsubstantiated musings of his own heart, he becomes like a wild beast, neither standing nor supported by anything, and accordingly, not sitting. This one, indeed, is said to walk in the counsel of the wicked. SELECTIONS FROM THE PSALMS 1.1.[16]

THE REJECTION OF GOD. HILARY OF POITIERS: The ungodly are those who despise searching for the knowledge of God, who in their irreverent mind take for granted that there is no Creator of the world, who assert that it arrived at the order and beauty that we see by chance, who in order to deprive their Creator of all power to pass judgment on a life lived rightly or in sin will have it that a person comes into being and passes out of it again by the simple operation of a law of nature. Thus all the counsel of these people is wavering, unsteady and vague and wanders about in the same familiar paths and over the same familiar ground, never finding a resting place, for it fails to reach any definite decision. They have never in their system risen to the doctrine of a Creator of the world, whether the world is for humanity or humanity for the world; the reason for death, its extent and nature. They press in ceaseless motion round the circle of this godless argument and find no rest in these imaginings. There are, besides, other counsels of the ungodly, that is, of those who have fallen into heresy. . . . Their reasoning ever takes the course of a vicious circle; without grasp or foothold to stay them, they tread their interminable round of endless indecision. Their ungodliness consists in measuring God not by his own revelation but by a standard of their choosing; they forget that it is as godless to make a god as to deny him; if you ask them what effect these opinions have on their faith and hope, they are perplexed and confused, they wander from the point and will-

---

[12]FC 46:158. [13]FC 48:4. [14]PG 23:76-77. [15]ACW 51:49. [16]PG 12:1085.

fully avoid the real issue of the debate. Happy is the one, then, who has not walked in this kind of counsel of the ungodly, who has not even entertained the wish to walk in it, for it is a sin even to think for a moment of things that are ungodly. HOMILY ON PSALM 1.7-8.[17]

THE DEVIL. DIDYMUS THE BLIND: The devil himself may be called the way of sinners. Let the one who stands in this way be warned lest he tarry there. Recall what the Scripture says: "Resist the devil, and he will flee from you."[18] For the one who will not stand in the devil's way will come to the Lord, who says, "I am the way."[19] Truly the one who follows this way, traveling the way to the end, will receive a reward. FRAGMENTS ON THE PSALMS 1.1.[20]

THE PATH OF NATURAL DISPOSITION. HILARY OF POITIERS: [The psalm here speaks of] those who abide in the church but do not obey its laws; such are the greedy, the drunken, the brawlers, the wanton, the proud, the hypocrites, liars, plunderers. No doubt we are urged toward these sins by the promptings of our natural instincts, but it is good for us to withdraw from the path into which we are being hurried and not to stand in it, seeing that we are offered so easy a way of escape. It is for this reason that the one who has not stood in the way of sinners is happy, for while nature carries him into that way, religious belief draws him back. HOMILY ON PSALM 1.9.[21]

A LASTING PERSISTENCE IN EVIL. BASIL THE GREAT: The "chair" here refers to steady and lasting persistence in the choice of evil. This we must guard against because the practice of assiduously occupying ourselves with sins engenders in our soul a certain condition that can scarcely be removed. An inveterate condition of the soul and the exercise of evil strengthened by time are hard to heal or even entirely incurable, since, for the most part, custom is changed into nature. Indeed, not to attach ourselves to evil is a request worth praying for. But there remains

a second way: immediately after the temptation to flee it as if it were a venomous sting, according to words of Solomon concerning the wicked woman: "Do not set your eye on her, but leap back; do not delay."[22] Now, I know that some in their youth have sunk down into the passions of the flesh and have remained in their sins until their old age because of the habit of evil. As the swine rolling about in the mire always smear more muck on themselves, so these bring on themselves more and more each day the shame of pleasure. Blessed is it, therefore, not to have had evil in your mind; but, if through the deceit of the enemy, you have received in your soul the counsels of impiety, do not stay in your sin. And, if you have experienced this, do not become established in evil. So then, "do not sit in the chair of pestilence." HOMILIES ON THE PSALMS 10.6 (Ps 1).[23]

COMPLICITY WITH THE WORLDLY POWERS. CLEMENT OF ALEXANDRIA: And "the chair of pestilences" will be the theaters and tribunals, or rather the compliance with wicked and deadly powers and complicity with their deeds. STROMATEIS 2.15.[24]

THE CONTAGION OF WORLDLY BUSINESS. HILARY OF POITIERS: Many, even God-fearing people, are led astray by the canvassing for worldly honors and desire to administer the law of the courts, though they are bound by those of the church. But although they bring to the discharge of their duties a religious intention, as is shown by their merciful and upright demeanor, still they cannot escape a certain contagious infection arising from the business in which their life is spent. For the conduct of civil cases does not suffer them to be true to the holy principles of the church's law, even though they wish it. And without abandoning their pious purpose they are compelled, against their will, by the

---

[17]NPNF 2 9:238*. [18]Jas 4:7. [19]Jn 14:6. [20]PG 39:1157. [21]NPNF 2 9:238*. [22]Prov 9:18 (only in LXX). [23]FC 46:161-62. [24]ANF 2:362.

necessary conditions of the seat they are prone to use, at one time invective, at another, insult, at another, punishment; and their very position makes them authors as well as victims of the necessity that constrains them, their system being as it were impregnated with the infection. Hence, this title, "the seat of pestilence," by which the prophet describes their seat, because by its infection it poisons the very will of the religiously minded. HOMILY ON PSALM 1.10.[25]

1:2 Delight in the Law

WHOLEHEARTED OBEDIENCE. JEROME: "Delight" refers to the fact that one wholeheartedly obeys the Lord's command. HOMILY ON PSALM 1.[26]

A MOTIVATION OTHER THAN FEAR. HILARY OF POITIERS: The majority of people are kept within the bounds of law by fear; the few are brought under the law by will. For it is the mark of fear not to dare to omit what it is afraid of, but of perfect piety to be ready to obey commands. This is why that one is happy whose will, not whose fear, is in the law of God. HOMILY ON PSALM 1.11.[27]

GRAFTING OUR WILLS ONTO GOD. SAHDONA: Let us too do this, meditating continuously on the things of God, and by means of the Lord's law, let our wills be grafted on to him. BOOK OF PERFECTION 61.[28]

FORMED BY THE WORD. THEODORE OF MOPSUESTIA: One learns to be bound by the law through continuous meditation so that one shapes himself by it. COMMENTARY ON PSALMS 1.2.[29]

MEDITATION LEADS TO ACTION. ORIGEN: [The blessed person] meditates on the law of the Lord day and night, not as one who entrusts the words of the law to his memory without works, but as one who by meditating performs works consistent with it, until through the disciplined meditation of the works that the law instructs, he is prepared for excelling in all the things that apply for living perfectly according to the law. SELECTIONS FROM THE PSALMS 1.2.[30]

MEDITATION MEANS PERFORMING THE LAW. HILARY OF POITIERS: Meditation in the law does not lie in reading its words but in pious performance of its injunctions; not in a mere perusal of the books and writings but in a practical meditation and exercise in their respective contents, and in a fulfillment of the law by the works we do by night and day, as the apostle says: "Whether you eat or drink, or whatsoever you do, do all to the glory of God."[31] HOMILY ON PSALM 1.12.[32]

REBUILDING WHAT ADAM DESTROYED. ARNOBIUS THE YOUNGER: The memory of the law of God overtakes [the blessed person's] own will. And day and night he models his behavior through meditation on divine law so that the life that Adam destroyed by his contempt, he himself may find by guarding it, remaining deep in the flowing water of the law, taking hold of the everlasting tree of life; so, finally, whatever he does will prosper. COMMENTARY ON THE PSALMS 1.[33]

CONTINUAL MEDITATION LEADS TO BLESSING. ORIGEN: Certainly, even if I shall not have been able to understand everything, if I am, nevertheless, busily engaged in the divine Scriptures and "I meditate on the law of God day and night" and at no time at all do I desist inquiring, discussing, investigating, and certainly, what is greatest, praying God and asking for understanding from him who "teaches humankind knowledge,"[34] I shall appear to dwell "at the well of vision." . . . You too, therefore, if you shall always search the prophetic visions, if you always

---

[25]NPNF 2 9:238. [26]FC 48:6**. [27]NPNF 2 9:239*. [28]CS 101:227. [29]CCL 88A:8. [30]PG 12:1088. [31]1 Cor 10:31. [32]NPNF 2 9:239. [33]CCL 25:4. [34]Ps 94:10 (93:10 LXX).

inquire, always desire to learn, if you meditate on these things, if you remain in them, you too will receive a blessing from the Lord and dwell "at the well of vision." For the Lord Jesus will appear to you also, "in the way," and will open the Scriptures to you so that you may say, "Was not our heart burning within us when he opened to us the Scriptures?"[35] But he appears to those who think about him and meditate on him and live "in his law day and night." HOMILIES ON GENESIS 11.3.[36]

ILLUMINED BY THE RADIANCE OF GOD.
ATHANASIUS: The splendid brilliance of God's grace never suffers an eclipse. No, it is always at hand to enlighten the inner thoughts of those who really want it. Great good comes to people who, enlightened by the grace of God, make it their habit to apply the truths of holy Scripture to their lives. They receive just such a blessing as the psalmist describes. . . . Those blessings come because the person who accepts God's grace is not illumined by mere physical light from the sun, the moon or even the whole host of stars. Rather, he glows all over with the radiant brilliance of God. FESTAL LETTERS 5.1.[37]

MEDITATION PREFERRED TO OTHER PURSUITS. CAESARIUS OF ARLES: When we sing, "Blessed is the one who shall meditate on the law of the Lord day and night," let us reject useless occupations, stinging jests, idle and wicked conversations, as the poison of the devil. Let us frequently read over and over again the divine lessons, or, if we cannot read them ourselves, let us often and eagerly listen to others read them. SERMON 75.3.[38]

THE ADVANTAGE OF NIGHTLY MEDITATION.
NICETAS OF REMESIANA: Meditation during the day is, of course, good, but that at night is better. During the day, there is the clamor of our many cares, the mental distraction of our occupations. A double preoccupation divides our attention. The quiet and solitude of the night make it a favorable time for prayer and most suitable for those who watch. With worldly occupations put aside and the attention undivided, the whole person, at night, stands in the divine presence. VIGILS OF THE SAINTS 8.[39]

MEDITATION ASSISTED BY CONVERSATION AND WRITING. AUGUSTINE: As for myself, I meditate on the law of God, if not day and night, at least during the few moments of time that I can, and lest my meditations escape from me through forgetfulness, I hold on to them by my pen. I am confident that God in his mercy will make me remain steadfast in all the truths that I regard as certain, but if I am minded otherwise in any point, he will make it known to me, either by his own secret inspirations, or through his own lucid words or through discussions with my brethren. For this do I pray, and I place this trust and my own desires in his hands, who is wholly capable of guarding what he has given and of fulfilling what he has promised. ON THE TRINITY 1.3.5.[40]

1:3 Like a Tree by Streams of Water

THE LIVING TREE OF WISDOM. HILARY OF POITIERS: In the book of Genesis, it is stated that there stands in the midst of the garden a tree of life and a tree of the knowledge of good and evil; next, that the garden is watered by a stream that afterwards divides into four heads. The prophet Solomon teaches us what this tree of life is in his exhortation concerning Wisdom: "She is a tree of life to all those that lay hold on her and lean on her."[41] This tree, then, is living; and not only living, but, furthermore, guided by reason; guided by reason, that is, insofar as to yield fruit in its own season. And this tree is planted beside the rills of water in the domain of the kingdom of God, that is, of course, in paradise, and in the place where the stream as it

---

[35]Lk 24:32. [36]FC 71:174-75. [37]*ARL* 90-91*. [38]FC 31:351. [39]FC 7:63. [40]FC 45:9. [41]Prov 3:18.

issues forth is divided into four heads. . . . This tree is planted in that place wither the Lord, who is Wisdom, leads the thief who confessed him to the Lord, saying, "Truly I say to you, today you will be with me in paradise." . . . The blessed person, then, will become like this tree when he or she shall be transplanted as the thief was, into the garden and set to grow beside the rills of water; and this planting will be that happy new planting that cannot be uprooted, to which the Lord refers in the Gospels when he curses the other kind of planting and says, "Every planting that my Father has not planted shall be rooted up."[42] This tree, therefore, will yield its fruits. HOMILY ON PSALM 1.14-15.[43]

LIKE CHRIST. JEROME: When Solomon says, "She is a tree of life to those who grasp her,"[44] he is speaking of Wisdom. Now, if wisdom is the tree of life, Wisdom itself, indeed, is Christ. You understand now that the one who is blessed and holy is compared with this tree, that is, with Wisdom. . . . He is, in other words, like Christ. HOMILY ON PSALM 1.[45]

CHRIST, STABLE IN A FLOOD OF TEMPORALITY. AUGUSTINE: What do you want? To have temporal things and to pass away together with time or not to love the world and to live forever with God? The river of temporal things carries [us] along, but like a tree growing near a river is our Lord Jesus Christ. He assumed flesh, died, rose again, ascended into heaven. He wanted, so to speak, to plant himself near the river of temporal things. Are you being swept headlong? Take hold of the wood. Does love of the world whirl you about? Take hold of Christ. For your sake was the temporal made that you may become eternal. HOMILIES ON 1 JOHN 2.10.2.[46]

STREAMS OF THE SPIRIT. THEODORET OF CYR: The streams from the divine Spirit resemble watering by rivers: just as they cause trees planted near them to flourish, so the spiritual

streams are the cause of bearing divine fruit. For this very reason Christ the Lord called his own teaching water. . . . Appropriately, then, blessed David compared the person devoted to the divine sayings with trees growing on riverbanks, ever green, bearing fruit in season. COMMENTARY ON THE PSALMS 1.7-8.[47]

THE WORDS AND SENSE OF SCRIPTURE. DIDYMUS THE BLIND: The tree is the wisdom of God; its fruit the mystical and spiritual sense of the Scriptures; the leaves covering its fruits are external words, which besides protecting the fruits display appropriate behavior, and they become the nourishment of good people, who are called beasts of burden on account of their own simplicity. FRAGMENTS ON THE PSALMS 1.3.[48]

FRUIT AND FOLIAGE. JEROME: This tree bears twofold: it produces fruit, and it produces foliage. The fruit that it bears contains the meaning of Scripture; the leaves, only the words. The fruit is in the meaning; the leaves are in the words. . . . Whoever reads sacred Scripture . . . with true spiritual insight gathers the fruit. . . . The leaves of this tree are by no means useless ["and whose leaves never fade"]. Even if one understands holy Writ only as history, he has something useful for his soul. HOMILY ON PSALM 1.[49]

FAITH AND WORKS. JOHN OF DAMASCUS: The soul watered by sacred Scripture grows fat and bears fruit in due season, which is the orthodox faith, and so is it adorned with its evergreen leaves, with actions pleasing to God, I mean. And thus we are disposed to virtuous action and untroubled contemplation by the sacred Scriptures. ORTHODOX FAITH 4.17.[50]

THE FRUIT OF WISDOM. METHODIUS: "A tree planted by the waterside, that will bring forth

---

[42]Mt 15:13. [43]NPNF 2 9:239-40*. [44]Prov 3:18. [45]FC 48:7. [46]FC 92:152. [47]FC 101:49. [48]PG 39:1160. [49]FC 48:8**. [50]FC 37:374*.

his fruit in due season"; that is, learning and charity and discretion are imparted in due time to those who come to the waters of redemption. BANQUET OF THE TEN VIRGINS 9.3.[51]

CHURCHES, THE FRUIT OF CHRIST. AUGUSTINE: That tree, therefore, is our Lord, who draws those who are in the way from the running waters, that is, from the peoples who sin. By drawing them into the roots of his discipline, he will bring forth fruit; that is, he will establish churches, but in due time, that is, after he has been glorified by his resurrection and ascension into heaven. Once the Holy Spirit had been sent to the apostles, and once they had been established in their faith in him and sent out to the peoples, he bore the churches as his fruit. EXPOSITIONS OF THE PSALMS 1.3.[52]

THE FRUIT OF IMMORTALITY. HILARY OF POITIERS: Now what, you ask, is this fruit that is to be dispensed? That assuredly of which this same apostle is speaking when he says, "And he will change our vile body, that it may be fashioned like his glorious body."[53] Thus he will give us those fruits of his that he has already brought to perfection in that one whom he has chosen to himself, who is portrayed under the image of a tree, whose mortality he has utterly done away and has raised him to share in his own immortality. HOMILY ON PSALM 1.15.[54]

A GLORIOUS RESURRECTION. CAESARIUS OF ARLES: O blessed cross, which makes people blessed! O cross, from which such great and wonderful fruits are gathered! The fruit of the cross is a glorious resurrection. This fruit of the wood is truly planted "near running water," for baptism is always joined to the cross. However, this wood produced "its fruit in due season," at the Lord's resurrection. It will do so again when he appears from heaven, "is seen on earth,"[55] and with dazzling sign of the cross preceding him, comes from above. SERMON 112.4.[56]

1:4 Like Dust Blown by the Wind

MADE LIKE DUST. HILARY OF POITIERS: The ungodly have no possible hope of having the image of the happy tree applied to them. The only lot that awaits them is one of wandering and winnowing, crushing, dispersion and unrest; shaken out of the solid framework of their bodily condition, they must be swept away to punishment in dust, a plaything of the wind. They shall not be dissolved into nothing, for punishment must find in them some stuff to work on, but ground into particles imponderable, unsubstantial, dry, they shall be tossed to and fro and make sport for the punishment that gives them no rest. Their punishment is recorded by the same prophet in another place where he says, "I will beat them small as the dust before the wind; like the mire of the streets I will destroy them."[57] HOMILY ON PSALM 1.19.[58]

INSUBSTANTIAL EXISTENCE. JEROME: Dust does not seem to have any substance, but it does, of course, have a kind of existence of its own. There is no body to it, yet what substance it does have is really by way of punishment. It is scattered here and there and is never in any one place; wherever the wind sweeps it, there its whole force is spent. The same is true of the wicked person. Once he has denied God, he is led by delusion wherever the breath of the devil sends him. HOMILY ON PSALM 1.[59]

DRIVEN BY EVERY TEMPTATION. CHRYSOSTOM: Even as chaff lies exposed to the gusts of wind and is easily caught up and swept along, so is also the sinner driven about by every temptation; for while a sinner is at war with himself and bears the warfare about with him, what hope of safety does he possess; betrayed as he is

---

[51]ANF 6:346. [52]WSA 3 15:68-69. [53]Phil 3:21. [54]NPNF 2 9:240. [55]Bar 3:38 (LXX). [56]FC 47:154-55. [57]Ps 18:42. [58]NPNF 2 9:241. [59]FC 48:10*.

at home, carrying with him that conscience that is a constant enemy? HOMILIES CONCERNING THE STATUES 8.4.[60]

1:5 The Wicked and the Judgment

NO STANDING. JEROME: Let us at this point consider the meaning of the words "therefore in judgment the wicked shall not stand." They shall not rise to be judged because they have already been judged, for "he who does not believe in me is already judged," "nor shall sinners in the assembly of the just." It does not say that sinners shall not rise again but that they shall not stand in the assembly of the just; they do not deserve to stand with those who are not to be judged. If they believed in me, says the Lord, they would rise up with those who do not have to be judged. HOMILY ON PSALM I.[61]

RESURRECTION TO PUNISHMENT. CYRIL OF JERUSALEM: They shall rise, though not to be judged, but to be sentenced. For God needs no lengthy scrutiny, but as soon as the wicked rise again, their punishment forthwith follows. CATECHETICAL LECTURES 18.14.[62]

TURNED BACK TO SHEOL. APHRAHAT: And even as the righteous who are perfected in good works shall not come into the judgment to be judged, so of the wicked also whose sins are many, and the measure of whose offenses is overflowing, it shall not be required that they should draw near to the judgment, but when they have risen again they shall turn back to Sheol. . . . All the nations that know not God their Maker are esteemed by God as nothingness and shall not come near to judgment, but as soon as they have risen shall turn back to Sheol. DEMONSTRATIONS 22.17.[63]

1:6 The Two Ways

VANISHING WICKEDNESS. JEROME: If the wicked perish, there is no chance for their repen-

tance. It does not say that the wicked shall perish but that the way of the wicked vanishes, that is, wickedness shall perish. Not the wicked but wickedness itself; not the one who was wicked will perish, but while he is repenting, wickedness vanishes. HOMILY ON PSALM I.[64]

THE KNOWLEDGE AND IGNORANCE OF GOD. ORIGEN: God is ignorant of evil deeds, not because he is unable to understand everything or to grasp it with his own intelligence (for it is wrong to think this way about God) but because those deeds are unworthy of his contemplation.
. . . God is ignorant of the way of the wicked, and he knows the way of the righteous. Further, who is the way of the righteous except the one who said, "I am the way" whom the Father knows? "No one has known the Son except the Father."[65] The distinction between the knowledge and ignorance of God is referred to in the prophets as "the memory and forgetfulness" of God. Often it is said in prayer: "Be mindful of me" and "Why have you forgotten our poverty?" Just as God removes sinners from his own memory, so does he again receive the repentant and become mindful of them. SELECTIONS FROM THE PSALMS 1.6.[66]

KNOWLEDGE AND EXISTENCE. AUGUSTINE: The Lord knows the way of the just but does not know the way of the ungodly. This does not mean that there is anything the Lord does not know, but he did say to sinners, "I never knew you."[67] However, to say "the way of the ungodly will perish" is substantially the same as saying, "The Lord does not know the way of the ungodly"; but it makes the point clearer that to be unknown to the Lord is to perish, and to be known by him is to remain. Thus being corresponds to God's knowledge and nonexistence to not being known. EXPOSITIONS OF THE PSALMS 1.6.[68]

---

[60]NPNF 1 9:397. [61]FC 48:12. [62]FC 64:127. [63]NPNF 2 13:408*. [64]FC 48:13. [65]Mt 11:27. [66]PG 12:1100. [67]Mt 7:23. [68]WSA 3 15:70.

2:1-12 THE LORD'S ANOINTED KING

When finding fault with the conspiracy . . . against the Savior

you have Psalm 2 . . . which accuses the impious

and those who act contrary to law.

ATHANASIUS ON THE INTERPRETATION OF THE PSALMS 14, 15 [OIP 66*]

¹*Why do the nations conspire,*
and the peoples plot in vain?
²*The kings of the earth set themselves,*
and the rulers take counsel together,
against the LORD *and his anointed, saying,*
³*"Let us burst their bonds asunder,*
and cast their cords from us."

⁴*He who sits in the heavens laughs;*
the LORD *has them in derision.*
⁵*Then he will speak to them in his wrath,*
and terrify them in his fury, saying,
⁶*"I have set my king*
on Zion, my holy hill."

⁷*I will tell of the decree of the* LORD*:*
He said to me, "You are my son,

today I have begotten you.
⁸*Ask of me, and I will make the nations your*
heritage,
and the ends of the earth your possession.
⁹*You shall break them with a rod of iron,*
and dash them in pieces like a potter's
vessel."

¹⁰*Now therefore, O kings, be wise;*
be warned, O rulers of the earth.
¹¹*Serve the* LORD *with fear,*
with trembling ¹²*kiss his feet,*
lest he be angry, and you perish in the way;
for his wrath is quickly kindled.

Blessed are all who take refuge in him.

a Cn: The Hebrew of 11b and 12a is uncertain

OVERVIEW: The second psalm begins carrying over the theme from the end of the first psalm (THEODORET). In fact, the first psalm can be taken as the inscription of the second psalm (GREGORY OF NYSSA), which speaks of the folly and ignorance of all nations joined in opposition to Christ (THEODORET, EUSEBIUS). By opposing Christ, they also oppose the Father (ORIGEN). But the saints understand the future victory of Christ, which understanding constitutes the Lord's laughter (AUGUSTINE). The anger of God is manifested in the human perception of the wrongness of sin, in the darkening of the mind of the sinner (AUGUSTINE) and in the retribu-tion that justly falls on the sinner (CASSIODO-RUS). However, we must remember that God's wrath is conditional on repentance (ORIGEN).

The Father refers the nations to Christ (JE-ROME), who, as the Word of God, the Creator, was sovereign already over them (THEODORE OF MOPSUESTIA), but as human, had received it by election (THEODORET). Some believe that the Father's address to the Son indicates that incar-nation (CYRIL OF ALEXANDRIA, THEODORET). Others believe that it signifies eternal genera-tion (ORIGEN, AUGUSTINE, CASSIODORUS), and yet others see a reference to his birth in those who come to know God (METHODIUS).

The Father's invitation to the Son to ask for the nations applies to the economy of the Son (Augustine) and signifies our salvation (Leo, Didymus), both Jews and Gentiles (Theodoret). He breaks them in order to reform them (Theodore of Mopsuestia), destroying the "old man" (Augustine), making them into an inheritance (Origen). The kings of the earth are instructed to serve the Lord (Augustine). We all are admonished to fear him at all times (Evagrius) through devotion, not coercion (Theodore of Mopsuestia), even in the choice of entertainment (Apostolic Constitutions). This is the key to holiness (Peter Chrysologus).

2:1-2 The Nations Rage

Theme Continued from the First Psalm. Theodoret of Cyr: Having concluded the first psalm with a reference to the ungodly, he opened the second in turn with this same reference so as to teach us that the aforementioned end of the ungodly lies in wait for both kings and rulers, Jews and Gentiles, who rage against the Savior. Commentary on the Psalms 2.1.[1]

An Inscription for the Second Psalm. Gregory of Nyssa: The first psalm lacks an inscription. For the aim of what is said in it is obvious to the readers, namely, that it is an introduction to philosophy in that it advises separation from evil, coming to be in the good and becoming like God so far as possible. . . . The second psalm, which predicts the mystery of the gospel, is then appended, that we might be without impiety. Consequently, in a sense, the first psalm is an inscription of the second, for the latter speaks of the one who through flesh was begotten today because of us. (Now "today" is a division of time, but because the Son is always from the Father and in the Father, he is also God.) It also speaks of those not ruled by a king, who had been listed among the Gentiles because they did not serve God. These lived under their own laws, or rather without laws, since they did not accept the divine law but cast the yoke from themselves. (Now by "yoke" he means the commandment.) But when the kingdom that excels everything comes on them, those who once were without a master become the inheritance of God through faith in the one who was begotten today. I mean this one who was appointed king over them. And when they themselves have been begotten, they too become kings. When the rod of iron, that is, the unchangeable power, smashed that which was made of earth and clay, it transformed them into the undefiled nature, having taught them that trusting in him alone is blessed. Although this is the meaning that we have expounded of this psalm, one who wishes can test our opinion by means of the divine words themselves to see if what we have said fits with the inspired Scripture. On the Inscriptions of the Psalms 2.8.74-75.[2]

The Folly of Opposing Christ. Theodoret of Cyr: [The words of the psalm] come from someone deploring and censuring folly. . . . Despite their conspiring together and hatching a tawdry plot for the murder of the Lord, their schemes all came to nothing, as they were unable to consign to oblivion the one crucified by them: on the third day he rose again and took possession of the world. Commentary on the Psalms 2.1.[3]

All Nations Joined in Opposition. Eusebius of Caesarea: The leaders of the nations throughout the whole world and the kings of the earth who have held dominion at various times have all been drawn into this impious alliance together, holding on to whatever insult or for whatever reason, or having suffered whatever offense, so that they devise treacheries, they enter into the wicked counsel against the Lord of the universe and God the King and against his anointed one. Commentary on Psalms 2.2.[4]

---

[1]FC 101:52. [2]GNTIP 143-44**. [3]FC 101:52. [4]PG 23:81.

CHRIST AND THE FATHER. ORIGEN: They rage, therefore, and dwell on worthless ideas and have gathered themselves and stand united together. Not only by their appearance have they moved the crowds against Christ, but whatever has been done by them is counted as if they had assailed the Father. So, it is said that these had turned against the Lord and his anointed. SELECTIONS FROM THE PSALMS 2.1-2.[5]

2:4 The Lord Laughs

HE LAUGHS THROUGH THE SAINTS. AUGUSTINE: None of this is to be understood in a bodily sense, as though God laughed with his cheeks or expressed mockery with his nose; it must be referred to the capacity that he gives to his saints. They foresee what is to come, that the name of Christ and his lordship will spread to future generations and be acknowledged among the nations; and so they are enabled to understand that those others have devised futile schemes. This capacity whereby such things are foreseen is God's laughter and derision. EXPOSITIONS OF THE PSALMS 2.3.[6]

2:5 In God's Wrath

GOD'S ANGER MANIFESTED AS EMOTION IN THE JUST. AUGUSTINE: The Lord God's anger and rage should not be thought of as any disturbance in his mind but as the power by which he most justly punishes, for the whole creation is subjected to him and at his service. . . . God's anger is the emotion that occurs in the mind of someone who knows God's law, when it sees that same law being transgressed by a sinner. Through this emotion in the souls of the just many things are avenged. God's anger could also reasonably be interpreted as the very darkening of the mind that befalls those who transgress God's law. EXPOSITIONS OF THE PSALMS 2.4.[7]

GOD'S ANGER MANIFESTED AS RETRIBUTION. CASSIODORUS: God judges calmly and

confounds without abandoning his fatherly love. He does not grow heated through some mounting emotion against the wicked but withdraws from them the impact of his grace. So, retribution to sinners is termed God's anger. The blessed Godhead does not experience emotions but continues always eternal and immovable. But such a change of mood befits human frailty, so that a person becomes sad after being glad, angry after being peaceable, hostile after being well-disposed. "Then shall he speak" marks the time when he shall come to judge the world. So the words *anger* and *rage* are rightly used, since obstinate sinners are accorded all that is appropriate to their deserts. EXPLANATION OF THE PSALMS 2.6.[8]

GOD'S WRATH CONDITIONAL ON REPENTANCE. ORIGEN: These are words of destruction that are pronounced in anger. Moreover, the evils that God had said he was going to inflict, he promises that he will withdraw if the listeners will become penitent. God in his anger spoke through Jonah to the Ninevites,[9] and since they repented in ash and sackcloth, they endured nothing of those things about which they had heard. Actually, God knew beforehand when he sent Jonah that they were going to repent if he sent Jonah for their deliverance. Right now he also is speaking deliverance to those sinners who are in his wrath. For it did not say, "He will punish those in his wrath even if they will repent." SELECTIONS FROM THE PSALMS 2.5.[10]

2:6 King on Zion

HE REFERS THEM TO CHRIST. JEROME: The first four verses are spoken by a prophet or an angel wondering why human rashness had risen up against the Son of God. From the fifth verse, though, the Lord himself responds, exhorting the Gentiles and all the people from the Jews

---

[5]PG 12:1104. [6]*WSA* 3 15:71*. [7]*WSA* 3 15:72*. [8]ACW 51:61. [9]Jon 3. [10]PG 12:1105.

who are going to believe in him, so that they may loosen the binding chains and cast off the heavy burden of the law that their own ancestors were unable to carry, so they may follow him whose yoke is easy, and burden light.[11] BRIEF COMMENTARY ON PSALMS 2.[12]

CHRIST'S KINGSHIP. THEODORET OF CYR: [This] verse . . . is expressed in human fashion: as God he possesses his kingship by nature, as human he receives it by election. COMMENTARY ON THE PSALMS 2.7.[13]

THE WORD OF GOD, ALREADY SOVEREIGN. THEODORE OF MOPSUESTIA: Truly, God did not establish the Word as King at that time, whose power did not just begin at a point but who was and always is powerful, who as in his nature had power to create whatever he wished; so also in his nature he had power rightly so to rule over all things that were made by him. COMMENTARY ON PSALMS 2.6.[14]

2:7 Begotten of God

AN ADDRESS PROPER TO THE INCARNATION. CYRIL OF ALEXANDRIA: The word *today* indicates the present time in which he was made in the flesh—he who nevertheless in his own nature was the Lord of everything. John testifies to this,[15] that he came among his own, calling the world his own. Having been called into a kingdom in accordance with his accustomed glory, he said, "I have been made king by him," that is, by God the Father. Furthermore, he fulfilled this by being made the Son in his humanity even if then he was the Son in his own nature. He smoothed the way for human nature to participate in adoption, and he called to himself people oppressed by the tyranny of sin. Just as we, since we are weighted down by curse and death, have received the evils of the transgressions of Adam like a certain inheritance handed across the generations to the whole universe from the ancestors, so also the splendid gifts of Christ flow down

to the generations of humankind into the whole universe. The Only Begotten receives them not wholly for himself but for us. He is fully God as to his nature, nor does he lack anything whatever. He himself becomes richer than all creation with good things from above. EXPOSITION OF THE PSALMS 2.7.[16]

THE WORD IS THE ONLY-BEGOTTEN SON. THEODORET OF CYR: To be sure, God the Word had the name "only-begotten Son" before the ages as connatural with his condition, yet while still possessing the title of the Son as God, he also receives it as human being. Hence in the present psalm he added the words [of this verse]. Now no one who believes the teaching of the divine Spirit would apply this verse to the divinity of Christ the Lord. In fact, let us listen in this regard to the God of all speaking through David, "From the womb before the morning star I begot you."[17] So as man he both receives this verse and hears what follows. COMMENTARY ON THE PSALMS 2.7.[18]

ETERNAL GENERATION. ORIGEN: There is no evening of God possible and, I think, no morning, but the time, if I may put it this way, which is coextensive with his unoriginated and eternal life, is today for him, the day in which the Son has been begotten. Consequently neither the beginning nor the day of his generation is to be found. COMMENTARY ON THE GOSPEL OF JOHN 1.204.[19]

THE ETERNAL GENERATION OF THE WISDOM OF GOD. AUGUSTINE: In eternity there is nothing that is past, as though it had ceased to be, nor future, as though not yet in existence; there is present only, because whatever is eternal always is. By this phrase, "today have I begotten you," the most true and catholic faith proclaims the eternal generation of the Power and Wisdom

---

[11]Mt 11:29. [12]CCL 72:181. [13]FC 101:55. [14]CCL 88A:13. [15]Jn 1:1, 11. [16]PG 69:721. [17]Ps 110:3. [18]FC 101:56. [19]FC 80:74.

of God, who is the only-begotten Son. EXPOSITIONS OF THE PSALMS 2.6.[20]

BEGOTTEN FROM ETERNITY. AUGUSTINE: Begotten from the eternal Father, begotten from eternity, begotten in eternity, with no beginning, with no ending, with no space of extension, because he is what is, because he himself is who is. HOMILIES ON 1 JOHN 2.5.[21]

THE NATIVITY. CASSIODORUS: "I have begotten you" signifies the nativity, of which Isaiah wrote, "Who shall declare his generation?"[22] He is Light from Light, Almighty from Almighty, true God from true God, from whom and through whom and in whom are all things. EXPLANATION OF THE PSALMS 2.8.[23]

BORN IN THOSE WHO COME TO KNOW GOD. METHODIUS: He willed that he who existed before the ages in heaven should be begotten on the earth—that is, that he who was before unknown should be made known. Now, certainly, Christ has never yet been born in those people who have never perceived the manifold wisdom of God—that is, has never been known, has never been manifested, has never appeared to them. But if these also should perceive the mystery of grace, then in them too, when they were converted and believed, he would be born in knowledge and understanding. BANQUET OF THE TEN VIRGINS 8.9.[24]

2:8 Ask of Me

ASK IN ORDER TO RECEIVE. ORIGEN: It may perhaps be a dogma of some kind that no one receives a divine gift who does not request it. The Father, indeed, through the psalm, urges the Savior to ask that it may be given to him, as the Son teaches us when he says, "The Lord said to me, You are my son; ask from me, and I will give you the Gentiles as your inheritance and the ends of the earth as your possession." And the Savior says, "Ask and it will be given to you . . .

for everyone who asks receives."[25] COMMENTARY ON THE GOSPEL OF JOHN 13.5.[26]

THIS APPLIES TO THE ECONOMY OF THE SON. AUGUSTINE: In contrast to the preceding verse, this one is to be understood in a temporal sense, of the manhood he took on himself, he who offered himself as a sacrifice to supersede all sacrifices and intercedes for us still.[27] The words "ask of me," then, may be referred to the whole temporal dispensation made for the benefit of the human race, namely, that the nations are to be joined to the name of Christ and so redeemed from death and become God's possession. "I will give you the nations as your heritage" means "May you possess them for their salvation, and may they bear for you spiritual fruit." EXPOSITIONS OF THE PSALMS 2.7.[28]

THIS IS OUR SALVATION. LEO THE GREAT: Therefore, let us rejoice in the day of our salvation, dearly beloved. We have been taken up through the new covenant into participation with him who was told by the Father through a prophet, "You are my Son; this day I have begotten you. Ask it of me, and I will give you the nations for your inheritance and the ends of the earth for your possession." Let us glory, therefore, in the mercy of the one adopting us. SERMON 29.3.[29]

WHAT IS GIVEN TO THE PEOPLE. DIDYMUS THE BLIND: The words, therefore, "Ask of me, and I will give to you," are spoken for our sake, not for the Son's. They indicate that something is given not to the Son but to the peoples who belong to him. FRAGMENTS ON THE PSALMS 2.8.[30]

JEWS AND GENTILES. THEODORET OF CYR: Now it is possible to discover an appropriate fulfillment for this prophecy, too: the number

[20]WSA 3 15:73*. [21]FC 92:149. [22]Is 53:8. [23]ACW 51:62. [24]ANF 6:338*. [25]Mt 7:7-8. [26]FC 89:70. [27]Rom 8:34. [28]WSA 3 15:73*. [29]FC 93:124. [30]PG 39:1160.

of the Jews who came to faith was not only the 12 apostles but was as well the 70 disciples, the 120 whom blessed Peter addressed in assembly,[31] the 500 to whom he appeared on one occasion after the resurrection according to the statement of the divinely inspired Paul,[32] the 3,000 and the 5,000 that the chief of the apostles made his catch through addressing them and the many myriads of whom the mighty James exclaimed, "You see, brother, what countless numbers of Jewish believers there are." These, to be sure, and in addition to them those of the Jews throughout the whole world who have come to faith he declares a holy people, and through them he takes possession of all the nations, thus fulfilling the prophecy in the words "Rejoice, nations, with his people." In addition to this, however, he fulfills also his own prophecy, which he made in regard to the Jews in the words, "Now, I have other sheep that do not belong to this fold. Those, too, I must gather; they will hear my voice, and there will be one flock, one shepherd."[33] This, too, he says in the present psalm. But it occurs to me to lament the faithlessness of the [unbelieving] Jews, who though hearing the prophecy that made specific mention of the ends of the earth, and realizing that none of their kings had had such sway, but only Christ the Lord, David's offspring in the flesh, blind the eyes of their mind according to the prophecy that says, "They grope about, as blind people do for the wall, and not as they will do who have the benefit of eyesight."[34] COMMENTARY ON THE PSALMS 2.9-10.[35]

2:9 The Rod and the Crushed Pot

CRUSHED TO BE RE-FORMED. THEODORE OF MOPSUESTIA: Are not, therefore, those words that were spoken by blessed David appropriately applied to the Lord whose kingdom extends to the farthest outposts of the earth and the whole world? [It is he] who, like the rod, threatens and punishes the broken condition of the nations and of the Jews, not in order to destroy them but in

order to bring them back together and reshape them, as when the old man is put off and the new man takes his place through the sacrament of baptism. David really said this: "just like a pot of clay you will break them," showing the parallel, since by their contrition there had been no destruction, but a renewal was about to follow. This is likened to the intention of every potter: that the vases, if they do not follow the will and hand of the one making them, while they are yet new and not hardened by the kiln, the potter breaks them and puts them back on the wheel to be re-formed. COMMENTARY ON PSALMS 2.9.[36]

DESTRUCTION OF THE OLD MAN. AUGUSTINE: You will dash to pieces in them earthly desires and the muddy preoccupations of the old man and whatever has been contracted or implanted from the slime of sin. EXPOSITIONS OF THE PSALMS 2.8.[37]

THE ROD OF CORRECTION. AUGUSTINE: Remember the rod of correction and discipline, and do not get conceited and proud when you have been filled with the good things of God's gifts and start grumbling against him; because in his anger he will shatter you with it like a potter's vessel. SERMON 366.6.[38]

CRUSHED TO BE AN INHERITANCE. ORIGEN: It is necessary to consider how the Father gave the nations to the Son as an inheritance and the ends of the earth as a possession. He says to him, "You will break them like a clay pot." For who gives an inheritance so that it may be broken by the heir? It must be demonstrated from Scripture, therefore, how the contrition of certain people proved so beneficial. We find in the fiftieth psalm, "Having brought a spiritual sacrifice to God, a contrite and humble heart God will not despise."[39] And it is said in another prophecy as instruction, "You will wail

---

[31]Acts 1:15. [32]1 Cor 15:6. [33]Jn 10:16. [34]Is 59:10. [35]FC 101:57-58. [36]CCL 88A:16. [37]WSA 3 15:73. [38]WSA 3 10:292*. [39]Ps 50:17 (50:19 LXX).

for the brokenness of your spirit."[40] There is a spirit within us, therefore, that it is necessary to destroy in order that it may become a contrite sacrifice to God. SELECTIONS FROM THE PSALMS 2.9.[41]

2:10-12 Warning to the Kings of the Earth

HOW KINGS SERVE THE LORD. AUGUSTINE: It is to your [you kings of the earth] advantage that you be subject to him by whom understanding and instruction are given to you. It is also to your advantage not to exercise lordship irresponsibly but to serve the Lord of all with reverence and rejoice in most certain and most pure blessedness while exercising due caution and consideration to avoid falling away from it through pride. EXPOSITIONS OF THE PSALMS 2.9.[42]

KINGS SHOULD HONOR GOD'S COMMANDMENTS. AUGUSTINE: How, then, do kings serve the Lord with fear except by forbidding and restraining with religious severity all acts committed against the commandments of the Lord? A sovereign serves God one way as man, another way as king: he serves him as man by living according to faith; he serves him as king by exerting the necessary strength to sanction laws that command goodness and prohibit its opposite. It was thus that Hezekiah served him by destroying the groves and temples of idols and the high places that had been set up contrary to the commandments of God; thus Josiah served him by performing similar acts; thus the king of the Ninevites served him by compelling the whole city to appease the Lord; thus Darius served him by giving Daniel power to break the idol and by feeding his enemies to the lions; thus Nebuchanezzar . . . served him when he restrained all his subjects from blaspheming God by a terrible penalty. It is thus that kings serve the Lord as kings when they perform acts in his service that none but kings can perform. LETTERS 185.19.[43]

SERVICE AT ALL TIMES. EVAGRIUS OF PONTUS: If you remember the Judge only when you are in difficulties as one who inspires fear and who is incorruptibly honest, then you have not as yet learned to "serve the Lord in fear and to rejoice in him with trembling." For understand this point well: one is to worship him even in spiritual relaxations and in times of good cheer with even more piety and reverence. CHAPTERS ON PRAYER 143.[44]

DEVOTION, NOT COERCION. THEODORE OF MOPSUESTIA: He wants devotion, not coercion . . . because to obey is more sublime than to yield simply to duty. COMMENTARY ON PSALMS 2.11.[45]

PRECAUTION IN ENTERTAINMENT. APOSTOLIC CONSTITUTIONS: Even your very rejoicings therefore ought to be done with fear and trembling, for a Christian who is faithful ought to repeat neither a heathen hymn nor an obscene song, because he will be obliged by that hymn to make mention of the idolatrous names of demons; and instead of the Holy Spirit, the wicked one will enter into him. CONSTITUTIONS OF THE HOLY APOSTLES 5.2.10.[46]

KEY TO HOLINESS. PETER CHRYSOLOGUS: He who remains in the fear of God remains in holiness. SERMON 80.[47]

---

[40]Is 65:14. [41]PG 12:1109. [42]WSA 3 15:74. [43]FC 30:160*. [44]CS 4:78. [45]CCL 88A:17. [46]ANF 7:442. [47]FC 17:130

3:1-8 PRAYER FOR DELIVERANCE

If persecuted by your own people,

and you have a whole crowd against you, say Psalm 3.

ATHANASIUS ON THE INTERPRETATION OF THE PSALMS 15 [OIP 66]

*A Psalm of David, when he fled
from Absalom his son.*

*¹O LORD, how many are my foes!
Many are rising against me;
²many are saying of me,
there is no help for him in God.*   Selah

*³But thou, O LORD, art a shield about me,
my glory, and the lifter of my head.
⁴I cry aloud to the LORD,
and he answers me from his holy hill.*
                                              Selah
⁵I lie down and sleep;

*I wake again, for the LORD sustains me.
⁶I am not afraid of ten thousands of people
who have set themselves against me round
about.*

*⁷Arise, O LORD!
Deliver me, O my God!
For thou dost smite all my enemies on the
cheek,
thou dost break the teeth of the wicked.*

*⁸Deliverance belongs to the LORD;
thy blessing be upon thy people!*   Selah

OVERVIEW: The third psalm makes reference to David, but it may be best to see it as having multiple references (JEROME), with some of the language especially suited to the Lord's passion and resurrection (AUGUSTINE). David's example shows that domestic trouble is a result of sin (ASTERIUS THE HOMILIST). However, the one who lives for Christ often has enemies without cause (DIDYMUS). Opposition to Christ, both past and present, sometimes takes the form of teachings that are opposed to his (ORIGEN). This is the first psalm in which we encounter the word Selah. Selah means either a change of thought (GREGORY OF NYSSA) or a change in rhythm and style (DIODORE).

The Lord is the glory of the saints (ORIGEN), who trust in God alone (THEODORET). He is our "head" who is lifted up (DIDYMUS). We have strength from our hope in him (THEODORE OF

MOPSUESTIA). Recalling the second psalm, the Lord hears from his holy mountain (EUSEBIUS) as faith turns to God without any delay (THEODORE OF MOPSUESTIA). The psalm goes on to speak of the resurrection of Christ (AUGUSTINE) and our resurrection with him (EUSEBIUS). The Father is the agent of resurrection, but Christ's own will is not excluded (AUGUSTINE).

An experienced faith does not despair of God's help (THEODORE OF MOPSUESTIA). Faith casts out fear (ORIGEN), as the Lord exemplifies, foreknowing the cross and the resurrection (CASSIODORUS), confident there would be no hindrance of the victory (EUSEBIUS). By use of a metaphor (CASSIODORUS), the psalmist calls on God to arise. The psalmist is confident he has been saved by grace through faith (EUSEBIUS) and that God has vindicated him by breaking the teeth of sinners, that is, their words and deeds (AMMONIUS OF ALEXANDRIA), their fleshly thoughts (EVAGRIUS), in fact, all their strength (THEODORET), as seen especially in their leaders against whom the church contends teeth to teeth (AUGUSTINE). God is our salvation and gives salvation to us (AUGUSTINE), which is received by faith (CASSIODORUS). The coming of the Son of God and his peace is our blessing (DIDYMUS, THEODORE OF MOPSUESTIA).

Superscription: *By David, in Flight from Absalom*

MULTIPLE REFERENTS. JEROME: This psalm can pertain to David or to Christ, and through him to all the saints. BRIEF COMMENTARY ON PSALMS 3.[1]

THE LORD'S PASSION AND RESURRECTION. AUGUSTINE: That this psalm should be understood as spoken in the person of Christ is strongly suggested by the words "I rested, and fell asleep, and I arose because the Lord will uphold me."[2] For this seems more in tune with the Lord's passion and resurrection than with the particular story in which we are told about David's flight from the face of his own son who was at loggerheads with him. EXPOSITIONS OF THE PSALMS 3.1.[3]

3:1-2 Many Foes

SIN BRINGS TROUBLE. ASTERIUS THE HOMILIST: It is shown in various statements and examples of holy Scripture that God has used domestic disputes, rebellion and multiple disasters in the punishment of sin. The purpose of David was to chastise and to edify life through the psalm, so that no one would do evil, or violate the law of God or experience what befalls a sinner. David was fleeing his son because he had acted unchastely; he was fleeing his son because he had violated purity in marriage; he was fleeing his son because he had departed from the law of God, which says, "You shall not kill; you shall

not commit adultery."[4] . . . Many today wage wars in their homes; one is opposed by his wife, another is besieged by his son; one is ruled by a brother, and another by a slave; and each one is in anguish and afflicted. He fights, wages war and is harassed by war, and no one can understand why. But if he had not planted the seeds of sin, it would have never happened that thorny plants and prickly bushes would grow up in his home; if he had not hidden the glare of his sins, his home would not burn. HOMILIES ON THE PSALMS 3.2.[5]

ENEMIES WITHOUT CAUSE. DIDYMUS THE BLIND: He who offers no grounds for hate and enmity may have enemies for no reason. Such are all who endure persecution because they live righteously for Jesus Christ.[6] To these the Savior says, "Blessed are you when people revile you and when liars speak evil against you on account of me."[7] This is what happened when David had many enemies for no reason such as Saul and Absalom and those who accompanied them. For they attacked without cause him who was a righteous man and had often shown them much goodness and gentleness. FRAGMENTS ON THE PSALMS 3.8.[8]

OPPOSITION TO CHRIST, THEN AND NOW. ORIGEN: We readily accept this psalm as spoken from the person of David, as we have noted in its title. According to history, certain men were hurting David, many of whom as their number increased were joining themselves to Absalom. . . . Those who were oppressing the Savior were Jews who were shouting, "Away with him; away with him!"[9] Judas the betrayer and Caiphas rose up against him. The ones who said that there was no deliverance of his life were the same ones passing by him at the time of his suffering who said, "Come down from the cross and we will believe you.". . . But, one may also understand this passage in this way: all the rulers and teachers of

---

[1]CCL 72:183. [2]Ps 3:5. [3]WSA 3 15:76. [4]Ex 20:13-14. [5]TLG 2061.001, 3.2.7. [6]2 Tim 3:12. [7]Mt 5:11. [8]PG 39:1164. [9]Jn 19:15.

subjects that are foreign to the decrees of Christ who have come against him. The people who cling to them and follow their teaching cause him trial. Finally, they who, neither teaching contrary matters nor instructed by false teaching, believe that there is no divine nature in the teaching of Christ, they say there is no salvation of the soul in God. They say that there is not anything that promises salvation either in the word of his teaching or the historical signs that he relates concerning his advent. Selections from the Psalms 3.2-3.[10]

Thoughts on the Meaning of Selah. Gregory of Nyssa: When the great David served as interpreter for the Spirit, he related in his song the things that he had previously learned, and if he was taught something additional while he was speaking, he submitted to the Spirit who was making the hearing of his soul resound and stopped the music, and when he was filled with these thoughts he related these matters, again entwining the words with the melody. One who has comprehended the term in a definition might say, then, that *diapsalma* is a pause that occurs suddenly in the midst of the singing of a psalm in order to receive an additional thought that is being introduced from God. Or, one might rather define it as follows. *Diapsalma* is a teaching from the Spirit that occurs in a mysterious manner in the soul, when the attention given to this new thought impedes the continuity of the song. . . . In the third psalm he spoke first about the distress and hardship that occurred when his enemies "rose up against" him. Then he separated that part with the *diapsalma* and put his trust in the one who was causing that sound of salvation to resound mysteriously in him and said, "But you, Lord, are my protector, my glory, and the lifter up of my head." Again, when he has stopped the music, saying, in accordance with that gracious voice that he has made his own, "I cried to the Lord with my voice, and he heard me from his holy mountain," he is taught

what the solution is for the hardship that is common to human ills. And after he has been taught the mystery related to the passion of the Lord in the sudden illumination of the Spirit, he assumes the character of the Lord and says, "I lay down and slept, and I was raised, because the Lord will help me." On the Inscriptions of the Psalms 2.10.115-16, 121-22.[11]

A Change in Rhythm and Style. Diodore of Tarsus: It is also necessary to indicate the difference between the term *diapsalma* and the song of the *diapsalma*, or in short what their meaning is. While *diapsalma* means a change of tune and alteration of rhythm, then, and not a shift in thought, as some commentators believed, so does song of the *diapsalma*, since frequently singers changed the tunes according to the availability of instruments. So it indicates alternation in styles and rhythms, not change in ideas. It is, in fact, ridiculous to mention anything else, though some commentators have come up with extraordinary notions, like the Spirit coming on the author at one time and withdrawing at another, which did not happen—perish the thought. I mean, the Holy Spirit did not grant the authors the grace of addressing the text in the manner the demons do to those unaware of what they are saying; rather, he implanted in their mind complete understanding, and on receiving this knowledge they gave voice to it to the extent of their capability, not uttering what they did not understand in the manner of the seers but having complete knowledge of the force of their words. As I said, therefore, the occurrences of *diapsalma* and songs of *diapsalma* are changes in rhythms and styles, not alterations in ideas. The movement of thought also reveals this: after the reference *diapsalma* you never find the following thought in opposition to what precedes, being instead sequential and consistent. Hence it is clear that the occurrence midstream of *diapsalma* involved no interruption to the

---

[10]PG 12:1120. [11]GNTIP 158-60.

thought of the text, instead perhaps altering the rhythm in keeping with the norms of music and rhythm applying at the time. COMMENTARY ON PSALMS 3.[12]

3:3 My Glory

THE GLORY OF THE SAINTS. ORIGEN: Certainly, people place their glory in various places, some in their country, some in family line, some in beauty, some in the strength of their bodies and in their skill of competing in the contest, being very elated they have overcome these people or those by their physical struggling. And why is it necessary to recount all the things through which those unknown gods are glorified, "whose glory is in their shame,"[13] as the apostle said? God is the glory of the saint who trusts him, glory, I say, not blindly credited but credited through faith that is reckoned as righteousness, through which one is enabled to see the signs of a present God and participate in his strength. So, God was the glory of Moses who loved the prophet so much that he revealed himself to the point of showing his face both before all the Hebrew people and before the Egyptians. God was the glory of the prophet Elijah, who revived the son of the widow and begged for the rain to be held back, and who continually was heard. God was speaking truth, therefore, when he said, "I will only honor them honoring me."[14] God is the glory of them who are magnified in their strength, which no one other than the Father places in them, who hand themselves over to him for sustaining their souls. SELECTIONS FROM THE PSALMS 3.4.[15]

TRUST IN GOD ALONE. THEODORET OF CYR: Many, in fact, are the enemies of every kind who assail me from all sides, but more numerous are those who trouble me by their mockery and their claims that I am bereft of your providence. Yet I know that you would not persist in ignoring me, despite my many failings. On the contrary, you will raise up the one who now humbles himself

for the sin he committed and make him appear stronger than his foes. . . . I have confidence neither in kingship nor in sovereignty; instead, I trust in you to be my glory, and I expect to be quickly raised up by your right hand. COMMENTARY ON THE PSALMS 3.2.[16]

OUR HEAD IS LIFTED UP. DIDYMUS THE BLIND: Since the psalm is spoken from the person of the Lord, it must be said that even the head of him who is lifted up is of God, since really his deity is made manifest to the faithful through external demonstration. The word *head* in this place indicates "chief." Christ, therefore, the chief of holy people, deservedly is their king, and it is his head that is lifted up. FRAGMENTS ON THE PSALMS 3.4.[17]

STRENGTH FROM HOPE. THEODORE OF MOPSUESTIA: The strength of a stable spirit that is greatly tested in adversity must be considered because, since it possesses hope, even amidst the greatest anguish it does not yield. Those, I say, who mock me say such things to increase my grief. I will not stop hoping in what I have believed because you, Lord, help me as I labor. You guard my step from the danger of evil. You restore my honor and worth. COMMENTARY ON PSALMS 3.4.[18]

3:4 God Answers from His Holy Hill

THE LORD OF THE SECOND PSALM. EUSEBIUS OF CAESAREA: The preceding psalm calls to mind this mountain when it says, "I have installed my king on mount Zion, my holy mountain." Christ was the one he was speaking of, and now David bears witness that he must be heard plainly by Christ from his holy mountain. Further, he says who is going to hear him except the Lord who has been installed as king upon Zion his holy mountain? Through this statement he

---

[12]WGRW 9:11. [13]Phil 3:19. [14]1 Sam 2:30. [15]PG 12:1121-24. [16]FC 101:60-61. [17]PG 39:1164. [18]CCL 88A:18.

[David], now alone, believed that he would be forgiven, that his glory would return and that his head would be lifted up. Commentary on Psalms 3.5.[19]

Faith Does Not Delay. Theodore of Mopsuestia: It is the greatest faith that allows no hesitation for seeking the help of God for himself and that approaches with confidence of his demand. Commentary on Psalms 3.5.[20]

3:5 Lying Down and Waking

This Must Refer to Christ. Augustine: The prophetic psalms are by no means silent on the subject of [Christ's] resurrection. . . . What other meaning can be taken from these words in Psalm 3, sung in the person of Christ? . . . For, unless one sees in this sleep the death, and in this awaking the resurrection of Christ thus prophesied, one is reduced to the silly supposition that the prophet wished to communicate to us the really remarkable news that he himself fell asleep and later on woke up! City of God 17.18.[21]

Revelation of Resurrection. Eusebius of Caesarea: As in the previous psalm so here the future is prophesied. . . . "I lie down, and I sleep" is spoken prophetically, namely, I will lie down, I will sleep, I will rise up, because you, Oh Lord, are my sustainer, my glory and the lifter of my head. . . . For "sleep" indicates death, concerning which the future is prophesied for us. It refers to the time of the life of the Savior, which when it was finished, prophecy came to an end; when, namely, the Son of man Christ descended even to hell and the Savior was clearly shown to the captives who were awaiting destruction; so as in the time of his resurrection from death many bodies of the saints who had been sleeping will live again with him, in whom was the likeness of the spirit of David. Commentary on Psalms 3.6.[22]

Christ's Will Not Excluded. Augustine:

Do not let these words, where he says, "since the Lord took me up," strike your minds as meaning that Christ himself did not raise up his own body. The Father raised him up, and he also raised himself up. How shall we prove to you that he raised himself up? Call to mind what he said to the Jews: "Pull down this temple, and in three days I will raise it up."[23] Sermon 305.3.[24]

3:6 Not Afraid

An Experienced Faith. Theodore of Mopsuestia: In this verse the psalmist is not moved by his own trials to the point of despairing of the help of God, nor is he dissuaded from a position of faith by words of reproach. He, having learned by experience the fullness of previous help, cries out most confidently after the kindnesses of God toward him through which he is freed from all of the entangling of his troubles: "I will not fear ten thousands surrounding me." Commentary on Psalms 3.7.[25]

Faith Casts Out Fear. Origen: The verse clearly teaches that the one who comes to the greatest virtue, to very great security, comes on account of faith in God. . . . The Savior, recognizing that thousands of the people of the circumcision were going to demand that he be crucified and knowing his own spirit of fearlessness (I say these things speaking in terms of the flesh), is able to say even these words. Selections from the Psalms 3.7.[26]

What the Lord Foreknew. Cassiodorus: He could not fear death, because he foreknew that it would last for only three days and that it would be of service to the world. Explanation of the Psalms 3.7.[27]

No Hindrance. Eusebius of Caesarea: He predicts that there are going to be many thou-

---

[19]PG 23:96. [20]CCL 88A:19. [21]FC 24:68-69. [22]PG 23:96. [23]Jn 2:19. [24]WSA 3 8:321. [25]CCL 88A:19. [26]PG 12:1129. [27]ACW 51:71.

sands of adversaries who will wish to hinder the resurrection of the saints because they are jealous of their salvation: which ones I will regard as nothing, he said. I have trusted my defender, the victor over death, who, after the bronze gates were torn down and the iron bolts thoroughly broken, opened the gates of death that had been closed for ages, and with those people known to him, from which number was David, he prepared for the resurrection life. COMMENTARY ON PSALMS 3.7.[28]

3:7 Arise, O Lord!

METAPHORICAL LANGUAGE. CASSIODORUS: Not that God is roused from sleep or rest, but the divine Scriptures in explanation of some matter often make metaphorical statements about God after our manner of behavior, a metaphor being an expression translated from its own sphere to one not its own. EXPLANATION OF THE PSALMS 3.8.[29]

SAVED BY GRACE THROUGH FAITH. EUSEBIUS OF CAESAREA: When he foresees his deliverance after death, he has faith that he has been saved by grace and that kindness has been granted. He is certain that this faith of some in the resurrection of the Savior is able to come to him, and consequently he prays that the resurrection of the Lord be hastened so that through it he himself will experience salvation. . . . Now, he says, you have broken the teeth of sinners; that is, their conversations and blasphemous words hurled against me you have stripped away. COMMENTARY ON PSALMS 3.8.[30]

THE WORDS AND DEEDS OF SINNERS. AMMONIUS OF ALEXANDRIA: He has struck his adversaries, he has broken the teeth of sinners; indeed, so that he may heal them again: "I will strike [he said], and again I will heal." He has broken the teeth of sinners, or, in other words, the wicked words and carnal actions, because he desires to destroy them in the inmost parts. Per-

haps he has called those same ones adversaries and sinners: since he has broken the teeth of all sinners who turned against Christ, but especially the Jews on account of unfaithfulness; those teeth about which in another psalm he says, "Those who devour my people as bread, and they do not call on the Lord."[31] He broke these teeth . . . when he arose from the dead. FRAGMENTS ON PSALMS 3.8.[32]

FLESHLY THOUGHTS. EVAGRIUS OF PONTUS: The teeth of sinners are thoughts foreign to reason coming to us on account of our nature by which our enemies approach us, just like using their teeth time after time again to devour our flesh. That is, those [are] things that spring forth from the flesh: "Manifest are the works of the flesh,"[33] as the apostle says. NOTES ON THE PSALMS 3.8.[34]

LOSS OF STRENGTH. THEODORET OF CYR: The phrase "breaking the teeth of sinners," that is to say, depriving them of all strength, is by comparison with wild beasts, which when bereft of their teeth are quite undaunting and open to attack. COMMENTARY ON THE PSALMS 3.4.[35]

TEETH TO TEETH. AUGUSTINE: The phrase "the teeth of sinners" can also be understood as those sinful leaders by whose authority a person is cut off from the community of those who live upright lives and is incorporated, so to speak, into those who live corruptly. Opposed to these teeth are the teeth of the church, by whose authority believers are cut clean away from the error of the heathen and of a whole range of heterodox opinions and are brought over into that society that is Christ's body. Peter was told to slaughter animals and eat them with teeth like this, which means to kill in the Gentiles what they were and changed it into what he himself was. . . . "You have broken the teeth of sinners," should,

---

[28]PG 23:97. [29]ACW 51:71. [30]PG 23:97, 100. [31]Ps 14:4 (13:4 LXX). [32]PG 85:1364. [33]Gal 5:19. [34]PG 12:1132. [35]FC 101:62.

therefore, be understood in the sense, "you have brought to nothing the chief sinners, by striking down all who oppose me without good cause." For it was the leaders who, according to the Gospel story, persecuted him, while the inferior rabble held him in honor. EXPOSITIONS OF THE PSALMS 3.7.[36]

3:8 Deliverance Belongs to the Lord

HE IS AND GIVES SALVATION. AUGUSTINE: He who gives salvation is called "the salvation of the Lord," and he is likewise our salvation who received him. ON THE TRINITY 5.14.15.[37]

RECEIVED BY FAITH. CASSIODORUS: By this one sentence he both enjoined on people what they must believe and promised what they can receive

from him. EXPLANATION OF THE PSALMS 3.9.[38]

THE COMING OF THE SON. DIDYMUS THE BLIND: What is the blessing to people who overcome unless it is the will of the Father concerning the coming of his Son into the world? FRAGMENTS ON THE PSALMS 3.9.[39]

PEACE. THEODORE OF MOPSUESTIA: What is this blessing of the Lord? Without a doubt it is peace, just as Scripture says in many places: "Peace be over Israel."[40] Through these words he wishes to show that in the place of blessing peace is conferred on the people. COMMENTARY ON PSALMS 3.9.[41]

---

[36]WSA 3 15:80-81. [37]FC 45:193. [38]ACW 51:72*. [39]PG 39:1164. [40]Ps 125:5 (124:5 LXX). [41]CCL 88A:20-21.

4:1-8 DELIVERANCE AND THANKSGIVING

If after being deeply troubled, you cried out to the Lord and your prayer was heard and now you wish to give thanks, sing Psalm 4.

ATHANASIUS ON THE INTERPRETATION OF THE PSALMS 15 [OIP 66]

To the choirmaster: with stringed instruments*. A Psalm of David.

¹Answer me when I call, O God of my right!
Thou hast given me room when I was in distress.
Be gracious to me, and hear my prayer.

²O men, how long shall my honor suffer shame?

How long will you love vain words, and seek after lies? Selah
³But know that the LORD has set apart† the godly for himself;
the LORD hears when I call to him.

⁴Be angry, but sin not;
commune with your own hearts on your beds, and be silent. Selah
⁵Offer right sacrifices,
and put your trust in the LORD.

^{6}There are many who say, "O that we might
     see some good!
  Lift up the light of thy countenance upon
     us, O LORD!"
^{7}Thou hast put more joy in my heart

than they have when their grain and wine
     abound.

^{8}In peace I will both lie down and sleep;
  for thou alone, O LORD, makest me dwell
     in safety.

* LXX *for the end*   † LXX *has made marvelous*

OVERVIEW: The title, "with instruments," indicates a hymn that symbolizes the measured harmony of thought and action (DIDYMUS). "For the end" indicates the victory or victories we have in Christ (ORIGEN, GREGORY OF NYSSA).

We need to give attention to how we pray (CHRYSOSTOM), noting that prayer is a matter of faith (ORIGEN) and that the righteous, that is, those who are partakers of Christ (ORIGEN), never have enough of prayer (THEODORET). David found relief through prayer and experienced a double grace: he was heard and was heard quickly (ASTERIUS THE HOMILIST). The resourcefulness of God met his need (CHRYSOSTOM) with a more generous providence (DIODORE). While the difficulty may remain, God sometimes grants the courage needed to face it (DIDYMUS), increased understanding of the situation (EVAGRIUS), an enlarged heart (AUGUSTINE), filled with joy by the presence of his Word (ORIGEN). Such mercies are granted by God's kindness, not on the basis of our merit (THEODORE OF MOPSUESTIA).

Many, however, are prone to deceitful thoughts about divine providence (DIODORE), focusing on nonrealities (CHRYSOSTOM) and seeking happiness in lies (AUGUSTINE). Lying is unbecoming to Christians (ASTERIUS THE HOMILIST). True blessing can only be found in truth (AUGUSTINE). And so, the only way to be truly happy in times of distress is to turn to the Lord (EUSEBIUS), identify with Christ in his death and rise in the blessedness of his life (AUGUSTINE). Not only will we be victorious in Christ, but distinguished in victory (THEODORET).

The voice God hears comes from the inner heart and seeks the things of God (ORIGEN). God

hears such prayer as often as we pray (THEODORE OF MOPSUESTIA). God does not hear inappropriate requests, for which we should be glad, and we should never be discouraged by what seems to be a delay (CHRYSOSTOM). It should be a rule for us to always repent of sin and seek God in prayer (ASTERIUS THE HOMILIST).

We should examine ourselves regarding anger (THEODORE OF MOPSUESTIA), recognizing that the providence of God is often beyond our understanding (DIODORE) and even when anger seems justified, moderation is just and beneficial for human society (LACTANTIUS). Those in ruling positions should especially take note (AMBROSE). There is a right and a wrong anger (CHRYSOSTOM), and there are two ways to understand the psalmist's injunction: do not sin in your anger at others, but also, turn your anger against your own sin and repent (AUGUSTINE, CASSIODORUS). We need to keep our mouths shut (AMBROSE), recognizing the better wisdom (AMBROSE), the Christian response of ending anger completely (JEROME).

The practice of nightly prayer is particularly helpful for avoiding future sins (BASIL). The bed becomes a bed of council (JOHN CASSIAN) where one examines the reason for one's actions (ORIGEN). The best gift we offer to God is a disposition of righteousness and the confidence of hope (CHRYSOSTOM). The hope is the hope of our inheritance (ORIGEN), and the sacrifice we offer is the imitation of Christ (CASSIODORUS).

Many blindly question whether there is any good in daily life (AUGUSTINE). But they are blind to the midday sun of God's providence (CHRYSOSTOM). There is a certain One who shows us God's goodness (DIDYMUS), who restores to us the radiance of God's image (BEDE) and illumines our understanding as we participate in the Light (ORIGEN). It fills our hearts with joy (ORIGEN). We rejoice in the blessings of his daily providence (DIODORE), carried by a deeper joy that goes beyond the material goods of that providence (CHRYSOSTOM). It is a joy and peace found only in Christ (AUGUSTINE), a sinless peace (CHRYSOSTOM), a peace that goes beyond the grave (EUSEBIUS, DIDYMUS).

Superscription: *Psalm of David*

A MEASURED HARMONY. DIDYMUS THE BLIND: The psalm is a hymn that is sung to an instrument, either a lyre or a psaltery. According to the spiritual or anagogical sense, the poem is a contemplation of truth that happens not only in the mind but also in music as with measured harmony. The psalm denotes actions that are done according to right reason; so as one sings he follows the way of an effective life; he sings who follows a life of contemplation. . . . Now the phrase "for the end" indicates that which is called the best because all pleasing things are appealing and must be desired. FRAGMENTS ON THE PSALMS 4, PROLOGUE.[1]

THOSE VICTORIOUS IN CHRIST. ORIGEN: Therefore, since Christ is referred to as David, the psalms that are titled "for the end" announce the end and victory of Christ. . . . Victory is granted to each one who is conquered by Christ; he overcomes the evil happening to him, and he is lifted from its midst as he is subjected to Christ. For Christ conquers no one who is unwilling but by persuasion since he is the Word of God. . . . Truly, since not only the songs of David but also of Asaph and even the sons of Korah are titled "for the end" it is not absurd for us to understand this is written about all the saints who receive the image of Christ. SELECTIONS FROM THE PSALMS 4.1.[2]

A SUCCESSION OF VICTORIES. GREGORY OF

NYSSA: After he has, at the right time, fled the one who has risen up against him (who is one in nature but becomes a multitude in evil alliance) and said, "Those who afflict me are multiplied, and many rise up against me," and everything that follows in the psalm, then the beginning of his victory occurs. . . . Victory is the end of every contest, . . . and when you once taste victory, successive victories are achieved against the enemies. ON THE INSCRIPTIONS OF THE PSALMS 2.11.143-44.[3]

4:1 *Answer Me; Hear My Call*

HOW TO PRAY. CHRYSOSTOM: Prayer is no small bond of love for God, developing in us the habit of converse with him and encouraging the pursuit of wisdom. . . . We are, however, not as aware as we should be of the benefit of prayer, for the reason that we neither apply ourselves to it with assiduity nor have recourse to it in accord with God's laws. Typically, when we converse with people of a class above us, we make sure that our appearance and gait and attire are as they should be and dialogue with them accordingly. When we approach God, by contrast, we yawn, scratch ourselves, look this way and that, pay little attention, loll on the ground, do the shopping. If on the contrary we were to approach him with due reverence and prepare ourselves to converse with him as God, then we would know even before receiving what we asked how much benefit we gain. . . . [In receiving prayer] God, after all, looks not for beauty of utterance or turn of phrase but for freshness of spirit; even if we say what just comes into our mind, we go away with our entreaties successful. . . . Often we do not even need a voice. I mean, even if you speak in your heart and call on him as you should, he will readily incline toward you even then. In this way was Moses also heard, in this way also Hannah. No soldier stands by to scare people away, no bodyguard to cut short

---

[1]PG 39:1165. [2]PG 12:1133. [3]*GNTIP* 167.

the proper moment; he is not the one to say, "Now is not a good time to make your approach, come back later." Rather, when you come, he stands listening, even if it is lunchtime, even if dinnertime, even if the worst of times, even if in the marketplace, even if on a journey, even if at sea, even if inside the courtroom before a judge, and you call on him, there is no obstacle to his yielding to your entreaty as long as you call on him as you should . . . being of sober mind and contrite spirit, approaching him in a flood of tears, seeking nothing of this life, longing for things to come, making petition for spiritual goods, not calling down curses on our enemies, bearing no grudges, banishing all disquiet from the soul, making our approach with heart broken, being humble, practicing great meekness, directing our tongues to good report, abstaining from any wicked enterprise, having nothing in common with the common enemy of the world—I mean the devil, of course. . . . This is the way you should be righteous; and being righteous you will be heard, since you have such an advocate. COMMENTARY ON THE PSALMS 4.2-3.[4]

A MATTER OF FAITH. ORIGEN: Invocation is not a matter of the voice, but it is posited . . . in solid faith. SELECTIONS FROM THE PSALMS 4.1.[5]

NEVER ENOUGH PRAYER. THEODORET OF CYR: Righteous people never have enough of prayer; instead, being in need and taking advantage of goodwill, they reap the fruit of prayer and continue offering supplication, realizing as they do the benefit coming from it. COMMENTARY ON THE PSALMS 4.2.[6]

PARTAKERS OF CHRIST. ORIGEN: The one who calls on the Lord must have true righteousness. Since Christ is righteous, the just person, the partaker of righteousness, must be a partaker of Christ. Lest saying "God of my righteousness" should give birth to pride, we can say this also: He has been made wisdom and righteousness for us, and he is our Redeemer. Consequently, to

say "God of my righteousness" would be as if you said, "God of my Lord." SELECTIONS FROM THE PSALMS 4.1.[7]

A DOUBLE GRACE. ASTERIUS THE HOMILIST: "You have made room for me in distress."[8] God has made room for [the psalmist] in two ways; one, because he heard his prayer, and two, because he heard quickly. It is a double grace not just to be heard but to be heard quickly. To be heard quickly and immediately in calamity is what he called "room," "In distress you made room for me." An unexpected calm disrupts the surge of calamity; the foaming sea is turned into a lake; the storms and tempests are changed into dew; enemies are made friends; and suppliants become givers of praise. "In distress you have made room for me." No longer as an infant do I open my mouth, for the providence of God, just like a mother, gives me food. "In distress you have made room for me." When I was longing for food, he filled me from the fruit of the earth of grain, wine and oil, so that not I alone but all those subordinate to me could enjoy them. HOMILIES ON THE PSALMS 5.13.[9]

THE RESOURCEFULNESS OF GOD. CHRYSOSTOM: The inventiveness and resourcefulness of God are demonstrated particularly in this, not only in his bringing on tribulations but also in providing great relief from it while they linger. This also demonstrates God's power; it renders the sufferers more resigned when there is space for consoling the distressed spirit; the distress is not relieved, stiffening as it does the lax spirit and ridding it of indifference. COMMENTARY ON THE PSALMS 4.3.[10]

A MORE GENEROUS PROVIDENCE. DIODORE OF TARSUS: There are therefore two forms of tribulation: we either inflict tribulations and sufferings on ourselves as a result of mismanage-

---

[4]CCOP 1:47-49*. [5]PG 12:1136. [6]FC 101:64. [7]PG 12:1136. [8]LXX. [9]TLG 2061.001, 5.13.3. [10]CCOP 1:49.

ment, or we fall foul of them despite our best intentions. The former tribulation requires us to show endurance and patience, the sufferers being aware that there is nothing harmful in what comes from God, and it is they themselves who reap the thorns they personally sow. The righteous request, by contrast, is a case of the latter tribulation of which we fall foul despite our best intention, when as often happens we are the victim of brigands, we suffer shipwreck or we come close to death by illness, in all of which cases the righteous request brings joy. It is in regard to them that David confirms that often when he was involved involuntarily in distress and begged God's assistance, he was not only rescued but even was vouchsafed more generous providence—the sense of given space, since though tribulation constricts and depresses the soul, relief and joy expand and elate it. COMMENTARY ON PSALMS 4.[11]

COURAGE. DIDYMUS THE BLIND: Instead of allaying the disaster or restraining evil deeds, God sometimes offers courage for bravely bearing the disaster. FRAGMENTS ON THE PSALMS 4.2.[12]

INCREASED UNDERSTANDING. EVAGRIUS OF PONTUS: Whenever we realize the reasons why we suffer and are tested, then our minds are greatly opened. NOTES ON THE PSALMS 4.2.[13]

AN ENLARGED HEART. AUGUSTINE: When I called, God, from whom my righteousness derives, heard me, says the psalmist . . . from the cramped conditions of sorrow [God] has led me into the broad open fields of joy and gladness. . . . [The psalmist's] heart does not live in a dingy little room, even though his persecutors pile in against him from without, trying their best to drive him into a corner. In grammatical terms there is a change of person, a sudden shift from the third, where the psalmist says "he heard" to the second, where he says, "You led me into spacious freedom." If it is not done simply for the sake of variety and elegance of style, I

wonder why he wanted in the first case to show everyone that he had been heard and in the second to address the one who heard him. Perhaps it was because after he had indicated how in the enlargement of his heart he had been heard, he preferred to talk with God; for this was another way of showing what it means to have our heart enlarged, to have God poured into our hearts already: it means that we can converse inwardly with him. EXPOSITIONS OF THE PSALMS 4.2.[14]

JOY THROUGH THE WORD. ORIGEN: The sense of joy and good cheer that comes to us in critical times from God by the cooperation and presence of the Word of God, who encourages and saves us, is called "room." ON PRAYER 30.1.[15]

NOT OUR MERIT. THEODORE OF MOPSUESTIA: One who seeks mercy from God shows clearly that he does not demand the fruit of his own merit and the debt of his own zeal but that he wishes to benefit from the patience and kindness of God. COMMENTARY ON PSALMS 4.2.[16]

4:2 Vain Words

DECEITFUL THOUGHTS. DIODORE OF TARSUS: Their deceit, in fact, was in claiming God does not exercise providence, and their futile thinking was the conviction that the judge does not exercise surveillance. This thought constantly overtakes sinners: they think they will not pay the penalty, rejecting the judge's role along with his providence. This is not so, however, he is saying, not so! COMMENTARY ON PSALMS 4.[17]

NON-REALITIES. CHRYSOSTOM: "Futile" is the word used of that thing that is empty, when there is something in name but nothing in substance. The Greeks have many names for their gods but not a trace of substance; so too in many other matters: wealth has a name but not a trace of

---

[11]WGRW 9:13-14. [12]PG 39:1165. [13]AnSac 2:452. [14]WSA 3 15:85-86. [15]OSW 162. [16]CCL 88A:22. [17]WGRW 9:14.

substance; glory has a name but not a trace of substance; power has a name, and the name remains unsupported by fact. So who would be so heedless as to go in search of bare names of things and pursue hollow things that one ought avoid? Are not the pleasures and prosperity of life things of that kind? Do they not all mislead and deceive? Even if you cite glory and wealth and power, they are all futility. Hence Ecclesiastes also said, "Vanity of vanities, all is vanity." This is the very reason the inspired author is distressed, seeing such absurdity in life. I mean, it is like this: if you saw someone avoiding the light to seek out darkness, you would say, "Why are you doing this strange thing?" So too the inspired author: "Why do you love futility and seek falsehood?" COMMENTARY ON THE PSALMS 4.6.[18]

THE LIES PEOPLE SEEK. AUGUSTINE: What are the lies you are seeking? I will tell you right away. You all want to be happy, I know. Find me someone, let him be a robber, a villain, a fornicator, a sorcerer, sacrilegious, defiled by every imaginable vice, up to his neck in misdeeds and crimes of all sorts, who does not want to live a happy life? I know you all want to live happy lives. But what is it that makes a person's life happy? That is something you are not all seeking after. You are seeking gold, because you imagine you will be happy with gold; but gold does not make one happy. Why seek after lies? Why do you want to get to the top in this world? Because you imagine you will be happy with honor from people and worldly triumphs; but worldly triumphs do not make one happy. Why seek after lies? And whatever else you may seek after here, when you seek it in a worldly way, when you seek it by loving earth, when you seek it by licking the dust of the earth, the reason you are seeking it is in order to be happy; but nothing at all that is of the earth will make you happy. . . . What you are seeking is deceptive; what you are seeking is lies. SERMON 231.4.[19]

UNBECOMING TO CHRISTIANS. ASTERIUS THE

HOMILIST: Let us flee from lying, brothers, as if it were a sword to the soul. . . . And just as in war allies are distinguished from enemies by the watch word, so also in the war of human affairs the friends of God are recognized by truthfulness and by not spreading falsehood; the liars slaughter themselves with the sword of their own tongue. The mouth that does not perjure or lie surely is pleasing to God in its speech. For if we respect the friend and family member who does not lie, and when he asks for something, we grant it, how much more God who has no respect for lying grants benefit to him. When he sees a pure and spotless truthful tongue, he receives his words just like a gift on a tray. . . . As purple and a crown befit the king, so not lying befits the Christian. So those close to him respect him, friends, neighbors and business associates: the demons fear him, the angels love him, and as they rejoice they open the gates of the kingdom of heaven to him. HOMILIES ON THE PSALMS 5.24.[20]

TRUE BLESSING. AUGUSTINE: Why do you wish to be blessed by the most worthless things? Truth alone makes people blessed, the truth by which all things are true. For vanity is the preserve of those who exercise vanity, and "all things are vanity. What more of wealth does a person gain by all his toil, all his labor under the sun?"[21] Why therefore are you shackled to the love of temporal things? Why do you pursue things that are ultimately inconsequential as if they were of paramount importance? This is no more than vanity and lying. For you want all those things that pass away like a shadow to stay with you on a permanent basis. EXPOSITIONS OF THE PSALMS 4.3.[22]

TURN TO THE LORD. EUSEBIUS OF CAESAREA: David seems to be speaking here of those who, when being tested and put through various

---

[18]CCOP 1:55-56. [19]WSA 3 7:21*. [20]TLG 2061.001, 5.24.1. [21]Eccles 1:2-3. [22]WSA 3 15:86-87.

trials, would rather do anything than find refuge in God. Why is it necessary, he asks, to be disturbed and upset at the conditions of the times? What makes you hand yourselves over to vanity, you heavy-hearted people? Why do you seek lies and leave the truth behind? Rather than being informed by these things, know that the Lord God is the one who watches and controls everything, the one who never ever deserts his own righteous ones but always does miraculous things for them. You yourselves, as the upright, know that the Lord is going to be near to you and me whenever you will call out to him. COMMENTARY ON PSALMS 4.3.[23]

HOW TO BE TRULY HAPPY. AUGUSTINE: Do you want to be happy? If you like, I will show you what will put it in your power to be happy. Continue with that text: "How long with a heavy heart? Why do you love futility, and seek after lies? Know." Know what? "That the Lord has magnified his holy one."[24] Christ has come to our miseries; he was hungry, he was thirsty, he was tired, he slept, he performed wonders, he suffered evils, he was scourged, crowned with thorns, smeared with spittle, slapped around and beaten, nailed to a tree, wounded with a lance, laid in a tomb; but on the third day he rose again, all toil at an end, death dead. There you are, fix your eyes on his resurrection. Because hasn't the Lord magnified his holy one, to the extent of raising him from the dead and giving him the honor of sitting at his right hand in heaven? He has shown you what you should savor, if you really wish to be happy. Here, you see, you simply cannot be. In this life you cannot be happy. Nobody can. . . . But [Christ] came down and . . . he took your bad things. . . . He promised us his life, but what . . . he did is even more unbelievable; he paid us his death in advance. As though to say, "I am inviting you to my life, where nobody dies, where life is truly happy, where food does not go bad, where it provides nourishment and undergoes no diminishment. There you are, that is where I am inviting you, to the region of

the angels, to the friendship of the Father and the Holy Spirit, to the everlasting supper, to be my brothers and sisters, to be, in a word, myself. I am inviting you to my life. . . . So now, while we are living in this perishable flesh, by a change of habits let us die with Christ, by a love of being just let us live with Christ. We are only going to receive the happy, blessed life, when we come to him who came to us and when we begin to be with him who died for us. SERMON 231.5.[25]

4:3 The Godly Set Apart

DISTINGUISHED IN VICTORY. THEODORET OF CYR: You see, he will not simply free me from the troubles that befall me but will also render me conspicuous and distinguished in victory; this, you see is the meaning of "made an object of wonder." COMMENTARY ON THE PSALMS 4.3.[26]

THE VOICE GOD HEARS. ORIGEN: Here is the great cry that reaches up to God. It is not that cry people make resulting from some intense release of air, but it is the pure and untouched outpouring of the words of the inner mind, which extend even to God. It must be realized there is a certain voice in the innermost heart which is not used as an organ of the body, but which a person, after he has entered his bedchamber and settled himself, cries out beyond his own body from the hidden gate of his feelings to him who alone is able to hear a voice of this type. Even if we do not read that Moses cried out with an audible voice, nevertheless it is said by God in Exodus: "Why do you cry to me?"[27] It is the voice of every exile who cries to God about having earthly and ever-changing affairs. The Savior excludes this cry for approaching the Father when he says: "Seek great things, and the small things will be added to you. Seek the heavenly, and the earthly will be added to you."[28] SELECTIONS FROM THE PSALMS 4.4.[29]

---

[23]PG 23:105. [24]Ps 4:3. [25]WSA 3 7:22-23*. [26]FC 101:65. [27]Ex 14:15. [28]Cf. Mt 6:33. [29]PG 12:1141.

AS OFTEN AS I PRAY. THEODORE OF MOPSUESTIA: When there is a burdensome care, however many times I call out to God, he does not delay to hear me: this establishes, therefore, as an example to me and others, his providence. However, it is the custom of those who are bound by their miseries, who are pushed into the folly of bitterness, to complain against God and to say that he shows no concern for the affairs of mortals, nor does he govern human life with reason. COMMENTARY ON PSALMS 4.4.[30]

WHEN GOD DOES NOT HEAR. CHRYSOSTOM: So, why is it, you ask, that many people are not heard? On account of the inappropriate requests they make. You see, in this case not to be heard is better than to be heard. So even if we were heard, we would not be happy about it; whereas even in the cases we were not heard, we would give praise even on that account. In other words, on the one hand, when we make inappropriate requests, we are better off for not getting them; on the other, when our asking is indifferent, God beguiles us into entreating him by delaying the response, which is no little gain. . . . So let us not desist when we are not heard, nor be distraught nor become numb, but persist with entreaty and request. God, after all, does everything for the best. COMMENTARY ON THE PSALMS 4.7.[31]

A RULE FOR US. ASTERIUS THE HOMILIST: In the preceding psalm [David] suffered persecution from Absalom. He was ashamed because he was fleeing from his son, and he did not have the inner strength to make war. Now comes the prayer that hangs the tyrant and protects the one oppressed by his tyranny. Should you ask how he will overcome Absalom, how he will cast him down like Goliath, he responds, "Armed with prayer." "When I called on him, the God of my righteousness heard me." His prayer is uttered, and the tyrant hangs in the tree. In the same way when I sin, God arouses himself against me, but when I repent, he offers himself stretched out and trampled for my correction. Likewise, when we sin, God will arouse

enemies against us. But, in our fight, the only thing we have to do is to seek the reasons for the conflict, and if we have sinned, correct it. If we do that, we will see the enemies fall before our eyes. It is, therefore, a rule for us that we do not avenge our enemies, because God will always stir them up against us on account of our sins. Do you wish to see the destruction of those opposing you: repent from your sins, and the enemies will fall. HOMILIES ON THE PSALMS 5.8.[32]

4:4 Be Angry but Do Not Sin

A QUESTION. THEODORE OF MOPSUESTIA: After he said, "Be angry," he added, "And sin not." I propose it in the form of a question, as if he had said, "Are you angry? Sin not." Although one struggles confused and trapped in the offense of a disturbed spirit because of present affairs, although there seem to be so many causes for indignation, nevertheless do not think that it is true what reason and discipline hand over to us, but the spirit disturbed by wrath presses on us. It is the greatest testimony that your own opinion lacks truth because those things that you know, that you speak, have not come from reason but from your experience. COMMENTARY ON PSALMS 4.5.[33]

BEYOND OUR UNDERSTANDING. DIODORE OF TARSUS: When you are angry, do not sin further by thinking there is no divine providence. Instead, realize that much of what happens surpasses your understanding, and it is better to submit to the one who is aware and capable of everything. After all, if we allow surgeons to burn and cut the sick person on account of their skill, and do not get upset at their art despite the pain of the operation, how much more when we fall foul of more grievous and trying events that God, like a skillful surgeon, either applies to us or allows, like burning or the knife, do

---

[30]CCL 88A:22-23. [31]CCOP 1:58. [32]TLG 2061.001, 58.1. [33]CCL 88A:23.

we not submit to such great skill by convincing ourselves that he does everything for our benefit, especially since nothing but good was likely to happen? So "Are you angry?" he asks; "do not sin." COMMENTARY ON PSALMS 4.[34]

MODERATION BENEFICIAL FOR HUMAN SOCIETY. LACTANTIUS: When he enjoined us to be angry and yet not to sin, it is plain that he did not tear up anger by the roots but restrained it, that in every correction we might preserve moderation and justice. . . . For he has enjoined those things that are just and useful for the interests of society. TREATISE ON THE ANGER OF GOD 21.[35]

ESPECIALLY APPLICABLE TO RULERS. AMBROSE: He is not commanding us to be angry but making allowances for human nature. The anger that we cannot help feeling we can at least moderate. So, even if we are angry, our emotions may be stirred in accordance with nature, but we must not sin, contrary to nature. If someone cannot govern himself, it is intolerable that he should undertake to govern others. LETTER 63.60.[36]

RIGHT AND WRONG ANGER. CHRYSOSTOM: He does not dismiss anger, note, for it is useful, nor does he eliminate wrath, this too proving helpful, after all, in dealing with wrongdoers and the negligent. Instead, he speaks of wrongful anger, irrational wrath. . . . In other words, it is all right to be angry for good reason, as Paul too was angry with Elymas, and Peter with Sapphira. Yet I would not class that as anger pure and simple but as right thinking, solicitude, good management. A father too is angry with his son, but out of care for him. In the former case the one settling scores gives way to anger rashly, whereas in the latter case the one who sets at right anothers' behavior is the mildest person of all. Because God, too, whenever he is said to be angry, is angry not to take personal vengeance but to correct us. Let us also, accordingly, imitate this. Taking action against people in this way, after

all, is divine, whereas the other way is human. God differs from us, however, not only in being angry for good reason but in the fact that anger in God is not a passion.

So let us too not be angry rashly. Anger, you see, has been instilled in us for a reason, not for sinning but for checking others in their sin, not for it to become a passion and an affliction but for it to prove a remedy for passions. . . . This is the kind of thing anger is, a useful instrument for stirring up our tardy spirits, for imparting energy to the soul, for rendering us more concerned in our reaction to the fate of the wronged, for moving us to action against conspirators. This is precisely the reason he says, "Be angry, and do not sin." COMMENTARY ON THE PSALMS 4.7-8.[37]

TWO WAYS TO UNDERSTAND IT. AUGUSTINE: "Be angry, and do not sin" can be understood in two ways. (1) Even if you are angry, do not sin. This means, even if there wells up a strong emotional reaction, which we cannot altogether help, because of our sinful inheritance, at any rate do not let reason and the mind collude with it. The mind has been reborn within and conformed with God. The upshot of this is that with the mind we serve the law of God, even if still in the flesh we serve the law of sin. (2) Go on, repent! That is, be angry with yourselves about past sins and do not sin anymore in the future. EXPOSITIONS OF THE PSALMS 4.6.[38]

DIFFERENT KINDS OF ANGER. CASSIODORUS: The anger that does not effect its indignation is pardonable; in the words of Scripture: "One who conquers his anger is better than one who takes a city."[39] So the injunction to control it is appended, so that if we are already angry we do not sin through impulsive rashness. Because of human frailty we cannot govern our hot emotions, but with the help of God's grace we

---

[34]WGRW 9:14-15*. [35]ANF 7:277. [36]LCC 5:274*. [37]CCOP 1:59-60. [38]WSA 3 15:88*. [39]Pr 16:32.

contain them with the discipline of reason. So the blessed prophet permitted what is normal conduct but forbade what is blameworthy, for if in our anger we are not restrained by reflecting on the Lord but happen to be frustrated in our purpose by some unavoidable obstacle, it is quite clear that we bear the guilt of the deed even if we cannot achieve what we desired. Some prefer to interpret the passage as meaning that we should be angry at our past sins so as to be able to avoid wickedness in the present, for we cannot avoid fresh faults unless we condemn old ones by laudable cursing of them. What is repentance but being angry with oneself, so that one is aghast at one's deeds and seeks self-torture so that the angry Judge may not afflict us instead? EXPLANATION OF THE PSALMS 4.5.[40]

KEEP OUR MOUTHS SHUT. AMBROSE: Let there be a door to your mouth, that it may be shut when need arises, and let it be carefully barred, that none may rouse your voice to anger, and you pay back abuse with abuse. You have heard it read today: "Be angry, and sin not." Therefore although we are angry (this arising from the motions of our nature, not of our will), let us not utter with our mouth one evil word, lest we fall into sin; but let there be a yoke and a balance to your words, that is, humility and moderation, that your tongue may be subject to your mind. Let it be held in check with a tight rein; let it have its own means of restraint, whereby it can be recalled to moderation; let it utter words tried by the scales of justice, that there may be seriousness in our meaning, weight in our speech and due measure in our words. DUTIES OF THE CLERGY 1.3.13.[41]

A BETTER WISDOM. AMBROSE: It is said that the greatest of the philosophers granted immunity from punishment to those crimes that had been committed through anger, but the divine Scripture says better: "Be angry, and sin not." It preferred rather to cut off sin than to excuse it. It is better to find praise for mercy in an occasion for indignation than to be incited by wrath toward vengeance. ON THE DEATH OF THEODOSIUS 14.[42]

THE CHRISTIAN RESPONSE. JEROME: To be angry is human; to put an end to one's anger is Christian. LETTER 130.13.[43]

NIGHTLY PRAYER. BASIL THE GREAT: When the day's work is ended, thanksgiving should be offered for what has been granted us or for what we have done rightly therein and confession made of our omissions, whether voluntary or involuntary, or of a secret fault, if we chance to have committed any in words or deeds, or in the heart itself; for by prayer we propitiate God for all our misdemeanors. The examination of our past actions is a great help toward not falling into like faults again; wherefore the psalmist says, "The things you say in your ears, be sorry for them on your beds." THE LONG RULES, Q 37.[44]

A BED OF COUNCIL. JOHN CASSIAN: Whatever you think of in your hearts when sudden and nervous excitements rush in on you, correct and amend with wholesome sorrow, lying as it were on a bed of rest, and removing by the moderating influence of counsel all noise and disturbance of wrath. INSTITUTES 8.9.[45]

THE REASON FOR OUR ACTIONS. ORIGEN: By these words he seems to teach that anyone lying on his bed ought to seek the reason within himself for those things that he has done throughout the day, and in light of those acts he has done against reason he ought to expose them and disapprove of them and feel their sting, for if this is done correctly from his bed he will not be drawn away from honest deeds. SELECTIONS FROM THE PSALMS 4.5.[46]

---

[40]ACW 51:76. [41]NPNF 2 10:3*. [42]FC 22:313. [43]NPNF 2 6:268. [44]FC 9:310. [45]NPNF 2 11:260. [46]PG 12:1144.

4:5 *Trust in the Lord*

THE BEST GIFT; THE BEST DISPOSITION.
CHRYSOSTOM: Seek after righteousness, make
an offering of righteousness: this is the greatest
gift to God, this an acceptable sacrifice, this an
offering of great appeal, not sacrificing sheep
and calves but doing righteous things. . . . This
sacrifice requires no money, no sword, no altar,
no fire; it does not dissolve into smoke and ashes
and smells; rather, the intention of the offerer
suffices. Poverty is no impediment to it nor
indigence a problem, nor the place nor anything
else like that; instead, wherever you are, you are
fit to offer sacrifice, you are priest, and altar,
and sword and victim. This, you see, is what
things of the mind and spirit are like. They enjoy
greater facility; they have no need of outside
prompting. . . . Whom is there left to fear if you
have God as your ally? No one. Now, this is no
little virtue, having confidence in him, putting
trust in him. But along with righteousness he
also asks this virtue of us, to put our trust in
him to hope in him, to place no confidence in
things of this life but rather detach ourselves
from everything and fix our minds on him. After
all, the things of the present life are like dreams
and shadows and have even less substance than
they do, appearing and departing at the same
time; when present they cause their possessors
awful worry. Hope in God, [by contrast], is immortal, unchangeable, immovable; it is subject
to no alteration, stands firm and steady and
renders unassailable the one who professes it in
all diligence and with a proper disposition. COM-
MENTARY ON THE PSALMS 4.9.[46]

THE HOPE OF OUR INHERITANCE. ORIGEN: If
you wish to explain what it is to hope in everything, we are going to say that it is nothing
other than to become an heir of the kingdom of
heaven, to receive comfort, to be called the children of God, to see God, to be satisfied by the
righteousness for which one hungers and thirsts,
to enjoy his abundant mercy and to live in all

the things which the true God and our Lord
and Savior Jesus Christ promised.[47] SELECTIONS
FROM THE PSALMS 4.5.[48]

IMITATION OF CHRIST. CASSIDORUS: If Christ
was sacrificed for us, how much more fitting it is
to offer ourselves as sacrifice to him, so that we
can rejoice in imitating our King! EXPLANATION
OF THE PSALMS 4.6.[49]

4:6 *The Light of God's Countenance*

BLIND QUESTIONING. AUGUSTINE: This is the
chatter, the daily questioning of all foolish and
unjust people. Some of them crave peace and
tranquility in this earthly life yet do not find
it because people are so tiresome. So blind are
they to what is really happening that they dare
to find fault with the way things are; wrapped
up in their sense of their own goodness, they
think the present times worse than the past. Or
again, there are those who entertain doubts or
despair of that future life that is promised to
us. They often say, "Who knows if it is true?
Who has ever come back from the dead to tell us
about these things?" . . . By way of reply to the
questioning of those who say "Who has anything
good?" . . . . the psalmist says, "The light of your
countenance is stamped on us, O Lord." This
light is the complete and true good of humankind; it is seen not with the eyes but with the
mind. The psalmist's phrase, "stamped on us,"
suggests a coin stamped with the king's picture. For the human individual has been made
in God's image and likeness, something that
each has corrupted by sinning. Therefore true
and eternal goodness is ours if we are minted
afresh by being born again. EXPOSITIONS OF THE
PSALMS 4.8.[50]

BLIND TO THE SUN AT MIDDAY. CHRYSOSTOM:
The speakers are those who, in some cases, dis-

---

[46]CCOP 1:62-63.   [47]Cf. 1 Cor 2:9.   [48]PG 12:1149.   [49]ACW 51:77*.
[50]WSA 3 15:89-90.

tort the providence of God; in other cases they are people given over to pleasure, indulgence and luxury, notoriety and naked power. In their lives of such things as these they ask, Where are the good things from God? I am in poverty, and illness and hardship, at death's door, the victim of contumely and abuse, while my neighbor enjoys the good life, luxury, influence, reputation and money. Some people look only for these things, bypassing things really worthwhile, as I say, virtue and a love of wisdom, whereas others, as I mentioned above, on those grounds distort the providence of God in asking, Where is God's providence? Our lives are in such a mess, most of us are in need and poverty and at the end of our tether. What evidence is there of loving care? Those saying this, you see, behave exactly like someone struggling to see the sun in the unwavering brightness of midday and calling the light in question. COMMENTARY ON THE PSALMS 4.9.[51]

A CERTAIN ONE. DIDYMUS THE BLIND: Many individuals read it in this way: "A certain one will show us good things." For it is not that the many show good things but that the One shows good things; that is, the only begotten Son of God. To those who understand it this way, the word *who* indicates a provider of a certain distinguished nature, an individual and a being singular in number. They use this witness: "A certain noble man."[52] For in this passage the word *certain* denotes someone who is especially distinguished. FRAGMENTS ON THE PSALMS 4.7.[53]

RADIANCE RESTORED IN CHRIST. BEDE: But because a human being lost this radiance of the divine countenance by sinning, it pleased God to assume the condition of a human countenance by being born in the flesh, in order that he might thereby teach us that we ought to be reborn in the Spirit. It pleased him to appear without sin in the likeness of sinful flesh so that he might cleanse us thoroughly from every sin and form again in us the distinctness of his image. HOMILIES ON THE GOSPELS 1.6.[54]

PARTICIPATION IN THE LIGHT. ORIGEN: Indeed, in the same way the rays of the sun touch the face of one who looks at it, and in fact it is impossible for one who stands near to the sun not to feel it, so also it must be understood that the individual who is fully a partaker of God is the one who has meditated on the law of the holy word and who has surrendered his mind to understanding God. Which, I believe, the prophet indicates in this place when he says, "The light of your countenance is manifested toward us, O Lord." The representation of the light that shines in your countenance is imprinted on us as it comes to us, and that very light is the expression of your countenance, so that one who is able to see the sign of the divine light that is manifested, immediately recognizes that God's light is made in us. I think that this mystery is also declared in Exodus when the face of Moses, as he is speaking intimately with God, is glorified to the point that the people of Israel are not able to turn toward his glory, and after he puts on a veil the servant of God makes a speech to the people. Thus every spirit that is drawn totally to God and that yields to his truth that is unknown to many is made a partaker of his divine nature; he advances beyond the comprehension of many so that as he puts on the veil he guides the less knowledgeable by offering to them the things that are for their understanding. Moreover, it is obvious from the words of Psalm 66 that the face of God, about which is spoken and that illumines the mind of the one who is able to receive its rays, is the reason for our understanding: "God have mercy on us, and bless us and let your face shine over us, so that we may know your way in the land, the salvation among all nations."[55] SELECTIONS FROM THE PSALMS 4.7.[56]

4:7 More Joy in My Heart

JOY OF THE HEART. ORIGEN: The meaning of

---

[51]CCOP 1:63. [52]Lk 19:12. [53]PG 39:1168. [54]CS 110:55. [55]Ps 67:1-2 (66:1-3 LXX). [56]PG 12:1164-65.

this little verse is consistent with the verses that precede it. For what else is the light of the countenance of the Lord over his righteous ones than a heart full of joy? That very thing which we feel through the sensation of joy becomes a partaker of his divinity when it contemplates God. SELECTIONS FROM THE PSALMS 4.7.[57]

DAILY PROVIDENCE. DIODORE OF TARSUS: The forms of your providence are inscribed and indelibly etched, as it were, on each person's heart; after all, who is the provider and who the supplier of what is needed from without for life? In fact, perhaps it was for this reason also that you put us in a state of need, so that we might not forget the provider of what we need and receive. After all, you were capable first of making us feel no need, and then of giving us some nourishment sufficient for several days; you were not prepared to do this, however, causing us instead to look for it each day so that you might have the opportunity for supply, and those receiving it daily might not forget you as the giver. So who will set at nought, he asks, the manifest signs of your providence, or prove totally unmindful of it? COMMENTARY ON PSALMS 4.[58]

JOY BEYOND DAILY PROVIDENCE. CHRYSOSTOM: He did not say simply, "You have made me the gift of joy" but "of heart," suggesting that the joy is not in external things, not in . . . gold or silver, not in clothing or groaning tables, not in the extent of sovereignty or the size of one's house. Such joy is not of heart but of eyes only. Many people with these possessions, at any rate, think life not worth living; they carry around with them in their soul a furnace of despondency, exhausted by the multitude of concerns and oppressed by unceasing apprehension. . . . If present realities give you joy, and you learn God's providence from them, gain a greater and deeper learning from future realities, for the reason that they are better, more stable and permanent. You see, if you believe God's providence takes the form of you being in wealth and pros-

perity, let your having wealth in heaven bring you much more to this conviction. If, however, you inquire, "Why is it that these things are kept in store in hope and are not immediately obvious?" I should give this reply, that we believers regard the objects of hope to be more obvious than those that are obvious; such, after all, is the certainty of faith. But if you were to inquire again, "Why is it that we do not gain rewards here and now?" I should give this reply, that the present is the time for struggles and contests, the future is the time for wreaths and laurels. And this is an effect of God's providence, the gathering together of difficulties and sweat in this brief and passing life, on the one hand, and on the other the continuance of laurels and wreaths throughout an everlasting and ageless eternity. COMMENTARY ON THE PSALMS 4.10.[59]

4:8 *Lying Down in Peace*

JOY AND PEACE FOUND ONLY IN CHRIST. AUGUSTINE: Joy is not to be sought outside oneself, by those who, still heavy in heart, love emptiness and chase falsehood. Rather, it is to be sought within, where the light of God's face is stamped. For Christ dwells in the inner person, as the apostle says; and to Christ belongs the capacity to see truth. . . . But to those who chase after temporal things, who are certainly many, know nothing to say other than, "Who has anything good to show us?" They cannot see the good things that are true and certain within themselves. . . . When the mind is given over to temporal pleasures, [when it] is always burning with desire and cannot be satisfied, when it is stretched this way and that by all sorts of conflicting and miserable thoughts, it does not allow itself to see the good that is uncompounded. . . . Such a mind, filled with countless images, is so distended by the rise and fall of temporal goods, that is to say, by the succession of its wheat, wine and olives, that it is incapable of fulfilling the

[57]PG 12:1165. [58]WGRW 9:15-16. [59]CCOP 1:64-65.

command, "Think about the Lord in goodness, and seek him in simplicity of heart."[60] For the proliferation of which we speak is at the opposite end of the spectrum from that simplicity. And that is why the person of faith rejoices and says, "In peace, in Being-Itself,[61] I will rest and fall asleep," leaving aside those many people who are completely fragmented by their desire for temporal things and ask, "Who has . . ." when all the time these things are to be sought on the inside, in the simplicity of heart, rather than on the outside, by using the eyes. Believers rightly hope for a complete separation of the mind from mortal things and for the opportunity to forget the miseries of this world. This is fittingly and prophetically described by the terms "rest" and "sleep," which is where the greatest peace can be disturbed by no commotion. But this is not within our grasp at present, in this life. Instead, it is something to be hoped for after this life. This is something that even the verbs themselves, which are in the future tense, show; for what is said is neither "I rested and fell asleep" nor "I rest and fall asleep" but "I will rest and fall asleep." Then this corruptible nature will be clothed in incorruption and this mortal nature will be clothed in immortality; then will death be swallowed up in victory. This is what lies behind the text, "If we hope for what we do not see, we wait for it in patience."[62] EXPOSITIONS OF THE PSALMS 4.8-9.[63]

AN UNEASY CONSCIENCE ROBS REST. CHRYsostom: Nothing, you see, is so calculated to bring peace as knowledge of God and possession of virtue, banishing afar conflict of the passions and not allowing one to be at odds with oneself. Unless . . . you enjoy this kind of peace, then no matter if you are at peace abroad and no enemy assaults you, you are more miserable than the most embattled people in the world. You see, neither Scythians, nor Thracians, nor Indians,

nor Moors nor any other hostile races are capable of mounting such a conflict as an uneasy conscience gnawing at your soul, as untamed desire, as love of money, lust for power, addiction to mundane affairs. . . . Jealous, slanderous, greedy and rapacious people, you see, carry around with them everywhere this warfare, bearing within them enemies lying in ambush. No matter where they retreat to, they cannot avoid conflict; even if they stay at home and go to bed, they are under attack from clouds of arrows, disturbances more violent than pounding seas, massacres and uproar and lamentation and other calamities more disastrous than those occurring in battle. Righteous persons, on the contrary, are not in this predicament; rather, in their waking hours they enjoy life, and in nighttime they take their rest with great satisfaction. COMMENTARY ON THE PSALMS 4.11-12.[64]

A PEACE BEYOND THE GRAVE. EUSEBIUS OF CAESAREA: Even if grief, calamities, temptations, disasters are not lacking to me in this present life, nevertheless there is a future time for me in which I will depart from the body and sleep in peace. COMMENTARY ON PSALMS 4.9-10.[65]

REST IN HOPE. DIDYMUS THE BLIND: I will lie down and rest as I await the future age and the reward of a right life, and as I have been made secure beyond every disturbance because of my hope. FRAGMENTS ON THE PSALMS 4.9-10.[66]

---

[60]Wis 1:1. [61]With respect to the phrase *"In pace, in idipsum, obdormiam et requiescam,"* the footnote in *WSA* explains: "The Latin seems to mean 'In peace, in the selfsame. . .'; but in his meditation on this psalm after his conversion, described in his *Confessions* IX,4,8-11, Augustine takes it to be a mysterious name for God, Being-Itself, evoking the revelation of the divine name to Moses, Ex 3:14" (*WSA* 3:15:91, note 16). [62]Rom 8:25. [63]*WSA* 3 15:90-91*. [64]CCOP 1:68, 70*. [65]PG 23:109, 112. [66]PG 39:1168.

5:1-12 PLEA FOR JUSTICE

When you see the evildoers planning to lie in wait for you,
and you wish your prayer to be heard, get up at dawn and say Psalm 5.

ATHANASIUS ON THE INTERPRETATION OF THE PSALMS 15 [OIP 66]

To the choirmaster: for the flutes.*
A Psalm of David.

¹*Give ear to my words, O LORD;*
give heed to my groaning.
²*Hearken to the sound of my cry,*
*   my King and my God,*
*   for to thee do I pray.*
³*O LORD, in the morning thou dost hear my*
*   voice;*
*   in the morning I prepare a sacrifice for*
*   thee, and watch.*

⁴*For thou art not a God who delights in*
*   wickedness;*
*   evil may not sojourn with thee.*
⁵*The boastful may not stand before thy eyes;*
*   thou hatest all evildoers.*
⁶*Thou destroyest those who speak lies;*
*   the LORD abhors bloodthirsty and deceitful*
*   men.*

⁷*But I through the abundance of thy steadfast*
*   love*
*   will enter thy house,*

I will worship toward thy holy temple
*   in the fear of thee.*
⁸*Lead me, O LORD, in thy righteousness*
*   because of my enemies;*
*   make thy way straight before me.*

⁹*For there is no truth in their mouth;*
*   their heart is destruction,*
their throat is an open sepulchre,
*   they flatter with their tongue.*
¹⁰*Make them bear their guilt, O God;*
*   let them fall by their own counsels;*
because of their many transgressions cast
*   them out,*
*   for they have rebelled against thee.*

¹¹*But let all who take refuge in thee rejoice,*
*   let them ever sing for joy;*
and do thou defend them,
*   that those who love thy name may exult in*
*   thee.*
¹²*For thou dost bless the righteous, O LORD;*
*   thou dost cover him with favor as with a*
*   shield.*

* LXX *over her that inherits*

OVERVIEW: The titles of Psalms are not super-fluous (JEROME) but are divinely inspired. In the case of this psalm, the church is in view as she is the one who will obtain the inheritance in the end (JEROME). That inheritance is to pos-sess God (AUGUSTINE), a blessing granted to the individual believer and to the church as a whole by grace (DIDYMUS).

God weighs our words, and so should we (ASTERIUS THE HOMILIST). Let us make sure we speak in a Christian manner, not like the devil (CHRYSOSTOM), invoking God's help to live a devout life (THEODORET). God recognizes the cry of his children, even in the midst of many voices (ASTERIUS THE HOMILIST). They address him in truth as one God, in the singular, even while distinguishing the persons of the Trinity (AUGUSTINE).

Our prayer begins with gratitude for the light that has dawned in our soul (DIDYMUS), the morning that brings forth from us a voice that God hears (JEROME), even though the world remains in darkness, awaiting the dawning of the world to come (AUGUSTINE, BEDE). We offer our prayers and deeds to God as the first fruits of each solar day (EUSEBIUS), washing our soul to enter his presence (CHRYSOSTOM).

Evil does not come from God (DIDYMUS). The unrepentant will not remain in his presence but will endure his hatred (JEROME). We are liars by nature (AUGUSTINE), and the deceit of the lying mouth kills, especially the deceit of heresy (JEROME). But we are saved by the grace of God (CHRYSOSTOM). We enter his presence by his mercy and then learn the fear of the Lord (ORIGEN), worshiping God in Christ (EVAGRIUS), progressing toward the perfection in which love casts out fear (AUGUSTINE). We pray for God's strength (ORIGEN), for the guidance of God's righteousness (CHRYSOSTOM) and for the true understanding of God's Word (JEROME).

Christ is not in the hearts of heretics (JEROME). Their mouths are dead—unable to speak God's praises (CAESARIUS). Like open graves (THEODORET, CHRYSOSTOM), they give forth the odor of death-bearing dogmas (EUSEBIUS) that keep the graveyard active, pulling others into the tombs (AUGUSTINE). But the ungodly will be driven out completely (AUGUSTINE).

We, however, look for a blessedness that comes from God, not from ourselves (CHRYSOSTOM). Consequently we boast in God, not in ourselves (CHRYSOSTOM), and we attain that blessedness by following in the way of Christ (JEROME) having Christ within us as a living companion (EUSEBIUS). For Christ is our shield of protection from destruction and our crown of blessing (JEROME), the only blessing that counts (CHRYSOSTOM). In this way, we are crowned with mercy and righteousness (CHRYSOSTOM), shielded by a gratuitous salvation (AUGUSTINE) not dependent on our merit (CASSIODORUS).

Superscription: *Over Her That Inherits*

TITLE NOT SUPERFLUOUS. JEROME: There are many who insist that the titles do not belong to the psalms but who really do not know why they hold such a view. If the titles were not found in all the manuscripts—Hebrew, Greek and Latin—their position would be tenable. Since, however, there are titles in the Hebrew books, and this one in particular marks the fifth psalm, I am amazed at the implication that there can be anything in Scripture without reason. If it be true that "not one jot or one title shall be lost from the Law," how much more shall not a word or a syllable be lost? HOMILY ON PSALM 5.[1]

THE CHURCH IN VIEW. JEROME: Who is she who is to obtain the inheritance? I believe it is the church, for it is the church who receives the inheritance. . . . David sings at the beginning that the church wins the inheritance at the end. . . . There are, however, several other interpretations. Many say that the psalm accords with the history of the people of Israel who long to return to Judea from Babylon, but they have failed to interpret "unto the end" and "for her that obtains the inheritance." We, then, by "combining spiritual with spiritual" shall endeavor with the help of your prayers to consider this psalm as applying to the church. HOMILY ON PSALM 5.[2]

THE POSSESSION OF GOD. AUGUSTINE: The title of the psalm is "For her who receives the inheritance." The feminine pronoun is used of the church, which receives eternal life as its inheritance through our Lord Jesus Christ so as to possess God and so as to be blessed by holding

---

[1]FC 48:15. [2]FC 48:15-16.

fast to him. . . . The voice in this psalm is that of the church called to its inheritance, so that it in turn may be the Lord's inheritance. EXPOSITIONS OF THE PSALMS 5.1.[3]

BECAUSE OF GRACE. DIDYMUS THE BLIND: Because of grace this hymn is sung, in behalf of the individual spirit or for the church called out for the divine inheritance, not a natural one but a spiritual one. FRAGMENTS ON THE PSALMS 5.1.[4]

5:1 Hear My Words, O Lord

GOD WEIGHS OUR WORDS, AND SO SHOULD WE. ASTERIUS THE HOMILIST: From the start God examines all the words that you speak, whether they are shameful, blasphemous or lying words; whether malicious, harmful or deceitful; or whether they are words of degradation, which through their deceit are able to overwhelm the one whom the lie injures. "You have loved words of destruction, a deceitful tongue."[5] . . . "Every careless word that people speak will return to them judgment."[6] How much more when you speak hurtful words do they become a hindrance and destruction to your spirit! God judges your cry: whether you have cried out against anyone unjustly, whether you have trumpeted unjust anger with your cry or whether you, overcome with such wrath, have called for the striking down of the innocent, like those who stoned Stephen: "Shouting with a loud voice, they covered their ears and in one spirit united against him they rushed him."[7] And their shout became a vehicle of murder. God, therefore, tests your words. . . . Therefore, since God will measure our words, let us give to him spiritual songs and canticles, hymns and psalms, becoming a sweet smell not by running to bars but by hastening to the church; not sunk in our drunkenness but adorned with sobriety; not dancing and being wanton like the Jews but glorifying the way of life of the apostles. . . . No one may walk into the royal dwelling leaping about; no one may stand before the king drunk. If such caution is

followed on earth, how much more caution is there for the heavenly state and the kingdom that exists there? Let us live lives worthy of that kingdom, rejoicing and happy in the grace and mercy of our Lord Jesus Christ to whom there is glory and power from now to infinite ages of ages. HOMILIES ON THE PSALMS 9.2.[8]

SPEAK LIKE A CHRISTIAN. CHRYSOSTOM: If you say, "Give ear to my words," utter those words that come from a gentle and loving person, containing nothing of the devil. . . . A supplicant, in fact, does not employ the language of an accuser. COMMENTARY ON THE PSALMS 5.2-3.[9]

WE NEED GOD'S HELP. THEODORET OF CYR: On all sides the church of God is buffeted by many huge waves, as likewise is each soul that embraces the devout life, but each survives and breasts the billows by constantly invoking the divine aid. This in fact is what the inspired Word also teaches, instructing us how it behooves us both to entreat and implore the God and King of all. COMMENTARY ON THE PSALMS 5.2.[10]

5:2 Crying Out to God

GOD RECOGNIZES THE CRY OF HIS CHILDREN. ASTERIUS THE HOMILIST: If one grants that indeed each animal recognizes the cry of its own offspring in the largest and most crowded flocks, that though a thousand calves may cry, the mother knows the cry of her own young, that though a thousand lambs may bleat, the female runs to the voice of her own and it does not fall, how much more among a thousand sinners crying out does God know the cry of the just and recognize him as the pure voice of his own child? HOMILIES ON THE PSALMS 10.5.[11]

THE ONE GOD OF INVOCATION. AUGUSTINE:

---

[3]*WSA* 3 15:93*. [4]PG 39:1168. [5]Ps 51:6 (LXX). [6]Mt 12:36. [7]Acts 7:57. [8]TLG 2061.001, 9.2.2. [9]CCOP 1:82-83. [10]FC 101:68-69. [11]TLG 2061.001, 10.5.9..

The Son is God, and the Father is God, and Father and Son together are one God. If we ask about the Holy Spirit, no other reply is possible than that he is God. And when Father, Son and Holy Spirit are spoken of all together, nothing other than one God is to be understood. Nonetheless, the Scriptures tend to use the title "king" of the Son. Therefore, in line with what Scripture says, "The way to the Father is through me,"[12] the order, "my king" and then "my God," is correct. However, the psalmist did not say "give heed" in the plural but in the singular. For it is not two or three gods that the catholic faith preaches but the Trinity itself, one God. It is not the case that the same Trinity can be spoken of now as the Father, now as the Son, now as the Holy Spirit, as Sabellius believed. No—the Father alone is the Father, and the Son alone is the Son, and the Holy Spirit alone is the Holy Spirit, and this Trinity is none other than the one God. EXPOSITIONS OF THE PSALMS 5.3.[13]

5:3 In the Morning God Hears

GRATITUDE FOR LIGHT FROM GOD. DIDYMUS THE BLIND: Think about the one on whom the sun of righteousness has arisen, expressing praise because of his grateful spirit to the author of the light. "In the morning," he says, "you will hear my voice." For to whom is it necessary to have gratitude for so much good, unless to you, Lord, who has brought the light to me, which is the source for the greatest illumination to me? FRAGMENTS ON THE PSALMS 5.4.[14]

THE MORNING OF OUR HEARTS. JEROME: After the shadows recede from my heart and the light of the true Sun has arisen, then you will hear me, and I will be able to stand before you as a servant. BRIEF COMMENTARY ON PSALMS 5.[15]

WHILE THE WORLD REMAINS IN DARKNESS. AUGUSTINE: How can it be that whereas the church said above, "Hear," as if it wanted to be heard immediately, now it says, "In the morning you will hear me," as opposed to "Hear"; and further says, "to you I will pray," rather than "to you I pray"? The same holds for what follows: "In the morning I will stand before you and I will see" rather than "I stand before you and see now." What is the point of this change? . . . Shrouded in darkness amid the storms of this age, the church realizes that it does not see what it longs for. . . . However, the church understands why it does not see, because the night is not yet over. The night represents the darkness that our sins have deserved. . . . . When it says now, "You will hear in the morning," the church means "in the morning I will understand that I have been heard. . . ." Injustice, ill will, falsehood, murder, deceit, and anything else of this sort are what constitute the night. Once this night has passed, morning comes, so that God may be seen. EXPOSITIONS OF THE PSALMS 5.4-5.[16]

THE MORNING OF THE WORLD. BEDE: When the night of this world is over, the morning of the world to come will begin to shine. . . . Then we shall no longer have any need of light from books, for the true Light of the world will appear and enlighten us. ON THE TABERNACLE 3.27.21.[17]

CONSECRATED BY THE FIRST FRUITS OF THE DAY. EUSEBIUS OF CAESAREA: The person "who inherits" (as in the title of the psalm) is consecrated by prayers and by service to God as the first fruits of his daily deeds. Moreover, it is a token of his innocence to go forth from his chamber cleansed by his pure prayers and to be able to say to God, "Early in the morning I will wait on you, and I will look up." COMMENTARY ON PSALMS 5.1-5.[18]

WASH YOUR SOUL EVERY MORNING. CHRYSOSTOM: Let those heed this who come to prayer

---

[12]Jn 14:6. [13]WSA 3 15:93-94. [14]PG 39:1169. [15]CCL 72:185. [16]WSA 3 15:94-95. [17]TTH 18:108. [18]AnSac 3:377.

only after countless activities. . . . "One must precede sunrise in giving you thanks," Scripture says, remember, "and entreat you before the dawning of the day."[19] Now, you would not tolerate someone inferior to you preceding you in giving homage to the emperor; in this case, however, while the soul pays homage you are asleep, and you yield pride of place to creatures and do not anticipate the whole of creation that is made for you. You do not give him thanks; instead, when you get up, you wash your face and hands but ignore the fact your soul is uncleansed. Do you not realize that as the body is cleansed with water, so the soul is with prayer? So wash your soul before your body. Many evil stains besmirch it; expunge them by prayer. If, in fact, we hedged our mouth around in this fashion, we should lay a fine foundation for daily life. COMMENTARY ON THE PSALMS 5.3.[20]

5:4 Evil May Not Stay with You

EVIL IS NOT FROM GOD. DIDYMUS THE BLIND: It is true that evil is not from God, as is the opinion of some who say that evil has a substantial reality. For from the mouth of the Most High, the one willing there only be good, good and evil do not go forth. FRAGMENTS ON THE PSALMS 5.6.[21]

5:5 God Hates Evildoers

THE UNREPENTENT. JEROME: Whom does God hate? The evildoer. But if we are all sinners and every sinner is hated by God, it would naturally follow that we are all hated by God. If, however, we are all hated by God, how is it that we have been saved by grace? . . . . The psalmist did not say those who have been guilty of wrongdoing, but those who are wrongdoers. Those who persevere in sin are those who are held in abhorrence by God, but those who abandon the ways of sin are loved by the Lord. . . . These words are intended for sinners who are persisting in sin. HOMILY ON PSALM 5.[22]

5:6 Those Who Lie

LIARS BY NATURE. AUGUSTINE: Of our own nature we are liars. However, if we wish to be truthful, let us have recourse to the Lord. By his help we are truthful; by our own nature we are liars. SERMON 257.2.[23]

THE DECEIT OF HERESY. JEROME: What Scripture says in the words "you destroy all who speak falsehood" we should interpret as referring to heretics, both from the forward movement of the psalm and from the order within the movement itself. The doer of evil has, indeed, killed his own soul; but the heretic—the liar—has killed as many souls as he has seduced. . . . . Every heretic is bloodthirsty, for every day he spills the blood of souls. . . . Deceitful is the right word. He is both a murderer and a practitioner of deceit. How is he deceitful? His words deliberately misrepresent the words of the Lord. . . . Just think of the condition of the heretic: the Lord abhors him! HOMILY ON PSALM 5.[24]

5:7 God's Steadfast Love

SALVATION ONLY BY GRACE. CHRYSOSTOM: Since, you see, the church has been gathered together out of such people—pagans, soothsayers, murderers, sorcerers, liars, cheats—it said, "you hate and abhor," indicating that it was not due to its righteousness and good deeds but to God's lovingkindness that it had been rescued from them and led into the precincts. So [the church] added, "I, on the contrary, in the abundance of your mercy, shall enter your house." I mean, in case someone should say, "So how is it that you, who are guilty of this and that, are saved?" it mentioned the manner of salvation: it was due to God's wonderful lovingkindness, to his ineffable goodness. COMMENTARY ON THE PSALMS 5.4.[25]

---

[19]Wis 16:28. [20]CCOP 1:83. [21]PG 39:1169. [22]FC 48:18-19. [23]FC 38:363. [24]FC 48:19-20. [25]CCOP 1:85*.

Mercy, Then Fear. Origen: Since evil and iniquity may not dwell with you, nor may they remain in your sight, I will enter into your house by your mercy. Then I will be able to say, "Early in the morning I will stand before you, and you will see me." And since I enter into your house by no other way than by your mercy, with great reverence that is called your fear [i.e., the fear of God], I will worship you, having walked in spirit and truth. Selections from the Psalms 5.8-9.[26]

Worship in Christ. Evagrius of Pontus: The holy temple of God is Christ, concerning which "God was in Christ reconciling the world to himself." In the fear of God each one turns away from evil; in fear he worships in the temple of the Lord that is Christ. Notes on the Psalms 5.8.[27]

Progress Toward Perfection. Augustine: The psalmist does not say, "I shall worship in your holy temple," but "I shall worship in the direction of your holy temple." This should be understood as suggesting not perfection itself but the advance toward perfection: the phrase "I shall enter your house" signifies perfection. But in order that this may happen the psalmist first says, "I shall worship in the direction of your holy temple." And perhaps he adds "in fear of you" because this is a great source of protection for those progressing toward salvation. But when each of us has arrived, the promise of Scripture will be fulfilled in us, "charity made perfect casts out fear."[28] Expositions of the Psalms 5.9.[29]

5:8 Lord, Lead Me in Righteousness

God's Strength. Origen: One who wishes to know and to act rightly has many adversaries. There are people and demons full of envy whom the good deeds of those acting uprightly torment. The prophet, when he understood this, did not allow himself to fight by his own strength against those who rose up against him, but he called on God to extend his hand by which he could escape unharmed from so many enemies, saying, "You, O Lord, lead me in your righteousness; then it will happen that my path may be directed in your sight." Selections from the Psalms 5.11.[30]

Guidance from God. Chrysostom: There is . . . a human righteousness that depends on external laws, but it is inferior, possessing nothing perfect and complete, arising from human deliberation. It is your righteousness, on the contrary, that I seek, that has come down from you and leads up to heaven. . . . The present life, you see, is a way on which guidance from on high is required. I mean, if we want to enter a city, we need someone to show us the way; much more if we are to travel to heaven do we have need of grace from above to point out and determine the way and guide us on it. There are many paths to lead us astray, after all. Hence let us hold God's right hand. Commentary on the Psalms 5.4-5.[31]

A True Understanding of Scripture. Jerome: What is this way of yours? The reading of holy Scripture. Direct my steps, therefore, lest I stumble in the reading of your Word through which I desire to enter your church, for everyone whose understanding of holy Writ is faulty falls down in the path of God. Homily on Psalm 5.[32]

5:9 No Truth in Their Mouth

Christ Not in Their Hearts. Jerome: Heretics do not have Christ, the Truth, on their lips because they do not have him in their heart. . . . Heretics are unhappy people; they are whited sepulchers, full of dead people's bones. . . . Arius, Eunomius and other heretics have tongues like

---

[26]PG 12:1169. [27]AnSac 2:455. [28]1 Jn 4:18. [29]WSA 3 15:98. [30]PG 12:1171. [31]CCOP 1:86-87*. [32]FC 48:20.

arrows, jaws like empty tombs. . . . "Open" is well said, for whenever anyone has been deceived enough to enter that tomb, the heretic is ready and draws him right in. The mouths of heretics are forever gaping. . . . They mean one thing in their heart; they promise another with their lips. They speak with piety and conceal impiety. They speak Christ and hide the Antichrist, for they know that they will never succeed with their seduction if they disclose the Antichrist. They present light only to conceal darkness; through light they lead to darkness. HOMILY ON PSALM 5.[33]

THE MOUTH OF THE DEAD. CAESARIUS OF ARLES: Truly, those jaws are like those of a dead person, for they never or only with difficulty deign to speak God's praises. SERMON 68.2.[34]

5:9 An Open Sepulcher

OPEN GRAVES. THEODORET OF CYR: When graves are filled in they keep the stench within, but when opened they release the awful smell. These people are like that, . . . spewing out words redolent of utter impiety and evil smells. Now, . . . these words . . . suggest blasphemy against God and lewd and licentious speech. COMMENTARY ON THE PSALMS 5.7.[35]

MOUTH AS GRAVE OR TREASURY. CHRYSOSTOM: Make sure your mouth is not a grave but a treasury. Treasuries, you know, differ markedly from graves: the latter corrupt what they receive; the former preserve it. Accordingly, keep for yourself the wealth that lasts forever, the search for wisdom, nothing fetid or rotting. COMMENTARY ON THE PSALMS 5.5.[36]

DEATH-BEARING DOGMAS. EUSEBIUS OF CAESAREA: Vain is the heart of the philosophers of alien ideas, about whom it is said, "The Lord knows the thoughts of the wise, that they are vain";[37] from their throats they spew out death-bearing dogmas as they teach the Word of God is not alive, and they bring forth lies and words

of death. COMMENTARY ON PSALMS 5.10-11.[38]

AN ACTIVE GRAVEYARD. AUGUSTINE: By telling lies and employing seductive flattery, people draw to themselves those whom they entice to sin, and they swallow them, so to speak, when they make them turn to their own style of life. When this happens the flatterers die through their sin, and so it is right to refer to those by whom they are drawn in as open graves; indeed, they themselves are somehow lifeless in that they lack the life of truth, and they gather into themselves the dead whom they have slain by lying words and empty hearts, making their victims into copies of themselves. EXPOSITIONS OF THE PSALMS 5.12.[39]

5:10 Let Them Fall

THE FALL OF HERESY. JEROME: Those who refuse to know the Father, let them experience the Judge. . . . And how? The answer follows: "Let them fall by their own devices." . . . Excellently said, . . . for heretics change or alter their doctrine from day to day. In fact, if a theologian learned in the Scriptures contends with them, overwhelming them with proof from the sacred books, what do they do but straightway look around in search of a new doctrine? They do not seek knowledge for the sake of salvation but look around for new doctrine to vanquish the opponent. . . . Let them fall by their own countless contrivances, and let them have but one recourse, you, my God. . . . You are, O Lord, sweet by nature, but sinners and heretics change the sweetness of your nature into bitterness of their evil devices. HOMILY ON PSALM 5.[40]

DRIVEN OUT COMPLETELY. AUGUSTINE: The point of the phrase "in accordance with the great number of their wrongdoings" is that they are to be driven out completely. The ungodly are driven

---

[33]FC 48:20. [34]FC 31:323*. [35]FC 101:71*. [36]CCOP 1:87. [37]Ps 94:11 (93:11 LXX). [38]PG 23:117. [39]WSA 3 15:99-100. [40]FC 48:21-22.

out from that inheritance in which God is possessed by understanding and vision. It is like the way in which diseased eyes are forced to shut by the dazzling brightness of the light. What brings joy to others is punishment to them. They, therefore, will not stand by in the morning and see. And that expulsion is a punishment as great as is the reward that is described in these terms: "my good is to hold fast to God."[40] EXPOSITIONS OF THE PSALMS 5.14.[42]

5:11 Exult in God

THE BLESSEDNESS THAT COMES FROM GOD. CHRYSOSTOM: Other joys, at any rate, are no better than flowing steams, no sooner seen than gone by. The happiness that is from God, by contrast, remains steady and has firm roots, is both ample and lasting, interrupted by no unforeseen circumstance but rendered more elevated by the very obstacles themselves. COMMENTARY ON THE PSALMS 5.5.[43]

BOASTING IN GOD. CHRYSOSTOM: Someone who takes pride in the things of this life is no different from people enjoying themselves in dreams. What human thing is it, after all, tell me, of such a kind as to permit one to boast? Strength of body? But that is not an achievement of our willing, and hence is no grounds for boasting, especially since the body weakens and collapses in a flash, and the strong person suffers from the effects of not using it properly. This can also be said of the bloom of youth and a shapely figure, of riches, of power, of luxury, and of all the things of this life. To boast in God, on the contrary, and in love for him, is a greater honor than all others and a distinction outshining diadems beyond telling, even if the one boasting is in prison. This honor is not interrupted by disease, by old age, by the pressure of affairs, by variety of seasons, by death itself, at which times instead it shines more brightly. COMMENTARY ON THE PSALMS 5.5-6.[44]

CHRIST, THE WAY TO OUR BLESSEDNESS. JEROME: Our beatitude is of the future, to which alone the promise refers. Let some rule with power; others possess wealth; still others receive honors and recognition. We, however, are miserable in this life in order to be happy in the next. Let us follow Christ our Lord. He who says he believes in Christ "ought himself also to walk, just as he walked."[45] Christ, the Son of God, "has not come to be served but to serve";[46] he did not come to command but to obey; he did not come to have his own feet washed but to wash the feet of his disciples; he did not come to strike others but to be struck; he did not give blows, but he received them; he did not crucify but was crucified; he did not destroy but himself suffered destruction; he was poor to make us rich; he was scourged for our sake, let us offer our cheek to the blows; let us lay bare our back to receive the stripes; let us imitate Christ. He who is struck with blows imitates Christ; he who strikes imitates the Antichrist. HOMILY ON PSALM 5.[47]

CHRIST IN US. EUSEBIUS OF CAESAREA: It is the goal of good people to receive the inheritance promised to them, to follow the Lord, to have him living within as a companion, in accordance with those things that were promised, saying, "I will live with them and walk among them, and I will be their God, and they will be my people."[48] COMMENTARY ON PSALMS 5.12.[49]

5:12 Covered as with a Shield

GOD IS OUR SHIELD. JEROME: God is our shield, he is our crown. He protects us as if he were a shield; as God he crowns us. He is our shield; he is our crown. . . . Let us give thanks to God, and let us beseech him in his good will to be our shield and crown that we may never depart from him and that we may follow him and declare with Jeremiah: "I was not weary of

---

[41]Ps 73:28. [42]WSA 3 15:101. [43]CCOP 1:88. [44]CCOP 1:89. [45]1 Jn 2:6. [46]Mk 10:45. [47]FC 48:23*. [48]2 Cor 6:16. [49]AnSac 3:379.

following you."[50] HOMILY ON PSALM 5.[51]

CROWNED WITH A SHIELD. JEROME: Does anyone really crown with a shield, you ask? Surely, he who crowns, crowns with flowers, or with gold or with other crowns. Now how does one crown with a shield? But the Lord's shield is a crown, for he surrounds us with his protection and defends us and so crowns us. HOMILY ON PSALM 5.[52]

ONLY THE LORD'S BLESSING COUNTS. CHRYSOSTOM: What harm, after all, could come to you from the mockery of human beings, even the whole world, when the Lord of the angels praises and extols you? Just as, consequently, should he not bless you, no matter if all the inhabitants of earth and sea sang your praises, it would do you no good. So make it the complete object of your attention that he extol you, that he bestow the crown. If this were the case, we should be the most exalted people of all, even if we were in poverty, if failing health, at death's door. COMMENTARY ON THE PSALMS 5.6.[53]

CROWNED WITH MERCY AND RIGHTEOUSNESS. CHRYSOSTOM: This victory wreath is woven of mercy, as David says elsewhere, "Who crowns you with mercy and compassion."[54] It is also woven of righteousness, as Paul says, "Hereafter there is set aside for me the wreath of righteousness."[55] It is also a wreath of grace, as another author says, "She will defend you with a wreath of graces."[56] Yet it is also a wreath of honor, as Isaiah says, "there will be the wreath of hope, woven of honor."[57] The wreath, you see, has all these attributes—lovingkindness, righteousness, grace, honor, comeliness. The gift, after all, comes from God, offering a grace of many hues. It is also a wreath proof against corruption, as Paul says, "Whereas their purpose

is to gain a corruptible wreath, ours is incorruptible."[58] COMMENTARY ON THE PSALMS 5.12.[59]

THE SHIELD OF SALVATION BY GRACE. AUGUSTINE: This is what blessing is: to glory in God and to be indwelt by God. Sanctification like this is granted to the righteous, but in order that they may become righteous, their calling comes first. It depends not on merits but on God's grace. "For all have sinned and are stripped of the glory of God."[60] "But those whom he called, he has also justified; and those whom he has justified, these he has also glorified."[61] Because, therefore, the calling does not derive from our merits but from God's kindness and mercy, the psalmist added the following statement: "Lord, you have encompassed us as with the shield of your good will." God's good will precedes our good will, in order that he may call sinners to repentance. EXPOSITIONS OF THE PSALMS 5.17.[62]

NOT BY OUR MERIT. CASSIODORUS: Let us note how sweetly and aptly this psalm ends, indicating with a single word the Lord's kindnesses that no volumes can explain. . . . Your "good will": since the Lord's call comes before all merit, and he does not find a thing deserving but makes it so, for that reason it is called gratuitous; otherwise it would be called just. So this is the good will that summons and draws us. We can think or perform nothing that benefits us without our obtaining it from the Author of goodness. As Paul says, "For we cannot think anything of ourselves, as of ourselves, but our sufficiency is from God."[63] EXPOSITIONS OF THE PSALMS 5.13.[64]

---

[50]Jer 17:16 (LXX). [51]FC 48:24*. [52]FC 48:29. [53]CCOP 1:89-90. [54]Ps 103:4. [55]2 Tim 4:8. [56]Prov 4:9. [57]Cf. Is 28:5. [58]1 Cor 9:25. [59]CCOP 1:90. [60]Rom 3:23. [61]Rom 8:30. [62]WSA 3 15:101-2. [63]2 Cor 3:5. [64]ACW 51:88.

6:1-10 PRAYER FOR HEALING

When you feel the Lord's displeasure,
if you see that you are troubled by this, you can say Psalm 6.

ATHANASIUS *On the Interpretation of the Psalms* 15 [OIP 66]

To the choirmaster: with stringed*
instruments; according to
The Sheminith. A Psalm of David.

¹*O* LORD, *rebuke me not in thy anger,*
nor chasten me in thy wrath.
²*Be gracious to me, O* LORD, *for I am*
languishing;
O LORD, *heal me, for my bones are*
troubled.
³*My soul also is sorely troubled.*
But thou, O LORD—*how long?*

⁴*Turn, O* LORD, *save my life;*
deliver me for the sake of thy steadfast love.
⁵*For in death there is no remembrance of thee;*
in Sheol who can give thee praise?

⁶*I am weary with my moaning;*
every night I flood my bed with
tears;
I drench my couch with my weeping.
⁷*My eye wastes away because of grief,*
it grows weak because of all my foes.

⁸*Depart from me, all you workers of evil;*
for the LORD *has heard the sound of my*
weeping.
⁹*The* LORD *has heard my supplication;*
the LORD *accepts my prayer.*
¹⁰*All my enemies shall be ashamed and sorely*
troubled;
they shall turn back, and be put to shame
in a moment.

* LXX *for the eighth*

OVERVIEW: The sixth psalm, in the Septuagint, bears the title "To the eighth," which is variously understood as the day of judgment (AUGUSTINE), the day of resurrection (GREGORY OF NYSSA) or the new age of spiritual circumcision (DIDYMUS). Perhaps it is best to leave it as an unexplained mystery (DIODORE).

The psalm opens with a reference to the anger of God, which should not be understood literally as a passion for us to imitate (JOHN CASSIAN) but rather as a figurative expression (CHRYSOSTOM), speaking of the effects of his discipline in us (ORIGEN). We prefer that he treat us like a father rather than a judge (THEODORET). We turn to the divine Physician (EUSE-BIUS) of our spirits (HESYCHIUS), of our reasoning (THEODORET). We may have to wait for the doctor (AUGUSTINE), but he truly is our greatest hope (CHRYSOSTOM).

The prayer that God turn to us entails our turning to him (DIDYMUS, AUGUSTINE), for deliverance requires our conversion (JEROME), which is granted to us not on our merits but by divine mercy (THEODORET) as is becoming of God (DIODORE). Now is the time for repentance; conversion is not possible after death (CHRYSOSTOM, THEODORET, AUGUSTINE, JEROME). Now is the time for cleansing; then the time for chastisement (GREGORY OF NAZIANZUS). The one who is mindful of God now knows him then

(DIDYMUS), for such zeal is idle in hades (GREGORY OF NYSSA).

Such repentance is a mourning that is blessed (CHRYSOSTOM), which recognizes that no one's sins are too great to be forgiven (CAESARIUS). It is repentance in Christ (JOHN OF DAMASCUS), in which one's heart is changed (PAULINUS OF NOLA) and one's longings are transferred from this world to the next (LEO). It raises the soul from its sick bed (AUGUSTINE). The righteous pray in the night vigils and nightly prayer possesses great power (ISAAC OF NINEVEH).

Anger clouds the soul (CAESARIUS). It blocks the light of good intent (GREGORY THE GREAT), even anger that seems legitimate (GREGORY THE GREAT). Opposition comes from enemies both human (AUGUSTINE) and spiritual (CHRYSOSTOM). Wisdom teaches us to respond quickly to the wounds of sin (CHRYSOSTOM). But, let us pray that our enemies may be changed (JEROME). For they who seek to harm us now will be ashamed forever (AUGUSTINE), in a judgment that comes quickly (AUGUSTINE). They ridicule us now, but Christians are confident in his mercy (THEODORET).

Superscription: *For the Eighth*

THE DAY OF JUDGMENT. AUGUSTINE: The phrase "about the eighth" seems obscure, though the remainder of this title is clearer. Some have taken it as pointing to the day of judgment, that is, the time of our Lord's second coming, when he will come to judge the living and the dead. . . . Then will come the number eight, the day of judgment, which assigns to each one's merits what is due. It will conduct the saints not to temporal activities but to eternal life, and the ungodly it will condemn forever. EXPOSITIONS OF THE PSALMS 6.1-2.[1]

THE DAY OF RESURRECTION. GREGORY OF NYSSA: All the diligence of the virtuous life looks to the next age, whose beginning, which succeeds perceptible time, which repeats itself in hebdo-

mads,[2] is designated octave. The inscription "for the octave" advises, therefore, that we not look to the present time, but that we look toward the octave. For whenever this transitory and fleeting time ceases, in which one thing comes to be and another is dissolved, and the necessity of coming to be has passed away, and that which is dissolved no longer exists, and the anticipated resurrection transforms our nature into another condition of life, and the fleeting nature of time ceases, and the activity related to generation and corruption no longer exists, the hebdomad too, which measures time, will by all means halt. Then that octave, which is the next age, will succeed it. The whole of the latter becomes one day, as one of the prophets says when he calls the life which is anticipated the great day. For this reason the perceptible sun does not enlighten that day, but the true light, the sun of righteousness, who is designated "rising" by the prophecy because he is never veiled by settings. ON THE INSCRIPTIONS OF THE PSALMS 2.5.52-53.[3]

SPIRITUAL CIRCUMCISION. DIDYMUS THE BLIND: This psalm is sung "for the end" because these are the most perfect contemplations concerning the eighth. . . . Just as he who is circumcised in the flesh has removed a certain part of his body, so also he who casts off every care of life is circumcised in his heart and is like the true pure ones who dwell earnestly on thoughts of the Lord. On the eighth day the circumcision is completed. FRAGMENTS ON THE PSALMS 6.1.[4]

A MYSTERY. DIODORE OF TARSUS: The practitioners of allegory . . . refer mention of "the eighth" to numerology, coming up with ideas as their trade suggests and causing the readers to go gray in the process of wearing themselves out over perfect and imperfect numbers. This not being the way to go, then, people with a more sober idea of "the eighth" claim instead it is the

---

[1]WSA 3 15:103, 105. [2]A hebdomad is a period of seven successive days—a week. [3]GNTIP 136-37. [4]PG 39:1173, 1176.

Lord's day since the eighth day is the same as the first. If this were the case, however, I still cannot understand why the psalm does not keep to hymns but instead involves confession and declaration of sin and is a petition for freedom from current misfortune, even though the title says "in hymns, a psalm of David." For this reason, then, we leave the whole title to those prepared to guess at it. COMMENTARY ON PSALMS 6.[5]

6:1 Not in Anger

NOT A PASSION TO IMITATE. JOHN CASSIAN: We have heard some people trying to excuse this most pernicious disease of the soul [anger] in such a way as to endeavor to extenuate it by a rather shocking way of interpreting Scripture: as they say that it is not injurious if we are angry with the brethren who do wrong, since, say they, God is said to rage and to be angry with those who either will not know him or, knowing him, spurn him, as here: "And the anger of the Lord was kindled against his people";[6] or where the prophet prays and says, "O Lord, rebuke me not in your anger, neither chasten me in your displeasure"; not understanding that while they want to open to people an excuse for a most pestilent sin, they are ascribing to the divine Infinity and Fountain of all purity a taint of human passion. INSTITUTES 8.2.[7]

SPEAKING FIGURATIVELY OF GOD. CHRYSOSTOM: When you hear of anger and rage in God's case, do not get the idea of anything typical of human beings; the words, you see, arise from considerateness. The divine nature, after all, is free of all these passions. COMMENTARY ON THE PSALMS 6.1.[8]

GOD'S DISCIPLINE OF US. ORIGEN: When we speak of God's wrath, we do not hold that it is an emotional reaction on his part but something that he uses in order to correct by stern methods those who have committed many terrible sins. That the so-called wrath of God and what is

called his anger has a corrective purpose, and that this is the doctrine of the Bible is clear from the words of Psalm 6: "Lord, do not rebuke me in your anger, nor correct me in your wrath." AGAINST CELSUS 4.72.[9]

LIKE A FATHER, NOT A JUDGE. THEODORET OF CYR: He does not beg to be uncensured but rather not to be censured in anger, nor does he plead to avoid discipline but not to suffer it with wrath. Discipline me like a father, he asks, not like a judge; like a physician, not like a torturer. Do not fit the punishment to the crime; instead, temper justice with lovingkindness. COMMENTARY ON PSALMS 6.2.[10]

6:2 Heal Me

THE DIVINE PHYSICIAN. EUSEBIUS OF CAESAREA: Every fault arises from weakness because the spirit is always inclined to a wicked disposition, on account of which it flees to the Savior and Healer, namely, the Son of God. For when one comes to the word and reason of God, he gives up his unreasonable actions; as wisdom frees the spirit from foolishness, justice from injustice, truth from lying. COMMENTARY ON PSALMS 6.2-4.[11]

SPIRITUAL BONES. HESYCHIUS OF JERUSALEM: According to the spiritual meaning, the bones are the companion virtues of a reasonable spirit that will draw one to discernment. There are steadfastness, discretion and the temperance that is strength according to God, justice, and, in short, absolutely every type of excellence, which, when they are not found in us (that is, properly provided and in order), it is inevitable that the spirit, since it does not have fitting strength, is thoroughly stirred up with those inordinate passions that are in it. LARGE COMMENTARY ON PSALMS 6.2.[12]

[5]WGRW 9:19. [6]Ps 106:40 (105:40 LXX). [7]NPNF 2 11:258*. [8]CCOP 1:95. [9]OCC 241. [10]FC 101:74*. [11]PG 23:120. [12]PG 93:1181.

RATIONAL BONES. THEODORET OF CYR: Under the influence of weakness, sin overcomes. After all, if the reasoning faculty within us were not weak, the passions would not rebel; to put it another way, provided the charioteer is firm and steers and controls the horses skillfully, there is no occasion for bucking. . . . He calls reasoning bones, since bones are naturally rather dense and support the body; speaking figuratively he gave the name "bones" to reasoning, by which the living being is steered. Disturbance in that faculty, he is saying, ruffled and shook me. Hence I beg to be allowed to enjoy your lovingkindness so as to receive healing through it. COMMENTARY ON THE PSALMS 6.3.[13]

WAITING FOR THE DOCTOR. AUGUSTINE: Here, obviously, is a soul wrestling with its own diseases but long untreated by the doctor, in order that it may be convinced how great are the evils into which it has launched itself by sinning. . . . God . . . is . . . a good persuader of the soul with regard to the evil it has occasioned for itself. EXPOSITIONS OF THE PSALMS 6.4.[14]

OUR GREATEST HOPE. CHRYSOSTOM: He constantly invokes this word *Lord* as though adducing some claim to pardon and grace. This, after all, is our greatest hope, his lovingkindness beyond telling, and the fact that he is such a one as to be ready to pardon. COMMENTARY ON THE PSALMS 6.5.[15]

6:4 Turn, O Lord

TWO SENSES OF GOD'S TURNING. DIDYMUS THE BLIND: We may understand the word *turn* in two ways. Sometimes the sense is this: Since you have turned your face away from me, I ask that now you return that mercy and show it to me. Sometimes the significance is this: Since my spirit has turned away into evil, may you, returning and calling that soul back to you (as "You have turned who are given to turning away"[16]) redeem my soul from repeated sins and from the

powers causing these evils. FRAGMENTS ON THE PSALMS 6.4, 5.[17]

GOD'S TURNING IS OUR TURNING. AUGUSTINE: In the act of turning itself, the soul prays that God also may turn to it, as Scripture says, "Turn to me and I shall turn to you, says the Lord."[18] Or perhaps "Turn, Lord" is to be understood to mean "make me turn," since the soul in the very act of turning experiences difficulty and hardship. . . . While we are turning ourselves . . . we find it a tough and uphill struggle to twist ourselves away from the gloom of earthbound desires, back to the serenity and tranquility of the divine light. In a difficult situation such as this we say, "Turn, Lord," that is, help us, so that there may be fully achieved in us the conversion that finds you ready and waiting, and offering yourself to those who love you for their enjoyment. And that is why, after saying, "Turn, Lord," he added, "and rescue my soul," as if enmeshed in the perplexities of this world and suffering the thorns of the longings that tear the soul apart, even as it strives to turn. "Save me," he says, because of your mercy." He understands that it is not on his own merits that he is being healed, because a righteous condemnation is most certainly due to the sinner who transgresses the commandment as laid down. Heal me, therefore, says the psalmist, not in proportion to what I in fact deserve but in proportion to your own abundant mercy. EXPOSITIONS OF THE PSALMS 6.5.[19]

THE NECESSITY OF CONVERSION. JEROME: Unless he converts my soul, he can not deliver it from danger. BRIEF COMMENTARY ON PSALMS 6.[20]

A MATTER OF MERCY. THEODORET OF CYR: Now, it was appropriate for him to add "for your mercy's sake": I am not trusting in myself, he is saying, nor do I attribute your help to my own

---

[13]FC 101:74. [14]WSA 3 15:106. [15]CCOP 1:101. [16]Cf. Jer 3:14, 22 (LXX). [17]PG 39:1177. [18]Zech 1:3. [19]WSA 3 15:106-7. [20]CCL 72:187.

righteousness; instead, I beg to be granted it on account of your mercy. COMMENTARY ON THE PSALMS 6.4.[21]

BECOMING OF GOD. DIODORE OF TARSUS: Treat me lovingly, not because I am worthy but because it becomes you to grant me this, such as I am.... Let this happen completely and quickly, since it becomes you to grant such a thing, merciful as you are, and to be ever mindful of me as a recipient of your kindness. COMMENTARY ON PSALMS 6.[22]

6:5 Death, Too Late

NOW IS THE TIME FOR REPENTANCE. CHRYSOSTOM: [When the psalmist says] "for in death there is no one to remember you," [he is] not implying that our existence lasts only as far as the present life: perish the thought! After all, he is aware of the doctrine of resurrection. Rather, it is that after our departure from here there would be no time for repentance. For the rich man praised God and repented, but in view of its lateness it did him no good. The virgins wanted to get some oil, but no one gave any to them. So this is what this man requests, too, for his sins to be washed away in this life so as to enjoy confidence at the tribunal of the fearsome judge. COMMENTARY ON THE PSALMS 6.4.[23]

ONLY THOSE ALIVE CAN REPENT. THEODORET OF CYR: It is not in death but in life that one recalls God. Likewise, confession and reform do not come to the departed in hades. God confined life and action to this life; there, however, he conducts an evaluation of performance. And in any case this is proper to the eighth day, giving no longer opportunity for preparation by good or bad deeds to those who have arrived at it; instead, whatever works you have sown for yourself you will have occasion to reap. For this reason he obliges you to practice repentance here, there being no practice of this kind of effort in hades. COMMENTARY ON THE PSALMS 6.5.[24]

NO REPENTANCE IN THE NEXT LIFE. AUGUSTINE: He understands also that now is the time for conversion, because when life is past, there remains only the settling of accounts in relation to what we deserve.... By "hell" the psalmist means the blindness of the mind that captures and envelopes the person who is sinning—that is dying.... It is from this death and this hell that the soul prays earnestly to be kept safe while it sets about its conversion to God and experiences all the difficulties that stand in its way. EXPOSITIONS OF THE PSALMS 6.6.[25]

REPENT WHILE YOU CAN. JEROME: While you are still in this world, I beg of you to repent. Confess and give thanks to the Lord, for in this world only is he merciful. Here, he is able to be compassionate to the repentant, but because there he is judge, he is not merciful. Here, he is compassionate kindness; there, he is judge. Here, he reaches out his hand to the falling; there, he presides as judge. HOMILY ON PSALM 105[106].[26]

THE TIME FOR CLEANSING. GREGORY OF NAZIANZUS: It is better to be punished and cleansed now than to be transmitted to the torment to come, when it is the time of chastisement, not of cleansing. For as he who remembers God here is conqueror of death (as David has most excellently sung), so the departed have not in the grave confession and restoration; for God has confined life and action to this world, and to the future the scrutiny of what has been done. ON HIS FATHER'S SILENCE, ORATION 16.7.[27]

DEATH AND THE KNOWLEDGE OF GOD. DIDYMUS THE BLIND: The saints are not only mindful of God as they hold on to this life but even more so when they are separated from this perishable body. What, therefore, does he say? No one who is mindful of you falls into that death that sin brings forth, that is, that death that separates

---

[21]FC 101:74 [22]WGRW 9:20-21. [23]CCOP 1:102. [24]FC 101:75. [25]WSA 3 15:107-8. [26]FC 48:234-35*. [27]NPNF 2 7:249-50.

the sinning spirit from a life of virtue. I desire to be mindful of you by turning toward your kindness. Save me, lest I be consumed in death when my prevailing weakness has turned against me and my spirit is thoroughly distraught. For it is also said, he is not mindful of you who dies; but he who is mindful of you does not fall into that death about which the Savior said: "He who hears my word will not see death in eternity."[28] FRAGMENTS ON THE PSALMS 6.6.[29]

IDLE IN HADES. GREGORY OF NYSSA: For he who has made the inheritance known has also mentioned the octave, which becomes both the boundary of the present time and the beginning of the age to come. Now the characteristic feature of the octave is that it no longer affords those who are in it opportunity to procure things good or bad, but one hands over instead the sheaves from whatever seeds he has sown for himself through his works. For this reason he prescribes here that the one who is exercised in the same victories effect repentance, as such zeal is idle in hades. ON THE INSCRIPTIONS OF THE PSALMS 2.11.146-47.[30]

6:6 Tears in Bed

THE BLESSING OF MOURNING. CHRYSOSTOM: Let those who have beds of silver listen to what the bed of the king was like: not jewel-encrusted or gilt but washed with tears. His were not nights of repose but nights of mourning and lamenting. Many cares would beset him at night, a time that all people devote to rest but that he would devote to confession, lamenting the more earnestly then. You see, while it is always good to weep, it is particularly so at night, when no one resists this wonderful experience, but given good will one is able to give free rein to it. Those who have tried what I speak of know the great elation stemming from such a flood of tears. Tears like this can extinguish an unquenchable fire, can stem the flood sweeping us to our condemnation. Hence Paul too wept night and day

for three years, correcting unnatural passions. Far from correcting our own, we give ourselves over to merriment and indulgence and bury the night in utter stupor. Some are sunk in a sleep resembling death, while others pass sleepless nights more dire than death, devising fraud and usury and other schemes at that time. Not so are sober people, tending their souls' welfare, applying their tears like a shower, promoting the growth of virtue. The bed that receives tears like that gives no access to any evil or licentiousness. The person who sheds such tears places no value on things of the earth and instead frees the soul from any siege, rendering the mind clearer than the sun. Do not think I am directing these remarks only to monks; in fact, the exhortation is for people in the world as well, and for them more than the others, they after all being in particular need of the remedy of repentance. The one uttering groans like this will rise with spirit in better condition than a calm haven, expelling every passion; such a one, filled with great joy, will approach the house of God in confidence, will converse with neighbors pleasantly, no anger lurking within, after all no lust inflamed, no hankering after possessions, no envy, nothing else of this kind. All these passions, you see, like savage beasts lurking in their dens, those groans and tears in the night succeeded in taming. COMMENTARY ON THE PSALMS 6.4.[31]

NOT BEYOND FORGIVENESS. CAESARIUS OF ARLES: Perhaps someone thinks that he has committed such grievous sins that he is beyond God's mercy. Let this be far from the thoughts of all sinners. Whoever you are, O man, you look at the multitude of your sins and do not see the almighty power of the divine Physician. Although God would like to show mercy because he is good, and he can because he is omnipotent, a person closes the door of divine mercy to his soul when he believes that God is either unwilling or unable to have pity on him. He does not believe

---

[28]Jn 8:51. [29]PG 39:1177. [30]GNTIP 167-68. [31]CCOP 1:103-4.

that God is good or almighty. No one should despair of divine mercy after a hundred sins, nor even after a thousand. Rather, he should show his confidence by hastening to regain God's favor without any delay. . . . David, who through divine mercy became both a king and a prophet, . . . was overtaken to such an extent that he committed both adultery and murder. However, he did not wait to take refuge in the healing of repentance in his old age. Immediately covering himself with a hairshirt and sprinkling his head with ashes, he repented with loud groaning and lamenting. Thus was fulfilled what he had said in the psalms: "Every night I will wash my bed; I will water my couch with my tears." SERMON 65.2.[32]

REPENTANCE IN CHRIST. JOHN OF DAMASCUS: So from all these and many other examples beyond count we learn the virtue of tears and repentance. Only the manner thereof must be noted—it must arise from a heart that hates sin and weeps, as the prophet David says. . . . Again the cleansing of sins will be wrought by the blood of Christ, in the greatness of his compassion and the multitude of the mercies of that God who says, "Though your sins be as scarlet, I will make them white as snow."[33] BARLAAM AND JOSEPH 11.97-98.[34]

A CHANGED HEART. PAULINUS OF NOLA: My heart of stone has no tears to summon. . . . Delicacies are my pleasure while my soul goes hungry. Who could furnish me with a spring for streams of tears, so that I might lament my deeds and days? For I need a river to lament the heavy strokes that I deserve for a life spent in sin. Break the stone that is my heart, saving Jesus, so that the inner me may be softened and a stream of devotion pour forth. POEMS 31.407.[35]

TRANSFERRED LONGINGS. LEO THE GREAT: In hell there is no amendment. No means of satisfaction can be given where no act of the will remains any longer, as David says in prophecy:

"Since in death there is no one who remembers you, who will give you thanks in hell?" Let us flee harmful pleasures, dangerous joys and desires that perish right away. What fruit is there, what use is there, in wanting these things incessantly, things that we must abandon even if they do not abandon us? Let the love of ephemeral things be transferred to incorruptible ones. Let hearts called to lofty things find their enjoyment in heavenly delights. SERMON 35.4.[36]

THE SICK BED OF THE SOUL. AUGUSTINE: What in this context is called the "bed" is where the sick and feeble mind rests, that is, in the gratifications of the body and in every worldly pleasure. Whoever tries to free himself from that delight bathes such pleasure in tears, for he sees that he is already condemning carnal longings; and yet his weakness is held captive by his delight and lies down in it willingly. The mind cannot rise from it unless it is healed. EXPOSITIONS OF THE PSALMS 6.7.[37]

NIGHTLY PRAYER. ISAAC OF NINEVEH: Prayer offered up at night possesses a great power, more so than the prayer of the day-time. Therefore all the righteous prayed during the night, while combating the heaviness of the body and the sweetness of sleep and repelling corporeal nature. . . . And for every entreaty for which they urgently besought God, they armed themselves with the prayer of night vigil, and at once they received their request. ASCETICAL HOMILIES 75.[38]

6:7 Wasting Away from Grief

ANGER CLOUDS THE SOUL. CAESARIUS OF ARLES: Listen to the psalmist tell how anger clouds the eye of the heart: "My eyes are dimmed," he says, "with sorrow." SERMON 148.2.[39]

LIGHT OF GOOD INTENT. GREGORY THE

---

[32]FC 31:312-13*. [33]Is 1:18. [34]LCL 34:165*. [35]ACW 40:322*. [36]FC 93:154. [37]WSA 3 15:108. [38]AHSIS 372. [39]FC 47:317.

GREAT: In quarrels the very light of the soul, the light of good intent, is blocked. Whence the psalmist says, "My eye is troubled because of anger." LETTER 11.46.[40]

EVEN LEGITIMATE ANGER PROBLEMATIC. GREGORY THE GREAT: There are many things that are allowed and legitimate, and yet we are to some extent defiled in the doing of them; as often we attack faults with anger and disturb the tranquility of our own mind. And, though what is done is right, yet it is not to be approved that the mind is therein disturbed. For instance, he had been angry against the vices of transgressors who said, "My eye is disturbed because of anger." For, since the mind cannot, unless it is tranquil, lift itself up to the light of contemplation, he grieved that his eye was disturbed in anger, because, though assailing evil doings from above, he still could not help being confused and disturbed from contemplation of the highest things. And therefore his anger against vice is laudable, and yet it troubles him, because he felt that he had incurred some guilt in being disturbed. LETTER 11.64.[41]

HUMAN ENEMIES. AUGUSTINE: By the phrase "in all my enemies" the psalmist is speaking of the men and women who refuse to turn to God. For even if these people do not know it, even if they are accommodating, even if they share, on the best of terms, the same meals and households and cities, without any obvious antagonism, and enjoy frequent social contacts in apparent cordiality, nonetheless by their aspirations they are opposed to those who are turning toward God, and hence they are enemies. For when one group loves and longs for this world and the other wishes to be freed from the world, who cannot see that the former is the enemy of the latter? If they could, they would be dragging them with them to their doom. And yet it is a very special gift to the way of God's commandments. For often as the mind strives to press ahead toward God, it is roughly handled while

on the road and loses its nerve. This is why it often fails to fulfill its good intention, for fear of offending those with whom it lives, who love and pursue other things that are good but nonetheless perishable and transient. Every sane person is separated from them, not geographically but in mind. Bodies are contained in particular places, but the mind's place is what it loves. EXPOSITIONS OF THE PSALMS 6.9.[42]

SPIRITUAL ENEMIES. CHRYSOSTOM: Our life is a struggle, and our existence beset with countless foes who prove to be stronger when we fall into sin. Hence we should do everything to escape their clutches and never come to terms with them; this, after all, is the surest path to insecurity. Paul touches on the horde of those enemies in saying, "Our wrestling is not with flesh and blood but with the powers and the authorities and the cosmic rulers of darkness of this age."[43] Since, then, the horde of enemies is of this kind, we must constantly be on the alert and avoid the assault of sin. COMMENTARY ON THE PSALMS 6.5.[44]

6:10 Quickly Ashamed

RESPOND QUICKLY TO THE WOUNDS OF SIN. CHRYSOSTOM: It is as if we saw someone about to fall down a cliff and stopped him with the words, "Fellow, where are you heading? A cliff lies in front of you," just so does this author demand that the evil people reverse their course. Likewise, too, unless you were quick to restrain a galloping horse, it would soon be lost. Likewise, too, when as frequently happens the poison of some serpent spreads through the whole of the body, physicians very promptly stop its spreading further, canceling its harmful effect. In exactly the same way do we behave, very promptly checking the evil in us lest it develop further and aggravate the ailment. The wounds of sin,

---

[40]NPNF 2 13:68. [41]NPNF 2 13:79. [42]WSA 3 15:110. [43]Eph 6:12. [44]CCOP 1:104-5.

you see, get worse when neglected, and the effects of disease and ill health do not stop short at wounds but even bring about undying death; similarly, if we dealt with small beginnings at the outset, greater consequences would not develop. . . . Accordingly, let us not be indifferent to the slightest sins but suppress them with great severity. COMMENTARY ON THE PSALMS 6.6.[45]

PRAYER FOR ENEMIES. JEROME: He prays not against his enemies but in their behalf so that they may be changed and may blush with shame at their sins; and they may blush not briefly but forcibly; not with delay but immediately. BRIEF COMMENTARY ON PSALMS 6.[46]

A FUTURE SHAME. AUGUSTINE: As to his saying, "Let them blush with shame and be thrown into confusion," I do not see how it can come about except on the day when the rewards of the just are revealed and the punishments of sinners too. For as things are, so far are the godless from blushing with shame that they never cease to insult us. What usually happens is that so successful are they with their mockery that they make the weak blush with shame at the name of Christ. . . . Take the case of someone who wishes to fulfill the sublime expectations of the commandments by sharing what he has, giving to the poor so that his righteousness may endure forever, selling off all his earthly possessions and distributing them to the needy so as to follow Christ . . . Such a person is a butt for the profane banter of the godless and is called insane by those who refuse to be restored to sanity. Often, in order to avoid being called insane by those who are beyond hope, he is afraid to act and puts off what the most trustworthy and

powerful of all physicians has ordered. These, then, are not the ones disposed to feel shame at the present time, the ones we wish would stop causing shame to us, calling us back, obstructing and hindering us on the journey we have already decided to make. But the time will come when they will be ashamed. EXPOSITIONS OF THE PSALMS 6.12.[47]

JUDGMENT COMES QUICKLY. AUGUSTINE: He adds "very quickly," for when everyone has already begun to think that the day of judgment will not come, when people say, "'Now we have peace,' sudden destruction will overtake them."[48] But whenever it does come, the very thing we had ceased to expect will in fact come very quickly. It is only when our hopes are fixed in this life that we can think of life as long. In fact, though, nothing seems to have gone by more quickly than the portion of our life that is already over. When, therefore, the day of judgment comes, sinners will realize how short is the whole of this transient life. The very thing they do not want, or rather do not believe will come, will seem to them not to have been at all slow in coming. EXPOSITIONS OF THE PSALMS 6.13.[49]

CONFIDENT IN GOD'S MERCY. THEODORET OF CYR: Let those who do not see their own iniquities and yet ridicule my failings mock me no longer. I won divine favor, in fact, and am confident that through my entreaties he will overlook my faults and make me a beneficiary of his pardon. COMMENTARY ON THE PSALMS 6.8.[50]

---

[45]CCOP 1:106-7. [46]CCL 72:188. [47]WSA 3 15:111. [48]1 Thess 5:3. [49]WSA 3 15:112. [50]FC 101:76.

7:1-17 GOD THE RIGHTEOUS JUDGE

When certain people plot against you, as did Achitophel against David,
and you are informed of this,
sing Psalm 7, and place your trust in God, who will deliver you.

Athanasius On the Interpretation of the Psalms 15 [OIP 66]

*A Shiggaion of David,
which he sang to the* Lord
concerning Cush a Benjaminite.

¹Lord my God, in thee do I take refuge;
save me from all my pursuers, and deliver
 me,
²lest like a lion they rend me,
 dragging me away, with none to rescue.

³O Lord my God, if I have done this,
 if there is wrong in my hands,
⁴if I have requited my friend with evil
 or plundered my enemy without cause,
⁵let the enemy pursue me and overtake me,
 and let him trample my life to the ground,
 and lay my soul in the dust.

 Selah

⁶Arise, O Lord, in thy anger,
 lift thyself up against the fury* of my
 enemies;
 awake, O my God;ᵇ thou hast appointed a
 judgment.
⁷Let the assembly of the peoples be gathered
 about thee;
 and over it take thy seatᶜ on high.
⁸The Lord judges the peoples;
 judge me, O Lord, according to my
 righteousness

and according to the integrity that is in me.

⁹O let the evil of the wicked come to an
 end,
 but establish thou the righteous,
thou who triest the minds and hearts,
 thou righteous God.
¹⁰My shield† is with God,
 who saves the upright in heart.
¹¹God is a righteous judge,
 and a God who has indignation every
 day.

¹²If a manᵈ does not repent, Godᵈ will whet
 his sword;
 he has bent and strung his bow;
¹³he has prepared his deadly weapons,
 making his arrows fiery shafts.
¹⁴Behold, the wicked man conceives evil,
 and is pregnant with mischief,
 and brings forth lies.
¹⁵He makes a pit, digging it out,
 and falls into the hole which he has made.
¹⁶His mischief returns upon his own head,
 and on his own pate his violence descends.

¹⁷I will give to the Lord the thanks due to his
 righteousness,
 and I will sing praise to the name of the
 Lord, the Most High.

b Or *for me*   **c** Cn: Heb *return*   **d** Heb *he*   * lxx *borders*   † lxx *help*

OVERVIEW: The seventh psalm carries an inscription that sets it in the time of Absalom's rebellion against David. But David's history contains mysteries of Christ (AUGUSTINE), and the psalm speaks of the struggle of the virtuous life (GREGORY OF NYSSA).

It begins with hope in God (CHRYSOSTOM) and then considers our primary enemy, the devil (AUGUSTINE, CHRYSOSTOM). God alone saves us (DIDYMUS). He is our true Savior (PSEUDO-ATHANASIUS), our one true help (CHRYSOSTOM).

When we ask God for deliverance, we must pray to be heard (CHRYSOSTOM), with a virtue found in the imitation of Christ (AUGUSTINE). The souls of sinners are trampled by the devil (BASIL), and their pride is shown to be vain (AUGUSTINE). God rises against their pride (DIDYMUS). He who was hidden in his secret plans (AUGUSTINE) rises in the faith of believers (JEROME), just as he rose literally in Christ's resurrection (GREGORY OF NYSSA). Many are thereby converted (BASIL), forming a chorus of praise to God (EUSEBIUS).

David speaks of his righteousness with respect to Absalom. But David is not claiming perfect righteousness (THEODORET). He is not boasting that he possesses an uncommon righteousness (BASIL). He speaks of a higher righteousness (AUGUSTINE) that means salvation (DIDYMUS).

God tests thoughts, desires and intentions (AUGUSTINE). He is our help (BASIL), granting us salvation and preservation (AUGUSTINE). His character is revealed in his judgment (AUGUSTINE, THEODORET). He is a just judge (EUSEBIUS). One should not be misled by his patience (BASIL, DIODORE).

Those who do not repent are warned of God's judgment (THEODORET, BASIL). The Lord, in his providence, uses both apostles and heretics as weapons for different purposes (AUGUSTINE). But some see the psalm speaking of the devil and his weapons (JEROME, EVAGRIUS).

The wicked open and dig pits for their own destruction (AUGUSTINE). It is instructive to note the difference in Scripture between digging a pit and digging a well (BASIL). Sin is harmful to the sinner (DIDYMUS). Ahithophel, in the Absalom narrative, is an example of this (EUSEBIUS). The sinner will be in bondage to sin (AUGUSTINE); even the devil cannot escape the recoiling effects of evil (JEROME).

The one who does not dig such pits will rejoice in thankfulness for salvation (EUSEBIUS). And we can praise the providence of God through which even the wicked fit into the order of his governance (AUGUSTINE).

Superscription: *Concerning the Word of Cush*

DAVID'S HISTORY CONTAINS MYSTERIES OF CHRIST. AUGUSTINE: The story from which this prophecy took its origin is easy to identify in the second book of Kings. For there, Hushai, the friend of King David, crossed over to the camp of Absalom, David's son, who was waging war against his father, to spy on Absalom's tactics and to report what he was plotting against his father at the instigation of Ahithophel. It is not the story itself that is due for consideration in this psalm. The prophet has drawn back the veil of mysteries from it, and if we have crossed over to Christ, let the veil be removed. EXPOSITIONS OF THE PSALMS 7.1.[1]

THE STRUGGLE OF THE VIRTUOUS LIFE. GREGORY OF NYSSA: That same adversary, Absalom, as if he has been born again from ourselves, prepares the war against us. Our sound judgment concerning the matter, or rather our alliance with God, turns him who is bloodthirsty against us back. For because he attributes the cause of the good things that have been accomplished for him through "the words of Cush" to God, he composes this thanksgiving. . . . It would be worthwhile to apply the figures of the story to the virtuous life, how the advice that

---

[1]WSA 3 15:113.

saves us becomes the strangling of the adversary; and this saving advice has been recorded, on the one hand, in the history, and on the other, in the psalm. INSCRIPTIONS OF THE PSALMS 2.11.148-49.[2]

7:1 Taking Refuge in God

HOPE IN GOD. CHRYSOSTOM: David wrote the psalm, offering songs of thanksgiving to God. . . . Not in Hushai, nor in human wisdom, nor in that man's shrewdness nor in my advice but "in you have I hoped." Let us therefore act likewise: even if some achievement comes to us through human beings, let us give thanks for them to God, both for the benefits that fall to us through our own means as well as through others. . . . See the wonderful frame of mind with which he speaks, which was customary with him. He did not say, note, "O Lord God," but "O Lord my God"; and elsewhere, "O God, my God, I look for you at break of day."[3] . . . This is the way God acts with righteous people, and being God of everyone equally he says he belongs to righteous people individually. "I am the God of Abraham, the God of Isaac, the God of Jacob."[4] COMMENTARY ON THE PSALMS 7.3.[5]

NUMBERS AND POWER NOT RELIABLE. DIODORE OF TARSUS: While my son trusts in numbers, weapons, horses and above all the audacity and frenzy of those with him, I hope in you alone, who are capable of saving me not only from him but also from all those conspiring with him against me. COMMENTARY ON PSALMS 7.[6]

7:2 Tearing Like a Lion

OUR PRIMARY ENEMY. AUGUSTINE: Therefore, after saying, in the plural, "Save me from all my persecutors," the psalmist went on to use the singular, saying, "lest he ever, like a lion, tear my soul." He did not say, "In case they tear," because he knows exactly which enemy, one violently opposed to the perfect soul, stands in his way.

EXPOSITIONS OF THE PSALMS 7.2.[7]

THE DEVIL IS A LION. CHRYSOSTOM: For proof that the devil is called a lion in Scripture, listen to it saying, "Your enemy the devil prowls around like a lion roaring and looking for someone to devour."[8] And this inspired author himself says elsewhere, "You will tread on the lion and the serpent."[9] This beast is wily, you see; but if we are on the alert, this lion and serpent will be less than dirt in importance, neither will it mount an assault against us directly, but if it does mount an assault, it will be trodden on. "Walk on snakes and scorpions,"[10] Scripture says, remember. He goes around in an awful rage, in fact, like a lion; but if he attacks those who have Christ, and his cross on their forehead, and the fire of the Spirit and the lamp that is never spent, he will not succeed even in looking them in the eye but will turn tail, not daring even to face about. And for you to learn that the words are not froth and bubble, consider, pray, the example of Paul. I mean, he too was human, but this lion had a such a healthy respect for him as to shun his garments and his shadow. Rightly so: he could not bear the fragrance of Christ emanating and ascending from him and had not the strength to raise his eyes to the lamp of his virtue. COMMENTARY ON THE PSALMS 7.3.[11]

GOD ALONE SAVES. DIDYMUS THE BLIND: Who is that one except he who says, "There is no one who can save except me,"[12] the one who has come to seek and to save that which has been lost[13] and to give his soul as a ransom for many?[14] These things show that God the Father saves through God the Son. Through this the deity of the Father and the Son must not be distinguished by the words above and must not be seen as different from one another. FRAGMENTS ON THE PSALMS 7.2.[15]

---

[2]*GNTIP* 168*. [3]Ps 63:1. [4]Ex 3:6. [5]CCOP 1:115. [6]WGRW 9:22. [7]WSA 3 15:115. [8]1 Pet 5:8. [9]Ps 91:13 (90:13 LXX). [10]Lk 10:19. [11]CCOP 1:116-17. [12]Is 45:21. [13]Lk 19:10. [14]Mt 20:28; Mk 10:45. [15]PG 39:1180.

GOD, THE TRUE SAVIOR. PSEUDO-ATHANASIUS: Cush is the one who went to Abasalom in the guise of a traitor, and brought to naught the counsel of Ahithophel and saved David from death. When David learned of these things, he knew that his Savior was not a man but God. EXPOSITION ON PSALMS 7.[16]

ONE TRUE HELP. CHRYSOSTOM: To be sure, he had assembled an army and had a large number with him; so why does he say, "with no one to ransom or save me"? Because he considers not even the whole world as help should he not enjoy influence from on high, nor does he think of it as solitude if he is alone, as long as he shares in help from God. COMMENTARY ON THE PSALMS 7.3.[17]

7:3 O Lord, My God

PRAY TO BE HEARD. CHRYSOSTOM: This must everywhere be our concern, not simply to pray but to pray in such a way as to be heard. It is not sufficient that prayer effects what is intended, unless we so direct it as to appeal to God. For the Pharisee too prayed and achieved nothing, and again the Jews prayed but God turned away from them in their prayer. They did not pray, you see, as they should have prayed. Hence we were bidden to pray the prayer most likely to be heard. . . . Being heard happens in this fashion: first, of course, worthiness to receive something; then, praying in accordance with God's laws; third, persistence; fourth, asking nothing earthly; fifth, seeking things to our real benefit; sixth, contributing everything of our own. COMMENTARY ON THE PSALMS 7.3.[18]

7:4 Repaying with Evil

IMITATION OF CHRIST. AUGUSTINE: When the perfect soul prays for the words of Hushai, the son of Jemini, it prays for the knowledge of that secret and that silence, which the Lord, who is merciful and kindly disposed toward us, effected for our salvation, enduring the plots of

his betrayer and bearing them with the utmost patience. It is as if he were to say to this perfect soul, explaining the meaning of the secret, "It was for you, ungodly sinner, that I endured my betrayer in deep silence and inexhaustible patience, so that your iniquities might be washed away by the shedding of my blood. Should you, then, not imitate me and, in your turn, refrain from rewarding evil with evil?" Perceiving and understanding what the Lord has done for him and by following his example advancing toward perfection, the psalmist says, "If I have repaid those who have paid me back with evil," that is, if I have not myself done what you, by doing it, taught me, "let me fall empty-handed before my enemies." EXPOSITIONS OF THE PSALMS 7.3.[19]

7:5 My Soul in the Dust

TRAMPLED TO THE GROUND. BASIL THE GREAT: The soul of the one who is just, severing itself from affection for the body, has its life hidden with Christ in God, so that it can say like the apostle: "It is now no longer I that live, but Christ lives in me. And the life that I now live in the flesh, I live in faith."[20] But the soul of the sinner and of one who lives according to the flesh and is defiled by the pleasures of the body is wrapped up in the passions of the flesh as in mud; and the enemy, trampling on this soul, strives to pollute it still more and, as it were, to bury it, treading on him who has fallen, and with his feet trampling him into the ground. HOMILIES ON THE PSALMS 11.3 (Ps 7).[21]

THE VANITY OF PRIDE. AUGUSTINE: This is the dust that the wind hurls forth from the face of the earth, that is to say, the vain and silly boastings of the proud, puffed up but without substance, like a handful of dust lifted high by the wind. . . . This particular vice of groundless boasting is the only vice there really is, or the

---

[16]CSCO 387:5. [17]CCOP 1:116*. [18]CCOP 1:117. [19]WSA 3 15:115. [20]Gal 2:20. [21]FC 46:169*.

one most to be avoided by those who are perfect. For the soul conquers last of all the very vice by which it fell first. "The starting point of all sin is pride," and "the starting point of human pride is rebellion against God."[22] EXPOSITIONS OF THE PSALMS 7.4.[23]

7:6 The Fury of Enemies

THE PRIDE OF OUR ENEMIES. DIDYMUS THE BLIND: So, it is spoken: He asks that God on high appear at the borders of his enemies. Then, he says, their iniquities that make them my enemies will end. Perhaps the boundaries of the enemies refer to the "pride" in which they have rejoiced. They think they are going to dwell with stability in the furthermost boundaries. FRAGMENTS ON THE PSALMS 7.6.[24]

GOD'S SLEEP, OUR IGNORANCE. AUGUSTINE: Arise, he says, using the word to mean "appear"; he employs a human and obscure expression, as though God were asleep, when really he is hidden and unrecognized in his secret plans. EXPOSITIONS OF THE PSALMS 7.5.[25]

ARISE IN THE FAITH OF MANY. JEROME: Arise, in order that a vast multitude may believe in you, for after you have risen, what else would we pray for? Return to the Father. "Above them on high be enthroned."[26] For whose sake? For the assembly of the peoples. In that you suffered, you suffered for us; in that you rose again, you rose for us; in that you ascended to the Father, ascend for us. "Above them on high be enthroned." "And no one has ascended into heaven except him who has descended from heaven: the Son of man who is in heaven."[27] HOMILY ON PSALM 7.[28]

RESURRECTION OF THE LORD; DEATH OF HIS ENEMIES. GREGORY OF NYSSA: The mass of adversaries cannot otherwise be destroyed, if the Lord has not risen on our behalf, and death must by all means precede the resurrection. He, then, who has revealed the resurrection of the

Lord has, at the same time, shown that which is bound up together with the resurrection, I mean, of course, the mystery related to the passion. For this reason, having been inspired by the indwelling of the Holy Spirit, he says, "Rise up, O Lord, in your anger; be exalted in the ends of my enemies." By "anger" he indicates the retributive power of the just judge, and by the rest he indicates the destruction of evil. For that which is perceived as contrary to the good, being only hostile by nature, is the evil whose end is destruction and a passing over into nonexistence. He, then, who said, "Be exalted in the ends of my enemies," predicts, through the evil of his enemies "being brought to an end," that the course to evil no longer remains in [his] life. ON THE INSCRIPTIONS OF THE PSALMS 2.10.125-26.[29]

7:7 Surrounded by the Peoples

MANY CONVERTED BY THE PUNISHMENT OF ONE. BASIL THE GREAT: "And a congregation of people shall surround you." It is evident that if one unjust person is chastened, many will be converted. Punish, therefore, the wickedness of this person, in order that a great congregation of people may surround you. HOMILIES ON THE PSALMS 11.4 (Ps 7).[30]

A CHORUS OF PRAISE. EUSEBIUS OF CAESAREA: "A great crowd of people will surround you" when you [Lord Jesus] root out your enemies, when the lie of the demons is destroyed, when the assembly of the elect is established and when it becomes the one who calls the nations. Then you, placed in the midst of it as if in a chorus, will bring a hymn to that church worthy of your Father, and so by you, O Lord, it is spoken: "I will tell your name to my brothers; I will praise you in the midst of the church." David proph-

---

[22]Sir 10:13, 12 (10:15, 14 Vg). [23]WSA 3 15:116-17. [24]PG 39:1180. [25]WSA 3 15:117. [26]Ps 7:7 (7:8 LXX). [27]Jn 3:13. [28]FC 48:31. [29]GNTIP 161. [30]FC 46:170-71.

esies all these things through the Holy Spirit, indicating a theophany of the Savior, things that are not to be passed over as for himself alone but for every race of humankind. COMMENTARY ON PSALMS 7.7-8.[31]

7:8 My Righteousness and Integrity

NOT PERFECT RIGHTEOUSNESS. THEODORET OF CYR: In these words the divine David has not left a testimony to his own righteousness: we hear him protesting the opposite, "because I acknowledge my lawlessness, and my sin is always before me"; and, "I said, 'I shall declare my lawlessness against myself to the Lord,'" but he calls it justice in the matter before us. I committed no wrong, in fact, he is saying, against Absalom, or Ahithophel or those arrayed in battle with them against me. So I beg to be judged in the light of this righteousness and innocence and not in the light of the faults previously committed by me. I ask for judgment on these current grounds and not for a payment of penalty at this time for other sins. COMMENTARY ON THE PSALMS 7.5.[32]

NOT BOASTING. BASIL THE GREAT: These words seem to contain some boastfulness and to be very much like the prayer of the Pharisee who was exalting himself, but, if one considers them reasonably, the prophet will be seen to be far from such a disposition. . . . "According to my justice" [means] according to that attainable by people and possible for those living in the flesh. "And according to my innocence," [in this] he names his innocence as if it were simplicity and ignorance of things useful to know according to the saying in the Proverbs: "The innocent believes every word." Since, therefore, we people through ignorance fall unguardedly into many sins, he entreats God and asks to meet with pardon because of his innocence. From this it is evident that these words show the humility of the speaker rather than arrogance. HOMILIES ON THE PSALMS 11.6 (Ps 7).[33]

A HIGHER RIGHTEOUSNESS. AUGUSTINE: "Judge me, Lord, according to my righteousness and my harmlessness, which are above me." . . . The addition "above me" can be understood as referring . . . to righteousness. . . . By such an addition the psalmist shows that the soul does not have its righteousness and innocency through itself but through God, who gives light and brightness. For of the soul he says in another psalm, "You, Lord, will light my lamp,"[34] and of John the Baptist it is said, "He was not himself in the light but came to bear witness about the Light";[35] and again, "He was a burning, shining lamp."[36] That Light, from which souls are lit like lamps, shines forth with its own dazzling splendor, not with one borrowed from someone else. This Light is Truth itself. When, therefore, the psalm says, "According to my righteousness and my innocence, which are above me," it is as though a burning, shining lamp were to say, "Judge me according to the flame that is over me, that is, not by that which I am of myself, but by that flame with which I shine when set on fire from you." EXPOSITIONS OF THE PSALMS 7.8.[37]

THE JUDGMENT THAT MEANS SALVATION. DIDYMUS THE BLIND: There is an important difference between human righteousness and that of God; the Psalmist wishes to be judged according to the righteousness of the Lord, knowing for sure that this will mean salvation for him. FRAGMENTS ON THE PSALMS 7.9.[38]

7:9 Testing Minds and Hearts

THOUGHTS, DESIRES AND INTENTIONS. AUGUSTINE: God sees the thoughts of everyone; this is what the word *heart* means. He also sees the things that give everyone pleasure: they are to be understood by the expression "inward parts." . . . God, therefore, examines our heart and explores carefully to see that it is where our

---

[31]AnSac 3:386. [32]FC 101:79. [33]FC 46:173-74. [34]Ps 18:28 (17:29 LXX). [35]Jn 1:8. [36]Jn 5:35. [37]WSA 3 15:120. [38]PG 39:1181.

treasure is, that is, in heaven. He examines also our inward parts and explores carefully to see that we do not capitulate to flesh and blood but rejoice in God. Thus he guides the just person's conscience in his own presence, guides it in the place where no human being sees; he alone sees who discerns what each person thinks and what causes each person delight. For delight is the object of our efforts: each of us strives by care and thought to attain our own delight. Therefore the one who examines the heart sees the things that we really care about. But he who explores our inward parts sees also the object of our striving and where we seek our joy, so that when he finds that our efforts do not incline toward the lust of the flesh, or toward the craving of the eyes or toward worldly ambition, all of which pass away like a cloud, but are raised upward to the joys of things eternal, which are disturbed by no changefulness, then God, who examines the heart and the inward parts, can direct the just. For our works, expressed in deeds and words, can be well known by other people, but only the God who examines the heart and the inward parts knows with what intention they are done and what we want to gain through them. EXPOSITIONS OF THE PSALMS 7.9.[39]

7:10 My Shield Is with God

HELP FROM THE LORD. BASIL THE GREAT: My help is not from wealth or from corporal resources or from my own power and strength nor from human ties of kinship, but "my help is from God." What assistance the Lord sends to those who fear him, we have learned elsewhere in a psalm that says, "The angel of the Lord shall encamp round about them that fear him and shall deliver them."[40] And in another place: "The angel who has delivered me."[41] HOMILIES ON THE PSALMS 11.7 (Ps 7).[42]

SALVATION AND PRESERVATION. AUGUSTINE: Medicine has two functions, one whereby in-

firmity is cured, the other whereby good health is maintained. . . . In the former case it is said, "Save me, Lord, because of your mercy." In the latter case, "my righteous help is from the Lord, who saves the upright in heart." Both in fact save us, but while the former effects the transition from sickness to health, the latter upholds us in that state of good health. Therefore in the former case the assistance is merciful, because the sinner has no merit of his own but still longs to be justified by believing in the one who justifies the ungodly. In the latter case, the assistance is just, because it is given to one who is already righteous. Therefore, the sinner who confessed, "I am weak," was right to say there, "Save me, Lord, because of your mercy," and the just person who said previously, "If I have repaid those who paid me back with evil," can say now, "My righteous help is from the Lord who saves the upright in heart." For if God dispenses the medicine by which in our weakness we are healed, how much more should he provide the means by which we are preserved once we are well? If Christ died for us when we were still sinners, how much more, now that we are justified, shall we be saved from God's wrath through him? EXPLANATIONS OF THE PSALMS 7.10.[43]

7:11 A Righteous Judge

GOD'S CHARACTER REVEALED. AUGUSTINE: He is just who will recompense each of us in proportion to our works. He is strong who, while himself most powerful, for our salvation endured even godless persecutors. He is long-suffering who did not, immediately after his resurrection, seize those who persecuted him, in order to punish them; instead he bore with them, in order that they might eventually turn from such impiety to salvation. And still he bears with them, reserving the final punishment until the final judgment and even today

---

[39]WSA 3 15:121. [40]Ps 34:7 (33:8 LXX). [41]Gen 48:16. [42]FC 46:176. [43]WSA 3 15:122.

still inviting sinners to repentance. Expositions of the Psalms 7.12.[44]

God Delays Wrath for a Time. Theodoret of Cyr: "God is a righteous judge, . . .
who does not give free rein to his wrath every
day." Instead, he also shows lovingkindness, by
which he bears people's faults for a longer time.
For whenever he sees people not reaping profit
from it, he gives them further opportunity with
the addition of threats, putting the punishments
off; but if they scorn the opportunity and persist
in sinning, he immediately brings on their ruin
in keeping with justice. Commentary on the
Psalms 7.6.[45]

God, the Just Judge. Eusebius of Caesarea: God alone is the just Judge, he alone is
the one who sees hearts. He gives to each one
according to his works. Truly, "man looks at the
outward appearance,"[46] but the Lord is a judge of
thoughts and the feelings of the spirit. There is
no judgment hidden from him. Commentary on
Psalms 7.10, 11.[47]

Do Not Be Misled. Basil the Great: Do
not be so poorly disposed toward God as to
think that he is too weak to avenge, for he is also
strong. What reason is there, then, that swift
vengeance is not inflicted on the sinner? Because
he is patient, "he is not angry every day." Homilies on the Psalms 11.7 (Ps 7).[48]

Respect God's Patience. Diodore of Tarsus: If long-suffering were not associated with
his justice, there would have been nothing to
stop him punishing day in day out, since sinners
always provide grounds for just punishment.
Sinners, however, should not for this reason be
disposed to indifference: those of right mind
rightly respect long-suffering as a threat and
take delay in wrath as an aggravation of punishment; this should also be the attitude of those on
whom the imposition of judgment does not fall
promptly. Commentary on Psalms 7.[49]

7:12-13 God's Weapons Prepared

God's Warning. Theodoret of Cyr: These
are not words of punishment, note, but of threat:
he said wield, not inflict; bent his bow, not fired
the arrow. And to teach us against whom he will
fire the arrows, he immediately attached the
words "he made his arrows into flaming shafts,"
that is, those taking combustible material of sin,
building with wood, hay and stubble, as the divine apostle says, will be struck with these fiery
arrows. Commentary on the Psalms 7.7.[50]

Polishing His Sword in Vengeance. Basil
the Great: Just as men who are polishing up
their arms indicate by this action the attack in
war, so Scripture, wishing to bespeak a movement
of God toward vengeance, says that he polishes
his sword. "He has bent his bow." . . . There is no
bowstring that stretches the bow of God, but a
punitive power, now strained tight, again loosened. Scripture threatens the sinner that future
punishments are prepared for him, if he remains
in his sin. Homilies on the Psalms 11.7 (Ps 7).[51]

Apostles and Heretics. Augustine: I
would happily understand [the bow in this verse]
as the holy Scriptures, where the rigidity of
the Old Testament is bent and subdued by the
strength of the New Testament, as by some sort
of bowstring. The apostles are launched from it
like arrows, or divine proclamations are hurled
from it. These arrows he has fashioned . . . to
make those who are struck by them blaze with
the love of God. . . . Once struck by these and
set on fire by them, you must blaze with so great
a love for the kingdom of heaven that you scorn
the tongues of all who block your path and want
to call you back from your fixed resolve. . . . But
the Lord is said to have prepared not only arrows
but also "implements of death in his bow." It
may be asked what the implements of death are.

---

[44]*WSA* 3 15:123 [45]FC 101:80. [46]1 Sam 16:7. [47]PG 23:125. [48]FC
46:177. [49]WGRW 9:23. [50]FC 101:80. [51]FC 46:177-78.

Perhaps they are heretics? For they, too, out of the same bow, that is, from the same Scriptures, leap into souls who are destined not to be set alight with love but to be destroyed by poisons, but this only because they deserve it. And so even that arrangement is to be attributed to divine providence, not because providence makes them sinners, but because it works them into an ordered framework after they have sinned. For by reading the Scriptures with a perverse hidden agenda because of sin, they are forced to understand them perversely. This itself is a punishment for sin. And yet by their death, the children of the catholic church are raised from sleep, as if pricked by thorns, and they progress to an understanding of the divine Scriptures. EXPOSITIONS OF THE PSALMS 7.14-15.[52]

THE WEAPONS OF THE DEVIL. JEROME: Many maintain that these words of the psalm refer to the devil; they mean, unless you will have been converted, unless you will have repented, you will be in the power of the devil. "He will bend and aim his bow." The devil always has his bow ready, and he is ever alert to shoot his arrows and strike us down. . . . They whose hearts are burning with lust and passion are the very ones whom the devil conquers. . . . The psalm did not say for those who are about to burn—that is, about to burn from his arrows. The hearts of those he sees already burning, no matter whose they are, are his target. HOMILY ON PSALM 7.[53]

THE DEVIL'S FLAMING ARROWS. EVAGRIUS OF PONTUS: The ones who are burning are those who have received the flaming arrows of the devil. NOTES ON THE PSALMS 7.14.[54]

7:15 Falling into a Pit

THE OPENING AND DIGGING OF PITS. AUGUSTINE: A pit [in earthly matters] is opened when compliance is given to the evil prompting of earthbound desires. And it is dug out, when, after consenting, we press on to putting the deception into practice. EXPOSITIONS OF THE PSALMS 7.17.[55]

PITS VERSUS WELLS. BASIL THE GREAT: We do not find the name of "pit" ever assigned in the divine Scriptures in the case of something good or a "well" of water in the case of something bad. As to the reason for the pits being assigned among the worse things and the wells among the better, we think it is this. The water in the pit is something acquired, having fallen from the sky; but in the wells, streams of water, buried before the places were dug out, are revealed when the heaps of earth covering them and the material of any sort whatsoever, lying on them, which is also all earth, have been removed. Now, it is as if there were a pit in souls in which the better things, changed and debased, fall down, when a person, having resolved to have nothing good and noble of his own, puts to flight the thoughts of the good and noble that have slipped into it, twisting them to evildoing and to contradictions of truth. And again, there are wells, when a light and a stream of water unimpaired in word and in doctrines break forth after the baser materials that had been covering it are removed. Therefore, it is necessary for each one to prepare a well for himself, in order that he may guard the command mentioned previously, which says, "Drink water out of your own cistern and the streams of your own well. Thus we shall be called the sons of those who have dug the wells, Abraham, Isaac and Jacob. But a pit must not be dug lest we fall into the hole, as it is said in this place, and so fail to hear the words written in Jeremiah in reproach of sinners, for, God says concerning them what we have briefly mentioned before: "They have forsaken me, the fountain of living water, and have digged to themselves cisterns, broken cisterns, that can hold no water." HOMILIES ON THE PSALMS 11.8 (Ps 7).[56]

---

[52]WSA 3 15:124-25*. [53]FC 48:32. [54]AnSac 2:458. [55]WSA 3 15:126-27. [56]FC 46:179-80.

THE HARM OF SIN. DIDYMUS THE BLIND: Truly, he sins first against himself, then he injures another; since sin is harmful and ruinous, foremost it harms and roughly handles the one sinning. ... "If the blind lead the blind, both will fall into the pit".[57] In this saying it must be realized that teachers and students become blinded by foolishness and wantonness. FRAGMENTS ON THE PSALMS 7.15.[58]

7:16 Violence Falls on the Sinner's Head

AHITHOPHEL, AN EXAMPLE. EUSEBIUS OF CAESAREA: These words seem to me to have been fulfilled literally in Ahithophel. At the time of the uprising of Cush, he was a man harboring envy, branded by disgrace, falling out as the watchman, who used his skill to be able to see ahead and predict future events that the affairs of Absalom would fail. Before he himself could be substituted by the men of David, he removed himself, and, withdrawing from the household, he hanged himself with a noose. While he gathered the seeds of evil in his thinking and devised against David whatever he had conceived in his thoughts, he brought forth the same seeds for his own destruction. . . . These words express the general opinion that as anyone plans evil in his spirit against his neighbor and wishes to harm others and builds a pit for their ruin, he does these things against himself, and his trouble will return on his own head. Each one will cause his own sentence on the day of judgment by his own deeds and will receive the fruits of his own labors. COMMENTARY ON PSALMS 7.15-17.[59]

THE BONDAGE OF SIN. AUGUSTINE: Because he himself did not wish to escape sin, he has been subjected to sin like a slave. . . . His iniquity will be "over him," since he is subject to his own iniquity. . . . It oppresses him and weighs him down and does not allow him to fly back to rest with the saints. This happens when in a wicked person reason is enslaved and lust holds the upper hand. EXPOSITIONS OF THE PSALMS 7.18.[60]

EVIL RECOILS. JEROME: Just as anyone who tosses a stone straight up into the air and is foolish enough not to move out of its way is struck on the head and wounded by his own stone, in the same way, the devil downs himself by his own arrogance; the pride that exalts him is the same pride that defeats him. "His mischief shall recoil on his own head." All the devil wants is to hold his head up high, but he cannot. Why can he not? Because his "mischief shall recoil on his own head" and crush him down. HOMILY ON PSALM 7.[61]

7:17 Giving Thanks to the Lord

ONE WHO DOES NOT DIG PITS. EUSEBIUS OF CAESAREA: He has built traps for no one. He has dug a pit for no one. He has despised iniquity. Knowing the future destruction of the wicked at judgment, he said, "I will give thanks to the Lord according to his righteousness," my righteous works having been brought forth at the tribunal; and "I will sing to the name of the Lord most high," bound by the hope that I am going to be received into the choir of those who are going to follow after salvation through him, through his merit. COMMENTARY ON PSALMS 7.18.[62]

THE PROVIDENCE OF GOD. AUGUSTINE: Whoever sees that what souls deserve is ordered by God in such a way that while each is given his due, the beauty of the whole is in no sense violated, praises God in all things. This is the confession not of sinners but of the righteous. . . . The psalmist says, "I will confess to the Lord in accordance with his justice," as if he were someone who saw that darkness was not created by God but set in a providential order. . . . There is no such thing as a nature consisting in darkness. For all nature, insofar as it is nature, must exist. . . . Therefore, whoever deserts the God by whom he was made and leans in the direction of that from which he was made, that is, toward

---

[57]Mt 15:14. [58]PG 39:1184. [59]AnSac 3:388. [60]WSA 3 15:127. [61]FC 48:32-33. [62]PG 23:125.

nothing, is darkened in this sin. And yet he does not perish completely but is given a place in the ordered hierarchy among the lowest. EXPOSITIONS OF THE PSALMS 7.19.[63]

---

[63]WSA 3 15:127-28.

8:1-9 THE GLORY OF THE LORD

As you see the grace of the Savior extended everywhere,

so many being saved, if you wish to raise your voice to the Lord,

sing Psalm 8; or you can use the same psalm

as well as 84 in thanksgiving for the vintage harvest.

ATHANASIUS ON THE INTERPRETATION OF THE PSALMS 16 [OIP 67]

To the choirmaster: according to The Gittith.*
A Psalm of David.

¹*O* LORD, *our Lord,*
how majestic is thy name in all the earth!

Thou whose glory above the heavens is
chanted
²*by the mouth of babes and infants,*
thou hast founded a bulwark because of
thy foes,
to still the enemy and the avenger.

³*When I look at thy heavens, the work of thy*
fingers,
the moon and the stars which thou hast
established;
⁴*what is man that thou art mindful of him,*

and the son of man that thou dost care for
him?

⁵*Yet thou hast made him little less than*
God,
and dost crown him with glory and
honor.
⁶*Thou hast given him dominion over the*
works of thy hands;
thou hast put all things under his feet,
⁷*all sheep and oxen,*
and also the beasts of the field,
⁸*the birds of the air, and the fish of the sea,*
whatever passes along the paths of the sea.

⁹*O* LORD, *our Lord,*
how majestic is thy name in all the earth!

* LXX *for the wine press*

OVERVIEW: The superscription of the eighth psalm in the Septuagint is "for the winepresses." The presses are the churches, in which the saved are separated from the lost (AUGUSTINE), in which the Word of God is processed (AUGUSTINE). Previously, there was one press in Jerusalem, but now there are many throughout the world (PSEUDO-ATHANASIUS). There are also presses of truth in everyday life (DIDYMUS).

The psalmist begins by acknowledging the marvelous Lord (HESYCHIUS) and his wonderful name (CHRYSOSTOM). But the glories we see are only the back parts of God (GREGORY OF NAZIANZUS). God imparts praise to those who are infants in faith (CASSIODORUS), in spite of the enemies of the faith (AUGUSTINE). His work is an effortless mystery (CHRYSOSTOM) by the uncontained God (CYRIL OF JERUSALEM). He gives stability to the cosmic order (JOHN OF DAMASCUS), giving proof of his existence (GREGORY OF NAZIANZUS), and showing the error of philosophers (CLEMENT OF ALEXANDRIA). But he gives special honor to humankind (EUSEBIUS), considered from both an earthly and heavenly perspective (AUGUSTINE). It makes one wonder (CHRYSOSTOM). We are lowly yet exalted (GREGORY OF NAZIANZUS), flesh but also spirit (JEROME).

Our glory is a humble glory (CASSIODORUS). But, by his providence (PRUDENTIUS), God exalts the lowly (THEODORET), extending his dominion over the heavens (EUSEBIUS), with no exemptions (CASSIODORUS, DIODORE), except the Father and the Son, in whom the exaltation takes place (AMBROSE). Animal mortals become real people when visited by the Lord (AMBROSE). Only the blind decline submission to him (BEDE). And so, the superscription fits the words of the psalm, as God's presses separate wine from grape skins, subjecting souls to Christ (AUGUSTINE).

Superscription: *For the Winepress*

THE CHURCHES AS WINEPRESSES. AUGUSTINE: We . . . take winepresses as referring to the churches, by the same line of reasoning as we understand the threshing floor in terms of the church, because whether on the threshing floor or in the winepress, what happens is that fruit is stripped of its covering. The coverings were necessary for two reasons: that the crop might come to life and that it might reach its maturity whether of the harvest or the vintage. The crop, therefore, is stripped bare of its coverings or supports. Grain is separated from the straw on the threshing floor; grapes are stripped of their skin in the winepress. The same process takes place in our churches, so that through the work of God's ministers good people may be sifted out by spiritual love from the crowd of worldly people gathered there with them, a crowd that has, nonetheless, been necessary to bring the good to birth and prepared them to receive the divine word. EXPOSITIONS OF THE PSALMS 8.1.[1]

PROCESSING THE WORD OF GOD. AUGUSTINE: The divine Word can also be understood as a grape. . . . When the divine Word takes over the sound of the human voice in order to speak and reach the ears of the hearers, the content of the Word is encased like wine within the sound of the voice, which, in turn, is like grape skins. In this way the grape reaches our ears as if it were coming into the place where the grapes are trodden, and there it is processed in such a way that while the sound penetrates the ears, the meaning is caught in the memory of those who hear, as it were in a vat, and trickles through into a rule of behavior and habit of mind. EXPOSITIONS OF THE PSALMS 8.2.[2]

FROM ONE TO MANY PRESSES. PSEUDO-ATHANASIUS: Previously for the worship associated with the law there was one winepress, the altar in Jerusalem. But after the calling of the Gentiles there were many winepresses, which are the churches among all peoples, which receive the fruits of those who do good deeds in them. . . . Henceforth not only in Judah as previously, but also in all the [region] under the sun, God is praised. EXPOSITION ON PSALMS 8.[3]

THE PRESSES OF EVERYDAY LIFE. DIDYMUS THE BLIND: One who tends the cluster of grapes also enjoys the clusters of truth on that vine,

---

[1]WSA 3 15:129. [2]WSA 3 15:129-30. [3]CSCO 387:6.

which are necessary to gather in due season and to collect into the winepresses, so that the wine by its compression may make the hearts of people glad;[4] and some press out doctrines of truth; others, spiritual works. Nor is there one winepress; indeed, there are many useful virtues, and a winepress is prepared for the individual fruit of each one, as those who are celibate bear their fruit in respect to the winepress of modesty, and those who keep the marriage bed pure [bear their own fruit], and so forth. Many are the presses of everyday life to which the teachings apply that press out different principles of truth. FRAGMENTS ON THE PSALMS 8.1.[5]

8:1 The Lord's Name Is Majestic

THE MARVELOUS LORD. HESYCHIUS OF JERUSALEM: The church says, "O Lord, our Lord." For after the recognition of Christ when one is freed from the slavery of idolatry, one begins to call on God and the Lord. Always the whole earth truly is full of the marvelous creations, the works of God. And even more marvelous the name of that One, namely, Christ, has been made wonderful among all the nations and foreign peoples through faith in him. LARGE COMMENTARY ON PSALMS 8.2.[6]

GOD'S WONDERFUL NAME. CHRYSOSTOM: "How wonderful your name." Through this name, in fact, death was dissolved, demons imprisoned in bonds, heaven opened, gates of paradise thrown wide, the Spirit sent down, slaves made free, enemies become sons, strangers become heirs, human beings become angels. Why speak of angels? God became man, and man became God; heaven accepted the nature from earth, earth accepted the one seated on the cherubim along with the angelic host. The wall was removed, the partition dissolved, what were separate were united, darkness was banished, light shone, death was swallowed up. COMMENTARY ON THE PSALMS 8.1.[7]

ONLY THE BACK PARTS OF GOD. GREGORY OF NAZIANZUS: The Majesty, or as holy David calls it, the Glory, is manifested among the creatures that it has produced and governs. These are the back parts of God, which he leaves behind him, as tokens of himself like the shadows and reflection of the sun in the water, which show the sun to our weak eyes, because we cannot look at the sun himself, for by his unmixed light he is too strong for our power of perception. ON THEOLOGY, THEOLOGICAL ORATION 2(28).3.[8]

8:2 A Bulwark Founded

IMPARTED PRAISE. CASSIODORUS: The sense here is: You are not only worthy of praise from the perfect who know you fully, but you are proclaimed by the mouths of infants and little ones . . . those who have begun to draw near to the Lord in newness of faith, so that this wisdom might be seen to be imparted from heaven rather than amassed by human effort. EXPLANATION OF THE PSALMS 8.3.[9]

ENEMIES OF FAITH. AUGUSTINE: By enemies . . . we ought in a general sense to understand all who forbid us to believe in things beyond our experience, while themselves promising certain knowledge. This is what all heretics do, and the same holds for those who among superstitious Gentiles pass for philosophers. It is not that the promise of knowledge is reprehensible in itself, but rather that they think that the step of faith can be bypassed, a step most conducive to salvation and necessary for us. Yet it is precisely by taking this step that the ascent must be made to any form of real certainty, which cannot be other than eternal. From this it is clear that they do not possess even that knowledge that they promise, while scorning faith, because they are completely unaware of the step that is useful and necessary as a means to it. Therefore "from the mouths of infants and nurslings our Lord has perfected

---

[4]Ps 104:15 (103:15 LXX). [5]PG 39:1184-85. [6]PG 93:1181. [7]CCOP 1:155. [8]NPNF 2 7:289*. [9]ACW 51:111*.

praise," first laying down through the prophet the rule "unless you believe, you will not understand"[10] and then later saying in his own person, "blessed are those who have not seen, yet will believe."[11] EXPOSITIONS OF THE PSALMS 8.6.[12]

8:3 The Work of God's Fingers

EFFORTLESS MYSTERY. CHRYSOSTOM: And why did he not say "your hands" instead of "your fingers"? To show that visible things are a work requiring the least power, and the extraordinary aspect of creation, namely, that the stars hang there without falling; at any rate, though the very nature of the foundations required, not that they be suspended above but lie below, still the excellent Architect and Creator produced a surprise in making most of the visible things surpass the logic of nature. COMMENTARY ON THE PSALMS 8.6.[13]

THE UNCONTAINED GOD. CYRIL OF JERUSALEM: Now this Father of our Lord Jesus Christ is not circumscribed to some place, nor is there heaven beyond him, but "the heavens are the work of his fingers," and "the whole earth is holden in the hollow of his hand."[14] He is in everything, and yet nothing contains him. Do not imagine that God is smaller than the sun or that he is as large as the sun. For, as he made the sun, he must have been already incomparably greater than the sun and more resplendent with light. He knows what is to come, and nothing equals him in power. He knows everything and does as he wills. He is not subject to any law of sequence, or genesis, or fortune or fate. He is perfect by every measure. He possesses unchangeably every kind of virtue, never less and never more, but ever in the same degree and manner. CATECHETICAL LECTURES 4.5.[15]

COSMIC STABILITY. JOHN OF DAMASCUS: By saying "founded" he meant the stability and immutability of the order and succession given them by God. ORTHODOX FAITH 2.7.[16]

PROOF OF GOD'S EXISTENCE. GREGORY OF NAZIANZUS: Our very eyes and the law of nature teach us that God exists and that he is the efficient and maintaining cause of all things: our eyes, because they fall on visible objects and see them in beautiful stability and progress, immovably moving and revolving, if I may so say; natural law, because through these visible things and their order it reasons back to their author. For how could this universe have come into being or been put together unless God had called it into existence and held it together? For everyone who sees a beautifully made lute and considers the skill with which it has been fitted together and arranged, or who hears its melody, would think of none but the lutemaker or the luteplayer, and would recur to him in mind, though he might not know him by sight. And thus to us also is manifested that which made and moves and preserves all created things, even though he is not comprehended by the mind. ON THEOLOGY, THEOLOGICAL ORATION 2(28).6.[17]

THE ERROR OF PHILOSOPHERS. CLEMENT OF ALEXANDRIA: How great is the power of God! His bare volition was the creation of the universe. For God alone made it, because he alone is truly God. By the bare exercise of volition he creates; his mere willing was followed by the springing into being of what he willed. Consequently the choir of philosophers are in error, who indeed most nobly confess that humanity was made for the contemplation of the heavens but who worship the objects that appear in the heavens and are apprehended by sight. . . . Let none of you worship the sun, but set your desires on the Maker of the sun; nor deify the universe, but seek after the Creator of the universe. EXHORTATION TO THE GREEKS 4.[18]

THE HONOR GIVEN TO HUMANKIND. EUSEBIUS OF CAESAREA: You are mindful of man, and you

---

[10]Is 7:9 (LXX). [11]Jn 20:29. [12]WSA 3 15:131-32*. [13]CCOP 1:165. [14]Cf. Is 40:12. [15]LCC 4:101-2. [16]FC 37:217. [17]LCC 3:139-40. [18]ANF 2:190.

have concern for him because you did not make him as if he were a small and worthless animal, but he is worthy of so much honor that he is celebrated with hymns from the mouths of infants and sucklings. COMMENTARY ON PSALMS 8.4-5.[19]

THE EARTHLY AND THE HEAVENLY. AUGUSTINE: Those who bear the image of the earthly man, who is not a son of man, can be called "men"; but those who bear the image of the heavenly man are more truly called "sons of men." For the former is also called the old man, the latter the new man; but the new is born from the old because spiritual regeneration is begun by a change of earthly and worldly life, and on that account the new man is called a son of man. Therefore "man" in this context is earthly, whereas the "son of man" is heavenly. The former is separated from God at a great distance; the latter is present with God. And that is why God remembers the one, as far away from him, but the other he comes to visit; and by his presence he illuminates him with his countenance. For "salvation is far from sinners,"[20] but "the light of your countenance is stamped on us, Lord."[21] EXPOSITIONS OF THE PSALMS 8.10.[22]

MAKES ONE WONDER. CHRYSOSTOM: "What is it about human beings?" . . . Taking full account of such marvelous care and such wonderful providence on God's part, and the arrangements he put in place for the salvation of the human race, [the psalmist] is struck with complete wonder and amazement as to why on earth God considered them worthy of attention. Consider, after all, that all the visible things were for their sake. For them the design implemented from the time of Adam up to his coming; for them paradise, commandments, punishments, miracles, retribution, kindnesses after the Law; for them the Son of God became human. What could anyone say of the future they are intended to enjoy? So all those things are going through his mind when he says, to be thought worthy of such wonderful privileges, what must the human being be? I mean, if

you consider what was done and is being done for their sake, and what they will enjoy afterwards, you will be stricken with awe, and then you will see clearly how this being is an object of such attention on God's part. COMMENTARY ON THE PSALMS 8.6-7.[23]

LOWLY YET EXALTED. GREGORY OF NAZIANZUS: Would that I might mortify my members that are on the earth! Would that I might spend all for the spirit, walking in the way that is narrow and trodden by few, not the way that is broad and easy! For what comes after this life is splendid and great, and our hope is greater than our worth. "What is man that you are mindful of him?" What is this new mystery concerning me? I am small and great, lowly and exalted, mortal and immortal, earthly and heavenly. I am connected with the world below, and likewise with God; I am connected with the flesh, and likewise with the spirit. I must be buried with Christ, rise with Christ, be joint heir with Christ, become the Son of God, even God himself. ON HIS BROTHER ST. CAESARIUS, ORATION 7.23.[24]

FLESH AND SPIRIT. JEROME: The psalmist is speaking here of the frailty of the body and of human weakness, and what does he say? If you consider his flesh, what is a person? If you consider his spirit, he is noble. Let us by no means scorn the flesh, but let us reject its works. Let us not despise the body that will reign in heaven with Christ. "Flesh and blood can obtain no part in the kingdom of God"; no, not flesh and blood of themselves, but the works of the flesh. "Flesh and blood can obtain no part in the kingdom of God." How, then, are they going to reign together with Christ; how shall we be seated together in heaven in Christ? HOMILY ON PSALM 143.[25]

8:5 A Little Lower Than Angels

---

[19]PG 23:129. [20]Ps 119:155 (118:155 LXX). [21]Ps 4:6. [22]WSA 3 15:134. [23]CCOP 1:167*. [24]FC 22:24. [25]FC 48:381.

HUMBLE GLORY. CASSIODORUS: From this point on the humility and glory of the Lord Savior is recounted. He made him less not to oblige him to serve but by the spontaneous wish of his devoted love; as Paul says, "He emptied himself, taking the form of a servant."[26] The next words are "a little less than the angels," because he took up the cross of salvation for all; it is in this sense that the Creator of angels was made less than the angels—a little less, because though he took on a mortal body, he had no sin. He was "crowned with glory and honor" when, after his most marvelous resurrection, God insofar as he was made man was exalted and received the belief of the entire world. EXPLANATION OF THE PSALMS 8.6.[27]

8:6 Dominion Over the Works of God's Hands

BY GOD'S PROVIDENCE. PRUDENTIUS:
From his Providence, humanity has received
All that he grasps with imperious hand:
All that the sky and the earth and the sea
Yields from the air and the waves and the
    fields,
This he subjects to me, me to himself.
HYMNS FOR EVERY DAY 3.36-40.[28]

EXALTING THE LOWLY. THEODORET OF CYR: And this is a precise demonstration of your lovingkindness and power, he is saying, imbuing the lowly nature of human beings with wisdom so that they might have control over not only the land creatures but also those that fly and that swim and that do both, use their skills to hunt those in the heights and in the depths, and keep under control those that pass through the air and those hidden in the water. . . . Uncreated nature alone, you see, is separate from this subjection as something free. The nature that receives existence from it, however, is subject whatever it be—visible or invisible—to Christ the Lord, both as God and as man. Such is the honor human nature received from the God of all. Hence, as a conclusion he used the same verse as at the beginning:

"O Lord, our Lord, how wonderful is your name in all the earth!" COMMENTARY ON THE PSALMS 8.6-7.[29]

DOMINION OVER THE HEAVENS. EUSEBIUS OF CAESAREA: When it is says, "You have set him over the works of your hand," clearly the word reveals that he is set over the heavens, a man established by the God of the universe. How and when are these future things unless when the kingdom of heaven is received as an inheritance according to the promises made and according to the word of the apostle: "The heir of God and the coheirs of Christ"?[30] So in this age, let the earthly creatures as oxen, cattle, beasts of burden, birds and fish, be subject to humankind. To humankind is reserved the life common to angels in the heavenly city of God, when people are received into the kingdom of heaven and appointed over the works of the hands of God, and they will be the rulers and protectors of all things of the heavens, the moon and stars and everything of the heavens above. The letter to the Hebrews considering this word treats the statement for the future age: "All things you have placed under his feet." For after the lower course of this life, whenever that new age comes in which the kingdom of heaven is awaited and following the glorious appearance of our Savior all things will be subjected, according to that witness that has been made by the promise from the Father to him: "Sit on my right, until I place your enemies a footstool under your feet." COMMENTARY ON PSALMS 8.6.[31]

NO EXEMPTIONS. CASSIODORUS: "You have subjected all things under his feet". . . . Just as nothing is outside God's work, so it is demonstrated that nothing is separated from the power of Christ, for he will judge the world. The expression "all things" suggests that neither the earthly nor the heavenly is exempted. EXPLANATION OF THE PSALMS 8.7.[32]

---

[26]Phil 2:7. [27]ACW 51:113. [28]FC 43:16. [29]FC 101:85-86. [30]Cf. Rom 8:17. [31]AnSac 3:390-91. [32]ACW 51:113-14*.

THE LORD'S AUTHORITY. DIODORE OF TARSUS: There is no work of God that is exempt from the authority of the one appointed Lord. COMMENTARY ON PSALMS 8.[33]

EXCEPT THE FATHER AND THE SON. AMBROSE: The Father is not "among" all things, for to him it is confessed that "all things serve you." Nor is the Son reckoned "among" all things, for "all things were made by him," and "all things exist together in him, and he is above all the heavens." The Son, therefore, exists not "among" but above all things, being, indeed, after the flesh, of the people, of the Jews, but yet at the same time God over all, blessed forever, having a name that is above every name, it being said of him, "You have put all things in subjection under his feet." But in making all things subject to him, he left nothing that is not subject, even as the apostle has said.[34] ON THE CHRISTIAN FAITH 4.11.140.[35]

VISITED BY THE LORD. AMBROSE: One who, by way of ignorance, pretended to the insensibility and lack of knowledge characteristic of a beast begins to be a human once he has been encompassed by the grace of God. Indeed, if he is capable of reason and of grace, he is proved human by that very fact, and thus he rejoices that he has been separated from the dumb animals and has been admitted into the company of humankind, which God visits and protects. For what are human beings except that the Lord is mindful of them and that they are visited by the Lord? THE PRAYER OF JOB AND DAVID 3.9.26.[36]

THE BLIND DECLINE. BEDE: What the psalmist said of the Father concerning our Lord as he rose from the dead, "You have put all things under his feet," is surely the same as what our Lord himself said to his disciples as he rose, "All power in heaven and on earth has been given to me."[37] Indeed, even before he rose from the dead, the angelic virtues in heaven knew that they were rightfully subject to the human nature they saw had been specifically assumed by their Maker. Blind human beings on earth, however, disdained to be brought into subjection to one they knew had put on mortality in common with themselves; they declined to understand the divine power in his miracles, since they discerned that there was human weakness present in his sufferings. HOMILIES ON THE GOSPELS 2.8.[38]

8:7 Sheep and Cattle

CONTEXT QUALIFIES MEANING. AUGUSTINE: So, then, in accordance with the simile of the winepresses, not only the grapes but also the husks are trodden under his feet. This means not only sheep and cattle, that is to say, the holy souls of the faithful, either in the people or among the clergy, but, what is more, beasts of pleasure also and birds of pride and fish of inquisitiveness. All these types of sinners we see here and now in the churches mixed up with the good and the holy. Let God work, then, in his churches and separate wine from grapeskins. Let us cooperate with God so that we may be wine or sheep or cattle, rather than husks or beasts of the field or fish that weave their way through the pathways of the deep. This is not to say that these words can be understood and explained only in this way, but this is what the present context dictates. Somewhere else they may have a different meaning. This rule of thumb is to be upheld in every allegory, that what is expressed through a simile should be judged in the light of the immediate context. Such is the teaching of our Lord and the apostles. EXPLANATIONS OF THE PSALMS 8.13.[39]

---

[33]WGRW 9:28. [34]Cf. Heb 2:8. [35]NPNF 2 10:280. [36]FC 65:384*. [37]Mt 28:18. [38]CS 111:71. [39]WSA 3 15:138.

9:1-20 CONFIDENCE IN GOD

When the enemy is being accused and creation saved,

do not take the glory for yourself,

but know that this is the victory of the Son of God,

and sing to him in the words of Psalm 9.

*To the choirmaster: according to
Muthlabben.* A Psalm of David.*

*¹I will give thanks to the LORD with my whole
heart;
I will tell of all thy wonderful deeds.
²I will be glad and exult in thee,
I will sing praise to thy name, O Most
High.*

*³When my enemies turned back,
they stumbled and perished before thee.
⁴For thou hast maintained my just cause;
thou hast sat on the throne giving righteous
judgment.*

*⁵Thou hast rebuked the nations, thou hast
destroyed the wicked;
thou hast blotted out their name for ever
and ever.
⁶The enemy have vanished in everlasting
ruins;†
their cities thou hast rooted out;
the very memory of them has perished.*

*⁷But the LORD sits enthroned for ever,
he has established his throne for judgment;
⁸and he judges the world with righteousness,
he judges the peoples with equity.*

⁹The LORD is a stronghold for the oppressed,

*a stronghold in times of trouble.
¹⁰And those who know thy name put their
trust in thee,
for thou, O LORD, hast not forsaken those
who seek thee.*

*¹¹Sing praises to the LORD, who dwells in
Zion!
Tell among the peoples his deeds!
¹²For he who avenges blood is mindful of them;
he does not forget the cry of the afflicted.*

*¹³Be gracious to me, O LORD!
Behold what I suffer from those who hate
me,
O thou who liftest me up from the gates of
death,
¹⁴that I may recount all thy praises,
that in the gates of the daughter of Zion
I may rejoice in thy deliverance.*

*¹⁵The nations have sunk in the pit which they
made;
in the net which they hid has their own foot
been caught.
¹⁶The LORD has made himself known, he has
executed judgment;
the wicked are snared in the work of their
own hands. Higgaion. Selah*

¹⁷The wicked shall depart to Sheol,

all the nations that forget God.
¹⁸For the needy shall not always be forgotten,
 and the hope of the poor shall not perish
 for ever.

¹⁹Arise, O LORD! Let not man prevail;
 let the nations be judged before thee!
²⁰Put them in fear, O LORD!
 Let the nations know that they are but men!
           Selah

*LXX concerning the hidden things of the Son † LXX The swords of the enemy have given way at the end

---

OVERVIEW: The superscription of the ninth psalm differs in the Hebrew and Greek texts. The Hebrew superscription may be read as "for the death" and refers to the death of the Son (JEROME). The Septuagint refers to "hidden things of the Son," which indicates the secret of the Son's death (THEODORET). This one psalm in Greek is divided into two (Psalms 9 and 10) in Hebrew (DIODORE).

The psalm begins with wholehearted confession (AUGUSTINE), characteristic of an undivided heart (THEODORET). The psalmist finds happiness in God (CHRYSOSTOM), rejoicing in Christ (AUGUSTINE), singing a lover's song (CHRYSOSTOM). By the mere gaze of his power (CHRYSOSTOM), God destroyed the psalmist's enemies (CHRYSOSTOM), including death itself, the final enemy (EUSEBIUS).

Righteous judgment is unique to God (CHRYSOSTOM) and is here spoken in reference to the present, not just the future (SALVIAN). By his Word alone, God rebukes the godless of the nations (CHRYSOSTOM), not just in the temporal age but into the eternal (AUGUSTINE), blotting out their names in judgment (CASSIODORUS), although we note that there is a gracious blot as well (ORIGEN). The enemies' swords, misguided opinions propagated by the devil (AUGUSTINE), have been broken by the gospel (JOHN OF DAMASCUS), converted for true religion (THEODORET). The cities of the enemy, the devil (AUGUSTINE), have undergone destruction (CHRYSOSTOM). He has no power against us (ANTHONY). God's judgment was first hidden in Christ and will be revealed openly in the future (AUGUSTINE). The psalm warns the wicked (DIDYMUS), for judgment works in the present as well in the future

(CHRYSOSTOM). However, for the righteous, the Lord is our refuge (EUSEBIUS), the best refuge one could have (CHRYSOSTOM). They come to know him personally (AUGUSTINE) and find him totally sufficient (CHRYSOSTOM). He never abandons (DIDYMUS) those who diligently seek him (CHRYSOSTOM).

God dwells in Zion (CHRYSOSTOM), where songs proclaim the Lord's deeds by which he alters the state of things (THEODORET), especially changing the nature of human beings by faith in the gospel (CLEMENT OF ALEXANDRIA). God will exact vengeance for murder (CHRYSOSTOM), and he will vindicate the martyrs (IRENAEUS). God hears the cry of the poor in spirit (PSEUDO-ATHANASIUS) who devote themselves to constant prayer (CHRYSOSTOM). The one who prays for mercy will be lifted up from the gates of death (DIDYMUS), even as Christ was raised from death (EUSEBIUS). He will be transferred to the gates of Zion (ORIGEN), which are the gates of praise (DIDYMUS). We rejoice in God's salvation (CHRYSOSTOM). Christ is the salvation in which we rejoice (CASSIODORUS). And we enter more deeply into that joy as our deeds conform to our faith (BEDE).

The wicked are caught in their own sin (DIDYMUS), their own snares (EUSEBIUS), their own corruption (AUGUSTINE). Vice is the weakness of the wicked (CHRYSOSTOM). They cannot free themselves from it (CASSIODORUS). The Lord will execute external punishment on them (CASSIODORUS). The diapsalma, at this point, indicates that a new psalm is about to begin (DIDYMUS). A terrible, eternal disgrace awaits (PACHOMIUS). They forgot God (CLEMENT OF ALEXANDRIA). They rejected Christ (ATHANASIUS), not able to see him from within themselves (ORIGEN). But God will not forget his own (DIODORE). The proud will be rebuked, the humble blessed (CAESARIUS). Wrong will be reversed (EUSEBIUS). Perfection comes through patience (CASSIODORUS), a key feature of God's providential plan (LEO). A final appeal considers God's judgment on Antichrist (CASSIODORUS) and the imposition of Christ's law on the nations (EUSEBIUS).

Superscription: *Hidden Things of the Son*

THE HEBREW INSCRIPTION. JEROME: There is a difference here in the Hebrew text. The Hebrew reading . . . means "for the death" . . . for the death, therefore, of the Son, as the Hebrew text has it. HOMILY ON PSALM 9.[1]

THE SECRET OF THE SON'S DEATH. THEODORET OF CYR: This psalm . . . contains a prophecy of Christ the Lord's victory over death: having bravely and vigorously conquered sin without giving death any occasion of capture, he brought to an end its dominion. Now, the Septuagint called this mystery "secret," since it escaped the notice of everyone, including the apostles themselves. The Evangelist is witness to this frequent statement of the Lord to them, "See, we are going up to Jerusalem, and the Son of man will be handed over to be crucified, and they will kill him, and on the third day he will rise"; and the Evangelist added, "And this was hidden from their eyes."[2] . . . It was proper, therefore, for the Septuagint to call the Son's death a secret. COMMENTARY ON THE PSALMS 9.1.[3]

TWO PSALMS IN HEBREW. DIODORE OF TARSUS: This ninth psalm has been divided into two in the Hebrew. That is likely to be the case, since this psalm seems to have two themes. Its first part contains thanksgiving for God's ransoming them from neighbors and enemies against the odds at different times, whereas the other part of the psalm levels a clear accusation against the disdainful treatment by the wealthy of the poor members of the people. COMMENTARY ON PSALMS 9.[4]

9:1 *Wholehearted Thanks*

WHOLEHEARTED CONFESSION. AUGUSTINE: Whoever entertains doubts about God's providence in any particular does not confess to God with a whole heart. Wholehearted confession is, rather, the mark of the person who already discerns the hidden things of the wisdom of God, and how great is his invisible reward, the person who says, "We even rejoice in our sufferings."[5] Such people understand that all the hardships that are imposed on the body either offer training to those who have turned to God, or warn them to turn or else prepare the stubborn for the final and just judgment; and so they see that all things that the foolish think happen somehow by chance and at random, without any divine direction, are to be referred to the guidance of divine providence. EXPOSITIONS OF THE PSALMS 9.2.[6]

AN UNDIVIDED HEART. THEODORET OF CYR: It is characteristic of the perfect to dedicate their whole heart to God and to consecrate their whole mind to him. "You shall love the Lord your God with your whole heart," Scripture says, "with your whole soul, with your whole strength and with your whole mind."[7] Those who divide their thoughts between mammon and God, between Christ and gold, between the present and the future life, cannot truthfully say, "I shall confess to you, O Lord, with all my heart." COMMENTARY ON THE PSALMS 9.2.[8]

9:2 *Gladness and Exultation*

HAPPINESS IN GOD. CHRYSOSTOM: This . . . is pleasure properly speaking; at least as far as all other things are concerned, they are pleasure in name only, bereft of substance. This lifts human beings above this world, this liberates the soul from the body, this gives it wings in heaven's direction, this elevates it above worldly things, this gives free-

---

[1]FC 48:35-36. [2]Cf. Lk 18:31-34. [3]FC 101:87-88. [4]WGRW 9:30. [5]Rom 5:3. [6]WSA 3 15:140-41. [7]Lk 10:27; cf. Deut 6:5. [8]FC 101:88.

dom from evil, and rightly so. . . . After all, people loving those other things are quickly if unwillingly brought to a point of oblivion since what they love perishes and wastes away. By contrast, this love is infinite, everlasting, possessing the greater pleasure and the greater gain; furthermore, the lover is encouraged by the fact that this will never be destroyed. COMMENTARY ON THE PSALMS 9.2.[9]

IN CHRIST ALONE. AUGUSTINE: Not now in this age, not in the pleasure of bodily caresses, not in the flavors of the palate and the tongue, not in sweet scents, not in pleasant sounds that fade away, not in beautifully colored objects, not in the vanities of human praise, not in matrimony and offspring that one day will die, not in the abundance of temporal riches, not in this world's getting, whether it extend in space or be prolonged in the succession of time; but "in you I will rejoice and exult," that is, in the hidden things of the Son, where the light of your face, O Lord, has been stamped on us. For indeed "you will hide them," says a psalmist, "in the hidden recess of your face."[10] EXPOSITIONS OF THE PSALMS 9.3.[11]

A LOVER'S SONG. CHRYSOSTOM: This is a particular habit of a lover. Those in love, you know, sing songs to their beloved; even if they are not in sight, they comfort themselves with the song. That is just what the inspired author does. Since it is not possible to see God, he composes songs to him, holding converse with him in song, stirring up desire and gaining the impression of seeing him—or, rather, stirring up the desire of many people through the singing of hymns and songs. In other words, just as lovers recite the praises of their beloved and bandy their names about, exactly so does he. COMMENTARY ON THE PSALMS 9.2.[12]

9:3 Enemies Perished Before God

THE GAZE OF GOD'S POWER. CHRYSOSTOM: Now, notice how he proclaims God's strength: "They will lose heart and perish before your face." Once more, on hearing "face," do not form an

impression of anything bodily. At this point, in fact, he is suggesting God's power, his manifestation, the facility of his strength. Just as he says elsewhere, "He gazes on the earth and makes it tremble," so here too he says the same thing. His gaze, you see, is sufficient to destroy his enemies. COMMENTARY ON THE PSALMS 9.3.[13]

THE DESTRUCTION OF DEATH. EUSEBIUS OF CAESAREA: These things, he said, I will assuredly do "when my enemies are turned back." But who is such an enemy unless it is death, the enemy of life about which it is said, "You knew the enemy death will be destroyed." Destruction will be Death's end when he is turned back. But "back" where, unless the return into the pristine condition when he did not exist? "For God did not make death, but through the envy of the devil, death entered into the world." When, therefore, as death is turned back, it will no longer be, then all the rest of the enemies will be enfeebled and the enemies of your Word will be destroyed before your face. COMMENTARY ON PSALMS 9.3-4.[14]

9:4 On the Throne

JUDGMENT UNIQUE TO GOD. CHRYSOSTOM: He speaks in rather human terms by mentioning throne and seat, whereas the phrase "giving right judgment" is customary with God and expresses something remarkable of his essence. I mean, it is not something you can say in connection with human beings. They do not consistently give right judgments, you see, even if they are righteous over and over, ignorant as they are of what is righteous, sometimes from incompetence, sometimes from laziness. God, on the contrary, is free of all these impediments; knowing and willing a righteous verdict, he delivers it. So the phrase "you have sat on your throne" means God has judged, prosecuted, taken vengeance. COMMENTARY ON THE PSALMS 9.3.[15]

---

[9]CCOP 1:181-82. [10]Ps 31:20 (30:21 LXX). [11]WSA 3 15:141. [12]CCOP 1:182. [13]CCOP 1:183. [14]AnSac 3:393. [15]CCOP 1:184*.

PRESENT JUDGMENT. SALVIAN THE PRESBYTER: The same prophet showed elsewhere the difference between the present and future judgment of God. What did he say to the Lord about the verdict of the immediate trial? You have sat on the throne, you who judge justice. And what of God's future and everlasting judgment? "He shall judge the people in justice."[16] By these words, he distinguished the time element between the present and the future judgments of God. To point to our present judgment, he wrote, "You judge," and to distinguish the future from the present he later added, "He shall judge." THE GOVERNANCE OF GOD 2.6.[17]

9:5 Rebuking the Nations

BY GOD'S WORD ALONE. CHRYSOSTOM: You see how he has no need of weapons—sword, bows, arrows; rather, those things are mentioned in more human fashion. After all, God has only to censure, and those destined for punishment perish. COMMENTARY ON THE PSALMS 9.3.[18]

THE TEMPORAL AND THE ETERNAL. AUGUSTINE: What is "the age of the age," if not that of which this age is a kind of image and shadow? The cycle of times that succeed each other, while the moon wanes and again waxes full, while the sun each year finds its height again, while the spring, or summer, or autumn or winter passes only to return—all this is a kind of imitation of eternity. But the age of this age is that which consists in unchangeable eternity. It is like a verse that exists in the mind and a verse that is spoken. The former is understood, the latter is heard; and the former regulates the latter. That is why the former is effective in art and endures, whereas the latter sounds in the air and is gone. Likewise the mode of being of this changeable world is defined by that unchangeable world, which is spoken of as "the age of this age." And for this reason the latter endures in the art, that is, in the wisdom and power of God; but the other is carried on through the providential administration of the created order. EXPOSITIONS OF THE PSALMS 9.7.[19]

THE BLOT OF JUDGMENT. CASSIODORUS: From this point on, the most sacred event of the second coming of the Lord is explained, when unbelieving nations will be rebuked and the devil with his tricks will perish forever; for his stormy subversion will not continue when with the Lord's help everything will be calm. . . . The meaning "forever" has been suitably explained also in "till the world," the world here signifying the Lord's future kingdom, which will be ended by no age or time. . . . So let heretics stop saying that at some time the devil and his followers can be brought back to grace, for they are clearly told that they are to be condemned "forever till the world after this world," so that not even a trace of their name can survive. EXPLANATION OF THE PSALMS 9.6.[20]

A GRACIOUS BLOT. ORIGEN: The expression "you have rebuked" indicates correction: "You have blotted out his name." God blotted out the name Abram, making it Abraham, and Sarai, calling her Sarah, and Simon, naming him Peter. And thus it follows, the name of those are blotted out whom he has rebuked. . . . Observe, however, that it is not said, You have blotted out their names from the book of the living . . . but from the pledges that had been signed in the book of debtors or in the book of the dead among the household of the wicked; thus he inscribes the dead, and he registers their names on the earth. The Savior will inscribe the names of his disciples in the heavens. SELECTIONS FROM THE PSALMS 9.6.[21]

9:6 Everlasting Ruins

MISGUIDED OPINIONS. AUGUSTINE: "The swords of the enemy have given way at the end."

---

[16]Ps 96:13 (95:13 LXX). [17]FC 3:66. [18]CCOP 1:184. [19]WSA 3 15:144*. [20]ACW 51:119. [21]PG 12:1188.

These swords . . . are to be understood as various misguided opinions by which the devil destroys souls. EXPOSITIONS OF THE PSALMS 9.8.[22]

BROKEN BY THE GOSPEL. JOHN OF DAMASCUS: From there by his grace [the apostles] were scattered abroad among all nations and preached the orthodox faith, baptizing them in the name of the Father, and of the Son and of the Holy Spirit, and teaching them to observe all the commandments of the Savior. So they gave light to the people that wandered in darkness and abolished the superstitious error of idolatry. Though the enemy chafes under his defeat and even now stirs up war against us, the faithful, persuading the fools and unwise to cling to the worship of idols, yet is his power grown feeble, and his swords have at last failed him by the power of Christ. BARLAAM AND JOSEPH 7.55.[23]

CONVERSION. THEODORET OF CYR: [The godless one] was stripped of his own weapons, having no supporters of his godlessness; instead, those who appointed themselves his instruments have now changed sides and taken up the fight against him. With the overthrow of godlessness practiced in them in former times, the cities took on the building up of true religion; it would have been impossible for them to develop true religion had not they overthrown godlessness first. COMMENTARY ON THE PSALMS 9.5.[24]

THE CITIES OF THE ENEMY. AUGUSTINE: "And you have destroyed their cities": the cities, clearly, in which the devil rules, where deceitful and fraudulent purposes have something approaching the status of government. This sovereignty is maintained by the services of various parts of the body acting as satellites and ministers, the eyes for curiosity, the ears for lewdness or whatever else of ill repute is willingly listened to, the hand for looting or any other outrage or atrocity, and the other parts enlisted in a similar way under this tyrannical regime, that is, in the service of these evil purposes. The ordinary people, so to

speak, of this city are all the self-indulgent desires and the unsettling emotions of the mind, whipping up insurrection within a person every day. Now where a king, a court, ministers and common people are to be found, there is a state. Such characteristics would not be found in evil states unless they occurred first in individual people, who are like elements and seed of city-states. God brought about the destruction of these states when he drove out their ruler, of whom it is said, "Now has the ruler of this world been cast out."[25] These kingdoms are laid waste by the word of truth, the wicked purposes are silenced, base desires are subdued, the activities of limbs and senses taken prisoner and handed over to the active service of justice and good works. This is to make sure that here and now "sin shall reign no more in our mortal body,"[26] as the apostle says, together with other suchlike things. Then the soul is given peace and the person concerned put in proper order so as to receive serenity and blessedness. EXPOSITIONS OF THE PSALMS 9.8.[27]

COMPLETE DESTRUCTION. CHRYSOSTOM: God's anger is like that, you see: it razes and destroys everything. Or what another translator teaches us in saying "deserts," implying that he razed not only their inhabited places but also their uninhabited places, and laid waste their cities. Such, in fact, is the way the righteous person waged war, such the way he put down his foes, not employing light and heavy weapons but enjoying grace from God. Hence for him the war was glorious and famous, and his victory overwhelming. COMMENTARY ON THE PSALMS 9.3.[28]

NO POWER AGAINST US. ANTHONY THE GREAT (VIA ATHANASIUS): Once someone knocked at the door of my cell. And when I went out, I saw someone who seemed massive and tall. When I asked, "Who are you?" he said, "I am Satan." I said, "What are you doing here?" And he asked,

---

[22]WSA 3 15:145. [23]LCL 34:97*. [24]FC 101:90. [25]Jn 12:31. [26]Rom 6:12. [27]WSA 3 15:145. [28]CCOP 1:184.

"Why do the monks and all the other Christians censure me without cause? Why do they curse me every hour?" When I replied, "Why do you torment them?" he said, "I am not the one tormenting them, but they disturb themselves, for I have become weak. Haven't they read that 'the swords of the enemy have failed utterly, and that you have destroyed their cities'? I no longer have a place—no weapon, no city. There are Christians everywhere, and even the desert has filled with monks. Let them watch after themselves and stop censuring me for no reason!" Marveling then at the grace of the Lord, I said to him, "Even though you are always a liar and never tell the truth, nevertheless this time, even if you did not intend to, you have spoken truly. For Christ in his coming reduced you to weakness, and after throwing you down he left you defenseless." On hearing the Savior's name, and being unable to endure the scorching from it, he became invisible. Now if even the devil confesses that he is able to do nothing, then we ought to treat him and his demons with utter contempt. For his part, the enemy with his dogs has treacheries of the sort I have described, but we are able to scorn them, having learned of their weakness. Therefore let us not be plunged into despair in this way, or contemplate horrors in the soul or invent fears for ourselves. . . . Let us consider in our soul that the Lord is with us, he who routed them and reduced them to idleness. Let us likewise always understand and take it to heart that while the Lord is with us, the enemies will do nothing to us. LIFE OF ANTHONY 41-42.[29]

9:7 The Lord Enthroned

THE HIDDEN AND OPEN JUDGMENT. AUGUSTINE: He prepared his seat when he himself was judged, for through his endurance and suffering, humankind won heaven, and God in man benefited those who believe. This is the Son's hidden working. But he will also come openly and clear for all to see in order to judge the living and the dead. EXPOSITIONS OF THE PSALMS 9.9.[30]

9:8 The Lord Judges the World

A WARNING TO THE WICKED. DIDYMUS THE BLIND: These words warn that we must withdraw from evil and impiety and pursue excellence and righteousness. For who being prudent, if he believes this, would not fear that he might fall into the hands of judgment and rightly and properly so on account of his own blameworthy conduct and wicked thoughts? Indeed, under such judgment he will not avoid the curse. FRAGMENTS ON THE PSALMS 9.8.[31]

PRESENT AND FUTURE JUDGMENT. CHRYSOSTOM: While the general judgment is reserved for that time, the particular is for this; after all, he puts many things into effect here and now lest the heedless form the impression that present realities do not fall under his providence. If, on the contrary, not everyone receives their crown in this life, do not be surprised. "He has prepared a day," remember, "on which he intends to judge the world," whereas for the present there is an arena, contest, struggles. Hence not everyone receives their just desserts; instead, rewards are reserved there for those who do well and punishments for those who fail. COMMENTARY ON THE PSALMS 9.4.[32]

9:9 A Stronghold

THE LORD OUR REFUGE. EUSEBIUS OF CAESAREA: The righteous who now seek you know that you are not going to abandon them in the time of judgment. Let them hope strongly in you, having patience in everything awaiting the prepared retribution. COMMENTARY ON PSALMS 9.10, 11.[33]

THE BEST REFUGE. CHRYSOSTOM: He did not say, note, "My armies have proved your refuge, or money or ramparts"; instead, "the Lord has proved a refuge for the poor." He personally established me in safety, he is saying; nothing, in fact, is equal

---

[29]LALM 62-63*. [30]WSA 3 15:146. [31]PG 39:1192. [32]CCOP 1:186. [33]PG 23:133.

to that refuge on the score of ease and security. The other refuges may be subject to scheming and cannot be found promptly and readily, but they are obstructed by time and place and countless circumstances; this, by contrast, you find close at hand, provided only you search for it diligently. "Even while I am talking to you, lo, I am at hand," remember; and "I am a God close by, not a God far off." [34] Consequently, there is no need of running around or traveling about; rather, those sitting at home can gain this refuge. COMMENTARY ON THE PSALMS 9.5.[35]

9:10 Those Who Know God's Name

PERSONAL KNOWLEDGE. AUGUSTINE: The name of God is by now spread far and wide, but knowledge of that name exists only when he is known, whose name it is: a name is not a name for its own sake but for the sake of that which it signifies. Scripture says, "The Lord is his name."[36] This means that whoever has willingly subjected himself to God as a servant has come to know this name. EXPOSITIONS OF THE PSALMS 9.11.[37]

TOTALLY SUFFICIENT. CHRYSOSTOM: Those who know you, he is saying, your support and assistance, have hope in you as sufficient anchor, sufficient assistance, impregnable tower, the one who not only promises relief from problems but also does not permit us to be alarmed by the problems even when present. COMMENTARY ON THE PSALMS 9.5.[38]

GOD NEVER ABANDONS US. DIDYMUS THE BLIND: Those who have a perfect knowledge of your name trust in no other thing. They are not abandoned by God. This word must be understood with wisdom and reverence, considering that one should not think that the person who lives rightly in his daily affairs is abandoned by God. One who thinks thus is deceived. Indeed, several of the impious have thus believed. Some say that Abel, who was killed, was abandoned, as also the prophets and apostles, for these individu-

als were afflicted continuously, and many of them even murdered by people. With this distinction made, we say that the person who is with God up to his last breath is not abandoned, even if he suffers innumerable wounds from his enemies. FRAGMENTS ON THE PSALMS 9.11.[39]

DILIGENTLY SEEK GOD. CHRYSOSTOM: So how can we seek God? When we earnestly direct our mind in that direction, when we free it from worldly interests. The seeker who drives out everything from the soul moves toward what is being sought. We must not simply seek but seek out. Those who seek out do not only take it on themselves to conduct the search but also enlist other aids to finding what is sought. But in the case of worldly things, we often do not find what we have sought for, whereas in the case of spiritual things this is impossible, as it is inevitable that the searcher makes the discovery. In fact, if we merely make the effort toward searching, God will not permit us to be rebuffed; hence he says, "Everyone who seeks finds."[40] COMMENTARY ON THE PSALMS 9.6.[41]

9:11 The Lord Lives in Zion

GOD IN ZION. CHRYSOSTOM: What do you mean? Does the one whose throne is heaven and his footstool earth, in whose hands are the bounds of the earth, dwell in Zion? Yes: he refers here to his dwelling, not for him to be circumscribed (his greatness, after all, is unbounded) but to indicate his affinity with the place and his feeling at home there with a view to winning the Jews over to him through this considerateness. . . . Now, in a spiritual sense Zion refers to the church: "You have approached Mount Zion," remember, "and church of the firstborn."[42] Rightly is the church called a mountain on account of being firm, solid and unshakeable. You

---

[34]Jer 23:23. [35]CCOP 1:187. [36]Jer 33:2; Amos 5:8. [37]WSA 3 15:147. [38]CCOP 1:188. [39]PG 39:1192-93. [40]Mt 7:8. [41]CCOP 1:189. [42]Cf. Heb 12:22-28.

see, just as it is impossible to shake a mountain, so too the church of God. COMMENTARY ON THE PSALMS 9.6.[43]

GOD'S EXPLOITS—AN ALTERATION OF REALITY. THEODORET OF CYR: A drastic alteration of circumstances took place in reality: ancient enemies became friends, those distant became close, slaves became sons, those ignorant became knowledgeable, those in darkness came to be in light, the dead in hope of life the poor became heirs of the kingdom of heaven, Jews came to be far away and Gentiles close at hand, sons became dogs, dogs sons. In short, the Savior's devices took on a divine seemliness: the gift of immortality was given through mortality, life through death, honor through dishonor, blessing through curse, salvation through a cross—these are the devices, these the exploits of our God. COMMENTARY ON THE PSALMS 9.8.[44]

GOSPEL PROCLAMATION. CLEMENT OF ALEXANDRIA: Those who are wild in respect of faith and polluted in life, not purified by the righteousness that is according to the law, are called wild beasts. But changed from wild beasts by the faith of the Lord, they become people of God, advancing from the wish to change to the fact. For some the Lord exhorts, and to those who have already made the attempt he stretches forth his hand and draws them up. "For the Lord dreads not the face of anyone, nor will he regard greatness; for he has made small and great and cares alike for all."[45] And David says, "For the heathen are fixed in the destruction they have caused; their foot is taken in the snare that they hid."[46] "But the Lord was a refuge to the poor, a help in season also in affliction."[47] Those, then, who were in affliction had the gospel seasonably proclaimed. And therefore it said, "Declare among the heathen his pursuits," that they may not be judged unjustly. STROMATEIS 6.6.[48]

9:12 God Remembers the Afflicted

VENGEANCE. CHRYSOSTOM: He also touches

on an important truth here: there is no murder committed that goes unpunished and is not fully avenged. Moses indicates as much in Genesis in the words "I will avenge your blood."[49] This is proof of God's boundless providence, of his intense care. Yet if he does not promptly take vengeance, do not be surprised: he gives the sinner the opportunity of repentance. COMMENTARY ON THE PSALMS 9.6.[50]

MARTYRS VINDICATED. IRENAEUS: Some . . . have proceeded to such a degree of temerity that they pour contempt on the martyrs and vituperate those who are slain on account of the confession of the Lord, and who suffer all things predicted by the Lord and who in this respect strive to follow the footprints of the Lord's passion, having become martyrs of the suffering One; these we do also enroll with the martyrs themselves. For when inquisition shall be made for their blood and they shall attain to glory, then all shall be confounded by Christ, who have cast a slur on their martyrdom. AGAINST HERESIES 3.18.5.[51]

9:13 Be Gracious to Me

THE CRY OF THE POOR IN SPIRIT. PSEUDO-ATHANASIUS: The Lord does not forget the cry of the poor, and especially of those who in the spirit ask of him vengeance for wrongs brought against them by demons. Those who pray that there may arise a Savior for those on earth in order to repress the second tyrannical man who waxed strong against us and to impose on us the spiritual law of the gospel, from which people who are rational may learn, no more to imitate senseless animals. They are also hastening to his coming, hoping for salvation. EXPOSITION ON PSALMS 9.[52]

CONSTANT PRAYER. CHRYSOSTOM: See him

---

[43]CCOP 1:189-90. [44]FC 101:91-92. [45]Wis 6:7. [46]Ps 9:15 (9:16 LXX). [47]Ps 9:9 (9:10 LXX). [48]ANF 2:492*. [49]Gen 9:5. [50]CCOP 1:190. [51]ANF 1:447. [52]CSCO 387:7.

given constantly to prayer: though freed from troubles and made secure, he does not cease from praying again in the words "have pity on me" and implores God for future benefits. You see, we always stand in need of God's providence, but especially at a time of freedom from troubles. I mean, another battle follows that is more difficult than the former, that against indifference and obtuseness; then it is that the devil comes panting more aggressively. And so it is especially after being freed from troubles that we have need of that grace so as to cope with good times more easily. COMMENTARY ON THE PSALMS 9.6.[53]

THE PRAYER FOR MERCY. DIDYMUS THE BLIND: For one who lives in this type of death and in the lusts of the world, with a depressed spirit, if he will perceive a sense of his own wrongdoing and the nature of divine goodness, let him say in the manner of a prayer: "Have mercy on me and see my humility," which I suffer from my enemies. They have humiliated me, drawing me down. You alone are able to lift me up from the gates of death because of your essential goodness. FRAGMENTS ON THE PSALMS 9.15.[54]

9:14 Praises in the Gates

CHRIST'S RESURRECTION. EUSEBIUS OF CAESAREA: David, . . . prophesying in the person of Christ, says somewhere of his resurrection after death: . . . "You who lift me up from the gates of death, that I may tell all your praises." I consider that not even the most obtuse can look these things in the face [and disregard them]. PROOF OF THE GOSPEL 3.2.101.[55]

FROM DEATH TO ZION. ORIGEN: In the Psalms the prophet gives thanks saying, "He who lifts me up from the gates of death that I may declare all your praises in the gates of the daughter of Zion." And from this we learn that it is never possible for anyone to be fit to declare the praises of God, unless he has been lifted up from the gates of

death and has come to the gates of Zion. COMMENTARY ON THE GOSPEL OF MATTHEW 12.13.[56]

THE GATES OF PRAISE. DIDYMUS THE BLIND: The gates of the daughter of Zion, being opposed to the gates of death, are praiseworthy deeds and the contemplation on the works of God done according to excellence and wisdom. FRAGMENTS ON THE PSALMS 9.15.[57]

REJOICING IN GOD'S SALVATION. CHRYSOSTOM: "I will rejoice in your salvation." This is my crown, this my diadem, erecting a trophy thanks to you, enjoying salvation thanks to you. Let us too in this manner seek not to be saved at any price, not to be freed at any price and in any fashion but in God's way. COMMENTARY ON THE PSALMS 9.7.[58]

THE SALVATION IN WHICH WE REJOICE. CASSIODORUS: The salvation of the Father is the Lord Christ, his Strength and Wisdom, who has given us eternal rest and salvation. So the prophet rightly proclaims that he rejoices in him, for there is no end of joy there. EXPLANATION OF THE PSALMS 9.15.[59]

DEEPER JOY. BEDE: We need to direct our whole intention, dearly beloved brothers, to learning the mysteries of the faith, and we need to show that our works accord with our faith. With all vigilance we need to beware of the multifarious and subtle snares of the gates of hell, so that, in accordance with the word of the psalmist, we may be worthy to be snatched from these [snares] by the Lord's aid and to announce his praises at the gates of the daughter of Zion, that is, to enter into the joys of the heavenly city. And we should not think that it is sufficient for our salvation if either in our faith or our acts we [merely] come up to the level of the undiscerning and untaught crowd, for whom there is prescribed in the sacred

---

[53]CCOP 1:191. [54]PG 39:1193, 1196. [55]POG 1:116. [56]ANF 9:457. [57]PG 39:1196. [58]CCOP 1:192. [59]ACW 51:123.

literature only one rule of believing and of living. But as often as the examples of those who have gone astray are made known to us, let us immediately turn away the eyes of our mind so that they may not see vanity,[60] and instead with attentive heart let us examine what truth itself discerns, following the example of blessed Peter. He rejected the false ideas of those who were in error, and with unhesitating words he delivered his confession of the hidden mystery of the faith he had come to recognize, and he kept [it] with unconquerable care in his heart. HOMILIES ON THE GOSPELS 1.20.[61]

9:15 The Pit They Made

THE WICKED CAUGHT IN THEIR OWN SIN. DIDYMUS THE BLIND: One is not held by the sin and unrighteousness of another; rather, each one will die in his own sin. The wicked, first harming themselves, strive deceitfully to drive others into the same curse. Secretly they build traps of deceit with their own plans and words, so they may seize someone unsuspecting. But by that very trap that they have hidden they are punished, for vindicators will keep those very ones they have caught. This punishment is done by the providence of God. For what other is the judgment of God than that the sinner is caught by his own deeds, because he holds the reason for his own condemnation for those who live unrighteously. This agrees with that which is said before: "He who has opened a pit for his neighbor will fall into it."[62] FRAGMENTS ON THE PSALMS 9.16.[63]

CAUGHT IN THEIR OWN SNARES. EUSEBIUS OF CAESAREA: Whenever they desire to wipe out and abolish the race of the faithful, they themselves are lured into their own calamity; and in the very snares they have concealed for the people of God they are caught, and "their foot will fall." COMMENTARY ON PSALMS 9.16-17.[64]

CAUGHT IN CORRUPTION. AUGUSTINE: Notice how the punishment is reserved for the sinner

from out of his own deeds. . . . "Their own foot has been caught in the very trap that they set." This hidden trap is deceitful scheming. The foot of the soul is properly understood as love. When it is misshapen, it is called concupiscence or lust; when it is well formed it is called love or charity. Love moves a thing in the direction toward which it tends. But the dwelling place of the soul is not in any physical space that the form of the body occupies, but in delight, where it rejoices to have arrived through love. Destructive pleasure follows greed; fruitful delight follows love. . . . The foot of sinners, that is, their love, is caught in the trap that they themselves hide. This is because when pleasure has followed deceitful action, when God has handed them over into the lusts of their heart, the pleasure already binds them in such a way that they do not dare to tear their love from it and apply it to useful objects. When they try to do so, they will suffer great inner pain, longing to pull their foot from the snare. Conquered by this pain, they refuse to withdraw from the harmful things they love. In the "trap that they have set," therefore, that is, in deceitful plotting, "their foot has been caught," for their love has led them to empty pleasure, from which pain results. EXPOSITIONS OF THE PSALMS 9.15.[65]

THE WEAKNESS OF THE WICKED. CHRYSOSTOM: Nothing . . . is so destructive as vice. In fact, nothing is weaker than the wicked; they are undone by their own weapons, as iron is by rust and wool by a moth—so too is the wicked person by vice. COMMENTARY ON THE PSALMS 9.15.[66]

CANNOT FREE THEMSELVES. CASSIODORUS: By "the Gentiles stuck fast" he means those . . . fastened by the nails, so to speak, of sins, so that they cannot free themselves from the harsh bonds that are seen to restrain them. . . . When we talk of persons taken, we mean those drawn tight by intricate deceit. "Foot" indicates mental

---

[60]Ps 119:37 (118:37 LXX). [61]CS 110:203. [62]Ps 7:15 (7:16 LXX). [63]PG 39:1195-1196. [64]AnSac 3:394. [65]WSA 3 15:150*. [66]CCOP 1:192.

steps and the debased longing that makes them advance toward evil. As Solomon says in Proverbs, "Their feet run to evil and make haste to shed blood."[67] EXPLANATION OF THE PSALMS 9.16.[68]

9:16 Snared in Their Own Works

ETERNAL PUNISHMENT. CASSIODORUS: The Lord shall be clearly observed to execute judgments when sinners are allotted the agony of eternal torture. In this life their crimes are uncontrolled, and accordingly they may be assumed to be left unpunished, but when the day of his appearance comes and the Lord Savior sits on the throne of his majesty, there will be universal recognition that his judgments are in session, when the human race by his decree will be divided on left and on right. To execute judgments means investigating the deserts of individuals without obfuscation. There follows the open declaration of this statement, for he states how it is known that the Lord truly executes judgments; that is, when the sinner is held tight in the noose of his own deeds and suffers worthy vengeance according to the nature of his acts. EXPLANATION OF THE PSALMS 9.16.[69]

A NEW PSALM BEGINS. DIDYMUS THE BLIND: For if the whole psalm is called a song because of its tone and force, then the term "song" would be placed at the beginning of [the psalm], as it is in a number of psalms. But here it is otherwise, and after the diapsalma he begins the song; the title is placed between the diapsalma and song. It is reasonable, therefore, that the following has the sense of a psalm. FRAGMENTS ON THE PSALMS 9.16.[70]

9:17 The Wicked Shall Depart

A TERRIBLE DISGRACE. PACHOMIUS: O what a terrible disgrace! In the world you went about praised as one of the elect, and when you arrive in the valley of Josaphat, the place of judgement, you are found naked, and all see your sins and ugliness laid bare to God and people. Woe to you at that moment! Where will you turn your face? Will you open your mouth? To say what? Your sins are etched into your soul, which is as black as a hair shirt. What will you do at that moment? Weep? There will be no one to accept your tears. Pray? No one to accept your prayers, for those to whom you are handed over are pitiless. How awful the moment when you hear the terrible, cutting voice, "Sinners, go to hell," and, "Depart from me, you damned, to the eternal fire prepared for the devil and his angels,"[71] and again, "I have detested those who transgress."[72] "I must wipe out of the city of the Lord all who commit iniquities."[73] INSTRUCTIONS 1.33.[74]

PRIOR KNOWLEDGE. CLEMENT OF ALEXANDRIA: They forget, plainly, him whom they formerly remembered and dismiss him whom they knew previous to forgetting him. There was then a dim knowledge of God also among the nations. STROMATEIS 6.8.[75]

REJECTION OF CHRIST. ATHANASIUS: When, by faith and knowledge, the Lord's people have embraced true life, they surely receive the joy of heaven. The wicked, however, since they do not care about the Lord's life, are rightly deprived of its blessings. For "let the wicked be taken away so that he shall not see the glory of the Lord."[76] In the end they, like everyone else, shall hear the universal proclamation of the promise, "Awake, sleeper, and rise up from the dead."[77] They shall rise and knock on the doors of heaven, saying, "Open to us."[78] The Lord, however, will rebuke them for rejecting knowledge of him and will tell them, "I do not know you."[79] And the Holy Spirit speaks against them, "The wicked shall be turned into hell, and all nations that forget God." FESTAL LETTERS 7.2.[80]

---

[67]Prov 1:16. [68]ACW 51:123*. [69]ACW 51:123-24. [70]PG 39:1196-97. [71]Mt 25:41. [72]Ps 101:3 (100:3 LXX). [73]Ps 101:8 (100:8 LXX). [74]CS 47:28. [75]ANF 2:495. [76]Is 26:10 (LXX). [77]Eph 5:14. [78]Mt 25:11. [79]Lk 13:25. [80]ARL 116.

UNABLE TO SEE. ORIGEN: They are shut off, he said, in that they, since they are turned in the opposite direction within, do not see the spirit of Jesus ascending and descending. SELECTIONS FROM THE PSALMS 9.18.[81]

9:18 Not Always Forgotten

NOT FORGOTTEN. DIODORE OF TARSUS: Even if by some permission his people suffered and were humbled, yet God will not forget his own forever. "The perseverance of the needy will not be lost forever"; instead, he trains his own in perseverance, and when he sees them persevering properly, the patience he produces in them is not without purpose. COMMENTARY ON PSALMS 9.[82]

THE PROUD REBUKED. CAESARIUS OF ARLES: All who are proud should realize that since the beginning of the world they have been, are and should be rebuked in all kinds of publications. However, in both the Old and New Testaments all the humble and mild have been, are and should be blessed, because God does not lie when he says, "God resists the proud but gives grace to the humble."[83] SERMON 49.2.[84]

THE REVERSAL OF WRONG. EUSEBIUS OF CAESAREA: In this life the wicked are raised up, in no sense comprehending their own wicked wrongdoing. But there will be a time of the judgment of God in which the crime that they have admitted will be overturned [in hades, when they are about to receive punishments; LXX]. Every person of God, however humbled in this life, whenever poor in spirit and however much he is trampled by the wicked so that it seems that God denies him by his forgetfulness, through it all is never rejected. "For the poor shall not be forgotten forever," and the patience that he brings to this life and his calm spirit will not follow the end without fruit. COMMENTARY ON PSALMS 9.18-19.[85]

PATIENCE. CASSIODORUS: If patience is lacking in the midst of any hardship, a soul cannot be perfect. Patience is the act of thanksgiving continually maintained in the fear of the Lord amid the troublesome difficulties of the world until death. EXPLANATION OF THE PSALMS 9.19.[86]

GOD'S PROVIDENTIAL PLAN. LEO THE GREAT: Let Christian kindness overflow in you, dearly beloved. As you desire the recurring seasons of the year to be filled with fruit, so let your hearts be generous in feeding the poor. Assuredly, God . . . could produce the necessary materials for them, since all things are his. He could distribute so much goods to them that they would need nothing from your generosity. Much of the matter of virtue would be lacking to them and to you, if their want did not drive them to the crown of patience or your abundance lead you to the glory of compassion. Divine Providence has wonderfully arranged it that there should be in the church both holy poor and good rich people, who in turn benefit each other from their very diversity. In order for the eternal and incorruptible rewards to be gained, those receiving give thanks to God, and those distributing give thanks to God, for as it is written, . . . "the patience of the poor will not perish forever," and "God loves a cheerful giver."[87] SERMON 89.6.1.[88]

9:19 Let Not Humankind Prevail

ANTICHRIST. CASSIODORUS: When the prophet was discussing the end of the world, he foresaw the coming of Antichrist in the clear light of his heart, and terrified by the magnitude of the danger, he cried aloud, "Arise, O Lord, let not humankind prevail." He is indeed a most wicked man whom the human condition cannot endure, who embodies such deceit or power that only God's strength can defeat his wickedness. EXPLANATION OF THE PSALMS 9.20.[89]

---

[81]PG 12:1189. [82]WGRW 9:33. [83]Jas 4:6. [84]FC 31:251. [85]AnSac 3:394-95. [86]ACW 51:125. [87]2 Cor 9:7. [88]FC 93:378. [89]ACW 51:125.

9:20 *Let the Nations Know*

THE NEW LAW OF CHRIST. EUSEBIUS OF CAE-SAREA: He urges God by his tolerance and the strength of his mercy and patience that he grant a time of trials of long duration to the people harass-ing him. Before he had prayed that the nations be judged in the sight of God; now he asks that a law-giver be appointed for the nations before the future judgment, so that they might learn they are people and not brute animals, for the law was hardly given to brutish animals. This law is not from Moses, who once had carried it from the midst of people; it is not about the law given to the Jews alone, nor does he wish that another law be awaited, as the law of the New Testament stretches over the whole earth. Indeed, Christ is the Lawgiver, and the Gospel message applies to the nations.[90] COMMENTARY ON PSALMS 9.20, 21.[91]

---

[90]See also Is 42:1-4. [91]PG 23:133.

10:1-18 PLEA FOR GOD'S JUDGMENT

In the Psalms we read how afflictions must be borne,
and what one should say both during and after the affliction.

ATHANASIUS ON THE INTERPRETATION OF THE PSALMS 10 [OIP 62]

[1]*Why dost thou stand afar off, O LORD?*
    Why dost thou hide thyself in times of
      trouble?
[2]*In arrogance the wicked hotly pursue the*
      poor;
    let them be caught in the schemes which
      they have devised.

[3]*For the wicked boasts of the desires of his*
      heart,
    and the man greedy for gain curses and
      renounces the LORD.
[4]*In the pride of his countenance the wicked*
      does not seek him;
    all his thoughts are, "There is no God."

[5]*His ways prosper at all times;*
    thy judgments are on high, out of his sight;
    as for all his foes, he puffs at them.

[6]*He thinks in his heart, "I shall not be moved;*
    throughout all generations I shall not meet
      adversity."

[7]*His mouth is filled with cursing and deceit*
      and oppression;
    under his tongue are mischief and iniquity.
[8]*He sits in ambush in the villages;*
    in hiding places he murders the innocent.

His eyes stealthily watch for the hapless,
    [9]*he lurks in secret like a lion in his covert;*
he lurks that he may seize the poor,
    he seizes the poor when he draws him into
      his net.

[10]*The hapless is crushed, sinks down,*
    and falls by his might.
[11]*He thinks in his heart, "God has forgotten,*

he has hidden his face, he will never see it.”

¹²*Arise, O LORD; O God, lift up thy hand;*
forget not the afflicted.
¹³*Why does the wicked renounce God,*
and say in his heart, “Thou wilt not call to
account”?

¹⁴*Thou dost see; yea, thou dost note trouble*
and vexation,
that thou mayst take it into thy hands;
the hapless commits himself to thee;
thou hast been the helper of the
fatherless.

¹⁵*Break thou the arm of the wicked and*
evildoer;
seek out his wickedness till thou find none.
¹⁶*The LORD is king for ever and ever;*
the nations shall perish from his land.

¹⁷*O LORD, thou wilt hear the desire of the*
meek;
thou wilt strengthen their heart, thou wilt
incline thy ear
¹⁸*to do justice to the fatherless and the*
oppressed,
so that man who is of the earth may strike
terror no more.

OVERVIEW: The tenth psalm speaks of conditions in which God seems to be absent (CASSIODORUS). The situation is such that evil is applauded (CHRYSOSTOM). The wicked are deceived by human praise (CASSIODORUS) regarding what constitutes divine blessing (DIDYMUS). Such is the condition of the disease of pride (MARTIN). The wicked person is unaware of God (DIODORE), caught up in a culpable self-deception (THEODORET), totally absorbed in vice (CHRYSOSTOM). Such is the peril of flattery (CHRYSOSTOM). The wicked one is caught in a corrupting ignorance (EUSEBIUS), totally defiled (AUGUSTINE), repeating the pattern of the devil (DIDYMUS). His mouth is filled with arrogant blasphemies (EUSEBIUS); his mind is caught up in fantasies (CHRYSOSTOM). The wicked one is most aptly described by images of wild beasts (CHRYSOSTOM), especially by the image of a lurking lion (DIDYMUS). The image aptly describes the final persecution enacted by the Antichrist (CASSIODORUS). The mouth of Antichrist expresses a double perversion—blasphemy and bitterness (CASSIODORUS) in contrast to the righteous one who praises God at all times (EVAGRIUS). The wicked go on their way in blind ignorance of God (AUGUSTINE).

The psalmist then appeals to the righteous judgment of God, symbolized by the uplifted hand (EUSEBIUS). The truth will prevail (CASSIODORUS). We know by faith that God keeps account of human behavior (THEODORET) and that it is good to be in the hands of God (CASSIODORUS). The spiritually poor and orphaned abandon themselves to him (DIDYMUS). But when divine forebearance does not lead to repentance, punishment follows (CHRYSOSTOM). Both the sinner and the wicked one will be broken (EVAGRIUS), and the arrogant will learn the precariousness of power (CHRYSOSTOM). God, who is before any beginning and after any end (GREGORY OF NYSSA), will reign in the human heart (DIDYMUS) and in the future, after Antichrist is defeated (CASSIODORUS). The effects of his power will be manifest (CASSIODORUS), and glory will go to God alone(EUSEBIUS).

10:1-2 *Standing Far Off*

AN APPARENT ABSENCE. CASSIODORUS: In his concern for the afflicted he says to the Lord in the fashion of human weakness, “Why have you retired afar off?” Not that God leaves a place and passes to another district, for he is wholly everywhere; but he is imagined to have retired, so to say, when he is slow to lend help. . . . We consider ourselves slighted if we are put off even for the shortest time, but his help is all the more fruitful when he accords us the consolations of great patience. EXPLANATION OF THE PSALMS 10.22.[1]

10:3 The Wicked One Boasts

EVIL APPLAUDED. CHRYSOSTOM: This is what the inspired author laments, that evil has so prevailed as to be something to be proud of and spoken openly about, and what is more regrettable, that it is shameless and not simply applauds itself for its achievements but also has others to applaud it. COMMENTARY ON THE PSALMS 10.9.[2]

DECEIVED BY HUMAN PRAISE. CASSIODORUS: When the evil person is praised, he is in high spirits, and the person who finds a fawning eulogizer does not think of self-correction. Next comes the exaltation of wickedness, so that the person known as an evildoer is blessed. Such a person is beguiled by spurious adulators and puffs himself up with the lofty pride of tyranny. This we must take as referring especially to Antichrist, who is so inveigled by the bands of deceivers that he proclaims himself not only as earthly king but also the God of all things. EXPLANATION OF THE PSALMS 10.24.[3]

DECEIVED ABOUT BLESSING. DIDYMUS THE BLIND: [The wicked] are chiefly of this type who lack wisdom and spiritual resources, nor do they hold to teachings of the faith correctly. They incur the judgment of wise providence when they praise the sinner indulging in his own desires. However, it becomes apparent enough that the sinner strives not for better things but for more pleasing and desirous ones. In addition to that mistake, they judge that they who have riches and human glory are taking part in blessing. Accordingly, they claim the wicked are blessed by God; but it is necessary to believe that blessing of God is granted to the religious. FRAGMENTS ON THE PSALMS 10.3.[4]

THE DISEASE OF PRIDE. MARTIN OF BRAGA: The disease of pride is acute; it poisons from

either side, and it wounds when least expected. For some boast of themselves because they are good, others because they are bad. Of the good who boast it is said, "For God has scattered the bones of those who are pleased with themselves." Of the evil who boast it is said, "For the wicked person is praised in the desires of his soul, and the worker of injustice shall be blessed." DRIVING AWAY VANITY 4.[5]

10:4 The Wicked One Does Not Seek God

UNAWARE OF GOD. DIODORE OF TARSUS: In his wish to give vent to his anger and desires, [a wicked person] becomes so caught up in his passion as to be unaware that there is someone who has an eye to human affairs. . . . He acts as if God were not surveying what happens. COMMENTARY ON PSALMS 10.[6]

CULPABLE SELF-DECEPTION. THEODORET OF CYR: The unbeliever and the sinner never keeps God before his eyes; instead, each day and at every moment he soils and sullies his paths, not believing there is any judgment. Well, what is the reason for this? . . . He completely despises your laws; he spends all his time in lawlessness. The unbeliever, in fact, belittles and vilifies the commands of God. COMMENTARY ON THE PSALMS 10.2.[7]

TOTALLY ABSORBED IN VICE. CHRYSOSTOM: Do you see the fruit of vice? Their light is extinguished, their thinking impaired, they are taken captive by wickedness. Just as the disabled person constantly falls into a pit, so too these people, since they do not have the fear of God before their eyes, are totally absorbed in vice— not a case of now in virtue and now in vice, but permanently in vice, mindful not of hell, or of the judgment to come or of accounts to be rendered. Instead, rejecting all these aids as though

---

[1]ACW 51:126. [2]CCOP 1:201. [3]ACW 51:127*. [4]PG 39:1200-1201. [5]FC 62:38-39. [6]WGRW 9:34. [7]FC 101:95.

bridle and bit, they are like a ship without ballast that is at the mercy of winds and fierce billows with no one to guide their thinking. Do you see the wicked in the actual condition of vice having to give an account? After all, what is worse than an unbridled horse, a ship without ballast, a maimed individual? Yet more miserable than all these is the person living in vice, having extinguished the light coming from the fear of God and given over to captivity. COMMENTARY ON THE PSALMS 10.9-10.[8]

10:5 Out of God's Sight

THE PERIL OF FLATTERY. CHRYSOSTOM: Do you see the folly? Do you see the unutterable ruin? Do you see the destruction gradually increasing? Do you see the things prized by the mindless, in reality full of deep misery, and now they sink from sight? Those people are applauded in their sins, commended in their wrongdoing. This is the first pitfall, sufficient to trip up the unwary. Hence it is much more necessary to welcome those who censure and correct us than those who applaud and flatter us to the point of destruction. The latter, in fact, prove the ruination of the stupid and impel them to worse evil—as though even by puffing up these sinners they led them on the way to folly. COMMENTARY ON THE PSALMS 10.10.[9]

A CORRUPTING IGNORANCE. EUSEBIUS OF CAESAREA: One who holds tight his sin readies himself for a great outpouring of anger; since he does not seek God in the least he is ensnared. Hence it is said, "Because of the greatness of his wrath he does not search" and "God is not in his sight." Indeed, so great is the power of the anger that fills his whole spirit that he has removed the natural ideas of God from his thinking. . . . One who does not put God before his eyes makes all the deeds of life as paths and ways befouled and polluted, since "God is not in his sight." In as much time the wicked one, who is without God, was walking successfully in this life so

that he dominated over his enemies, even in so much time is his wickedness, which overcame his enemies, punished. COMMENTARY ON PSALMS 10.25-26.[10]

TOTAL DEFILEMENT. AUGUSTINE: Whoever knows what gives joy or delight in the soul knows how great an evil it is to be abandoned by the light of truth. People consider physical blindness, which means the withdrawal of daylight, a great evil. Just imagine, then, how great the punishment people suffer who, while their sins are a roaring success, are led to the point where God is no longer in their field of vision and where their ways are defiled all the time, which means that their thoughts and machinations are absolutely filthy! EXPOSITIONS OF THE PSALMS 10.23.[11]

THE PATTERN OF THE DEVIL. DIDYMUS THE BLIND: This is the reason why the sinner provokes the Lord, because he does not keep him before his eyes, because he turns himself away from God. The one who sins conducts himself in this way. Concerning all of this, God says, "They have shown me their backs and not their faces."[12] Cain, the offspring of this wickedness, "departed from the face of the Lord God."[13] That is, he turned himself away from him. Inasmuch as these words are spoken about people being sinners, even more so do they speak about the devil. "His ways are profaned at all times." For of which people are the ways profaned for all time, since even the wicked often live with much honesty? He enters without permission to draw people to corrupt deeds and even to deny the providence of God. And so he persuades many to believe that the world is without the direction of God, and later he falls away from right ideas concerning the governing of God and the knowledge of judgment. FRAGMENTS ON THE PSALMS 10.5.[14]

---

[8]CCOP 1:202. [9]CCOP 1:202. [10]AnSac 3:398. [11]WSA 3 15:153. [12]Cf. Jer 18:17. [13]Gen 4:16. [14]PG 39:1202.

10:6 *Thoughts in the Heart*

ARROGANT BLASPHEMY. EUSEBIUS OF CAE-SAREA: So bold is the person who does not look on God or recognize his judgment that he does not consider within himself his own audacious wicked deeds, believing that he will rejoice forever in his prosperity. His mouth swells up with blasphemies and irreverence. At length, the arrogant one blares out with fierce confidence countless blasphemies and curses, asserting that there is no God, nor does he look down on us, nor will he judge, COMMENTARY ON PSALMS 10.27-31.[15]

CAUGHT UP IN FANTASIES. CHRYSOSTOM: What could be more stupid than this attitude in a human being, subject to death, caught up in affairs of the moment, subject to countless changes, to come up with such fantasies? Now, where did this spring from? From stupidity. You see, whenever a heedless person enjoys great prosperity, prevails over his enemies, is praised and admired, he proves more to be pitied than anyone. In fact, by not expecting any change he does not even cope with prosperity sensibly; but on falling on hard times he is disturbed and upset, being out of practice and heedless. . . . These people . . . once corrupted, have no regard for human limitations but consider their state immovable on account of their success—the basis of ultimate folly and destruction and the occasion of utter ruin. COMMENTARY ON THE PSALMS 10.10.[16]

10:7-10 *Lurking Like a Lion*

WILD BEASTS. CHRYSOSTOM: Just as the inspired author describes them as a wild beast, so he talks about them in those terms, making a show of their tricks, ambushes, schemes. What could be more pitiful than this, what could be more desperate, to feel the need of the possessions of the poor? So shall we call these people rich, tell me? . . . Do you see their moral bankruptcy and cruelty? Moral bankruptcy, because

they lust after the goods of the poor; cruelty, because far from being moved by their plight they aggravate their penury when they should pity it and ameliorate it. Still, they do not get up to this with impunity: when they exert their power, when they seem to prevail, when they think they are unassailable, then it is they perish, so that the inventiveness of God, the patience of the poor, the errors of these miscreants and the forbearance of God's long-suffering may come to light. Hence it is that justice does not follow close on their heels, since God in his long-suffering summons them to repentance; but when they profit nothing from the long-suffering, then he admonishes them with retribution. COMMENTARY ON THE PSALMS 10.10.[17]

A LURKING LION. DIDYMUS THE BLIND: He lies in wait in secret, like a lion in his den or a savage lion in his cave so that he may drag off the poor by crafty speech and, equally often, by their deeds. After he has caught him in the trap he will draw him to apostasy. Wild beasts are threatening, and especially so the lion. Often, therefore, lying in wait, while he discusses fasting, he openly persuades them to greed; and addressing modesty, he introduces them to a certain appearance of luxury. Thus, he pushed Eve deceptively in the garden to commit transgression, saying she was going to be equal to God. Thus he lured Judas by greed. FRAGMENTS ON THE PSALMS 10.8.[18]

THE FINAL PERSECUTION OF ANTICHRIST. CASSIODORUS: Initially the persecution of the church was merely violent, when pagans attempted to force Christians to sacrifice to idols by use of proscriptions, tortures and beatings. The second kind of persecution is by guile, which is now employed by heretics and false Christians. The final form is still to come, and it is predicted here that it will come through Antichrist. Noth-

---

[15]AnSac 3:399. [16]CCOP 1:203. [17]CCOP 1:203-204. [18]PG 39:1204-5.

ing will be more dangerous than this, for it will be extremely violent through the power of that unique kingdom, and through miraculous events it will mislead "so as to deceive," as the Lord says in the Gospel, "if possible even the elect."[19] So the word *lion* denotes violence, and the expression "in his den," guile, and thus both Antichrist's vices are suggested by the individual expressions. EXPLANATION OF THE PSALMS 10.29-30.[20]

A TWOFOLD PERVERSION. CASSIODORUS: His wickedness is described as embracing twofold perversion, for on his lips he shall have blasphemous cursing when he shall falsely claim to be the Son of God, and bitterness when he shall proclaim the death penalty for those who resist him and shall order those who refused to adore him as deity to proceed to execution. On his lips will lie his public utterances, but under his tongue, as the psalmist says, he will keep the most savage thoughts, so that since he himself is destroyed he may hasten to destroy everything. EXPLANATION OF THE PSALMS 10.28.[21]

CONTRAST WITH THE RIGHTEOUS. EVAGRIUS OF PONTUS: [By contrast] the righteous person praises God at all times. NOTES ON THE PSALMS 9[10].28-29.[22]

10:11-12 God Has Forgotten

BLIND IGNORANCE OF GOD. AUGUSTINE: The human mind seems to prosper in the midst of its iniquities and thinks that it is being spared, whereas it is instead being blinded and kept on hold for the final and timely punishment.... The people who maintain that God does not see them to the very end are those who assert that he does not concern himself with human and earthly affairs. This earth is like the end, in that it is the last element in which men and women work according to a very definite order, though they are unable to see the ordered pattern of their labors, for this belongs particularly to the hidden things of the Son. EXPOSITIONS OF THE PSALMS 10.29.[23]

10:12 Lift Up Your Hand

THE UPLIFTED HAND OF GOD. EUSEBIUS OF CAESAREA: Through these words he asks that whenever the forbearance and kindness of God are being set in motion, and he is stirred to judgment against the wicked, in which judgment the uplifted hand of God, he will judge each one. With the figure of the lifted hand he indicates the power of divine judgment that seems to rest on and humble one until he sets in place justice against the wicked. When, however, he begins to exercise his power, giving to each one according to his merit, then he is said to be exalted. Wherefore you will not be forgetful of your poor who are poor in spirit, knowing that everything is under your hand and it is granted that none flee beyond it. . . . Do not yourselves seek revenge, O beloved, but give space to your wrath. "Vengeance is from me, I will repay, says the Lord." COMMENTARY ON PSALMS 10.33-35.[24]

10:14 God Sees

TRUTH WILL PREVAIL. CASSIODORUS: He will find that he who he hoped was forgetful is mindful, and he will come to the realization that his innumerable actions, which he thought were not remembered because his sins were so many, are taken into account. EXPLANATION OF THE PSALMS 10.34.[25]

WE KNOW BY FAITH. THEODORET OF CYR: Even if those living in impiety claim countless times, he is saying, that you are not looking at human affairs, we know that you are studying and considering their crimes and requiring due penalty of them. COMMENTARY ON THE PSALMS 10.6.[26]

CONSIGNED TO GOD. CASSIODORUS: The person consigned to him is robbed of no advantages, for being left to the devoted Prince is the same as

---

[19]Mt 24:24. [20]ACW 51:129. [21]ACW 51:128. [22]AnSac 2:463. [23]WSA 3 15:156. [24]AnSac 3:400. [25]ACW 51:130. [26]FC 101:96-97.

being exposed to all blessings. EXPLANATION OF THE PSALMS 10.35.[27]

THE SPIRITUALLY POOR AND ORPHANED. DIDYMUS THE BLIND: The poor abandon themselves to you. You will care for his deliverance so that you may make him rich in heavenly goods. So also, the orphan is helped, protected and nourished like a son. It is important to understand here that the orphan is one whose father is the devil because of iniquity but who has cast him out through the practice of repentance. FRAGMENTS ON THE PSALMS 10.12-15.[28]

WHEN FORBEARANCE DOES NOT LEAD TO REPENTANCE. CHRYSOSTOM: What is the meaning of "up to the point of their being given into your hands"? It is a rather human expression, but what it means is this: You bide your time, you are forbearing, with the result that they are given over to the excess of wickedness. You are capable, of course, of destroying and subduing them from the outset; yet beyond telling is the ocean of your forbearance, observing them, not pursuing them but awaiting their movement to repentance. If, however, they prove unresponsive, then you will punish them when they profit nothing from your long-suffering. COMMENTARY ON THE PSALMS 10.11.[29]

10:15 The Wicked and the Evildoer

THE SINNER AND THE WICKED. EVAGRIUS OF PONTUS: The sinner is the one who sins out of lust and weakness; the wicked one is he who follows after evil with a deliberated plan. NOTES ON THE PSALMS 9[10].36.[30]

THE PRECARIOUSNESS OF POWER. CHRYSOSTOM: Let no one be arrogant about the pinnacle of power or be puffed up; it is a precarious and risky position and topples the careless with great ease. COMMENTARY ON THE PSALMS 10.11.[31]

10:16 King Forever and Ever

BEFORE ANY BEGINNING. GREGORY OF NYSSA: Therefore we define him to be earlier than any beginning and exceeding any end. AGAINST EUNOMIUS 1.42.[32]

THE KINGDOM OF THE HEART. DIDYMUS THE BLIND: The land of God is the good heart; from this land the nations perish when they are driven by whatever destruction of mind and every evil thought. . . . No sinner is allowed to walk in this land, for the righteous alone possess it. It is said by a good man: "I believe I will see the goodness of the Lord in the land of the living."[33] FRAGMENTS ON THE PSALMS 10.16.[34]

THE FUTURE KINGDOM. CASSIODORUS: Once the universal calamity has been expunged, the psalmist passes to the order of future events, for once Antichrist has been slain, the eternal, holy, generous kingdom of the Lord will come. Wicked evil is allowed to run far ahead so that the Lord's kingdom for which we long may be more welcome when attained, for in it the blessed now become untroubled and take rest. The traps that a holy person is compelled to endure in this world are no longer feared. EXPLANATION OF THE PSALMS 10.37.[35]

10:17 God Will Hear

EFFECTS OF GOD'S POWER. CASSIODORUS: "Your ear has heard." We must regularly note that in God there are no physical parts, but the effect of the power by which he hears is called his ear, that by which he sees his eye, that by which he performs his hand. Let these words be stored in your memory, that we may not seem to weary you by repeating them if they have often to be restated. EXPLANATION OF THE PSALMS 10.38.[36]

GLORY ONLY TO GOD. EUSEBIUS OF CAESAREA:

---

[27]ACW 51:131. [28]PG 39:1205. [29]CCOP 1:205. [30]AnSac 2:464. [31]CCOP 1:206. [32]NPNF 2 5:98. [33]Ps 27:13 (26:13 LXX). [34]PG 39:1205. [35]ACW 51:132*. [36]ACW 51:132.

The Lord has heard the desires of the poor.
. . . They have suffered misfortune and endured
affliction in this life, but he who is king of the
ages and judge will vindicate them "lest people
boast on the earth." COMMENTARY ON PSALMS
10.38-39.[37]

[37]AnSac 3:400.

11:1-7 TRUST IN THE LORD

If anyone wishes to disturb you, hold on strongly to your
confidence in the Lord and say Psalm 11.

ATHANASIUS ON THE INTERPRETATION OF THE PSALMS 16 [OIP 67]

*To the choirmaster.** *Of David.*

[1]*In the* LORD *I take refuge; how can you say
     to me,
"Flee like a bird to the mountains;*[e]
[2]*for lo, the wicked bend the bow,
     they have fitted their arrow to the string,
     to shoot in the dark at the upright in heart;*
[3]*if the foundations are destroyed,
     what can the righteous do"?*

[4]*The* LORD *is in his holy temple,*
the LORD'*s throne is in heaven;
     his eyes behold, his eyelids test, the children
     of men.*
[5]*The* LORD *tests the righteous and the wicked,
     and his soul hates him*[†] *that loves violence.*
[6]*On the wicked he will rain coals of fire and
     brimstone;
     a scorching wind shall be the portion of
     their cup.*
[7]*For the* LORD *is righteous, he loves righteous
     deeds;
     the upright shall behold his face.*

e Gk Syr Jerome Tg: Heb *flee to your mountain, O bird*   * LXX To the end   † LXX *he hates his own soul*

OVERVIEW: The eleventh psalm encourages all
who are wronged to hope in God (THEODORET).
It is a call to ascend to God in our hearts (ARNO-
BIUS THE YOUNGER), an exhortation to spiritual
heroism (PSEUDO-ATHANASIUS). We face a choice
of refuge (CHRYSOSTOM). But we are secure only
in the Lord (DIODORE), and the power of hope in
the Lord is great (CHRYSOSTOM). There is really
nowhere else to go (CHRYSOSTOM). We must not
succumb to flittering minds (CASSIODORUS) but
exercise the wings of the soul (AMBROSE). Faith
is needed in light of the strategies of the enemy
(JEROME, CYRIL OF JERUSALEM).

The wicked destroy the natural knowledge
of God in the soul (EUSEBIUS); heretics destroy
the Word by false interpretation (CASSIODORUS).
None of this, however, escapes God's knowledge
(THEODORET). God is all-seeing (CHRYSOSTOM).
He looks on all for mercy or for judgment
(EUSEBIUS). Let us choose the favored position
(EVAGRIUS). By humility, let us maintain the
unity of the temple of the Lord (AUGUSTINE).

Wickedness is self-destructive (CHRYSOSTOM). It kindles the flame of wrath (CAESARIUS) and turns one into his own murderer (FULGENTIUS). True self-esteem hates iniquity (EVAGRIUS) and embraces the Word of God (CAESARIUS).

The psalmist next speaks of the punishment of blasphemers (AUGUSTINE), who receive justice, not mercy (FULGENTIUS). They drink a cup of judgment instead of a cup of blessing (DIDYMUS). The righteousness of God renders his judgment unchanging (APOSTOLIC CONSTITUTIONS). Human righteousness before God must be given by God, as a gift (CASSIODORUS), formed in us from Christ, who is himself ultimate justice (ORIGEN).

Superscription: *To the End*

HOPE IN GOD. THEODORET OF CYR: Pursued by Saul, the divine David uttered this psalm to those urging him to secure his salvation by flight. It is suitable, however, for every wronged person placing hope in God. Now, "to the end" occurs in the title for the reason that it contains a prophecy of God's righteous judgment and the punishment to be imposed on the lawless. COMMENTARY ON THE PSALMS 11.1.[1]

LET US ASCEND IN OUR HEARTS. ARNOBIUS THE YOUNGER: This psalm refers to David when, like a sparrow, he sought a hiding place in an inaccessible mountain, when sinners have bent their bows against him, whether Saul, Absalom, or innumerable enemies. But let us drawing on the counsels of the saints hear these words for our building up, and making the ascent in our heart let us move onto the mountain "from the valley of weeping."[2] COMMENTARY ON PSALMS 11.[3]

SPIRITUAL HEROISM. PSEUDO-ATHANASIUS: [The psalmist] sings this psalm after he prevailed over the power of the enemy. It exhorts to heroism befitting the saints who with confidence in the Lord blunt the arrows of sinners, the evil demons. EXPOSITION ON PSALMS 11.[4]

11:1 *Taking Refuge in the Lord*

A CHOICE OF REFUGE. CHRYSOSTOM: Those who trust in the things of this life are in no better situation than the sparrow, which relies on the wilderness and is prey to all. People who put their hope in money are like that. Just as the sparrow is snared by children with bird lime and trap and countless other devices, so too the wealthy by friend and foe. They are much more vulnerable than a sparrow, with many to set traps for them and, more immediately, evil tendencies of their own. They are migrants, constantly reacting to developments, fearful of the long arm of the law and the emperor's wrath, the wiles of flatterers and the deceit of friends. In time of war their fear is greater than anyone's, in time of peace they suspect treachery, their wealth never being secure of proof against loss. Hence they are always taking to flight and migrating, searching out wilderness and eyries, preferring the dark and looking for the black of night in noontime, adopting disguises to achieve it. Good people, on the contrary, are quite different. "The ways of their righteous shine like the sun,"[5] remember. I mean, far from opting for scheming and lawlessness, their souls are at rest. . . . How then is this darkness to be dissipated? By separating yourself from all these things and coming to depend on hope in God, sinner though you be ten times over. . . . This is remarkable, in fact, that even sinners who cling to this anchor are invincible. It is, you see, a particular mark of an option for God that though weighed down by such awful evils they are still buoyed up by his lovingkindness. In other words, as the one trusting in man is doubly cursed, so the one trusting in God is blessed. So tear yourself away from all these things, and cling to this anchor. . . . Let us come before him, and remain ever with our eyes on him. COMMENTARY ON THE PSALMS 11.3.[6]

---

[1]FC 101:99. [2]Ps 84:6 (83:7 LXX). [3]CCL 25:13. [4]CSCO 387:7. [5]Pr 4:18. [6]CCOP 1:213-14*.

THE POWER OF HOPE IN THE LORD.

SECURE ONLY IN GOD. DIODORE OF TARSUS: Even if movement is necessary, he is saying, nevertheless let it be known that I do not hope to secure safety from those with whom I am constantly in opposition except by hoping in God, who can provide me with safety in every place. COMMENTARY ON PSALMS 11.[7]

THE POWER OF HOPE IN THE LORD. CHRYSOSTOM: Great is the power of hope in the Lord, invincible citadel, unassailable rampart, insuperable reinforcement, tranquil haven, impregnable tower, irresistible weapon, unconquerable power capable of discovering a refuge where none seems possible. COMMENTARY ON THE PSALMS 11.1.[8]

NOWHERE ELSE TO GO. CHRYSOSTOM: I have the Lord of the universe as my ally. The one who without difficulty created everything everywhere is my leader and support, and you would send me to the wilderness and provide for my safety in the desert? After all, surely the help from the desert does not surpass the one capable of anything with complete ease? COMMENTARY ON THE PSALMS 11.1.[9]

FLITTERING MINDS. CASSIODORUS: Here the psalmist speaks of those whose most random inclination bears them off to the loftiest region of earth. So those who in fickleness of wavering mind turn to most wicked doctrines are rightly considered similar to them. EXPLANATION OF THE PSALMS 11.2.[10]

WINGS OF THE SOUL. AMBROSE: The soul has wings by which it can raise itself free from the earth. But this movement of the wings is not of something constructed of feathers but a continuing series of good works, like those of the Lord of whom it is well said, "And in the shadow of your wings I shall take refuge." In the first place, the hands of our Lord fixed on the cross were extended like something in flight, and, second, the actions of God are like a refreshing shadow of eternal salvation that can regulate the conflagra-

tion raging in our world. ON VIRGINITY 18.116.[11]

11:2 The Wicked Bend the Bow

FAITH IS NEEDED. JEROME: Sinners or rebels have ready burning arrows that must be repelled with the shield of faith. In their quivers, they carry darts to shoot at the just, not in the daytime, not in the glimmering night when the moon comfortingly tempers the darkness, but when the night is deep and the darkness groping. HOMILY ON PSALMS 10[11].[12]

FAITH IS STRONG PROTECTION. CYRIL OF JERUSALEM: Though the enemy is unseen, we have our faith as a strong protection, according to the saying of the apostle: "In all things taking up the shield of faith, with which you may be able to quench all the fiery darts of the most wicked one."[13] Oftentimes a fiery dart of desire of base indulgence is discharged by the devil; but faith, representing to us the Judgment and cooling the mind, extinguishes the dart. CATECHETICAL LECTURES 5.4.[14]

11:3 Foundations Destroyed

DESTRUCTION OF NATURAL KNOWLEDGE. EUSEBIUS OF CAESAREA: That which you have framed they have pulled down. Those were the seeds of the best ideas grafted by nature, which God impresses on each person, placing within their spirit the knowledge that is called natural. COMMENTARY ON PSALMS 11.4-6.[15]

FALSE INTERPRETATION. CASSIODORUS: Heretics . . . have destroyed the Lord's law when by false interpretations they strive to rend the holy Scriptures, which are prophetic utterances from the Lord for our salvation. EXPLANATION OF THE PSALMS 11.4.[16]

---

[7]WGRW 9:36. [8]CCOP 1:209. [9]CCOP 1:210. [10]ACW 51:135. [11]AOV 51*. [12]FC 57:5-6. [13]Eph 6:16. [14]FC 61:141. [15]AnSac 3:402. [16]ACW 51:136.

11:4 God's Eyes Behold People

NONE OF THIS ESCAPES GOD'S KNOWLEDGE.
THEODORET OF CYR: So while they practice their
evil ways against me, you, the righteous Judge,
seated on your heavenly throne and making your
own special appearance in the temple on earth,
view the whole world, though sufficient for you
is a mere glance of your eyes to learn about all
human affairs. You know precisely the doings
of the righteous and the unrighteous, and you
measure out repayment for work done. COMMEN-
TARY ON THE PSALMS 11.3.[17]

GOD IS ALL-SEEING. CHRYSOSTOM: Do you see
a ready ally, a well-prepared aid, present everywhere, seeing everything, gazing on all things,
having as his particular role—even if no one
requests it—to exercise providence and care,
to pursue wrongdoers, to assist the wronged,
to award recompense to the virtuous, to assign
punishment to sinners? He is, therefore, ignorant of nothing; his eyes in fact look attentively
on the whole world. He is not simply aware of
things, however; he also wants to correct them.
. . . If, in fact, he is righteous, he will not simply
overlook these happenings. He rebuffs the
wicked; he praises the righteous. COMMENTARY
ON THE PSALMS 11.2.[18]

MERCY OR JUDGMENT. EUSEBIUS OF CAE-
SAREA: He alone is judge of all, and the only
true judge. What has the Lord done against the
wicked who have drawn up a battle line against
him, who rise up against the righteous? In his
own temple, standing in the house of the heavens and sitting immovable on his royal throne,
he overlooks nothing of the earthly creation
with his gaze, and when he looks at the poor,
he gives them the grace of his eyes. Those eyes
are understood to be the merciful rewards of
his gaze, through which he looks on the poor
with generosity. His eyelids are the providence
by which he judges, by which he discerns, by
which he thoroughly searches deeds. Now since

all stand in his judgment, it is said, "The Lord
tries the just and unjust." COMMENTARY ON
PSALMS 11.4-6.[19]

CHOOSE THE FAVORED POSITION. EVAGRIUS
OF PONTUS: If the eyes of God look on the poor,
let us be numbered among the poor, so that the
eyes of the Lord may look down on us. If the rich
do not become poor, very little will the eyes of
the Lord look on them. NOTES ON THE PSALMS
10[11].4.[20]

THE TEMPLE OF THE LORD. AUGUSTINE: The
Lord is in this holy temple. It consists of many
members, each carrying out its own duties and
functions built together by love into one structure. Any who separate themselves from this fellowship for the sake of their own pre-eminence
violate its unity. EXPOSITIONS OF THE PSALMS
11.7.[21]

11:5 Hating Those Who Love Violence

WICKEDNESS IS SELF-DESTRUCTIVE. CHRY-
SOSTOM: Wickedness, after all, is the soul's
enemy, its foe and ruination, and so the wicked
person pays the penalty even before punishment
is imposed. Do you see how he shows on every
score that his adversaries . . . are hoisted on their
own weapons by which they protect themselves,
consumed by them and damaging themselves?
COMMENTARY ON THE PSALMS 11.2.[22]

THE FLAME OF WRATH. CAESARIUS OF ARLES:
I do not think that anyone who keeps precious
garments locked up in a chest would agree to
enclose within it either a live coal or any kind of
spark. Why is this, brothers? Because he would
be afraid that the clothing that he wears to a
feast may be burned. I ask you, brothers, if a
person does not want to put a spark of fire in his
chest of clothes, why does he not fear to kindle

---

[17]FC 101:100. [18]CCOP 1:212. [19]AnSac 3:402. [20]AnSac 2:464-65. [21]WSA 3 15:166. [22]CCOP 1:212-13.

the flame of wrath in his soul? We know clearly and plainly why this happens. We do not put fire into a chest of clothes because we love our garments; but we do not extinguish the fire of wrath because we not only fail to love our soul but even harbor hatred for it. This is according to what is written: "The lover of violence hates his own soul." SERMON 227.5.[23]

SELF-MURDER. FULGENTIUS OF RUSPE: If a murderer is one who hates his brother, what is he who, loving iniquity, hates his own soul? And if the one who hates his brother does not have eternal life remaining in him, how will he who ends this life in the love of iniquity and hatred of his own soul be able to attain the forgiveness of sins through which one attains life? ON THE FORGIVENESS OF SINS 2.7.1.[24]

TRUE SELF-ESTEEM. EVAGRIUS OF PONTUS: If the one who values iniquity hates his own life, then the one who hates iniquity esteems his own life. NOTES ON THE PSALMS 10[11].5.[25]

SOULS THAT LOVE INIQUITY. CAESARIUS OF ARLES: If, then, you hate your own soul by loving iniquity, do you wonder that you hate the Word of God, which wishes well to your soul? SERMONS 145.1.[26]

11:6 Fire and Brimstone

THE BLESSING AND JUDGMENT OF PREACHING. CASSIODORUS: "Rain" refers to preachers' words pouring from heaven that serve as showers for the truly devoted but become fiery snares for the unfaithful. The first group yields fruit through understanding well the words; the second chokes their souls with the noose of perversity by interpreting them wrongly. EXPLANATION OF THE PSALMS 11.7.[27]

THE PUNISHMENT OF BLASPHEMERS. AUGUSTINE: This is the punishment and the death of those through whom the name of God is blas-

phemed. It means that, to begin with, they are ruined by the fire of their own lusts. Next, they are cast out from the company of the blessed because of the stench of their evil works. Finally, they are whisked away and overwhelmed, and they suffer unspeakable punishments. This is the portion of their cup, unlike the cup of the righteous, which is called "your brimming cup, intoxicating and lovely," for they will be inebriated by the rich abundance of your house. EXPOSITIONS OF THE PSALMS 11.11.[28]

JUSTICE, NOT MERCY. FULGENTIUS OF RUSPE: Eternal life will be given in the future only to the one to whom forgiveness of sins has been given in this world. Only he will receive the forgiveness of sins here who renounces his sins and hastens to the highest and true God with true conversion of heart. For that will not be a time of forgiveness but of retribution. There mercy will not justify the sinner, but justice will distinguish the just and the sinner. This is written in the psalm: "The Lord tests the righteous and the wicked." And, so that he might show that in iniquity lies the destruction, not the salvation, of the soul, he goes on the say, "He who loves iniquity hates his own soul." Lest they who persist in iniquity to the end of the present life promise themselves mercy, it is said subsequently concerning God: "On the wicked he will rain coals of fire and sulphur; a scorching wind shall be the portion of their cup. For the Lord is righteous; he loves righteous deeds; the upright shall behold his face." . . . Whoever, hearing these things, is unwilling to seek the mercy of God through conversion in the present time, will never be able to find it in the future life. ON THE FORGIVENESS OF SINS 6.1-2.[29]

THE CUP OF JUDGMENT VERSUS THE CUP OF BLESSING. DIDYMUS THE BLIND: Harsh

---

[23]FC 66:167*. [24]FC 95:156. [25]AnSac 2:465. [26]FC 47:306. [27]ACW 51:137. [28]WSA 3 15:168. [29]FC 95:154*.

punishments are often denoted in Scripture by the word *cup*. . . .[30] So it follows that even in this place "cup" denotes the punishment to be poured out, especially, the fullness of this cup is fire, sulphur and a stormy wind, whose symbols were written in Genesis, the type of punishment inflicted by the Lord on Sodom and Gomorrah. Besides fire and sulphur, there is also in the cup the stormy wind. The fire indicates threatening flames; sulphur, the force by which more fire is burned; and, finally, the wind illustrates the certain whirlwind of temptations; chiefly we are able to learn this from the writing of Isaiah.[31] . . . Let us flee impiety, so that there is no cup of this type for us, and we may live righteously; so that we may drink to drunkenness that which is the best. From which also it is said: "The Lord is my portion and my cup."[32] Because the Lord is just and loves justice, he shows his face to the upright. FRAGMENTS ON THE PSALMS 11.7.[33]

11:7 The Lord Is Righteous

UNCHANGING JUDGMENT. APOSTOLIC CONSTITUTIONS: As to the ungodly, if you give all the world to the poor, you will not benefit him at all. For to whom the Deity was an enemy while he was alive, it is certain he will be so also when he is departed; for there is no unrighteousness with him. For "the Lord is righteous and has loved righteousness." CONSTITUTIONS OF THE HOLY APOSTLES 8.4.43.[34]

A RIGHTEOUSNESS GIVEN BY GOD. CASSIODORUS: "His countenance beheld righteousness," that is, the righteousness that he himself grants in his kindness, for humanity of itself possesses nothing worthy; it has only what it has obtained from the Lord, the bestower of all things. EXPLANATION OF THE PSALMS 11.8.[35]

ULTIMATE JUSTICE. ORIGEN: The ultimate justice itself is Christ, "who was made wisdom for us from God, and justice, and sanctification and redemption."[36] The justice in each person, however, is formed from that justice, so that many justices come into existence in those who are saved; wherefore it has also been written, "The Lord is just and has loved justice." COMMENTARY ON THE GOSPEL OF JOHN 6.40.[37]

---

[30]Is 51:17; Jer 25:15. [31]Is 21:1-2. [32]Ps 16:5 (15:5 LXX). [33]PG 39:1209-12. [34]ANF 7:498*. [35]ACW 51:138. [36]1 Cor 1:30. [37]FC 80:179.

12:1-8 PRAYER FOR PROTECTION

When you see the arrogance of the crowd and evil spreading everywhere
so that there seems to be no one left who is pleasing to God
take refuge in the Lord and say Psalm 12.
ATHANASIUS ON THE INTERPRETATION OF THE PSALMS 16 [OIP 67]

To the choirmaster: according to The Sheminith.* A Psalm of David.

[1]*Help, LORD; for there is no longer any that is godly;*
for the faithful have vanished from among the sons of men.
[2]*Every one utters lies to his neighbor;*

with flattering lips and a double heart they
    speak.

³May the LORD cut off all flattering lips,
    the tongue that makes great boasts,
⁴those who say, "With our tongue we will
    prevail,
    our lips are with us; who is our master?"

⁵ "Because the poor are despoiled, because the
    needy groan,
    I will now arise," says the LORD;

"I will place him in the safety for which he
    longs."
⁶The promises of the LORD are promises that
    are pure,
    silver refined in a furnace on the ground,
    purified seven times.

⁷Do thou, O LORD, protect us,
    guard us ever from this generation.
⁸On every side the wicked prowl,
    as vileness is exalted among the sons of
    men.

*LXX For the end. For the eighth.

OVERVIEW: The twelfth psalm speaks of deliverance into the eighth day (CASSIODORUS), on deliverance from wickedness and the revelation of Christ's salvation (PSEUDO-ATHANASIUS). The Lord alone is the true Savior (CASSIODORUS, EUSEBIUS). But regard for truth is in danger of extinction (THEODORET) because of the failure of righteousness (EVAGRIUS). The problem is in the heart (VALERIAN), the problem of a double heart (AUGUSTINE). Deceit endangers the soul (VALERIAN). The psalmist prays against this sin, that sinners may be converted (CHRYSOSTOM, CASSIODORUS) through a salvific destruction of the base things of the soul (ORIGEN). The problem is an unthinking arrogance (THEODORET) that refuses to acknowledge that all things are from God (CHRYSOSTOM). All blessing is in Christ (AUGUSTINE). The Father is revealed in the Son (CASSIODORUS). The words of the Lord are true, exceedingly pure (DIODORE), containing nothing false (EUSEBIUS), containing no lies (ORIGEN). They are tested and proved true through hardship (AUGUSTINE). They purify the soul and give one access to God (ATHANASIUS). Divine protection is all by grace, now and forever (THEODORET). He helps us here and glorifies us there (CASSIODORUS), no matter the opposition (DIODORE). The wicked are excluded from the eighth day (CASSIODORUS), but the righteous emerge superior through God's care (DIODORE).

Superscription: *For the End . . . the Eighth*

DELIVERANCE INTO THE EIGHTH DAY. CASSIODORUS: As has already been explained in Psalm 6, "eighth" refers to our eternal rest, for this world does not experience an eighth day. Once the seventh day is finished, it always returns to the first. In these seven days, the number is plural, but eighth is taken as singular because it does not change with any successor. So the psalm's purport must be explained so that the words of the heading can be more easily understood by realization of its purpose. The prophet, then, begs that this world's wickedness be destroyed, so that the great truth of the future promise may be attained. EXPLANATION OF THE PSALMS 12.1.[1]

DELIVERANCE FROM AN EVIL GENERATION. PSEUDO-ATHANASIUS: The prophet prays in this psalm to be delivered from the evil generation, of which at the time of our Savior Christ's dispensation the Lord said, "The people of Nineveh will stand in judgment with this generation and will condemn it."[2] For how are they not guilty and worthy to be effaced, in that they vainly conspired against the truth? . . . Because of the wretchedness of the wicked and

---

[1]ACW 51:139. [2]Mt 12:41; Lk 11:32.

the groaning of the poor in spirit, he promises that he will rise and make his salvation clearly manifest to all people, as also his pure words, silver tested and proved by the earth, which is purified sevenfold. And not only will he save [us] from the impious who encircle [us], but he will also increase for us immortal life like his hill, after renewing the body of our abasement in the form of his glory, as it is written. EXPOSITION ON PSALMS 12.[3]

12:1 Help, Lord

MY LORD, MY SAVIOR. CASSIODORUS: Since he saw this world oppressing souls in many ways, he asked the Lord to be saved. He knew that true healing could be found with God. EXPLANATION OF THE PSALMS 12.2.[4]

ONLY ONE DELIVERER. EUSEBIUS OF CAESAREA: There is no righteous one left anywhere, he said, who can become the author of my deliverance. Truly I lack a Savior, and since there is none, you yourself, Lord, be my Savior. COMMENTARY ON PSALMS 12.2-3.[5]

MANY EXPRESSIONS OF ONE TRUTH. AUGUSTINE: The truth by which the souls of the saints are enlightened is one in number, but because there are many souls, it is possible to speak of many expressions of the truth in them, just as there are many images of the one face in a hall of mirrors. EXPOSITIONS OF THE PSALMS 12.2.[6]

12:2 A Double Heart

REGARD FOR TRUTH IN DANGER. THEODORET OF CYR: Regard for truth is in danger of being snuffed out, with everyone, you might say, suffering from distrust in one another. . . . They pretend friendship and perform the actions of enemies. . . . Some use their lips to direct falsehood into their neighbor's heart; others return the compliment. COMMENTARY ON THE PSALMS 12.2.[7]

NO RIGHTEOUSNESS, NO TRUTH. EVAGRIUS OF PONTUS: First the righteous fail, then the truth is diminished. Not only is there no truth among the righteous, there is no holiness among honest people. Now, since the righteous have failed, truth is diminished. Perhaps the poverty of righteous people is the reason why so many heresies have shot up. NOTES ON THE PSALMS 11[12].2.[8]

A HEART PROBLEM. VALERIAN OF CIMIEZ: We shall take care to have nothing base spring from our hearts, nothing blasphemous fly from our lips, nothing harmful harbored in our thought. The prophet condemns not only what offends the ears but also the attitude that some people cherish in their minds. "With deceitful lips and with a double heart they have spoken evil things." Deliberations, too, then should be listed among the faults of an insolent tongue. Whatever you speak in your heart you are confessing to the Lord, because God is the Searcher of hearts. Since you cannot hide even your thought from him, can that which you shout aloud remain hidden from him or excused? Reflect on this. HOMILY 5.7.[9]

A DOUBLE HEART. AUGUSTINE: There is a double heart there, not a simple one; it is not what it has within itself that it utters outwardly. The double heart, once upon a time, received this damning judgment: "Deceitful lips in heart and heart have spoken evil." It should have been enough to say, "In the heart they have spoken evil." How are lips deceitful? What is deceit? When one thing is done openly, another covered up. Deceitful lips mean a not simple heart; and because it is not a simple heart, that is why "in heart and heart"; that is why "in heart" twice over; because it is a double heart. SERMON 133.4.[10]

12:3 Flattering Lips

---

³CSCO 387:8. ⁴ACW 51:140. ⁵AnSac 3:403. ⁶WSA 3 15:170. ⁷FC 101:102. ⁸AnSac 2:466. ⁹FC 17:335*. ¹⁰WSA 3 4:334.

DANGEROUS DECEPTION. VALERIAN OF CIMIEZ: We find many who occasionally mix poison with sweet words in one and the same conversation and enter into conflicts by feigned persuasions to peace. What can be more unfortunate or dangerous than the case of those people who with all the ardor of their deceitful tongues plot against someone's life? Why do they fail to consider the prophet's psalm, which states, "May the Lord destroy sinful lips." Do you perceive under what a curse one lives who is contriving one plan in his heart and placing another on his tongue? HOMILIES 5.5.[11]

PRAYER AGAINST THE SIN. CHRYSOSTOM: Do you see the solicitude of the inspired author, how he prays for them? The remark is not against them, no, but on their behalf. He did not ask for them to be destroyed, note, but for the evil to be done away with. He did not say "the Lord will destroy them," note, but the "deceitful lips." Again, he asks for the destruction not of their being but of their tongue, their folly, their deceit, and for an end to be put to their arrogance. COMMENTARY ON THE PSALMS 12.1-2.[12]

CASSIODORUS: Note his piety as he says this, for he inveighs not against people, for many of them were to be converted, but against the vices themselves. EXPLANATION OF THE PSALMS 12.4.[13]

SALVIFIC DESTRUCTION. ORIGEN: When the Lord wipes out those things that are base, he will destroy those very things, so that when those things that have come on a person unexpectedly have been destroyed, the foremost creation of God whom the baser things had overtaken may take up the higher things. SELECTIONS FROM THE PSALMS 12.4.[14]

12:4 We Will Prevail

UNTHINKING ARROGANCE. THEODORET OF CYR: With mouths agape they heedlessly utter whatever occurs to them, scornful of divine long-suffering and giving no thought to their falling under the lordship of God. COMMENTARY ON THE PSALMS 12.3.[15]

ALL THINGS FROM GOD. CHRYSOSTOM: "Our lips are our own; who is our master?" These are words of insane and deranged people. For this very reason Paul says the opposite to them in the words, "You are not your own; you were bought at a price,"[16] and bids them not to live for themselves. Your lips are not yours, he is saying, but the Lord's. He it was, in fact, who made them, who fitted you together, who breathed life into you. But you—what do you have? Not all that we have, by contrast, is ours; for even the possessions we have others have entrusted to us, and the land we lease others have given to us. Exactly so has God let these things out on lease to you, not for you to bear thorns but to convert the seed into something useful; not for you to make folly flourish by them, not for deceit but for humility, benediction and love. He gave you eyes, not to indulge in unrestrained gazing but to embellish them with temperance; and hands, not for striking but for giving alms. COMMENTARY ON THE PSALMS 12.2.[17]

12:5 The Lord Will Arise

BLESSING IS IN CHRIST. AUGUSTINE: This . . . should be taken as spoken in the person of God the Father who deigned to send his Son for the sake of the poor and needy, that is, those who suffered need and poverty in lacking spiritual good things. . . . He is understood to have put into Christ whatever relates to the taking away of the wretchedness of the poor and the relief of the destitute who are groaning. EXPOSITIONS OF THE PSALMS 12.6.[18]

THE FATHER IN THE SON. CASSIODORUS: "I will arise" is a metaphorical statement to the

---

[11]FC 17:333*. [12]CCOP 1:218*. [13]ACW 51:141*. [14]PG 12:1200. [15]FC 101:102. [16]1 Cor 6:19-20. [17]CCOP 1:218*. [18]WSA 3 15:171.

effect that he who knows no human weakness of prostration rises up; but "I will arise" means I shall appear and be manifest in the Son, for their strength is one and their majesty undivided. The Father appears and is manifest in the Son, as Christ says in the Gospel: "He who sees me sees the Father also."[19] EXPLANATION OF THE PSALMS 12.6.[20]

12:6 Silver Refined by Fire

EXCEEDINGLY PURE. DIODORE OF TARSUS: Since he said that the Lord's sayings are pure and unmixed with falsehood, he goes on to say that as silver brought into contact with fire is found to be purified of every defilement, so also such commands of God emerge sincere and unaffected by falsehood. The phrase "seven times" means repeatedly, his meaning being that it is exceedingly pure and untainted with falsehood. COMMENTARY ON PSALMS 12.[21]

NOTHING FALSE. EUSEBIUS OF CAESAREA: In the same manner silver is purified by fire after it is drawn through the flame two or three times, nor is that enough, but again and again being purged thoroughly by the furnace, never will it have any false or foreign material, so also the words of the Lord genuinely spoken are full of truth, as pure and undefiled, including no falsehood. COMMENTARY ON PSALMS 12.7.[22]

NO LIES. ORIGEN: Although they may be beautiful, the words of those who stand apart from Christ are not pure but interspersed with innumerable lies; the words of the Lord alone are pure, in which there is no lie mixed, and they are true as silver purged and proven in the furnace. When anything is declared with them, it is never to be rejected in doubt. SELECTIONS FROM THE PSALMS 12.7.[23]

TESTED THROUGH HARDSHIP. AUGUSTINE: "The words of the Lord are pure words." By "pure" he means without any alloy of deceit.

These words of the Lord are words tested and proved through hardships, "purified seven times": by fear of God, by devotion, by knowledge, by fortitude, by deliberation, by understanding, by wisdom. EXPOSITIONS OF THE PSALMS 12.7.[24]

ACCESS TO GOD. ATHANASIUS: When Israel had left Egypt, God forbade the people to even touch the mountain where he was giving the Law, because they were far from being "on fire" for the Lord. He did, however, call the blessed Moses to that mountain. Moses was totally committed to him and clung to his grace, so God said, "Let Moses alone draw near."[25] So Moses climbed up the mountain into the cloud, and although that mountain smoked with the heat and presence of the Lord, Moses was unharmed. Rather, through "the words of the Lord, which are pure silver refined in a furnace," he came down more pure than when he went up. FESTAL LETTERS 3.4.[26]

12:7 Lord, Protect Us

ALL BY GRACE. THEODORET OF CYR: Guarded by your grace we shall not only escape the wiles of the present generation but shall also be provided with everlasting salvation. COMMENTARY ON THE PSALMS 12.4.[27]

HELP HERE AND GLORY THERE. CASSIODORUS: He consoles us here in our tribulations and in heaven sets us in everlasting freedom from anxiety. He helps us here and glorifies and crowns us there. So the most devoted Creator both preserves us in this world lest we perish and blesses us in the next so that we can be wholly free of wretchedness. EXPLANATION OF THE PSALMS 12.8.[28]

NO MATTER THE OPPOSITION. DIODORE OF

[19]Jn 14:9. [20]ACW 51:142. [21]WGRW 9:39. [22]AnSac 3:405. [23]PG 12:1201. [24]WSA 3 15:171. [25]Ex 24:2. [26]ARL 73. [27]FC 101:103. [28]ACW 51:143.

TARSUS: Even if the godless and demons and agitators surround us, even if they besiege us and cut us off, you will render us superior with your help. COMMENTARY ON PSALMS 12.[29]

12:8 The Wicked Prowl

THE WICKED, EXCLUDED FROM THE EIGHTH DAY. CASSIODORUS: "The wicked walk round about," so that they can never reach the right path, for circuitous routes are always invested with evil manners. . . . They cannot attain the repose of the eighth day, for they are always revolving backwards like wheels. EXPLANATION OF THE PSALMS 12.9.[30]

SUPERIOR. DIODORE OF TARSUS: When you care for us, even if we are abandoned among those guilty of hostility and scheming, we emerge superior on account of the care of the Most High. COMMENTARY ON PSALMS 12.[31]

[29]WGRW 9:40. [30]ACW 51:144. [31]WGRW 9:40.

13:1-6 WAITING ON THE LORD

Though the plot of the enemies lasts a very long time,
do not lose heart, as though God had forgotten you,
but call on the Lord, singing Psalm 13.
ATHANASIUS ON THE INTERPRETATION OF THE PSALMS 16 [OIP 67]

To the choirmaster. A Psalm of David.

¹How long, O LORD? Wilt thou forget me for ever?
How long wilt thou hide thy face from me?
²How long must I bear pain[f] in my soul,
and have sorrow in my heart all the day?
How long shall my enemy be exalted over me?

³Consider and answer me, O LORD my God;

lighten my eyes, lest I sleep the sleep of death;
⁴lest my enemy say, "I have prevailed over him";
lest my foes rejoice because I am shaken.

⁵But I have trusted in thy steadfast love;
my heart shall rejoice in thy salvation.
⁶I will sing to the LORD,
because he has dealt bountifully with me.

f Syr: Heb hold counsels

OVERVIEW: The thirteenth psalm was expressed by David after his sin with Bathsheba as a prayer for reconciliation (DIODORE). He contemplates the danger of being forgotten by God (HESYCHIUS). This is a human way of speaking about God (AUGUSTINE). He longs for the appearing of Christ (CASSIODORUS). Most important, one should know the meaning of being forgotten by God (CHRYSOSTOM), which results in a life of anxiety and sorrow (CHRYSOSTOM). In contrast, one should learn to trust in God's plan (ORIGEN).

Divine abandonment is a form of discipline (Chrysostom). But the light of God's help dispels the darkness (Theodoret). The power of illumination comes from God (Eusebius). God is undivided light (Gregory of Nazianzus) who causes the sleeping heart to awake (Cassiodorus). He opens the eyes of the heart (Augustine), the eyes of the mind (Origen), restoring proper sight (Cyril of Alexandria, Diodore). Sin opposes the Spirit (Eusebius). It constitutes a step into the enemy's trap (Cassiodorus). It makes our enemy strong (Chrysostom). But the psalmist trusts in God's mercy, not in his own merit (Theodoret). He knows that salvation is through faith (Pseudo-Athanasius). This is not the boasting of pride (Augustine) but a hope-filled soul (Chrysostom) exalting in the love of God (Cassiodorus). Confident hope with gratitude receives the favor of God (Chrysostom).

13:1 *Will You Forget Me?*

Prayer for Reconciliation. Diodore of Tarsus: The psalm's theme, in fact, is clear: it is uttered on the part of David himself when he suffered the effects of the sin with Bathsheba. On falling foul of every harsh, grievous and painful incident on that account, remember, he then identified the sin as the cause, especially on hearing that "the Lord has taken away your sin."[1] You see, while he received the gift as coming from a loving Lord, he thought it behooved him not to forget the sin but instead to advance in virtue with the degree of determination he required to be preserved from committing such a sin against so good a lord. But on being caught up in the events involving Absalom in particular, he believed the outcome was God's abandoning him and realized the sin was most of all to blame. He therefore asks God to be completely reconciled to him and not forsake him but to lift the weight of misfortune that was proving too heavy for the strength of the sufferer. Commentary on Psalms 13.[2]

The Danger of Being Forgotten. Hesychius of Jerusalem: The forgetfulness of God [would be] a very serious thing, even temporarily. It would mean death, the loss of immortality. Large Commentary on Psalms 13.1.[3]

A Human Way of Speaking. Augustine: How long will you turn your face away from me? God no more turns away his face than he forgets, but Scripture adopts our human idiom. God is said to turn away his face as long as he refuses knowledge of himself to a soul whose spiritual eyes are not yet pure. Expositions of the Psalms 13.1.[4]

The Incarnate Face. Cassiodorus: He asks for the appearance of Christ, whom he had long foreseen in spirit. For his face is that which could appear before bodily eyes, which that holy man uttering this general sentiment rightly desired to see, for that face by its manifestation from heaven deigned to save the world. Explanation of the Psalms 13.1.[5]

The Meaning of Being Forgotton. Chrysostom: Whence comes his knowledge that God had forgotten him, does the text say? Since he knew also when he remembered him, and he was wise enough to know what forgetting meant and what remembering. Not like the majority of people, who, when they are wealthy, when they enjoy a good reputation with people, when everything goes favorably for them, when they better their foes, then think God remembers them. Hence neither do they understand when it is God forgets them. They do not recognize the sign of God's remembering, you see, nor do they grasp the sign of his forgetting. . . . Nothing, after all, brings remembrance by God so much as doing good, being sober and watchful, practicing virtue; likewise, nothing prompts forgetting so much as living in sin and giving oneself to greed

---

[1]2 Sam 12:13. [2]WGRW 9:40-41. [3]PG 93:1184. [4]WSA 3 15:173. [5]ACW 51:146.

and rapacity. So for your part, dearly beloved, when you are in trouble, do not say, "God has forgotten me," but when you are living in sin and everything is going favorably for you. After all, if you knew this, you would quickly abandon evil things. COMMENTARY ON THE PSALMS 13.1.[6]

13:2 Sorrow in My Heart

ANXIETY AND SORROW. CHRYSOSTOM: Just as the sailor on leaving port wanders in every direction and the person deprived of light bumps into many things, so too the one who encounters God's forgetting is caught up constantly in worries and cares and sorrows. COMMENTARY ON THE PSALMS 13.1.[7]

LEARN TO TRUST IN GOD'S PLAN. ORIGEN: At first this one makes many plans in his soul, but in the end [see v. 5], he rests in the great plan of God for everyone, whose spirit is in the root of Jesse. SELECTIONS FROM THE PSALMS 13.2.[8]

13:3 Lighten My Eyes

ABANDONMENT A FORM OF DISCIPLINE. CHRYSOSTOM: Just as when God defends us and stands by us, everything damaging is removed from us, so when he keeps his distance and forgets us, our soul is cut in two, our heart plunged in sorrow, those who do harm fall on us and life becomes craggy and precipitous. Now, this is allowed to happen for our advantage, so that through the whole of it those more indifferent people may be goaded into becoming more zealous and return to the condition from which they fell. "Your falling away will instruct you, after all," Scripture says, "and your wickedness censure you."[9] And so even abandonment by God is a form of providence. You see, when the one who exercises providence and care is slighted, he ignores and abandons us to some extent so that at that point indifference may be expelled and the negligent may turn more zealous. COMMENTARY ON THE PSALMS 13.1.[10]

DISPELLING THE DARKNESS. THEODORET OF CYR: By night I am overwhelmed by my problems, in the grip of discouragement like a kind of sleep. But if the light of your assistance shines, it will disperse the darkness of trouble and put an end to the sleep of discouragement. If, however, you delay your help, I am afraid the sleep will turn into death, as the distress becomes stronger than my resolve. COMMENTARY ON THE PSALMS 13.3.[11]

THE DIVINE POWER OF ILLUMINATION. EUSEBIUS OF CAESAREA: The face of God, full of light, is a certain power looking to confer gifts, by which each partaker will be enlightened, as if they were enjoying the rays of the sun. But if one has turned away, his spirit lives in the shadows without light; because the eyes within, namely, the thoughts of the mind, can see nothing. When one persists in sin, more and more shadows come, because deep within him the face of God remains turned away. COMMENTARY ON PSALMS 13.3-5.[12]

UNDIVIDED LIGHT. GREGORY OF NAZIANZUS: If you are blind and unenlightened, lighten your eyes that you sleep not in death. In God's Light see light, and in the Spirit of God be enlightened by the Son, that threefold and undivided Light. ON HOLY BAPTISM, ORATION 40.34.[13]

THE SLEEPING HEART. CASSIODORUS: The eyes . . . of the heart sleep in death when the light of faith is buried, and they are closed through pleasure of the flesh; for this is the sleep in which the enemy delights. EXPLANATION OF THE PSALMS 13.4.[14]

THE EYES OF THE HEART. AUGUSTINE: We must understand the eyes of the heart here: he is praying that they may not be closed by the pleasurable myopia of sin. EXPOSITIONS OF THE PSALMS 13.3-5.[15]

---

[6]CCOP 1:224-25*. [7]CCOP 1:225. [8]PG 12:1204. [9]Jer 2:19. [10]CCOP 1:225-26. [11]FC 101:105*. [12]PG 23:144. [13]NPNF 2 7:372. [14]ACW 51:147. [15]WSA 3 15:174.

EYES OF THE MIND. ORIGEN: Is God a light to enlighten the eyes of the body or the eyes of the intellect? The prophet says of the latter, "Enlighten my eyes lest I sleep in death." I think it is clear to everyone that we would not say that God performs the work of the sun and assigns to another the task of enlightening the eyes of those who will not sleep in death. God, therefore, enlightens the mind of those whom he judges to be worthy of personal enlightenment. But if God illuminates the mind according to the statement "The Lord is my light,"[16] then we must assume that he is apprehended by the intellect and is invisible and incorporeal, because he is the light of the mind. COMMENTARY ON THE GOSPEL OF JOHN 13.135-37.[17]

PROPER SIGHT. CYRIL OF ALEXANDRIA: The right sight of the eyes hidden within is to be able to see plainly and subtly, insofar as is allowed, whatever considerations there may be concerning the words of God. "For we see through a mirror in an obscure manner and we know in part,"[18] but "he who discloses the recesses of the darkness"[19] sends the light of truth to those who wish to gain a knowledge concerning him rightly. It is necessary therefore that we prostrate ourselves before God saying, "Give light to my eyes that I may not sleep in death," for to slip away from the rightness of holy doctrines would be nothing else except to sleep in death, and we depart from this rightness when we do not follow the divinely inspired Scriptures. LETTER 55.3.[20]

SEEING THE GOOD BEHIND TRIBULATION. DIODORE OF TARSUS: Since the misfortunes and the tribulations render the sun, which is a source of pleasure to everyone, dim and faint to me, he is saying, free me from the misfortune so that I may see good things as they naturally are and not as the tribulations represent them. COMMENTARY ON PSALMS 13.[21]

13:4 Lest Enemies Rejoice

SIN OPPOSES THE SPIRIT. EUSEBIUS OF CAESAREA: As we sin, the adversary becomes haughty and domineering over us, and we are pressed down by our sin; this is really the nature of sin, to cast down and to oppress the spirit. COMMENTARY ON PSALMS 13.1-4.[22]

STEPPING INTO THE DEVIL'S TRAP. CASSIODORUS: A person must step into the devil's trap if he withdraws by a single step from the Lord's strength. EXPLANATION OF THE PSALMS 13.5.[23]

ASSISTING THE ENEMY. CHRYSOSTOM: What is the meaning of "I have prevailed over him"? That even if he is not absolutely strong, yet he has proved strong against me. Our defeat clothes him in strength, makes him look strong, powerful and invincible. Do you see that when we sin, not only do we shame and destroy ourselves and fall headlong into death, but also we declare to be strong and powerful the foes by whom we are defeated. And not only this: we also bring them to a state of joy and exultation. Bless me! What stupidity! What madness! To be of assistance ourselves to our enemies and make their soul rejoice and exult through the pain and distress they cause us! See how absurd it is. Whereas we should conquer the enemy ("His swords have finally failed," remember, "and the godless has been destroyed"[24]), whereas we should conquer, we are beaten; and not only this, but we make him appear powerful and strong. Nor does the extent of our madness and extreme derangement stop at this point: We prove the cause of bringing him to a state of joy and exultation. Sin in reality is the height of madness and extreme evil. . . . Let us . . . give thought and expend effort lest we puff the enemy up, lest we show him to be strong, lest we give him joy; instead, let us do the opposite, make him humble, lowly, weak, dejected, gloomy. You see, if he were to

---

[16]Ps 27:1 (26:1 LXX). [17]FC 89:96. [18]1 Cor 13:12. [19]See Job 12:22. [20]FC 77:16. [21]WGRW 9:41. [22]AnSac 3:405. [23]ACW 51:147. [24]Cf. Ps 9:6.

see sinners reforming, all these things would happen together. COMMENTARY ON THE PSALMS 13.1-2.[25]

13:5 Trusting in God's Steadfast Love

MERCY, NOT MERIT. THEODORET OF CYR: It is clear also from this that he uttered this psalm after the sin: he relies not on his righteousness but on mercy and says it is in this that he trusts. COMMENTARY ON THE PSALMS 13.4.[26]

SALVATION THROUGH FAITH. PSEUDO-ATHANASIUS: In this I trust, that I shall receive forgiveness of my sin, in that I hope in your mercy through which you have worked salvation for all people. EXPOSITION ON PSALMS 13.[27]

NOT THE BOAST OF PRIDE. AUGUSTINE: When a righteous person has not been shaken but has stood firm in the Lord, he or she must not claim credit for it; pride itself may shake such persons loose, even while they are boasting of not being shaken. EXPOSITIONS OF THE PSALMS 13.6.[28]

A HOPE-FILLED SOUL. CHRYSOSTOM: Do you see a hope-filled soul? He asked, and before receiving he gives thanks as though having received, sings praise to God and achieves all

that had been anticipated. COMMENTARY ON THE PSALMS 13.2.[29]

THE LOVE OF GOD. CASSIODORUS: The love of God is, so to say, a spring shower of virtues, beneath which a blessed longing germinates and holy action bears fruit. In this world it is patient in adversity and controlled in prosperity, powerful in humility and most joyful in affliction, kindly to enemies and overcoming evil people with its blessings. Even creatures of heaven are fired by it, becoming a renewing flame, a longing that swells and brings salvation. EXPLANATION OF THE PSALMS 13.1.[30]

13:6 Singing to the Lord

CONFIDENT HOPE WITH GRATITUDE. CHRYSOSTOM: Hope in God's mercy, have no doubts, and you will gain your request completely; once gained, however, do not prove ungrateful for the favor and unappreciative but make a record of the kindness and offer it as a thanksgiving song to the Lord. COMMENTARY ON THE PSALMS 13.3.[31]

---

[25]CCOP 1:226-27. [26]FC 101:105. [27]CSCO 387:8. [28]WSA 3 15:174. [29]CCOP 1:228. [30]ACW 51:145*. [31]CCOP 1:229*.

14:1-7 NONE SEEK GOD

When you hear some people blaspheming against the providence of God,
do not make common cause with them in their impiety,
but on the other hand, intercede with God, saying Psalm 14.

ATHANASIUS ON THE INTERPRETATION OF THE PSALMS 16 [OIP 67]

To the choirmaster.* Of David.

*¹The fool says in his heart, "There is no God."
  They are corrupt, they do abominable deeds,
  there is none that does good.*

*²The LORD looks down from heaven upon the children of men,
  to see if there are any that act wisely,
  that seek after God.*

*³They have all gone astray, they are all alike corrupt;
  there is none that does good,
  no, not one.*

*⁴Have they no knowledge, all the evildoers
  who eat up my people as they eat bread,
  and do not call upon the LORD?*

*⁵There they shall be in great terror,
  for God is with the generation of the righteous.*

*⁶You would confound the plans of the poor,
  but the LORD is his refuge.*

*⁷O that deliverance for Israel would come out of Zion!
  When the LORD restores the fortunes of his people,
  Jacob shall rejoice, Israel shall be glad.*

* LXX *To the end*

OVERVIEW: The fourteenth psalm carries the superscription "Unto the End" in the Septuagint. A christological reference is implied (AUGUSTINE), although some see a historical reference in the later history of Israel (DIODORE). Atheism is illogical (ASTERIUS THE HOMILIST). Yet, there are many forms of atheism (EUSEBIUS), and Scripture records a history of fools (ASTERIUS THE HOMILIST). Christ revealed the existence of God by his power and grace (JOHN OF DAMASCUS), but some come to know him only by the experience of his judgment (THEODORET). Corruption follows the denial of God (ATHANASIUS), which entails the denial of his Word (CASSIODORUS). They are sick, yet they refuse medicine (ASTERIUS THE HOMILIST), which is given only in Christ (CASSIODORUS).

The psalm speaks figuratively of God looking down from heaven, which refers to the grace by which God makes himself known (ASTERIUS THE HOMILIST). Humankind is turned away (ASTERIUS THE HOMILIST) in profound ignorance (ASTERIUS THE HOMILIST), which shows just how much Christ is needed (EUSEBIUS). Those who never come to know God's grace will be overtaken by fear (DIODORE). But God is over the righteous (ASTERIUS). Even Israel will be converted from its former ignorance (EUSEBIUS) in fulfillment of the Word of God (AUGUSTINE).

Superscription: *To the End*

CHRIST, THE END. AUGUSTINE: There is no need to repeat again and again what is meant by "to the end," "for Christ is the end of the law," bringing justification to everyone who believes, as the apostle Paul says.[1] EXPOSITIONS OF THE PSALMS 14.1.[2]

A HISTORICAL SITUATION. DIODORE OF TARSUS: The theme refers to Sennacherib at the time when he sent the Rabshakeh to prevail on the inhabitants of Jerusalem, make war on them, take them captive and make them slaves of the king of the Assyrians, namely, Sennacherib. COMMENTARY ON PSALMS 14.[3]

14:1 Fools Deny God

ILLOGICAL. ASTERIUS THE HOMILIST: "There is no God." There is no foundation, then how does the building stand? There is no keel, then how does the ship stabilize? There is no captain, then how is the ship readied? There is no builder, then how is the house built? There is no architect, then who founded the city? There is no farmer, then how do the fields bear their bundles? There is no music, then how can there be the harmony on the lyre of the world? There is no one to foresee, then how does foreknowledge permeate everything? There is no charioteer, then how is the chariot of the four elements driven? There is no sculptor, then how are statues of people in the world crafted? There are no builders of arches, then who has built the arch of heaven for you? There is no gold worker, then who has placed the golden disc sun in heaven as on a table? There is none who brings a torch, then who gave the moon of the night to you as a silver torch? There is none who brings light, and who has given to you a light with clear splendor? There is none who alone makes great lights, then who has put the ascending lamps of the stars in the sky for you? . . . Is there no Creator about whom the creature testifies? HOMILIES ON THE PSALMS 25.8.[4]

FORMS OF ATHEISM. EUSEBIUS OF CAESAREA: Some have denied that there is a divine spirit altogether. They have openly professed that God is not the ruler of everything, that his name is nothing but empty and that he is of no substance. Others worship gods who do not exist, denying him who is God alone. Some suggest that indeed there is a God in name, but they contend that he does not oversee earthly matters or look on human affairs. In summary, therefore, all these people have come together into the single position of atheism (godlessness), believing that there is no God. Since they are not bold enough to announce this openly, they persuade themselves in their hearts, being foolish and senseless in the matter of truth, that God does not exist. (A natural understanding about God and the innate seeds of the instinct drive all of them to confess a recognition of God; they are not so bold to deny this fact with their lips, so they pretend to recognize him not as the only God but as an innumerable plurality.) . . . Their godless position is brought to light from their works (as indeed a tree is judged by its fruit), with their villainy and a way of living like it. They have poisoned their own spirit, betraying it to their bodies with whatever corruption, and as men act in madness with men and through whatever other monstrous and abominable acts, they defile their own selves. In this way it was shown that even if they mustered ten thousand gods, even if they blared out with their lips and confessed God governs all things, in their hearts, and really in their minds, there is not the least recognition of God. Such, therefore, was the life of these people before the advent of our Savior. COMMENTARY ON PSALMS 14.1.[5]

A HISTORY OF FOOLS. ASTERIUS THE HOMILIST: It was the fool who said through Pharoah, "I have not known this God"; and the depth of the sea became a tomb for him. The fool said through Sennecharib, "God is not able to snatch Hezekiah from my hands," and he was killed by

---

[1]Rom 10:4. [2]WSA 3 15:175. [3]WGRW 9:41-42. [4]TLG 2061.001, 25.8.2. [5]AnSac 3:407-8.

his sons. The fool said through Nebuchadnez-zar, "Who is this God who can snatch you from my hand? Who is the most powerful of men?" . . . Judas the denier of God was destroyed by a noose because he had deemed God as a man to be betrayed. HOMILIES ON THE PSALMS 25.17.[6]

REVEALED BY CHRIST. JOHN OF DAMASCUS: The fact that God exists is not doubted by those who accept the sacred Scriptures—both the Old and New Testaments, I mean—or by the majority of the Greeks, for, as we have said, the knowledge of God's existence has been revealed to us through nature. However, since the wickedness of the evil one has so prevailed over people's nature as even to drag some of them down to the most unspeakable and extremely wicked abyss of perdition and to make them say that there is no God, . . . then the Lord's disciples and apostles, made wise by the all-Holy Spirit, did by his power and grace show signs from God and draw up those people alive in the net of their miracles from the depths of the ignorance of God to the light of his knowledge. ORTHODOX FAITH 1.3.[7]

LEARNING BY EXPERIENCE. THEODORET OF CYR: [Like the Assyrian army in the days of Hezekiah], all will come to know through experience the one fighting against them; fear will strike them from a source they did not expect. I mean, who would have thought they would be destroyed by an angel? That God cares for the Jews? Those who mocked the counsel of poor and lowly Hezekiah for trusting in God rather than arms will realize that the one who made himself dependent on God enjoyed a hope that was not disappointed. COMMENTARY ON THE PSALMS 14.2.[8]

CORRUPTION FOLLOWS. ATHANASIUS: This statement [about fools] is directly followed by one pointing out that their actions correspond with their thoughts: "They are corrupt, and their behavior is evil." The unrighteous person corrupts his body in every possible way: stealing,

committing adultery, cursing, getting drunk, and doing similar things. . . . Count on it: those who are fools in their thoughts will do wicked deeds. As the Lord said [to the Pharisees], "How can you speak good things when you are evil?"[9] And they truly were evil, because their thoughts were wicked. FESTAL LETTERS 9.8, 12.6.[10]

FALLEN AWAY FROM SCRIPTURE. CASSIODO-RUS: "They are corrupt and are become abominable in their desires." They are corrupt because in abandoning the sanity of the Scriptures they have demonstrably fallen into sinful thoughts. The punishment for sin follows next; disfigured by their most wicked reluctance to believe, they became abominable to the Lord through their errors. EXPLANATION OF THE PSALMS 14.1.[11]

SICK YET REFUSING MEDICINE. ASTERIUS THE HOMILIST: They are corrupt—wounded and rotten, smelling rank, seeping foulness and poison, not seeking medicine. They become abominable like pigs rolling in the mud of sin; like dogs returning to vomit, they run with rage. . . . Because they have despised the thinking of God, pious people despise them. They are corrupt like worm-infested garments, as rusted iron, as those who have touched death and the ashes of dead bones. . . . "There is no one who does good, not one."[12] Not Herod killing innocent babies, not the Jew who called Jesus Beelzebub when he cast out demons, not the one endeavoring to keep the law perfectly, not priests acting dishonorably, not scribes writing for naught, not Pharisees pressing and pushing rules, not Sadducees debating, not Judas selling him, not the master boxing the slave's ear, not Pilate condemning him, not the people shouting. . . . "There is no one who speaks good," when all the disciples fled as they abandoned him. John ran off naked. Peter denied him, the disciples fled, the spear of doubt pierced the soul of Mary. There was no one who

---

[6]TLG 2061.001, 25.17.3. [7]FC 37:168. [8]FC 101:107. [9]Mt 12:34. [10]ARL 155, 193. [11]ACW 51:150. [12]Ps 14:3 (13:3 LXX).

showed the fruit of love in his suffering. . . . Even after his death, the soldier pierced his side. . . . Surely he has visited us and wants to save, but none desires to be shown the medicine. HOMILIES ON THE PSALMS 25.19.[13]

MUST GAIN CHRIST. CASSIODORUS: We cannot do good unless through his mercy we have gained Christ. When we reach him and do not abandon him, every good is undoubtedly performed. This is the end promised in the heading of the psalm. EXPLANATION OF THE PSALMS 14.1.[14]

14:2 The Lord Looks at Humankind

HOW THE LORD LOOKS DOWN. ASTERIUS THE HOMILIST: When you hear the Lord looks down from heaven, think not of his divine and incorporeal nature that he has bowed and bent down, or has bent his knee or nodded his head, but realize his visitation, forgiveness and kindness. Although he is said to have a head, ears, eyes, mouth and hands, and to sit and to rise, yet he is not altogether constituted of members and parts. So he does not literally look down but shows his own mercy. He looks down from heaven, not through fences and gates in the sky, but because from heaven he has visited humankind. . . . He sees them to serve them and to embrace them as a friend. . . . He appears to them who have faith in him in order that he may see who is sick and who needs the doctor and who is poor and who requires Christ, the storehouse of the Father. . . . Then after they see the Lord of the prophets has looked down from heaven so that he may see, . . . they say, "It is not enough, Lord, that you look down from heaven. Descend. . . . Come, . . . Son of the Father. Seek what is made in your image." HOMILIES ON THE PSALMS 25.25.[15]

14:3 Corrupt and Straying

TURNED AWAY. ASTERIUS THE HOMILIST: Everywhere they all have turned to tyranny. They no longer cling to the prophets. Come, King, appear, and they will fear your authority. All have turned from the ways of the prophets. Come, O Way, and lead back those who have wandered away. . . . Humankind was created right by God, . . . but they have turned away by choice to evil. . . . They have turned away from their right nature. . . . "There is no one who does good, no, not one." From head to foot, from rich to poor, the whole world grows sick. HOMILIES ON THE PSALMS 25.27.[16]

WHAT THEY DO NOT KNOW. ASTERIUS THE HOMILIST: What do they know? That God is an avenger. He is coming as judge of the living and the dead. They know that he is going to return to each one according to his works. . . . And what do they not know? That God looks down from heaven. What do they not know? That those who do evil displease him. What do they not know? They do not wish to know the ways of God. . . . And now there are wars, pestilence and volcanoes [earthquakes]. Many never come to their senses concerning their sins, and they are punished with threatening evils. What do they not know? The will of God, his good and celestial promises, his treasures, the delights of paradise, eternal life. HOMILIES ON THE PSALMS 25.33.[17]

THE NEED FOR CHRIST. EUSEBIUS OF CAESAREA: It was right to show openly the magnitude of the disease that lingered with sinister purpose for all people before the advent of the Savior: as it was manifested to all, his sojourn on earth became straightforwardly necessary. As all have sinned, all lacked the glory of God, and now they are all justified by his grace. COMMENTARY ON PSALMS 14.3.[18]

14:5 Great Terror

---

[13]TLG 2061.001, 25.19.6. [14]ACW 51:150*. [15]TLG 2061.001, 25.25.1. [16]TLG 2061.001, 25.27.6. [17]TLG 2061.001, 25.33.5. [18]PG 23:145.

FEAR COMES. DIODORE OF TARSUS: Such people will never learn from experience what a harsh thing it is to do wrong to the Lord's people, so bitter are they toward us as to wish to treat us like a meal of bread. . . . Since they are ready to swallow us raw, then, and do not have the Lord before their eyes, fear will overtake them from a quarter where they do not expect it. COMMENTARY ON PSALMS 14.[19]

14:6 The Lord a Refuge

GOD OVER THE RIGHTEOUS. ASTERIUS THE HOMILIST: Like the general over the soldiers and the king over the senate, God is over the generation of the righteous. . . . If God is in the midst of two or three, how much more is he found in the generation of the righteous where there is a battle-free life, a lack of sadness, rest and inheritance and a kingdom without end. HOMILIES ON THE PSALMS 25.40.[20]

IGNORANCE OF THE SAVIOR. EUSEBIUS OF CAESAREA: These words that are now put forth can be understood in my opinion in light of the Jews trying to upset the plan of the Savior, because they thought that he was lacking power. They did not consider carefully the treasure of his divinity. So they always contradicted his teaching, and the power of his miracles they misrepresented as not from divine power but as having been worked through some other source. COMMENTARY ON PSALMS 14.6.[21]

14:7 Deliverance for Israel

THE SALVATION OF ISRAEL. AUGUSTINE: "Who will give Israel salvation out of Zion?" We must supply, "other than the one whose humility you have despised?" For he himself will come in glory to judge the living and the dead and to usher in the kingdom of the just. This would mean that, as by his coming in humility blindness fell on part of Israel until the full tally of the Gentiles should come in, so, by that glorious coming, the rest of the prophecy may come true and all Israel be saved. For the apostle takes as reference to the Jews that testimony of Isaiah where it is said, "From Zion shall come the one who will turn away ungodliness from Jacob,"[22] as though it were an answer to the question in this psalm, "Who will give Israel salvation out of Zion?" EXPOSITIONS OF THE PSALMS 14.8.[23]

---

[19]WGRW 9:43. [20]TLG 2061.001, 25.40.3. [21]PG 23:148. [22]Rom 11:26. [23]WSA 3 15:178.

15:1-5 THE BLAMELESS

If you wish to learn what sort of person is
a citizen of the kingdom of heaven, sing Psalm 15.

ATHANASIUS *ON THE INTERPRETATION OF THE PSALMS* 16 [OIP 67]

A Psalm of David.

¹*O Lord, who shall sojourn in thy tent?*
  Who shall dwell on thy holy hill?

²*He who walks blamelessly, and does what is*
    right,
  and speaks truth from his heart;
³*who does not slander with his tongue,*
  and does no evil to his friend,
    nor takes up a reproach against his
    neighbor;
⁴*in whose eyes a reprobate is despised,*
  but who honors those who fear the LORD;
who swears to his own hurt and does not
    change;
⁵*who does not put out his money at interest,*
    and does not take a bribe against the
    innocent.

He who does these things shall never be
  moved.

OVERVIEW: The fifteenth psalm presents ten virtues that model the Ten Commandments (CASSIODORUS) and that characterize the life of the one who sojourns in the tent of God, the tent of cleansing (ARNOBIUS THE YOUNGER), the tent of faith (AUGUSTINE). This is the way of life that belongs to the redeemed (THEODORET). The blamelessness we read about in this psalm was first found in Christ (CASSIODORUS). It comes to us as God's work in the soul (RULE OF ST. BENEDICT). So, although we are justified by faith not by works, works follow justification in the life of the believer (AUGUSTINE).

The psalmist focuses first on justice, since it is the mother of all virtues (JEROME). Next, true speech comes from truth in the heart (AUGUSTINE), and we note here the progression in the psalm from heart to tongue to deed (THEODORET). Christ is the example, who purely transmitted the Word of God (CASSIODORUS). But how do we detect the truth in the words of others? If we practice humility, we can distin-guish truth from flattery (MARTIN).

Doing no evil to a neighbor is a compre-hensive statement. It covers both business and private life (AMBROSE). Such is possible only by grace (JEROME). Complete instruction in virtue honors even the lowly who fear the Lord (DIODORE). The words of such a person are like the oath of God—his promises will be fulfilled (CASSIODORUS). The Scripture speaks of two kinds of currency: preaching, which is given with the expectation of return, and the lending of money at interest (CASSIODORUS). The problem with lending money at interest is that it lacks kindness (LEO). Indebtedness destroys lives—that of the bor-rower and of the lender (BASIL). It has brought about the failure of entire nations (AMBROSE). Finally, this psalm speaks of a perfect life— perfect in small things as well as great things (AUGUSTINE).

15:1 Your Tent

THE TEN COMMANDMENTS. CASSIODORUS: [This psalm] is not, like some of the psalms, wrapped, so to say, in profundity, but the Lord replies to the prophet's questioning following the mode of the Decalogue, saying that one reaches the hall of his blessedness through ten virtues. . . . This is the great divine decalogue, the spiritual psaltry of ten chords. Here is the truly crowning number that only he could fulfill who with his Father laid low the sins of the world. Let us continually pray to his omnipotence that we who cannot of ourselves perform such acts as are enjoined on us may do them by being enriched with his gift. EXPLANATION OF THE PSALMS 15.1, 5.[1]

THE TENT OF CLEANSING. ARNOBIUS THE YOUNGER: All the defiled approach the tabernacle of the Lord, and there they are made undefiled. Jesus alone, undefiled, having entered the uncorrupted tabernacle, has freed us from the defilement of the flesh and has given us holiness. COMMENTARY ON PSALMS 15.[2]

THE TENT OF FAITH. AUGUSTINE: Although the word *tent* is used sometimes to denote an everlasting habitation, strictly speaking a tent is something associated with war. Hence soldiers are referred to as tent companions, because their tents are grouped together. This interpretation receives further backing from the words "who will sojourn?" For we do battle with the devil for a time, and we need a tent in which to regain our strength. This points in particular to faith under this temporal dispensation established for us within time by our Lord's incarnation. EXPOSITIONS OF THE PSALMS 15.1.[3]

THE LIFE OF THE REDEEMED. THEODORET OF CYR: Since the psalm before this also prophesied salvation for the inhabitants of Jerusalem and forecast the return of those already made captive, it is right for him to introduce exhortation in this psalm and propose a way of life proper for them to live who are under God's command and

enjoying such wonderful assistance. COMMENTARY ON THE PSALMS 15.1.[4]

15:2 *Walking Blamelessly*

FOUND IN CHRIST. CASSIODORUS: The Lord Christ . . . entered the temple at Jerusalem free from sins. Whereas others had entered the house of God for purification, he was the only One to enter in such a way as to stand before the Father's face without blemish. So the law did not bestow anything on him, but as the best legislator he fulfilled the law. EXPLANATION OF THE PSALMS 15.2.[5]

GOD'S WORK IN THE SOUL. BENEDICT: Brothers, let us hear the Lord's answer to the question, an answer that shows the way to the heavenly tabernacle. . . . He who drives the tempter and his temptations far from his heart, defeats his malice and dashes his rising thoughts against the Rock Christ. He who fears the Lord without growing proud of his virtue and humbly acknowledges that what is good in him does not proceed from himself. He who gives God his due and with the prophet blesses the work of God in himself: "Not to us, O Lord, not to us, but to your name give the glory."[6] The apostle Paul found nothing of his own to boast of in his preaching: "By the grace of God [says he] I am what I am,"[7] and again, "He who glories, let him glory in the Lord."[8] RULE OF ST. BENEDICT, PROLOGUE.[9]

WORKS FOLLOW FAITH. AUGUSTINE: When the apostle says that in his opinion a person is justified through faith without the works of the Law, he does not intend by this decision to express contempt for the commandments and the works of justice by the profession of faith but to inform anyone that he can be justified by faith even if he has not previously fulfilled the works

---

[1]ACW 51:156, 160. [2]CCL 25:16. [3]WSA 3 15:179. [4]FC 101:111. [5]ACW 51:157. [6]Ps 115:1 (113:9 LXX). [7]1 Cor 15:10. [8]2 Cor 10:17. [9]LCC 12:292*.

of the Law; for they follow when one has been justified and do not come before for one to be justified. FAITH AND WORKS 14.21.[10]

THE MOTHER OF ALL VIRTUES. JEROME: Note exactly what the psalmist is saying: "And does justice." Now, the Holy Spirit did not say, one who practices chastity, who applies wisdom, who exercises fortitude. Yet these are excellent virtues indeed. Wisdom, for example, is of great advantage to us; fortitude is valuable in resisting persecution; finally, temperance and chastity are indispensable in preventing us from losing our souls. Justice alone is the great virtue and the mother of them all. Someone may ask, "How is justice greater than all the other virtues?" The other virtues gratify the one who possesses them; justice does not give pleasure to the one possessing it but instead pleases others. If I am wise, wisdom delights me; if I am brave, my fortitude comforts me; if I have been chaste, my chastity is my joy. On the contrary, justice does not benefit the one who has it but all the wretched who do not have it. Suppose that some poor person has a quarrel with my brother; suppose that my brother is powerful and with his power crushes the other one, I mean, the stranger to me, the poor and wretched person. Of what avail is my wisdom to the poor person? Of what avail my courage? My chastity, how does it help the poor person? Justice is the virtue that benefits him, for I do not regard the person of my brother but judge according to truth. Justice knows no brother, it knows no father, it knows no other; it knows truth; it is not a respecter of persons; it imitates God. HOMILY ON PSALM 14[15].[11]

TRUTH IN THE HEART. AUGUSTINE: Some have the truth on their lips and yet do not have it in their heart. Suppose someone were to give false directions deliberately, knowing full well that on the road in question there were brigands, and were to say, "If you go this way, you will be safe from brigands," and then it turned out that in fact there were no brigands to be found there. Our imaginary person would have spoken the truth, but not in his heart. He was thinking otherwise, and he spoke the truth unwittingly. Therefore, it is insufficient to utter the truth unless it also exists in the heart. "Who has not practiced deceit with his tongue." Deceit is practiced with the tongue when one thing is professed with the lips and another is concealed in the breast. EXPOSITIONS OF THE PSALMS 15.3.[12]

HEART, TONGUE AND DEED. THEODORET OF CYR: It is necessary, he is saying, for such a one to rid himself of evil and be free of all blame, and to practice every virtue studiously. . . . He must keep free of falsehood not only his tongue but also his mind, and be rid completely of the double deceit so that on their part no harm results to their neighbor. Now, it was very logical for him to make mention first of the heart, then of the tongue and then of the deed: word precedes action; and thinking, word. COMMENTARY ON THE PSALMS 15.2.[13]

PURE TRANSMISSION OF GOD'S WORD. CASSIODORUS: He attests in the Gospel that he was without guile in all he said by the words "Whatsoever I have heard from my Father I have made known to you."[14] What could be more pure and simple than that the unchangeable truth should pass to people's ears untainted by any addition or suppression in its unadulterated integrity? "Nor has done evil to his neighbor." . . . [This virtue is] again demonstrated in the Lord: He not only harmed no one but also endured all things patiently. EXPLANATION OF THE PSALMS 15.3.[15]

PROTECTION AGAINST FLATTERY. MARTIN OF BRAGA: The prophet David said that it was better for him to be corrected or advised by a just person than to be praised by any flatterer. It was right that he should denote the flat-

---

[10]FC 27:247*. [11]FC 48:40*. [12]WSA 3 15:179-80. [13]FC 101:111. [14]Jn 15:15. [15]ACW 51:157-58.

terer with the name of "sinner," since his is the greatest and most detestable crime in the sight of God—to hold one thing in his heart, speak another with his lips. Of such he also says in another psalm: "His words are smoother than oil, but they are drawn swords."[16] Of the just person he says, "He speaks the truth in his heart and works not deceit with his tongue." Although in these ways any subtle remarks of people, even without the pleasing sensations of praise, may draw your credulous mind to agreement, turn rather to the deeds of our Lord Jesus Christ in the Gospels, and you will find that the Lord of lords left us to a great example of sacred humility amid the praises of people. Practice humility, then, take it for your mistress, set it as your guide when flatterers entice. Humility will tell you just how much of the things that people ascribe to you in praise is really yours and how long it will last. Humility does not let you be attentive to lies. EXHORTATION TO HUMILITY 3.[17]

TRUTH IN BUSINESS. AMBROSE: In everything, therefore, good faith is seemly, justice is pleasing, due measure in equity is delightful. But what shall I say about contracts, and especially about the sale of land, or agreements or covenants? Are there not rules just for the purpose of shutting out all false deceit and to make him whose deceit is found out liable to double punishment? Everywhere, then, does regard for what is virtuous take the lead; it shuts out deceit, it expels fraud. Wherefore the prophet David has rightly stated his judgment in general, saying, "He has done no evil to his neighbor." Fraud, then, ought to be wanting not only in contracts, in which the defects of those things that are for sale are ordered to be recorded (which contracts, unless the vendor has mentioned the defects, are rendered void by an action for fraud, although he has conveyed them fully to the purchaser), but it ought also to be absent in all else. Candor must be shown, the truth must be made known. DUTIES OF THE CLERGY 3.10.66.[18]

ONLY BY GRACE. JEROME: This is a noble thing to say. Never, says the psalmist, has a neighbor murmured against him; never, he says, has he found occasion for his disparagement. This virtue is beyond . . . human power; it exists by the grace of God. "By whom the reprobate is despised." Mark what it says: "By whom the reprobate is despised." Even if he is an emperor, even if he is a governor, if he is a bishop, if he is a priest, . . . whoever he is, if he is evil, he is nothing in the sight of the saint. HOMILY ON PSALM 14[15].[19]

15:4 Honoring Those Who Fear the Lord

EVEN THE LOWLY. DIODORE OF TARSUS: Whoever abhors the wicked, even if they are very rich, while "honoring those who fear the Lord," even if they are very lowly and poor, will live in honor and respect. There is therefore need to consider how in the apparent reply of God complete instruction in virtue emerges, the intention being for a person first to attend to piety and righteousness, then to keep one's distance from all wicked behavior, and after this not to admire the deportment of the rich if piety does not accompany wealth. . . . One should have especial regard for the poor provided they did not have a change of heart for the worse as a result of poverty but rather continued to be devoted to a godly way of life. COMMENTARY ON PSALMS 15.[20]

GOD'S OATH. CASSIODORUS: Swearing in human terms means promising something by calling God to witness. But when God . . . makes the promise, it is more appropriate to say that the swearing lay in his promising, for the word *swear* means "to speak justly." Now a person speaks justly when what he promises is fulfilled. God's swearing, then, means promising and fulfilling. EXPLANATION OF THE PSALMS 15.4.[21]

---

[16]Ps 55:21 (54:22 LXX). [17]FC 62:53. [18]NPNF 2 10:78. [19]FC 48:41-42. [20]WGRW 9:45. [21]ACW 51:158-59*.

15:5 *Not Putting Out Money at Interest*

TWO KINDS OF MONEY LENDING. CASSIODO-RUS: In the holy Scriptures money is clearly understood in two senses. One is the metal money that we are absolutely forbidden to put out to usury, because it is the vice of greed to seek to demand what you know you have not lent. The Lord Christ had this money, and he gave it to Judas to be paid out to the poor. This he has not put out to usury, since with devoted generosity he donated it to the poor for our instruction. The other kind is that which we are persuaded through the gospel teaching to put out to usury, namely, most holy preaching and divine teaching. EXPLANATION OF THE PSALMS 15.5.[22]

THE PROFIT THAT LACKS KINDNESS. LEO THE GREAT: The evil of usury must be shunned, and the profit that lacks all human kindness must be avoided. The means for unjust and grievous gain is increased, but the essence of the soul is worn down, since usury in money is the ruin of the soul. The holy prophet David showed what God thinks about the people of this kind when he says, "Lord, who will dwell in your tent, or who will rest on your holy mountain?" Those are taught by the reply of the divine voice, and those know that they have a part in eternal rest if, among the other rules of a holy life, "they do not give their own money at usury." They are shown to be strangers to the "tent" of God and foreign to his "holy mountain" if they seize a deceitful profit for their money by usury, and, while they want to be rich through another's loss, they are worthy to be punished by eternal penury. But you, dearly beloved, who have believed the promises of the Lord with your whole heart, flee the foul leprosy of avarice and make a holy and wise use of God's gifts. Since you enjoy his generosity, take care that you may be able to have companions of your joy. The things that are supplied to you are lacking to many, and in their need the material has been given to you for imitating the divine goodness, so that through you

the divine goodness might pass over to others. As you give out your temporal goods well, you are acquiring eternal. SERMON 17.3-4.[23]

USURY DESTROYS LIVES. BASIL THE GREAT: We advise the poor . . . to persevere in their terrible situations rather than to accept the misfortunes that come from the payment of interest. But if you [who are rich] obey the Lord, what need is there of these words? What is the counsel of the Master? "Lend to those from whom you do not hope to receive in return."[24] "And what sort of a loan is this," one might ask, "to which there is no hope of a return attached?" Consider the force of the Lord's statement, and you will admire the kindness of the Lawmaker. Whenever you have the intention of providing for a poor person for the Lord's sake, the same thing is both a gift and a loan, a gift because of the expectation of no repayment but a loan because of the great gift of the Master who pays in his place. . . . "He who has mercy on the poor lends to God."[25] Do you not wish to have the Lord of the universe answerable to you for payment? . . . Give the money, since it is lying idle, without weighing it down with additional charges, and it will be good for both of you. There will be for you the assurance of its safety because of his custody; for him receiving it, the advantage from its use. And, if you are seeking additional payment, be satisfied with that from the Lord. He himself will pay the interest for the poor. Expect kindly acts from him who is truly kind. This interest, which you take, is full of extreme inhumanity. You make profit from misfortune, you collect money from tears, you strangle the naked, you beat the famished; nowhere is there mercy, no thought of relationship with the sufferer; and you call the profits from these things humane! Woe to you who say that the bitter is sweet and the sweet bitter, and who call inhumanity by the name of humanity.[26]

---

[22]ACW 51:159. [23]FC 93:65-66. [24]Cf. Lk 6:35. [25]Prov 19:17. [26]Cf. Is 5:20.

. . . "People do not gather grapes from thorns or figs from thistles,"[27] or humanity from interest. Every "bad tree bears bad fruit."[28] Some are collectors of a hundredfold and some collectors of tenfold, names horrible indeed to hear; monthly exactors, they attack the poor according to the cycles of the moon, like those demons that cause epileptic fits. It is wicked lending for both, for the giver and for the receiver, bringing loss to the one in money and to the other in soul. . . . It is not evident for whom you collect. It is indeed apparent who he is who weeps because of the interest, but it is doubtful who he is who is to enjoy the abundance that comes from it. In fact, it is uncertain whether you will not leave to others the gift of wealth, but the evil of injustice you have treasured up for yourself. "And from him who would borrow of you, do not turn away,"[29] and do not give your money at interest, in order that, having been taught what is good from the Old and the New Testament, you may depart to the Lord with good hope, receiving there the interest from your good deeds, in Christ Jesus our Lord, to whom be glory and power forever. Amen. HOMILIES ON THE PSALMS 12.5 (Ps 15).[30]

THE FAILURE OF NATIONS. AMBROSE: What is more cruel than to lend money to one who has none and then to exact double the amount? If one cannot pay the simple amount, how will he pay double? . . . Nations have often failed because of usury, and this has been the cause of public calamity. LETTER 19.[31]

PERFECT IN LITTLE THINGS. AUGUSTINE: These are no great achievements! But people who are incapable of even these are much less able to speak the truth in their hearts, to refrain from practicing deceit with their tongues, to profess the truth outwardly just as it is in their hearts, to have on their lips "a yes that is yes and a no that is no,"[32] to avoid harming their neighbors (that is, anyone) or reject a slanderous accusation against a neighbor. Such are the qualities of the perfect, in whose sight the spiteful has been reduced to nothing. Yet the psalmist concludes his enumeration of even these small-scale acts by declaring, "whoever acts so will not be moved forever," suggesting that such person will proceed to those greater things in which powerful and unshakeable stability may be gained. EXPOSITIONS OF THE PSALMS 15.5.[33]

---

[27]Mt 7:16. [28]Mt 7:17. [29]Mt 5:42. [30]FC 46:190-91*. [31]FC 26:175 (Letter 35 in this edition). [32]Mt 5:37. [33]WSA 3 15:180

16:1-11 FAITHFULNESS TO THE LORD

Psalm 16 reveals [the Savior's] resurrection from the dead.

ATHANASIUS *On the Interpretation of the Psalms* 26 [OIP 72]

A Miktam of David.

¹*Preserve me, O God, for in thee I take refuge.*
  ²*I say to the* LORD, *"Thou art my Lord;*
  I have no good apart from thee."ᵍ*

³*As for the saints in the land, they are the*
    noble,
  in whom is all my delight.

⁴*Those who choose another god multiply their*
    sorrows;ʰ
  their libations of blood I will not pour out
  or take their names upon my lips.

⁵*The* LORD *is my chosen portion and my cup;*
  thou holdest my lot.
⁶*The lines have fallen for me in pleasant*
    places;

yea, I have a goodly heritage.

⁷*I bless the* LORD *who gives me counsel;*
  in the night also my heart instructs me.
⁸*I keep the* LORD *always before me;*
  because he is at my right hand, I shall not
  be moved.

⁹*Therefore my heart is glad, and my soul*
    rejoices;
  my body also dwells secure.
¹⁰*For thou dost not give me up to Sheol,*
  or let thy godly one see the Pit.

¹¹*Thou dost show me the path of life;*
  in thy presence there is fulness of joy,
  in thy right hand are pleasures for
  evermore.

g Jerome Tg: The meaning of the Hebrew is uncertain   h Cn: The meaning of the Hebrew is uncertain   * LXX *because my goods are nothing to you*

OVERVIEW: The sixteenth psalm is a prophecy about Christ (PSEUDO-ATHANASIUS) in two themes; deliverance and thanksgiving (CASSIODORUS). In response, we thank God for the gift of salvation (CASSIODORUS). The psalm opens with a request for protection (THEODORET) and an acknowledgment that all good things come from God (CASSIODORUS, THEODORET). Our own goods are nothing to God. He has no possible need of anything from us (AMBROSE). All our goods are his already (AUGUSTINE). Whatever we give to him, he gives back to us (JEROME). When we worship him, we are the beneficiaries, not he himself (AUGUSTINE).

Our inheritance is the understanding of God (EVAGRIUS), or more fully, the Lord is our inheritance (AUGUSTINE). We are to live now so as to possess the Lord (JEROME). He is everything for us (LEANDER). Let us express our love for him (AUGUSTINE). The measure of our inheritance depends on our capacity for God (EVAGRIUS). The measure of Christ's inheritance is the full company of the redeemed (CASSIODORUS), and his passion for their salvation remained strong even in the nighttime of his suffering (JEROME). The path of righteousness is the line of sight fixed on God (CASSIODORUS). We have the responsibility to set the Lord before us (JEROME).

Christ's position at the right hand reveals the equality of worth he shares with the Father (HESYCHIUS).

The psalm goes on to speak of the resurrection of the flesh (ORIGEN). It was not just his soul, but his body had hope (JEROME). He speaks here as man, not as God (CYRIL OF ALEXANDRIA), of the salvation of his humanity through the presence of the Word (ATHANASIUS). He saved what he assumed (GREGORY OF NYSSA). We avoid an improper view of Christ's body by understanding the meaning of "corruption" (JOHN OF DAMASCUS). Christ goes on to express his hope of resurrection (THEODORET) in a way that reveals the fact of his human soul (CASSIODORUS). Obviously, this is not just David speaking here (AUGUSTINE). While not excluding other referents, the words are more applicable to the Lord (DIODORE). As such, they serve as a refutation to major heresies (THEODORET).

The psalm ends in an expression of joy overflowing (CASSIODORUS, THEODORET). He who is the way learned the way (JEROME). And that way comes from him to us (MAXIMUS OF TURIN).

16:1 Preserve me

CHRIST IN THE PSALM: AN OVERVIEW.
PSEUDO-ATHANASIUS: The words in [this psalm] are sung as if by the person of Christ, who although he is noble as Lord by nature and has under his feet creation as a handmaid, yet he asks to be preserved by the Father as the head of the body of the church. . . . He made those sanctified by the Spirit a marvel in the land—in his church—teaching them the will of the Father as an angel of mighty counsel. They hastened to hear the preaching, not through blood [sacrifices] or practices of the law to please God, but through praise and bloodless sacrifice. Nor with names that befit their former works did he say, I shall call them, that is, idolaters and polytheists and atheists; but called and holy and pious, and who have a share in the Lord. Because the latter was obedient to the Father to death—which

he calls a cup—for this reason he gave him as a portion and inheritance to the Gentiles. And he binds it to him with cords—fetters of spiritual life. . . . He is on [the Father's] right hand in that we gain through his hands his heavenly Father as helper, and like a rod of power he has supported our weakness. Therefore he also says to him: My flesh will reside in hope. The hope, then, is that his flesh will again assume the soul that was constituted. For his soul was not left in Sheol, nor did his body see the corruption of the grave. . . . For these things are granted us in him as the head and firstborn of the resurrection and because we have grown rich with his poverty. And again we shall be in unfading delights, which the saints will receive on the day of his manifestation from him who is the Father's right hand. EXPOSITION ON PSALMS 16.[1]

CHRIST IN TWO THEMES. CASSIODORUS: The person of the Lord Savior is introduced throughout the psalm. In the first theme, in accord with his acceptance of human form, he . . . [asks] the Father to be saved, because he has always put his hope in him. By this he does not in any sense lessen his divinity but reflects the nature of his humanity. . . . In his second theme he gives thanks to the Father, who by appearing at his right hand has by the power of his omnipotence overcome the wickedness of this world. He maintains that because of this his soul has been freed from hell, and he recounts that after the glory of the resurrection he has been set among the delights at his right hand. EXPLANATION OF THE PSALMS 16.1.[2]

THE GIFT OF SALVATION. CASSIODORUS: Let us meditate on the immensity of the gift of salvation that this psalm offers for our instruction. It gives us confidence in sufferings and promises eternal glory in hope, so that through this teaching of our future happiness we do not fear the hardships of the present. This is heavenly

---

[1]CSCO 387:10. [2]ACW 51:161.

schooling, learning for life, the lecture hall of truth, and most indubitably a unique discipline that occupies its pupils with thoughts that bear fruit, not with the flattery of empty words. Explanation of the Psalms 16.11.[3]

PROTECTION OF THE INCARNATE LORD. THEODORET OF CYR: The psalm is spoken in the person of the Savior but is spoken from the viewpoint of his humanity, as are also many other such statements that we find in the sacred Gospels. . . . In this psalm also he asks to be protected and is protected by himself: while he asks as a human being, as God he grants the request, his own Father of course being pleased and cooperating. COMMENTARY ON THE PSALMS 16.2.[4]

16:2 No Good Apart from God

RECIPIENT OF GOOD THINGS. CASSIODORUS: He attributes all things to him who has bestowed them, and not to himself who received what was bestowed. EXPLANATION OF THE PSALMS 16.2.[5]

GRACE. THEODORET OF CYR: The abundance of good things, he is saying, comes to me from your grace. COMMENTARY ON THE PSALMS 16.3.[6]

16:2 My Goods Are Nothing to You

NO POSSIBLE NEED. AMBROSE: Who has ever given him anything, since "from him, and through him and in him"[7] are all things? The fount of life is that highest Good that bestows the substance of life on all, because it has life abiding in itself. It receives from no one as though it were needy; it lavishes goods on all and borrows from others nothing for itself, for it has no need of us. It says, too, in the person of humankind: "You do not need my goods." What is more lovely than to approach him and cling to him? What pleasure can be greater? What else can he desire who sees and tastes freely of this fount of living water? what realms? what powers?

what riches? when he sees how pitiable are the conditions of kings, how changeable the status of their power, how short the span of this life, in how great bondage even sovereigns must live, since they live at the will of others and not their own. LETTER 29.[8]

ALL MY GOODS ARE GOD'S GIFTS. AUGUSTINE: What in any case are my goods, if not what I have been given by you? And how can the one by whom every good is given be in need of any good? SERMON 331.2.[9]

GOD GIVES BACK TO US. JEROME: God, the omnipotent, does not need our goods, nor do our virtuous acts contribute to the perfection of God, since increase is impossible to him. But whatever we produce by toil and bring forth in labor, that he exacts and takes from us in order to give back to us what he has received. HOMILY ON PSALM 15[16].[10]

WE ARE THE BENEFICIARIES. AUGUSTINE: It is man, not God, who benefits from the whole economy of worship. CITY OF GOD 10.5.[11]

IN OUR INTEREST. AUGUSTINE: God does not derive any benefit from our worship, but we do. When he reveals or teaches how he is to be worshiped, he does so in our own highest interest, with absolutely no need of anything for himself. All such sacrifices are symbolic; they are a representation of certain things by which our attention is aroused to study or understand or reflect on the realities represented by them. LETTER 102.3.[12]

16:5 The Lord Is a Chosen Portion

UNDERSTANDING GOD. EVAGRIUS OF PONTUS: The inheritance is the contemplation of the pres-

---

[3]ACW 51:167. [4]FC 101:113-14. [5]ACW 51:162. [6]FC 101:114. [7]See Rom 11:36. [8]FC 26:444-45 (Letter 79 in this edition). [9]WSA 3 9:191. [10]FC 57:18*. [11]FC 14:123. [12]FC 18:160.

ent and future ages; the inheritance of Christ is the understanding of God. NOTES ON THE PSALMS.[13]

OUR INHERITANCE IS THE LORD. AUGUSTINE: Let the others choose earthly and temporal portions to enjoy; the share of the saints is the Lord eternal. Let others drink deep of death-dealing pleasures; the Lord is the cup allotted to me. When I say "my," I include the church, because where the Head is, there the body is too. I will gather together their assemblies to be my inheritance, and as I drink deep of the cup I will forget their old names. "You are he who will restore to me my inheritance," that the glory I had with you before the existence or the world may be known to these also whom I set free. You will not restore to me what I never lost, but you will restore to those who have lost in the knowledge of that bright glory. Yet because I am among them, "you will restore it to me." EXPOSITIONS OF THE PSALMS 16.5.[14]

POSSESS THE LORD. JEROME: He who in his own person is the Lord's portion, or has the Lord for his portion, must so bear himself as to possess the Lord and to be possessed by him. He who possesses the Lord and who says with the prophet, "The Lord is my portion," can hold to nothing beside the Lord. For if he holds to something beside the Lord, the Lord will not be his portion. LETTER 52.5.[15]

GOD IS EVERYTHING TO YOU. LEANDER OF SEVILLE: See, my blessed sister, how much you have achieved; see to what a high peak you have attained, how you have found the grace of many benefits in one and the same Christ. He is, indeed, your true Bridegroom, he is also your brother, he is likewise your friend, he is your inheritance, he is your reward, he is God and the Lord. You have in him a Bridegroom to love: "For he is fair in beauty above the sons of men."[16] He is a true brother for you to hold, for by adoption you are the daughter of him whose natural

Son Christ is. He is a friend of whom you need not doubt. . . . You have in him the inheritance that you may embrace, for he is himself the portion of your inheritance. You have in him the reward that you may recognize, for his blood is your redemption. You have in him God by whom you may be ruled, the Lord to fear and honor. THE TRAINING OF NUNS, PROLOGUE.[17]

I LOVE YOU, LORD. AUGUSTINE: [The psalmist is saying] "O Lord, why give me some other inheritance? Whatever you give, it isn't worth much. You be my inheritance; I love you, I love you with all I am, with all my heart, with all my soul, with all my mind I love you. What can it mean to me, anything you give me apart from yourself?" That is to love God freely, to hope in God for God, to hasten to be filled with God, to be satisfied with him. He, after all, is enough for you; apart from him, nothing is enough for you. SERMON 334.3.[18]

16:6 A Goodly Heritage

THE MEASURE OF OUR CAPACITY. EVAGRIUS OF PONTUS: If the line is measured, how is it written the Gospel of John: "For God gives the Spirit without measure"[19] and "I will pour out my spirit on you."[20] Perhaps by chance it is called "measure" not in terms of knowledge itself but on account of him who receives it, because its receptivity cannot be greater. The rain itself also may exceed the measure, yet it is measured in that vessel in which it is received. NOTES ON THE PSALMS 15[16].6.[21]

THE COMPANY OF THE REDEEMED. CASSIODORUS: After the ancient fashion, an inheritance was meted out by lines on the earth, so that an individual could obtain an amount of land by measurement, in accordance with the amount bestowed and the person's status. So

---

[13]PG 12:1213. [14]WSA 3 15:183. [15]NPNF 2 6:91. [16]Ps 45:2 (44:3 LXX). [17]FC 62:185. [18]WSA 3 9:206. [19]Jn 3:34. [20]Joel 2:28. [21]PG 12:1213.

in the Old Testament Moses is said to have ordered Joshua to distribute the land inheritance to Israel's sons of promise by means of lines. So he now aptly used the word *lines*, because he was relating the breadth and glory of his inheritance. . . . The inheritance of Christ is the predestined multitude of saints. EXPLANATION OF THE PSALMS 16.6.[22]

16:7 In the Night

EVEN IN THE NIGHT. JEROME: What the Lord is saying . . . is this: My knowledge, deepest thought and the inmost desire of my heart was with me, not only in my heavenly mansions but also when I dwelled in the night of this world and in darkness; it remained in me as man, and it instructed me and never left me, so that whatever the weakness of the flesh was unable to achieve, divine thought and power accomplished. HOMILY ON PSALM 15[16].[23]

16:8 The Lord Always Before Me

THE PATH OF RIGHTEOUSNESS. CASSIODORUS: By explaining his action, he passes on to the unique remedy by which to avoid sins, for the person who with mental eye always gazes on the Lord in no way turns toward sins. So when truth dwells in the mind, it chastises the entry of falsehood. EXPLANATION OF THE PSALMS 16.8.[24]

OUR RESPONSIBILITY. JEROME: Consider here that it is always in our power to set the Lord before us. The one who resembles the Savior in his integrity places God at his right side and says, he is at my right hand to keep me steadfast. The just person places the Lord at his right hand because he keeps his eyes on him whom he follows, but the sinner casts the word of the Lord behind him. . . . For the Lord Savior, or through the Lord Savior for his saints, God is always standing at the right side. The just person has, in fact, no left side, and in whatever directions he turns, "the angel of the Lord encamps round

about those who fear him and delivers them."[25] HOMILY ON PSALM 15[16].[26]

THE RIGHT HAND. HESYCHIUS OF JERUSALEM: Do you see the equal worth of the Son with the Father? Sometimes the Son is said to stand or to sit on the right; now they grant the right to the Father, so that you may say that there is one power, that of the Father (the begetter) and that of the begotten (the Son), even if now he is humbled on account of the flesh. LARGE COMMENTARY ON PSALMS 16.7.[27]

16:9 Joy and Security

RESURRECTION OF THE FLESH. ORIGEN: "My flesh will rest in hope." The Lord Jesus Christ says these words, whose flesh is the first to rest in hope. Crucified, made the first fruit of the dead and having been taken into heaven after the resurrection, he carried the earthly body with him so that even the heavenly powers were awestruck and terrified seeing the flesh ascending into heaven. Concerning Elijah it was written that he was taken up into heaven; and about Enoch, that he was translated. Now, however, it is said that Jesus ascended into heaven. Let him be offended who so wishes at our word. I, however, guard it will all faith because just as Christ is the first fruit from the dead, so also he is the first to carry his flesh to heaven. SELECTIONS FROM THE PSALMS 16.9.[28]

HIS BODY HAD HOPE. JEROME: There are some who, from the fact that the Lord entered through closed doors, adduce proof that a different body arose from that which died. Let these heretics hear what the Lord recounts in this verse. . . . Most certainly, after the Savior suffered and died, that body was laid in the tomb that had been alive; that same body, therefore, that had been lying lifeless and dead in the tomb rose from the

---

[22]ACW 51:164. [23]FC 57:28. [24]ACW 51:165. [25]Ps 34:7 (33:8 LXX). [26]FC 57:29. [27]PG 93:1186. [28]PG 12:1215-16.

dead. If, moreover, that same body arose from the dead in the Lord, how do some come to the conclusion that, though it was wonderful and spiritual, it was not a human body? We are not saying that we deny the body of Christ assumed that glory that we believe we also are going to receive as saints, for then indeed, this corruptible body will put on incorruption, and this mortal body will put on immortality.[29] Just as before the Lord suffered his passion, when he was transformed and glorified on the mountain, he certainly had the same body that he had had down below, although of a different glory, so also after the resurrection, his body was of the same nature as it had been before the passion but of a higher state of glory and in more majestic appearance. HOMILY ON PSALM 15[16].[30]

AS MAN, NOT AS GOD. CYRIL OF ALEXANDRIA: Let us see [Jesus] . . . in his suffering as man but not suffering as God, and in his dying in the flesh but being greater than death, and in not remaining . . . in the tomb as we do and not being held fast by the gates of the underworld together with the other dead. . . . For he rose again, despoiling death and "saying to the prisoners: Come out, to those in darkness: Show yourselves,"[31] and he ascended to his Father above in the heavens to a position inaccessible to people, having taken on himself our sins and being the propitiation for them. LETTER 41.13.[32]

BECAUSE OF THE WORD. ATHANASIUS: We die not by our own choice but by necessity of nature and against our will. However, the Lord, being himself immortal yet having mortal flesh, had power, as God, to separate from his body and to take it back again, when he would. . . . For it was fitting that the flesh, corruptible as it was, should no longer after its own nature remain mortal, but because of the Word who had put it on, should abide incorruptible. For as he, having come in our body, was conformed to our condition, so we, receiving him, partake of the immor-

tality that is from him. DISCOURSES AGAINST THE ARIANS 3.28.57.[33]

CHRIST SAVED WHAT HE ASSUMED. GREGORY OF NYSSA: [Christ's] Godhead, alike before taking flesh and in the flesh and after his passion, is immutably the same, being at all times what it was by nature and so continuing forever. But in the suffering of his human nature the Godhead fulfilled the dispensation for our benefit by severing the soul for a season from the body, yet without being itself separated from either of those elements to which it was once for all united, and by joining again the elements that had been thus parted, so as to give to all human nature a beginning and an example that it should follow of the resurrection from the dead, that all the corruptible may put on incorruption, and all the mortal may put on immortality,[34] our firstfruits having been transformed to the divine nature by its union with God . . . the Lord, reconciling the world to himself by the humanity of Christ, apportioned his work of benevolence to people between his soul and his body, willing through his soul and touching them through his body. AGAINST EUNOMIUS 2.13.[35]

THE MEANING OF CORRUPTION. JOHN OF DAMASCUS: The word destruction (phthora) has two meanings. [First], it means human sufferings such as hunger, thirst, weariness, piercing with nails, death—that is separation of the soul from the body—and the like. In this sense, we say that the Lord's body was destructible, because he endured all these things freely. Destruction, however, also means the complete dissolution of the body and its reduction to the elements of which it was composed. By many this is more generally called corruption (diaphthora). This the Lord's body did not experience, as the prophet David says [in this psalm]. . . . Therefore, it is impious to say with the insane Julian and Gaianus that before the

---

[29]See 1 Cor 15:53. [30]FC 57:33-34. [31]Is 49:9. [32]FC 76:175-76*.
[33]NPNF 2 4:425**. [34]See 1 Cor 15:53. [35]NPNF 2 5:127.

resurrection the Lord's body was indestructible in the first sense. For, if it was thus incorruptible, then it was not consubstantial with us, and the things such as the hunger, the thirst, the nails, the piercing of the side and death that the gospel says happened did not really happen but only seemed to. But if they only seemed to happen, then the mystery of the incarnation is a hoax and a stage trick; it was in appearance and not in truth that he was made man and in appearance and not in truth that we have been saved. But far be it, and let those who say this have no part in salvation. We, however, have gained and shall obtain the true salvation. Moreover, in the second sense of the word *destruction,* we confess that the Lord's body was indestructible, that is to say, incorruptible, even as has been handed down to us by the inspired fathers. ORTHODOX FAITH 3.28.[36]

16:10 Not Given Up to Sheol

THE HOPE OF RESURRECTION. THEODORET OF CYR: So at this place, too, Christ the Lord in human fashion says, "Constantly supported by the divine nature, I am in the midst of my saving passion and find gladness in the hope of resurrection. My soul, you see, will not be abandoned in hades, nor will my flesh suffer natural corruption. I shall achieve a rapid resurrection and return to life, giving all people a glimpse of this path." COMMENTARY ON THE PSALMS 16.7.[37]

CHRIST'S HUMAN SOUL. CASSIODORUS: Where are the misguided Apollinarians who say that the Lord Christ had not a rational soul? See how he himself cries out and gives thanks to the Father because his soul is not in the usual way left abandoned in hell but is glorified by swift resurrection and has passed to the kingdom of heaven. EXPLANATION OF THE PSALMS 16.10.[38]

NOT DAVID. AUGUSTINE: Who save him who rose on the third day was in a position to say that his flesh rested in hope, that his soul, not left in hell, would swifty return to reanimate

his flesh, that his flesh would not undergo corruption as other corpses rot away? Surely, no one can maintain that all of this was verified in David, king and prophet! CITY OF GOD 17.18.[39]

HERESY REFUTED. THEODORET OF CYR: This psalm refutes the folly of Arius, of Eunomius and of Apollinaris: the former ones said God the Word assumed a body without a soul, whereas Apollinaris called the body that was assumed ensouled though denying it a rational soul; I do not know where he found his doctrine of these two souls—the divine Scripture nowhere teaches it. Yet the all-Holy Spirit through blessed David made undisguised mention of a soul, thus giving clear refutation of each heresy. COMMENTARY ON THE PSALMS 16.8.[40]

THE LITERAL WORDS OF PETER IN ACTS. DIODORE OF TARSUS: Blessed Peter in the Acts of the Apostles took these words as applied to the Lord. . . . He did not, however, take the words as though he were undermining their factual basis, but as more applicable to the Lord than to those of whom they were said, especially since it was also in the case of the Lord that the outcome of the events more appropriately brought out these words than in the case of those who live for a while but later are consigned to death—the Israelites themselves, I mean. Nothing therefore prevents either the factual basis being preserved or these words being understood of the Lord. COMMENTARY ON PSALMS 16.[41]

16:11 Fullness of Joy

JOY OVERFLOWING. CASSIODORUS: Filling to the brim is adding to fullness, and he who does so pours into a vessel already full. That joy fills in such a way that it is all preserved forever. The verse also shows that all just people in that blessed state will be filled with the joy of the Lord's pres-

---

[36]FC 37:333-34. [37]FC 101:117. [38]ACW 51:165. [39]FC 24:71. [40]FC 101:118. [41]WGRW 9:48.

ence, and he attests that he can be filled among them because he is the Lord. But let us examine a little more carefully why he says here that he will be filled with delights at the right hand of the Father, whereas earlier he said, "For he is at my right hand, that I be not moved." The fact is that in this world, in which he suffered scourgings in the flesh that he assumed, was struck with slaps and was spattered with spittle yet defeated by none of its hardships, it was fitting to say that the Lord was always seen at his right hand. He overcame the opposition of the world because he moved not an inch from contemplation of the Father. There he has now laid aside the hardships of this world, and his humanity is filled with the glorification of his whole majesty and rules united to the Word with the Father and the Holy Spirit forever. "Even to the end" signifies perfection and eternity, for his glory abides in its perfection and will be limited by no season. EXPLANATION OF THE PSALMS 16.11.[42]

HAVING BECOME IMMUNE TO SUFFERING.

THEODORET OF CYR: He will be in unceasing joy, having become immune to suffering, to change, to death, even in his human nature. As God, you see, this was always the case, and of course even in his human nature once formed in the womb it was easy to provide him with this. But he allowed the nature he had assumed to travel through the sufferings so as by these means to loose the sway of sin, put a stop to the tyranny of the devil, undo the power of death and provide all people with the basis of a new life. So as man he assumes both incorruption and immortality. COMMENTARY ON THE PSALMS 16.8.[43]

HE LEARNED THE WAY. JEROME: He who is the Way and the Life said that he had learned the ways to life; he had learned in what way people would follow him who said he is the Way and the Life. . . . The body he had received—and in his body, the entire human race—rejoiced that the divinity of the Son was made known to it. That is why he rejoices, he says, and has the fullness

of joy with the Father . . . and his delight is full and perfect and his happiness ineffable because he sits at the right hand of the Father. . . . This is his delight, this his happiness to the end of the divine decree . . . because the Lord suffered and rose from the dead and entered heaven as victor in order to establish humanity at the right hand of the Lord. HOMILY ON PSALM 15[16].[44]

FROM HIM TO US. MAXIMUS OF TURIN: This, indeed, is said of the person of the Savior in the resurrection—of him who, when after his death he returned from the depths to the heights, began to make known the path of life, which previously had been unknown. The path of life was unknown before Christ because until then it had never been trodden on by anyone who had risen from the dead. But when the Lord rose, that path, now known, was worn smooth by the feet of a multitude, about whom the holy Evangelist says, "The bodies of many of the saints rose with him and entered into the holy city."[45] And so, when the Lord says in his own resurrection, "You have made known to me the paths of life," we also are able to say to the Lord, "You have made known to us the paths of life." For he who has shown us the way to life has himself made known to us the paths of life. He made the paths of life known to me when he taught me faith, mercy, justice and chastity; by these roads one arrives at salvation. And although in the dissolution of our body the shadow of death encompasses us, nonetheless life does not desert its own steps, and by the power of Christ we walk swiftly through the midst of the very jaws of hell. This is why the holy prophet says, "And if I should walk in the midst of the shadow of death I shall fear no evil, for you are with me."[46] The Lord says this more clearly when he speaks of the believer: "But whoever believes in me shall not die, and although he die he shall live."[47] SERMON 14.1. [48]

---

[42]ACW 51:166-67. [43]FC 101:117-18. [44]FC 57:35-36. [45]Mt 27:52-53. [46]Ps 23:4. [47]Jn 11:25. [48]ACW 50:248*. The authenticity of this sermon is doubtful.

17:1-15 PRAYER FOR PROTECTION

When you are in difficulty as enemies circle around you
threatening your life, say Psalm 17.

ATHANASIUS ON THE INTERPRETATION OF THE PSALMS 17 [OIP 67]

A Prayer of David.

¹*Hear a just cause, O LORD; attend to my cry!*
    Give ear to my prayer from lips free of
        deceit!
²*From thee let my vindication come!*
    Let thy eyes see the right!

³*If thou triest my heart, if thou visitest me by*
        night,
    if thou testest me, thou wilt find no
        wickedness in me;
    my mouth does not transgress.
⁴*With regard to the works of men, by the word*
        of thy lips
    I have avoided the ways of the violent.
⁵*My steps have held fast to thy paths,*
    my feet have not slipped.

⁶*I call upon thee, for thou wilt answer me, O*
        God;
    incline thy ear to me, hear my words.
⁷*Wondrously show thy steadfast love,*
    O savior of those who seek refuge
    from their adversaries at thy right hand.

⁸*Keep me as the apple of the eye;*
    hide me in the shadow of thy wings,

⁹*from the wicked who despoil me,*
    my deadly enemies who surround me.

¹⁰*They close their hearts to pity;*
    with their mouths they speak arrogantly.
¹¹*They track me down; now they surround me;*
    they set their eyes to cast me to the ground.
¹²*They are like a lion eager to tear,*
    as a young lion lurking in ambush.

¹³*Arise, O LORD! confront them, overthrow*
        them!
    Deliver my life from the wicked by thy
        sword,
¹⁴*from men by thy hand, O LORD,*
    from men whose portion in life is of the
        world.
May their belly be filled with what thou hast
        stored up for them;
    may their children have more than enough;
    may they leave something over to their
        babes.

¹⁵*As for me, I shall behold thy face in*
        righteousness;
    when I awake, I shall be satisfied with
        beholding thy form.

OVERVIEW: The seventeenth psalm is a continuous prayer, instructive for us in its application to Christ (CASSIODORUS). It begins with a plea for careful consideration praying in the words of Scripture (EUSEBIUS). Appeal is made on the basis of having been tried and found true, both in David's case (THEODORET) and in Christ's case, although Christ is the only one who is wholly pure (EUSEBIUS). The psalmist expresses confidence that God already knows the situation and the desires of his heart (DIODORE). We need to be careful not to find fault with others

(BABAI). The avoidance of sin is difficult, but Christ has shown the way (CASSIODORUS). The hard life of discipleship is made easier by charity (AUGUSTINE). The Word of God is itself the path we follow (CASSIODORUS), by God's help (JOHN CASSIAN), and we are confident of future reward (EVAGRIUS). Even so, in our case, it is by grace that God hears us (CASSIODORUS).

Understanding that he is the savior of those who seek refuge in him, we must remain faithful (AMBROSE), trusting in God, not ourselves (PSEUDO-ATHANASIUS). As such, we enjoy a ring of protection just like the apple of the eye (THEODORET). We are overshadowed by the wings of mercy and love (CASSIODORUS), an apt metaphor for God's help (CHRYSOSTOM). This is the source of courage in our daily walk (LEO), as we beware the devil and the bait of impure thoughts (HESYCHIUS, EVAGRIUS). Against him, we brandish the sword of the Word of God (EUSEBIUS) and of a righteous soul (PSEUDO-ATHANASIUS). The unrighteous will be punished according to the plan and wisdom of God (DIODORE), for they leave the wrong kind of inheritance for their children (HESYCHIUS). But we will be satisfied with God (AUGUSTINE), fully satisfied (BEDE). Anticipation of this satisfaction leads us to wonder what God must truly be like (AUGUSTINE).

17:1 Hear My Prayer

A CONTINUOUS PRAYER. CASSIODORUS: Whereas other psalms contain brief prayers for help mingled with various topics, this is a supplication through virtually the whole of its composition. Hence it is rightly designated as such beforehand, since its purpose is wholly directed toward zeal for prayer. EXPLANATION OF THE PSALMS 17.1.[1]

PRAYER IN THE WORDS OF SCRIPTURE. EUSEBIUS OF CAESAREA: We speak fully and clearly when we use words taken from divine Scripture. . . . The righteous person alone cleanses his tongue, lips and the voice itself from using more

common words, as one acquainted with that verse: "You will give an account of every careless word on the day of judgment."[2] The ears of God do not hear words offered from lying lips, but they receive any word offered from a cleansed tongue accustomed to meditating on divine words. COMMENTARY ON PSALMS 17.1.[3]

17:3 God Tries the Heart

DAVID TRIED AND TRUE. THEODORET OF CYR: Although many times [David had] Saul in his grasp, he refrained from doing away with him and instead rendered good for evil; hence he recalled even the night in which he did this, when by night he saved the sleeping Saul from death and allowed no one to deal him a lethal blow. Now, in a figurative manner he calls his disasters "nights" on account of the gloom of discouragement, as likewise he refers to the test as burning: "you examined me by fire," he says, "and no wrong was found in me." In other words, just as you would test gold of some sort, you found me unadulterated, O Lord; so far be it from me to harm the enemy that I even kept my tongue free of abuse against him, and what he continues to do I refrained from mentioning. COMMENTARY ON THE PSALMS 17.2.[4]

CHRIST ALONE PURE. EUSEBIUS OF CAESAREA: Who can with confidence say, "I am pure from sins"? Christ alone is truly and properly able to say these words. . . . When gold is tested by fire, it remains pure and shining. According to Isaiah, out of all people since the beginning of the age, Christ alone "did not sin, nor was there any deceit found in his mouth."[5] COMMENTARY ON PSALMS 17.3.[6]

GOD ALREADY KNOWS. DIODORE OF TARSUS: Even before I make the request, my predicament does not escape you, nor are you ignorant of

---

[1]ACW 51:167. [2]Mt 12:36. [3]PG 23:159. [4]FC 101:119-20. [5]Is 53:9. [6]PG 23:161.

all the designs in my heart that I experience in the night and ponder by day. COMMENTARY ON PSALMS 17.[7]

DO NOT FIND FAULT. BABAI: Excuse yourself from unprofitable and empty conversation, and be wary in your heart of complaining against others, for they are your brothers, and maybe the complaint will rebound on yourself. Do not find fault with anyone in your mind, and do not make your tongue impure by accusing your neighbor. For the words "the deeds of people have not passed my mouth in the utterance of the lips" are trustworthy. LETTER TO CYRIACUS 55.[8]

17:4 Avoiding the Ways of the Violent

THE WAY CHRIST TROD. CASSIODORUS: The path of avoidance of sins is hard, and the ascent is always difficult, whereas when we slip toward vices, it is an easy downhill path. But the Lord Christ, set before people's eyes in this world, demonstrated the canons of total meekness and self-discipline, so he rightly says that by reason of the Lord's commands he has walked with spotless feet on the hard ways of people. EXPLANATION OF THE PSALMS 17.4.[9]

MADE EASIER BY CHARITY. AUGUSTINE: What the Lord has commanded seems hard and harsh, that any who wish to follow him should deny themselves. But nothing can be hard and harsh that is commanded by one who helps us to do what he commands. You see, both these things are true, both what is said to him in the psalm: "Because of the words of your lips I have kept to hard ways";[10] and what he himself said, "My yoke is easy, and my burden is light."[11] The fact is, whatever is hard in the commandments is made easy by charity. SERMON 96.1.[12]

17:5 Hold Fast to God's Paths

THE PATHS OF GOD'S WORD. CASSIODORUS: "In the paths," that is, "in your commandments";

these are the truly right ways, and if we follow them as dedicated people we attain the rewards of our heavenly land. EXPLANATION OF THE PSALMS 17.5.[13]

BY GOD'S HELP. JOHN CASSIAN: Never by our sole diligence or zeal or by our most tireless efforts can we reach perfection. Human zeal is not enough to win the sublime rewards of blessedness. The Lord must be there to help us and to guide our hearts toward what is good. Every moment we must join in the prayer of David: "Direct my footsteps along your paths so that my feet do not move astray" and "He has settled my feet on a rock and guided my footsteps"[14]— all this so that the invisible guide of the human spirit may direct back toward love of virtue our free will, which in its ignorance of the good and its obsession with passion is carried headlong into sin. CONFERENCES 3.12.[15]

FUTURE REWARD. EVAGRIUS OF PONTUS: Even if now [the way] is full of pain and without joy, later it will bear the fruit of righteousness for those who have been trained in it. NOTES ON THE PSALMS 16[17].3,4.[16]

17:6 God Will Answer

THE GRACE OF BEING HEARD. CASSIODORUS: Human weakness cannot approach the Father by its own power. The Father hears when he mercifully shows his indulgence and bestows his clemency beforehand so as to receive the prayers of suppliants. EXPLANATION OF THE PSALMS 17.6.[17]

17:7 Savior of Those Who Seek Refuge

REMAIN FAITHFUL. AMBROSE: It becomes Christians to pray for peace and quiet but not to abandon steadfast faith and truth even at the

---

[7]WGRW 9:49. [8]CS 101:155. [9]ACW 51:170*. [10]LXX. [11]Mt 11:30. [12]WSA 3 4:29. [13]ACW 51:170. [14]Ps 40:2 (39:3 LXX). [15]JCC 93. [16]PG 12:1217. [17]ACW 51:171.

peril of death. For the Lord is our Leader, "who will save them that put their hope in him." LETTER 20.14.[18]

TRUST WHOLLY IN GOD. PSEUDO-ATHANASIUS: He teaches us that even if we are virtuous, we should trust not in ourselves but in God, and that we should pray to him that like the pupil of the eye he protect the mind—our soul's eye—from evil of the opposing powers. EXPOSITION ON PSALMS 17.[19]

17:8 Preserve Me

THE PROTECTION OF THE EYE. THEODORET OF CYR: His prayer is to enjoy such protection as does the apple of the eye, which has eyelids as a kind of rampart and eyelashes for a palisade; it also has eyebrows as mounds, conducting the stream of sweat to the temples and warding off from the faculty of sight any harm from that source. COMMENTARY ON THE PSALMS 17.3.[20]

THE WINGS OF MERCY AND LOVE. CASSIODORUS: The Father's protection is compared with wings. Mercy and love are, as it were, the Father's wings by which he asks to be protected. The comparison derives from birds, which guard their dear brood by spreading out their wings. EXPLANATION OF THE PSALMS 17.8.[21]

A METAPHOR FOR HELP. CHRYSOSTOM: The written words say that God has wings. . . . But we will not on that account say that God's spiritual and indestructible essence is winged. . . . What, then, are we to understand by the wings? The help, security, shelter, defense and unconquerable aid that God gives us. AGAINST THE ANOMOEANS 8.4[22]

THE SOURCE OF COURAGE. LEO THE GREAT: This should be the careful consideration of wise people, that since the days of this life are short and the time uncertain, death should never be unexpected for those who are to die. Those who

know that they are mortal should not come to an unprepared end. Therefore this, which has been proclaimed by the voice of the prophet, should be taken up in the hearts of those praying, so that it may be said, not with the lips only but also with the heart. . . . For we are always in need of divine help. This is the unconquerable courage of human devotion, that we always have a protector without whom we are not able to be brave. SERMON 90.4.1.[23]

17:12 Like a Lion

THE BAIT OF IMPURE THOUGHTS. HESYCHIUS OF JERUSALEM: The demons surround our mind and try to entangle it like a wild beast, . . . and the richest baits are sinners who themselves have been allured by desires. LARGE COMMENTARY ON PSALMS 17.9.[24]

THE DANGER OF IMPURE THOUGHTS. EVAGRIUS OF PONTUS: Through impure thoughts our adversary like a lion overcomes our mind. NOTES ON THE PSALMS 16[17].12.[25]

17:13 By the Sword

THE SWORD OF GOD'S WORD. EUSEBIUS OF CAESAREA: That sword will be the "word of God living and more active than any double edged sword,"[26] here in the place of a straight sword, which is entrusted to my spirit for driving out the enemies. COMMENTARY ON PSALMS 17.13, 14.[27]

THE SWORD OF A RIGHTEOUS SOUL. PSEUDO-ATHANASIUS: The soul of each of the righteous—clearly of those who pull sinners from impiety to piety—is as a sharpened sword against the spirits of evil. This sword, O our Lord, which you sharpened against your en-

---

[18]LCC 5:212. [19]CSCO 387:11. [20]FC 101:120. [21]ACW 51:172. [22]FC 72:214. [23]FC 93:382. [24]PG 93:1185. [25]PG 12:1221. [26]Heb 4:12. [27]PG 23:164.

emies, save from the enemies of your hand. EXPOSITION ON PSALMS 17.[28]

17:14 *What Is Stored Up*

THE PUNISHMENTS GOD KNOWS BEST. DIODORE OF TARSUS: Since I do not know how to ask for manifest punishment of them, whereas you are aware, having as you do hidden treasuries of wisdom, inflict on them the punishments you best know. COMMENTARY ON PSALMS 17.[29]

THE WRONG INHERITANCE. HESYCHIUS OF JERUSALEM: Here the psalmist is not criticizing the children's food, as some would think (for those things that enter the mouth do not make a person unclean[30]), but he regards those to whom God has given many offspring unwise when they leave behind them not excellence but their evils as an inheritance. LARGE COMMENTARY ON PSALMS 17.14.[31]

17:15 *Satisfied with Beholding God*

WE WILL BE SATISFIED. AUGUSTINE: Why talk about those treasures of wisdom and knowledge, about those divine riches, if not because they are what suffices us? And why talk about that multitudinous sweetness, if not because it is what satisfies us? . . . In one of the psalms somebody, one of us, or in us, or for us says to him, "I will be satisfied when your glory is revealed." . . . He will convert us and show us his face, and "we shall be saved";[32] we shall be satisfied, and it will suffice us. SERMON 194.3.[33]

SATISFACTION WHEN CHRIST APPEARS. AUGUSTINE: When shall we be satisfied? . . . "When your glory is revealed." Now though, the glory of our God, the glory of our Christ, is concealed; and with it is concealed ours also. But "when Christ appears, your life, then you too will ap-

pear with him in glory."[34] SERMON 255.5.[35]

FULLY SATISFIED. BEDE: In the [present] life we need the light of the sacred Scriptures and the refreshment of the heavenly sacraments, but in the future we shall have no need of such aids. According to the word of the psalmist, whoever appears there will be fully satisfied with justice when the glory of the Lord is made manifest. HOMILIES ON THE GOSPELS 2.25.[36]

WHAT GOD MUST BE LIKE. AUGUSTINE: What this future glory will be like, however, how richly it will flourish, with what splendor it will blaze out, while we can sing its praises, we cannot possibly explain. Why not? Because we read, "Eye has not seen, nor ear heard, nor has it come up into the human heart, what things God has prepared for those who love him."[37] So if that is what has to be said about the eternal good things of heaven, . . . what must God himself be, who has prepared such great and wonderful things? What, I repeat, must almighty God be like? What but unfathomable, inexpressible, incomprehensible, surpassing all things, beyond all things, apart from all things? He excels, after all, every one of his creatures; he goes far beyond everything he has made; he surpasses the whole universe. I mean, if you are looking for greatness, he is greater; if for beauty, he is more beautiful still; if for delightfulness, he is still more delightful; if for splendor, he is more brilliant; if for justice, he is more just; if for strength, he is stronger; if for fatherly care, he is kinder. Reason, after all, in no way allows us to equate the thing made with its maker or the work with its craftsman. SERMON 384.1.[38]

---

[28]CSCO 387:11. [29]WGRW 9:51. [30]Cf. Mt 15:17-18. [31]PG 93:1188. [32]Ps 80:3. [33]*WSA* 3 6:54. [34]Col 3:4. [35]*WSA* 3 7:161. [36]CS 111:265. [37]1 Cor 2:9. [38]*WSA* 3 10:383*.

18:1-50 THANKSGIVING

When you have been saved from your enemies
and delivered from your pursuers, sing Psalm 18.

ATHANASIUS *On the Interpretation of the Psalms* 17 [OIP 67]

To the choirmaster. A Psalm of David the servant of the LORD, who addressed the words of this song to the LORD on the day when the LORD delivered him from the hand of all his enemies, and from the hand of Saul. He said:

¹*I love thee, O LORD, my strength.*
²*The LORD is my rock, and my fortress, and my deliverer,*
 my God, my rock, in whom I take refuge,
 my shield, and the horn of my salvation, my stronghold.
³*I call upon the LORD, who is worthy to be praised,*
 and I am saved from my enemies.

⁴*The cords of death encompassed me,*
 the torrents of perdition assailed me;
⁵*the cords of Sheol entangled me,*
 the snares of death confronted me.

⁶*In my distress I called upon the LORD;*
 to my God I cried for help.
From his temple he heard my voice,
 and my cry to him reached his ears.

⁷*Then the earth reeled and rocked;*
 the foundations also of the mountains trembled
 and quaked, because he was angry.
⁸*Smoke went up from his nostrils,*
 and devouring fire from his mouth;

glowing coals flamed forth from him.
⁹*He bowed the heavens, and came down;*
 thick darkness was under his feet.
¹⁰*He rode on a cherub, and flew;*
 he came swiftly upon the wings of the wind.
¹¹*He made darkness his covering around him,*
 his canopy thick clouds dark with water.
¹²*Out of the brightness before him*
 there broke through his clouds
 hailstones and coals of fire.
¹³*The LORD also thundered in the heavens,*
 and the Most High uttered his voice,
 hailstones and coals of fire.
¹⁴*And he sent out his arrows, and scattered them;*
 he flashed forth lightnings, and routed them.
¹⁵*Then the channels of the sea were seen,*
 and the foundations of the world were laid bare,
at thy rebuke, O LORD,
 at the blast of the breath of thy nostrils.

¹⁶*He reached from on high, he took me,*
 he drew me out of many waters.
¹⁷*He delivered me from my strong enemy,*
 and from those who hated me;
 for they were too mighty for me.
¹⁸*They came upon me in the day of my calamity;*

but the LORD was my stay.
^{19}He brought me forth into a broad place;
  he delivered me, because he delighted
    in me.

^{20}The LORD rewarded me according to my
  righteousness;
  according to the cleanness of my hands he
    recompensed me.
^{21}For I have kept the ways of the LORD,
  and have not wickedly departed from my
    God.
^{22}For all his ordinances were before me,
  and his statutes I did not put away from me.
^{23}I was blameless before him,
  and I kept myself from guilt.
^{24}Therefore the LORD has recompensed me
  according to my righteousness,
  according to the cleanness of my hands in
    his sight.

^{25}With the loyal thou dost show thyself loyal;*
  with the blameless man thou dost show
    thyself blameless;
^{26}with the pure thou dost show thyself pure;
  and with the crooked thou dost show thyself
    perverse.
^{27}For thou dost deliver a humble people;
  but the haughty eyes thou dost bring down.
^{28}Yea, thou dost light my lamp;
  the LORD my God lightens my darkness.
^{29}Yea, by thee I can crush a troop;
  and by my God I can leap over a wall.
^{30}This God—his way is perfect;
  the promise of the LORD proves true;
  he is a shield for all those who take refuge
    in him.

^{31}For who is God, but the LORD?
  And who is a rock, except our God?—
^{32}the God who girded me with strength,
  and made my way safe.
^{33}He made my feet like hinds' feet,
  and set me secure on the heights.
^{34}He trains my hands for war,

so that my arms can bend a bow of
  bronze.
^{35}Thou hast given me the shield of thy
  salvation,
  and thy right hand supported me,
  and thy help^i made me great.
^{36}Thou didst give a wide place for my steps
  under me,
  and my feet did not slip.
^{37}I pursued my enemies and overtook them;
  and did not turn back till they were
    consumed.
^{38}I thrust them through, so that they were
  not able to rise;
  they fell under my feet.
^{39}For thou didst gird me with strength for the
  battle;
  thou didst make my assailants sink under
    me.
^{40}Thou didst make my enemies turn their
  backs to me,
  and those who hated me I destroyed.
^{41}They cried for help, but there was none to
  save,
  they cried to the LORD, but he did not
    answer them.
^{42}I beat them fine as dust before the wind;
  I cast them out like the mire of the streets.

^{43}Thou didst deliver me from strife with the
  peoples;^{j}
  thou didst make me the head of the
    nations;
  people whom I had not known served me.
^{44}As soon as they heard of me they obeyed
  me;
  foreigners came cringing to me.
^{45}Foreigners lost heart,
  and came trembling out of their fastnesses.

^{46}The LORD lives; and blessed be my rock,
  and exalted be the God of my salvation,
^{47}the God who gave me vengeance
  and subdued peoples under me;
^{48}who delivered me from my enemies;

*yea, thou didst exalt me above my
        adversaries;
thou didst deliver me from men of violence.*

⁴⁹*For this I will extol thee, O* LORD, *among*

        *the nations,
        and sing praises to thy name.*
⁵⁰*Great triumphs he gives to his king,
        and shows steadfast love to his anointed,
        to David and his descendants for ever.*

i Or *gentleness* j Gk Tg: Heb *people* * LXX *With the holy you will be holy*

OVERVIEW: The eighteenth psalm is a hymn of victory (EUSEBIUS), a remembrance of God's kindness composed by David toward the end of his life (DIODORE).

The psalm begins with a profession of love for God, a recognition that he is everything to me (DIODORE). Christ reminds us that the one who loves the Lord is the one who hears and does his words (ARNOBIUS THE YOUNGER). This is the one who trusts not in himself but trusts God fully (AUGUSTINE). David overcame his enemies by the help of God (EUSEBIUS), and we are reminded that our horn of salvation is none other than the cross of Christ (JEROME). Praise is powerful (NICETAS) and contributes to future faith (ARNOBIUS THE YOUNGER). But we must remember to praise God, not ourselves (AUGUSTINE). Faith is the guiding compass in the storms of life (EUSEBIUS), and the prayer of faith is heard by God (ARNOBIUS THE YOUNGER). In the rest of the psalm, David recounts how God has met his every need (DIODORE).

The words of the psalm remind us of how Christ has shaken the systems of the world (EUSEBIUS), shaking and confusion being effects of his anger (DIODORE). The darkness of smoke indicates the mystery of his dispensation (PSEUDO-ATHANASIUS). In his compassionate kindness (JEROME), he descended to us for our salvation (PSEUDO-GREGORY THAUMATURGOS). His flight in the heavens indicates his ascension (EUSEBIUS) and the fact that he is unknowable, being above our knowledge, except by love (AUGUSTINE). His covering of darkness indicates that the infinite things of God are unknown, yet the Father has revealed himself in Christ (ORIGEN). The covering of darkness indicates his

incarnation (AUGUSTINE), the reasons for which remain obscure (ORIGEN, JEROME), so that we are unable to fully contemplate him (JEROME).

The clouds and hailstones refer to the preaching of the Word (AUGUSTINE), sent forth after his ascension and by which he drives away demonic delusion (EUSEBIUS). He sent out his Evangelists (AUGUSTINE) and the lightning of understanding (EVAGRIUS). He laid bare the secrets of the earth, showing that there is only One who must be feared (DIODORE). He delivers us solely by his grace (EUSEBIUS), rendering us blameless in Christ (ARNOBIUS THE YOUNGER). He is known as holy, because he makes us holy (AUGUSTINE) and is holy with the holy (ARNOBIUS THE YOUNGER). Therefore, let us be holy, especially bishops in the handling of the Word (APOSTOLIC CONSTITUTIONS). To the crooked, he will show perversity for the sake of their correction (CLEMENT OF ALEXANDRIA).

Human nature is such that true enlightenment must come from God (AUGUSTINE). That enlightenment came when the true Light entered the lamp of David (EUSEBIUS). It is the oil of his grace that feeds his light in us (ARNOBIUS THE YOUNGER), and we must be careful not to quench the light (THEODORE OF ALEXANDRIA). By God's strength, I overcome the walls of enemies and the wall of heaven (EUSEBIUS), the wall of sin (AUGUSTINE), the wall of human will (POEMEN). He is the supreme Protector (EUSEBIUS), the One who strengthens and disciplines me (EUSEBIUS) and directs me heavenward (AUGUSTINE), which is our peculiar domain (EUSEBIUS). He disciplines me (EVAGRIUS) with divine reproof (AUGUSTINE), enabling me to walk correctly (EUSEBIUS). I can pursue my enemies (ARNOBIUS

THE YOUNGER) because he pursued me (JE-ROME) by grace (EUSEBIUS)—a promise for one to believe with humility (EVAGRIUS). He girds our desires so that we are not hindered BY them (AUGUSTINE), and our assailants find themselves assailed in return (EVAGRIUS). We gain the sight of victory (ARNOBIUS THE YOUNGER).

David is now honored by the Gentiles (EUSEBIUS), a people formerly ignorant of God (TERTULLIAN) from whom many have become God's people by faith (IRENAEUS) through the hearing of the preached word (AUGUSTINE), subdued by the use of Christ's weapon, the cross (ARNOBIUS THE YOUNGER). David's praise leads to the honor of his greater Son (EUSEBIUS), and while blessing passed to many of David's off-spring, only One retains it forever (DIODORE).

18:1 I Love You, Lord

A HYMN OF VICTORY. EUSEBIUS OF CAESAREA: David has consecrated this hymn of triumph on the occasion of his victory over his enemies and opponents to the Author of all victories. David is called a victor, that is, "he is made a victor," because he achieved victories. . . . The psalm is inscribed "for the end" chiefly because it is pro-claimed in the last years of his life and after all his deeds that were accomplished in history; or because it announces the prophecy of things that are going to happen in the future age; or, third, because the reader is told about those things that happened in the last part of this hymn, at the end of which is the call of the Gentiles and a prophecy about Christ. COMMENTARY ON PSALMS 18.1.[1]

A REMEMBRANCE OF GOD'S KINDNESS. DIO-DORE OF TARSUS: This psalm has a title con-sistent with the theme, as can be found also in [2 Samuel]. Blessed David uttered it in thanks-giving, in fact, toward the end of his life when reminding himself of all the favors he had been granted by God throughout his life. It is typical of pious people, you see, to keep constantly in mind God's kindnesses done to them, and espe-cially at the time of death it seems right to them to number them, both out of gratitude and also to teach those coming later how great is God's providence and lovingkindness toward those hoping in him. COMMENTARY ON PSALMS 18.[2]

THE LORD IS EVERYTHING TO ME. DIODORE OF TARSUS: The phrase "I shall love" does not mean I shall love you from this point on since you always provided me with many things; rather, the tense has been changed, and the meaning is, my love and affection for you, my master, were always right and proper. I felt benevolence and longing for God, in fact, for he proved to be everything to me in time of need—strength in war, steadfastness in endurance, ref-uge in misfortune, rescuer from all the schemers. So while even the opening of the psalm sufficed as a perfect hymn of praise, anyone with love for God repeatedly adopts the same sentiments as an intense form of thanksgiving when occupied in recalling God's graces. In a range of texts, in fact, he seems to recite and go over the same sentiments in the process of recalling every event from childhood to old age in which God pro-vided him with help and support. COMMENTARY ON PSALMS 18.[3]

THE ONE WHO LOVES THE LORD. ARNOBIUS THE YOUNGER: Let us ask the Lord and say, "Who is he who loves you?" He will respond to us through his Gospel and say, "He who hears my words and does them, this is the one who loves me."[4] COMMENTARY ON PSALMS 18.[5]

THE ONE WHO TRUSTS GOD FULLY. AUGUS-TINE: Take care not to let trust in your own strength steal on you, for you are human, and "cursed be everyone who puts his hope in man."[6] But put your trust fully and with your whole heart in God, and he will be your strength;

---

[1]PG 23:168. [2]WGRW 9:51-52. [3]WGRW 9:52. [4]Jn 14:21. [5]CCL 25:20-21. [6]Cf. Jer 17:5.

trust him lovingly and gratefully and say to him humbly and faithfully, "I will love you, O Lord, my strength," because that very charity of God, when it is perfected in us, "casts out fear."[7] LETTER 218.[8]

18:2 The Lord Is My Rock

BY THE HELP OF GOD. EUSEBIUS OF CAESAREA: Christ is the rock. When David built his own house on the rock, he was like the wise man.[9] . . . In such a way, he is made superior to all his enemies. He becomes faithful, not by hope or by training but by the help of God, established in all types of defenses and in the horn of salvation. COMMENTARY ON PSALMS 18.2, 3.[10]

THE HORN OF THE CROSS. JEROME: Unless one has a horn with which to rout his enemies, he is not worthy to be offered to God. That is why the Lord is described as a horn to those who believe in him; and it was with the horns of the cross that he routed his enemies. On the cross he confounded the devil and his entire army. To be sure, Christ was crucified in his body, but on the cross, it was he who was crucifying there the devils. It was not a cross; it was a symbol of triumph, a banner of victory. His whole purpose in mounting the cross was to lift us up from earth. I think the cross of the Savior was the ladder that Jacob saw. On that ladder, angels were descending and ascending; on that ladder, that is, the cross, the Jews were descending and the Gentiles ascending. . . . Others may have many horns; I have only one. "But as for me, God forbid that I shall glory save in the cross of the Lord, through whom the world is crucified to me, and I to the world."[11] HOMILY ON PSALM 91[92].[12]

18:3 Worthy to Be Praised

THE POWER OF PRAISE. NICETAS OF REMESIANA: Praise issuing from a pure conscience delights the Lord, and so the same psalmist exhorts us, "Praise ye the Lord because a psalm is good;

to our God be joyful and comely praise."[13] With this in mind, aware of how pleasing to God is this ministry, the psalmist again declares, "Seven times a day I have given praise to you."[14] To this he adds a further promise: "And my tongue shall meditate your justice, your praise all the day long."[15] Without doubt, he had experience of the good to be derived from this work, for he reminds us [in the psalm before us]: "Praising I will call on the Lord, and I shall be saved from my enemies." It was with such a shield of praise to protect him that as a boy [David] destroyed the great power of the giant Goliath, and, in many other instances, came out victorious over the invaders. LITURGICAL SINGING 8.[16]

PRESENT PRAISE, FUTURE FAITH. ARNOBIUS THE YOUNGER: He is my refuge, he is my liberator; as I praise and call on him I will be safe from my enemies. Let me say this in the present so that I may not doubt it in the future. COMMENTARY ON THE PSALMS 18.[17]

PRAISE GOD, NOT YOURSELF. AUGUSTINE: There you have something you can do. Praising, call—but remember it is the Lord you praise and call on. Because if you praise yourself, you will not be saved from your enemies. Praising, call on the Lord, and you will be saved from your enemies. SERMON 67.6.[18]

18:6 Calling on the Lord

FAITH, THE GUIDING COMPASS. EUSEBIUS OF CAESAREA: Stirred by the onrush of injustices and surrounded by the rest of the evils which are recounted above, when he realizes that he is beset by danger, he flees to the gate of his deliverance. He says, therefore, "In my distress I called on the Lord, and to my God I cried." Thereby he teaches that one wanders least from the path

---

[7]1 Jn 4:18. [8]FC 32:97-98*. [9]See Mt 7:24-27. [10]PG 23:168. [11]Gal 6:14. [12]FC 48:170-71. [13]Ps 147:1 (146:1 LXX). [14]Ps 119:164 (118:164 LXX). [15]Ps 35:28 (34:28 LXX). [16]FC 7:71. [17]CCL 25:21. [18]WSA 3 3:218*.

when he is full of such faith, for "hope does not disappoint."[19] COMMENTARY ON PSALMS 18.5-7.[20]

THE PRAYER OF FAITH IS HEARD. ARNOBIUS THE YOUNGER: While the groans of death, the injustices, griefs, and snares, surround me, I called out to him in faith. He heard my voice from his holy temple, and my cry reached his ears. COMMENTARY ON THE PSALMS 18.[21]

GOD MET EVERY NEED. DIODORE OF TARSUS: Having made his introduction to this point, from now on he recounts more descriptively how many dangers he encountered and how God against the odds rendered him always superior to the schemers. He also recounts the dangers in a very figurative manner, as also the help of God, the greater the difficulties, the greater the lovingkindness rescuing him from such awful dangers. COMMENTARY ON PSALMS 18.[22]

18:7 The Earth Reeled

CHRIST HAS SHAKEN THE WORLD SYSTEMS. EUSEBIUS OF CAESAREA: When the Son of God journeyed on the earth in the time of his incarnation, whoever worshiped the natural elements of this earth were shaken and trembled, and everywhere his reputation became familiar to the ears of Greeks and barbarians; and truly those things he called the foundations of the mountains have trembled and quaked. . . . The mountains were all the lofty thoughts that were directed against the knowledge of God, namely, certain adversarial powers that through the long span of the ages had led all who dwelled on the earth into error and the worship of multiple gods. "The foundations of the mountains," that is, loftier plans and thoughts, when they had realized the strength of the Lord, "were disturbed and shaken because he is angry with them." COMMENTARY ON PSALMS 18.8.[23]

EFFECTS OF GOD'S ANGER. DIODORE OF TARSUS: The effect of God's hearkening and being

moved to wrath was that everything together was reduced to alarm and confusion, their common master being enraged. COMMENTARY ON PSALMS 18.[24]

18:8 Smoke Went Up

A MYSTERIOUS DISPENSATION. PSEUDO-ATHANASIUS: In this and the following verses, he posits as a sign the smoke, which in his descent from heaven he made as darkness under his feet; it indicates the incomprehensibility of his dispensation. And in his ascension, he flew on the wings of the Spirit, as on cherubim, that is, the cloud that received him. And because in his church, which is his tabernacle, he mysteriously dwells and operates, he says, "He set darkness as his hiding place." Again, because the remarks about him are made obscurely in the holy prophets, he writes, "Dark waters in the clouds of the airs," which he showed to be clear and obvious when he openly came to earth. EXPOSITION ON PSALMS 18.[25]

18:9 God Bowed the Heavens

IN HIS COMPASSIONATE KINDNESS. JEROME: Because we are little and lowly and unable to lift ourselves up to him, the Lord stoops down to us and in his compassionate kindness deigns to hear us. In fact, because we are people and cannot become gods, God became man and inclined himself, as it is written: "He inclined the heavens and came down." HOMILY ON PSALM 114(116A).[26]

FOR OUR SALVATION. PSEUDO-GREGORY THAUMATURGUS: With the purpose of saving the race of people and fulfilling the covenant that was made with our ancestors, Christ has once "bowed the heavens and come down." And thus he shows himself to us as we are capable of receiving him, in order that we might have

---

[19]Rom 5:5. [20]PG 23:168-69. [21]CCL 25:21. [22]WGRW 9:52. [23]PG 23:169. [24]WGRW 9:53. [25]CSCO 387:12. [26]FC 48:286.

power to see him, and handle him and hear him when he speaks. And on this account did God the Word consider it proper to take to himself the flesh and the perfect humanity by a woman, the holy Virgin; and he was born a man, in order that he might discharge our debt and fulfill even in himself the ordinances of the covenant made with Abraham, in its rite of circumcision and all the other legal appointments connected with it. Homily 2.[27]

18:10 God Flew

The Descending and Ascending Christ. Eusebius of Caesarea: Secretly and with mysterious reckoning he represents his incarnation through [images of] darkness and thick clouds. At last he returns to the same place from whence he had set forth: and he ascends into the heavens with the cherubim and flies, although he had not descended with those cherubim, without the cherubim he himself bowed the heavens and descended. On his return it is said, "And he mounted on cherubs, and he flew," with the body he had assumed. Commentary on Psalms 18.11-13.[28]

Unknowable Except by Love. Augustine: He was raised above the full range of knowledge, so that no one should come to him by any means other than love, for the fulfillment of the law is love. And without delay he showed those who love him that he is ultimately unknowable, to prevent them from thinking that he is to be understood by the sort of thoughts we have in our bodily state. Expositions of the Psalms 18.11.[29]

18:11 Darkness Is God's Covering

Revealed in Christ. Origen: It is said of God in the eighteenth psalm that "God made darkness his hiding place." This is a Hebrew way of showing that the ideas of God that people understand in accordance with their

merits are obscure and unknowable, since God hides himself as if in darkness from those who cannot bear the radiance of the knowledge of him and who cannot see him, partly because of the defilement of the mind that is bound to a human "body of humiliation,"[30] partly because of its restricted capacity to comprehend God. . . . Moreover, our Savior and Lord, the Logos of God, shows the depth of the knowledge of the Father, and that, although a derived knowledge is possessed by those whose minds are illuminated by the divine Logos himself, absolute understanding and knowledge of the Father is possessed by himself alone in accordance with his merits, when he says, "No one has known the Son save the Father, and no one has known the Father save the Son, and him to whom the Son will reveal him."[31] Neither can anyone worthily know the uncreated and firstborn of all created nature[32] in the way that the Father who begat him knows him; nor can anyone know the Father in the same way as the living Logos who is God's wisdom and truth. By participation in him who took away from the Father what is called darkness, which he made "his hiding place," and what is called his covering, "the great deep," thus revealing the Father, anyone whatever who has the capacity to know him may do so. Against Celsus 6.17.[33]

The Covering of Flesh. Augustine: When God wished to appear visibly to people and desired also to teach them in person what he had first laid down in the law, he tempered the force, the power of the divine, by taking on the human and "made the darkness his cover round about him," when he concealed himself in the tent of the flesh. Sermon 371.2.[34]

Reasons Obscure. Origen: The reasons of the divine dispensation and providence are most obscure. For "God made darkness his hiding

---

[27]ANF 6:65*. [28]PG 23:172. [29]WSA 3 15:191. [30]Phil 3:21. [31]Mt 11:27; Lk 10:22. [32]Col 1:15. [33]OCC 330-31. [34]WSA 3 10:313.

place." Those desiring audaciously and rashly to examine this darkness and appropriating for themselves one thing from another have fallen headlong into the dense "darkness" of errors. Homilies on Exodus 4.7.[35]

God Is Unfathomable. Jerome: This verse suggests the ineffable dispensation of God and our inability to comprehend his wisdom. As with these eyes of ours we cannot look into an unfathomable depth, neither are we able to contemplate the majesty or the wisdom of God. Homily on Psalm 103[104].[36]

Unable to Contemplate. Jerome: There is no doubt but that the clouds and darkness round about him were the body that the Lord Savior deigned to assume. . . . He appeared just as he willed to appear and not in accordance with his divine nature. "He made darkness the cloak about him." If God is light, how is light able to dwell in darkness? In that passage, darkness represents our imperfect knowledge and our infirmity, for we cannot gaze on his majesty. If human eyes cannot, in fact, look on the rays of the sun of this world, a creature, our fellow slave, how much more are there shades and darkness round about the Sun of Justice that he may not be observed or looked on by us? Homily on Psalm 96[97].[37]

18:12 Clouds, Hailstones and Coals of Fire

The Preaching of His Word. Augustine: "In advance of the lightning of his presence," in preparation, that is, for the brightness of his manifestation, "his clouds have passed over," for the preachers of his Word are no longer confined within the borders of Judea but have crossed over to the nations. "Hailstones and fiery coals": by this figure of speech we should understand reproofs, which batter hard hearts like hail. But if the well-cultivated and receptive soul of a godly mind receives reproofs, the hardness of the hail is dissolved into water, because the terror

of a reproof, charged with lightning and frozen hard, is dissolved into nourishing doctrine, while hearts come back to life when kindled by the fire of love. Expositions of the Psalms 18.13.[38]

He Drives Away Demonic Delusion. Eusebius of Caesarea: He came down and then ascended with the cherubim after he thundered in the heaven. . . . Against the Egyptian sorcerers the Lord who flies on the cherubim sends forth hailstones and coals of fire. I think, also, that those vengeful acts against skillful wicked powers are called hailstones and coals of fire. Those acts, therefore, appointed for punishment and revenge and directed in the secret way of the will of God against the demons who had brought the superstition of multiple gods, were driving away all those demons. Therefore, all their oracles cease, their prophecies are denied, their temples are deserted, their sacred objects are robbed by invisible and hidden forces, as the Lord does all these things after his ascension into the heavens. Commentary on Psalms 18.14.[39]

18:14 God Sends Out Arrows

He Sent Out Evangelists. Augustine: He sent out his Evangelists to fly on straight courses, on wings of strength, using not their own powers but those of the one by whom they were sent; and he scattered those to whom they were sent, that to some among them the Evangelists might be the savor of life leading to life but to others the stench of death leading to death.[40] Expositions of the Psalms 18.15.[41]

The Lightning of Understanding. Evagrius of Pontus: When we compare spiritual things with spiritual things, we flash forth lightnings, indicating the knowledge advancing from them. Notes on the Psalms 17[18].15, 16.[42]

---

[35]FC 71:270*. [36]FC 48:224*. [37]FC 57:110*. [38]WSA 3 15:191-92. [39]PG 23:173. [40]See 2 Cor 2:16-17. [41]WSA 3 15:192. [42]PG 12:1229.

18:15 Foundations Laid Bare

Only One to Fear. Diodore of Tarsus: He presents him as a general come to the aid of his own man, mentioning as arrows all the missiles indiscriminately—hail, coals, things that are naturally used as missiles. . . . In fear of the one appearing and the missiles and lightning flashes, the earth bared itself in all directions so as even to reveal its hidden secrets, springs, and anything else hidden in its depths. "At your rebuke, Lord." The exclamatory remark emphasized nicely that creation has no one else to dread in this way except the author of creation himself. Commentary on Psalms 18.[43]

18:19 God Delivered Me

By His Grace. Eusebius of Caesarea: "He will deliver me because he has pleasure in me"; indeed, it was not that I had repented, or had been convicted concerning my sin or had a prophet sent to me, but it was because he took pleasure to deliver me. And I know and I am absolutely persuaded that in the day of his judgment of the righteous no mention will be made of my sin and the crimes that I committed in the day of my misery. Commentary on Psalms 18.20-21.[44]

18:23 Blameless Before God

Blameless in Christ. Arnobius the Younger: I will be blameless with him, with that very one who, himself blameless, suffered on the cross for our iniquities. Commentary on Psalms 18.[45]

18:25 With the Holy, You Will Be Holy

Holy by Grace. Augustine: There is a deeply hidden sense in which you are known as holy with the holy, because you make them holy. Expositions of the Psalms 18.26.[46]

Holy with the Holy. Arnobius the

Younger: We agree with common opinion, "He will be like the one with whom he is joined." Indeed, this statement is very true, but it does not apply to the interpretation of the present verse. In this verse, if you wish to make the plain sense of the hymn, you will remember what the Lord said through the prophet to the people: If you walk upright in my sight, I will walk upright with you; if you walk turned from my ways, I will be turned from you. The psalmist speaks to this statement: With the holy, you will be holy; with the innocent, innocent, and et cetera. Commentary on Psalms 18.[47]

Therefore Be Holy. Apostolic Constitutions: Therefore, O bishop, together with your subordinate clergy, endeavor rightly to divide the Word of truth. For the Lord says, "If you walk cross-grained to me, I will walk cross-grained to you." . . . Walk therefore in holiness, that you may rather appear worthy of praise from the Lord than of complaint from the adversary. Constitutions of the Holy Apostles 2.6.43.[48]

18:26 With the Crooked

For the Sake of Correction. Clement of Alexandria: By perverse, he means he will chastise sinners. For his natural uprightness . . . and his goodness toward those who believe obediently are immovable and unshakable. . . . Therefore, he treats them severely in the hope that perhaps he might curb their impulse toward death. Christ the Educator 85-86.[49]

18:28 God Lightens the Darkness

Enlightened by God. Augustine: Since our light does not come from ourselves, it is you, Lord who will light my lamp. . . . Of ourselves we are darkness by reason of our sin, but you, my God, "will enlighten my darkness." Exposi-

---

[43]WGRW 9:54. [44]PG 23:176-77. [45]CCL 25:21-22. [46]WSA 3 15:194. [47]CCL 25:22. [48]ANF 7:416*. [49]FC 23:76.

tions of the Psalms 18.29.[50]

THE GRACE OF ENLIGHTENMENT. AUGUSTINE: Examine human nature: it is born and increases, it learns these customs of people. What does [this nature] know except earth, of the earth? It speaks human things, it knows human things, it understands human things. Carnal itself, [this nature] judges carnally, it surmises carnally. Let the grace of God come, let it enlighten a person's darkness, as [the psalmist] says. . . . Let grace take possession of the human mind and turn it to its own light; immediately it begins to say what the apostle says: "Yet not I, but the grace of God with me"[51] and "And it is no longer I that live, but Christ lives in me."[52] TRACTATES ON THE GOSPEL OF JOHN 14.6.2.[53]

THE TRUE LIGHT IN THE LAMP OF DAVID. EUSEBIUS OF CAESAREA: "I will bring forth a horn to David; I have prepared a lamp for my anointed."[54] The lamp is prepared for Christ, having arisen from the seed of David, for who other could it be than the offspring who has come forth from the succession of David according to the flesh; in what way does Christ who came into the womb of David become the ray of his own excellence and the light shining brightly for all people? Why in the aforesaid words does David speak prophetically: "Because you will light my lamp, Lord"? He says, "You yourself, Lord, who are the true light, having been united with the lamp coming forth from me in a certain mysterious way, are going to light that very lamp. Even the shadows with which I was once covered you will scatter entirely so that their memory does not enter my mind. COMMENTARY ON PSALMS 18.29, 30.[55]

OIL OF GRACE. ARNOBIUS THE YOUNGER: Just as the eye is the lamp of the body, so the lamp of the soul is the mind, in which, unless Christ has poured the oil of his grace, there will not be light within. The prophet, therefore, proclaims that his lamp is lighted by the Lord. COMMENTARY ON THE PSALMS 18.[56]

DO NOT QUENCH THE LIGHT. THEODORE OF TABENNESI: Let us not allow what is according to the flesh to persecute what is according to the spirit; neither let us, using the body as a pretext, quench the lamp that has been lit in us. We must therefore not contradict to the point of thinking or of speaking contrary to the faith in the holy Scriptures. But "those whom he loves, God chastises";[57] he afflicts and puts them to the test in everything to see "whether they will keep his commandments or not."[58] Yet, what God is looking for in us are "the fruits of the Holy Spirit";[59] we must not be negligent concerning them, for it is about them that we shall be questioned. INSTRUCTIONS 3.40.[60]

18:29 God Gives Strength

THE WALLS OF ENEMIES. EUSEBIUS OF CAESAREA: Truly I have known that I am going to cross over that heavenly wall built by your strength and power; and then situated in a safe place, I will receive salvation from you. Or, in this way: I, whom they try to close out by surrounding me in order to stop me, will cross and leap over all the fortifications of the enemies, both fence and wall. COMMENTARY ON PSALMS 18.29-30.[61]

THE WALL OF SIN. AUGUSTINE: Not by my own efforts shall I be delivered, but by you. . . . Again, it is not by my own strength but in my God that I shall leap over the wall that sins have built between humankind and the heavenly Jerusalem. EXPOSITIONS OF THE PSALMS 18.30.[62]

THE WALL OF HUMAN WILL. POEMEN: A person's will is a brazen wall and a stone hurled between himself and God. If one puts it aside, he can say the words of the psalm: "In my God

---

[50]WSA 3 15:194. [51]1 Cor 15:10. [52]Gal 2:20. [53]FC 79:69*. [54]Ps 132:17 (131:17 LXX). [55]PG 23:178, 180. [56]CCL 25:22. [57]Heb 12:6. [58]Deut 8:2. [59]Gal 5:22. [60]CS 47:116. [61]PG 23:180. [62]WSA 3 15:194*.

I shall go over a wall" and "as for my God, his way is undefiled." If righteousness assists the will, then a person does good. SAYINGS OF THE FATHERS 10.60.[63]

18:30 God Is A Shield

THE SUPREME PROTECTOR. EUSEBIUS OF CAESAREA: What, moreover, do those oracles tried in the fire of the Lord teach? That he himself is the protector of all the ones hoping in him and that there is no God except our Lord, and there is none strong except our God; and rightly is it said that he is the protector of all hoping in him since none is able to be found who is able to stand against such and so great a protector. COMMENTARY ON PSALMS 18.31-32.[64]

18:32 Girded with Strength

STRENGTHENED AND DISCIPLINED BY GOD. EUSEBIUS OF CAESAREA: He builds me up with his own strength and weapons, and he affirms by his grace my mortal and human strength; just like one having his limbs undergirded by his own strength, I will stand against my enemies. But as it is said above, "My God, his way is perfect," so also wishing me to be likened to his own image, he has made my way blameless by teaching, admonitions and discipline of whatever type he wishes, and he has refined and perfected my way or settled life. COMMENTARY ON PSALMS 18.33-34.[65]

18:33 Secure On the Heights

DIRECTED HEAVENWARD. AUGUSTINE: "He who made my feet perfect like a deer's," who had made my love perfect, to leap over the thorny, dark entanglements of this world, "he will set me on the high places." He will direct my gaze to my heavenly habitation, that I may be filled with all the fullness of God. EXPOSITIONS OF THE PSALMS 18.34.[66]

OUR PECULIAR DOMAIN. EUSEBIUS OF CAE-

SAREA: The same deer is swift in course as are also the righteous of God who look heavenward, not earthward, who seek the sublime; and this from a single love of the celestial kingdom. David ascribes his likeness to that of the righteous, strengthened by the grace of God, when he adds "and setting me on high places." Although there are others who try to draw us into the valleys of iniquity and lead us away, our God, like an overseer of our struggles, when he has determined that we are good runners, stirs us to suitable excellence, and his grace fulfills that very thing. Not in our excellence are we established in our high places; but truly by its very nature the celestial is the abode for the soul; and those high places are not foreign but are peculiar to us. COMMENTARY ON PSALMS 18.33-34.[67]

18:35 Support from God's Right Hand

DISCIPLINED BY THE RIGHT HAND. EVAGRIUS OF PONTUS: He who sits on the right of the Father corrects us with discipline, and accordingly he teaches us. For he directs the spirit with a right foundation; true understanding leads one into fullness. NOTES ON THE PSALMS 17[18].36.[68]

DIVINE REPROOF. AUGUSTINE: Your reproof, by not allowing me to deviate, has guided me to relate whatever I do to the goal of union with you. EXPOSITIONS OF THE PSALMS 18.36.[69]

18:36 A Wide Place

THE ABILITY TO WALK. EUSEBIUS OF CAESAREA: "You have made room for my steps under me," the steps, namely, by which I cross from iniquity to moral excellence, from things perceived by my senses to those perceived by my mind, from the present to the future age, the steps that from the beginning seemed arduous and narrow to me because I was walking in

---

[63]LCC 12:117*. [64]PG 23:180. [65]PG 23:180. [66]WSA 3 15:195. [67]PG 23:181. [68]PG 12:1237. [69]WSA 3 15:195.

a crooked way; but having progressed beyond them, I took notice of the widened places. For one who advances with every step and attains the end, having been drawn to the wide space, will not feel that narrowness, labor and grief that he had known in his advance. . . . He who follows Jesus follows hard his footsteps because he progresses on the worn and oft traveled way from Jesus Christ. COMMENTARY ON PSALMS 18.37.[70]

18:37 Pursuing Enemies

PURSUIT OF ENEMIES. ARNOBIUS THE YOUNGER: Not only do we avoid the ones pursuing us as we flee, but we pursue our enemies, and we seize them, and we do not turn back until they fail. COMMENTARY ON THE PSALMS 18.[71]

GOD PURSUED ME. JEROME: The mind must not through disbelief in the promised blessings give way to despair; and the soul once marked out for perdition must not refuse to apply remedies on the ground that its wounds are past curing. . . . Lo, I hear his promise: "I will pursue mine enemies and overtake them; neither will I turn again till they are consumed," so that I, who was once your enemy and a fugitive from you, shall be laid hold of by your hand. Cease not from pursuing me till my wickedness is consumed. LETTER 122.1.[72]

PURSUIT BY GRACE. EUSEBIUS OF CAESAREA: This is done for me through your grace, so that my feet are not ensnared nor am I cut off by the nets of my enemies or by the offenses that they had cast. COMMENTARY ON PSALMS 18.38.[73]

A PROMISE TO BELIEVE. EVAGRIUS OF PONTUS: If you pray against your passions or the demons that assail you recall to mind [this verse]. . . . You are to say this at the appropriate moment, thus arming yourself against your adversary with

humility. CHAPTERS ON PRAYER 135.[74]

18:39 Strength for the Battle

GOD GIRDS OUR DESIRES. AUGUSTINE: Tightly and strongly you have bound up the loosely flowing desires of my flesh, that I may not be hindered by them in battle. EXPOSITIONS OF THE PSALMS 18.40.[75]

ASSAIL THE ASSAILANTS. EVAGRIUS OF PONTUS: If fighters find themselves being assailed and assailing in return, and if the demons fight against us, then they too when they assail us will be assailed by us in return. Scripture says, "I will assail them, and they will not be able to stand";[76] and again, "Those who assail me and are my enemies, they have weakened and fallen."[77] PRAKTIKOS 72.[78]

18:40 Enemies Turn Their Backs

THE SIGHT OF VICTORY. ARNOBIUS THE YOUNGER: We will see the backs of our enemies fleeing, not the faces of ones pursuing us. COMMENTARY ON THE PSALMS 18.[79]

18:43 People Not Known

DAVID HONORED BY GENTILES. EUSEBIUS OF CAESAREA: He truly sees with his mind's eye that all the peoples throughout the whole world of the human race, whether barbarians or Greek, or of whatever accent or language, carry David respectfully in their memory, and they all speak his name with honor, who lift up his words through all the churches of Christ; and does anyone not assert the truth in these very words, if he attentively considers the people gathered from the nations, known by no sign to David, as they perform their duties of service with Davidic hymns and canticles, and as they

[70]PG 23:181, 184. [71]CCL 25:23. [72]NPNF 2 6:226*. [73]PG 23:184. [74]CS 4:77. [75]WSA 3 15:196. [76]Cf. Ps 18:37-38 (17:38-39 LXX). [77]Ps 27:2 (26:2 LXX). [78]GAC 109-10*. [79]CCL 25:23.

hear the song repeated and recite it, receiving the psalms entrusted by him that were written from the long ages back. COMMENTARY ON PSALMS 18.44-46.[80]

A People Formerly Ignorant. TERTULLIAN: "A people," he says. . . . But what is the "people" that was ignorant of God, but ours, who in days bygone knew not God? And who, in the hearing of the ear, gave heed to him, but we, who forsaking idols, have been converted to God? AN ANSWER TO THE JEWS 3.[81]

His People by Faith. IRENAEUS: We are not all the children of God: those only are so who believe in him and do his will. And those who do not believe and do not obey his will are sons and angels of the devil, because they do the works of the devil. And that such is the case he has declared in Isaiah: "I have begotten and brought up children, but they have rebelled against me."[82] And again, he says that these children are aliens: "Strange children have lied unto me."[83] According to nature, then, they are [his] children, because they have been so created; but with regard to their works, they are not his children. AGAINST HERESIES 4.41.2.[84]

18:44 They Obeyed

Hearing the Preached Word. AUGUSTINE: Though they did not see me with their own eyes, by receiving my preachers they have heard me and obeyed me. EXPOSITIONS OF THE PSALMS 18.45.[85]

18:48 Delivered from Enemies

His Weapon, the Cross. ARNOBIUS THE YOUNGER: All these things will happen to us through him who placed his arms on the cross as a bow in the sky, and daily he intercedes for us. COMMENTARY ON THE PSALMS 18.[86]

Praise from David and Honor to His Son.

EUSEBIUS OF CAESAREA: Just as David after the advent of our Savior is able to be presented just as if he were alive and living among people, and he sings praises to the God of the universe among all the peoples through his own writings, canticles and hymns, so also he who has come from his seed, to whom these words refer that we now explain, with like reasoning when he overcomes the ones lying in wait for him, he may rightly say, "You will exalt me above the ones rising against me." And he leaves them behind, and he shares his own truth and grace to all peoples; even now he himself, being present everywhere on the earth and in the midst of them resting their hope in him, is made known through his church. COMMENTARY ON PSALMS 18.50-51.[87]

18:50 To David and His Descendants

The Offspring of David. DIODORE OF TARSUS: Since by the Holy Spirit he understood that God's promises were not confined to him alone but would pass also to his offspring, so he spoke in this way here with particular reference to Christ's life. The outcome, in fact, showed that David's offspring, blessing and sanctifying the nations, referred to no one other than the Lord of all. The blessing affected the offspring without restriction, after all, and following David, remember, there were many famous descendants of his in each generation (Christ himself thought to be the one proven to be famous and great)— first Solomon, then Uzziah, then Hezekiah, then Josiah—yet none emerged as more precisely realizing the force of the promise than Christ alone, and after him there was no one, nor is there anyone to whom the blessing of the promises would be thought to refer. After all, with Judah in captivity and the tribes intermingled, and no clarity as to who was descended from whom, it is now obvious that the fulfillment of the promise

[80]AnSac 3:415. [81]ANF 3:154-55. [82]Is 1:2. [83]Ps 17:45 LXX. [84]ANF 1:525. [85]WSA 3 15:196. [86]CCL 25:23. [87]PG 23:185.

rested with Jesus himself, to whom in this case as well both the prayer and the prophecy allude, "To David and his offspring forever." I mean, those of the company of Hezekiah, even if they seemed to enjoy some grace from God, did not do so forever, death befalling each one with the result that they were not the subject of blessing forever. COMMENTARY ON PSALMS 18.[88]

---

[88]WGRW 9:58-59*.

19:1-14 GOD'S SELF-REVELATION

As you wonder at the order of creation, the grace of providence and the sacred prescriptions of the Law, sing Psalm 19.

ATHANASIUS *On the Interpretation of the Psalms* 17 [OIP 67]

To the choirmaster. A Psalm of David.

[1]*The heavens are telling the glory of God;*
  and the firmament proclaims his
      handiwork.
[2]*Day to day pours forth speech,*
  and night to night declares knowledge.
[3]*There is no speech, nor are there words;*
  their voice is not heard;
[4]*yet their voice[k] goes out through all the earth,*
  and their words to the end of the world.

In them he has set a tent for the sun,
[5]*which comes forth like a bridegroom leaving*
      his chamber,
  and like a strong man runs its course with
      joy.
[6]*Its rising is from the end of the heavens,*
  and its circuit to the end of them;
  and there is nothing hid from its heat.

[7]*The law of the LORD is perfect,*
  reviving the soul;
the testimony of the LORD is sure,
  making wise the simple;
[8]*the precepts of the LORD are right,*
      rejoicing the heart;
the commandment of the LORD is pure,
  enlightening the eyes;
[9]*the fear of the LORD is clean,*
  enduring for ever;
the ordinances of the LORD are true,
  and righteous altogether.
[10]*More to be desired are they than gold,*
  even much fine gold;
sweeter also than honey
  and drippings of the honeycomb.

[11]*Moreover by them is thy servant warned;*
  in keeping them there is great reward.
[12]*But who can discern his errors?*
  Clear thou me from hidden faults.
[13]*Keep back thy servant also from*
      presumptuous sins;
  let them not have dominion over me!
Then I shall be blameless,
  and innocent of great transgression.

[14]*Let the words of my mouth and the*
      meditation of my heart
  be acceptable in thy sight,
  O LORD, my rock and my redeemer.

---

k Gk Jerome Compare Syr: Heb *line*

OVERVIEW: The nineteenth psalm presents three laws in harmony with one another (THEODORET). It also presents a rebuke to atheism (DIODORE).

The psalm begins proclaiming that God, as designer of the heavens, is known by his design (THEODORET). The creation is not by chance (EUSEBIUS). Rather, created things are servants for our instruction (LEO). It is the spectacle of creation that speaks (CHRYSOSTOM), drawing a response from us that glorifies the Creator (JOHN OF DAMASCUS). Nevertheless, many have stumbled into idolatry (CHRYSOSTOM), even though the message of creation rebukes idolaters (ATHANASIUS). Anyone who misses this message fails in the first article of faith (ORIGEN). But those, like the apostles, who become heavenly themselves join in the testimony (ORIGEN) and become in turn a more excellent firmament (AMBROSE). God is revealed especially in the order of things (THEODORET, DIODORE). For it is clear that Reason rules through the natural order (EUSEBIUS). This order forms the primal music of the cosmos (GREGORY OF NYSSA). This natural revelation constitutes a message (GREGORY OF NYSSA) of the Lord's greatness (ORIGEN). His providence is a message of his love (CHRYSOSTOM) in a book open to all (CHRYSOSTOM), declared in a universal language (DIODORE). The tent pitched in the sun reminds us that the Lord took a form revealed in the light of the sun (AUGUSTINE), or, from another point of view, in the light of the Sun of righteousness (ARNOBIUS THE YOUNGER). The sun in the sky is a key witness to the creator (CYRIL OF JERUSALEM, CHRYSOSTOM). But the words here have special reference to Christ, the Bridegroom, who came forth as God incarnate from the womb of Mary (NOVATIAN, AUGUSTINE, FULGENTIUS, AUGUSTINE). Testimony to him has gone throughout the world (EUSEBIUS, AMBROSE). The seeds of divine knowledge have been spread to all (JEROME). We all require the heat of divine grace (CAESARIUS). He is the inextinguishable light (AUGUSTINE).

The psalm turns to the Mosaic law (THEO-

DORET), which corresponds to the natural law (DIODORE). God's talk corresponds to his own walk (CASSIODORUS). It leads us to the fear of the Lord, the right fear, that is (CASSIODORUS), which leads in turn to the right effect (CLEMENT OF ALEXANDRIA). It is an enduring fear (AUGUSTINE). So, the light he gives is desirable (CLEMENT OF ALEXANDRIA), being sweet to the mind (CASSIODORUS). But one must have a healthy appetite to enjoy it (CHRYSOSTOM), renouncing lesser goods (BASIL). Suffering cannot compare with the reward we receive (ARNOBIUS THE YOUNGER). The psalmist warns of voluntary and involuntary sins (DIODORE). He speaks of original sin (CASSIODORUS), of evil thoughts (JEROME), of countless small sins (CAESARIUS) and warns against boasting (AUGUSTINE, LEO). Only God's testing reveals these sins (AUGUSTINE). Only by God's Spirit can we hope to overcome them (GREGORY OF NYSSA). Concluding the three parts of the psalm (THEODORET), the psalmist closes on the theme of grace (CASSIODORUS, JEROME).

19:1 The Heavens Tell the Glory of God

THE HARMONY OF THREE LAWS. THEODORET OF CYR: We learn three kinds of divine laws from blessed Paul. One unwritten kind he said was given to human beings in creation and nature: "From the creation of the world," he says, "his invisible attributes have been understood and seen in created things";[1] and again, "For when the Gentiles, who do not have the law, practice the obligations of the law instinctively, despite having no law they are a law to themselves."[2] . . . Another law was provided in writing through the mighty Moses: "The Law was added because of transgressions," he says, "ordained through angels in the hand of a mediator."[3] He knew also a third one imposed after these, the law of grace: "For the law of the Spirit of life," he says, "has set me free from the law of sin and

---

[1]Rom 1:20. [2]Rom 2:14. [3]Gal 3:19.

death."[4] Blessed David in this psalm teaches human beings the harmony between these, following the same order: first, the one the Creator preaches in creation; then the one given through Moses, instilling a greater knowledge of the Creator to those willing to attend; after that, the law of grace, perfectly purifying souls and freeing them from the present destruction. This in fact is the reason the psalm also refers us "to the end," naming the New Testament in the end. Commentary on the Psalms 19.1.[5]

A Rebuke to Atheists. Diodore of Tarsus: This nineteenth psalm is doctrinal: just as the fourth, also being doctrinal, censures those claiming that existing things do not benefit from providence, so too the present psalm levels an accusation against those who claim . . . that existing things were made by no one, instead coming to be by themselves. Necessarily following on this is the view that these things also do not merit providence: with no admission of the Creator, the provider is also not acknowledged by them, either. Commentary on Psalms 19.[6]

Designer Known by the Design. Theodoret of Cyr: If you observe a most mighty and magnificent building, you admire the builder; and if you see a skillfully and beautifully designed ship, you think of the shipwright; and at the sight of a painting the painter comes to mind. Much more, to be sure, does the sight of creation lead the viewers to the Creator. Commentary on the Psalms 19.2.[7]

Creation Not by Chance. Eusebius of Caesarea: This verse serves as a lesson on how the great work of God is declared. People who have been blinded in the eyes of their minds have expelled from the natural order the hidden and invisible divine essence, which is incorporeal and uncreated, and cannot be touched in any way or recognized with carnal eyes. With a godless and wicked mouth they say that there is no God, that nothing excellent of a corporeal nature exists beyond its temporary appearance, and that the whole universe came together in a certain momentary and accidental coalescence and gathering of parts that previously existed by chance and without purpose. Thus, it was necessary in the present work by means of a psalm that the writer should prove through plain demonstration God's omniscience and creative power. The nature of mortals is insignificant and fragile, the thoughts of people, foolish, and our reasoning uncertain. Therefore, we are no match for declaring the divine glory. For these worthy words and reflections about God cannot be proclaimed with human voices or with tongues or lips of flesh. If one who has the facility of a strong mind could hear that powerful and most worthy teaching that comes from the heavens, he would direct his mind and mount up to attend to those things, embracing them completely in himself, celebrating his Creator and the Maker of the universe with hymns and songs. For those heavens above us and those elements present in the firmament attest to a nature capable of being understood by and realized through the senses. They ascribe glory to God, not through any human language but through their adornment, by their very creation, through their ordered movement they teach his immeasurable majesty. . . . Whoever, therefore, thinks that such beauty and magnitude adorned itself or that the heavens created themselves, and then ascribes their harmonious and ordered motions to some process devoid of any divine power, is foolish and wicked. Therefore, those of sound mind confess that the part is a unified whole, and not only do they hear the cry of the heavens but also the proclamation from that very work together announcing glory to God, their Maker and Creator. Commentary on Psalms 18[19].2.[8]

Servants for Our Instruction. Leo the Great: All nature serves the Word of God for our instruction. Through all the turning points

---

[4]Rom 8:2. [5]FC 101:133. [6]WGRW 9:59. [7]FC 101:134. [8]PG 23:185, 188.

of the year, as if through the four Gospels, we learn from the unceasing trumpet both what we should preach and what we should do. . . . What is there through which the truth does not speak to us? Its voice is heard in the day, it is heard in the night, and the beauty of all things, established by the work of one God, does not cease to put into the ears of our hearts a ruling order, to let us see the "invisible things of God through those which have been made intelligible to us,"[9] and it is subject not to the creatures but to the Creator of all things. SERMON 19.2.[10]

THE SPECTACLE ITSELF. CHRYSOSTOM: How . . . do they declare it? Voice they have none; mouth they possess not; no tongue is theirs! How then do they declare? By means of the spectacle itself. For when you see the beauty, the breadth, the height, the position, the form, the stability thereof during so long a period; hearing as it were a voice, and being instructed by the spectacle, you adore him who created a body so fair and strange! The heavens may be silent, but the sight of them emits a voice that is louder than a trumpet's sound, instructing us not by the ear but through the medium of the eyes, for the latter is a sense which is more sure and more distinct than the former. HOMILIES CONCERNING THE STATUES 9.4.[11]

OUR RESPONSE. JOHN OF DAMASCUS: "The heavens show forth the glory of God" not by speaking in a voice audible to sensible ears but by manifesting to us through their own greatness the power of the Creator, and when we remark their beauty, we give glory to their Maker as the best of all artificers. ORTHODOX FAITH 2.6.[12]

MANY HAVE STUMBLED. CHRYSOSTOM: Nevertheless, many have stumbled at it and in contrary directions to one another. And some have admired it so much above its worth as to think it God, while others have been so insensible of its beauty as to assert it to be unworthy of God's creating hand and to ascribe the greater

share in it to a certain evil matter. And yet God provided for both points by making it beautiful and great that it might not be deemed alien from his wisdom, yet defective and not sufficient to itself that it might not be suspected to be God. HOMILIES ON 2 CORINTHIANS 21.4.[13]

A REBUKE TO IDOLATORS. ATHANASIUS: Creation . . . points to God as its Maker and Artificer, who reigns over creation and over all things, even the Father of our Lord Jesus Christ; whom would-be philosophers turn from to worship and deify the creation that proceeded from him, which yet itself worships and confesses the Lord whom they deny on its account. For if people are awestruck at the parts of creation and think that they are gods, they might well be rebuked by the mutual dependence of those parts; which moreover makes known and witnesses to the Father of the Word, who is the Lord and Maker of these parts also, by the unbroken law of their obedience to him, as the divine law also says [in this verse of the psalm]. . . . The proof of all this is not obscure but is clear enough in all conscience to those the eyes of whose understanding are not wholly disabled. AGAINST THE HEATHEN 27.3-5.[14]

FIRST ARTICLE OF FAITH. ORIGEN: If someone, hypothetically, should seem to believe in Jesus but should not believe that the God of the law and of the gospel is one, whose glory the heavens declare, since they were made by him, and the work of whose hands the firmament proclaims, since it is their work, this person would be deficient in the greatest article of faith. COMMENTARY ON THE GOSPEL OF JOHN 32.190.[15]

THOSE WHO ARE HEAVENLY. ORIGEN: Any who are perfect, who have been made heavenly or have become [part] of heaven, "declare the glory of God," as it says in the psalm. For this

---

[9]Rom 1:20. [10]FC 93:70. [11]NPNF 1 9:401*. [12]FC 37:214. [13]NPNF 1 12:378*. [14]NPNF 2 4:18. [15]FC 89:378.

reason in brief also the apostles who were of heaven were sent to declare the glory of God and received the name of Boanerges, "which is the sons of thunder,"[16] that by the power of thunder we might believe them truly to be heavens. HOMILIES ON GENESIS 1.13.[17]

ANOTHER FIRMAMENT. AMBROSE: As heaven is lighted with the splendor of the stars, so do people shine with the light of their good works, and their deeds shine before their Father in heaven. The one is the firmament of heaven on high; the other is a similar firmament of which it is said, "On this rock I will build my church."[18] The one is a firmament of the elements, the other of virtues, and this last is more excellent. LETTER 43.[19]

19:2 Day to Day, Night to Night

GOD REVEALED BY THE NATURAL ORDER. THEODORET OF CYR: The ordained succession of night and day illustrates the boundaries set by the Creator . . . the visible things are inanimate, being a kind of mask that teaches everyone to be led from visible things to the invisible God and to offer singing to him . . . by putting forth neither words nor verbal expressions but the norm, and demonstrating their own order, they summon all land and sea to the divine singing. COMMENTARY ON THE PSALMS 19.3.[20]

ORDER AND THE ONE WHO ORDERS. DIODORE OF TARSUS: Now, where there is order there is also proof of the one determining order, and there too denial of being self-made, since what is not done by anyone cannot show order. All these visible things surely illustrate order. So he is saying, "They announce some pattern and cry aloud the order of the orderer and the folly of the notion of being self-made." COMMENTARY ON PSALMS 19.[21]

REASON RULES THROUGH ORDER. EUSEBIUS OF CAESAREA: The days and the nights teach those people who desire to be taught what ineffable wisdom, what incomprehensible power God has, who has measured out the intervals of time for them. If there were no one who would determine the space and the intervals for the seasons, but they existed in a thoughtless and unconsidered way by chance, it would happen that the days would not be ordered in equal spaces through the ages and there would be a confusion of things, and likewise the times of the nights would pass by chance or happenstance. Even the state of related matters would be disordered because of thoughtless chance, and confusion would follow the confused matter; but . . . reason rules the right order, and wisdom administers harmony and order. There are mutual changes and alterations; for the days, as the nights yield, are longer, and then the nights claim their space, rightfully due and given mutually, having been increased by winter and season. These things, I say, are not only voiced, but as they announce the knowledge of God to people they declare that most wise order of all things constituted by God. So the voices of the days and nights, by their very work being done, call out to them who are able to hear as their teaching reaches all ears. And the universe that is inhabited by people is replete with songs of this type and like choruses. COMMENTARY ON PSALMS 19.3.[22]

19:3 No Speech

PRIMAL MUSIC. GREGORY OF NYSSA: The accord and affinity of all things with one another that is controlled in an orderly and sequential manner is the primal, archetypal, true music. It is this music that the conductor of the universe skillfully strikes up in the unspoken speech of wisdom through these ever-occurring movements. ON THE INSCRIPTIONS OF THE PSALMS 1.3.21.[23]

19:4 Through All the Earth

[16]Mk 3:17. [17]FC 71:64-65. [18]Mt 16:18. [19]FC 26:258 (Letter 49 in this edition). [20]FC 101:134-35. [21]WGRW 9:60. [22]PG 23:189. [23]GNTIP 90*.

A MESSAGE NONETHELESS. GREGORY OF NYSSA: Yet, how can such declaring and showing forth be other than words, and how is it that no voice addresses itself to the ear? Is the prophet contradicting himself, or is he stating an impossibility, when he speaks of words without sound, and declaration without language and announcement without voice? Or, is there not rather the very perfection of truth in his teaching, which tells us, in the words that I have quoted, that the declaration of the heavens and the word shouted forth by the day, is no articulate voice or language of the lips but is a revelation of the power of God to those who are capable of hearing it, even though no voice is heard? . . . The very heavens, he says in displaying the wisdom of him who made them, all but shout aloud with a voice, and, though without voice, proclaim the wisdom of their Creator. For we can hear as it were words teaching us: "O mortals, when you gaze on us and behold our beauty and magnitude and this ceaseless revolution, with its well-ordered and harmonious motion, working in the same direction and in the same manner, turn your thoughts to him who presides over our system, and, by aid of the beauty that you see, imagine to yourselves the beauty of the invisible Archetype. For in us there is nothing without its Lord, nothing that moves of its own proper motion, but all that appears or that is conceivable in respect to us depends on a Power who is inscrutable and sublime." This is not given in articulate speech but by the things which are seen, and it instills into our minds the knowledge of divine power more than if speech proclaimed it with a voice. ANSWER TO EUNOMIUS' SECOND BOOK.[24]

THE LORD'S GREATNESS. ORIGEN: Behold the Lord's greatness. "The sound of his teaching has gone out into every land." Our Lord Jesus has been spread out to the whole world, because he is God's power. . . . The power of the Lord and Savior is with those who are in Britain, separated from our world, and with those who are in Mauretania and with everyone under the sun who has believed in his name. Behold the Savior's greatness. It extends to all the world. HOMILIES ON THE GOSPEL OF LUKE 6.9.[25]

GOD'S PROVIDENCE AND LOVE. CHRYSOSTOM: The providence of God is clearer than the sun and its rays. On every occasion and in every place you will see clear and abundant evidence of this providence—in the desert, on cultivated and uncultivated land, on land and sea, wherever you go. This evidence is old and new. Voices are raised from every side that sound more clearly than the voices of our reason, and they tell of God's care to one who wishes to hear. . . . Our tongue is known only to those who share our language, not to those of other tongues; but the voice of creation is audible to all peoples who dwell in the inhabited world. Those of good judgment regard as sufficient God's proclamation, without the demonstration of deeds. It reveals not only his providence but also his abundant love for us; for he does not merely take thought for us but is also our lover, and he loves us boundlessly with an inconceivable love. It is a love that knows no emotion, but it is most warm and intense, noble, insoluble, unquenchable. ON PROVIDENCE 5.2.[26]

A BOOK OPEN TO ALL. CHRYSOSTOM: The Scythian, barbarian, Indian, Egyptian and everyone who walks on the earth shall hear this voice; for not by means of the ears but through the sight, it reaches our understanding. And of the things that are seen, there is one uniform perception; and there is no difference, as is the case with respect to languages. On this volume the unlearned, as well as the wise, shall be alike able to look; the poor person as well as the rich person; and wherever anyone may chance to come, there looking upward toward the heavens, he will receive a sufficient lesson from the view of them. HOMILIES CONCERNING THE STATUES 9.5.[27]

---

[24]NPNF 2 5:272-73. [25]FC 94:27. [26]MFC 17:49. [27]NPNF 1 9:401*.

UNIVERSAL LANGUAGE. DIODORE OF TARSUS: The voices of visible creation . . . are equally clear to everyone, both Greeks and barbarians, giving everyone the one message, that they were made by someone and do not exist of themselves. COMMENTARY ON PSALMS 19.[28]

MANIFEST IN THE SUN'S LIGHT. AUGUSTINE: The sun's maker could only be seen by the sun's light, because he "set his tabernacle in the sun." He who was before the sun that he made, before the day star and all stars, before all angels, the true Creator (for all things were made by him, and without him was nothing made[29]), that he might be seen by the eyes of flesh that see the sun, set his own tabernacle in the sun—showed his flesh in manifestation by this light. HOMILIES ON 1 JOHN 1.2.[30]

THE SUN OF RIGHTEOUSNESS. ARNOBIUS THE YOUNGER: The Lord placed his own tabernacle in the sun. Not in that sun that, by arranging the days, directs the measure of the hours according to the seasons, but "the sun of righteousness,"[31] which, having been brought forth from the virginal womb in the splendor of eternal life has shone the true light to minds, and he has stepped forth from the Virgin just like the bridegroom from the bridal chamber. He rejoiced as a strong man running his course, and in every way he walked blameless on the way in the law of the Lord, having stepped forth from the highest heaven. Not from the seed of people, but from the word of the Father, who is in the highest of the heavens, his course is also the highest, not from the rising in the east, or as from the highest to the lowest points, but from highest to the highest and from excellence to excellence, and from the highest to the highest there will not be one who may hide himself from his heat. COMMENTARY ON THE PSALMS 19.[32]

19:5 Like a Bridegroom

THE WITNESS OF THE SUN. CYRIL OF JERUSALEM: Consider the apt disposition of the sun, or rather of him whose ordering determined its course; how in summer it is higher in the heavens and makes the days longer, thereby giving people good time for their works, while in winter it contracts its course that the cold season might not be too long and that the nights, becoming longer, might serve as the repose of people and for the fruitfulness of the earth's products. See too how the days give way to each other in due order, lengthening in summer, growing shorter in winter, but in spring and autumn affording mutually equal intervals; and the nights likewise, so that the psalmist says, "Day pours out word to day, and night to night imparts knowledge." For to the heretics, who have no ears, they all but shout, and by their good order they say that there is no other God save their Creator, who fixed their bounds and laid out the universe. CATECHETICAL LECTURES 9.6.[33]

THE SUN AND ITS CREATOR. CHRYSOSTOM: The sun renders the day brighter, shedding its rays like flashing lights and day by day revealing its own beauty in full bloom: as soon as it appears at dawn, it awakes the whole human race to the discharge of their respective duties. . . . Do you see how [in the psalm] he revealed to us both the sun's beauty and its speed of movement? That is, in saying, "Its span extends from one corner of heaven right to the other corner of heaven," it indicated to us how in one moment of time it traverses the whole world and scatters its rays from end to end, making its great resources available. It not only supplies heat to the earth but also dries it up, and not only dries it up but enkindles it and supplies us with many different resources, so marvelous a body is it, quite beyond one's power to describe adequately. I mention this to you and sing the praises of this heavenly body so that you may not stop short there, dearly beloved, but proceed further and transfer your

[28]WGRW 9:61. [29]Jn 1:3. [30]LCC 8:260-61*. [31]Mal 4:2. [32]CCL 25:24-25. [33]FC 61:188.

admiration to the Creator of the heavenly body. After all, the greater the sun is shown to be, so much the more marvelous is the revelation of the Creator. HOMILIES ON GENESIS 6.10-11.[34]

CHRIST THE BRIDEGROOM. NOVATIAN: He it is who "comes forth as a bridegroom from his bridal chamber." For he [returns] even to the height; "since no one has ascended into heaven except him who has descended from heaven, the Son of man who is in heaven."[35] He repeats this very same fact when he says, "Father, glorify me with the glory that I had with you before the world existed."[36] If this Word descended from heaven as a bridegroom to take on our flesh, so that in taking flesh he might ascend again as Son of man to that place where, as Son of God, the Word had descended, then assuredly, because of a mutual bond, the flesh bears the Word of God, and the Son of God assumes the weakness of the flesh. He ascends with his spouse, the flesh, to the same place from which he had descended without the flesh and receives now that glory that he is shown to have had before the creation of the world. This proves, without the least doubt, that he is God. Nevertheless, since the world itself is said to have been created after him, it is evident that it was created through him. This fact itself gives proof of the glory and the authority of the divinity that is in him, through whom the world was made. ON THE TRINITY 13.4-5.[37]

THE INCARNATE ONE CALLED FOR OUR RETURN. AUGUSTINE: But our very life came down to earth and bore our death, and killed death with the very abundance of his own life. And thundering, he called us to return to him into that secret place from which he came forth to us—coming first into the virginal womb, where the human creature, our mortal flesh, was joined to him that it might not be forever mortal—and came "as a bridegroom coming out his chamber, rejoicing as a strong man to run a race." For he did not delay but ran through the world, cry-

ing out by words, deeds, death, life, descent, ascension—crying aloud to us to return to him. And he departed from our sight that we might return to our hearts and find him there. For he left us, and behold, he is here. He could not be with us long, yet he did not leave us. He went back to the place that he had never left, for "the world was made by him."[38] In this world he was, and into this world he came, to save sinners. To him my soul confesses, and he heals it, because it had sinned against him. O mortals, how long will you be so slow of heart? Even now after life itself has come down to you, will you not ascend and live? CONFESSIONS 4.12.19.[39]

THE INSEPARABLE UNION OF NATURES. FULGENTIUS OF RUSPE: The only-begotten God . . . has joined and united the divine and human nature in the unity of his person in such a way that they cannot in any way be separated from him. For in the one person of the only-begotten God, who "like a bridegroom comes out from his wedding canopy," the union of each nature remains inseparable. LETTER 14.11.[40]

CLOTHED IN CLAY, HE CURES OUR CLAY. AUGUSTINE: He came in the flesh intending to cleanse the vices of the flesh. He came, clothed in healing human clay, to cure our interior eyes that our outer earthy vesture had blinded, so that, with soundness of vision restored, we who had before been darkness might become a shining light in the Lord and so that the Light might no longer shine in darkness but might be clearly envisaged by those perceiving it. For this purpose, he came forth as a bridegroom from his chamber and "has rejoiced as an athlete to run the course." Comely as a bridegroom, strong as a giant; amiable and terrible, severe and serene; beautiful to the good, stern to the evil—remaining in the bosom of his Father, he took possession of the womb of his mother. In this bridal

---

[34]FC 74:83. [35]Jn 3:13. [36]Jn 17:5. [37]FC 67:53. [38]Jn 1:10. [39]LCC 7:87*. [40]FC 95:511.

chamber, that is, in the womb of the Virgin, he united human to divine nature. The Word was made flesh for us so that coming forth from his mother, he might dwell among us, and so that, going forth to his Father, he might prepare a dwelling place for us. SERMON 195.3.[41]

19:6 Nothing Hidden from Its Heat

THE WITNESS OF THE SON. EUSEBIUS OF CAESAREA: By heavenly power and co-operation, like a sun ray, the saving Word quickly illumined the whole earth. Straightway, in accordance with the divine Scripture, the voice of its inspired Evangelists and apostles "went forth to the whole earth and their words to the end of the world." And then in all the cities and villages, churches were quickly established, filled with multitudes of people, like a teeming threshing floor, and all those souls, bound through hereditary succession and original error by the ancient disease of idolatrous superstition, on being set free as it were from terrible masters and finding release from most difficult bondage by the power of Christ through both the teaching of his disciples and their wonderful works, rejected all demoniacal polytheism and confessed that there was one God alone, the Creator of all things, and this One they honored with the rites of true piety through inspired and rational worship that was implanted by our Savior in the life of people. ECCLESIASTICAL HISTORY 2.3.[42]

THE BENIGN LIGHT OF CHRIST. AMBROSE: Christ fills his world with copious lights, since "his going out is from the end of heaven, and his circuit even to the end of it, and there is no one who can hide himself from his heat." Benignly he gives light to all, wishing not to repel the foolish but to correct them and desiring not to exclude the hard of heart from the church but to soften them. Hence . . . Christ in the Gospel invites them, saying, "Come to me, all you who labor, and are burdened, and I will give you rest. Take my yoke on you, and learn from me, for I am meek and humble of heart."[43] ON HIS BROTHER SATYRUS 2.117.[44]

THE SEEDS OF DIVINE KNOWLEDGE. JEROME: "And there is not one who may hide himself from his heat." Really there is none who does not have the seeds of the knowledge of God. BRIEF COMMENTARY ON PSALMS 19.[45]

THE HEAT OF DIVINE GRACE. CAESARIUS OF ARLES: As often as water is contracted by excessive cold, if the heat of the sun comes on it, it becomes melted; when the same sun departs, the water again becomes hard. Similarly the charity of many people freezes because of the excessive coldness of their sins, and they become as hard as ice; however, when the warmth of divine mercy comes on them again, they are melted. Surely that is the heat of which it is written, "Nothing escapes its heat." SERMON 101.4.[46]

INEXTINGUISHABLE LIGHT. AUGUSTINE: Someone lights a lamp. . . . That lamp, as far as regards the little flame that shines there, that fire has light in itself. . . . When the lamp was not there, your eyes were inactive and saw nothing. Now they, too, have light, but not in themselves. Accordingly, if your eyes turn away from the lamp, they are darkened. If they turn toward it, they are enlightened. But that fire, as long as it exists, emits light; if you wish to take the light away from the fire, you extinguish it also at the same time; for without light it cannot remain in existence. But the light, Christ, is inextinguishable and co-eternal to the Father, always glowing, always shining, always burning; for if he did not burn, would it be said in the psalm, "There is no one who can hide from his heat"? TRACTATES ON THE GOSPEL OF JOHN 22.10.1.[47]

19:7 The Law of the Lord

[41]FC 38:42-43*. [42]FC 19:91*. [43]Mt 11:28-29. [44]FC 22:252. [45]CCL 72:196. [46]FC 47:101. [47]FC 79:206*.

THE MOSAIC LAW. THEODORET OF CYR: He calls the Mosaic law Law, testimony, judgments, command, decrees. . . . It is called Law in that it regulates and prescribes the best way of life; testimony in testifying against sinners and highlighting the punishment for transgression; judgments in teaching what is right, forbidding what is wrong and declaring virtuous people righteous; command in commanding what is to be done and giving orders authoritatively; decrees in revealing the divine verdicts and teaching what goods the observant will enjoy and to what punishments the transgressor will be consigned . . . the law of God, being free of every fault, corrects people's souls and makes them faultless; the testimony gives wisdom to the immature and simple by frightening them; the judgments gladden the heart by revealing the basis of judgment; the command gives light to the mind's eye, teaching what constitutes service to the God of all. While piety and the fear of God, in suggesting observance of these, procure enjoyment of the eternal good, it was right for him to speak of the fear of God as pure—that is, free from blame—for the reason that human fear is blameworthy, being synonymous with dread. Now, he called the decrees true and justified on account of their conferring on people both honors and warranted punishments. In conclusion, he said these are worth more than gold and precious stones and sweeter than honey—not to all human beings, however, but to those truly human, whose life is not comparable with the brute beasts. COMMENTARY ON THE PSALM 19.5-6.[48]

CORRESPONDING LAWS. DIODORE OF TARSUS: What the written law does by teaching its intentions to those with a knowledge of writing the law in nature does by teaching those with an understanding eye that there is a Creator of visible realities. COMMENTARY ON PSALMS 19.[49]

GRACE. AUGUSTINE: The law cannot be fulfilled except by spiritual persons, and there cannot be such save by grace. The more one is assimilated to the spiritual law, the more one attains to a spiritual disposition, and the more one fulfills the law. The more one delights in it, the less one is afflicted by its burdensomeness and the more one is quickened by its light. . . . When grace forgives sins and infuses a spirit of charity, righteousness ceases to be hard and becomes even pleasant. ON VARIOUS QEUSTIONS TO SIMPLICIAN 1.1.7.[50]

19:8 Right Precepts

THE WALK AND TALK OF GOD. CASSIODORUS: They are truly right, because he is known to have acted precisely as he taught, whereas those whose actions differ from their words manifest no right justice. EXPLANATION OF THE PSALMS 19.9.[51]

19:9 Fear of the Lord

THE RIGHT FEAR. CASSIODORUS: The fear of God is not panicky consternation but untroubled commitment, the terms of which are changed by no transient alteration but continue to concentrate on it with the sincerity of a good conscience. Human fear changes with time and is not holy because it cannot be productive, whereas fear of God contains no disturbance. Though one rightly fears his Maker, he knows that the Judge is truly merciful to those who beseech him; so the person who is found both to fear and to love dwells in all holiness. Fear of the Lord is love mixed with apprehension; in secular contexts it is called reverence. EXPLANATION OF THE PSALMS 19.10.[52]

THE RIGHT EFFECT. CLEMENT OF ALEXANDRIA: Accordingly [this] is said [in the psalm] . . . For those who from fear turn to faith and righteousness remain forever. STROMATEIS 7.12.[53]

---

[48]FC 101:136-37. [49]WGRW 9:62. [50]LCC 6:379. [51]ACW 51:199. [52]ACW 51:200. [53]ANF 2:546.

ENDURING FEAR. AUGUSTINE: As for that fear that is holy, enduring forever, if it can exist in the world to come—and how else can we interpret "enduring forever"?—it will not be a fear deterring us from an evil that might befall us but a fear preserving us in a good that can never be lost. For in a state where love of possessed good is utterly unchangeable, there, if I may put it thus, fear of all evil will be perfectly at peace. What "holy fear" really means is a will so fixed that we shall necessarily refuse to sin and guard against it, not out of worry or weakness lest we fall, because our love is perfectly at peace. CITY OF GOD 14.9.[54]

19:10 To Be Desired

DESIRABLE LIGHT. CLEMENT OF ALEXANDRIA: "Sweet is the Word that gives us light, precious above gold and gems; it is to be desired above honey and the honeycomb." For how can it be other than desirable, since it has filled with light the mind that had been buried in darkness and given keenness to the "light-bringing eyes" of the soul? For just as, had the sun not been in existence, night would have brooded over the universe notwithstanding the other luminaries of heaven, so, had we not known the Word and been illuminated by him, we should have been nowise different from fowls that are being fed, fattened in darkness and nourished for death. Let us then admit the light that we may admit God; let us admit the light and become disciples to the Lord. EXHORTATION TO THE GREEKS 11.[55]

SWEET TO THE MIND. CASSIODORUS: Whereas honey and the comb sweeten only the palate, God's judgments bring total sweetness to people's minds. EXPLANATION OF THE PSALMS 19.11.[56]

A HEALTHY APPETITE. CHRYSOSTOM: [The words of God, the prophet says,] are "desirable above gold and a very precious stone, and sweeter than honey and the honeycomb," but they are so only to those in sound health. Therefore he added, "For your servant keeps them." And elsewhere again, after saying that they are sweet, he added, "to my palate." "How sweet to my palate," he says, "are your promises." And he goes on to insist on their excellence by the words "sweeter than honey and the honeycomb to my mouth,"[57] because he was in very sound health. Well, then, let us not on our part approach these words in ill health, but let us receive nourishment from them, after having restored our souls to health. HOMILIES ON THE GOSPEL OF JOHN 1.[58]

RENUNCIATION OF LESSER GOODS. BASIL THE GREAT: Renunciation [is] . . . the severance of the bonds of this material and transient life and freedom from human concerns, whereby we render ourselves more fit to set out on the road leading to God. It is the unhindered impulse toward the possession and enjoyment of inestimable goods, "more to be desired than gold and many precious stones." In short, it is the transference of the human heart to a heavenly mode of life, so that we can say, "But our conversation is in heaven."[59] Also—and this is the chief point—it is the first step toward the likeness to Christ, who, being rich, became poor for our sake.[60] Unless we attain to this likeness, it is impossible for us to achieve a way of life in accord with the gospel of Christ. THE LONG RULES, Q.8.[61]

19:11 Great Reward

SUFFERING CANNOT COMPARE. ARNOBIUS THE YOUNGER: In the guarding of the precepts of God there is so much reward, that "the sufferings of this time are not worth (comparing) to the future glory that will be revealed to us."[62] COMMENTARY ON THE PSALMS 19.[63]

19:12 Hidden Faults

---

[54]FC 14:371-72. [55]ANF 2:203. [56]ACW 51:201*. [57]Ps 119:103 (118:103 LXX). [58]FC 33:8-9*. [59]Phil 3:20. [60]2 Cor 8:9. [61]FC 9:256-57. [62]Rom 8:18. [63]CCL 25:25.

VOLUNTARY AND INVOLUNTARY SELF. DIO-
DORE OF TARSUS: Having given instruction in
regard to devotion, at this point he proceeds to
speak of the sins in respect of human beings and
puts people on the alert so as to realize what is
an involuntary sin and what voluntary, and how
they differ from each other, and further into
how many types involuntary sin is divided. He
employs an admirable division, first dividing sin
into two, voluntary and involuntary. After this
he divides the involuntary sin into three, since
for example we fall when compelled, or through
weakness or when mislead; or we do something
when an incident occurs that is more influential
than good intentions, or we prove too weak to
overcome the power of lust and fall into sin, or
in many cases we make a judgment with the
best of intentions but by some deception we are
inveigled into doing the opposite. COMMENTARY
ON PSALMS 19.[64]

ORIGINAL SIN. CASSIODORUS: Whereas human
errors transgress in three ways, by thought,
word and deed, he confines this boundless sea
of sins to brief compass and attests that it wells
forth from two sources. Secret sin is that termed
"original," in which we are conceived and born
and by which we sin with secret longing, as
when we desire our neighbor's property, or long
for vengeance on our enemies, or wish to become
more eminent than the rest, or seek more suc-
culent food or commit similar sins that sprout in
and steal on us in such a way that they seem hidden from many before they take effect. If they
do become obvious to anyone . . . we must yet
realize that there are many sins of which we are
wholly ignorant, whose sources and deceptions
we cannot realize. So in the phrase "Who can
understand sins?" we must additionally interpret
this as all sins. EXPLANATION OF THE PSALMS
19.13.[65]

EVIL THOUGHTS. JEROME: It is not my will
to conceive sin; I do not want to entertain bad
thoughts, and yet I do; I do not want to enter-

tain evil, and, like a captive against my will, I
am drawn into evil reflections. Because it is not
in my power either to think or not to think evil,
that is why I declare, "Surely they are wanton
sins that come into my heart," but since I cannot
seem to avoid them, I plead, "Cleanse me from
my unknown faults." Unprovoked they come, but
because I harbor them, I beg the Lord, "From
wanton sin especially restrain your servant."
Why am I saying all this? Because the prophet
said, "I shall please the Lord"; not "I please" but
"I shall please," for no matter how much I strive
here, I cannot be a perfect man, a just man.
Consequently, the apostle also says, "We know
in part, and we prophesy in part," and "We see
now through a mirror in an obscure manner."[66]
HOMILY ON PSALM 114[116A].[67]

COUNTLESS SMALL SINS. CAESARIUS OF ARLES:
Very often sins creep up on us through thoughts
or desires or speech or action, as the result of
necessity, through weakness or out of forgetfulness. If a person thinks only of serious sins and
strives to resist only these but has little or no care
about small sins, he incurs no less danger than if
he committed more serious offenses. Therefore
let us not think little of our sins because they are
slight, but let us fear them because they are many.
Drops of rain are small, but because they are
very many, they fill rivers and submerge houses,
and sometimes by their force they even carry off
mountains. Concerning these it is written: "He
who scorns little things will fall little by little";[68]
and again: "Who can detect failings?" Who
is there who guards his heart with such great
vigilance that no idle word ever proceeds from
his lips? However, an account must be rendered
for this on the day of judgment. Who is there
who does not lie? . . . Who is there from whose
mouth an evil word does not sometimes issue? . . .
Who could even count the sins that we consider
small or almost nonexistent, even though sacred

---

[64]WGRW 9:63. [65]ACW 51:201-2. [66]1 Cor 13:9, 12. [67]FC 48:291.
[68]Sir 19:1.

Scripture testifies that we are going to be severely punished for them? For this reason, with God's help and in accord with the text of Solomon, ["The just person falls seven times in a day and rises again,"[69]] let us keep our hearts with all watchfulness. SERMON 234.4.[70]

WARNING AGAINST BOASTING. AUGUSTINE: However great a person's righteousness may be, he ought to reflect and think, lest there should be found something blameworthy that has escaped indeed his own notice, when that righteous King shall sit on his throne, whose cognizance no sins can possibly escape, not even those of which it is said, "Who understands his transgressions?" "When, therefore, the righteous King shall sit on his throne, who will boast that he has a pure heart? Or who will boldly say that he is pure from sin?"[71] Except perhaps those who wish to boast of their own righteousness and not glory in the mercy of the Judge. ON THE PERFECTION OF HUMAN RIGHTEOUSNESS 14.33.[72]

BE CAREFUL. LEO THE GREAT: Although in any time there are many who lead an innocent life, and very many commend themselves to God by their habitual performance of good deeds, we should not however trust in the integrity of our conscience to such a point that we think that human weakness, living among scandals and temptations, can meet nothing that will harm it. The chief of prophets says, "Who will boast that they have pure hearts or that they are cleansed from sin?"[73] [Here in this psalm] he says, "From my hidden faults cleanse me, O Lord, and from dangerous ones spare your servant." SERMON 44.1.[74]

TESTING. AUGUSTINE: You must know then, dearly beloved, that God's testing is not aimed at his getting to know something he was ignorant of before but at bringing to light what was hidden in a person, by means of a test, which is a kind of interrogation. People are not as well known to themselves as they are to their Creator,

nor do the sick know themselves as well as the doctor does. A person is sick; he is suffering, the doctor is not suffering, and the patient is waiting to hear what he is suffering from from the one who is not suffering. That is why a man cries out in a psalm, "From my hidden ones cleanse me, O Lord." There are things in a person that are hidden from the person in whom they are. And they will not come out, or be opened up or discovered, except through tests and trials and temptations. If God stops testing, it means the master has stopped teaching. SERMON 2.3.[75]

BY THE SPIRIT. GREGORY OF NYSSA: So wicked and hard to cure and strong are those things possessed in the depths of our souls that it is not possible to rub them out and to remove them through human efforts and virtue alone unless through prayer we take the power of the Spirit as an ally and, in this way, conquer the evil that is playing the tyrant within us, as the Spirit teaches us through the voice of David: "Cleanse me from my unknown faults." ON THE CHRISTIAN MODE OF LIFE.[76]

19:14 My Rock and Redeemer

THREE PARTS TO THE PSALM. THEODORET OF CYR: [The psalm] instructs us first on creation and providence; in the middle, on the Law; and finally, on grace. COMMENTARY ON THE PSALMS 19.9.[77]

GRACE. CASSIODORUS: He calls God his helper in goodly things and his redeemer from evil ones, so that none may attribute to his own merits what he has obtained from the generosity of heaven. EXPOSITIONS OF THE PSALMS 19.15.[78]

JEROME: The third division is one of praise that teaches the impossibility of the Law, and

---

[69]Prov 24:16. [70]FC 66:203. [71]Prov 20:8-9. [72]NPNF 1 5:171*. [73]Prov 20:9. [74]FC 93:190. [75]WSA 3 1:177-78*. [76]FC 58:137. [77]FC 101:138*. [78]ACW 51:203.

since through transgressing it more sin had appeared in the world, the grace of the gospel has been made complete; nor is anyone able to be freed from the filthiness of his thinking except

through the advent of the Holy Spirit. BRIEF COMMENTARY ON PSALMS 19.[79]

[79]CCL 72:196.

20:1-9 PRAYER FOR VICTORY

When you see others in affliction,
comch them by praying with them in the words of Psalm 20.
ATHANASIUS ON THE INTERPRETATION OF THE PSALMS 17 [OIP 67]

To the choirmaster. A Psalm of David.

[1]*The LORD answer you in the day of trouble!*
  The name of the God of Jacob protect you!
[2]*May he send you help from the sanctuary,*
  and give you support from Zion!
[3]*May he remember all your offerings,*
  and regard with favor your burnt
    sacrifices!   Selah

[4]*May he grant you your heart's desire,*
  and fulfil all your plans!
[5]*May we shout for joy over your victory,*
  and in the name of our God set up our
    banners!

May the LORD fulfil all your petitions!

[6]*Now I know that the LORD will help his*
    anointed;
  he will answer him from his holy heaven
  with mighty victories by his right hand.
[7]*Some boast of chariots, and some of horses;*
  but we boast of the name of the LORD our
    God.
[8]*They will collapse and fall;*
  but we shall rise and stand upright.

[9]*Give victory to the king, O LORD;*
  answer us when we call.[1]

l Gk: Heb *give victory, O LORD, let the King answer us when we call*

OVERVIEW: The twentieth psalm is taken to be a prayer through Christ to God (EUSEBIUS). It begins with a plea from clean hearts (CASSIODORUS). Our memory is stirred by our appeal to God's memory (AUGUSTINE), and we align our minds with the intention of Christ (AUGUSTINE). His victory, then, becomes our victory (AUGUS-

TINE), and made righteous in him, we rejoice in the salvation of God (EVAGRIUS). We continue in ongoing intercession (AUGUSTINE), raised to the mountain of God by a humble heart (AUGUSTINE). We are empowered by his salvation (CASSIODORUS), because of our chosen object of trust (THEODORET). And so, we see greater triumphs than those commonly recognized (CASSIODO-RUS). Others will fall in the trap of desire, the pit of death (CASSIODORUS), but we shall rise by grace (CASSIODORUS). Our victory comes when the Savior returns (EUSEBIUS). We rise because he has risen (ARNOBIUS THE YOUNGER). Our prayer is heard in Christ (AUGUSTINE).

20:1 May God Answer You

A PRAYER THROUGH CHRIST. EUSEBIUS OF CAESAREA: This entire psalm voices a prayer as spoken by holy people to the person of Christ. For since for our sakes and on our behalf he received insult when he became man, we are taught to join our prayers with his as he prays and supplicates the Father on our behalf, as one who repels both visible and invisible attacks against us. PROOF OF THE GOSPEL 4.16.5.[1]

A PLEA OF CLEAN HEARTS. CASSIODORUS: By saying "in the day of tribulation," he denotes the time of greatest affliction in which we beg the Lord with great longing. We do not pay lip service but rather beg from clean hearts for what we ask to be granted us in those circumstances. EXPLANATION OF THE PSALMS 20.2[2]

20:3 May God Remember

GOD'S MEMORY, OUR MEMORY. AUGUSTINE: "May he remember all you sacrificed" and make us mindful of all the tortures and insults you bore for our sake . . . may he turn into resurrection joy that cross on which you were offered up in your entirety to God. EXPOSITIONS OF THE PSALMS 20.4.[3]

20:4 Fulfilling All Your Plans

THE INTENTION OF CHRIST. AUGUSTINE: Yes, may he fulfill not only your intention to lay down your life for your friends, so that the seed, by dying, might spring again more abundantly, but also your intention that . . . the entry of the

whole Gentile world should be facilitated. EXPOSITIONS OF THE PSALMS 20.5.[4]

20:5 Joy for Victory

GOD'S VICTORY, OUR VICTORY. AUGUSTINE: "We shall rejoice in your salvation," rejoice that death will not harm you, for so you will show us that it will not harm us either. EXPOSITIONS OF THE PSALMS 20.6.[5]

OBJECTS OF JOY. EVAGRIUS OF PONTUS: People rejoice in riches, or in glory or in nobility of birth, but the righteous in the salvation of God. NOTES ON THE PSALMS.[6]

ONGOING INTERCESSION. AUGUSTINE: "May the Lord grant all your requests"—all of them, not only the petitions you offered on earth but those also by which you intercede for us in heaven. EXPOSITIONS OF THE PSALMS 20.7.[7]

20:6 God Answers from Heaven

HUMBLE HEART. AUGUSTINE: Sometimes people run off to a mountain to pray, as though God will be able to hear them better from there. Do you want to make contact with God in your prayer? Humble yourself. But again, just because I have said, "Do you want to make contact with God? Humble yourself," do not take it literally and materialistically and go off down to underground vaults and there start beseeching God. Do not go seeking either caverns or mountains. Have lowliness in your heart, and God will give you all the high altitude you want. He will come to you and be with you in your bedroom. SERMON 45.7.[8]

SALVATION POWER. CASSIODORUS: The salvation established by the Son is recognized as our power, for that salvation is neither weakened

---

[1]POG 1:205*. [2]ACW 51:204. [3]WSA 3 15:215. [4]WSA 3 15:215. [5]WSA 3 15:216. [6]PG 12:1247. [7]WSA 3 15:216. [8]WSA 3 2:256.

by diseases nor wounded by pains, but it makes us powerful by guarding us with its everlasting existence. EXPLANATION OF THE PSALMS 20.6-7.[9]

20:7 Boasting of God's Name

OBJECTS OF TRUST. THEODORET OF CYR: They trusted in horses and chariots, he is saying, and enjoyed no benefit from them but were caught up in unseen entanglements and collapsed. We, by contrast, invoked divine assistance, and won salvation in visible manner and emerged superior to the adversaries. COMMENTARY ON THE PSALMS 20.4.[10]

GREATER TRIUMPHS. CASSIODORUS: There were two types of triumph among the ancients: one was the greater, celebrated in chariots and called a laureled triumph, the other, the lesser, called an ovation. But the psalmist leaves such things to worldly people and maintains that he has been exalted in the Lord's name. It is not chariots or the horse that exalt, though they are seen to glorify with distinctions in this world, but the Lord's name that in the end leads to eternal rewards. EXPLANATION OF THE PSALMS 20.8.[11]

20:8 They Shall Fall

THE PIT OF DEATH. CASSIODORUS: Those who trust in human distinctions have been caught in the noose of their base desires and have fallen into the pit of death. EXPLANATION OF THE PSALMS 20.9.[12]

WE RISE BY GRACE. CASSIODORUS: A Christian is said to rise again in two senses; first, when in this world he is freed by grace from the death of vices and is justified by God. . . . Second, there is the general resurrection, at which the just will attain their eternal rewards. Here both meanings are clearly appropriate, and he used the words "we are set upright," because in any resurrection the faithful rise from humility and are exalted to divine rewards. EXPLANATION OF THE PSALMS 20.9.[13]

THE FUTURE RISE AND FALL. EUSEBIUS OF CAESAREA: They say these things will happen in the time of the advent of that Savior. Then all the powers of the adversaries and those hidden and secret enemies of God who have turned their backs on the Savior will be laid low. All who receive that Savior will rise from the first fall. Therefore, Simeon says, "Behold, this child is destined to cause the rising and falling of many,"[14] namely, the ruin of his enemies and adversaries and the resurrection of those who, having fallen once, have been rescued by him. COMMENTARY ON PSALMS 20.8-10.[15]

WE RISE BECAUSE HE IS RISEN. ARNOBIUS THE YOUNGER: We will rise upright as others are collapsing, because our King is saved, and arising from the dead he ascends into the heavens, and as he sits on the right hand of God the Father he hears us in the day we call him. To him be glory forever. Amen. COMMENTARY ON THE PSALMS 20.[16]

20:9 Answer When We Call

HEAR US IN CHRIST. AUGUSTINE: "And hear us on the day we call on you." As Christ now offers sacrifice on our behalf, hear us on the day we call on you. EXPOSITIONS OF THE PSALMS 20.10.[17]

---

[9]ACW 51:206. [10]FC 101:140. [11]ACW 51:207. [12]ACW 51:207. [13]ACW 51:207*. [14]Lk 2:34. [15]PG 23:197. [16]CCL 25:26. [17]WSA 3 15:217*.

21:1-13 THANKSGIVING FOR VICTORY

Psalm 21 reveals Christ's kingdom, and the power of his judgment,
and his coming again in the flesh to us and the summoning of the nations.

ATHANASIUS ON THE INTERPRETATION OF THE PSALMS 26 [OIP 72]

To the choirmaster. A Psalm of David.

¹*In thy strength the king rejoices, O LORD;*
and in thy help how greatly he exults!
²*Thou hast given him his heart's desire,*
and hast not withheld the request of
his lips. Selah
³*For thou dost meet him with goodly blessings;*
thou dost set a crown of fine gold upon his
head.
⁴*He asked life of thee; thou gavest it to him,*
length of days for ever and ever.
⁵*His glory is great through thy help;*
splendor and majesty thou dost bestow upon
him.
⁶*Yea, thou dost make him most blessed for*
ever;
thou dost make him glad with the joy of thy
presence.
⁷*For the king trusts in the LORD;*
and through the steadfast love of the Most

High he shall not be moved.

⁸*Your hand will find out all your enemies;*
your right hand will find out those who hate
you.
⁹*You will make them as a blazing oven*
when you appear.
The LORD will swallow them up in his wrath;
and fire will consume them.
¹⁰*You will destroy their offspring from the*
earth,
and their children from among the sons of
men.
¹¹*If they plan evil against you,*
if they devise mischief, they will not
succeed.
¹²*For you will put them to flight;*
you will aim at their faces with your bows.

¹³*Be exalted, O LORD, in thy strength!*
We will sing and praise thy power.

OVERVIEW: The twenty-first psalm speaks of a salvation yet to come (PSEUDO-ATHANASIUS) and puts before us the divine and human aspects of Christ (CASSIODORUS). David begins the psalm by rejoicing in the Lord (EUSEBIUS). Hope is birthed in mercy (EUSEBIUS), and Christ's desires are granted by his Father (AUGUSTINE). The crown of the Lord is the church (JEROME), and the Lord is the crown of reason (EVAGRIUS). Through him, we receive the crown of grace (AUGUSTINE, CASSIODORUS). Christ prayed not

only for himself but also for the church (AUGUSTINE), and his prayer was answered (ARNOBIUS THE YOUNGER). We receive eternal life as a gift of grace (IRENAEUS). Our salvation is his glory (ARNOBIUS THE YOUNGER), his blessing forever (AUGUSTINE)—a blessing in response to his faith (ARNOBIUS THE YOUNGER).

The psalm then turns to the judgment of Christ (ARNOBIUS THE YOUNGER). But we are reminded that enemies may yet be converted (CASSIODORUS). The unsaved face a fire within and without (AUGUSTINE), the punishment of hell (CASSIODORUS). Their words, teachings and writings will be destroyed (EUSEBIUS). The plot against Christ failed (CASSIODORUS). Sinners are turned away from, even as the saved are turned to, Christ (AMBROSE). The exaltation of Christ is revealed (THEODORET, DIODORE) and proclaimed by our words and deeds (CASSIODORUS).

21:1 The King Rejoices

FOR SALVATION YET TO COME. PSEUDO-ATHANASIUS: Friends of David also delivered this psalm, as if he were now pleased for the salvation that was born from his seed for the world; this was a glorious crown for him, and length of days and glory and magnificence, and delight and joy and hope and unshakeable grace. EXPOSITION ON PSALMS 21.[1]

DIVINE AND HUMAN ASPECTS OF CHRIST. CASSIODORUS: Our belief that is conducive to salvation is that there are two natures, divine and human, in Jesus Christ, and they continue in one person unchangeably for ages without end. This statement should be repeated frequently, because regularly hearing and believing it brings life.... In the initial narrative of this psalm the prophet's words are addressed to God the Father concerning the Lord's incarnation. The second describes his various virtues and glory, beginning with his suffering and continuing to the point at which by his own gift he attained the dominion and peak of all things. In the third, the prophet also turns to the Lord Christ, and here like those who yearn he prays that what he knows is to come will take place at the judgment. EXPLANATION OF THE PSALMS 21.1.[2]

DAVID REJOICED IN THE LORD. EUSEBIUS OF CAESAREA: I think that these words had been prophesied by those who had spoken long before David. Since David had learned from the lofty oracles that those words were looking not only at the strength of his own salvation but also that

which was going to come forth from his seed, concerning which he said he would rejoice and praise with enthusiasm. Having been assured of those things and the enemies having been thoroughly subjugated with mighty power, to you, God, the author of the victory, he grants the prize of his victory. And he rejoices and praises as he is snatched from the snares of the enemies, nor does he rejoice so much in his own deliverance as in that salvation sent from you. As he seeks your deliverance with lofty vows from his own lips, he will entreat you often for the advent of his deliverance; his prayer frequently uttered, he never fails in hope, nor will his request be in vain. COMMENTARY ON PSALMS 21.2.[3]

21:2 Heart's Desires

HOPE BIRTHED IN MERCY. EUSEBIUS OF CAESAREA: Having prophesied the promises made earlier to David, he then explains the reason why these things are going to happen. For what is that reason unless hope in God in which the one who has received mercy does not falter and in that very hope granted by God most high he does not waver from a firm and steady foundation? COMMENTARY ON PSALMS 21.3-7.[4]

CHRIST'S DESIRE GRANTED BY THE FATHER. AUGUSTINE: He longed to eat the Passover, to lay down his life when he willed and to take it up again when he willed; and all these you have granted to him. EXPOSITIONS OF THE PSALMS 21.3.[5]

21:3 A Crown of Gold

THE CROWN OF THE LORD. JEROME: The crown of the Lord is the church gathered from the various nations, about which Paul in the person of the believers says, "My joy and my crown."[6] BRIEF COMMENTARY ON PSALMS 21.[7]

---

[1]CSCO 387:14. [2]ACW 51:208-9. [3]PG 23:197, 200. [4]PG 23:200. [5]WSA 3 15:218. [6]Phil 4:1. [7]CCL 72:197.

THE CROWN OF REASON. EVAGRIUS OF PONTUS: Christ is the crown of the rational nature. NOTES ON THE PSALMS.[8]

THE CROWN OF GRACE. AUGUSTINE: And what is here more fitly understood than that very desire of good of which we are speaking? For good begins then to be longed for when it has begun to grow sweet. But when good is done by fear of penalty, not by the love of righteousness, good is not yet well done. Nor is that done in the heart that seems to be done in the act, when a person would rather not do it if he could evade it with impunity. Therefore the "blessing of sweetness" is God's grace, by which is caused in us that what he prescribes to us delights us, and we desire it—that is, we love it; in which if God does not precede us, not only is it not perfected but it is not even begun, from us. For if without him we are able to do nothing, we are able neither to begin nor to perfect, because to begin, it is said, "His mercy shall prevent me";[9] to finish, it is said, "His mercy shall follow me."[10] AGAINST TWO LETTERS OF THE PELAGIANS 2.21.[11]

ADORNED WITH GOD'S GRACE. CASSIODORUS: Humanity is ever adorned by the anticipatory grace of the Godhead, since no one offers God anything first. All that is good has been granted to us by the kindness of heaven. EXPLANATION OF THE PSALMS 21.4.[12]

21:4 Asking Life from God

HE PRAYED FOR HIMSELF AND THE CHURCH. AUGUSTINE: He prayed for his resurrection . . . and you answered his prayer. . . . Long endurance for the church he asked, throughout this present age, and then eternity for evermore. EXPOSITIONS OF THE PSALMS 21.5.[13]

CHRIST'S PRAYER ANSWERED. ARNOBIUS THE YOUNGER: He sought life; he lived as a man. Having been limited in life, in death he received length of days not just to old age but to eternity.

COMMENTARY ON PSALMS 21.[14]

A GIFT OF GRACE. IRENAEUS: It is the Father of all who imparts continuance forever and ever on those who are saved. For life does not arise from us nor from our own nature, but it is bestowed according to the grace of God. AGAINST HERESIES 2.34.3.[15]

21:5 Great Glory

SALVATION, THE GLORY. ARNOBIUS THE YOUNGER: Great is his glory. In what way is it great? Not in the assumption of deity but in the salvation of humanity. COMMENTARY ON THE PSALMS 21.[16]

21:6 Blessed Forever

THE BLESSING GIVEN TO CHRIST. AUGUSTINE: This is the blessing that you will give him forever and ever . . . with the vision of your face you will delight his human nature, which he has lifted up to you. EXPOSITIONS OF THE PSALMS 21.7.[17]

21:7 The King Trusts in the Lord

A BLESSED FAITH. ARNOBIUS THE YOUNGER: For that reason you placed glory and great honor on him, and you gave him eternal blessing, because he hoped in the Lord and in his mercy he was not deeply disturbed. COMMENTARY ON PSALMS 21.[18]

21:8 Finding Out All Enemies

THE JUDGMENT OF CHRIST. ARNOBIUS THE YOUNGER: From the place [of exaltation] the Father says to his Son, "Let your hand be found by all your enemies; let your right, which

[8]PG 12:1249. [9]Ps 59:10. [10]Ps 23:6. [11]NPNF 1 5:401*. [12]ACW 51:210*. [13]WSA 3 15:218. [14]CCL 25:27. [15]ANF 1:411. [16]CCL 25:27*. [17]WSA 3 15:219. [18]CCL 25:27.

received the nails on the cross, find those who hated you; discard them as earthen vessels in a fire in the time of your appearance. Then in your wrath you will throw them into disorder, and the fire will devour them." Commentary on the Psalms 21.[19]

Enemies May Be Converted. Cassiodorus: These people are called enemies only so long as they are beguiled by the enticements of the devil. Once they return to the Lord Christ, they are called servants, children and friends. Explanations of the Psalms 21.9.[20]

21:9 Fire Will Consume Them

A Fire Within and Without. Augustine: You will set them on fire within, as consciousness of their impiety burns them. After being convicted by their own consciences and thrown into confusion by the Lord's vengeance, they will be given over to eternal fire to be devoured. Expositions of the Psalms 21.10.[21]

The Punishment of Hell. Cassiodorus: An oven is a fashioned vessel of bronze, circular in shape, for baking loaves. . . . Sinners are aptly compared with it, for at the judgment to come they will be tortured with both mental grief and the pain of punishment, for having lived in opposition to the Lord's laws with unbending minds. The time of the Lord's anger is the day of judgment when the Son of man will be visible to all, but only the just look on him by contemplation of his divinity. . . . Earlier the psalmist in praising the Lord Christ . . . described the Lord's distinction and glory in the diverse nature of graces. Now . . . he says that the Lord's enemies will be afflicted by various punishments, so they were to be rendered as grisly as he was to be made marvelous. . . . The sentence they will receive is to be devoured by undying flames. No delay ensues at the Lord's command; his decision is no sooner made than it is carried out. Explanation of the Psalms 21.10.[22]

21:10 Their Offspring Destroyed

Words, Teachings, Writings. Eusebius of Caesarea: But the seed of the godless and the fruit of the wicked are their words, teachings and unrighteous writings, which they have disseminated through people after they are forgotten. God, being good, scatters each one and destroys them from the midst so that neither the fruit nor the seed of the wicked remains. Commentary on Psalms 21.11.[23]

21:11 They Will Not Succeed

Failure of the Plot Against Christ. Cassiodorus: We use the verb *divert* to express the idea of repelling evils that threaten some group onto a different company innocent of any wickedness that might merit such a fate. This clearly happened in the case of the Lord's passion, for since the Jews believed that the Roman Empire would encompass their destruction if they accepted the Lord Savior as King, they are seen to have diverted on him the evils that they thought would befall themselves from Roman vengeance. "They devised a plan" with the words, "It is expedient that one man should die for all."[24] "Which they were unable to establish": in other words, to complete their design. All unknowingly they spoke the truth; it was necessary that one man should die for all. The words were true, but they were uttered with evil aspirations, and so they will suffer punishment for such a deed because their consciences were not pure. Explanation of the Psalms 21.12.[25]

21:12 Put to Flight

Sinners, Not the Saved. Ambrose: "Turned away" [is] an expression properly applied to the sinner, for "Cain went out from the face of the Lord,"[26] and the psalmist says, "You will make

---

[19]CCL 25:27. [20]ACW 51:212. [21]WSA 3 15:219. [22]ACW 51:212-13. [23]PG 23:201. [24]Cf. Jn 11:50. [25]ACW 51:213*. [26]Gen 4:16.

them turn their back." One who is righteous does not turn away from the Lord but runs to meet him and says, "My eyes are ever toward the Lord."[27] And when the Lord said, "Whom shall I send?" Isaiah offered himself of his own accord and said, "Behold, here I am."[28] JOSEPH 3.9.[29]

21:13 Be Exalted, O Lord

THE REVELATION OF EXALTATION. THEODORET OF CYR: Not for being lowly is God exalted, nor does he receive what he does not possess; instead, what he possesses he reveals . . . your exaltation is revealed in your ineffable power, which we shall continue to celebrate and sing, recounting your marvelous works. COMMENTARY ON THE PSALMS 21.8.[30]

EXALTED. DIODORE OF TARSUS: Exalted though

you are, then, you are shown to be more exalted through your power and in outdoing all the arrogant, as by inflicting the blow on them from on high. For this reason we shall not cease singing your praises always. COMMENTARY ON PSALMS 21.[31]

WORDS AND DEEDS. CASSIODORUS: Singing entails uttering the Lord's words with the lips, and praising means fulfilling with constancy the divine commands by good works. These are the two things demanded of us in every way: faithfully to sing the Lord's praises with our lips and to carry out his commands by our deeds. EXPLANATION OF THE PSALMS 21.14.[32]

---

[27]Ps 25:15 (24:15 LXX). [28]Is 6:8. [29]FC 65:193*. [30]FC 101:144. [31]WGRW 9:69. [32]ACW 51:214.

22:1-31 LAMENT IN SUFFERING

In Psalm 22 he speaks in the person of the Savior
about the manner of his death. . . . The psalmist places all these teachings
in front of us because the Lord suffered all this
not on his own account but for us.

ATHANASIUS *ON THE INTERPRETATION OF THE PSALMS* 7 [OIP 59]

To the choirmaster: according to *The Hind of the Dawn. A Psalm of David.*

[1]*My God, my God, why hast thou forsaken me?*
  Why art thou so far from helping me, from the words of my groaning?
[2]*O my God, I cry by day, but thou dost not answer;*

and by night, but find no rest.

[3]*Yet thou art holy,*
  enthroned on the praises of Israel.
[4]*In thee our fathers trusted;*
  they trusted, and thou didst deliver them.
[5]*To thee they cried, and were saved;*
  in thee they trusted, and were not disappointed.

[6]*But I am a worm, and no man;*
scorned by men, and despised by the people.
[7]*All who see me mock at me,*
they make mouths at me, they wag their heads;
[8]*"He committed his cause to the LORD; let him deliver him,*
let him rescue him, for he delights in him!"

[9]*Yet thou art he who took me from the womb;*
thou didst keep me safe upon my mother's breasts.
[10]*Upon thee was I cast from my birth,*
and since my mother bore me thou hast been my God.
[11]*Be not far from me,*
for trouble is near
and there is none to help.

[12]*Many bulls encompass me,*
strong bulls of Bashan surround me;
[13]*they open wide their mouths at me,*
like a ravening and roaring lion.

[14]*I am poured out like water,*
and all my bones are out of joint;
my heart is like wax,
it is melted within my breast;
[15]*my strength is dried up like a potsherd,*
and my tongue cleaves to my jaws;
thou dost lay me in the dust of death.

[16]*Yea, dogs are round about me;*
a company of evildoers encircle me;
they have pierced[m] *my hands and feet—*
[17]*I can count all my bones—*
they stare and gloat over me;
[18]*they divide my garments among them,*
and for my raiment they cast lots.

[19]*But thou, O LORD, be not far off!*
O thou my help, hasten to my aid!
[20]*Deliver my soul from the sword,*
my life[n] *from the power of the dog!*
[21]*Save me from the mouth of the lion,*
my afflicted soul[o] *from the horns of the wild oxen!*

[22]*I will tell of thy name to my brethren;*
in the midst of the congregation I will praise thee:
[23]*You who fear the LORD, praise him!*
all you sons of Jacob, glorify him,
and stand in awe of him, all you sons of Israel!
[24]*For he has not despised or abhorred*
the affliction of the afflicted;
and he has not hid his face from him,
but has heard, when he cried to him.

[25]*From thee comes my praise in the great congregation;*
my vows I will pay before those who fear him.
[26]*The afflicted*[p] *shall eat and be satisfied;*
those who seek him shall praise the LORD!
May your hearts live for ever!

[27]*All the ends of the earth shall remember*
and turn to the LORD;
and all the families of the nations
shall worship before him.[q]
[28]*For dominion belongs to the LORD,*
and he rules over the nations.

[29]*Yea, to him*[r] *shall all the proud of the earth bow down;*
before him shall bow all who go down to the dust,
and he who cannot keep himself alive.
[30]*Posterity shall serve him;*
men shall tell of the Lord to the coming generation,
[31]*and proclaim his deliverance to a people yet unborn,*
that he has wrought it.

m Gk Syr Jerome: Heb *like a lion* **n** Heb *my only one* **o** Gk Syr: Heb *thou hast answered me* **p** Or *poor* **q** Gk Syr Jerome: Heb *thee* **r** Cn: Heb *they have eaten and*

OVERVIEW: The superscription of the twenty-second psalm speaks of the dawn, the end of shadowy gloom (MAXIMUS OF TURIN), the time of salvation (JEROME). This psalm is recited at the paschal service (CASSIODORUS). By a prophetic locution, it opens to us the plan of God (LEO), prophesying to us about Christ (EUSEBIUS). In it Christ speaks for our sakes (PSEUDO-ATHANASIUS). In it we see our old selves crucified with him (AUGUSTINE).

The psalm opens presenting to us the Son of God who suffered according to the flesh (CYRIL OF ALEXANDRIA, AMBROSE). He was forsaken as our representative (GREGORY OF NAZIANZUS, EUSEBIUS, THEODORET). His cry was heard at the proper time (EUSEBIUS). God's faithfulness was known from the examples of the ancestors (AUGUSTINE) who trusted in God rather than themselves (AUGUSTINE). Christ exemplifies that trust. For our sakes (AMBROSE), our great God also became small (AUGUSTINE). The language here may refer to his unique generation (EPHREM) or to his lowliness (THEODORET). Even now, many treat him in a lowly manner (EUSEBIUS). But he took on our weakness (CYRIL OF ALEXANDRIA) and gave us an example of humility (CLEMENT OF ROME) in words that constitute a clear gospel text (CASSIODORUS). Speaking as man (AMBROSE), he appeals to God's providence (DIODORE). Like his Father, he would also become the helper of the helpless (EUSEBIUS).

The psalm then speaks explicitly of the sufferings of the cross. It describes the audacity and frenzy of Christ's enemies (THEODORET). It turns to the disjointed condition of his bones, which will experience a future reunion, in his case and in ours (ORIGEN). We hear of great distress (DIODORE), a great suffering that only made him stronger (ARNOBIUS THE YOUNGER). It was a Lion that laid down in the dust (CYRIL OF JERUSALEM). Around him, children turned into dogs (THEODORET), bad dogs at that (EUSEBIUS). The whole scene was foul, a foulness from which beauty would come (AUGUSTINE). He was subjected to hardened stares (CASSIODORUS), blank stares (AUGUSTINE). The prophecy gives even the details of how his garments would be divided (CHRYSOSTOM), showing that the future is present to God (AMBROSE) and symbolizing as well how heretics and enemies of Christ would divide up the Scriptures (MAXIMUS, EUSEBIUS).

The prayer for deliverance of his soul extends to the whole body of Christ (AUGUSTINE). He speaks to us as a brother by grace (AMBROSE), of a hymn (EUSEBIUS), a sweet praise fitting for those who fear the Lord (CASSIODORUS), for those who receive a gracious hearing (BEDE)—a praise that comes from God (AUGUSTINE). The truly poor are blessed (CASSIODORUS) with a wonderful gift of life from God (CLEMENT OF ALEXANDRIA), a gift that reaches the whole world (THEODORET). For it is not the proud who will rule (AUGUSTINE). All nations (EUSEBIUS) will be his kingdoms (CASSIODORUS). Illustrious teachers (BEDE) will proclaim him, the justice of the Father (CASSIODORUS). Christ, and Christ alone, is truly presented to us in this psalm (THEODORET).

Superscription: *According to the Hind of the Dawn*

END OF SHADOWY GLOOM. MAXIMUS OF TURIN: The rising of the dawn always precedes the rising of the sun, and before the sun's clear brightness casts its light on the earth, dawn puts an end to the darkness of the night. Gradually, when the shadowy gloom has been driven away, a certain form and light is bestowed on all things. And although the world had lain in confusion, as if under one cover of darkness, with the arrival of the dawn different things take shape in the variety of their forms. That is to say, that although all things had been blind, now the eyes of all are restored. For night, so to speak, removes the world's eyes and dawn restores them. SERMON 29.1.[1]

---

[1]ACW 50:70.

SALVATION AT DAWN. JEROME: At daybreak on the third day we were filled with your kindness when your Son rose from the dead. In the evening, he descended for our sake into the shadows of death to draw us forth at daybreak. Accordingly, at that hour of dawn, we experienced the fullness of your kindness. It is in this sense that Psalm 22 is entitled "For the protection at dawn." Your kindness has always been manifest to your faithful servants, but never has it been so clear and lavish, as when the Redeemer of all rose from the dead for the salvation of each and every one. HOMILY ON PSALM 89[90].[2]

PASCHAL PSALM. CASSIODORUS: This is the psalm that the church solemnly chants at the paschal service. . . . This psalm alone ought to have been enough to inspire belief in the passion that Truth so obviously claimed about himself. EXPLANATION OF THE PSALMS 22.32.[3]

PROPHETIC LOCUTION. LEO THE GREAT: What human ears did not yet know as about to be done, the Holy Spirit was announcing as accomplished. King David, whose offspring Christ is according to human lineage,[4] preceded the day of the Lord's crucifixion by more than eleven hundred years. He had suffered none of these tortures that he mentions as having been inflicted on himself. Because the Lord—who was going to take the suffering flesh from David's stock—spoke through his mouth, the history of the crucifixion has rightly been prefigured in the person of David. David bore in himself the bodily origin of the Savior. Truly David suffered in Christ, because Jesus was truly crucified in the flesh of David. All the things, therefore, that the wickedness of Jews inflicted on the "Lord of Majesty"[5] had been fully predicted. Prophetic locution was interwoven not so much concerning future things as concerning those past. What else, then, did these things open up to us except the unchanging order of God's eternal plan? With God, things that are going to be discerned have already been decided, and future things

have already been accomplished. SERMON 67.1-2.[6]

A PROPHECY OF CHRIST. EUSEBIUS OF CAESAREA: The psalm refers to Christ and no one else, for its contents harmonize with none other but him. . . . But if any one would apply them to some other person, whether king, prophet or other godly man among the Jews, let him prove if he can how what is written is in harmony with him. For who of those who were ever born of women has attained such heights of virtue and power, as to embrace the knowledge of God with unchanging reason, with unruffled soul and with sober mind, and to fasten all his trust on God, so as to say, "You are he that took me out of my mother's womb, my hope from my mother's breasts. I was cast on you from my mother; from my mother's womb you are my God." And who that has ever been so cared for by God has also become "a reproach of people" and "the outcast of the people"? By what bulls and calves can we suppose such a man to have been surrounded? And in what suffering was he "poured out like water"? How were "all his bones loosened"? How was "he brought into the dust of death," and being brought into the dust of death how does he say those words still and live and speak? Who are "the dogs" that surround him, that are other than the beforenamed "bulls and calves"? What gathering of evil people pierced his feet as well as his hands, stripped him of his raiment, divided some of it among themselves and cast lots for the remainder? What was the sword, the dog and the lion? . . . And how . . . after being brought into the dust of death, can he promise to proclaim his Father's name, not to all, but only to his brothers? Who are the brothers, and what church is it of which this sufferer says, "In the midst of the church I will hymn you," adding, not the one Jewish nation but "all the earth shall understand, and turn to the Lord, and all the kindreds of the nations shall worship before him"? It is for you yourself to test every

---

[2]FC 57:81**. [3]ACW 51:234*. [4]Rom 1:3. [5]1 Cor 2:8. [6]FC 93:291.

expression in the psalm and see if it is possible to apply them to any chance character. You will find them only applicable to our Savior, who is most true and most to be trusted and who applied the words of the psalm to himself, as the Evangelists bear witness. Proof of the Gospel 10.8.491-92.[7]

For Our Sakes. Pseudo-Athanasius: The psalm is sung by Christ as in the person of all humanity. It narrates what he endured from the Jews when he bore the cross for our sake. He asks that the Father turn his face to us, and remove from us sin and the curse and teach us to be humble-minded, just as he was humbled for our sake. And that from the womb and the breasts we cast ourselves onto God; and that when troubles are near, we may pray that he help us. Exposition on Psalms 22.[8]

Our Old Self. Augustine: The words of this psalm are spoken in the person of the crucified one. . . . He speaks consistently in the character of our old self, whose mortality he bore and that was nailed to the cross with him.[9] Expositions of the Psalms 22.1.[10]

22:1 My God, My God, Why Have You Forsaken Me?

According to the Flesh. Cyril of Alexandria: We confess that he, the Son begotten of God the Father and only-begotten God, though being incapable of suffering according to his own nature, suffered in his own flesh for our sake, according to the Scriptures. And he made his own the sufferings of his own flesh in his crucified body impassibly, for by the grace of God and for the sake of all he tasted death[11] by having surrendered to it his own body although by nature he was life and was himself the resurrection.[12] In order that by his ineffable power, after having trampled on death in his own flesh first, he might become "the firstborn from the dead"[13] and "the first fruits of those who have fallen

asleep"[14] and in order that he might prepare the way for the rise to immortality for the nature of people,[15] by the grace of God, as we said just now, for the sake of all he tasted death, but on the third day he came back to life after despoiling hell. Letter 17.11.[16]

He Suffers as Man. Ambrose: Seeing, then, that he took on himself a soul he also took the affections of a soul, for God could not have been distressed or have died in respect of his being God. . . . As being man, therefore, he speaks, bearing with him my terrors, for when we are in the midst of dangers we think ourself abandoned by God. As man, therefore, he is distressed, as man he weeps, as man he is crucified. On the Christian Faith 2.7.56.[17]

Our Representative. Gregory of Nazianzus: It was not he who was forsaken, either by the Father or by his own Godhead, as some have thought, as if it were afraid of the passion and therefore withdrew itself from him in his sufferings (for who compelled him either to be born on earth at all or to be lifted up on the cross?). But . . . he was in his own person representing us. For we were the forsaken and the despised, but now by the sufferings of him who could not suffer, we have been taken up and saved. Similarly, he makes his own our folly and our transgressions and says what follows in the psalm, for it is very evident that the twenty-second refers to Christ. On the Son, Theological Oration 4(30).5.[18]

Why Did the Father Forsake Him? Eusebius of Caesarea: It is to impel us to ask why the Father forsook him, that he says, "Why have you forsaken me?" The answer is, to ransom the whole human race, buying them with him precious blood from their former slavery to their invisible tyrants, the unclean demons and the

---

[7]POG 2:216-17*. [8]CSCO 387:14-15. [9]Rom 6:6. [10]WSA 3 15:221. [11]Heb 2:9. [12]Acts 4:2. [13]Col 1:18. [14]1 Cor 15:20. [15]1 Cor 15:53. [16]FC 76:85-86*. [17]NPNF 2 10:230. [18]NPNF 2 7:311.

rulers and spirits of evil. And the Father forsook him for another reason, namely, that the love of Christ himself for people might be set forth. For no one had power over his life, but he gave it willingly for people, as he teaches us himself in the words, "No one takes my life from me: I have power to lay it down, and I have power to take it again."[19] Proof of the Gospel 10.8.495-96.[20]

He Speaks for Us. Theodoret of Cyr: Just as the one who was a fount of righteousness assumed our sin, and the one who was an ocean of blessing accepted a curse lying on us and scorning shame endured a cross, so too he uttered the words on our behalf. Commentary on the Psalms 22.3.[21]

22:2 You Do Not Answer

The Proper Time. Eusebius of Caesarea: He is surely showing his surprise here that the Father does not hear him; he regards it as something strange and unusual. But the Father reserved his hearing until the fit time that he should be heard. That time was the hour of dawn, of the resurrection from the dead, when to him it could be more justly said than to any, "In a time accepted I heard you, and in a day of salvation I succored you. Behold, now is the accepted time; behold, now is the day of salvation."[22] Proof of the Gospel 10.8.496.[23]

22:4 Examples from the Past

The Son Hopes in His Father. Augustine: We know how many of our ancestors who hoped in God were rescued by him; we have read about them. . . . How could he fail with regard to his only Son and not hear him as he hung on the cross? Expositions of the Psalms 22.6.[24]

22:5 In You They Trusted

Not in Themselves. Augustine: They hoped in you, and their hope did not deceive them,

because they did not place it in themselves. Expositions of the Psalms 22.6.[25]

22:6 I Am a Worm

For Our Sakes. Ambrose: He became all these things so that he might dull the sting of our death, that he might take away our state of slavery, that he might wipe away our curses, sins and reproaches.[26] Letter 46.[27]

Our God. Augustine: Understand your God. That is what he is, this one so great and so small, "a worm and no man," and yet through him humankind was made. Sermon 380.2.[28]

His Unique Generation. Ephrem the Syrian: By the word *worm* did the Spirit foreshow him in a parable, because his generation was without marriage. Hymns on the Nativity 1.[29]

His Lowliness. Theodoret of Cyr: I am like a worm, he is saying, seen to be worthless and become a laughingstock. Now, some claimed that by "worm" is suggested also the birth from a virgin, as it is not by intercourse that it comes into existence; but I believe only lowliness is indicated here. Commentary on the Psalms 22.6.[30]

Even Now. Eusebius of Caesarea: Wonder not if this was said of and fulfilled by the passion of the Savior, for even now he is a reproach among all people who have not yet received faith in him! Proof of the Gospel 10.8.499.[31]

22:7 Seeing and Mocking

Our Weakness Became His Own. Cyril of Alexandria: Just as we say that the flesh became [the Word's] very own, in the same way

---

[19]Jn 10:18. [20]POG 2:221*. [21]FC 101:147. [22]2 Cor 6:2. [23]POG 2:222*. [24]WSA 3 15:231*. [25]WSA 3 15:222. [26]Cf. 1 Cor 15:55. [27]FC 26:138 (Letter 27 in this edition). [28]WSA 3 10:362*. [29]NPNF 2 13:223. [30]FC 101:148. [31]POG 2:224*.

the weakness of that flesh became his very own in an economic appropriation according to the terms of the unification. So, he is "made like his brothers in all things except sin alone."[32] Do not be astonished if we say that he has made the weakness of the flesh his own along with the flesh itself. He even attributed to himself those external outrages that came on him from the roughness of the Jews, saying through the voice of the psalmist: "They divided my garments among them and cast lots for my clothes,"[33] and again: "All those who saw me sneered at me, they wagged their tongues, they shook their heads." On the Unity of Christ.[34]

22:8 Committing His Cause to the Lord

The Lord's Example. Clement of Rome: You see, dear friends, the kind of example we have been given. And so, if the Lord humbled himself in this way, what should we do who through him have come under the yoke of his grace? 1 Clement 16.[35]

A Gospel Text. Cassiodorus: These words are in fact an exact Gospel text, for when Christ hung on the cross the Jews said, "He hoped in the Lord: let him deliver him, since he will have him."[36] How unchanging is the divine dispensation! We surely seem to be reviewing the Gospel here rather than a psalm, since these things were fulfilled so authentically that they seem already enacted rather than still to come. Explanation of the Psalms 22.9.[37]

22:10 You Have Been My God

Speaking as Man. Ambrose: He and the Father are One, and the Father is his Father by possession of the same nature. . . . Speaking as the Son, he called God his father, and afterward, speaking as man, named him as God. Everywhere, indeed, we have witness in the Scriptures to show that Christ, in naming God as his God, does so as man. "My God, my God, why have

you forsaken me? And again: "From my mother's womb you are my God." In the former place he suffers as a man; in the latter it is a man who is brought forth from his mother's womb. And so when he says, "From my mother's womb you are my God," he means that he who was always his father is his God from the moment when he was brought forth from his mother's womb. On the Christian Faith 1.14.91-92.[38]

22:11 None to Help

Appeal to Providence. Diodore of Tarsus: He did well to focus his attention on providence in general, asking . . . "Who is the one who shaped me in the womb, who is the one who brought me from the womb, who is the one who nourished me at maternal breasts and brought me to this stage of life?" Having anticipated my needs and provided me with such benefits when I contributed nothing, then, will you now cut me adrift when I both perceive your kindness and am able to give thanks? What, then? "Do not keep your distance from me, because tribulation is nigh, because there is no one to help me": as you provided all these benefits . . . therefore, now too, when they all advance against me with intrigues and you are the only one left for my salvation, lend help. Commentary on Psalms 22.[39]

Helper of the Helpless. Eusebius of Caesarea: It is surely the very climax of affliction to have no helper. For Christ went for the salvation of the souls in hades that had so long awaited his arrival. He went down to shatter the gates of brass, and to break the iron bonds and to let them go free that before were prisoners in hades, which was indeed done, when many bodies of the saints that slept arose and entered with him into the true holy city of God. Proof of the Gospel 10.8.501.[40]

---

[32]Heb 2:17. [33]Ps 22:18. [34]OUC 107*. [35]LCC 1:51-52. [36]Mt 27:43. [37]ACW 51:220-21. [38]NPNF 2 10:216*. [39]WGRW 9:71. [40]POG 2:226-27*.

22:12 Bulls Surround Me

AUDACITY AND FRENZY. THEODORET OF CYR:
The psalm describes in advance the attacks of
the chief priests, the scribes and the Pharisees,
who in imitation of the audacity of bulls and
the frenzy of lions hemmed in Christ the Lord.
COMMENTARY ON THE PSALMS 22.8.[41]

22:14-15 Distress and Death

A FUTURE REUNION. ORIGEN: [We know] that
even if . . . all the bones of Christ appear to be
scattered in persecutions and afflictions by the
plots of those who wage war against the unity of
the temple by persecutions, the temple will be
raised up and the body will arise on the third day.
COMMENTARY ON THE GOSPEL OF JOHN 10.229.[42]

GREAT DISTRESS. DIODORE OF TARSUS: He
mentions what is typical of people worried and
distressed: since all worry affects the heart, he
did well to add "my heart was melted like wax,"
my mind having no stability or composure or
sound hope; instead, under pressure from the
threats and depressing expectations my thoughts
dissolved like wax. Next, as happens also with
those in distress, "my strength was dried up like
a potsherd": all my condition left me, depression
reducing me to great dryness. COMMENTARY ON
PSALMS 22.[43]

MADE STRONGER. ARNOBIUS THE YOUNGER:
As much as his brokenness seems without cure,
so much more praiseworthy then is his recovery.
And, likewise, the more the work of the potter is
fired, the better and more solid will the work be
found. COMMENTARY ON THE PSALMS 22.[44]

LION IN THE DUST. CYRIL OF JERUSALEM: You
have often heard also the words of the psalm:
"To the dust of death you have brought me
down." Think also of the prophecy of Jacob in
the Scriptures: "He lay down and couched as
a lion, and as a lion's whelp; who will disturb

him?"[45] Similarly in Numbers: "Lying down he
has slept as a lion, and as a lion's whelp."[46] CAT-
ECHETICAL LECTURES 14.3.[47]

22:16 Encircled by Evildoers

DOGS AND SONS. THEODORET OF CYR: After
the passion those former "dogs" took on the
status of children through faith, whereas those
who once had enjoyed the care shown to children
received the name of dogs for raging against the
Lord. . . . Blessed Paul cries out about them,
"Beware of the dogs, beware of the evildoers.
Beware of mutilation."[48] COMMENTARY ON THE
PSALMS 22.10.[49]

THE DOGS WHO OPPOSE CHRIST. EUSEBIUS
OF CAESAREA: The dogs that surrounded him
and the council of the wicked were the rulers
of the Jews, the scribes and high priests and the
Pharisees, who spurred on the whole multitude
to demand his blood against themselves and
against their own children. Isaiah clearly calls
them dogs when he says, "You are all foolish
dogs, unable to bark."[50] For when it was their
duty, even if they could not acquire the character
of shepherds, to protect like good sheepdogs
their master's spiritual flock and the sheep of
the house of Israel, and to warn by barking, and
to fawn on their master and recognize him, and
to guard the flock entrusted to them with all
vigilance and to bark if necessary at enemies
outside the fold, they preferred like senseless
dogs, yes, like mad dogs, to drive the sheep wild
by barking, so that the words aptly describe
them that say, "Many dogs have surrounded me;
the council of the wicked has hemmed me in."
And all who even now conduct themselves like
them in reviling and barking at the Christ of
God in the same way may be reckoned their kin;
yes, they who like those impious soldiers crucify

[41]FC 101:149. [42]FC 80:305. [43]WGRW 9:71. [44]CCL 25:28.
[45]Gen 49:9. [46]Num 24:9. [47]FC 64:33**. [48]Phil 3:2. [49]FC
101:150*. [50]Is 56:10.

the Son of God and put him to shame have a character very like theirs. Yes, all who today insult the body of Christ, that is, the church, and attempt to destroy the hands and feet and very bones are of their number. PROOF OF THE GOSPEL 10.8.505-6.[51]

THE WISDOM OF GOD. CASSIODORUS: In the case of the Lord Savior's body, when it was fastened with nails and pierced by a lance, it yielded for us fruit that would abide forever. So we do not now fear to say that God suffered in the flesh, that God died for the salvation of all. So Father Augustine in his usual brilliant manner preached these words: "It was a long-standing fact that humankind should die. But so that it should not always happen to humankind, a new event occurred, that God died."[52] So too Paul says, "But we preach Christ, and him crucified."[53] So that you might not think, as some mad people believe, that the Virgin's Son was some other, he added, Christ, "who is the power of God and the wisdom of God; for the foolishness of God is wiser than people, and the weakness of God is stronger than people."[54] For what seems so foolish and feeble to unbelievers as when they hear that God, God's Son, was both crucified and buried? "But it pleased God by the foolishness of our preaching to save them that believe,"[55] for the Lord's incarnation is the wondrous height of his mercy, a gift beyond calculation and a mystery beyond understanding. From it either salvation sprouts for right-thinking minds or death is begotten for perverted intelligences. EXPLANATION OF THE PSALMS 22.17.[56]

22:17 *Staring and Gloating*

FROM FOULNESS COMES BEAUTY. AUGUSTINE: The passion of our Lord signifies our time, the period in which we weep here. Scourges, bonds, insults, spittle, a crown of thorns, wine mixed with gall, vinegar on a sponge, reviling, abuse, finally the cross itself, the sacred limbs hanging on the wood [of the cross]—what do all these

sufferings signify for us except the period through which we are passing, the time of sorrow, the time of mortality, the time of trial? It is a foul period, but let that foulness of the dung be in the field, not in the house. Let grief arise on account of one's sins, not on account of frustrated desires. A foul period, if used to advantage, is a fertile period. What has a more unpleasant odor than a field that has been covered with dung? It was a beautiful field before it received this load of manure; it was first reduced to foulness so that it might come to fertility. Foulness, therefore, is a mark of this time; let that foulness, however, be for us a period of fertility. Furthermore, let us see with the prophet who says, "We have seen him." What is he like? "There is no beauty in him or comeliness."[57] Why is this? Ask another prophet. "They have numbered all my bones." They have numbered his bones as he hung on the cross. A foul sight, the sight of one crucified; but that foulness produced beauty. What beauty? That of the resurrection, because he is "beautiful above the sons of people."[58] SERMON 254.5.[59]

HARDENED STARES. CASSIODORUS: They did not act in a momentary or offhand way. He says rather that they "looked and stared," and their stony hearts were not softened by miracles. Rocks were rent, the earth trembled, the sun hid itself in the garb of darkness so as not to witness so great a crime, yet sadly enough their wickedness remained immovable in its sacrilege, and their eyes unbending. EXPLANATION OF THE PSALMS 22.18.[60]

BLANK STARES. AUGUSTINE: They looked on but did not understand; they watched but did not see. They had eyes to see his body but no discerning heart to reach the Word. EXPOSITIONS OF THE PSALMS 22.19.[61]

---

[51]POG 2:231*. [52]Augustine *Sermon* 350.1 (PL 39.1533). [53]1 Cor 1:23. [54]1 Cor 1:24-25. [55]1 Cor 1:21. [56]ACW 51:225-26*. [57]Is 53:2. [58]Ps 45:2 (44:3 LXX). [59]FC 38:346*. [60]ACW 51:226. [61]WSA 3 15:234.

22:18 Garments Divided

Detailed Prophecy. Chrysostom: Now, the soldiers divided his garments among themselves, but not his tunic. Notice how they frequently caused prophecies to be fulfilled by their wicked deeds. I say this for this detail had been foretold of old. Furthermore, even though there were three crucified, the prophecy was fulfilled only with reference to Christ. Why, indeed, did they not do this in the case of the other two, but only with regard to this One alone? Kindly notice, too, the exactness of the prophecy. The prophet declared not only that they divided the garments among themselves but also that they did not divide them. Thus, the soldiers divided some of Christ's garments into parts, but they did not divide the tunic; on the contrary, they settled its possession by lot. Homilies on the Gospel of John 85.[62]

The Future Present to God. Ambrose: To God the things that are to come are present, and for him who foreknows all things, they are as though they were past and over; as it is written, "Who has made the things that are to be." On the Christian Faith 1.15.97.[63]

Prophecies and Teachings of Scripture. Maximus of Turin: These garments are the prophecies and the lessons of the heavenly Scriptures by which the sacrament of Christ the Lord was announced. The adversaries of the Savior (that is, the wicked heretics who daily lay impious hands on him as the soldiers did[64]) . . . willfully divide these prophecies among themselves and scatter the garments of the one body in different places, and as they strip the Lord, they clothe him in their own false teachings. Sermon 29.4.[65]

Christ's Garment at Calvary. Eusebius of Caesarea: They divide his garments among them and cast lots on his vesture, when each individual tears and destroys the glory of his Word, I mean the words of the holy Scriptures, now this way, now that, and when they take up opinions about him from misleading schools of thought such as godless heretics invent. Proof of the Gospel 10.8.506.[66]

22:20 Deliver My Soul

The One Soul of Christ's Body. Augustine: Let each one also think this about his own life, that he may hate in it that private affection that is undoubtedly transitory and may love in it that union and sense of sharing of which it was said, "They had one soul and heart toward God."[67] Thus, your soul is not your own but is shared by all the brothers whose souls are also yours, or, rather, whose souls form with yours not souls but one soul, the single soul of Christ, of which the psalm says that it is delivered from the hand of the dog. From this it is an easy step to contempt of death. Letter 243.[68]

22:22 To My Brothers

A Brother by Grace. Ambrose: He is the Lord by nature but a brother by grace. On the Patriarchs 4.17.[69]

The Hymn of the Brothers. Eusebius of Caesarea: He says that he will tell the name of his Father first to the apostles, who he calls his brothers. And after them, with swift progress, he promises that he will teach the hymn of his Father to the church founded in his name throughout all the world. It is just as if some supreme teacher of philosophy should give a course of instruction in the midst of his pupils for them to hear and understand, that he in the midst of the church says, "I will hymn your praise," that the church, learning and hearing his words, might in fit manner sing back the praises,

---

[62]FC 41:430-31. [63]NPNF 2 10:217*. [64]Cf. Mt 26:50. [65]ACW 50:72. [66]POG 2:231-32. [67]Acts 4:32. [68]FC 32:221-22*. [69]FC 65:251.

no longer of the demons but of the one almighty God, by him that preached him. PROOF OF THE GOSPEL 10.8.508.[70]

22:23 Praise the Lord!

SWEET PRAISE. CASSIODORUS: Now that he has recounted the Lord's passion at considerable length, he passes to the third section, so that the hearts of the faithful should not be dismayed by enduring sadness. Here he addresses his devoted ones, asking that they acknowledge the Lord's ordering of events and praise him, thronging to proclaim him with universal joy, for through his passion has come salvation for the faithful and life for the just. Now let us observe how sweet is the declaration of feeling in the fear of the Lord. Human fear brings forth not praise but abuse, but fear of the Lord is just and right, and so it begets praise, confesses love, fires the flames of charity. EXPLANATION OF THE PSALMS 22.24.[71]

22:24 The Lord Has Heard

A GRACIOUS HEARING. BEDE: He does not reject or scorn the prayer of the poor when we entreat him for what he himself loves, but he graciously hears; and he will grant us to see his good things in the land of the living,[72] Jesus Christ our Lord, who lives and reigns with the Father in the unity of the Holy Spirit, God throughout all ages of ages. HOMILIES ON THE GOSPELS 2.25.[73]

22:25 Praise in the Congregation

PRAISE FROM GOD. AUGUSTINE: The circumcision of the heart [refers to] the will that is pure from all unlawful desire; [it] comes not from the letter, inculcating and threatening, but from the Spirit, assisting and healing. Such doers of the law have their praise . . . not of people but of God, who by his grace provides the grounds on which they receive praise, of

whom it is said, "My soul shall make its boast of the Lord,"[74] and to whom it is said, "My praise shall be of You." ON THE SPIRIT AND THE LETTER 13.[75]

22:26 The Afflicted Satisfied

THE BLESSED POOR. CASSIODORUS: Realize that by "poor" he meant those who scorned the enticements of this world with the richest contempt; not the wealthy, stuffed with this world's happiness, but the poor, those hungry for God's kingdom. . . . The poor praise the Lord; the rich exalt themselves. The rich accumulate treasures on earth; the poor grow rich with heavenly abundance. Their resources differ, but their mentalities are totally at odds. In short, the rich derive their wealth from the world, the poor from God. . . . The poor possess what they can never lose; the rich hold what not only the dead but even the living often lose. EXPLANATION OF THE PSALMS 22.27.[76]

A GIFT FROM GOD. CLEMENT OF ALEXANDRIA: To inquire, respecting God, if it tends not to strife but to discovery, is salutary. For it is written in David, "The poor eat and shall be filled; and they shall praise the Lord that seek him. Your heart shall live forever." For they who seek him after the true search, praising the Lord, shall be filled with the gift that comes from God, that is, knowledge. And their soul shall live; for the soul is figuratively termed the heart, which ministers life: for by the Son is the Father known. STROMATEIS 5.1.[77]

22:27 The Ends of the Earth

THE WHOLE WORLD. THEODORET OF CYR: Not one nation or even two, but countless

---

[70]POG 2:234*. [71]ACW 51:229-30. [72]Ps 27:13 (26:13 LXX). [73]CS 111:267-68*. [74]Ps 34:2 (33:3 LXX). [75]NPNF 1 5:88*. [76]ACW 51:231. [77]ANF 2:447*.

numbers of all those in the world will run to him, and will enthusiastically receive the rays of the knowledge of God. COMMENTARY ON THE PSALMS 22.16.[78]

22:28 Dominion Belongs to the Lord

NOT THE PROUD. AUGUSTINE: Sovereignty belongs to the Lord, not to the proud, and lordship over the nations is his. EXPOSITIONS OF THE PSALMS 22.29.[79]

ALL NATIONS. EUSEBIUS OF CAESAREA: In these words he very aptly proclaims the glorious works after his resurrection, which are fulfilled in the calling of people from all nations and by the election of people from the ends of the earth, the results of which being visible to all eyes afford evidence of the truth of the words of the psalm. And we, too, are the poor, who like beggars in the things of God, the word of salvation nourishes with spiritual bread, the life-giving food of the soul, and affords eternal life. PROOF OF THE GOSPEL 10.8.510.[80]

HIS KINGDOMS. CASSIODORUS: God shall have dominion over the nations, for the kingdom is the Lord's. Kingdoms belong not to nations but to the Lord, who both changes and preserves kings by his power, and he who is known clearly to be the Lord of this world is to be adored everywhere. EXPLANATION OF THE PSALMS 22.29.[81]

22:31 Proclaiming Deliverance

ILLUSTRIOUS TEACHERS. BEDE: The saints who are aflame with desire for heavenly things are fittingly called "the heavens," as the psalmist says, "And the heavens will proclaim his justice to a people yet to be born," which is to say, "And the most illustrious teachers will proclaim, with mind, voice and action, his justice to a people, who, coming recently to the faith, desire to be born in him." HOMILIES ON THE GOSPELS 2.17.[82]

PROCLAIM HIM. CASSIODORUS: The Son of God is the justice of the Father. So justice is to be preached to the people who are to believe in God, who abandon the death brought by sins and advance to life, who by God's kindness are born of faith in such a way as to deserve to live forever. EXPLANATION OF THE PSALMS 22.32.[83]

ONLY CHRIST. THEODORET OF CYR: We see none of this happening to David or to any of his successors. Only Christ the Lord, on the contrary, who is of David according to the flesh, God the Word who became man, who though of David's line took the form of a slave; he filled all earth and sea with the knowledge of God, after all, and persuaded those who were once in error and offered adoration to idols to adore the true God instead of false gods. COMMENTARY ON THE PSALMS 22.18.[84]

---

[78]FC 101:153. [79]WSA 3 15:226. [80]POG 2:235*. [81]ACW 51:232. [82]CS 111:166. [83]ACW 51:233*. [84]FC 101:155.

23:1-6 GOD'S PROTECTION

When you see yourself shepherded and guided safely by the Lord,
rejoice in the words of Psalm 23.

ATHANASIUS ON THE INTERPRETATION OF THE PSALMS 17 [OIP 67]

A Psalm of David.

¹*The Lord is my shepherd, I shall not want;*
  ²*he makes me lie down in green pastures.*
He leads me beside still waters;
  ³*he restores my soul.*
*He leads me in paths of righteousness*ᵘ
  for his name's sake.

⁴*Even though I walk through the valley of the*
    *shadow of death,*ᵛ
  I fear no evil;

for thou art with me;
  thy rod and thy staff,
  they comfort me.

⁵*Thou preparest a table before me*
  in the presence of my enemies;
thou anointest my head with oil,
  my cup overflows.
⁶*Surely*ʷ *goodness and mercy*ˣ *shall follow me*
  all the days of my life;
and I shall dwell in the house of the LORD
  *for ever.*ʸ

s Heb *the waters of rest*   t Or *life*   u Or *right paths*   v Or *the valley of deep darkness*   w Or *Only*   x Or *kindness*   y Or *as long as I live*

OVERVIEW: The twenty-third psalm transitions to the joys of resurrection life (ARNOBIUS THE YOUNGER), enumerating the kindness we receive from the Lord (CASSIODORUS) and setting forth for our contemplation the heavenly sacraments (AMBROSE). Attention is focused on the Lord, the right shepherd (AUGUSTINE), the One who feeds the sheep (THEODORET). Acknowledgment of him is an act of complete dependence (AUGUSTINE). The Lord leads to pastures that feed the soul (AUGUSTINE), to the waters of baptism (AUGUSTINE, THEODORET, CASSIODORUS), because of what he did for us on the cross (ARNOBIUS THE YOUNGER). We receive righteousness for his name's sake, not by our merit (AUGUSTINE). The Lord illumines our darkness (AUGUSTINE), enabling us to walk through rather than remain in it (ORIGEN). We have assurance of salvation in Christ (CASSIODORUS). Faith eliminates fear (EVAGRIUS) because of the indwelling presence of Christ (AUGUSTINE).

The psalm goes on to speak of the support and guidance we have from him (THEODORET). He corrects us out of love (JEROME) and consoles us even in the pain of correction (CASSIODORUS). When threatened by his judgment, we look to him mercy (ORIGEN). The psalm then speaks to the food he gives us (AUGUSTINE), a spiritual table even in the midst of trials (ORIGEN). Symbolically, the psalm shows us the Lord's table (EUSEBIUS), which gives us the true food of the Word of God (ORIGEN, AMBROSE). His cup sobers the mind and spirit (CYPRIAN, CASSIODORUS), granting us the grace of love (FULGENTIUS). He is our head that was anointed (CASSIODORUS). The table is a blessing for us but punishment for them (THEOPHILUS OF ALEXANDRIA). The Lord's lovingkindness does not wait for our requests (THEODORET). His mercy precedes and follows us (AUGUSTINE, CASSIODORUS), putting us in the position of always receiving grace from him (AMBROSE). We find his blessings in the church (ARNOBIUS THE YOUNGER) and in the kingdom to come (CASSIODORUS).

23:1 The Lord Is My Shepherd

THE JOY OF RESURRECTION. ARNOBIUS THE YOUNGER: We have in the previous psalm the tribulation of the passion. In this one let us receive the joy of the resurrection. COMMENTARY ON THE PSALMS 23.[1]

THANKSGIVING FOR TEN KINDNESSES. CASSIODORUS: Through the whole psalm it is the most faithful Christian, reborn of water and the Holy Spirit, who speaks; he has laid aside the old age of the first man. He gives thanks that through the Lord's generosity he has been led from the desert of sin to the region of pasture and the water of rebirth. We must also observe that just as previously he accepted the Ten Commandments of the Law, so here he rejoices that he has been enriched by ten kindnesses. They are not reported in separate verses but recounted in brief phrases. EXPLANATION OF THE PSALMS 23.1.[2]

HEAVENLY SACRAMENTS. AMBROSE: How often have you heard Psalm 23 and not understood it! See how it is applicable to the heavenly sacraments: "The Lord feeds me, and I shall want nothing; he has set me in a place of pasture; he has brought me on the water of refreshment; he has converted my soul. He has led me on the paths of justice for his own name's sake. For though I should walk in the midst of the shadow of death, I will fear no evils, for you are with me. . . . Your rod is power, the staff suffering, that is, the eternal divinity of Christ, but also corporeal suffering; the one created, the other redeemed. You have prepared a table before me against them that afflict me. You have anointed my head with oil; and my chalice that inebriates me, how goodly it is!" ON THE SACRAMENTS 5.3.13.[3]

THE RIGHT SHEPHERD. AUGUSTINE: Since my shepherd is the Lord Jesus Christ, I shall not lack anything. EXPOSITIONS OF THE PSALMS 23.1-2.[4]

THE ONE WHO FEEDS THE SHEEP. THEODORET OF CYR: Having said in the psalm before this, "The needy eat and will be filled, and those who seek him out will praise the Lord," and again, "All the prosperous of the earth ate and adored him,"[5] here he suggests the provider of such food and calls the feeder shepherd. This in fact is the name Christ the Lord also gave himself: "I am the good shepherd, I know my own, and I am known by my own."[6] It is also what he called himself through the prophet Ezekiel.[7] So here, too, all who enjoyed the saving food cry out, "The Lord shepherds me, and nothing will be wanting for me": this shepherd regales those shepherded by him with enjoyment of good things of all kinds. COMMENTARY ON THE PSALMS 23.1.[8]

COMPLETE DEPENDENCE. AUGUSTINE: When you say, "The Lord is my shepherd," no proper grounds are left for you to trust in yourself. SERMON 366.2.[9]

23:2 Green Pastures and Still Waters

FOOD FOR THE SOUL. AUGUSTINE: The pastures that this good shepherd has prepared for you, in which he has settled you for you to take your fill, are not various kinds of grasses and green things, among which some are sweet to the taste, some extremely bitter, which as the seasons succeed one another are sometimes there and sometimes not. Your pastures are the words of God and his commandments, and they have all been sown as sweet grasses. These pastures had been tasted by that man who said to

---

[1]CCL 25:29-30. [2]ACW 51:235. [3]FC 44:312*. [4]WSA 3 15:244. [5]Ps 22:26, 29 (21:27, 30 LXX). [6]See Jn 10:3-4. [7]Ezek 34:23. [8]FC 101:156. [9]WSA 3 10:289*.

God, "How sweet are your words to my palate, more so than honey and the honeycomb in my mouth!"[10] SERMON 366.3.[11]

THE WATER OF REBIRTH. THEODORET OF CYR: He hints at the water of rebirth, in which the baptized person longs for grace and sheds the old age of sin and is made young instead of being old. COMMENTARY ON THE PSALMS 23.2.[12]

THE WATERS OF BAPTISM. AUGUSTINE: He nurtured me beside the water of baptism, where those who have lost their soundness and strength are made new. EXPOSITIONS OF THE PSALMS 23.1-2.[13]

THE REFRESHING WATER OF BAPTISM. CASSIODORUS: "The water of refreshment" is the baptismal font by which the soul, barren through the parching effect of sin, is watered by heavenly gifts to bear good fruits. EXPLANATION OF THE PSALMS 23.2.[14]

BECAUSE OF WHAT THE LORD DID FOR US. ARNOBIUS THE YOUNGER: The Lord leads me. That is the word of the one who the church, settled in a place of pasture and drawn from the water of reflection, has received, the one who is made complete from the suffering of the Lord. When the stream flows, it pours forth from deep veins, there freshness, there pleasantness, there renewal. These things will happen to me because he has transformed my soul through his suffering. COMMENTARY ON THE PSALMS 23.[15]

23:3 Righteousness for His Name's Sake

NOT BY OUR MERIT. AUGUSTINE: "He has converted my soul." This is a confession rightly to boast about. . . . You will make it truly . . . and with an unalterable conscience, if you say it, not on account of your merits but for the sake of his name. SERMON 366.4.[16]

GUIDING ALONG THE NARROW PATH. AUGUS-

TINE: He has guided me along the narrow paths of his righteousness, where few people walk; and this not for any merit of mine but for the sake of his own name. EXPOSITIONS OF THE PSALMS 23.3.[17]

23:4 Guidance and Comfort

A LAMP IN A DARK PLACE. AUGUSTINE: As long as you remain in this present life, you are walking in the midst of vices, of worldly pressures, which are the shadow of death. Let Christ shine in your heart, who lights the lamp of our minds with the love of God and neighbor; and you will not fear any evils, since he is with you. SERMON 366.5.[18]

WALKING, NOT SITTING. ORIGEN: To walk in the midst of the shadow of death is not the same as to sit in the shadow of death; one who sits in the shadow of death is firmly fixed in that shadow and strengthened in evil. On account of this, he is in darkness and lacks mercy so that the light may rise for him. He who does not sit, but who passes or walks through the midst of the shadow of death, not standing and hurrying across, does not walk alone because the Lord goes through with him. SELECTIONS FROM THE PSALMS 23.4.[19]

ASSURANCE OF SALVATION. CASSIODORUS: The shadow of death is . . . the devil, who sets snares for us in the darkness so that we may lose our way in the fog that he draws around us and fall headlong into eternal death. But this fate is not feared by one who is truly faithful, even if in his reliance on divine mercy he presumes to walk amid those snares. EXPLANATION OF THE PSALMS 23.4.[20]

FAITH ELIMATES FEAR. EVAGRIUS OF PONTUS:

---

[10]Ps 119:103 (118:103 LXX). [11]WSA 3 10:290. [12]FC 101:156. [13]WSA 3 15:244. [14]ACW 51:236. [15]CCL 25:30. [16]WSA 3 10:290-91. [17]WSA 3 15:244. [18]WSA 3 10:291-92. [19]PG 12:1260. [20]ACW 51:237-38*.

One who cultivates pure prayer will hear noises, crashings, voices and tormenting screams that come from the demons; yet he will not suffer collapse or surrender his thoughts if he says to God, "I shall fear no evil, for you are with me." Chapters On Prayer 97.[21]

Christ in Me. Augustine: I shall not be afraid of evil happenings, because you live in my heart through faith; you are with me now to ensure that when this shadow of death has passed away, I may be with you. Expositions of the Psalms 23.4.[22]

Support and Guidance. Theodoret of Cyr: "Your rod and your staff comforted me": with one he supports my weakness, with the other he guides toward the right way. You would not be wrong, however, to apply this to the saving cross: by its seal and remembrance we are rid of the hostile demons and guided to the true path. This is the meaning of "your rod and your staff comforted me": the cross is assembled from two rods, with the upright staff confirming and directing those who believe in him and strengthening those who are weak, and using the crossbar as a rod against the demons. Commentary on the Psalms 23.3.[23]

Correction a Sign of Love. Jerome: He whom the Lord loves, he corrects. Brief Commentary on Psalms 23.[24]

Consolation. Cassiodorus: The "rod" denotes the justice and strength of the Lord Savior. As he says in another psalm, "The scepter of your kingdom is the rod of justice."[25] "Staff" indicates the support he provides for us. With the aid of a staff the foot is firmly planted and the whole body of those who lean on it from above is poised.... The psalmist says that he has been consoled by these two things.... There is no doubt that the staff consoles, for it is always used to aid human weakness, but what shall we say of the rod, which strikes, beats and corrects

our vices through the Judge's severity? Obviously this too consoles the faithful when it brings improvement and leads people to the Lord's path. We rightly say that everything that helps us consoles us, even if it brings passing pain for our correction. Explanation of the Psalms 23.4.[26]

Look to His Mercy. Origen: Scripture is a witness that "rod" speaks of punishments and scourges. If you have sinned and you see the rod of God threatening you, know that the mercy of God will not be far from you. Selections from the Psalms 23.4.[27]

23:5 A Table Prepared

The Progress of Divine Care. Augustine: The time for the rod has passed, that time when I was small and animal-like and was instructed amid the flocks in the pasture; now after that era of the rod I have begun to be guided under your staff, and now you have prepared a table before me, so that I may be no longer fed on milk like a baby, but as an adult eat solid food and be strengthened against those who oppress me. Expositions of the Psalms 23.5.[28]

The Table in the Midst of Trial. Origen: Just as certain rewards are given to the contender in mighty contests, so also in any trial, when that which afflicts is nearby and the powers of the adversaries bring tribulation, know that a spiritual and intellectual table is prepared on account of this trial. Therefore, however many times you will be afflicted, equally many times a spiritual table is placed before you. Fix firm your eyes attentive only to my tables, and, giving thanks, you may say with the apostle, "Not I alone, but we are made glorious in tribulation."[29] Selections from the Psalms 23.5.[30]

---

[21]GAC 203. [22]WSA 3 15:244. [23]FC 101:157. [24]CCL 72:200. [25]Ps 45:6 (44:7 lxx). [26]ACW 51:238*. [27]PG 12:1260, 61. [28]WSA 3 15:244-45. [29]Cf. Rom 5:3. [30]PG 12:1261.

THE LORD'S TABLE. EUSEBIUS OF CAESAREA: In place of the ancient sacrifices and whole burnt offerings the incarnate presence of Christ . . . was offered. And this very thing he proclaims to his church as a great mystery expressed with prophetic voice. . . . As we have received a memorial of this offering that we celebrate on a table by means of symbols of his body and saving blood according to the laws of the new covenant, we are taught again by the prophet David to say, "You have prepared a table before me." . . . Here plainly the mystic chrism and the holy sacrifices of Christ's table are meant, by which we are taught to offer to almighty God through our great High Priest all through our life the celebration of our sacrifices, bloodless, reasonable and well-pleasing to him. PROOF OF THE GOSPEL 1.10.39.[31]

TRUE FOOD. ORIGEN: This bread that God the Word declares is his body is the word that feeds souls, word proceeding from God the Word and bread from heavenly Bread. It has been placed on the table about which was written, "You have prepared a table in my sight against those who afflict me." And this drink that God the Word declares is his blood is the word that gives drink and wonderfully intoxicates the hearts of those who drink. This is the cup concerning which was written, "and your intoxicating cup, how glorious it is!" Also, this drink is the fruit of the true Vine, who said, "I am the true vine,"[32] and it is the blood of that Grape that produced this drink when it was cast into the winepress of the passion, just as the bread too is the word of Christ, made from that Wheat that "falling into the earth . . . produces much fruit."[33] For God the Word was not saying that the visible bread that he was holding in his hands was his body, but rather the Word, in whose mystery the bread was to be broken. He was not saying that the visible drink was his blood, but the Word, in whose mystery the drink was to be poured out. For what else could the body and the blood of God the Word be except the Word that nourishes and the Word

that "makes glad the heart"?[34] COMMENTARY ON THE GOSPEL OF MATTHEW 26.26-28.[35]

THE BREAD AND CUP OF THE FEAST. AMBROSE: "You have prepared a banquet in my sight." This banquet consists of the living Bread,[36] the Word of God. At this banquet there is the oil of sanctification, poured richly over the head of the just. This oil strengthens the inner senses. It does away with the oil of the sinner that fattens the head.[37] In this banquet, too, you have the cup that inebriates: "how excellent" it is, or "how powerful," for the Greek has *kratiston*, meaning most mighty, strong or powerful. Surely it is a powerful cup that washes away every stain of sin. COMMENTARY ON TWELVE PSALMS 35.19.[38]

THE CUP THAT SOBERS. CYPRIAN: The inebriation of the cup and of the blood of the Lord is not like the inebriation coming from worldly wine, since the Holy Spirit says in the psalm, "Your cup that inebriates," and adds, "how excellent it is,"[39] because the cup of the Lord inebriates in such a way that it makes people sober, that it brings minds to spiritual wisdom, that from the taste for this world each one returns to the knowledge of God. And, as the mind is relaxed by that ordinary wine and the soul is eased and all sadness is set aside, so, when the blood of the Lord and the lifegiving cup have been drunk, the memory of the old man[40] is set aside, and there is induced forgetfulness of former, worldly behavior, and the sorrowful and sad heart, which was formerly pressed down with distressing sins, is now eased by the joy of the divine mercy. This can delight the one who drinks in the church of the Lord, but only if what is drunk keeps to the truth of the Lord. LETTER 63.11.[41]

THE LORD'S BLOOD. CASSIODORUS: [The cup]

[31]POG 1:60-61*. [32]Jn 15:1. [33]Jn 12:24-25. [34]Ps 104:15 (103:15 LXX). [35]MFC 7:187-88. [36]Jn 6:51. [37]Ps 141:5 (140:5 LXX). [38]ACTP 47. [39]Ps 22:5. [40]Eph 4:22. [41]FC 51:210**.

is the Lord's blood, which inebriates in such a way that it cleanses the mind, preventing it from wrongdoing, not leading it to sins. This drunkenness makes us sober; this fullness purges us of evils. He who is not filled with this cup fasts in perennial need. EXPLANATION OF THE PSALMS 23.5.[42]

SATED WITH BLESSINGS. CASSIODORUS: It is a drunkenness that brings blessedness, a satiety that brings salvation; the more abundantly it is drunk, the more it begins to bestow satiety on people's minds. EXPLANATION OF THE PSALMS 64(65).10.[43]

THE CUP OF LOVE. FULGENTIUS OF RUSPE: The word *cup* is to be understood as the perfect grace of charity by which the strength for undergoing suffering for the name of Christ is infused. This is given in such a way that even if the opportunity by which anyone may undergo suffering for Christ is lacking, there is still such great strength in the heart by a divine gift that nothing is lacking for putting up with punishment, scorning life and undergoing death for the name of Christ. This is well understood in that text in the psalm where it is said, "My cup overflows," and he had just said before, "You anoint my head with oil." What must be understood by "head anointed with oil" except a mind strengthened by the gift of the Holy Spirit? The shining quality of this oil is the unconquerable fortitude of spiritual grace by which the holy drunkenness is poured into the inner depths of the heart so that every affection of the heart, overcome, is consigned to oblivion. Filled with this drunkenness, the spirit learns to rejoice always in the Lord and to consign to contempt whatever he loved in the world. We drink this drunkenness when, having received the Holy Spirit, we possess the grace of perfect charity that drives out fear. LETTER 14.42.[44]

CHRIST ANOINTED FOR US. CASSIODORUS: The "head" of the faithful is the Lord Christ,

rightly described as anointed with oil since he does not dry up through the aridity of the sinner. EXPLANATION OF THE PSALMS 23.5.[45]

BLESSING FOR YOU, PUNISHMENT FOR THEM. THEOPHILUS OF ALEXANDRIA: I am the true vine,[46] . . . intoxicating like the most powerful antidote, joy, against the grief that sprouted in Adam. Behold, I have prepared a table for you over against those who afflict you. Opposite Eden I settled Adam, who had violated that celebrated place, that by his seeing the delight no longer permitted he might suffer a ceaselessly smoldering distress. Again, over against those who afflict you have I given you a table, life-giving and joy-creating, which offers in exchange for distress unspeakable joy before those who have envied you. Eat the bread that renews your nature. Drink the wine, the exultation of immortality. Eat the bread that purges away the old bitterness, and drink the wine that eases the pain of the wound. This is the healing of your nature; this is the punishment of the one who did the injury. SERMON ON THE MYSTICAL SUPPER.[47]

23:6 Goodness and Mercy

THE LORD'S LOVINGKINDNESS. THEODORET OF CYR: Providing these good things is your ineffable lovingkindness, not awaiting our request but closely following us like fugitives, anticipating our needs, giving us a share in salvation, providing residence in the divine dwellings, one in the present life, one in the future. COMMENTARY ON THE PSALMS 23.4.[48]

MERCY THAT PRECEDES AND FOLLOWS. AUGUSTINE: In the sacred Eloquence we read, "His mercy goes before me," and, "His mercy shall follow me." It predisposes a person before he wills, to prompt his willing. It follows the act of willing, lest one's will be frustrated. Otherwise, why are

---

[42]ACW 51:239. [43]ACW 52:102*. [44]FC 95:557-58 [45]ACW 51:239. [46]Jn 15:1. [47]MFC 7:152. [48]FC 101:158.

we admonished to pray for our enemies, who are plainly not now willing to live piously, unless it is that God is even now at work in them and in their wills? Or again, why are we admonished to ask in order to receive, unless it is that he who grants us what we will is he through whom it comes to pass that we will? We pray for enemies, therefore, that the mercy of God should go before them, as it goes before us; we pray for ourselves that his mercy shall follow us. ENCHIRIDION 9.32.[49]

MERCY'S PROTECTION. CASSIODORUS: Though the Lord's mercy always goes before us, he says here that it "will follow me." It follows particularly to protect, but it precedes to bestow grace. If it merely followed, no one would observe its gifts, and if it merely preceded, none could keep what is bestowed. The ambushes laid by the devil . . . are quite formidable, and without the presence of the Lord's mercy our human frailty is most easily deceived. It is precisely when a person believes that he has outflanked a vice that he is more easily lulled by rash ignorance. So it is vitally necessary that the Lord's grace should precede us and his mercy follow us always. EXPLANATION OF THE PSALMS 23.6.[50]

WE ALWAYS RECEIVE. AMBROSE: When do you not have something that you owe to God? Or when are you without a gift of God, since your daily enjoyment of living is from God? "For what have you, that you have not received?" Therefore, because you always receive, always call on God;

and since what you have is from God, always acknowledge that you are his debtor. I prefer that you pay your debts rather through love than as one forced to do so. ON THE DEATH OF THEODOSIUS 22.[51]

BLESSINGS GIVEN IN THE CHURCH. ARNOBIUS THE YOUNGER: What he now has, let us look within the church. He has a rod with which he warns the delinquent ones. He has a staff by which he succors the penitent. He has a table where he gives bread to the believing. He has oil with which he anoints the head of those being present for freedom of conscience. He has a cup from which he will drink preaching the word in such a way that when it is the third hour of the day he is thought to be drunk in his preaching.[52] He has mercy that follows him all the days of his life so he may dwell the length of his days in the house of the Lord, praising the Lord Jesus Christ who rules forever. Amen. COMMENTARY ON THE PSALMS 23.[53]

EVERLASTING BLESSING. CASSIODORUS: This is the full perfection of all blessings. . . . "The house of the Lord" denotes the Jerusalem to come, which continues without uncertainty "to length of days," for it is lasting blessedness and joy without end. EXPLANATION OF THE PSALMS 23.6.[54]

---

[49]LCC 7:359*. [50]ACW 51:239-40. [51]FC 22:317*. [52]Cf. Acts 2:13-15. [53]CCL 25: 30. [54]ACW 51:240*.

24:1-10 APPROACHING GOD

As you wonder at the order of creation,
the grace of providence and the sacred prescriptions
of the Law, sing . . . Psalm 24.

ATHANASIUS ON THE INTERPRETATION OF THE PSALMS 17 [OIP 67]

A Psalm of David.*

¹*The earth is the LORD's and the fulness
    thereof,
    the world and those who dwell therein;*
²*for he has founded it upon the seas,
    and established it upon the rivers.*

³*Who shall ascend the hill of the LORD?
    And who shall stand in his holy place?*
⁴*He who has clean hands and a pure heart,
    who does not lift up his soul to what is
    false,
    and does not swear deceitfully.*
⁵*He will receive blessing from the LORD,
    and vindication from the God of his
    salvation.*

⁶*Such is the generation of those who seek him,
    who seek the face of the God of Jacob.*ᶻ
                                            Selah

⁷*Lift up your heads, O gates!
    and be lifted up, O ancient doors!
    that the King of glory may come in.*
⁸*Who is the King of glory?
    The LORD, strong and mighty,
    the LORD, mighty in battle!*
⁹*Lift up your heads, O gates!
    and be lifted up,ᵃ O ancient doors!
    that the King of glory may come in.*
¹⁰*Who is this King of glory?
    The LORD of hosts,
    he is the King of glory! Selah*

z Gk Syr: Heb *thy face, O Jacob*   a Gk Syr Jerome Tg Compare verse 7: Heb *lift up*   * LXX adds *on the first day of the week*

OVERVIEW: The twenty-fourth psalm in the Septuagint carries the superscription "On the first day," which is the Lord's day, that is, the day of the Lord's resurrection (AUGUSTINE, CASSIODORUS). It is also identified as the day of his ascension (PSEUDO-ATHANASIUS). The earth is the Lord's, not ours (GREGORY OF NYSSA). It is his by virtue of his having created it (THEODORET). But it has become his again through the preaching of the gospel (AUGUSTINE) and will be revealed as such in the kingdom to come (PSEUDO-ATHANASIUS).

The next section addresses the character of those who belong to him (CASSIODORUS). The hill envisioned refers to the Lord's righteousness (AUGUSTINE). We stand there only on Christ (ORIGEN). Such a one has his soul settled on eternity (AUGUSTINE), exhibiting purity in intention and action (THEODORET). Unlike Judas (EVAGRIUS), his speech is without deceit (CASSIODORUS), which reminds us to carefully weigh our words (CALLISTUS). God's blessing comes to us based on his mercy (THEODORET, CASSIODORUS). Such are those who have been changed by his grace (ORIGEN), those who have been reborn (AUGUSTINE).

The psalm then speaks of the entry of the King of glory. This could not have been said of Solomon (JUSTIN MARTYR). The everlasting Word enters the temple gateway (PRUDENTIUS) announced by angels accompanying him (HIP-POLYTUS), being revealed to angels in heaven (THEODORET). Humankind has been redeemed for heaven (TERTULLIAN). The Lord opened the way for us (ATHANASIUS), and we are exalted in him (ATHANASIUS). Let us then ascend with Christ (GREGORY OF NAZIANZUS). Let us enter through heaven's gate with him (JEROME). Let us be like him (ARNOBIUS THE YOUNGER). He enters heaven as the Lord of powers (EUSE-BIUS), a spiritual victor (TERTULLIAN), clad in scarlet garments (ORIGEN). Because of this, the way for us is now open (AUGUSTINE), both the way out of death and the way into heaven (AUGUSTINE). It is he himself who comes thus (BEDE): Christ, the Son of God (ARNOBIUS THE YOUNGER), the One who glorifies us (CAS-SIODORUS).

Superscription: *A Psalm of David*

THE LORD'S DAY. AUGUSTINE: This is a psalm for David, dealing with the glorification and resurrection of our Lord, which took place early in the morning on the first day of the week, now called the Lord's day. EXPOSITIONS OF THE PSALMS 24.1.[1]

THE FIRST DAY OF THE WEEK. CASSIODORUS: "The first day of the week" indicates the Lord's day, the first after the sabbath, the day on which the Lord rose from the dead. It is rightly called the Lord's day because of the outstanding nature of the miracle or because on that day he stabilized the world, for by rising again on it he is seen to lend succor to the world and is declared also its Maker. Because the whole psalm is sung after the resurrection, this heading has been set before it to inform the hearts of the faithful with the appropriate indication. EXPLANATION OF THE PSALMS 24.1.[2]

THE ASCENSION. PSEUDO-ATHANASIUS: In this psalm he preaches about the ascension of our Lord and teaches the Gentiles how they

may become worthy of the heavenly tabernacles. EXPOSITION ON PSALMS 24.[3]

24:1 *The Earth Is the Lord's*

THE LORD'S, NOT OURS. GREGORY OF NYSSA: The foolish person counts as his own possession that which never actually belongs to him, seemingly ignorant in his greed that "the earth is the Lord's, and the fullness thereof," for "God is king of all the earth." It is the passion of having that gives people a false title of lordship over that which can never belong to them. "The earth," says the wise preacher, "abides forever,"[4] ministering to every generation, first one, then another, that is born on it. But people, though they are so little even their own masters that they are brought into life without knowing it by their Maker's will, and before they wish are withdrawn from it, nevertheless in their excessive vanity think that they are its lords; that they, now born, now dying, rule that which remains continually. ON VIRGINITY 4.[5]

THE CREATOR. THEODORET OF CYR: He is Lord of the whole world. He is its Lord, however, not by wresting authority or by depriving anyone else of lordship but by personally creating it and leading it from nonbeing into being. COMMENTARY ON THE PSALMS 24.2.[6]

PREACHED TO ALL NATIONS. AUGUSTINE: This is true, for the Lord, now glorified, is preached to all nations to bring them to faith, and the whole world thus becomes his church. EXPOSITIONS OF THE PSALMS 24.2.[7]

THE COMING KINGDOM. PSEUDO-ATHANASIUS: This verse teaches about God's kingdom to come, in which he will reign over all. And in order to make known that as maker and natural Lord he will reign over it, he said [in the next

---

[1]WSA 3 15:246. [2]ACW 51:241. [3]CSCO 387:16. [4]Eccles 1:4. [5]NPNF 2 5:349*. [6]FC 101:159. [7]WSA 3 15:246.

verse], "He is its foundations." EXPOSITON ON PSALMS 24.[8]

24:3 Who Shall Stand?

SECOND SECTION. CASSIODORUS: Once he has briefly taught us that all creation is the Lord's since he established it, he now begins the second section with a question, and in answer explains the necessary character of those who wish to call themselves his. EXPLANATION OF THE PSALMS 24.3.[9]

HILL OF RIGHTEOUSNESS. AUGUSTINE: Who will ascend to the towering heights of the Lord's righteousness? EXPOSITIONS OF THE PSALMS 24.3.[10]

STAND ON CHRIST. ORIGEN: Where should you stand, you who seek sanctification from God? The writer says, "You have established my feet on the rock." "Christ was the rock." Let us learn about the one who follows these promises. SELECTIONS FROM THE PSALMS 24.3.[11]

24:4 Clean Hands and a Pure Heart

SETTLED ON ETERNITY. AUGUSTINE: Who, then, will climb up there and stay there? Only a person innocent in action and pure in thought. "One who has not received his soul in vain," that is, a person who has not consigned his or her soul to the things that pass away but realizes that it is immortal and longs for a settled and changeless eternity. "Or sworn deceitfully to a neighbor": such a person's dealings with others are free from deceit, just as the things of eternity are simple and straightforward. EXPOSITIONS OF THE PSALMS 24.4.[12]

PURE INTENTIONS AND ACTIONS. THEODORET OF CYR: It is appropriate, he is saying, for him who desires to ascend that mountain both to purify his soul of idle thoughts and to keep his hands away from such pursuits. He put "hands" in place of pursuits, and by "heart" he implied desires: with the latter we form our intentions, and by the former we put them into action. COMMENTARY ON THE PSALMS 24.4.[13]

NOT LIKE JUDAS. EVAGRIUS OF PONTUS: Truly Judas ascended onto the mountain of the Lord, but he did not stand in his holy place. He was not innocent in hands or pure in heart, but a thief who was taking the money. NOTES ON THE PSALMS 23[24].4.[14]

NO DECEIT. CASSIODORUS: Swearing truthfully was certainly not forbidden in the Old Testament, but because a pretext for perjury often occurs to human beings through mental weaknesses, in the New Testament it states that it is more profitable that we should not swear at all. . . . One swears deceitfully if he intends to act differently from his promise, not regarding it as perjury if he willfully misleads one who makes the mistake of trusting him. EXPLANATION OF THE PSALMS 24.4.[15]

WEIGH YOUR WORDS. CALLISTUS OF ROME [DUB.]: Let no one speak deceitfully to his neighbor. The mouth of the malevolent is a deep pit. The innocent person, while he believes easily, falls readily; but though he falls, he rises; and the shuffler, with all his arts, goes headlong to ruin, from which he can never rise or escape. Therefore let everyone weigh well his words, and let him not say to another what he would not say to himself. EPISTLE 2.5.[16]

24:5 Blessing and Vindication

BLESSING BASED ON MERCY. THEODORET OF CYR: Now, it was quite appropriate for him to associate mercy with blessing: even what are thought rewards are given to human beings only

---

[8]CSCO 387:16. [9]ACW 51:242. [10]WSA 3 15:246. [11]PG 12:1265. [12]WSA 3 15:246. [13]FC 101:160. [14]PG 12:1268. [15]ACW 51:243*. [16]ANF 8:617*.

on account of divine lovingkindness. I mean, all the righteousness of human beings is not nearly sufficient for gifts bestowed by God and certainly not for those yet to come, which even surpass human imagining. COMMENTARY ON THE PSALMS 24.4.[17]

BLESSING COMES THROUGH GOD'S KINDNESS. CASSIODORUS: It is the future Judge who blesses; he who could have imposed irreversible damnation forgives. So he wanted us to acknowledge the deserving kindness of this magnanimous concession of the Lord. . . . Next comes mercy, so that the blessing may appear to have come not through human deserts but through the Lord's kindness, for there is no person who does not need pity to be shown him. Sins are conceded so that a crown may ensue, just as freedom cannot be bestowed unless slavery has first been removed. So our Lord Christ is the savior by whom blessedness is granted and also sins are loosed. We should not be disturbed because he first said, "He shall receive a blessing from the Lord," and later added, "And mercy from God his savior," whereas in the order of events he would first pardon our sins and then the gifts of his blessing would follow. You frequently find this variation with mercy placed first. . . . This figure is called *anastrophe* or inversion, when we express and idea in the reverse order. EXPLANATION OF THE PSALMS 24.5.[18]

24:6 Those Who Seek God

THOSE WHO HAVE BEEN CHANGED. ORIGEN: No one seeking the face of God will see his face and live, . . . unless he or she has been changed. SELECTIONS FROM THE PSALMS 24.6.[19]

THOSE WHO HAVE BEEN REBORN. AUGUSTINE: It speaks of them as a "generation" because those who seek him are born like this. "Of those who seek the face of the God of Jacob." They are seeking the face of the God who gave first place to the one born later. EXPOSITIONS OF THE PSALMS 24.6.[20]

24:7 Lift Up Your Heads, O Gates!

NOT SAID OF SOLOMON. JUSTIN MARTYR: Solomon was not the Lord of hosts. But, when our Christ arose from the dead and ascended into heaven, the heavenly princes chosen by God were ordered to open the gates of heaven that the King of glory might enter and sit at the right hand of the Father until he makes his enemies his footstool.[21] Now, when these heavenly princes saw that he was in appearance without beauty, honor or glory, and not recognizing him, they asked, "Who is this King of glory?" And the Holy Spirit, either in his own name or in the Father's, answered, "The Lord of hosts. He is the King of glory." But I am sure that everyone will admit that none of the gatekeepers of the temple at Jerusalem ever said of Solomon (though he was ever so glorious a king) or of the ark of testimony, "Who is this King of glory?" DIALOGUE WITH TRYPHO 36.[22]

A TEMPLE GATEWAY. PRUDENTIUS:
Learn what our temple is, if you would know;
It is one that no artisan has built,
A structure not of riven fir or pine,
Nor reared with blocks of quarried marble fair.
Its massive weight no columns high support
Beneath the arches of a gilded vault.
By God's Word it was formed, not by his voice,
But by the everlasting Word, the Word made flesh.[23]
This temple is eternal, without end,
This you attacked with scourge and cross and gall.
This temple was destroyed by bitter pains.[24]
Its form was fragile from the Mother's womb,
But when brief death the Mother's part dissolved,

[17]FC 101:160. [18]ACW 51:243-44. [19]PG 12:1268. [20]WSA 3 15:247. [21]Ps 110:1 (109:1 LXX). [22]FC 6:203. [23]Jn 1:14. [24]Mk 14:58; Jn 2:19-21.

The Father's might restored it in three
　　days.
You have beheld my saving temple rise
On high, surrounded by an angel throng.[25]
The everlasting gates uphold its roof;
Through lofty towers the glorious stairs
　　arise,
And at the top appears a shining path.
THE DIVINITY OF CHRIST 518-36.[26]

ANNOUNCED BY ANGELS. HIPPOLYTUS: He
comes to the heavenly gates: angels accompany
him, and the gates of heaven were closed. For
he has not yet ascended into heaven. Now first
does he appear to the powers of heaven as flesh
ascending. Therefore to these powers it is said
by the angels, who are the couriers of the Savior
and Lord, "Lift up your gates, you princes; and
be lifted up, you everlasting doors; and the King
of glory shall come in. FRAGMENTS ON THE
PSALMS 24.[27]

A REVELATION TO ANGELS. THEODORET OF
CYR: Let no one wonder, I ask you, on hearing
of the ignorance of the invisible powers: they
have neither advance knowledge nor complete
knowledge—only the divine nature has that
knowledge. Angels and archangels, however,
and the other companies of the invisible powers know as much as they are taught, for which
reason the divine apostle also, speaking of them,
said, "So that to the principalities and authorities in the heavenly places the wisdom of God
in its rich variety might now be made known
through the church."[28] Now, if they came to
learn the divine wisdom more precisely through
the life of the church, there is nothing out of
order for the powers on high to be ignorant even
of the mystery of Christ's ascension when they
see the human nature and do not perceive the
divinity concealed in it. . . . No human being
had ever passed through [the eternal gates]; but
when God the Word became human and took up
our first fruits, he both led the way up to heaven
and took his place at the right hand of majesty in

the highest places, above every principality, authority, dominion and every name that is named,
not only in this age but also in the age to come.
COMMENTARY ON THE PSALMS 24.6-7.[29]

REDEEMED FOR HEAVEN. TERTULLIAN: God
spared not his own Son for you,[30] letting him
become a curse for us; for "cursed is he who hangs
on a tree";[31] . . . that he might redeem us from
our sins. The sun was darkened on the day of
our redemption;[32] hell lost its right to us, and we
were enrolled for heaven. The eternal gates were
lifted up that the King of glory, the Lord of might,
might enter in, and humankind, born of the earth,
destined for hell, was purchased for heaven. ON
FLIGHT IN TIME OF PERSECUTION 12.2.[33]

HE OPENED THE WAY FOR US. ATHANASIUS:
It was not the Word himself that needed an
opening of the gates, being Lord of all; nor were
any of his works closed to their maker; but we
it was that needed it, whom he carried up by his
own body. For as he offered it to death on behalf
of all, so by it he once more made ready the way
up into the heavens. ON THE INCARNATION 25.[34]

EXALTED IN HIM. ATHANASIUS: The Word, being the image of the Father and immortal, took
the form of a servant, and as man he underwent
death for us in his flesh, that thereby he might
offer himself for us through death to the Father.
Likewise also, as man, he is said because of us
and for us to be highly exalted, that as by his
death we all died in Christ, so again in Christ
himself we might be highly exalted, being raised
from the dead and ascending into heaven, "where
the forerunner Jesus has entered for us, not into
the figures of the true, but into heaven itself,
now to appear in the presence of God for us."[35]
But if no Christ has entered into heaven itself
for us, even though he was previously and always

---

[25]Cf. Acts 1:10. [26]FC 52:22-23. [27]ANF 5:170*. [28]Eph 3:10. [29]FC
101:161-62. [30]Rom 8:32. [31]Gal 3:13. [32]Mt 27:45. [33]FC 40:299*.
[34]LCC 3:80. [35]Heb 6:20; 9:24.

Lord and Framer of the heavens, then it is for us, therefore, that the present exaltation is written. And as he himself, who sanctifies all, also says that he sanctifies himself to the Father for our sakes, not that the Word may become holy but that he himself may in himself sanctify all of us, in like manner we must take the present phrase, "He highly exalted him"—not that he himself needed to be exalted, for he is already the highest, but that he may become righteousness for us, and that we may be exalted in him and may enter the gates of heaven, which he has also opened for us, the forerunners saying, "Lift up your gates, O you rulers, and be lifted up, you everlasting doors, and the King of glory shall come in." For here also the gates were not shut on him who is the Lord and Maker of all, but because of us this too is written, to whom the door of paradise was shut. And therefore in a human relation, because of the flesh that he bore, it is said of him, "Lift up your gates," and "shall come in," as if a man were entering; but in a divine relation on the other hand it is said of him, since "the Word was God," that he is the "Lord" and the "King of glory." Such our exaltation the Spirit foreannounced in the eighty-ninth psalm, saying, "And in your righteousness shall they be exalted, for you are the glory of their strength."[36] And if the Son is Righteousness, then he is not exalted because he himself was in need, but it is we who are exalted in that Righteousness, which is he.[37] DISCOURSES AGAINST THE ARIANS 1.41.[38]

LET US ASCEND WITH CHRIST. GREGORY OF NAZIANZUS: If he ascend up into heaven, ascend with him. Be one of those angels who escort him or one of those who receive him. Bid the gates be lifted up, or be made higher, that they may receive him, exalted after his passion. Answer to those who are in doubt because he bears up with him his body and the tokens of his passion, which he did not have when he came down, and who therefore, inquire, "Who is the King of glory?" that it is the Lord strong and mighty, as in all things that he has done from time to time and does, so now in

his battle and triumph for the sake of humankind. And give to the those who doubt the question the twofold answer. And if they marvel and say as in Isaiah's drama who is this that comes from Edom and from the things of earth? Or how are the garments red of him that is without blood or body, as of one that treads in the full winepress?[39] Set forth the beauty of the array of the body that suffered, adorned by the passion and made splendid by the Godhead, than which nothing can be more lovely or more beautiful. ON HOLY EASTER, ORATION 45.25.[40]

LET US ENTER THROUGH THIS GATE. JEROME: As our Lord ascends to the Father in triumph, he issues commands to the angels saying, "Open to me the gates of justice; I will enter them and give thanks to the Lord."[41] These are the gates of which in the twenty-fourth psalm the angels were speaking while they were preparing for the entrance of the Lord: "Lift up, O gates, your lintels; reach up, you ancient portals, that the King of glory may come in!" Aptly are the gates commanded to lift up high and raise aloft their portals, since, in accordance with the dispensation and mystery of the flesh and in conformity with the victory of the cross, he reenters heaven mightier than he had come down on earth. "This gate is the Lord's; the just shall enter it."[42] Through this gate, Peter has entered, and Paul, and all the apostles and martyrs, and today the saints continue to go in; through this gate, the thief was the first to pass with the Lord. Have faith, therefore, and be hopeful for your own entrance. HOMILY 94, ON EASTER SUNDAY.[43]

LET US BE LIKE HIM. ARNOBIUS THE YOUNGER: Now it is said to that one: Open the gates for your leaders. Cast away the example of Adam who is your leader according to the flesh, and lift up the eternal doors holding the power-

---

[36]Ps 89:17-18 (88:18-19 LXX). [37]1 Cor 1:30. [38]NPNF 2 4:330**. [39]Is 63:2. [40]NPNF 2 7:432*. [41]Ps 118:19 (117:19 LXX). [42]Ps 118:20 (117:20 LXX). [43]FC 57:251*.

ful and mighty king of glory, powerful in battle, overcoming faults and their offsprings, worthless of spirit. Therefore, lift up the gates for your leaders. "Just as we have borne the likeness of the earthly man, so shall we bear the likeness of the heavenly man."[44] COMMENTARY ON THE PSALMS 24.[45]

24:8 The Lord, Strong and Mighty

LORD OF POWERS. EUSEBIUS OF CAESAREA: Lord of Sabaoth is translated "Lord of powers." And he is the captain of the powers of the Lord, whom also the divine powers salute as Lord of Sabaoth in Psalm 24, foretelling his return from earth to heaven. . . . In the Hebrew he is here again called Lord of Sabaoth. And since he is the King of glory, and by his sojourn here the whole earth would be filled with his glory, both in the psalm and in the prophecy the fulfillment is rightly placed in the present: in the prophecy in the words, "The whole earth is full of his glory," in the psalm at the beginning where it says, "The earth is the Lord's and the fullness thereof, the world and all that dwell therein." PROOF OF THE GOSPEL 7.1.311-12.[46]

A SPIRITUAL VICTOR. TERTULLIAN: Christ must be understood to be an exterminator of spiritual foes, who wields spiritual arms and fights in spiritual strife. . . . It is of such a war as this that the psalm may evidently have spoken: "The Lord is strong, the Lord is mighty in battle." For with the last enemy death did he fight, and through the trophy of the cross he triumphed. AGAINST MARCION 4.20.[47]

24:9 Be Lifted Up, O Ancient Doors!

SCARLET GARMENTS. ORIGEN: But after he had destroyed his enemies through his passion, the Lord, who is mighty in battle and strong, . . . goes, bearing victory and trophies, with the body that arose from the dead. . . . Certain powers say, "Who is this that is coming from Edom, with

scarlet garments from Bosra, so beautiful?" And those escorting him say to those stationed at the gates of heaven, "Lift up your gates, and the King of glory will come in." COMMENTARY ON THE GOSPEL OF JOHN 6.287-88.[48]

THE WAY NOW OPEN. AUGUSTINE: The way lies open now from earth to heaven. Let the prophet's trumpet sound again: get rid of your gates, yes, even you heavenly princes, you who have erected gates in the minds of people who worship the host of heaven. "But you, everlasting gates, lift yourselves up," gates of everlasting righteousness, love and purity, through which a soul loves the one true God and refuses to prostitute itself to many so-called gods. "And the King of glory will enter." The King of glory will make his way in, to interced for us at the Father's right hand. EXPOSITIONS OF THE PSALMS 24.9.[49]

24:10 Who Is This King of Glory?

TWO GATES. AUGUSTINE: Now this is said twice in one and the same psalm . . . in a way that might be thought superfluous and unnecessary. But in the repetition of the same words pay attention to how they end, and notice why it is said twice. It is as if, you see, to the one who rises again once and ascends once, gates are opened twice, both those of hell and those of heaven. It is a new thing, after all, God present in hell; it is a new thing, a man taken up into heaven. At each moment, at each point, princes are terrified: "Who is this King of glory?" How can we tell this? Listen to the reply given to each. The first questioners are told, "The Lord, the valiant and mighty, the Lord mighty in war." What sort of war? Undergoing death for mortals, suffering alone for all, the Almighty not resisting and yet conquering death in dying. Great indeed, then, is the King of glory, even in the netherworld. This is also repeated to the heavenly powers.

[44]1 Cor 15:49. [45]CCL 25:31. [46]POG 2:50-51. [47]ANF 3:379. [48]FC 80:246. [49]WSA 3 15:247-48.

... But because he lifts up a man also with him to heaven, it is as if he is not recognized there either, and they ask, "Who is this king of glory?" But there, because he is no longer a contender but the winner, because he is not fighting but celebrating his triumph, the reply here is not "The Lord mighty in war," but "The Lord of hosts, he is the King of glory." SERMON 377.1.[50]

HE HIMSELF COMES. BEDE: With the report of his resurrection, already accomplished, going ahead of him, the Lord of hosts and the King of glory himself at length appeared and made clear with what great might he had overcome the death he had temporarily tasted. HOMILIES ON THE GOSPELS 2.9.[51]

CHRIST THE SON OF GOD. ARNOBIUS THE YOUNGER: Who is the King of glory? Christ, the Son of God, he is the King of glory, casting off the prince of shame. He lifts high the eternal

gates of the holy universal church, having cast down the temple of idols just as the gates of their prince the devil. If you should ask, "Who is that King of glory?" the apostle will answer, "The King of all for their salvation, Christ, Son of God, who rules forever." COMMENTARY ON THE PSALMS 24.[52]

THE ONE WHO GLORIFIES US. CASSIODORUS: The King of glory is none other than he who makes glorious those who glorify him—in the Lord's own words, "Those who glorify me, I will glorify"—and he who assigns power and strength and the other gifts to each individual as he will. EXPLANATION OF THE PSALMS 24.9.[53]

---

[50]WSA 3 10:352. [51]CS 111:78. [52]CCL 25:31-32. [53]ACW 51:245-46.

25:1-22 PRAYER FOR FORGIVENESS

When enemies surround you, lift up your soul to God in Psalm 25,
and you will see these evildoers put to flight.

ATHANASIUS *ON THE INTERPRETATION OF THE PSALMS* 17 [OIP 67]

A Psalm of David.

¹*To thee, O* LORD, *I lift up my soul.*
²*O my God, in thee I trust,*
    let me not be put to shame;
    let not my enemies exult over me.
³*Yea, let none that wait for thee be put to*
        shame;

let them be ashamed who are wantonly
        treacherous.

⁴*Make me to know thy ways, O* LORD;
    teach me thy paths.
⁵*Lead me in thy truth, and teach me,*
    for thou art the God of my salvation;
    for thee I wait all the day long.

⁶Be mindful of thy mercy, O LORD, and of thy
　　steadfast love,
　for they have been from of old.
⁷Remember not the sins of my youth, or my
　　trangressions;
　according to thy steadfast love remember
　　me,
　for thy goodness' sake, O LORD!

⁸Good and upright is the LORD;
　therefore he instructs sinners in the way.
⁹He leads the humble in what is right,
　and teaches the humble his way.
¹⁰All the paths of the LORD are steadfast love
　　and faithfulness,
　for those who keep his covenant and his
　　testimonies.

¹¹For thy name's sake, O LORD,
　pardon my guilt, for it is great.
¹²Who is the man that fears the LORD?
　Him will he instruct in the way that he
　　should choose.
¹³He himself shall abide in prosperity,

and his children shall possess the land.
¹⁴The friendship of the LORD is for those who
　　fear him,
　and he makes known to them his covenant.
¹⁵My eyes are ever toward the LORD,
　for he will pluck my feet out of the net.

¹⁶Turn thou to me, and be gracious to me;
　for I am lonely and afflicted.
¹⁷Relieve the troubles of my heart,
　and bring me[b] out of my distresses.
¹⁸Consider my affliction and my trouble,
　and forgive all my sins.

¹⁹Consider how many are my foes,
　and with what violent hatred they hate me.
²⁰Oh guard my life, and deliver me;
　let me not be put to shame, for I take refuge
　　in thee.
²¹May integrity and uprightness preserve me,
　for I wait for thee.

²²Redeem Israel, O God,
　out of all his troubles.

Or *The troubles of my heart are enlarged; bring me*

OVERVIEW: The twenty-fifth psalm is an alphabetic psalm (CASSIODORUS). David prays that he may trust in God alone (ARNOBIUS THE YOUNGER). This involves an exchange of trust, from himself to God (AUGUSTINE). David prays that he will not be the object of his enemies' laughter (CASSIODORUS). Having in mind many examples of faith (THEODORET), he waits on God (CASSIODORUS). David asks to know God's ways, that is, the plans and deeds of God (THEODORE OF MOPSUESTIA). These are the right choices of life (AMBROSE), the narrow paths of the Lord (AUGUSTINE). He teaches us to believe and wait (CASSIODORUS), waiting on mercy (AUGUSTINE) and walking in the paths he walked (ARNOBIUS THE YOUNGER). His mercy is ever present to us (AUGUSTINE), and it is by mercy that we receive grace, not by our merits (CASSIODORUS). God's

mindfulness is his presence, which he extends to us (EVAGRIUS). David asks that God remember him but not his sin (THEODORET). He asks that God remember God's own goodness, not what is due to David (AUGUSTINE, DIODORE).

God's law is a gift of his goodness (CASSIODORUS), given for our benefit (DIODORE), and by it, the gentle are taught (EVAGRIUS). In all his dealings with us, mercy is constant (THEODORE OF MOPSUESTIA). He instructs the humble (AUGUSTINE), those who are meek and mild (CASSIODORUS). These are his ways (THEODORE OF MOPSUESTIA), known to us from Scripture (THEODORET), even though the sinner may be abandoned to his weakness for a while (JEROME).

The third section of the psalm highlights the fear of the Lord (CASSIODORUS). The one who fears the Lord has a spiritual inheritance

(PSEUDO-ATHANASIUS), receiving blessings even before the resurrection (CASSIODORUS). Fear yields hope (CASSIODORUS), and looking toward God is the disposition of knowledge (EVAGRIUS) by which pitfalls are avoided (CASSIODORUS). Forgiveness is needed not just for the past but also for the present (AUGUSTINE). Enemies are everywhere (AUGUSTINE), but the church prays for the lost (CASSIODORUS). Patience is the source of hope (EVAGRIUS), and deliverance is by faith (AUGUSTINE). Motivated by hope to a life of integrity (THEODORE OF MOPSUESTIA), loving others by God's strength (CASSIODORUS), redeemed within and without (AUGUSTINE), the peace of David extends to the whole of Israel (THEODORET).

25:1 To You, O Lord

AN ALPHABETIC PSALM. CASSIODORUS: This is the first psalm set in the frame of the Hebrew alphabet. . . . Through the whole book there are two types of these psalms. The first is that clearly containing the whole alphabet, like Psalms 111, 112 and 119. . . . The second type deletes certain letters; . . . examples are the present psalm and Psalms 34, 37 and 145. . . . Here we must be aware that this psalm omits the sixth and nineteenth letters. . . . The alphabetic arrangement is found to be not unusual in the divine Scriptures, for Jeremiah bewailed the captivity of Jerusalem by lamentations extending over the alphabet four times, thus teaching us that the sacred use of letters unfolds for us also mysteries of heavenly matters. . . . Throughout the whole psalm the church prays in marvelous supplication with the figure known as *ethopoeia* that it should not appear before God's eyes as a figure despised by its enemies. In the first section, [the church] demands that it may know the Lord's intentions and his ways; this part contains five letters of the alphabet we mentioned. In the second section, [the church] asks for his kindnesses that he bestowed on the holy ancestors from the beginning of the world; this

embraces six further letters. In the third place, [the church] says that those who keep the Lord's commands deserve eternal rewards, and it attests that it remains constant in this one desire; here the remaining nine letters are incorporated. EXPLANATION OF THE PSALMS 25.1.[1]

TRUSTING IN GOD ALONE. ARNOBIUS THE YOUNGER: From all earthly profit, from all the things of this world that seem good, raising my spirit, let me come to you, Lord; I have been lifted up, now not trusting in money, or house, or business, or military might or in my abilities, but I search while trusting in you, so that I will not be ashamed when I depart from this body. . . . I have lifted my spirit to you so that my spirit may dwell on good things. COMMENTARY ON THE PSALMS 25.[2]

25:2 Not Put to Shame

EXCHANGE OF TRUST. AUGUSTINE: O my God, I have been brought to this point of bodily weakness because I trusted in myself. . . . But now I trust in you, so let me be shamed no longer. EXPOSITIONS OF THE PSALMS 25.2.[3]

THE LAUGH OF AN ENEMY. CASSIODORUS: Enemies laugh when they see that the trust of just people is not fulfilled. . . . Laughing is usually the characteristic of one well-disposed, but laughing at an individual is always the trait of a foe. EXPLANATION OF THE PSALMS 25.2-3.[4]

25:3 Those Who Wait on God

EXAMPLES OF FAITH. THEODORET OF CYR: I have a sufficient basis for hope, he is saying, in those who already believe in you and enjoy your aid. You are in the habit of showing care for them, while confounding those given to lawlessness. COMMENTARY ON THE PSALMS 25.2.[5]

---

[1]ACW 51:246-48*. [2]CCL 25:32. [3]WSA 3 15:249. [4]ACW 51:248*. [5]FC 101:163.

WAITING IN COURAGEOUS FASHION. CAS-
SIODORUS: Waiting on God in [courageous] fashion entails expecting him while enduring evils,
so that when he comes at his judgment he may
render what the spirit of the committed person
was seeking. EXPLANATION OF THE PSALMS 25.4.[6]

25:4 God's Ways and Paths

GOD'S PLANS AND DEEDS. THEODORE OF
MOPSUESTIA: As he refers by "way" to people's
actions and exploits (as in that verse, "I have
run in the way of your commands," as if to say, I
determined to do and observe your commands),
so he calls God's "way" whatever God deigns to
do by creating or arranging. So "teach me your
paths" means "make me rejoice in your acting
and planning." COMMENTARY ON PSALMS 25.4.[7]

RIGHT CHOICES. AMBROSE: Now the ways of
the Lord are, we may say, certain courses taken
in a good life, guided by Christ, who says, "I am
the way, and the truth and the life." The way,
then, is the surpassing power of God, for Christ
is our way, and a good way, too, is he, a way that
has opened the kingdom of heaven to believers.
Moreover, the ways of the Lord are straight, as
it is written: "Make your ways known to me, O
Lord." Chastity is a way, faith is a way, abstinence is a way. There is, indeed, a way of virtue,
and there is a way of wickedness; for it is written, "And see if there is any way of wickedness in
me." ON THE CHRISTIAN FAITH 3.7.51.[8]

NARROW PATHS. AUGUSTINE: They are not the
wide paths that lead many to perdition; train
me in your narrow ways that are known to few.
EXPOSITIONS OF THE PSALMS 25.4.[9]

25:5 Waiting for God

BELIEVE AND WAIT. CASSIODORUS: There
are two factors that make good Christians: the
first that we believe that God is our Savior, the
second that we must await his recompense with

patience all our lives. EXPLANATION OF THE
PSALMS 25.5.[10]

WAITING ON MERCY. AUGUSTINE: Let me shun
errors, "and teach me," for of myself I know
nothing but falsehood. . . . Turned out of paradise by you and wandering to a far-off country,
I cannot return by my own strength unless you
come to meet me in my wandering, for my return
has been waiting on your mercy throughout the
whole stretch of earthly time. EXPOSITIONS OF
THE PSALMS 25.5.[11]

WALKING IN THE PATHS GOD WALKED.
ARNOBIUS THE YOUNGER: Since as you lead,
Lord, your ways to life are found, which you
have walked, make them known to me, so that
through those very ways I may walk, and teach
me your paths so that I may proceed on them.
And as I do this very thing you direct me in your
truth and lead me, because you are my God of
salvation. COMMENTARY ON THE PSALMS 25.[12]

25:6 Mindful of God's Mercy

EVER-PRESENT MERCY. AUGUSTINE: You have
never been without them [your mercies]. You did
indeed subject sinful humans to frustration, but
you subjected them in hope; you did not abandon them but supported them with the many
great comforts of your creation. EXPOSITIONS OF
THE PSALMS 25.6.[13]

NOT BY OUR MERITS. CASSIODORUS: In these
words a noble and orthodox sentiment seems
to shine forth on us, for no one attains God's
grace by his own merits. By speaking of God's
"mercy, which is at the beginning of the world,"
the church continually praises the Lord as the
donor of mercies who does not as a prior step
take up people's deserving deeds but grants first

---

[6]ACW 51:248*. [7]WGRW 5:249*. [8]NPNF 2 10:250*. [9]WSA 3
15:249. [10]ACW 51:249. [11]WSA 3 15:249. [12]CCL 25:32. [13]WSA
3 15:250.

his own gifts. Truly all heresies have taken their origin from an execrable notion, and we are given to understand here how destructive the Pelagian evil is from its being clearly refuted with such insistence. EXPLANATION OF THE PSALMS 25.6.[14]

THE MINDFULNESS OF GOD. EVAGRIUS OF PONTUS: When people remember, they stir up within themselves the thoughts of things they had known before. But God, when he is mindful of the rational nature, is in that very nature. It is said that he is mindful of him into whom he comes. NOTES ON THE PSALMS.[15]

25:7 Remember Not the Sins of My Youth

NOT MY SIN, BUT ME. THEODORET OF CYR: In those expressions what he was asking for was this: According to your great mercy, remember me; remember not my sin but me in loving fashion. COMMENTARY ON THE PSALMS 25.3.[16]

NOT WHAT IS DUE ME. AUGUSTINE: Please do remember me, not in the anger of which I am worthy, but in your mercy, which is worthy of you, and this "because of your goodness, O Lord," not because of what is due to me, Lord, but because of your own goodness. EXPOSITIONS OF THE PSALMS 25.7.[17]

THE YOUTHFUL SINS OF ISRAEL IN EGYPT. DIODORE OF TARSUS: By "youthful sin" he refers to the people's sins in Egypt, where they committed idolatry, remember. So now, he is saying, remember not those sins but your lovingkindness, by which even then you were kind to them in their ignorance and had mercy on them of your own accord even without being asked; and so now, too, exercise such care and lovingkindness for your own sake. COMMENTARY ON PSALMS 25.[18]

25:8 God Instructs Sinners

A GIFT OF DIVINE GOODNESS. CASSIODORUS:

The Lord is sweet because while excelling all in kindnesses he still awaits the conversion of the sinner, for "he rains on the just and the unjust," granting life to those who deserved to be blotted out. . . . He is righteous because after numerous rebukes and extremely long delays he opposes evil people, humbles the proud and wicked, so that they may finally become wise and repent of their having sinned. As for his establishing a law, this was a particular mark of sweetness and righteousness, for he did not wish those people to sin whom he preferred to correct by the proclamation of the law. But so that none might believe that this came as a punishment emanating from harshness, he expounded the purpose of the law that he introduced, the law of goodness and sweetness. "On the way," that is, in the present life, where the law by which we are warned to live righteously is established. EXPLANATION OF THE PSALMS 25.8.[19]

FOR OUR BENEFIT. DIODORE OF TARSUS: How is it, if God is naturally loving and merciful, that he allowed some people to be subjected to punishments? David added "and upright" to bring out that justice accompanies goodness. He goes on, in fact, "Hence he will legislate for sinners in the way": for this reason, that justice also is an attribute of his, "he will legislate for sinners in the way," that is, he will correct sinners so as to bring them to uprightness. In regard to sinners, he is saying, God gives evidence of justice, whereas in regard to others it is goodness. . . . Nevertheless, whether people are punished or enjoy happy outcomes, they find everything happening to their own benefit, provided the mind is set on God and does not waver. COMMENTARY ON PSALMS 25.[20]

THE GENTLE ARE TAUGHT. EVAGRIUS OF PONTUS: If someone has mastered irascibility, he has mastered the demons, but if someone is a slave to

---

[14]ACW 51:249-50*. [15]PG 12:1272. [16]FC 101:164. [17]WSA 3 15:250. [18]WGRW 9:78. [19]ACW 51:251*. [20]WGRW 9:78-79*.

this passion, he is a complete . . . stranger to the ways of our Savior, since the Lord is said to teach the gentle his ways.[21] ON THOUGHTS 13.[22]

MERCY IS CUSTOMARY WITH GOD. THEODORE OF MOPSUESTIA: Mercy is customary with God; righteousness is his constant concern. Often, in fact, he obscures sin with a show of his goodness, and he does not submit individuals' behavior to harsh scrutiny; rather, when he sees some people persisting in their errors without amendment, he applies the rigor of justice and chastises them for the purpose of correcting them, and by the bitterness of the blows he brings the errant ones back to a life of discipline. COMMENTARY ON PSALMS 25.8.[23]

25:9 God Teaches the Humble

INSTRUCTING THE HUMBLE. AUGUSTINE: [God] will teach his ways not to those who want to run on ahead, as if they could rule themselves better than he can, but to those who do not strut about with their heads in the air or dig in their heels, when his easy yoke and light burden are set on them. EXPOSITIONS OF THE PSALMS 25.9.[24]

MEEK AND MILD. CASSIODORUS: The term "meek" excludes the proud and the puffed up. . . . "The mild" are the converse of the proud, who with a freedom harmful to themselves kick against the soft yoke and the light burden; God will teach those who do not grumble but do what they acknowledge as commands. The difference between mild and meek seems to be this: the meek are those untroubled by any flame of wildness, constantly abiding in gentleness of mind, whereas the mild (*mansueti*) are so called because they are tamed by hand (*manu sueti*), in other words, bearing injuries and not returning evil for evil. EXPLANATION OF THE PSALMS 25.9.[25]

25:10 Steadfast Love and Faithfulness

THESE ARE GOD'S WAYS. THEODORE OF MOP-

SUESTIA: These are the ways of the Lord. Now, he habitually links truth and mercy, as if to say, this is God's work, this his way, this his action, to accord secure and true salvation to those he has chosen. COMMENTARY ON PSALMS 25.10.[26]

KNOWN FROM SCRIPTURE. THEODORET OF CYR: Those constantly reared on the sacred Words have a precise knowledge from them that all the dispensations of God our Savior are tempered with mercy and truth: to some, who repent of sins committed, he extends mercy and pardon; others unconquered he proclaims and crowns as champions of virtue, giving his verdict with truth, while admittedly on those caught up in lawlessness and not taking advantage of repentance he inflicts punishments in terms of the standard of truth. COMMENTARY ON THE PSALMS 25.5.[27]

25:11 Great Guilt

ABANDONED FOR AWHILE. JEROME: Although the mercy of God mitigated the truth of his judgment, nevertheless, because David was bold enough to make such statements, he was abandoned to his weakness for awhile, and, as you say, to the freedom of his will. AGAINST THE PELAGIANS 2.19.[28]

25:12 Fearing the Lord

EMPHASIS ON FEAR. CASSIODORUS: In the third section, there is particular emphasis on who it is that fears the Lord or with what gift the Lord blesses him. EXPLANATION OF THE PSALMS 25.12.[29]

25:13 Possessing the Land

THE SPIRITUAL INHERITANCE. PSEUDO-ATHA-

---

[21]Cf. Ps 25:9 (24:9 LXX). [22]GAC 162*. [23]WGRW 5:251. [24]WSA 3 15:250*. [25]ACW 51:251. [26]WGRW 5:251. [27]FC 101:165. [28]FC 53:324-25. [29]ACW 51:252*.

NASIUS: The person who fears the Lord, his seed—which is good works—will cause him to inherit the spiritual land, which he will acquire by humility and labor with the forgiveness of sins. EXPOSITION ON PSALMS 25.[30]

BEFORE THE RESURRECTION. CASSIODORUS: When the just strip off their bodies, the perfect blessedness promised to saints at the resurrection is not immediately granted; however, . . . his soul can "dwell in good things," for even if there is still a postponement of those rewards that "eye has not seen, nor ear heard, neither have they entered into the heart of man," they still at this time feast on the unshakeable delight of home in their future reward. EXPLANATION OF THE PSALMS 25.13.[31]

25:14 The Friendship of the Lord

FEAR YIELDS HOPE. CASSIODORUS: Fear of people breeds lack of confidence, but fear of God yields the support of hope. EXPLANATION OF THE PSALMS 25.14.[32]

25:15 Eyes Turned to the Lord

THE DISPOSITION OF KNOWLEDGE. EVAGRIUS OF PONTUS: One who says and does everything so that he may know God always has the eyes of his soul toward the Lord. If one does not receive the spirit of the adoption of the children, he is not made a brother of Christ, nor is the power of the holy made effectual in him; let him say that he is an only child and poor in riches having been deprived of knowledge. NOTES ON THE PSALMS 24[25].16.[33]

AVOIDING PITFALLS. CASSIODORUS: One who does not watch the ground before his feet is likely to run into snares or fall into open wells. But the statement here is remarkable and true, that we shall walk circumspectly and guide our feet if we continually raise our eyes to the Lord, for such gazing makes us strangers to all stum-

bling. EXPLANATION OF THE PSALMS 25.15.[34]

25:18 Forgive All My Sins

FORGIVENESS NOW. AUGUSTINE: I ask you to forgive me not only the sins of my youth and ignorance committed before I believed but also those that I commit even now when I am living by faith, whether through weakness or the dark clouds that obscure this life. EXPOSITIONS OF THE PSALMS 25.18.[35]

25:19 Consider My Enemies

ENEMIES EVERYWHERE. AUGUSTINE: Not only outside, but within, at the very heart of the church, enemies are not lacking. "With wicked hatred they hate me," hating me even though I love them. EXPOSITIONS OF THE PSALMS 25.19.[36]

PRAYER FOR THE LOST. CASSIODORUS: In saying "Look on my enemies," the church prays for their return, for God converts without delay those whom he looks on; for example, in the Gospel the Lord looked on Peter, and he wept. . . . One might perhaps believe that a few could be held of little account, but the loss of many could not be endured without the greatest grief. EXPLANATION OF THE PSALMS 25.19.[37]

25:20 Deliver Me

THE SOURCE OF HOPE. EVAGRIUS OF PONTUS: Hope does not shame. She is the daughter of uprightness, and uprightness is the offspring of patience, and patience is birthed really in trials that the virtues receive from the enemy and by which the understanding of God is cut off. NOTES ON THE PSALMS 24[25].20.[38]

DELIVERED BY FAITH. AUGUSTINE: Guard my

[30]CSCO 387:17. [31]ACW 51:253*. [32]ACW 51:253*. [33]PG 12:1272. [34]ACW 51:253*. [35]WSA 3 15:252. [36]WSA 3 15:252. [37]ACW 51:254-55*. [38]PG 12:1273

soul from sliding into imitation of them, and deliver me from this confused situation where they are mixed in with me. . . . If they chance to rise up against me, let me not be shamed, because I have put my trust not in myself but in you. EXPOSITIONS OF THE PSALMS 25.20.[39]

25:21 *Wait for God*

LOVE BY HIS STRENGTH. CASSIODORUS: The church says that the innocent and upright have adhered to the church because it waited on the Lord; otherwise it could not love such people if it was not seen to be confident of such strength. EXPLANATION OF THE PSALMS 25.21.[40]

MOTIVATED BY HOPE. THEODORE OF MOPSUESTIA: Placing my hope in you, I took pains to be such a person that innocent people might associate with me and take pleasure in my company. COMMENTARY ON PSALMS 25.21.[41]

25:22 *Out of All One's Troubles*

REDEEMED WITHIN AND WITHOUT. AUGUSTINE: Redeem your people, O God, whom you have prepared for the vision of yourself. Redeem them from all the troubles they endure, not only from without but also from within. EXPOSITIONS OF THE PSALMS 25.22.[42]

PEACE THROUGH THE KING'S SALVATION. THEODORET OF CYR: Prayer offered to God befits a king: it is appropriate for one appointed to rule to exercise complete care of his subjects. This is surely the reason that blessed David offered prayer not only for himself but also for a people entrusted to him, especially as the salvation of the one who reigns wisely and well constitutes the welfare of the whole people. The verse implies something else as well, however. Israel was divided, in the time of Saul, of Mephibosheth and of Absalom. Consequently, if I were to enjoy your aid, he is saying, and prove stronger than my adversaries, Israel itself would obtain peace by putting an end to civil strife and would revel in your good things. COMMENTARY ON THE PSALMS 25.10.[43]

---

[39]WSA 3 15:252. [40]ACW 51:255*. [41]WGRW 5:255. [42]WSA 3 15:253*. [43]FC 101:168.

26:1-12 PRAYER FOR VINDICATION

If [enemies] persist and, with hands red with blood, try to drag you down
and kill you, remember that God is the proper judge
(for he alone is righteous while that which is human is limited)
and so say the words of [Psalm] 26.

ATHANASIUS *ON THE INTERPRETATION OF THE PSALMS* 17 [OIP 67]

A Psalm of David.

¹*Vindicate me, O LORD,*

for I have walked in my integrity,
and I have trusted in the LORD without
wavering.
²*Prove me, O LORD, and try me;*
test my heart and my mind.
³*For thy steadfast love is before my eyes,*
*and I walk in faithfulness to thee.*ᶜ

⁴*I do not sit with false men,*
nor do I consort with dissemblers;
⁵*I hate the company of evildoers,*
and I will not sit with the wicked.

⁶*I wash my hands in innocence,*
and go about thy altar, O LORD,
⁷*singing aloud a song of thanksgiving,*
and telling all thy wondrous deeds.

⁸*O LORD, I love the habitation of thy house,*
and the place where thy glory dwells.
⁹*Sweep me not away with sinners,*
nor my life with bloodthirsty men,
¹⁰*men in whose hands are evil devices,*
and whose right hands are full of bribes.

¹¹*But as for me, I walk in my integrity;*
redeem me, and be gracious to me.
¹²*My foot stands on level ground;*
in the great congregation I will bless the LORD.

c Or *in thy faithfulness*

OVERVIEW: The twenty-sixth psalm is appropriately placed in context in the life of David (THEODORET) but can also be applied to the ideal of the perfect Christian (CASSIODORUS). The psalmist makes his appeal expressing confidence in God (THEODORET), without any doubt (THEODORE OF MOPSUESTIA), certain of God's mercy (CASSIODORUS). Here is the source of Christian faith (ARNOBIUS THE YOUNGER). Life has its appointed sorrows (ORIGEN), which God employs for a remedial purpose (CASSIODORUS). The psalmist's appeal is that God reveal him to himself (AUGUSTINE). By faith, the psalmist is pleasing to God (CASSIODORUS), led by mercy, not by merit (AUGUSTINE), pleasing God in God (EVAGRIUS). Both present and future grace are in view (FULGENTIUS). The psalmist seeks justice for mercy's sake (JEROME). The psalmist avoids the council of the wicked (CASSIODORUS) and the vain as well (CASSIODORUS), thereby resisting the devil (CAESARIUS). He approaches the rational altar (EVAGRIUS) and undergoes a spiritual washing (CASSIODORUS), washing being a symbol of purity (CYRIL OF JERUSALEM). The psalm ends reflecting on the beauty of God's house (CASSIODORUS) and the ransom—the Lord's blood—

that frees us to enjoy it (AUGUSTINE, CASSIODORUS).

Superscription: *A Psalm of David*

CONTEXT IN THE LIFE OF DAVID. THEODORET OF CYR: In my view the divine David uttered this psalm also with himself in mind. . . . I consider he is employing these words when pursued by Saul and forced to live among foreigners; seeing their involvement in impiety, superstition and every kind of lawlessness, he shunned their assemblies and the feasts celebrated in honor of the demons. COMMENTARY ON THE PSALMS 26.1.[1]

THE PERFECT CHRISTIAN. CASSIODORUS: The whole of this text is to be applied to the theme of the perfect Christian who by the Lord's generosity continues with committed mind in his church, winning praise for his different merits and consoling himself with God's kindnesses. But since the hymn is described as such, we must ascribe it to Christ the Lord through the power of our understanding. EXPLANATION OF THE PSALMS 26.1.[2]

26:1 Vindicate Me

CONFIDENT IN GOD. THEODORET OF CYR: I appeal to you, O Lord, to act as judge of the justice of my cause: I know you are God, I placed my hopes in your providence, and I am confident I shall not fall into the hands of my pursuers. COMMENTARY ON THE PSALMS 26.2.[3]

CERTAIN OF GOD'S MERCY. CASSIODORUS: The request for judgment seems indeed to be hazardous, but separation from evil people, which takes place at the Lord's scrutiny, is acknowledged to be fittingly sought by one who is truly deserving. So we have here not pride in what he deserves, which is abominable, but a just request from a faithful servant asking to be separated from the exceedingly wicked, so that he may not share the portion of evil people. The psalmist demands

judgment because he is certain of the Lord's mercy. As Paul has it, "As to the rest, there is laid up for me a crown of justice, which the Lord, the just Judge, will render to me in that day."[4] He walks in his innocence because, as he says later, he puts his trust in the Lord, and the presumption he shows is not in his own powers but in God's generosity. There follows a beautiful proof of this assertion, for he maintains that he is not weakened in his trust in the Lord. This is in fact the "innocence" of which he spoke earlier, in other words, confidence in the Lord's power that no weakness of sin can weigh on him. EXPLANATION OF THE PSALMS 26.1.[5]

WITHOUT ANY DOUBT. THEODORE OF MOPSUESTIA: It is not to be read, as some commentators claim, "Judge me, Lord," for if it is read "Judge me," it gives quite a different sense, as though to say, condemn me, as also in Psalm 5 he appealed in the words "Condemn them, Lord," which is not appropriate for a suppliant to ask for in his own case. So it is to be read as "Give me a just verdict" . . . because I did not swerve from my innocent purpose, nor did I have any doubts about the hope I placed in you. COMMENTARY ON PSALMS 26.1.[6]

THE FAITH OF A CHRISTIAN. ARNOBIUS THE YOUNGER: Two things give faith to the Christian, that he has the mercy of God before his eyes and that he accepts the truth of the universal faith. COMMENTARY ON THE PSALMS 26.[7]

26:2 Try Me

APPOINTED SORROWS. ORIGEN: If need be, we will not only partake of the blessings of life but bear its appointed sorrows as a trial to our souls. For in this way is divine Scripture accustomed to speak of human afflictions, by which, as gold is tried in the fire, so the human spirit is tried and

---

[1]FC 101:169. [2]ACW 51:256. [3]FC 101:169. [4]2 Tim 4:8. [5]ACW 51:257*. [6]WGRW 5:257. [7]CCL 25:33.

is found to be worthy either of condemnation or of praise. . . . We are therefore prepared and are ready to say, "Try me, O Lord, and prove me; purge my reins and my heart." AGAINST CELSUS 8.56.[8]

REMEDIAL PURPOSE. CASSIODORUS: "Prove and try" is said not out of presumption but as a demand that it be done to bring about an improvement; for when God examines and tries us, he makes us aware of our sinning and helps us attain the reward of repentance. EXPLANATION OF THE PSALMS 26.2.[9]

REVEAL ME TO MYSELF. AUGUSTINE: Lest even one of my secret sins elude my scrutiny, examine me, Lord, and try me. Reveal me not to yourself, from whom nothing lies hidden, but to myself and others. "Sear my affections and my heart." Apply a remedial purge, like fire, to my desires and my thoughts, "because your mercy is before my eyes." EXPOSITIONS OF THE PSALMS 26.3.[10]

26:3 God's Love and Faithfulness

PLEASING TO GOD BY FAITH. CASSIODORUS: He could not forget his mercy; he continually regards this as an aid to him, because he always sets before his eyes the kindnesses that have been bestowed. . . . "In your truth" means "In your Christ," for he says, "I am the way, the truth and the life." Otherwise he cannot be pleasing to the Lord unless he has been strengthened by such belief. EXPLANATION OF THE PSALMS 26.3.[11]

LED BY MERCY. AUGUSTINE: It is your mercy, not my own merits, that has led me to such a life; let me keep your mercy before my eyes, that I may not be consumed in your purging fire. "And in your truth I have become pleasing to you," for though my own falsehood displeased me, your truth has given me pleasure, and so with it and in it I have myself become acceptable and pleasing to you. EXPOSITIONS OF THE PSALMS 26.3.[12]

PLEASING GOD IN GOD. EVAGRIUS OF PONTUS: If Christ our God is truth, as indeed he said, "I am the Truth"[13] and if David in truth was pleasing to God, surely David was pleasing to God in God. NOTES ON THE PSALMS 25[26].3.[14]

PRESENT AND FUTURE GRACE. FULGENTIUS OF RUSPE: The grace of justification is given in the present time, but the grace of glorification is saved as a future grace. The one is of faith, the other of sight. Paul says that now "we walk by faith, not by sight."[15] What the saints believe now, then they will see. . . . The just person living by faith says with trusting faith, "I believe that I shall see the good things of the Lord in the land of the living." This, therefore, is the order of divine redemption and reward in humankind so that, having been justified, he believes now what, having been glorified, he will receive then. LETTER TO MONIMUS 1.11.5.[16]

JUSTICE FOR MERCY'S SAKE. JEROME: He seeks justice so that he may tell of mercy. BRIEF COMMENTARY ON PSALMS 25[26].[17]

26:4 Avoiding the Wicked

THE COUNCIL OF THE WICKED. CASSIODORUS: He now lists what he has achieved through the Lord's kindnesses, for this was the basis of his claim that he was approved. "I have not sat in the council of vanity"; he does not lend assent to the discussions of the wicked by any association with their plans. It can happen by some chance that a holy person attends a council of the wicked at which unfitting or empty proposals are made, yet while he has cognizance of these he does not associate himself with them or linger with any delight in them, but instead either he argues against an evil proposal or quits it. So whereas earlier the psalmist said that he had not

[8]ANF 4:661*. [9]ACW 51:257*. [10]WSA 3 15:254. [11]ACW 51:258*. [12]WSA 3 15:254. [13]Jn 14:6. [14]PG 12:1273. [15]2 Cor 5:7. [16]FC 95:202*. [17]CCL 72:200.

sat with the wicked, now he claims that he has not gone in with those who are very wicked; first he avoided their discussions, and later he forsook their actions. "Going into" crime means beginning some reckless action, for the going in signifies the commencement of the activity that the holy person claims is alien to his moral sense. EXPLANATION OF THE PSALMS 26.4.[18]

26:5 The Company of the Wicked

THE VAIN AND THE WICKED. CASSIODORUS: It would not have been enough for the holy person to have avoided the evil council without also hating the assembly of those who are cunning in every way. Hatred connotes division, just as love connotes partnership. Just as the psalmist said earlier that he had not sat in the council of vanity, so now he claims that he does not sit with the wicked, for both must be utterly forsaken. The vain and the wicked are different from each other. The vain are those concerned with transient interests who spend their time in empty discourse; but the wicked are the heretics who seek to devalue the divine Scriptures with treacherous questions, as the apostle Peter says: "Wresting them to their own destruction and perdition."[19] So he rightly warns that both groups be avoided, because the first loves empty things and the second implants weapons of subversion. EXPLANATION OF THE PSALMS 26.5.[20]

RESISTING THE DEVIL. CAESARIUS OF ARLES: Do not be malicious toward one another, for the Lord detests this vice, as he says: "I hate the assembly of evildoers." Let us, then, amend vices of the flesh, dearly beloved, for the sake of beauty of soul, in which there is the image of Christ. I speak the truth, brothers, that if we want to observe all these things, we will also say to the one who is tempting us: Do not persuade me, devil, to defile the image of my God by listening to you. He suffered for me, he was covered with spittle for me, he was struck with blows on the cheek for me, he was scourged for me, he was

hung on a cross for me. This the servant of God should say to his tempter: Truly you will not persuade me to do what you are urging. SERMON 238.2.[21]

26:6 Going to the Altar

A SPIRITUAL WASHING. CASSIODORUS: Whoever makes spotless his own deeds through eagerness for a goodly life with others washes his hands among the innocent. He did well to add "among the innocent," because guilty people also can wash their hands, as Pontius Pilate did when in fouling his soul by wicked betrayal of the Lord. . . . But whoever washes his hands in the tears that render satisfaction washes his hands in the spiritual sense. EXPLANATION OF THE PSALMS 26.6.[22]

THE RATIONAL ALTAR. EVAGRIUS OF PONTUS: Our mind is the rational altar on which we burn all irrational thoughts with the fire sent from the Father. . . . When the soul reflects on itself, it encompasses the altar of God, nor does it seek a corner of corruption. . . . Contemplation is the altar of corporeal and incorporeal things by which my mind is cleansed. One who embraces it, that is, learning, declares all the marvels of God. NOTES ON THE PSALMS 25[26].6.[23]

SYMBOL OF PURITY. CYRIL OF JERUSALEM: You have seen the deacon who gives to the priest water to wash, and to the presbyters who stand around God's altar. He gave it not at all because of bodily defilement; it is not that, for we did not enter the church at first with defiled bodies. But the washing of hands is a symbol that you ought to be pure from all sinful and unlawful deeds; for since the hands are a symbol of action, by washing them, it is evident, we represent the purity and blamelessness of our conduct. Did you not hear the blessed David opening this

---

[18]ACW 51:258-59*. [19]2 Pet 3:16. [20]ACW 51:259*. [21]FC 66:222*. [22]ACW 51:259. [23]PG 12:1273, 1276.

very mystery and saying, "I will wash my hands in innocence, and so will I compass your altar, O Lord"? The washing therefore of hands is a symbol of immunity from sin. MYSTAGOGICAL LECTURES 5.2.[24]

26:8 The Habitation of God

THE BEAUTY OF GOD'S HOUSE. CASSIODO-RUS: "The beauty of your house" means not splendor of walls or most expensive tableware but the most blessed nature of those actions in which the whole church rejoices: namely, the glad rendering of psalms, the piety of prayers, the most humble devotion of the Christian people. Previously he spoke of the church as a whole, and now he comes to the saints in whom God's glory is known to dwell. Of them Paul says, "For the temple of God is holy, which you are."[25] By his mention of "the dwelling place," he was pointing to the secret region of the human heart; and he adds the wonderful phrase "of your glory," for wherever he dwells there is glory, since he makes glorious whatever place he designs to dwell in, and the majesty of the lodging grows with the merits of the Guest. EXPLANATION OF THE PSALMS 26.8.[26]

26:11 Redeem Me

THE LORD'S BLOOD. AUGUSTINE: May the immense ransom price of my Lord's blood purchase perfect freedom for me, and amid the perils of this life may your mercy not forsake me. EXPOSITIONS OF THE PSALMS 26.11.[27]

THE BLOOD OF DELIVERANCE. CASSIODORUS: "Redeem me," in other words, free me with precious blood at your coming, for by it the world was delivered when held subject to sins. "And have mercy on me," that is, in this world, where you spare those who faithfully entreat you. EXPLANATION OF THE PSALMS 26.11.[28]

---

[24]FC 64:191-92**. [25]1 Cor 3:17. [26]ACW 51:260. [27]WSA 3 15:256. [28]ACW 51:261.

27:1-14 PRAYER OF DEVOTION

If you experience the harsh and vehement attacks of the enemy,
and they crowd against you, despising you as one who is not anointed
[cf. LXX heading], and on this very account they fight against you,
do not succumb to these attacks but sing Psalm 27.

ATHANASIUS ON THE INTERPRETATION OF THE PSALMS 17 [OIP 67]

A Psalm of David.*

¹The LORD is my light and my salvation;
  whom shall I fear?
The LORD is the stronghold[d] of my life;
  of whom shall I be afraid?

²When evildoers assail me,
  uttering slanders against me,[e]
my adversaries and foes,
  they shall stumble and fall.

³Though a host encamp against me,
  my heart shall not fear;
though war arise against me,
  yet I will be confident.

⁴One thing have I asked of the LORD,
  that will I seek after;
that I may dwell in the house of the LORD
  all the days of my life,
to behold the beauty of the LORD,
  and to inquire in his temple.

⁵For he will hide me in his shelter
  in the day of trouble;
he will conceal me under the cover of his tent,
  he will set me high upon a rock.

⁶And now my head shall be lifted up
  above my enemies round about me;

and I will offer in his tent
  sacrifices with shouts of joy;
I will sing and make melody to the LORD.

⁷Hear, O LORD, when I cry aloud,
  be gracious to me and answer me!
⁸Thou hast said, "Seek ye my face."
  My heart says to thee,
"Thy face, LORD, do I seek."
  ⁹Hide not thy face from me.

Turn not thy servant away in anger,
  thou who hast been my help.
Cast me not off, forsake me not,
  O God of my salvation!
¹⁰For my father and my mother have forsaken me,
  but the LORD will take me up.

¹¹Teach me thy way, O LORD;
  and lead me on a level path
  because of my enemies.
¹²Give me not up to the will of my adversaries;
  for false witnesses have risen against me,
  and they breathe out violence.

¹³I believe that I shall see the goodness of the
  LORD
  in the land of the living!
¹⁴Wait for the LORD;
  be strong, and let your heart take courage;
  yea, wait for the LORD!

d Or *refuge* e Heb *to eat up my flesh* * Some versions of the LXX add *before he was anointed*

OVERVIEW: The twenty-seventh psalm in the Septuagint carries the superscription "before he was anointed," which raises the question to which of David's anointings should the psalm be referred (CASSIODORUS). Others relate it to later times (DIODORE). The Lord who is light is the source of our enlightenment (GREGORY OF NYSSA), our help in the darkness of trouble (DIODORE). Fear of the Lord casts out all other fear (CASSIODORUS), including the fear of demons (ORIGEN). We are confident through divine enablement (LEO).

David gives thanks for the fall of his adversaries (DIODORE, THEODORET), adversaries of his flesh but not of his soul (AMBROSE). He has confidence based on experience (THEODORET), confidence of an uncreated liberty (ORIGEN), a confidence exhibited by Christ (ORIGEN). Two types of warfare can be thought of here—active and contemplative (EVAGRIUS). Salvation is found in the Lord's house (THEODORET). We should, like David, long to dwell in the Lord's house (BEDE), while not forgetting the present house, the church (BEDE). Our grace-giving head, the Lord Jesus, is lifted up (BEDE), and no other sacrifices are pleasing to God (DIODORE). We seek in him the face of mercy (ARNOBIUS THE YOUNGER), preferring even the face of correction to abandonment (DIODORE).

We ask that the Lord not only teach us but also guide us (THEODORET), knowing that the law was given for our benefit (ARNOBIUS THE YOUNGER). We ask not to be given up to our adversaries but that the Lord improve us (DIODORE). We become strong waiting for God's promises (THEODORET), maintaining doctrinal strength (EVAGRIUS), enabled by God, not by our own strength (FULGENTIUS), strengthened by the Holy Spirit (CYRIL OF JERUSALEM) so that we labor in the Lord (CYRIL OF ALEXANDRIA).

Superscription: *A Psalm of David*

THE SECOND ANOINTING OF DAVID. CASSIODORUS: The history of this heading is revealed in greater detail in the book of Kings. When Saul sinned before God, David was anointed into the kingship in the presence of his father by the holy prophet Samuel.[1] However, the heading does not refer to that anointing but is seen rather to commemorate a second anointing, when after Saul's persecutions he was advanced to the kingship by the prayer of the people,[2] for it is clear that he wrote this psalm in witness of those events. If you care to concentrate your attention on the first anointing, you read that he composed no psalm before it, so it remains for us to understand the reference here as to the second anointing. EXPLANATION OF THE PSALMS 27.1.[3]

CONCERNING HEZEKIAH. DIODORE OF TARSUS: The twenty-seventh, twenty-eighth, twenty-ninth and thirtieth psalms have the same theme, composed from the viewpoint of blessed Hezekiah and directed against the Assyrians. The inspired author David prophesied and adopted this theme on the other's part, using his very words in prophecy and displaying his feelings. The four have a certain change and difference from one another, which commentary on each psalm will mention: the twenty-seventh and twenty-ninth are triumphal odes on the destruction of the Assyrians alone, whereas the twenty-eighth and thirtieth make reference also to Hezekiah's illness and recovery. COMMENTARY ON PSALMS 27.[4]

27:1 *Light and Salvation*

THE SOURCE OF LIGHT. GREGORY OF NYSSA: He is called a light by David, and from there the light of knowledge shines in people who are enlightened. AGAINST EUNOMIUS 2.15.[5]

THE LIGHT OF GOD'S HELP. DIODORE OF TARSUS: Tribulation caused the Israelites to live in darkness, as it were, whereas the Lord's support

---

[1]Cf. 1 Kings 16:13. [2]Cf. 2 Kings 5:2. [3]ACW 51:262. [4]WGRW 9:82. [5]NPNF 2 5:133*.

proved a light and help to them. COMMENTARY ON PSALMS 27.[6]

FEAR CASTS OUT FEAR. CASSIODORUS: "Whom shall I fear?" means "I shall fear no one"; fear of the Lord had ensured that he could fear no other. EXPLANATION OF THE PSALMS 27.2.[7]

NO FEAR OF DEMONS. ORIGEN: Christians have nothing to fear, even if demons should not be well-disposed to them; for they are protected by the supreme God, who is well pleased with their piety and who sets his divine angels to watch over those who are worthy of such guardianship, so that they can suffer nothing from demons. He who by his piety possesses the favor of the Most High, who has accepted the guidance of Jesus, the "angel of the great counsel,"[8] being well contented with the favor of God through Christ Jesus, may say with confidence that he has nothing to suffer from the whole host of demons. AGAINST CELSUS 8.27.[9]

ENABLEMENT FROM GOD. LEO THE GREAT: In rendering service to the grace of God, we are not only made subject to our King through obedience but are even joined to him through the will. If we are of one mind with him (willing what he wills, disapproving of what he disapproves), he himself will bring us victory in all our battles. He who has given the "will" will bestow also the ability. In this way can we "cooperate" with his works, speaking that prophetic utterance in the exultation of faith: "The Lord is my light and my salvation. Whom shall I fear? The Lord is the defender of my life. Of whom shall I be afraid?" SERMON 26.4.2.[10]

27:2 Evildoers

THE FALL OF MY ADVERSARIES. DIODORE OF TARSUS: Having referred to the victory in the introduction, he states these two clauses by way of narrative; lest he seem to be giving thanks needlessly, he introduces as well the reason for

thanksgiving in the words "When some enemies assembled against me who were so fierce and unrelenting as even to take a piece of me, as it were, then in particular I clearly sensed God's help, with their fall and our conquest." COMMENTARY ON PSALMS 27.[11]

VICTIMS OF THEIR OWN SCHEMES. THEODORET OF CYR: Those who stole an advantage over me in their pursuit like wild animals and their attempts to make a meal of me while still alive, far from doing me any harm, were themselves the victims of total destruction. COMMENTARY ON THE PSALMS 27.3.[12]

ENEMIES OF FLESH. AMBROSE: David says that he does not fear, because the enemy were eating up his flesh but not his soul. CONCERNING REPENTANCE 1.14.77.[13]

27:3 Confidence in God

CONFIDENT THROUGH EXPERIENCE. THEODORET OF CYR: Having such wonderful experience of assistance, he is saying, even should two or three times the number of enemies try to attack me, I would brave the difficulties, armed with this hope. COMMENTARY ON THE PSALMS 27.3.[14]

UNCREATED LIBERTY. ORIGEN: You see steadfastness and vigor of the soul that keeps the commandments of God and has the confidence of uncreated liberty. HOMILIES ON LEVITICUS 16.6.1.[15]

THE CONFIDENCE OF CHRIST. ORIGEN: It may be that these words are spoken by the prophet of no one else but the Savior, who feared no one because of the light and salvation given from the Father and who was afraid of no one because of

---

[6]WGRW 9:82. [7]ACW 51:264*. [8]Is 9:6. [9]ANF 4:649. [10]FC 93:108. [11]WGRW 9:82. [12]FC 101:174. [13]NPNF 2 10:342. [14]FC 101:174. [15]FC 83:272.

the protection with which God shielded him. And his heart was not at all fearful when the entire host of Satan encamped against him. His heart, filled with sacred teachings, hoped in God when war rose up against him. Exhortation to Martydom 29.[16]

Active and Contemplative Warfare. Evagrius of Pontus: One who follows the active life wages war by his own virtues with alien virtues. One who follows the contemplative life using true dogmas destroys every thought opposed to the knowledge of God. Notes on the Psalms 26[27].3.[17]

27:4 Dwelling in the House of the Lord

Salvation in the Lord's House. Theodoret of Cyr: Having enjoyed such beneficence, he is saying, I seek from my benefactor not wealth or influence, royalty or glory, but constant attendance in the divine temple, contemplation of the divine beauty there and inspection of everything happening in accordance with law. I have . . . already secured salvation from that source and escaped the hand of my pursuers. This the mighty David both asked for and received from the munificent God: he brought back the divine ark, erected another more wonderful tabernacle and assembled the different choirs of singers. You could gain a more precise knowledge of this from the books of Chronicles. Commentary on the Psalms 27.4.[18]

Longing for God's House. Bede: Let us strive with all our strength of soul to arrive there. Let us make our way there by the inward affection of our heart. Let us long [to arrive] there. Let us beg all together, and let us beg individually, of the Maker of that house, that we may dwell in his house all days of our life. Homilies on the Gospels 2.4.[19]

Remember the Present House. Bede: The Lord, born a human being among human beings,

did what God, by divine inspiration through [his] angels, prescribed for human beings to do. He himself kept the law that he gave in order to show us, who are human beings pure and simple, that whatever God orders is to be observed in everything. Let us follow the path of his human way of life if we take delight in looking on the glory of his divinity, if we want to dwell in his eternal home in heaven all the days of our lives, if it delights [us] to see the Lord's will and to be shielded by his holy temple. And lest we be forever buffeted by the wind of wickedness, let us remember to frequent the house, the church of the present time, with the requisite offerings of pure petitions. Homilies on the Gospels 1.19.[20]

27:6 Sacrifices and Singing

Our Grace-Giving Head. Bede: The Lord Christ is the head of all the saints, in himself always remaining equal and indivisible, to be sure, but distributing the grace of his Spirit to each one of those who are elect, according to their capacity for receiving. For this reason, not only to the whole church in general but also to each of its members in particular is it permissible to proclaim with confidence that prophetic [word]: "And now he has lifted up my head above my enemies." On the Tabernacle 2.9.[21]

Praise Satisfies God. Diodore of Tarsus: God takes more satisfaction in the praise in these sacrifices than in the slaughter of animals. Commentary on Psalms 27.[22]

27:8-9 Seeking God's Face

The Face of Mercy. Arnobius the Younger: In this place, the lover of God, not seeking any other type of purity but desiring the beauty of Christ alone, in those words which lovers are

---

[16]OSW 60. [17]PG 12:1277. [18]FC 101:174*. [19]CS 111:40*. [20]CS 110:188-89. [21]TTH 18:84*. [22]WGRW 9:83.

accustomed to say to those whom they love, cries out in the heart, "My heart says to you, as to your face, do not turn your face from me or turn away your servant in anger." I have done such things by which you, rightly angered, have turned away from me, having been justly angered by my desires, but be my merciful helper, do not turn away from me or look down on me, God of my salvation. COMMENTARY ON THE PSALMS 27.[23]

THE FACE OF CORRECTION. DIODORE OF TARSUS: What is it that I am asking? For you not to keep silent if ever I sin as a human being or dismiss without concern my situation, leaving me unschooled in better ways. Instead, correct and reform me in a loving way. . . . Do not put me beyond your care. COMMENTARY ON PSALMS 27.[24]

27:11 Teach Me Your Way

GUIDE AND TEACH. THEODORET OF CYR: In place of "Guide me by law," Aquila and Theodotion said, "Illuminate," whereas Symmachus has, "Give me a glimpse of your way." . . . Become for me in your own person both lawgiver and guide, giving me a glimpse of the path leading to you. COMMENTARY ON THE PSALMS 27.7.[25]

FOR MY BENEFIT. ARNOBIUS THE YOUNGER: Give the law to me concerning your way, show what you wish, what you do not wish, what you love, what you hate. I will offend if I do not learn what I ought. And since my enemies are eager for nothing other except that I would offend you, I ask this, that you direct me on the right way on account of my enemies. COMMENTARY ON THE PSALMS 27.[26]

27:12 Do Not Give Me Up

IMPROVE ME. DIODORE OF TARSUS: You do two things at the same time, making me better and not giving the foe an occasion for taunting or

for thinking that they will be able to harm me against your will. COMMENTARY ON PSALMS 27.[27]

27:14 Be Strong

WAITING FOR GOD'S PROMISES. THEODORET OF CYR: The mind adorned with virility, he is saying, and by means of it getting the better of the onset of misfortunes, is strengthened, and gains the victory and awaits the divine promises, to which it becomes the heir, the body also co-operating. Now, he calls the life looked forward to "land of the living" insofar as it is separated from death and free of corruption and sadness. COMMENTARY ON THE PSALMS 27.8.[28]

THE STRONG HEART. EVAGRIUS OF PONTUS: The strong heart is that which is not filled with false doctrines or impure thoughts. NOTES ON THE PSALMS 26[27].14.[29]

DIVINE ENABLEMENT. FULGENTIUS OF RUSPE: In your zeal for good works and your contempt of human praise, be careful lest you wish to assign the good that you do, not to the grace of God but to your own strength. Hold firmly that there can be no ability in you for good will or good works unless you received it by the free gift of divine mercy. Know, therefore, that it is God working in you both to will and to do, for a good will. Accordingly, work out your salvation in fear and trembling. Humble yourself in the sight of God that he may exalt you. Ask from him the beginning of a good will. Ask from him the effects of good works. Seek from him the gift of perseverance. Do not think at any time that you can either will or do anything good, once his assistance has ceased. Ask him to turn away your eyes lest they see vanity; ask him to show you the way in which you should walk; petition him to direct your steps according to his word and let no wickedness rule over

---

[23]CCL 25:34-35. [24]WGRW 9:84. [25]FC 101:176. [26]CCL 25:35. [27]WGRW 9:84. [28]FC 101:177. [29]PG 12:1281, 1284.

you. Pray to him that he direct the works of your hands for you. "Be strong and let your heart take courage; wait for the Lord." LETTER 2.36.[30]

STRENGTHENED BY THE HOLY SPIRIT. CYRIL OF JERUSALEM: [The Holy Spirit] is called Comforter, because he comforts and encourages us and "helps our weakness. For we do not know what we should pray for as we ought, but the Spirit himself pleads for us with unutterable groanings,"[31] that is, clearly, to God. Often a person for Christ's sake is treated with contumely and unjustly dishonored; martyrdom is at hand, tortures on every side, fire, swords, wild beasts and the abyss; but the Holy Spirit gently whispers, "Wait for the Lord," for your present sufferings are slight, while your rewards will be great; endure for a little while, and you will be with the angels forever. "The sufferings of the present time are not worthy to be compared with the glory to come that will be revealed in us."[32] He portrays for the person the kingdom of heaven and even gives him a glimpse of the paradise of pleasure; and the martyrs, who must present their bodily countenances to their judges, are in spirit already in paradise, despise what appear to be hardships. CATECHETICAL LECTURES 16.20.[33]

LABOR IN THE LORD. CYRIL OF ALEXANDRIA: Great and distinguished successes are brought to completion not without labors. No doubt it is necessary that for every good thing sweat must be caused first. And no wonder if we see that such occurs in great matters, since common and inferior ones are full of care and come to pass through labors. But even in labor we have learned to say, "Be strong, and be of stout heart and wait for the Lord." For we have taken heart that a glorious result attends zealous actions aimed at virtue, and we shall find that our reward from God is the gift of spiritual courage. LETTER 25.1.[34]

---

[30]FC 95:309. [31]Rom 8:26. [32]Rom 8:18. [33]FC 64:88*. [34]FC 76:108.

28:1-9 PLEA FOR DIVINE ASSISTANCE

If you suffer from the weakness of nature as the plots against you
grow more shameless so that you have scarcely any rest,
then cry out to the Lord, in Psalm 28.
ATHANASIUS ON THE INTERPRETATION OF THE PSALMS 17 [OIP 67-68]

A Psalm of David.

[1]*To thee, O* LORD, *I call;*
my rock, be not deaf to me,
lest, if thou be silent to me,

I become like those who go down to the Pit.
[2]*Hear the voice of my supplication,*
as I cry to thee for help,
as I lift up my hands
towards thy most holy sanctuary.[f]

³*Take me not off with the wicked,*
  with those who are workers of evil,
who speak peace with their neighbors,
  while mischief is in their hearts.
⁴*Requite them according to their work,*
  and according to the evil of their deeds;
requite them according to the work of their
    hands;
  render them their due reward.
⁵*Because they do not regard the works of the*
    Lord,
  or the work of his hands,
he will break them down and build them
    up no more.

⁶*Blessed be the Lord!*
  for he has heard the voice of my
    supplications.
⁷*The Lord is my strength and my shield;*
  in him my heart trusts;
so I am helped, and my heart exults,
  and with my song I give thanks to him.

⁸*The Lord is the strength of his people,*
  he is the saving refuge of his anointed.
⁹*O save thy people, and bless thy heritage;*
  be thou their shepherd, and carry them
    for ever.

f Heb *thy innermost sanctuary*

Overview: The twenty-eighth psalm is viewed by many as speaking of Christ in the time of his passion (Eusebius, Augustine, Arnobius the Younger). Some see a later reference to Hezekiah (Diodore) or refer it to David or an example of faith for us (Theodoret). The psalm begins with an appeal to God, our source of victory (Diodore). It reminds us to seek the Word of God (Origen), even as the Word was ever-present in Christ (Augustine), for the consequence of divine silence is death (Theodoret). The psalmist raises his hands to God, and we raise the hands of our deeds (Origen) in the direction of God's revelation (Theodoret). We avoid duplicity in our speech (Theodoret), remembering that simplicity characterizes those filled with the Spirit (Bede). The psalmist prays for justice, not revenge (Theodoret), a hard lesson for those who cannot learn otherwise (Jerome). We bless the Lord though Christ who dwells within us (Augustine). He renews us even as he was renewed (Maximus). He is the strength of those who trust in him (Augustine), proving to be the strength even of his own words (Arnobius the Younger), just as the Father was his strength (Eusebius). Being in him, we receive his blessings (Jerome). David, thus, proves to be an example for us (Theodoret).

The Lord raises us and saves his people forever (Pseudo-Athanasius).

Superscription: *A Psalm of David*

Christ. Eusebius of Caesarea: The psalm we are considering also refers to Christ, including the prayer of Christ that he prayed at the time of his passion. Proof of the Gospel 4.16.185.[1]

The Mediator. Augustine: The speaker here is the Mediator himself, strong . . . in the conflict of his passion. Expositions of the Psalms 28.1.[2]

The Son Is Fully Human, Fully Divine. Arnobius the Younger: We confess the Son of God, fully God, fully man, whom we think this psalm speaks of in his own inner man, in which he cries that he who committed no sins not be handed over with sinners. Commentary on the Psalms 28.[3]

Hezekiah. Diodore of Tarsus: The twenty-eighth psalm, as was remarked, makes mention

---

[1]POG 1:206*. [2]WSA 3 15:291. [3]CCL 25:35.

both of the illness and the recovery of Hezekiah himself: when the victory went to his head, human as he was, illness chastised him. But he was also freed from it, and he gives thanks for both. COMMENTARY ON PSALMS 28.[4]

DAVID, AN EXAMPLE OF FAITH. THEODORET OF CYR: He sings this psalm in the person of those who have come to faith in Christ, and with entreaty he calls on Christ for assistance.... The psalm was spoken by David when he was pursued by Saul and was the object of schemes on the part of those who seemed to be friends but betrayed him and tried to reveal his whereabouts to Saul, like Doeg[5] and Ziphites[6] and many others in addition to them. This psalm ... and in fact the psalms before it as well, are suited to everyone encountering calamities of this kind: like blessed David it is possible for the person intent on persevering both to petition God and thereby to secure his providence. COMMENTARY ON THE PSALMS 28.1.[7]

28:1 Lord, I Call to You

GOD, THE SOURCE OF VICTORY. DIODORE OF TARSUS: I shall attribute the fact of the victory not to my virtue but to you, the God who proved its source for me. COMMENTARY ON PSALMS 28.[8]

SEEK THE WORD OF GOD. ORIGEN: Frequently, in Scripture, the righteous are said to have called out to God. Each one tries to beseech God with a cry, and I may say with an unusual cry. He goes to his bedroom closet, locks the door and calls out to God: "Do not be silent before me." It was written of Moses, Aaron and Joshua the son of Nun. Indeed, they were the worthy ones to whom God spoke. He spoke through the prophets whenever the people stood before God. Let us not think that God speaks to us externally, for those righteous thoughts that are in our hearts are the words we speak and the voice through which God speaks to us. Understand this when Scripture says that God spoke to this

one or that. Thus Scripture testifies, "Blessed is the one whose help is from you...."[9] We have this help through which the word of God is received. Holy is that one ... who hears the word of the Lord and does it. SELECTIONS FROM THE PSALMS 28.1.[10]

THE WORD EVER PRESENT IN CHRIST. AUGUSTINE: To you, Lord, I have cried; O my God, do not sever from my humanity that unity that binds your Word to me.... It is because the eternity of your Word never ceases to unite itself to me that I am not like the rest of humankind. They are born into the deepest misery of this world, where because your word is not known, it is as if you are silent. EXPOSITIONS OF THE PSALMS 28.2.[11]

CONSEQUENCE OF DIVINE SILENCE. THEODORET OF CYR: If you keep silence with me and deprive me of your help, I shall immediately be consigned to death, which he called "pit," since the grave is dug like a pit. COMMENTARY ON THE PSALMS 28.1.[12]

28:2 Lifting Up Hands

THE HANDS WE RAISE. ORIGEN: Often, we communicate by the lifting of hands, as when Moses' arms were lifted up and Israel was victorious. When his hands were down, the Amalekites won.... Our hands are our deeds of piety. If we store treasures in heaven, we have hands lifted to God and overcome the enemy. When, therefore, I raise my hands to God, I lift my spirit to him through my uplifted hands. Amalek is conquered by me. So, it is needful to lift your hands to God. The temple of God is his glory. SELECTIONS FROM THE PSALMS 28.2.[13]

THE PLACE OF REVELATION. THEODORET OF

---

[4]WGRW 9:85. [5]1 Sam 22:9. [6]1 Sam 23:19-20. [7]FC 101:178. [8]WGRW 9:85. [9]Ps 146:5 (145:5 LXX). [10]PG 12:1284. [11]WSA 3 15:291. [12]FC 101:178. [13]PG 12:1285.

CYR: Though the temple was not yet built, he gives the name "temple" to the tabernacle in which he prayed, distant from it in body but directing his mind there. Likewise also when blessed Daniel in Babylon prayed, he opened the windows facing Jerusalem,[14] not under the impression that God was confined there but from his knowledge that the divine manifestation occurred there. COMMENTARY ON THE PSALMS 28.2.[15]

28:3 The Wicked Who Speak

DUPLICITY. THEODORET OF CYR: The prayer of blessed David is to have no truck with those who practice duplicity: he calls abhorrent those who say one thing but mean another. COMMENTARY ON THE PSALMS 28.2.[16]

SIMPLICITY. BEDE: It is good that the Spirit descended upon the Lord in the form of a dove, so that the faithful may learn that they cannot be filled with his Spirit unless they are simple, unless they possess true peace with their brothers, which is signified by the kiss of doves. Ravens also have kisses, but they tear flesh (which a dove does not do at all), signifying those "who speak peace with their neighbor, but wicked things are in their hearts." A dove, which by nature is innocent of the tearing of the flesh, most suitably fits those innocents who pursue peace and sanctity with everyone. HOMILIES ON THE GOSPELS 1.15.[17]

28:4 Repay Them

JUSTICE, NOT REVENGE. THEODORET OF CYR: Let no one think, however, that the righteous person is cursing his enemies: the words are a mark not of cursing but of a just verdict. "Grant them their due repayment," he says, meaning, May they fall foul of their own schemes, which they hatch against one another. This is said also in the seventh psalm, "Their trouble will come back on their own head, and their wrong will come down on top of them."[18] COMMENTARY ON THE PSALMS 28.3.[19]

A HARD LESSON. JEROME: Because they do not understand through blessings, they will understand through suffering. BRIEF COMMENTARY ON PSALMS 28.[20]

28:6 Blessed Be the Lord

CHRIST CONFESSES IN US. AUGUSTINE: Amid such grievous suffering the Lord helps me, and with immortality he protects me when I rise again. . . . Now that the fear of death has been done away with, those who believe in me will confess to him, not constrained by fear under the law but freely and in harmony with the law. And since I am in them, I shall confess to him. EXPOSITIONS OF THE PSALMS 28.6-7.[21]

28:7 The Lord Is Strength and Shield

RENEWED STRENGTH. MAXIMUS OF TURIN: Notice how he expresses himself: he does not say "flourished" but "flourished anew," for something does not flourish anew unless it had flourished before. But the flesh of the Lord flourished when first it came forth from the Virgin Mary's unsullied womb, as the prophet Isaiah says: "A shoot shall come forth from the root of Jesse, and a flower shall spring up from his root."[22] It flourished anew, however, when, the flower of the body having been cut by the Jews, it sprouted from the sepulcher with the renewed glory of the resurrection, and like a flower it breathed forth on everyone an odor as well as the splendor of immortality—spreading around the odor of good works with its sweetness, manifesting the incorruptibility of an eternal divinity with its splendor. SERMON 55.2.[23]

28:8 The Strength of His People

THE PEOPLE WHO TRUST IN GOD. AUGUS-

---

[14]Dan 6:10. [15]FC 101:179. [16]FC 101:179. [17]CS 110:151. [18]Ps 7:16 (7:17 LXX). [19]FC 101:179. [20]CCL 72:201-2. [21]WSA 3 15:292. [22]Is 11:1. [23]ACW 50:134.

TINE: This does not refer to the people which was ignorant of God's righteousness and tried to establish its own.[24] Rather, it refers to a different people that did not look to itself for its strength but knew instead that the Lord would be its strength as it contends with the devil in the difficulties of this life. EXPLANATIONS OF THE PSALMS 28.8.[25]

THE STRENGTH OF GOD'S WORDS. ARNOBIUS THE YOUNGER: All that he suffered, he suffered by his own will, as he said, "I have the power to lay down my spirit and to take it back."[26] And he also said, freely I will confess him. He himself is the strength of his own people because he fulfills his words by his deeds. He said that he was going to suffer and he suffered, that he was going to die and he died, that he was going to arise and he arose from the dead, overcoming weakness of fear and giving strength to a most eager will. Because he is the protector of the salvation of his own anointed, because without a doubt he is "God in Christ, reconciling the World to himself,"[27] saving his own people by bringing deliverance to spirit and body, and by blessing the nations, his own inheritance, by freeing them from demonic subjection, so that the Son of God, with the Father and Holy Spirit, may extol them and rule forever. COMMENTARY ON THE PSALMS 28.[28]

THE WORKS OF CHRIST AND THE FATHER. EUSEBIUS OF CAESAREA: This teaches us that all the wonders of Christ written in the holy Scriptures, done for our salvation, whether teachings or writings, or the mysteries of his resurrection now referred to, were all done by the will and power of the Father defending his own Christ as with a shield in all his marvelous and saving words and works. PROOF OF THE GOSPEL 4.16.185.[29]

BLESSINGS COME TO US. JEROME: Whoever is baptized in Christ is his anointed. BRIEF COMMENTARY ON PSALMS 28.[30]

28:9 Save Your People

DAVID, AN EXAMPLE. THEODORET OF CYR: The prayer for the people befits the king as well: it is also admirable about mighty David that though pursued also by the people, who waged war on him along with Saul, he offered supplication on their behalf to God. He foresaw their future conversion, you see, and had regard not for the injustice but for the servitude to come. COMMENTARY ON THE PSALMS 28.5.[31]

GOD SAVES HIS PEOPLE. PSEUDO-ATHANASIUS: He aids and saves the people that were anointed for inheritance and the priestly kingdom, and he tends and exalts them forever, showing us to be raised up and glorified in future infinite ages. EXPOSITION ON PSALMS 28.[32]

---

[24]Rom 10:3. [25]*WSA* 3 15:292**. [26]Jn 10:18. [27]Col 1:20. [28]CCL 25:36. [29]*POG* 1:206-7*. [30]CCL 72:202. [31]FC 101:180. [32]CSCO 387:18.

29:1-11 THE POWER OF GOD

If in a spirit of gratitude you wish to teach
how one should make a spiritual offering to the Lord, sing Psalm 29.
ATHANASIUS *ON THE INTERPRETATION OF THE PSALMS* 17 [OIP 68]

*A Psalm of David.**

¹*Ascribe to the* LORD, *O heavenly beings,*ᵍ
ascribe to the LORD *glory and strength.*
²*Ascribe to the* LORD *the glory of his name;*
worship the LORD *in holy array.*

³*The voice of the* LORD *is upon the waters;*
the God of glory thunders,
the LORD, *upon many waters.*
⁴*The voice of the* LORD *is powerful,*
the voice of the LORD *is full of majesty.*

⁵*The voice of the* LORD *breaks the cedars,*
the LORD *breaks the cedars of Lebanon.*
⁶*He makes Lebanon to skip like a calf,*

and Sirion like a young wild ox.

⁷*The voice of the* LORD *flashes forth flames*
of fire.
⁸*The voice of the* LORD *shakes the wilderness,*
the LORD *shakes the wilderness of Kadesh.*

⁹*The voice of the* LORD *makes the oaks to*
*whirl,*ʰ
and strips the forests bare;
and in his temple all cry, "Glory!"

¹⁰*The* LORD *sits enthroned over the flood;*
the LORD *sits enthroned as king for ever.*
¹¹*May the* LORD *give strength to his people!*
May the LORD *bless his people with peace!*

g Heb *sons of gods*   h Or *makes the hinds to calve*   * Some versions of the LXX add *on the occasion of the solemn assembly of the tabernacle*

OVERVIEW: The title of the twenty-ninth psalm, speaking of a completion or perfection, points to the perfection of the church (AUGUSTINE), the completion of God's temple (ARNOBIUS THE YOUNGER). The psalm begins with an exhortation to think rightly about the nature of things (BASIL). This brings glory to God, as does bearing the divine message (THEODORET) and bringing others to the Lord (BEDE). We worship rightly when we worship among the faithful (PSEUDO-ATHANASIUS) as well as in a sanctified heart (AUGUSTINE) without distraction (BASIL).

The Lord's voice was manifest on the waters at the baptism of Jesus (ARNOBIUS THE YOUNGER) and is extended as the voice of Christ over the nations (AUGUSTINE, THEODORET) converting them into spiritual waters of eternal life (BASIL). Empowered by the Spirit (THEODORET), weak people become magnificent (BASIL). Idols are overthrown (THEODORET), as is false glory (BASIL), and the proud are humbled (AUGUSTINE). True believers are invincible in their faith (THEODORET). The Lord's voice passes through the fires of human hatred (AUGUSTINE) and extinguishes the burning arrows of evil (EVAGRIUS). The fire of God is divided between present illumination and future punishment (BASIL).

The Lord's voice shakes the wildness out of the human soul (BASIL), shaking the unbelieving peoples into faith (AUGUSTINE, JEROME). Churches take the place of idols (THEODORET). We need to take heed to speak properly of God's glory (BASIL) and praise him for spiritual gifts (AUGUSTINE). Individually and collectively, we are God's temple (AUGUSTINE). He washes away sin (ARNOBIUS THE YOUNGER) as he makes a new creation (THEODORET). Renewing the soul for his dwelling (BASIL), God sits enthroned in his people (PSEUDO-ATHANASIUS).

Superscription: *A Psalm of David*

PERFECTION OF THE CHURCH. AUGUSTINE: This is a psalm of the strong-armed Mediator concerning the perfection of the church in this world, where it wages war within time against the devil. EXPOSITIONS OF THE PSALMS 29.1.[1]

COMPLETION OF THE TEMPLE. ARNOBIUS THE YOUNGER: The title is mindful of the completion of the temple. The completion of the temple is the end of the world, in which children of God bring to God the offspring of rams. The offspring of rams are the lambs who are placed on the right so that, offering glory and honor and the glory of his name in righteous works which they do, they may worship the Lord, no longer a building made by hands but his holy courts, that is in Christ Jesus, "in whom dwells the fullness of divinity."[2] COMMENTARY ON THE PSALMS 29.[3]

29:1 Ascribe Glory to the Lord

RIGHT THINKING. BASIL THE GREAT: Everyone who discusses divine matters in an orderly way so as always to hold the correct opinion concerning the Father, the Godhead of the Only-begotten and the glory of the Holy Spirit, brings glory and honor to the Lord. And, because his providence penetrates even to the smallest things, he increases the glory who is able to give the reasons for which all things

were created and for which they are preserved, and also for which, after this present stewardship, they will be brought to judgment. He who is able himself to contemplate each individual creature with clear and unconfused thoughts and, after having contemplated them himself, is able to present to others also the facts concerning the goodness of God and his just judgment, he is the one who brings glory and honor to the Lord and who lives a life in harmony with this contemplation. For, the light of such a person shines before others, since by word and work and through mighty deeds of every kind the Father in heaven is glorified. HOMILIES ON THE PSALMS 13.2 (Ps 29).[4]

BEAR THE DIVINE MESSAGE. THEODORET OF CYR: You who are entrusted with the divine message, he is saying, and are called children of God, bear the divine message everywhere with all enthusiasm, transform those reared on nonsense into rational people and offer them first to God; then through them present the worship and the hymns, celebrating the benefactor in the divine dwellings. This resembles what was said by the Savior to the sacred apostles, "Go, make disciples of all the nations, baptizing them in the name of the Father and the Son and the Holy Spirit."[5] COMMENTARY ON THE PSALMS 29.4.[6]

BRING OTHERS TO THE LORD. BEDE: Surely the holy teachers are often understood by the word *rams*, since they are the leaders of flocks that follow the Lord. Hence the psalmist says in a pleasing manner: "Bring to the Lord, O children of God, bring to the Lord the offspring of rams," which is clearly to say, "Bring to the Lord, O angels of God to whom the responsibility for this task has been delegated, bring to the Lord in heaven the spirits of the faithful who, through imitation of the blessed apostles' life and faith, have proved worthy to become

---

[1]WSA 3 15:294. [2]Col 2:9. [3]CCL 25:36. [4]FC 46:196. [5]Mt 28:19. [6]FC 101:183*.

their offspring." On the Tabernacle 2.4.[7]

29:2 Worshiping the Lord in Holiness

Worship among the Faithful. Pseudo-Athanasius: He commands us to worship the Lord in his holy court, teaching that it is not allowed to worship outside the church which holds the orthodox faith. Exposition on Psalms 29.[8]

Worship in Your Heart. Augustine: Worship the Lord in your heart, a heart widened and sanctified; for you are his regal and holy habitation. Explanations of the Psalms 29.2.[9]

Worship without Distraction. Basil the Great: Many assume an attitude of prayer, but they are not in the court because of the wandering of their mind and the distraction of their thoughts coming from vain solicitude.... He who makes his belly a god, or glory, or money, or anything else that he honors more than all things neither adores the Lord nor is in the holy court, even though he seems to be worthy of the visible assemblies. Homilies on the Psalms 13.3 (Ps 29).[10]

29:3 The Lord's Voice on the Waters

The Baptism of Jesus. Arnobius the Younger: When Jesus was baptized, after the heavens opened and the Holy Spirit came down as a dove, the Father spoke over the waters saying, "You are my Son."[11] The God of majesty thundered, that is, he spoke profoundly over the waters, that is, over the nations so that they would be made complete in virtue and in the magnificence of Christ Jesus. And each one stood apart from the rebellious and rejoiced. Commentary on the Psalms 29.[12]

Christ over the Nations. Augustine: "The Lord's voice over the waters": this means the voice of Christ over the nations.... From the cloud of his flesh the God of majesty has struck

fear by his preaching of repentance. "The Lord is over many waters," for this same Lord Jesus, having made his pronouncement over the peoples and greatly terrified them, converted them to himself and made them his dwelling. Expositions of the Psalms 29.3.[13]

The Thunder of the Gospel. Theodoret of Cyr: Now, the verse forecasts the voice emanating from heaven at the Jordan, "This is my Son, the Beloved, in whom I am well pleased."[14] He called it "thunder" as coursing to the whole world through the sacred Gospels. Commentary on the Psalms 29.4.[15]

Spiritual Waters. Basil the Great: The waters are also the saints, because rivers flow from within them, that is, spiritual teaching that refreshes the souls of the hearers. Again, they receive water that springs up to eternal life, wherefore it becomes in those who receive it rightly "a fountain of water, springing up unto life everlasting."[16] On such waters, then, is the Lord. Homilies on the Psalms 13.4 (Ps 29).[17]

29:4 The Voice of Power

Empowered by the Spirit. Theodoret of Cyr: From this he prophesies the power imparted to the apostles.... The narrative of the Acts also teaches us things in harmony with this: we learn from there how at his ascension Christ the Lord addressed his holy disciples in the words, "Stay in this city until you have been clothed with power from on high."[18] Ten days later on the feast of Pentecost, "there came a sound from heaven like that of a violent wind blowing."[19] ... Now, he gives the name "voice" to the grace of the Spirit filling the apostles with power and might and rendering puny people magnificent. Commentary on the Psalms 29.5.[20]

---

[7]TTH 18:63. [8]CSCO 387:19. [9]WSA 3 15:294. [10]FC 46:198. [11]Lk 3:22. [12]CCL 25:36-37. [13]WSA 3 15:294. [14]Lk 3:22. [15]FC 101:183. [16]Jn 4:14. [17]FC 46:201-2. [18]Lk 24:49. [19]Acts 2:6. [20]FC 101:183-84*.

MAGNIFICENT PEOPLE. BASIL THE GREAT: The voice of the Lord is not in the weak and dissolute soul but in that which vigorously and powerfully achieves the good. . . . Magnificence is virtue extraordinarily great. One who performs great actions becomingly . . . hears himself called magnificent. When the soul is not enslaved by the pride of the flesh but assumes a greatness and dignity proper to it because of its awareness of its attributes received from God, in this soul is the voice of the Lord. Therefore, they who entertain noble thoughts of God, contemplating sublimely the reasons for creation, and being able to comprehend to a certain extent at least the goodness of God's providence, and who besides are unsparing in their expenditures and are munificent in supplying the needs of their brothers, these are the magnificent people in whom the voice of the Lord dwells. . . . No difficult conditions will grieve the magnificent person; nor, in short, will any suffering greatly trouble him, nor will the sins of paltry and contemptible little people move him, nor the impurity of the flesh humble him. He is almost inaccessible to the humiliating passions, which cannot even look on him because of the loftiness of his mind. . . . Those, then who give great glory to God, elevate his magnificence. HOMILIES ON THE PSALMS 13.4 (Ps 29).[21]

29:5 The Lord Breaks the Cedars

DESTRUCTION OF IDOLS. THEODORET OF CYR: He signals through these words the overthrow of the idols: since the idols' precincts in ancient times were on high places, providing no fruit to their worshipers, he likened them to "the cedars of Lebanon," which though lofty do not naturally bear edible fruit. COMMENTARY ON THE PSALMS 29.5.[22]

FALSE GLORY. BASIL THE GREAT: The cedar is at times praised by Scripture as a stable tree, free from decay, fragrant, and adequate for supplying shelter, but at times it is attacked as

unfruitful and hard to bend, so that it offers a representation of impiety. . . . The Lord is said to break those vainly puffed up and magnifying themselves in the things of this world that are considered exalting, wealth, glory, power, beauty of body, influence or strength. . . . Just as the cedars, which are lofty in themselves, because they are produced on a high mountain become more conspicuous through the added height of the mountain, so also those leaning on the perishable things of the world are cedars indeed through their false glory and vanity of mind; and they are called cedars of Libanus because they are glorying in the elevation that belongs to another and are raised up to their false glory by the earth and earthly circumstance, as if by the summit of Libanus. HOMILIES ON THE PSALMS 13.5 (Ps 29).[23]

THE LORD HUMBLES THE PROUD. AUGUSTINE: The Lord will grind down in repentance those who lift themselves high in the brilliant distinction of earthly rank, since to their confusion he has chosen to reveal his godhead to the most insignificant of this world. EXPOSITIONS OF THE PSALMS 29.5.[24]

29:6 The Lord Makes Lebanon Skip

INVINCIBLE. THEODORET OF CYR: The people who believe, freed from that error [idolatry] and called beloved for that reason, will be invincible and unconquerable in being rid of polytheism and worshiping one Godhead. COMMENTARY ON THE PSALMS 29.6.[25]

29:7 The Voice Flashes Fire

THE VOICE PASSES THROUGH FIRE. AUGUSTINE: This is the voice of the Lord who passed through the fiercely burning hatred of those who jostled him, without any harm to himself,

---

[21]FC 46:202-3*. [22]FC 101:184. [23]FC 46:203. [24]WSA 3 15:295.
[25]FC 101:184.

or cut through the raging anger of his persecutors, some of whom said, "Perhaps this really is the Messiah?" while others said, "No, it couldn't possibly be. He is leading the people astray";[26] in this way he cut through their mad uproar, so as to bring some over within the reach of his love and leave others in their malice. EXPOSITIONS OF THE PSALMS 29.7.[27]

THE VOICE EXTINGUISHED FIRE. EVAGRIUS OF PONTUS: The voice of the Lord extinguishes the burning arrows of evil. That voice is the spiritual teaching that calls the ones believing in Christ grounded in wisdom. NOTES ON THE PSALMS 28[29].7.[28]

A DIVIDED FIRE. BASIL THE GREAT: Although fire seems to human intelligence to be incapable of being cut or divided, yet by the command of the Lord it is cut through and divided. I believe that the fire prepared in punishment for the devil and his angels is divided by the voice of the Lord, in order that, since there are two capacities in fire, the burning and the illuminating, the fierce and punitive part of the fire may wait for those who deserve to burn, while its illuminating and radiant part may be allotted for the enjoyment of those who are rejoicing. Therefore, the voice of the Lord divides the fire and allots it, so that the fire of punishment is dark, but the light of the state of rest remains unkindled. HOMILIES ON THE PSALMS 13.6 (Ps 29).[29]

29:8 The Voice Shakes the Wilderness

WILDERNESS SOULS. BASIL THE GREAT: The thick woods, the woody souls in which, like some wild beasts, the varied passions of sins lurk, are cleared out by that word, which is "keener than any two-edged sword."[30] HOMILIES ON THE PSALMS 13.7 (Ps 29).[31]

SHAKEN UNTO FAITH. AUGUSTINE: This is the voice that stirred to faith the peoples who were once without hope and without God in

the world, where no prophet, no preacher of the word of God was to be found, so that it was as though no humans lived there. EXPOSITIONS OF THE PSALMS 29.8.[32]

THE SOULS WHERE GOD DWELLS. JEROME: The souls that were in the desert by yielding to faults are moved to words of repentance, so that leaving those faults they become the habitation of God. BRIEF COMMENTARY ON PSALMS 29.[33]

THE DESERT CHURCH BECOMES FRUITFUL. JEROME: The desert was the church that, at first, had no children. By the preaching of Christ, this wilderness "was shaken" and "came to labor and gave birth, and there was born in a single day an entire nation." She who before was called the "wilderness of Cades," the desert of holiness—inasmuch as she had been barren of virtues—begins "to bring forth stags" and send out in throngs holy people who kill the serpents on earth, contemptuous of their poisons. While they are running throughout the world proclaiming the gospel of Christ, "in his temple all say 'Glory' " to God! HOMILY ON THE EPIPHANY AND PSALM 28.[34]

29:9 They Cry, "Glory"

CHURCHES IN PLACE OF IDOLS. THEODORET OF CYR: Now, he called "woods" the idols' precincts as being utterly fruitless; these are the kinds of woods or coppices that the best woodcutters are accustomed to chop down, leaving the earth bare of them, and they plant fruitbearing trees and sow seeds of edible crops. The cultivators of the world did this, too: pulling up idols' precincts by the roots, they planted the divine churches in their place. COMMENTARY ON THE PSALMS 29.8.[35]

---

[26]Jn 7:12, 26, 41. [27]WSA 3 15:295. [28]PG 12:1292. [29]FC 46:206. [30]Heb 4:12. [31]FC 46:208. [32]WSA 3 15:295-96. [33]CCL 72:203. [34]FC 57:230-31*. [35]FC 101:186.

SPEAK OF GOD'S GLORY. BASIL THE GREAT:
One who is in the temple of God does not speak
out abuse or folly or words full of shameful matters, but "in his temple all shall speak his glory."
. . . This one duty, referring glory to the Creator,
belongs to every army of heavenly creatures.
Every creature, whether silent or uttering sound,
whether celestial or terrestrial, gives glory to the
Creator. But wretched people who leave their
homes and run to the temple, as if to enrich
themselves somewhat, do not lend their ears to
the words of God; they do not possess a knowledge of their nature; they are not distressed,
although they have previously committed sin;
they do not grieve at remembering their sins,
nor do they fear the judgment; but, smiling and
shaking hands with one another, they make the
house of prayer a place of lengthy conversation,
pretending not to hear the psalm that solemnly
protests and says, "In the temple of God all
shall speak his glory." You not only do not speak
his glory, but you even become a hindrance to
the other, turning his attention to yourself and
drowning out the teaching of the spirit by your
own clamor. See to it that you do not at some
time leave condemned along with those blaspheming the name of God instead of receiving a
reward for glorifying him. You have a psalm; you
have a prophecy, the evangelical precepts, the
preachings of the apostles. Let the tongue sing,
let the mind interpret the meaning of what has
been said, that you may sing with your spirit,
that you may sing likewise with your mind. Not
at all is God in need of glory, but he wishes you
to be worthy of winning glory. Therefore, "what
a person sows, he will also reap."[36] Sow glorification, that you may reap crowns and honors and
praises in the kingdom of heaven. This statement, "In his temple all shall speak his glory,"
was made not unfittingly in a digression, because
some in the temple of God talk endlessly until
their tongue aches; and these enter without
profit. HOMILY ON PSALM 13.8 (Ps 29).[37]

PRAISE FOR SPIRITUAL GIFTS. AUGUSTINE:
In his church every one born again to an eternal
hope praises God for the gift that he or she has
received from the Holy Spirit. EXPOSITIONS OF
THE PSALMS 29.9.[38]

29:10 The Lord Sits Enthroned

THE LORD'S TEMPLE. AUGUSTINE: Therefore,
God dwells in each one singly as in his temples,
and in all of them gathered together as in his
temple. As long as this temple, like the ark of
Noah, is tempest-tossed in this world, the words
of the psalm are verified: "The Lord dwells in
the flood," although, if we consider the many
people of the faithful of all races whom the
Apocalypse describes under the name of waters, they can also be appropriately meant by
"the Lord dwells in the flood."[39] But the psalm
goes on: "And the Lord shall sit as king forever,"
doubtless in that very temple of his, established in eternal life after the tempest of this
world. Thus, God, who is everywhere present
and everywhere wholly present, does not dwell
everywhere but only in his temple, to which,
by his grace, he is kind and gracious, but in his
indwelling he is received more fully by some, less
by others. LETTER 187.38.[40]

THE LORD WASHES AWAY SIN. ARNOBIUS
THE YOUNGER: The Lord lives in the flood, that
is, in water that washes away faults, and in that
same water, the King sits forever. There he gives
strength to the people, the ones believing him.
He blesses his people in peace. COMMENTARY ON
THE PSALMS 29.[41]

A NEW CREATION. THEODORET OF CYR: He
will build a world that is inundated with the
torrent of iniquity, will restore it and will make
it a new creation. Hence blessed Paul also cries
aloud, "If anyone is in Christ, he is a new creation."[42] COMMENTARY ON THE PSALMS 29.9.[43]

---

[36]Gal 6:7. [37]FC 46:209-10*. [38]WSA 3 15:296. [39]Rev 17:15. [40]FC
30:252*. [41]CCL 25:37. [42]2 Cor 5:17. [43]FC 101:186.

THE RENEWED SOUL. BASIL THE GREAT: God sits in the soul that shines from its washing, as if he were making it a throne for himself. HOMILIES ON THE PSALMS 13.8 (Ps 29).[44]

ENTHRONED IN HIS PEOPLE. PSEUDO-ATHANASIUS: God dwells in the flood, that is, in the multitude of those who believed in Christ, who [as it says in the next verse] gives power to his people and blesses it in peace. For we are strengthened in Christ, who also gave us his peace. EXPOSITION ON PSALMS 29.[45]

---

[44]FC 46:211. [45]CSCO 387:19

30:1-12 PRAISE FOR HEALING

In dedicating your house—that is, your soul, which welcomes the Lord,
and the bodily house in which you dwell corporeally—
rejoice and sing Psalm 30.

ATHANASIUS ON THE INTERPRETATION OF THE PSALMS 17 [OIP 68]

A Psalm of David.
A Song at the dedication of the Temple.

¹*I will extol thee, O LORD, for thou hast drawn me up,*
and hast not let my foes rejoice over me.
²*O LORD my God, I cried to thee for help,*
and thou hast healed me.
³*O LORD, thou hast brought up my soul from Sheol,*
*restored me to life from among those gone down to the Pit.*ⁱ

⁴*Sing praises to the LORD, O you his saints,*
and give thanks to his holy name.
⁵*For his anger is but for a moment,*
and his favor is for a lifetime.
Weeping may tarry for the night,
but joy comes with the morning.

⁶*As for me, I said in my prosperity,*
"I shall never be moved."
⁷*By thy favor, O LORD,*
thou hadst established me as a strong mountain;
thou didst hide thy face,
I was dismayed.

⁸*To thee, O LORD, I cried;*
and to the LORD I made supplication:
⁹*"What profit is there in my death,*
if I go down to the Pit?
Will the dust praise thee?
Will it tell of thy faithfulness?
¹⁰*Hear, O LORD, and be gracious to me!*
O LORD, be thou my helper!"

¹¹*Thou hast turned for me my mourning into dancing;*

> thou hast loosed my sackcloth
>   and girded me with gladness,
> ¹²that my soul[j] may praise thee and not

> be silent.
> O LORD my God, I will give thanks to thee
>   for ever.

i *Or that I should not go down to the Pit*   j *Heb that glory*

OVERVIEW: The psalm follows the previous one, extending the thought from the completion of God's dwelling place to the dedication to everlasting peace (AUGUSTINE). Using the dedication of the historical temple as a type, the psalm points forward to the work of Christ renewing souls and fitting them into the church (THEODORET, PSEUDO-ATHANASIUS, JEROME, BASIL). The whole Christ speaks in the psalm (AUGUSTINE). The holy one (AMBROSE) rejoices in the gift of life given by the mercy of God (THEODORET). We are exalted in Christ (ORIGEN) from the lowest condition (AUGUSTINE). Only the truly righteous truly praise God, singing his praises from their hearts (BASIL). They remember his mercy (EVAGRIUS).

The Scripture speaks of divine wrath as punishment (THEODORE OF MOPSUESTIA) and of its effect as ignorance (EVAGRIUS). But we know that his will is life (PSEUDO-ATHANASIUS), and Scripture gives us the typology of reversal (THEODORET). Ours is only a momentary sorrow (AUGUSTINE) as we anticipate resurrection joy (ARNOBIUS THE YOUNGER). Just like material prosperity, there is a prosperity that comes to the soul (BASIL). To obtain it, divine grace is needed (PSEUDO-ATHANASIUS, BASIL). When God's providential face is turned away, we suffer (AUGUSTINE). We pray that his face may shine on us (BASIL). We acknowledge that all good comes from God (DIODORE), and we cry out for great and heavenly things (BASIL), knowing that Christ prays for us (AUGUSTINE). We are secure in Christ (AMBROSE) and are responsible for increasing the profit of his grace (ATHANASIUS). The garment of sin and mourning has been replaced with the joy of resurrection (AUGUSTINE, BASIL), the knowledge of which leads to action (EVAGRIUS). Secure in God's love for us (THEODORET), we have an everlasting testimony (AUGUSTINE) of a never-forgotten mercy (BASIL).

Superscription: *Dedication of the Temple*

THE PREVIOUS AND PRESENT PSALM. AUGUSTINE: In the previous psalm the completion of that tent in which we live in our time of warfare was celebrated, but now we have the dedication of the house that will abide in everlasting peace. EXPOSITIONS OF THE PSALMS 30.1.[1]

SOLOMON, CHRIST AND THE CHURCH. THEODORET OF CYR: Blessed David did not build the divine temple, nor do the verses of the psalm fit the builder. So by "reconsecration of the house" he refers to the restoration of human nature that Christ the Lord accomplished by accepting death on behalf of us, destroying death and giving us hope of resurrection. COMMENTARY ON THE PSALMS 30.1.[2]

A PSALM AFTER BEING SAVED FROM SIN. PSEUDO-ATHANASIUS: He sings this psalm after he was saved from sin and his soul was renewed by repentance. . . . And he gives thanks and prays for the future, that he may be in safety and be established as a type of virtue for the others. EXPOSITION ON PSALMS 30.[3]

PASSION, RESURRECTION, CONSUMMATION. JEROME: The dedication of the house of David is understood as the resurrection of the Savior, in which all bodies are dedicated. . . . This psalm is about the time of the passion, the resurrection and the consummation of the age. BRIEF COMMENTARY ON PSALMS 30.[4]

---

[1]*WSA* 3 15:297. [2]FC 101:187. [3]CSCO 387:19-20. [4]CCL 72:203.

THE BODY AND MUSIC. BASIL THE GREAT: The physical structure of the body is, speaking figuratively, a harp and an instrument harmoniously adapted for the hymns of our God; and the actions of the body that are referred to the glory of God are a psalm, whenever in an appropriate measure we perform nothing out of tune in our actions. Whatever pertains to lofty contemplation and theology is a canticle. . . . Accordingly, since this was entitled "A psalm of a canticle," we believe that the expression suggests action following contemplation. This psalm of a canticle, according to the title, embraces certain words of the dedication of the house. And the speech, in its material form, seems to have been delivered in the time of Solomon, when the renowned temple was raised, and to have been adapted to the harp; but, in its spiritual meaning, the title seems to signify the incarnation of the Word of God and to make known the dedication of a house, which same house had been constructed in a novel and incredible manner. We have found many things in this psalm announced by the Lord in person. Or, perhaps, it is proper to consider the house as the church built by Christ; just as Paul writes in his letter to Timothy: "In order that you may know how to conduct yourself in the house of God, which is the church of the living God."[5] The dedication of the church must be understood as the renewal of the mind, which takes place through the Holy Spirit in each individually, of those who make up the body of the church of Christ. It is a divine and musical harmony, which includes not words that gladden the ear but those that calm and soften the wicked spirits that trouble souls that are exposed to harm. HOMILIES ON THE PSALMS 14.1 (Ps 30).[6]

30:1 Extolling the Lord

THE WHOLE CHRIST. AUGUSTINE: So now it is the whole Christ who speaks. . . . You have given them no joy at my expense, those who throughout the world have constantly attempted to crush me with every kind of persecution.

EXPOSITIONS OF THE PSALMS 30.2.[7]

30:2 Healing from the Lord

THE HOLY ONE. AMBROSE: The more anyone strives toward the Lord, the more he exalts the Lord and is himself exalted. On this account also the psalmist says, "I will extol you, O Lord, because you have upheld me." One who is holy extols the Lord; the sinner brings him low. ISAAC, OR THE SOUL 7.57.[8]

BY GOD'S MERCY. THEODORET OF CYR: Human nature did not beseech God and look for reprieve from destruction; rather, it constantly fell to wailing and weeping, with death in view and no expectation of resurrection. Accordingly, the psalmist made mention of the tears and laments that occur with the sick and dying to show the ineffable lovingkindness of God . . . [by which,] without being invoked and seeing only the wailing, he took pity on what was happening and gave a reprieve from death. COMMENTARY ON THE PSALMS 30.2.[9]

30:3 God Restores to Life

EXALTED IN CHRIST. ORIGEN: No one is able to exalt God unless God has lifted him up. For we are lifted up on high through the cross of Christ, who said, "When I will have been lifted up, I will draw all to me."[10] We exalt the Lord who himself exalted the Father, and as much as he has been in him, he shows the Father to the ones who believe. He teaches that there are certain invisible enemies of the human spirit who envy the salvation handed over to them by God. They lie in wait, and they observe whether an error, fall or mishap should happen, which, if it would, straightway they mock that salvation as if joyful with the wrongdoing, against which mockery he bears up with strength if they will see that

---

[5]1 Tim 3:15. [6]FC 46:213-14. [7]WSA 3 15:297. [8]FC 65:47*. [9]FC 101:188. [10]Jn 12:32.

salvation illuminated by divine steps. He thanks God because God did not allow him to be cast away but corrected him from his fall. One who realizes this clearly exalts God and protects the worthy teaching that comes from God. Such a person lives a life of wisdom and keeps his spirit in all excellence. He exalts the one who lives within him. SELECTIONS FROM THE PSALMS 30.2.[11]

FROM THE LOWEST CONDITION. AUGUSTINE: You have rescued me from the condition of profound blindness and the lowest slime of corruptible flesh. EXPOSITIONS OF THE PSALMS 30.4.[12]

30:4 Praise the Lord

SINGING FROM THE HEART. BASIL THE GREAT: One does not sing to the Lord by simply uttering the words of the psalm with his mouth, but all who send up the psalmody from a clean heart and who are holy, maintaining righteousness toward God, these are able to sing to God, harmoniously guided by the spiritual rhythms. How many stand there, coming from fornication? How many from theft? How many concealing in their hearts deceit? How many lying? They think they are singing, although in truth they are not singing. For the Scripture invites the saint to the singing of psalms. "A bad tree cannot bear good fruit,"[13] nor a bad heart utter words of life. Therefore, "make the tree good and its fruits good."[14] Cleanse your hearts, in order that you may bear fruit in the spirit and may be able, after becoming saints, to sing psalms intelligently to the Lord. HOMILIES ON THE PSALMS 14.3 (Ps 30).[15]

REMEMBER GOD'S MERCY. EVAGRIUS OF PONTUS: All who are mindful of the mercy of God confess him. NOTES ON THE PSALMS 29[30].5.[16]

30:5 Joy Comes with the Morning

THE WRATH OF PUNISHMENT. THEODORE OF

MOPSUESTIA: By "wrath" he refers to punishment and retribution, by "wrath" the divine Scripture meaning not only the initial response but also lasting anger. So by "wrath" he refers to the awful process of vengeance, and by "anger" the effect it rightly has on sinners, the terms being interchanged as usual. . . . He takes vengeance when angered and is beneficent by purpose and intention. COMMENTARY ON PSALMS 30.6.[17]

IGNORANCE. EVAGRIUS OF PONTUS: In the same way that wrath arises from the indignation of God, so even life is generated from his will. If "life" indicates knowledge, . . . then wrath denotes lack of knowledge. Death is a turning from life. Wrath, then, indicates death, a deprivation of contemplation. NOTES ON THE PSALMS 29[30].6.[18]

GOD'S WILL IS LIFE. PSEUDO-ATHANASIUS: In God's wrath is anger, but in his will is life, because his will is life. . . . He is led to anger because of our sin. And although mourning will continue all night, in the morning he makes for us a rejoicing, when through repentance we strip off the burden of evil. EXPOSITION ON PSALMS 30.[19]

BIBLICAL TYPES. THEODORET OF CYR: Now, things turned out like this both in the case of Hezekiah and in the case of the salvation of everyone. After the Assyrians applied those awful threats and moved the city to weeping, they sustained the blow at night, and in the morning they filled with good cheer those whom they had forced to weep. The divine Isaiah brought Hezekiah the sentence of death in the evening, and towards morning brought him in turn the good news of life. And it happened likewise in the case of the salvation of everyone: the sacred apostles and the believers along with them lamented the

---

[11]PG 12:1292. [12]WSA 3 15:297. [13]Mt 7:18. [14]Mt 12:33. [15]FC 46:217-18. [16]PG 12:1293. [17]WGRW 5:273. [18]PG 12:1293. [19]CSCO 387:20.

passion of the Lord, but toward morning the women came and brought the joy of the resurrection. COMMENTARY ON THE PSALMS 30.3.[20]

MOMENTARY SORROW. AUGUSTINE: We weep only until that morning of resurrection gladness, looking to the joy that blossomed in advance in the early-morning resurrection of the Lord. EXPOSITION I OF PSALM 30.6.[21]

RESURRECTION JOY. ARNOBIUS THE YOUNGER: The world was cursed by the death of Adam, but life is revealed in the rising from the dead. Weeping will tarry till evening. . . . But we will have joy in the morning. In the early rising, as the shadows of the earth are ended and the time of morning rising arrives, the beauty of our faith stands. COMMENTARY ON THE PSALMS 30.[22]

30:6 In Prosperity

PROSPERITY OF THE SOUL. BASIL THE GREAT: As the prosperity of a city is dependent on the supply of goods for sale in the market, and as we say that a country is prosperous that produces much fruit, so also there is a certain prosperity of the soul when it has been filled with works of every kind. It is necessary first for it to be laboriously cultivated and then to be enriched by the plentiful streams of heavenly waters, so as to bear fruit thirtyfold, sixtyfold and a hundredfold and to obtain the blessing that says, "Blessed shall be your barns and blessed your stores."[23] One, therefore, who is conscious of his own constancy, will say with sure confidence and will strongly maintain that he will not be turned away by any opponent, like a full field that the Lord has blessed. HOMILIES ON THE PSALMS 14.5 (Ps 30).[24]

30:7 By the Lord's Favor

THE NEED FOR GRACE. PSEUDO-ATHANASIUS: Without your power I cannot rise from my fall. Bring it to pass that the grace of my soul shine out again, not averting your face as previously.

EXPOSITION ON PSALMS 30.[25]

BEAUTY AND THE BLESSED NATURE. BASIL THE GREAT: They who are engaged in the examination of the reason for virtues have said that some of the virtues spring from contemplation and some are noncontemplative . . . beauty and strength are noncontemplative virtues since they follow from the contemplative. . . . But, for this, namely, that beauty may exist in the soul and also the power for the fulfillment of what is proper, we need divine grace. . . . For I was beautiful according to nature but weak, because I was dead by sin through the treachery of the serpent. To my beauty, then, which I received from you at the beginning of my creation, you added a strength that is appropriate for what is proper. Every soul is beautiful that is considered by the standard of its own virtues. But beauty, true and most lovely, that can be contemplated by him alone who has purified his mind, is that of the divine and blessed nature. One who gazes steadfastly at the splendor and graces of it receives some share from it, as if from an immersion tingeing his own face with a sort of brilliant radiance. . . . Moses also was made resplendent in face by receiving some share of beauty when he held converse with God. Therefore, one who is conscious of his own beauty utters this act of thanksgiving: "O Lord, in your favor, you gave strength to my beauty." HOMILIES ON THE PSALMS 14.5 (Ps 30).[26]

GOD'S PROVIDENTIAL FACE. AUGUSTINE: When from time to time you averted your face from me in my sin, I became distressed, as the light by which I knew you was withdrawn from me. EXPOSITIONS OF THE PSALMS 30.8.[27]

MAY GOD'S FACE SHINE ON US. BASIL THE GREAT: God is said to turn away his face when

---

[20]FC 101:189*. [21]WSA 3 15:298. [22]CCL 25:38. [23]Deut 28:5. [24]FC 46:220*. [25]CSCO 387:20. [26]FC 46:220-21*. [27]WSA 3 15:298.

in times of troubles he permits us to be delivered up to trials, in order that the strength of him who is struggling may be known. . . . We pray always for the face of God to shine on us, in order that we may be in a state becoming to a holy person, gentle and untroubled in every way, because of our readiness for the good. "I am ready," he says, "and am not troubled."[28] HOMILIES ON THE PSALMS 14.6 (Ps 30).[29]

30:8 Crying to the Lord

ACKNOWLEDGE GOD. DIODORE OF TARSUS: I acknowledge the one responsible and shall not be reluctant to admit that all the good things I have are from you. COMMENTARY ON PSALMS 30.[30]

CRY FOR GREAT THINGS. BASIL THE GREAT: Crying out to the Lord is the sole privilege of one who desires great and heavenly things. But if anyone asks God for trifling and earthly things, he uses a small and low voice, which does not reach to the height or come to the ears of the Lord. HOMILIES ON THE PSALMS 14.6 (Ps 30).[31]

CHRIST PRAYS FOR US. AUGUSTINE: I hear the voice of your firstborn, my Head who is to die for me, as he prays, "To you, Lord, I will cry, and with my God I will plead." EXPOSITIONS OF THE PSALMS 30.9.[32]

30:9 What Gain in My Death?

SECURITY IN CHRIST. AMBROSE: God first predestined us and then called us. . . . Can he abandon those whom he has honored with his mighty benefits even to the point of their reward? . . . Can Christ then condemn you, when he redeemed you from death and offered himself on your behalf, and when he knows that your life is what was gained by his death? Will he not say, "What profit is there in my blood," if I condemn the one whom I myself have saved? . . . Can he give a sentence that is very harsh when he prays continually that the grace of reconciliation with

the Father be granted us? JACOB AND THE HAPPY LIFE 1.6.26.[33]

INCREASING THE PROFIT OF GRACE. ATHANASIUS: The Lord's descent to earth was not useless, for it gained the whole world! Nevertheless, even after his coming in the flesh, sinners would rather be without his flesh than profit by it. You see, he took pleasure in our salvation and thought of it as a distinctive victory for himself. [By contrast], he considered our destruction a sad loss. . . . He praised those who doubled the grace he gave, both the one who made ten talents from five and the one who made four talents from two. Both of them had done the right thing and had profited from it. But he threw out the one who hid the talent.[34] FESTAL LETTERS 6.4-5.[35]

30:11 Sackcloth Removed

A CHANGED GARMENT. AUGUSTINE: You have torn up the sacking that cloaked my sins, the sad garb of my mortal state, and have clothed me in the first robe, the raiment of undying happiness. EXPOSITIONS OF THE PSALMS 30.12.[36]

THE JOY OF MOURNING. BASIL THE GREAT: The joy of God is not found in just any soul but, if someone has mourned much and deeply his own sin with loud lamentations and continual weepings, as if he were bewailing his own death, the mourning of such a one is turned into joy. . . . The mourning garment, which he put on when bewailing his sin, is torn, and the tunic of joy is placed around him and the cloak of salvation, those bright wedding garments, with which if one is adorned, he will not be cast out from the bridal chamber. HOMILIES ON THE PSALMS 14.7 (Ps 30).[37]

FROM UNDERSTANDING TO ACTION. EVAGRIUS

---

[28]Ps 119:60-61 (118:60-61 LXX). [29]FC 46:222. [30]WGRW 9:90. [31]FC 46:222*. [32]WSA 3 15:298. [33]FC 65:136*. [34]Mt 25:26-30. [35]ARL 103*. [36]WSA 3 15:299. [37]FC 46:224*.

OF PONTUS: Mourning turns to joy and the understanding of God to action. NOTES ON THE PSALMS 29[30].12.[38]

30:12 *Praising God Forever*

GOD'S LOVE FOR US. THEODORET OF CYR: We have a basis of high repute in the evidence given by the God of all of his great affection for us: "God so loved the world," Scripture says, "that he has given his only-begotten Son so that all who believe in him may not perish but have eternal life."[39] "O Lord my God, I shall confess to you forever": not only in the present life but also after the resurrection I shall offer hymns to you, constantly recounting your extraordinary and ineffable gifts. COMMENTARY ON THE PSALMS 30.6.[40]

AN EVERLASTING TESTIMONY. AUGUSTINE:

This is my glory, Lord my God, that forever I may confess to you that nothing I have derives from myself but that all good things are from you, who are God, all in all. EXPOSITIONS OF THE PSALMS 30.12.[41]

NEVER-FORGOTTEN MERCY. BASIL THE GREAT: When you granted me pardon because of my repentance and led me back into glory, taking away the shame of my sins, for this I shall give praise to you for all eternity. In fact, what space of time could be so great, that it could produce in my soul forgetfulness of such mighty benefits? HOMILIES ON THE PSALMS 14.8 (Ps 30).[42]

---

[38]PG 12:1297. [39]Jn 3:16. [40]FC 101:191. [41]WSA 3 15:299. [42]FC 46:225.

31:1-24 PRAYER FOR RESCUE

When you see yourself hated and persecuted by all your relatives and friends
because of the truth, do not be downcast either for them or for yourself;
and when all your acquaintances turn away from you,
do not be frightened, but withdraw from them
and keep your eyes fixed on the future, singing Psalm 31.
ATHANASIUS *ON THE INTERPRETATION OF THE PSALMS* 18 [OIP 68]

To the choirmaster. A Psalm of David.

¹In thee, O LORD, do I seek refuge;
let me never be put to shame;
in thy righteousness deliver me!
²Incline thy ear to me,
rescue me speedily!

Be thou a rock of refuge for me,
a strong fortress to save me!

³Yea, thou art my rock and my fortress;
for thy name's sake lead me and guide me,
⁴take me out of the net which is hidden for me,
for thou art my refuge.

---

⁵*Into thy hand I commit my spirit;*
  thou hast redeemed me, O LORD, *faithful*
    God.

⁶*Thou hatest*ᵏ *those who pay regard to vain*
    idols;
  but I trust in the LORD.
⁷*I will rejoice and be glad for thy steadfast*
    love,
  because thou hast seen my affliction,
  thou hast taken heed of my adversities,
⁸*and hast not delivered me into the hand of*
    the enemy;
  thou hast set my feet in a broad place.

⁹*Be gracious to me, O* LORD, *for I am in*
    distress;
  my eye is wasted from grief,
  my soul and my body also.
¹⁰*For my life is spent with sorrow,*
  and my years with sighing;
*my strength fails because of my misery,*ˡ
  and my bones waste away.

¹¹*I am the scorn of all my adversaries,*
  *a horror*ᵐ *to my neighbors,*
an object of dread to my acquaintances;
  those who see me in the street flee from me.
¹²*I have passed out of mind like one who is*
    dead;
  I have become like a broken vessel.
¹³*Yea, I hear the whispering of many—*
  terror on every side!—
as they scheme together against me,
  as they plot to take my life.

¹⁴*But I trust in thee, O* LORD,
  I say, "Thou art my God."

¹⁵*My times are in thy hand;*
  deliver me from the hand of my enemies
    and persecutors!
¹⁶*Let thy face shine on thy servant;*
  save me in thy steadfast love!
¹⁷*Let me not be put to shame, O* LORD,
  for I call on thee;
let the wicked be put to shame,
  let them go dumbfounded to Sheol.
¹⁸*Let the lying lips be dumb,*
  which speak insolently against the righteous
  in pride and contempt.

¹⁹*O how abundant is thy goodness,*
  which thou hast laid up for those who fear
    thee,
and wrought for those who take refuge in thee,
  in the sight of the sons of men!
²⁰*In the covert of thy presence thou hidest them*
  from the plots of men;
thou holdest them safe under thy shelter
  from the strife of tongues.

²¹*Blessed be the* LORD,
  for he has wondrously shown his steadfast
    love to me
  when I was beset as in a besieged city.
²²*I had said in my alarm,*
  *"I am driven far*ⁿ *from thy sight."*
But thou didst hear my supplications,
  when I cried to thee for help.

²³*Love the* LORD, *all you his saints!*
  The LORD *preserves the faithful,*
  but abundantly requites him who acts
    haughtily.
²⁴*Be strong, and let your heart take courage,*
  all you who wait for the LORD!

k With one Heb Ms Gk Syr Jerome: Heb *I hate*   l Gk Syr: Heb *iniquity*   m Cn: Heb *exceedingly*   n Another reading is *cut off*

OVERVIEW: In the thirty-first psalm David gives expression to his experience while speaking prophetically of Christ (JEROME) and focusing especially on the passion and resurrection of the Lord (CASSIODORUS). The psalm begins with a wonderful expression of the gift of righteousness (AUGUSTINE) accomplished by a marvelous heavenly exchange (CASSIODORUS). Righteousness here encompasses all virtues, fulfilled in Christ (Evagrius). God hears through his mercy (Augustine) and rescues the one who hopes in him (Arnobius the Younger). The psalmist appeals for God's sake, not for his own (Theodoret), knowing his strength and refuge are in God (Augustine), and he is led through faith and works (Evagrius).

We must beware the double trap of the enemy (Augustine). We see here David's deliverance (Theodoret) and the deliverance of Christ (Cassiodorus). Here we have the words Christ uttered from the cross (Theodore of Mopsuestia). We may understand "spirit" here as mind (Evagrius), but the spirit that was given up on the cross was beyond comparison (Cassiodorus). Faith in anything less than God is futile (Augustine) and is rejected by God (Theodoret), whereas hope in the Lord is secure (Cassiodorus). The Lord rejoices with the humility appropriate to incarnation (Cassiodorus).

Understanding the reasons for temptation provides a "broad plane" of freedom (Evagrius), as does charity in one's soul (Augustine). Looming dangers may trouble the soul but not lead to despair (Cassiodorus). We must beware of anger (Augustine, John Cassian) and of wrath (Evagrius) and learn humility from our condition (Clement of Rome). Christ became for us an object of reproach (Cassiodorus) and in the opinion of many was destined to be lost and forgotten (Theodoret). He was abandoned (Cassiodorus) and considered useless (Augustine). But he kept his hope in the Lord (Cassiodorus), and our hope is fixed in Christ (Augustine). Our times are in the hands of the Lord (Diodore). Some enemies we pray for and some we pray against (Augustine). The Lord shows us his face, not his back (Pseudo-Athanasius). His regard is sufficient for our salvation (Diodore) as we call on him in faith (Cassiodorus). Silence is the way to avoid lying (Evagrius), and eventually all blasphemers will be silenced (Augustine).

The psalm goes on to speak of the revelation of God's blessings (Theodoret), the revelation of his sweetness (Cassiodorus), but this is given according to God's timing (Augustine). Faith is necessary (Augustine) and finds a mercy greater than our sins (Cyril of Jerusalem). The blessings to come to us are hidden now (Arnobius the Younger). In the meantime, he helps in ways hidden from the knowledge of others (Gregory of Nyssa). The Lord surrounds us with his love (Theodoret) and extends his mercy through the widest circles of human society (Augustine). He revealed his blessings especially to and from Jerusalem (Cassiodorus). David's situation was that he suffered when he turned aside from righteousness (Theodoret). We learn that we must heed the Lord (Theodoret). We are to love the Lord and love each other as friends (Cassiodorus), knowing that God punishes arrogance above every other sin (Diodore). We take comfort in the certain judgment of God (Arnobius the Younger) and stay strong in the power of the Lord (Cassiodorus).

Superscription: *A Psalm of David*

David and the Lord. Jerome: The whole psalm is understood about David according to history and about the Lord according to prophecy. Brief Commentary on Psalms 31.[1]

The Passion and Resurrection of the Lord. Cassiodorus: Throughout the psalm the words spoken are those of the Lord Savior. Initially he begs the Father that he may be freed from overhanging ills, and then he rejoices that he has undoubtedly been heard. In the second part he returns to his passion, and in a splendid narration by means of diverse allusions he describes what occurred. Third, he offers thanks in general for himself and for his faithful people, since God has bestowed the gifts of his mercy on the whole church. He also warns the saints to

---

[1] CCL 72:203.

continue in the Lord's love now that they have earlier heard both the rewards of the good and the punishments of the wicked. EXPLANATION OF THE PSALMS 31.1.[2]

31:1 Save Me by Your Righteousness

THE GIFT OF RIGHTEOUSNESS. AUGUSTINE: There is a justice that belongs to God but becomes ours as well when it is given to us. It is called God's justice to ensure that humans do not imagine that they have any justice as from themselves. . . . The Jews, on the contrary, assumed that they were able to achieve perfect justice by their own efforts, and in consequence they tripped over the stumbling stone, the rock of scandal, and failed to recognize the grace of Christ. . . . The reason why they did not recognize God's grace was that they did not want to be saved gratis. For who is saved gratis? Everyone in whom the Savior has found nothing to crown but only what he must condemn, one in whom he has found nothing that deserves rewards but only what merits torments. . . . Why call it "grace"? Because it is given gratis. And why is it given gratis? Because there were no preceding merits on your part; God's benefits forestalled you. . . . With this in mind, "in you, O Lord, have I put my trust," not in myself. "Let me not be shamed forever," because I trust in him who does not shame me. "In your justice set me free, and rescue me." Because you have found in me no justice of my own, set me free in yours; let me be freed by what renders me just, what makes a godless person godly, what enables a blind person to see, what raises up one who is falling, what makes a mourner rejoice. That is what sets me free; I do not liberate myself. "In your justice set me free, and rescue me." EXPOSITIONS OF THE PSALMS 31.6.[3]

THE HEAVENLY EXCHANGE. CASSIODORUS: He rightly implored the Lord's justice, for he knew that he was to suffer through unjust people. What a truly marvelous, heavenly exchange! He

accepted death and gave salvation in return. He endured injustices and conferred distinctions; he shouldered pain and bestowed safety. He is both unique and wholly devoted, for he proffered sweetness when he obtained bitterness. EXPLANATION OF THE PSALMS 31.2.[4]

CHRIST AND ALL VIRTUES. EVAGRIUS OF PONTUS: Not only does God free us into righteousness but also into temperance, fortitude and love. He uses "righteousness" to embrace all virtues. Perhaps he understands "Christ" for "righteousness." "He is made wisdom to us by God and our righteousness and sanctification and redemption."[5] NOTES ON THE PSALMS 30[31].2.[6]

31:2 Rescue Me

HOW GOD HEARS US. AUGUSTINE: God bends his ear to us when he pours down his mercy on us. What greater mercy could there be than that he should send his only Son, not to live with us, but to die for us? EXPOSITIONS OF THE PSALMS 31.7.[7]

THE ONE WHO HOPES IN GOD. ARNOBIUS THE YOUNGER: God rescues and frees the one who puts his hope in him. He bends his ear to them, and he snatches them . . . so that they are saved. COMMENTARY ON THE PSALMS 31.3.[8]

31:3 God Is My Rock

FOR HIS SAKE. THEODORET OF CYR: Now, through all the verses occurring here, at any rate, we learn the measure of his prudence: his appeal for divine assistance is made on the basis not of his own virtue but of God's name and of God's righteousness and because he hoped in him. COMMENTARY ON THE PSALMS 31.3.[9]

---

[2]ACW 51:290. [3]WSA 3 15:325-27. [4]ACW 51:290-91*. [5]1 Cor 1:30. [6]PG 12:1297, 1300. [7]WSA 3 15:327*. [8]CCL 25:39. [9]FC 101:193.

Strength and Refuge. Augustine: You are for me both fortitude to endure my persecutors and my place of refuge so that I can leave them behind. Expositions of the Psalms 31.4.[10]

God's Leading. Evagrius of Pontus: He leads through right faith and works and nourishes through his own understanding. Notes on the Psalms 30[31].4.[11]

31:4 Freed from the Net

The Double Trap of the Enemy. Augustine: The enemy's trap is stretched out ready; there are twin loops in it, error and terror: error to entice, terror to break and grip us. You must shut the door of greed against error and the door of fear against terror; and then you will be led clear of the trap. Expositions of the Psalms 31.10.[12]

David's Deliverance. Theodoret of Cyr: By this he indicated the plot of Ahithophel, which he put into operation against him, as we have spoken about previously.[13] . . . After frequently encountering many disasters I was freed from them by your aid—thus I entrust my soul to your providence. He calls providence here once again "hands." Commentary on the Psalms 31.4.[14]

Christ's Deliverance. Cassiodorus: The snare was indeed hidden by the enemy, but it was not to be hidden from Christ, for he did not fall into death by deception but knowingly undertook it to free us. So the Jews hid the snare for Christ because they thought that he was only a man, and they plotted to destroy him by secret ambush. So he says that he is to be brought out of it, in other words, swiftly raised to the realms of heaven by the kindly gift of the resurrection. Explanation of the Psalms 31.5.[15]

31:5 Into God's Hand

Words from the Cross. Theodore of Mopsuestia: Now, it is to be noted that the Lord cited this verse when on the cross, not that it was said of him in prophetic manner, as some commentators think, but because these words suited him when exposed to the risk of death and passion. So he cited this verse at the time when his soul was separated from his body, and [he] rightly entrusted it to the Father so that he might restore it to his body when it was in need of it at the time of the resurrection. Commentary on Psalms 31.6.[16]

Spirit Means Mind. Evagrius of Pontus: Here *spirit* indicates mind. The mind that clings to God is one spirit. Notes on the Psalms 30[31].6.[17]

Such a Spirit. Cassiodorus: Let us consider why the words that the Gospel text utters are set here. . . . Undoubtedly this is so that you may realize that here too the same man was speaking who was to say the same words when set on the cross many centuries later. "Into your hands" means "Into your truth, where you always perform kind and just deeds." So he commends to the Father that treasure beyond reckoning, that soul that did the Father's will with equal dedication. So it was right that such a spirit be commended to One so great to raise it. Then he attests that he was redeemed. But let us see at what price; it was that stated by Paul: "He emptied himself, taking the form of a servant."[18] You see how great the price was, that he lowered his majesty to the level of human flesh. He emptied himself to fill things human with things heavenly. Explanation of the Psalms 31.6.[19]

31:6 Trusting in the Lord

Futile Trust. Augustine: If you put your trust in money, you are paying futile regard to vain things; if you put your trust in high office

---

[10]WSA 3 15:316. [11]PG 12:1300. [12]WSA 3 15:329. [13]Cf. Ps 7:1. [14]FC 101:193. [15]ACW 51:292. [16]WGRW 5:275-77*. [17]PG 12:1300. [18]Phil 2:7. [19]ACW 51:292.

or some exalted rank in human government, you are paying futile regard to vain things. . . . When you put your trust in all these, either you expire and leave them all behind, or they will crumble while you are still alive, and what you trusted will have let you down. . . . For my part, I do not put my trust in empty things as they do or pay futile regard to them; I have put my trust in the Lord. EXPOSITIONS OF THE PSALMS 31.12.[20]

REJECTED BY GOD. THEODORE OF MOPSUESTIA: You hated them and rebuffed those paying constant attention to doing wrong; far from doing evil in the heat of passion, they involve themselves in the practice of evil as though an obligation (the sense of "paid constant attention"). By "futile things" he refers to the wrongdoing. By "in vain" he means that they got no benefit from their involvement in evildoing because of his hating and punishing them and not allowing them to bring to completion the object of their efforts. COMMENTARY ON PSALMS 31.7.[21]

SECURE IN THE LORD. CASSIODORUS: "I will hope in the Lord," in whom there is nothing empty, . . . but everything remains secure and whole. EXPLANATION OF THE PSALMS 31.7.[22]

31:7 Rejoicing in the Lord

THE HUMILITY OF CHRIST. CASSIODORUS: Let us also be aware of who says that his humility has been regarded. It is he who both created and keeps in being heaven and earth, he to whom the heavenly powers minister. But there was humility in the most High because humanity perfected at the very conception was truly joined to him. EXPLANATION OF THE PSALMS 31.8.[23]

31:8 Set in a Broad Place

UNDERSTANDING TEMPTATION. EVAGRIUS OF PONTUS: The reasons of temptation, when they are realized, provide a broad plane for the soul. NOTES ON THE PSALMS 30[31].9.[24]

THE BROAD PLANE OF FREEDOM. AUGUSTINE: You have not imprisoned me with no possible hope for liberty; you have not handed me over to the endless power of the devil. . . . The charity that is in me has been released from cramping fear and can walk unhindered forever into the broad stretches of freedom, for I know my Lord's resurrection and the promise of my own. EXPOSITIONS OF THE PSALMS 31.9.[25]

31:9 In Distress

TROUBLED, BUT NOT DESPAIRING. CASSIODORUS: When the flesh saw that dangers threatened it, the result was that it was troubled with panic. Note that he often says that he was troubled but nowhere that he despaired; this was said by him so that the heavenly Master could show us this formula for imitation. Anxiety cultivates the human race in close acquaintance, but despair could not emanate from divine sanctity. EXPLANATION OF THE PSALMS 31.10.[26]

BEWARE OF ANGER. AUGUSTINE: Before we go off into darkness, our eye is confused by anger, and we must be careful that anger does not develop into hatred and blind us. EXPOSITIONS OF THE PSALMS 31.4.[27]

THE POISON OF ANGER. JOHN CASSIAN: The deadly poison of anger has to be utterly rooted out from the inmost corners of our soul. For as long as this remains in our hearts and blinds with its hurtful darkness the eye of the soul, we can neither acquire right judgment and discretion nor gain the insight that springs from an honest gaze or ripeness of counsel, nor can we be partakers of life, or retentive of righteousness or even have the capacity for spiritual and true light: "for," says one, "my eye is disturbed by reason of anger." INSTITUTES 8.1.[28]

---

[20]*WSA* 3 15:331. [21]*WGRW* 5:277. [22]ACW 51:293. [23]ACW 51:293. [24]PG 12:1300. [25]*WSA* 3 15:317. [26]ACW 51:295. [27]*WSA* 3 15:337. [28]NPNF 2 11:257*.

Beware of Wrath. Evagrius of Pontus: Nothing darkens the mind like unbridled wrath. Notes on the Psalms 30[31].10.[29]

31:10 Sorrow and Sighing

Learn Humility. Clement of Rome: Let your children take part in the instruction that is in Christ, let them learn how powerful with God is humility, how strong is a pure love, how the fear of him is beautiful and great and saves those who live in it in holiness with a pure mind. For he is a searcher of thoughts and desires; his breath is in us, and when he wills, he will take it away. 1 Clement 21.[30]

31:11 An Object of Reproach

Christ, an Object of Reproach. Cassiodorus: Christ the Lord though innocent and stainless was regarded as a reproach among those who contaminated themselves with wicked sin. . . . A reproach suggests an extremely loathsome deed, which was clearly ascribed to the Lord Savior by the wicked when they said, "This man is not of God, who keeps not the sabbath,"[31] and elsewhere, You are "a Samaritan and have a devil."[32] Explanation of the Psalms 31.12.[33]

31:12 Gone from Memory

Lost and Forgotten. Theodoret of Cyr: Everyone has given me up for lost, he is saying, like a vessel mislaid or a corpse occupying a tomb. He brought out the degree of forgetfulness by reference to the worthless vessel: just as when lost it vanishes from the memory of the losers for reason of its worthlessness, he is saying, so too am I in their estimation like someone nonexistent and have become deserving of no esteem. Commentary on the Psalms 31.7.[34]

Christ Abandoned. Cassiodorus: Those who did not believe the Scriptures saw the Lord nailed to the cross and retired from his divine presence, hoping that their expectation was ended by his death. Likewise, heretics, who hear the divine Scriptures in the church and see glorious events, break away to wicked preaching, fleeing from the truth in which they wholly refuse to allow themselves to continue. . . . "An abandoned vessel" is one that is broken and without essential use, and it is always thrown away; so when Jesus died he was believed by the faithless to be disposable like an abandoned vessel. What more humbling statement can be made than that the almighty Majesty should be compared with frail jars? But realize that this was the belief of mad people. In fact there always existed in him a unique omnipotence and a marvelous divine fullness. Explanation of the Psalms 31.13-14.[35]

Useless. Augustine: I seemed to myself to be of no use any longer for the Lord's purposes, living on in this world but winning no one over to him, since they were all afraid to be associated with me. Expositions of the Psalms 31.13.[36]

31:14 You Are My God!

The Hope of Christ. Cassiodorus: The order of the phrases is marvelous and most sacred. When his enemies . . . put their hope in their strength, he says that he trusted the Lord, for he knew that their power was nonexistent and that they would kill themselves rather than him by such plots. . . . The Lord Christ says, "You are my God," but he speaks from the standpoint of the humanity that he assumed and that as he later says was subject to both time and death. He does not, as his enemies thought, state that his life was to be ended by their persecution, but he places his life's times in the Lord's power; for we exist through his creation, wax strong through his dispensation and also pass on at his command. So it was necessary that he kept his hope implanted in the Lord, for he knew that his life

---

[29]PG 12:1301. [30]FC 1:28. [31]Jn 9:16. [32]Jn 8:48. [33]ACW 51:296*. [34]FC 101:194. [35]ACW 51:296-97*. [36]WSA 3 15:318.

and death were in his power. EXPLANATION OF
THE PSALMS 31.15-16.[37]

MY HOPE IN CHRIST. AUGUSTINE: You have
undergone no change, so you will not fail to save
me, though you discipline me. EXPOSITIONS OF
THE PSALMS 31.15.[38]

31:15 In Your Hands

IN THE LORD'S HANDS. DIODORE OF TARSUS:
He says "my lot" in the sense of all my relief and
all my tribulation. Since everyone has times
when they are distressed and times when they
are also made happy, he means, "my lot," the
times allotted to me for being made glad and for
being distressed, all these are "in your hands"
and capable of being changed as you wish. COM-
MENTARY ON PSALMS 31.[39]

PRAYING FOR AND AGAINST ENEMIES. AU-
GUSTINE: We have to distinguish between
enemies for whom we must pray and enemies
against whom we must pray. Human enemies,
of whatever kind, are not to be hated, lest when
a good person hates a bad person who is causing trouble, the result is two bad people. A good
person must love even the bad person he or she
has put up with, so that at any rate there is only
one who is bad. The enemies against whom we
need to pray are the devil and his angels.
. . . Even when human enemies assail us, it is
only as the instruments of these evil spirits.
When the apostle Paul warns us how careful
we must be to guard against those enemies, he
is speaking to God's servants who are being harassed, and probably by the factions and dishonesty and hostility of human beings; yet he says to
them, "It is not against flesh and blood that you
have to struggle"—not against human enemies,
then—"but against principalities and powers
and the rulers of this world."[40] EXPOSITIONS OF
THE PSALMS 31.2.[41]

31:16 God's Favor

YOUR FACE, NOT YOUR BACK. PSEUDO-
ATHANASIUS: In this I trust, that I shall be saved
if you make your face to shine on me, hiding
your back from me. EXPOSITION ON PSALMS 31.[42]

SUFFICIENT SALVATION. DIODORE OF TARSUS:
Since it seemed as though God had turned away
from them and was angry with them, he asks
for reconciliation: Only have regard to me, he is
saying, and it is sufficient for my salvation. COM-
MENTARY ON PSALMS 31.[43]

31:17 Calling on the Lord

CALLING IN FAITH. CASSIODORUS: By saying,
"Save me in your mercy," he denies his own merit.
He continually says the same things for our
instruction and is never sated with the confession
that he loves, for the sweetness of the truth knows
no satiety. He further adds, "Let me not be confounded, Lord, for I have called on you." What a
wonderful, perfect proclamation, containing as it
does both a prayer of humility and the impenetrable constancy of belief! So he asks that he be not
ignored and confounded. But how does he believe
that he is heard? "For I have called on you"; calling
in faith is an act deserving rather than injurious,
since he can in no way be deceived because of his
presumption that he is heard by him. EXPLANA-
TION OF THE PSALMS 31.18.[44]

31:18 Lying Lips

STOP TALKING. EVAGRIUS OF PONTUS: One
who speaks falsely receives mercy when he becomes silent. He gives up deceit. NOTES ON THE
PSALMS 30[31].19.[45]

A FUTURE SILENCE. AUGUSTINE: When will
such lips be struck dumb? In this age? Never.
Daily they rant against Christians, especially

---

[37]ACW 51:297-98*. [38]WSA 3 15:318. [39]WGRW 9:96. [40]Eph
6:12. [41]WSA 3 15:347-48. [42]CSCO 387:20. [43]WGRW 9:96.
[44]ACW 51:298*. [45]PG 12:1301.

the lowly ones; they blaspheme daily; every day they bark their insults. . . . "Where is your God? What do you worship? What do you see? You believe, yet you have a hard life; your hard life is certain, but what you hope for is far from certain." But when that certainty for which we hope has become real, those lying lips will be struck dumb. EXPOSITIONS OF THE PSALMS 31.5.[46]

31:19 The Lord's Abundant Goodness

REVELATION OF GOD'S BLESSINGS. THEODORET OF CYR: Now, the verse has this sense: You hide the rewards and prizes for those who fear you, O Lord, many and great and marvelous though these are, and instead you allow them to struggle with sweat and tears. Yet there comes the time when you reveal the rewards, giving cheer to the athletes. . . . Then he described in detail the providence in their favor. . . . Your appearance suffices, he is saying (he calls it "presence"), for them to be freed from all human disturbance and commotion, and to conceal them as though admitted to the precincts of some tabernacle and render them invisible. COMMENTARY ON THE PSALMS 31.10.[47]

REVELATION OF GOD'S SWEETNESS. CASSIODORUS: The Lord's sweetness is revealed by many rewards. He is sweet when he corrects, sweet when he spares, sweet when he promises eternal rewards to believers. But you must realize that he is sweet only to those who taste his savor; the sweetness cannot reach those who have not deserved to taste him. EXPLANATION OF THE PSALMS 31.20.[48]

GOD'S TIMING. AUGUSTINE: This is the voice of the prophet, exclaiming in wonder as he discerns how abundant and how varied are the expressions of your sweetness, O Lord. You dearly love even those you discipline, but to ensure that they do not relax their guard and behave carelessly, you hide the sweetness of that love from those who will profit by fearing you. . . . You have

shown the perfection of your sweetness to those who trust in you, for you do not withhold it from those who persevere in hoping for it to the end. EXPOSITIONS OF THE PSALMS 31.20.[49]

FAITH IS NECESSARY. AUGUSTINE: From the law comes our fear of God, from faith our hope in him; but grace is hidden from those who are in fear of punishment. The soul that labors under that fear, not yet victorious over evil concupiscence and still held in the stern ward of that same fear, must take refuge by faith with the mercy of God, that he may grant what he commands, impart the sweet savor of grace and by his Holy Spirit make the delight of his precepts greater than the attraction that obstructs the keeping of them. Thus that "countless sum of his sweetness," the law of faith that is the love of him written and shed abroad in our hearts, is perfected to them that hope in him, so that the healed soul may work that which is good, not in fear of punishment but through love of righteousness. ON THE SPIRIT AND THE LETTER 51.[50]

MERCY GREATER THAN OUR SINS. CYRIL OF JERUSALEM: The sum of your sins does not surpass the magnitude of God's mercies. Your wounds are not beyond the healing skill of the great Physician. Only surrender to him with faith, tell the Physician of your malady. Repeat the words of David: "I said, I will confess against myself my iniquity to the Lord," and in like manner will be verified the second part of the verse: "And you forgave the wickedness of my heart."[51] CATECHETICAL LECTURES 2.6.[52]

31:20 Safe in God's Shelter

HIDDEN NOW. ARNOBIUS THE YOUNGER: Although the just suffer trials in this age, a greater sweetness awaits them, if they persevere to the future, which the Lord hides meanwhile for those

[46]WSA 3 15:351. [47]FC 101:195-96. [48]ACW 51:300. [49]WSA 3 15:319. [50]LCC 8:235-36. [51]Ps 32:5 (31:5 LXX). [52]FC 61:99-100.

who fear him. He does not wish to show it in this age, so he may complete it for the ones hoping in him in the presence of those who mock them. Now he hides them in the secret of his presence from the vexation of people.... Then he magnifies his mercy when he prepares a fortified city, which angels surround, the mother city of holy Jerusalem. COMMENTARY ON THE PSALMS 31.[53]

HIDDEN HELP. GREGORY OF NYSSA: God's abounding goodness aids us in a hidden way, and in the present life it is not clearly evident. For every objection of unbelievers would be removed, could we actually see what we only hope for. But our hopes await the ages to come, so that there may then be revealed what at present our faith alone apprehends. ADDRESS ON RELIGIOUS INSTRUCTION 17.[54]

31:21 Blessed Is the Lord

SURROUNDED BY LOVE. THEODORET OF CYR: He surrounded and enclosed me in his habitual lovingkindness, he is saying, as the inhabitants encircle a city with a strong rampart. COMMENTARY ON THE PSALMS 31.11.[55]

THE WIDEST CIRCLES OF HUMAN SOCIETY. AUGUSTINE: Blessed may the Lord be, because after the church had undergone the discipline of such bitter persecutions, he made his mercy wonderful all around the world, through the widest circles of human society. EXPOSITIONS OF THE PSALMS 31.22.[56]

JERUSALEM. CASSIODORUS: By "the surrounded city" we must understand the physical Jerusalem, set in the midst of nations and known to exist as the temple of faith. The nations that lay round it deserved to obtain from it the guidelines of Christian teaching; it was as though the clearest of springs had been opened up, and they were irrigated with the gifts of heavenly life. So in this city the Lord has "shown his wonderful mercy," for it was there that he deigned to teach,

to perform miracles and to suffer for people's salvation. There too he revealed the glory of his resurrection, so it was rightly said that he shows his wondrous power in Jerusalem, where he decided to reveal such mighty mysteries. EXPLANATION OF THE PSALMS 31.21.[57]

31:22 Driven from God's Sight

DAVID'S SITUATION. THEODORET OF CYR: This psalm is likely to have been spoken by blessed David at the time of being pursued by Absalom. . . . I thought that on falling into sin, he is saying, I was far from your care; but you took account of my humble words and did not despise me in my need. Now, he rightly called his sin "departure": after treading the way of righteousness he left it and turned aside; but he stumbled and fell foul of bloodthirsty brigands. This very thing reveals David's virtue: he was not in the habit of sinning, but departing a little from his chosen course he suffered that awful slide. COMMENTARY ON THE PSALMS 31.1, 11.[58]

31:23 Love the Lord

HEED THE LORD. THEODORET OF CYR: You who pass through the present life with divine hope, strengthen your souls with bravery and heed the directions of the pilot, traveling wherever he leads. COMMENTARY ON THE PSALMS 31.12.[59]

LOVE AS FRIENDS. CASSIODORUS: When he has sung this hymn in return for the kindnesses bestowed on him, he urges the saints to love the Lord, so that his members may love the Donor of such great kindness by acknowledging that it has been bestowed on their Head. He bids them love as friends now, not as servants; it is the role of servants to fear, of friends to love. EXPLANATION OF THE PSALMS 31.24.[60]

---

[53]CCL 25:39-40. [54]LCC 3:294-95. [55]FC 101:196. [56]WSA 3 15:320. [57]ACW 51:301-2*. [58]FC 101:192-96. [59]FC 101:197. [60]ACW 51:302.

PUNISHMENT OF THE PROUD. DIODORE OF TARSUS: He repays extraordinarily those who are guilty of arrogance so as to bring out that God loathes this transgression more than every other sin. COMMENTARY ON PSALMS 31.[61]

31:24 Be Strong

TAKE COMFORT. ARNOBIUS THE YOUNGER: There will be a judgment in which the Lord will require truth and he will repay the haughty. Be strong; flag not; let your heart be comforted. Be secure, you who hope in the Lord. COMMENTARY ON THE PSALMS 31.[62]

STAY STRONG. CASSIODORUS: Herein the power of the whole psalm and the usefulness of the sacred passion is summarized. . . . In other words, he urged the hearts of the faithful not to be frightened by the sufferings foretold but to strengthen themselves for that glorious imitation that they knew had been inaugurated for the healing and salvation of the world. . . . So this is an exhortation to good people, urging them not to withdraw themselves from a good course through weakness of the flesh. . . . Those who sustain their spirits are lent strength if they fortify their hope in the Lord's power. EXPLANATION OF THE PSALMS 31.25.[63]

---

[61]WGRW 9:97. [62]CCL 25:40. [63]ACW 51:303*.

32:1-11 CONFESSION AND FORGIVENESS

When you see people being baptized and ransomed
out of a generation that is perishing,
and you are in wonder at the lovingkindness of God toward the human race,
then sing to them Psalm 32.

ATHANASIUS ON THE INTERPRETATION OF THE PSALMS 18 [OIP 68]

A Psalm of David. A Maskil.

¹*Blessed is he whose transgression is forgiven,*
whose sin is covered.
²*Blessed is the man to whom the* LORD
imputes no iniquity,
and in whose spirit there is no deceit.

³*When I declared not my sin, my body wasted*
away

through my groaning all day long.
⁴*For day and night thy hand was heavy upon*
me;
my strength was dried up° as by the heat
of summer. Selah

⁵*I acknowledged my sin to thee,*
and I did not hide my iniquity;
I said, "I will confess my trangressions to the
LORD*";*

---

then thou didst forgive the guilt of my sin.
Selah

[6]*Therefore let every one who is godly*
offer prayer to thee;
at a time of distress,[p] *in the rush of great*
waters,
they shall not reach him.
[7]*Thou art a hiding place for me,*
thou preservest me from trouble;
thou dost encompass me with deliverance.[q]
Selah

[8]*I will instruct you and teach you*
the way you should go;
I will counsel you with my eye upon you.
[9]*Be not like a horse or a mule, without*
understanding,
which must be curbed with bit and bridle,
else it will not keep with you.

[10]*Many are the pangs of the wicked;*
but steadfast love surrounds him who trusts
in the Lord.
[11]*Be glad in the Lord, and rejoice, O*
righteous,
and shout for joy, all you upright in
heart!

o Heb obscure **p** Cn: Heb *at a time of finding only* **q** Cn: Heb *shouts of deliverance*

Overview: One needs to think carefully about the thirty-second psalm (Cassiodorus), for it points forward to the New Testament (Theodoret) and gives us an understanding of grace (Augustine, Theodore of Mopsuestia).

The psalmist speaks of the great blessing of the forgiveness of sins (Theodoret), by which sins are completely gone (Ambrose) and we receive free access to heaven (Cyril of Jerusalem). The reception of this grace begins with the acknowledgment of sin (Cassiodorus) and comes by trusting only in God (Augustine), knowing that one cannot hide from God (Cassiodorus). Calling on God keeps the spirit young (Evagrius). Knowing that God knows (Cassiodorus), the psalmist acknowledges his sin (Evagrius), personally (Augustine, Evagrius), bringing it out into the open (Origen), confessing it (Caesarius). He receives absolution from God (Cassiodorus) as a prompt response (Diodore) even though some consequences remain (Theodoret). The confession of sin may be offered in prayer (Cassiodorus). One must seize the present time (Diodore), for the opportunity for confession is limited (Augustine). There is only one way—the way of Christ (Augustine). God is our refuge (Augustine, Cassiodorus), the way of true joy (Athanasius).

The true understanding of sin is given only as a gift from God (Cassiodorus). We have need of this understanding (Pseudo-Athanasius, Diodore) because of the irrational motions of the human spirit (Evagrius). Sin has left people in bestial ignorance (Ambrose, Augustine, Caesarius), so that they must be disciplined by tribulation and judgment (Arnobius the Younger). God pursues those who pursue other gods (Ephrem), and we pray that he will break and correct them (Augustine). But the fool requires many blows (Ambrose). Thus we see the difference between punishment for those who trust in themselves or in false gods and mercy that surrounds those who trust in the Lord (Arnobius the Younger, Pseudo-Athanasius, Augustine). All people stand in need of grace (Theodoret). So, we rejoice in the Lord, not in ourselves (Theodoret, Cassiodorus) and through the gift of a right heart, we glorify the Lord (Arnobius the Younger).

Superscription: *A Psalm of David*

Think Carefully about This Psalm. Cassiodorus: Let us read [this psalm] carefully, and let us lament through remorse of heart, for what psalm is to be pondered over more eagerly than that in which sins are forgiven by the words of so great a Judge? The psalm has this outstanding and unique feature, that whereas other psalms of penitents in their peroration exult through the impulse of heaven-sent remorse, in this one the Lord, who is addressed with great longing, himself promises mercy and joy. EXPLANATION OF THE PSALMS 32.11.[1]

NEW TESTAMENT GRACE. THEODORET OF CYR: This psalm looks forward to the grace of the New Testament. COMMENTARY ON THE PSALMS 32.1.[2]

FOR UNDERSTANDING GRACE. AUGUSTINE: This is a psalm about God's grace and about our being justified by no merits whatever on our own part but only by the mercy of the Lord our God. . . . The title of the psalm is "For David himself, for understanding," so this is a psalm that promotes understanding. The first stage of understanding is to recognize that you are a sinner. The second stage of understanding is that when, having received the gift of faith, you begin to do good by choosing to love, you attribute this not to your own powers but to the grace of God. EXPOSITION 2 OF PSALM 32.1, 9.[3]

DO NOT TRUST IN YOUR OWN MERIT. THEODORE OF MOPSUESTIA: [Blessed David] teaches people, even if they are righteous, that they ought not trust in the merit of their actions nor attribute to themselves any good work. Rather, whatever good work they perform they should ascribe to divine grace and confess that God's mercy is necessary for them, and [they] should believe themselves blessed if they deserve to have God well disposed toward them. COMMENTARY ON PSALMS 32.1.[4]

32:1 Sin Is Covered

THE BLESSING OF FORGIVENESS. THEODORET

OF CYR: I class as enviable and blessed those who by the Lord's lovingkindness receive forgiveness of sins apart from their works. To them, in fact, he exercises such generosity as not only to forgive them but also cover over their sins so that no trace of them remains. COMMENTARY ON THE PSALMS 32.1.[5]

COMPLETELY GONE. AMBROSE: The expression "pardoning sins" applies to their forgiveness, for he takes them away altogether, and what he remembers not are as though they did not exist. LETTER 70.[6]

FREE ACCESS TO HEAVEN. CYRIL OF JERUSALEM: May God at length grant you to see that night when darkness is turned into day, of which it was said "the darkness hides not from you, but the night shall shine as the day."[7] Then let the gate of paradise be opened to each man and each woman among you. Then may you enjoy waters that bear Christ and have his sweet savor. Then may you receive his name of Christian, and the capacity for heavenly things. And even now, I pray you, lift up the eyes of your mind: take thought now of angelic choirs, and God the master of the universe enthroned, with his only-begotten Son sitting on his right hand, and his Spirit with him, while thrones and dominations do him service, and likewise each man and woman of you as being in a state of salvation. Even now imagine that your ears catch those lovely strains wherewith the angels acclaim you saved. "Blessed are those whose transgressions are forgiven and whose sins are covered" when, as stars of the church, you enter paradise with glorious body and radiant soul. CATECHETICAL LECTURES, PROCATECHESIS 15.[8]

32:2 No Deceit

---

[1]ACW 51:313. [2]FC 101:198**. [3]WSA 3 15:362, 371. [4]WGRW 5:279*. [5]FC 101:198*. [6]FC 26:240 (Letter 45 in this edition). [7]Ps 139:12 (138:12 LXX). [8]LCC 4:74-75*.

ACKNOWLEDGMENT OF SIN. CASSIODORUS: Since he is a sinner, he does not proclaim himself to be most holy, a sickness to which human nature is especially addicted, but acknowledges his sins and continually perseveres in making humble satisfaction. He who is displeasing to himself pleases the Lord, for when we impugn ourselves we seek the truth, but when we seek to praise ourselves our words are falsehood. EXPLANATION OF THE PSALMS 32.2.[9]

TRUSTING ONLY IN GOD. AUGUSTINE: The person of God is one of that number of the blessed of whom it was foretold: "Blessed is the one to whom the Lord has not imputed sin, and in whose mouth is no guile." For he confesses even sins of the just, asserting that they rather put their hope in the mercy of God than trust in their own justice, and therefore there is no guile in his mouth, or, indeed, in the mouths of all those to whose truthful humility or humble truth he bears witness. AGAINST JULIAN 2.8.29.[10]

32:3 Not Confessing Sin

WE CANNOT HIDE FROM GOD. CASSIODORUS: No one should think that what he stores away hidden in the depths of his conscience is concealed from the Lord. EXPLANATION OF THE PSALMS 32.3.[11]

HOW SPIRITS AGE. EVAGRIUS OF PONTUS: Strong spirits do not wax old from continual shouting to God, but they are renewed from day to day. From silence they wax old, entangling people who are corrupted through false desires. NOTES ON THE PSALMS 31[32].3.[12]

32:4 The Heaviness of God's Hand

A HEAVY HAND. CASSIODORUS: The hand that scourges is oppressive to the sinner, and the avenging hand is weighty. "Day and night" denotes continuous time, so that hand was rightly felt to be heavy since it did not cease from oppressive punishment. He would not happily have been humiliated if the hand of the Godhead had not oppressed him. EXPLANATION OF THE PSALMS 32.4.[13]

32:5 God Forgave

KNOWING THAT GOD KNOWS. CASSIODORUS: Foolish people . . . believe that God remains ignorant of their actions. . . . Those who are aware that he knows all things clearly abase themselves to humble confession and prayers of repentance so as not to suffer a hostile Judge when they could have him as merciful Advocate. EXPLANATION OF THE PSALMS 32.5.[14]

ACKNOWLEDGMENT. EVAGRIUS OF PONTUS: A righteous person accuses himself at the beginning of his speech.[15] NOTES ON THE PSALMS 31[32].5, 6.[16]

PERSONALLY. AUGUSTINE: God created me with free will; if I have sinned, it is I myself who have sinned, so my business is not simply to declare my unrighteousness to the Lord but to declare it against myself . . . . Why this emphasis, "I myself"? It would have been enough to write "I said." But the emphasis is deliberate: I said it *myself*. I, I myself, not fate, not my horoscope, not the devil either, because he did not compel me, but I consented to his persuasion. EXPOSITIONS OF THE PSALMS 32.16.[17]

TEARS AND FORGIVENESS. EVAGRIUS OF PONTUS: Pray first to receive tears, so that through compunction you may be able to mollify the wildness that is in your soul, and, having confessed against yourself your transgression to the Lord, you may obtain forgiveness from him. CHAPTERS ON PRAYER 5.[18]

---

[9]ACW 51:306. [10]FC 35:90-91*. [11]ACW 51:307*. [12]PG 12:1301. [13]ACW 51:307. [14]ACW 51:308. [15]Prov 18:17 (LXX). [16]PG 12:1304. [17]WSA 3 15:378. [18]GAC 193.

Brought into the Open. Origen: People had evil thoughts. They were revealed to bring them into the open and destroy them. Once they had been killed and are dead, they would cease to exist. He who died for us would kill them. For, as long as such thoughts were hidden and not brought out into the open, it was quite impossible to kill them. Thus, if we ourselves have sinned, we ought to say, "I made my sin known to you, and I have not hidden my iniquity. I said, 'Against myself shall I proclaim my injustice to the Lord.'" Homilies on the Gospel of Luke 17.8.[19]

Confession. Caesarius of Arles: Just as we can never be without the wounds of sins, so we should never lack the remedy of confession. God wants us to confess our sins, not because he himself cannot know them but because the devil longs to find something to charge us with before the tribunal of the eternal Judge and wants us to defend rather than to acknowledge our sins. Our God, on the contrary, because he is good and merciful, wants us to confess them in this world so we will not be confounded by them later on in the world to come. If we confess our sins, he spares us; if we acknowledge them, he forgives. Sermon 59.1.[20]

Absolution. Cassiodorus: He suddenly absolved his sins, for he regards the piety of a prayer as if it were the outcome of an action. The penitent said in his heart that he would not keep silent before the Lord about his past deeds; then, just as if he had revealed all, he was absolved of what he wished to confess, and rightly, since it is the will alone that absolves or punishes anyone. "I will pronounce" means "I will state publicly, that my devoted and faithful confession may draw others to imitate me." From his self-accusation follows the saving remedy, for since the guilty man did not spare himself, the Judge spared him. Explanation of the Psalms 32.5.[21]

A Prompt Response. Diodore of Tarsus: Just as I sinned and was punished, so I acknowl-edged it and was saved. . . . He wishes to bring out also the promptness of God's lovingkind-ness, saying, I shall confess, that is, I resolved to confess the fault to the Lord, and your pardon anticipated my confession. Commentary on Psalms 32.[22]

Some Consequences Remain. Theodoret of Cyr: When David said, "I have sinned against the Lord," Nathan replied, "The Lord has put away your sin, you will not die."[23] He did, how-ever, threaten to fill his house with calamities of all kinds; here too likewise, "You put away the impiety of my sin": immediately after perpetrat-ing such things, he is saying, I should have been consigned to death according to the law, but you applied your lovingkindness and did not so consign me, keeping my treatment to moderate censure. Commentary on the Psalms 32.3.[24]

32:6 Offer Prayer

By Prayer. Cassiodorus: One who is not a stranger to sins ought to involve himself in prayers of entreaty. What a saving cure! To with-stand all sinners' diseases, different remedies are offered them when sick; but if this one antidote is taken with a pure heart, the poisons of all sins are overcome. Explanation of the Psalms 32.6.[25]

Time for Confession. Diodore of Tarsus: Immediately after the sin is a fitting time for confession . . . since a sin that lingers is en-trenched. Commentary on Psalms 32.[26]

A Limited Time. Augustine: No one must assume that when the end comes suddenly, as it did in Noah's day, an opportunity will remain for the confession by which we may draw near to God. Expositions of the Psalms 32.6.[27]

---

[19]FC 94:74*. [20]FC 31:290. [21]ACW 51:308. [22]WGRW 9:99. [23]2 Sam 12:13. [24]FC 101:199. [25]ACW 51:309*. [26]WGRW 9:99. [27]WSA 3 15:360.

One Way. Augustine: The many waters are the variety of doctrines. God's doctrine is one. There are not many waters but one single water, whether we think of the water of baptism or the water of salutary doctrine. . . . The many other waters are the many teachings that pollute human souls. . . . Swimmers in this flood of many waters do not draw near to God. . . . What is the real water, the water that wells up from the most secret inner spring, from the pure channel of truth? Yes, what is that water, my brothers and sisters? It is the water that teaches us to confess the Lord. . . . This is the water that urges us to confess our sins, the water that humbles our hearts, the water of a way of life that leads to salvation, of those who abase themselves, do not presume on themselves at all and refuse any proud attribution of their achievements to their own strength. You will not find this water in any of the books of the pagans, whether Epicurean, Stoic, Manichean or Platonist. You will find throughout those books excellent precepts of morality and self-improvement, but nowhere humility like this. The way of humility comes from no other source; it comes only from Christ. It is the way originated by him who, though most high, came in humility. What else did he teach us by humbling himself and becoming obedient even to death, even to the death of the cross?[28] What else did he teach us by paying a debt he did not owe, to release us from debt? What else did he teach us, he who was baptized though sinless, and crucified though innocent? What else did he teach us, but this same humility? He had every right to say, "I am the way, and the truth and the life."[29] By this humility, then, we draw near to God, because the Lord is close to those who have bruised their hearts; but amid the flood of many waters, amid the torrent of those who exalt themselves in opposition to God and peddle proud blasphemies, no one will draw near to him. Expositions of the Psalms 32.18.[30]

32:7 A Hiding Place

God, My Refuge. Augustine: Let those others take refuge with their gods, or with their demons, or in their own strength or in defending their sins. As for me, I have no refuge in this flood except yourself, my refuge from the distress that besets me. Expositions of the Psalms 32.19.[31]

Refuge from Danger. Cassiodorus: A "refuge" is a place to which people flee to avoid dangers. But this penitent did not flee to trackless deserts, to a fortified camp or to human help, but to God, who could scatter the spiritual foes surrounding him. Explanation of the Psalms 32.7.[32]

True Joy. Athanasius: He caused a light to shine at the prayer of the psalmist, who said, "My Joy, deliver me from those who surround me"; this being indeed true rejoicing, this being a true feast, even deliverance from wickedness, to which a person attains by thoroughly adopting an upright conversation and being approved in his mind of godly submission toward God. Festal Letters 14.1.[33]

32:8 God Will Instruct

The Gift of Understanding. Cassiodorus: Sinners do not have understanding except when the Lord grants it in merciful kindness to the converted, for understanding spells good action and the directing of one's prayers to the Lord's commands. This is the very understanding that the truth of the psalm heading revealed and that the Lord's power mercifully poured on repentant people. Explanation of the Psalms 32.8.[34]

32:9 Not Without Understanding

The Need for Understanding. Pseudo-Athanasius: People have special need of

---

[28]Phil 2:8. [29]Jn 14:6. [30]WSA 3 15:380-81. [31]WSA 3 15:381. [32]ACW 51:309. [33]NPNF 2 4:542*. [34]ACW 51:310*.

[understanding], for when they have lost it, they become like horses and mules. Thus he says: I was turned to misery when thorns were thrust in me—that is, the sin that tormented him. On that account he says to God: I have shown you my sin, and my lawlessness I did not hide from you; and you removed my wickedness. The first duty of repentance is for a person to confess his sin, according to [the saying]: God will have mercy on him who confesses his sins and abandons them. EXPOSITION ON PSALMS 32.[35]

THE IMPORTANCE OF REASON. DIODORE OF TARSUS: The person with understanding and reason perceives the sin, whereas the one without understanding does not perceive it, not wanting to. COMMENTARY ON PSALMS 32.[36]

IRRATIONAL MOTIONS. EVAGRIUS OF PONTUS: He calls the irrational movement of spirit "horse" and "mule." Intellect is rational thinking and judgment. NOTES ON THE PSALMS 31[32].9.[37]

BESTIAL IGNORANCE. AMBROSE: Why do you dishonor yourself by surrendering to the allurements of the body, a slave to the whims of appetite? Why do you deprive yourself of the intelligence with which the Creator has endowed you? Why do you put yourself on the level of the beasts? To dissociate yourself from these was the will of God, when he said, "Do not become like the horse and the mule, which have no understanding." SIX DAYS OF CREATION 6.3.10.[38]

THE SOUL NEEDS UNDERSTANDING. AUGUSTINE: To have a soul and not to have an understanding, that is, not to use it or to live according to it, is a beast's life. For there is in us something bestial by which we live in the flesh, but it must be ruled by the understanding. For the understanding rules from above the impulses of the soul when it moves itself according to the flesh and desires to pour itself out immoderately into carnal delights. TRACTATES ON THE GOSPEL OF JOHN 15.19.2.[39]

THE FATE OF THE DISSIPATED SOUL. CAESARIUS OF ARLES: Our Lord admonishes us through the prophet: "Be not senseless like horses or mules.". . . As the ass or mule is tied to a grindstone with his bodily eyes weakened or closed with rages, so the dissipated soul has the eyes of its mind put out by the filth of its life, and through the errors of its thoughts is guided, as it were, around the turning millstone through laborious compassion, without its own sight and working with that of another. [A dissipated person] stands on the road of sinners, fettered with the bonds of his passions. He is his own prison, filled with the darkness of his error, stiff with the squalor of his conscience, enduring within himself the imprisonment of a mill. He turns the rock of his heart, which has been hardened by perseverance in iniquity, like a grindstone, making flour for his enemy out of the corrupt grain of his soul. SERMON 120.3.[40]

TRIBULATION AND JUDGMENT. ARNOBIUS THE YOUNGER: He gives instruction to us, and thus he teaches us on the way by which we walk so that he may fix his eyes upon us and so that we do not become as a horse or a mule. Those reluctant to draw near will have their jaws restrained with a rein of tribulation and a curb of judgment. COMMENTARY ON THE PSALMS 32.[41]

PURSUED BY GOD. EPHREM THE SYRIAN: The one who was God pursued the nations who pursued gods that were not gods at all. And [using] words like bridles, he turned them away from many gods [and brought them] to one. HOMILY ON OUR LORD 5.1.[42]

BROKEN AND CORRECTED. AUGUSTINE: We need not wonder if after the bit has been inserted the whip is also used. The sinner wanted to be like an unbroken animal and so must be subdued with bit and whip; and let us hope

---

[35]CSCO 387:21. [36]WGRW 9:99. [37]PG 12:1304. [38]FC 42:233. [39]FC 79:89. [40]FC 47:196*. [41]CCL 25:41. [42]FC 91:280*.

that he or she can be broken in. The fear is that such persons may resist so obstinately that they deserve to be left in their unbroken state and allowed to go their own sweet way. . . . May such people, when the whip catches them, be corrected and subdued, as the psalmist tells us he too was tamed. Expositions of the Psalms 32.23.[43]

Many Blows. Ambrose: Fools are not free. . . . Many blows are necessary that their wickedness be controlled. Training, not harshness, exacts this. Besides, "he who spares the rod hates his son,"[44] since each one is punished more heavily for his sins. The weight of sin is heavy, the stripes for crimes are heavy; they weigh like a heavy burden; they leave scars on the soul and make the wounds of the mind fester.[45] Letter 37.[46]

32:10 Steadfast Love

Punishment Versus Mercy. Arnobius the Younger: Many are the punishments of sinners, but those who hope in the Lord, he will surround with his mercy. Commentary on the Psalms 32.[47]

Mercy Found in the Lord. Pseudo-Athanasius: Even if there are many scourges of the sinner, yet mercy will surround one who trusts in the Lord, and the just will rejoice because their boast is in the Lord. Exposition on Psalms 32.[48]

Confession and Trust. Augustine: Those who refuse to confess their sins to God and want to be their own rulers find plenty to scourge them. . . . Those who trust in the Lord and submit themselves to his rule find his mercy all around them. Expositions of the Psalms 32.10.[49]

The Need for Grace. Theodoret of Cyr: All people, even if adorned with the works of virtue, stand in need of divine grace; hence the divine apostle also shouts aloud, "By grace you are saved through faith; this is not of your doing—it is God's gift."[50] Commentary on the Psalms 32.6.[51]

32:11 Be Glad in the Lord

In the Lord, Not in Ourselves. Theodoret of Cyr: So let no one rejoice in his or her own achievements but rather exult in God and find satisfaction in that. This is in keeping with the apostolic statements, "Let the one who boasts boast in the Lord."[52] Commentary on the Psalms 32.7.[53]

Joyful in the Lord. Cassiodorus: The just must "be glad in the Lord," not in themselves, for one who is joyful in himself is deceived by false presumption . . . whereas one who is glad in the Lord enjoys delight without end. Explanation of the Psalms 32.11.[54]

Glorify the Lord. Arnobius the Younger: You of good will come to the Lord. Rejoice and exalt in the Lord, you righteous ones, and glorify our Lord Jesus Christ in a right heart. Commentary on Psalms 32.[55]

---

[43]WSA 3 15:383. [44]Prov 13:24. [45]Ps 38:5-6 (37:6-7 lxx). [46]FC 26:301* (Letter 54 in this edition). [47]CCL 25:41. [48]CSCO 387:21. [49]WSA 3 15:360. [50]Eph 2:8. [51]FC 101:201. [52]2 Cor 10:17. [53]FC 101:201*. [54]ACW 51:312*. [55]CCL 25:41.

33:1-22 THE SOVEREIGNTY OF GOD

When you are gathered together with people who are righteous
and upright of life, sing with them Psalm 33.

ATHANASIUS ON THE INTERPRETATION OF THE PSALMS 18 [OIP 68]

[1]Rejoice in the LORD, O you righteous!
  Praise befits the upright.
[2]Praise the LORD with the lyre,
  make melody to him with the harp of ten
    strings!
[3]Sing to him a new song,
  play skilfully on the strings, with loud
    shouts.

[4]For the word of the LORD is upright;
  and all his work is done in faithfulness.
[5]He loves righteousness and justice;
  the earth is full of the steadfast love of the
    LORD.

[6]By the word of the LORD the heavens were
    made,
  and all their host by the breath of his
    mouth.
[7]He gathered the waters of the sea as in a
    bottle;
  he put the deeps in storehouses.

[8]Let all the earth fear the LORD,
  let all the inhabitants of the world stand in
    awe of him!
[9]For he spoke, and it came to be;
  he commanded, and it stood forth.

[10]The LORD brings the counsel of the nations
    to nought;
  he frustrates the plans of the peoples.
[11]The counsel of the LORD stands for ever,
  the thoughts of his heart to all generations.
[12]Blessed is the nation whose God is the LORD,
  the people whom he has chosen as his
    heritage!

[13]The LORD looks down from heaven,
  he sees all the sons of men;
[14]from where he sits enthroned he looks forth
  on all the inhabitants of the earth,
[15]he who fashions the hearts of them all,
  and observes all their deeds.
[16]A king is not saved by his great army;
  a warrior is not delivered by his great
    strength.
[17]The war horse is a vain hope for victory,
  and by its great might it cannot save.

[18]Behold, the eye of the LORD is on those who
    fear him,
  on those who hope in his steadfast love,
[19]that he may deliver their soul from death,
  and keep them alive in famine.

[20]Our soul waits for the LORD;
  he is our help and shield.
[21]Yea, our heart is glad in him,
  because we trust in his holy name.
[22]Let thy steadfast love, O LORD, be upon us,
  even as we hope in thee.

OVERVIEW: Rejoice in the Lord, not in human conditions (BASIL). In order to rejoice like this, submit the will to God (AUGUSTINE). To rejoice in the Lord is to rejoice in wisdom (EVAGRIUS). Its object is an everlasting joy (AUGUSTINE). The harp by which we make melody to God is our own selves (CASSIODORUS), the harp of our bodily actions (BASIL) empowered by love (AUGUSTINE). The new song is the new covenant sung by new people (AUGUSTINE). The loud shout comes from their unity and harmony by the Spirit (BASIL). The work of God is firm and permanent (THEODORE OF MOPSUESTIA), and we attribute all to the providence of God (BASIL). It is typical of God to show both kindness and justice (DIODORE, THEODORE), and we see an order in which kindness is followed by justice in the case of the unrepentant (HESYCHIUS, BASIL). These are two realities in God (AUGUSTINE). But we especially note that he is full of mercy (CASSIODORUS) and that the present time is the time for mercy (AUGUSTINE).

The Lord created all things immediately by his Word and his Spirit (THEODORET, HILARY OF POITIERS). Some see only metaphor here (THEODORE OF MOPSUESTIA). But most see a clear reference to the Trinity (JEROME, CASSIODORUS, NICETAS), in fact, the very rule of truth concerning God's act in creation (IRENAEUS). Specifically, we see the equal dignity of the divine Spirit (BASIL, JOHN OF DAMASCUS, ORIGEN). Nevertheless, many have fallen into the error of idolatry (CLEMENT OF ALEXANDRIA). The rationale of divine providence is hidden in the depths of God (BASIL), but we move in the direction of understanding when we praise him in all things (EVAGRIUS). Humanity especially needs to be brought under the divine will (CASSIODORUS).

The counsel of the nations is contrary to the will of God (EVAGRIUS), as is seen especially in the matter of the Lord's passion (BASIL). Such is the mystery of Christ (CASSIODORUS). The Lord's counsel prevails (THEODORE OF MOPSUESTIA). His plan is unchanging (AUGUSTINE, FULGENTIUS), which is a blessing for his people (THEODORET, THEODORE OF MOPSUESTIA). The Lord himself is our true happiness (AUGUSTINE). The Lord is the lofty spectator who sees and knows all (BASIL) and especially looks on us in grace (CASSIODORUS) from his human vantage point (AUGUSTINE). It is not that he is ignorant of anything (THEODORET). Rather, he has formed us individually (THEODORE OF MOPSUESTIA) according to his purpose (CASSIODORUS), knowing us completely, even to the intentions of our hearts (AUGUSTINE, THEODORE OF MOPSUESTIA). Demons, however, do not have this knowledge (EVAGRIUS). Consequently, only he can truly help us (ORIGEN, CHRYSOSTOM).

True help comes only from heaven (HESYCHIUS, BASIL). Consequently, we need to recognize God as God (AUGUSTINE), for no one is safe apart from God (ARNOBIUS THE YOUNGER). Specifically, we hope in his mercy (ARNOBIUS THE YOUNGER, BASIL, AUGUSTINE). Watchfulness is precisely his relationship with us (SALVIAN). He grants us salvation in the present and in the future (PSEUDO-ATHANASIUS, CASSIODORUS), teaching us the virtue of patience (CASSIODORUS) as he shields us with his protection (THEODORE). The Lord thus sustains us (ARNOBIUS THE YOUNGER) with higher delights (EVAGRIUS). We rejoice in him, not in ourselves (AUGUSTINE).

33:1 Rejoice in the Lord

REJOICE IN GOD. BASIL THE GREAT: "Rejoice," therefore, "in the Lord, O you righteous," not when the interests of your home are flourishing, not when you are in good health of body, not when your fields are filled with all sorts of fruits, but when you have the Lord—such immeasurable Beauty, Goodness, Wisdom. Let the joy that is in him suffice for you.... For the just person, the divine and heavenly joy is lasting, since the Holy Spirit dwells in him once and for all. "But the firstfruit of the Spirit is charity, joy, peace."[1]

---

[1]Gal 5:22.

Therefore, "rejoice in the Lord, O you just." The Lord is like a place capable of containing the just, and there is every reason for one who is in him to be delighted and to make merry. Moreover, the just person becomes a place for the Lord when he receives God in himself . . . . Let us, then, who are in the Lord and who, as much as we are able, observe closely his wonders, so draw joy to our hearts from the contemplation of them. HOMILIES ON THE PSALMS 15.1 (Ps 33).[2]

THE WILL OF THE RIGHTEOUS. AUGUSTINE: Who are the upright? Those who direct their hearts in accordance with the will of God. If human frailty unsettles them, divine tranquility consoles them, for although they may privately in their mortal hearts want something that serves their present purpose, or promotes their business or meets their immediate need, once they have understood and recognized that God wants something different, they prefer the will of One better than themselves to their own, the will of the Almighty to that of a weakling, the will of God to that of a human being. As God is infinitely above his human creatures, so is God's will far above the will of men and women. This is why Christ took the mantle of humanity, set us an example, taught us how to live and gave us the grace to live as he taught. To this end let his human will be seen. In his human will he embodied ours in advance, since he is our Head and we all belong to him as his members, as you know well. "Father," he said, "if it is possible, let this cup pass from me."[3] . . . "See yourself reflected in me," Christ says, because you have the capacity to want something on your own account that is at variance with God's will. This is natural to human frailty, characteristic of human weakness and difficult for you to avoid. But when it happens, think immediately about who is above you. Think of God above you, and yourself below him, of him as your Creator and yourself as his creature, of him as Lord and yourself as servant, of him as almighty and yourself as weak. Correct yourself, subject yourself

to his will, and say, "Not what I will, but what your will be done, Father."[4] EXPOSITIONS OF THE PSALMS 33.2.[5]

REJOICE IN WISDOM. EVAGRIUS OF PONTUS: The Lord is wise, so by rejoicing in the Lord, the righteous rejoice in wisdom. NOTES ON THE PSALMS 32[33].1.[6]

EVERLASTING JOY. AUGUSTINE: Let the unjust dance for joy in this world, by all means; but when this world comes to an end, there will be an end to their dancing. Let the just dance for joy in the Lord, for the Lord abides forever, and so will the exultation of the just. EXPOSITIONS OF THE PSALMS 33.1.[7]

33:2 The Harp of Ten Strings

WE ARE THE HARP. CASSIODORUS: The harp and psaltery lie within us, or rather we ourselves are the instruments when like them we sing through the quality of our actions by means of the Lord's grace. EXPLANATION OF THE PSALMS 33.2.[8]

THE BODILY HARP. BASIL THE GREAT: It is necessary to praise the Lord on the harp; that is, to render harmoniously the actions of the body. Since, indeed, we sinned in the body, "when we yielded our members as slaves of sin, to lawlessness,"[9] let us give praise with our body, using the same instrument for the destruction of sin. Have you reviled? Bless. Have you defrauded? Make restitution. Have you been intoxicated? Fast. Have you made false pretensions? Be humble. Have you been envious? Console. Have you murdered? Bear witness, or afflict your body with the equivalent of martyrdom through confession. And then, after confession you are worthy to play for God on the ten-stringed psaltery. For it is necessary, first, to correct the actions of our body, so that we per-

---

[2]FC 46:227-28*. [3]Mt 26:39. [4]Mt 26:39. [5]*WSA* 3 15:392-93. [6]PG 12:1304. [7]*WSA* 3 15:392. [8]ACW 51:316. [9]Rom 6:19.

form them harmoniously with the divine Word and thus mount up to the contemplation of things intellectual. . . . One, therefore, who observes all the precepts and makes, as it were, harmony and symphony from them, this one, I say, plays for God an a ten-stringed psaltery. HOMILIES ON THE PSALMS 15.2 (Ps 33).[10]

EMPOWERED BY LOVE. AUGUSTINE: Take up the psaltery and sing psalms to God on this psaltery with its ten strings. There are ten commandments in the law, and in these ten commandments you find the psaltery. . . . All these commandments are from God. They were granted to us as the gift of divine wisdom and are trumpeted from heaven. Pluck your psaltery, then, and fulfill the law, for the Lord your God came not to supersede it but to bring it to perfect fulfillment.[11] . . . For the Lord will grant sweetness and our earth shall yield its fruit, so that you are enabled to carry through by love what you found difficult when your motive was fear. EXPOSITIONS OF THE PSALMS 33.6.[12]

33:3 Sing a New Song

NEW PEOPLE SING IT. AUGUSTINE: Strip off your oldness; you know a new song. A new person, a New Covenant, a new song. People stuck in the old life have no business with this new song; only those who are new persons can learn it, renewed by grace and throwing off the old, sharers already in the New Covenant, which is the kingdom of heaven. All our love yearns toward that, and in its longing our love sings a new song. Let us sing this new song not with our tongues but with our lives. EXPOSITIONS OF THE PSALMS 33.8.[13]

THE LOUD SHOUT. BASIL THE GREAT: The loud noise is a certain inarticulate sound, when those who are fighting side by side in a war shout out in unison with each other. Sing, then, in harmony and in agreement and in union through charity. HOMILIES ON THE PSALMS 15.3 (Ps 33).[14]

33:4 All God's Work

FIRM AND PERMANENT. THEODORE OF MOPSUESTIA: Everything done by [God] is firm and permanent. The insertion of both these phrases was necessary in the light of the foregoing: he had to recommend thanksgiving and show the justice of the victory and the permanence of the gift so that the thanksgiving and hymn singing to him would emerge as a response to both, the provision of just assistance and the gift of abiding beneficence. He is saying, then, that both these features characterize what is done by God, and if either is missing, the level of thanksgiving could be diminished. That is to say, if the assistance were unjust, it would not be appropriate to offer thanks on their behalf, even though thanks are due for what is received, or if it underwent rapid change, it thus would be unnecessary to give thanks for good things that do not last. COMMENTARY ON PSALMS 33.4B.[15]

THE PROVIDENCE OF GOD. BASIL THE GREAT: "If you see the heavens," he says, "and the order in them," they are a guide to faith, for through themselves they show the Craftsman; and, if you see the orderly arrangement about the earth, again through these things also your faith in God is increased. In fact, it is not by acquiring knowledge of God with our carnal eyes that we believe in him, but by the power of the mind we have perceived the invisible God through visible things. Therefore, "all his works are done with faithfulness." Even if you consider the stone, it also possesses a certain proof of the power of its Maker. Likewise, if you consider the ant or the gnat or the bee. Frequently in the smallest objects the wisdom of the Creator shines forth. He who unfolded the heavens and poured out the boundless expanses of the seas, he it is who hollowed out the very delicate sting of the bee like a tube, so that through it the poison might

---

[10]FC 46:229-30*. [11]Mt 5:17. [12]WSA 3 15:398-99. [13]WSA 3 15:400*. [14]FC 46: 231. [15]WGRW 5:289-91.

be poured out. Therefore "all his works are done with faithfulness." Do not say, "This happened by chance" and "that occurred accidentally." Nothing is casual, nothing indeterminate, nothing happens at random, nothing among things that exist is caused by chance. And do not say, "It is a bad mishap," or "it is an evil hour." These are the words of the untaught. "Are not two sparrows sold for a farthing?[16] And yet not one of them will fall"[17] without the divine will. How many are the hairs of your head? Not one of them will be forgotten.[18] Do you see the divine eye, how none of the least trifles escapes its glance? HOMILIES ON THE PSALMS 15.3 (Ps 33).[19]

33:5 Righteousness and Justice

TYPICAL OF GOD. DIODORE OF TARSUS: This is typical of God, both to show lovingkindness and to judge—to show lovingkindness for those who hope in him and to condemn those who trust in themselves. COMMENTARY ON PSALM 33.[20]

GRACE AND RIGHTEOUSNESS. THEODORE OF MOPSUESTIA: Grace and righteousness are characteristic of what is done by God. In other words, he said that loving is characteristic of him, speaking perhaps excessively and meaning that not only does what has been done in the past have these two characteristics, but also he is very fond of doing such things as happen to have these two characteristics. COMMENTARY ON PSALMS 33.5A.[21]

KINDNESS, THEN JUDGMENT. HESYCHIUS OF JERUSALEM: He places kindness before judgment because God uses kindness, then judgment against those who continue in sin. LARGE COMMENTARY ON PSALMS 33.5.[22]

THE MERCIFUL JUDGE DESIRES REPENTANCE. BASIL THE GREAT: The Judge wishes to have mercy on you and to share his own compassion. . . . But if he sees your heart unrepentant, your mind proud, your disbelief of the future life and your fearlessness of the judgment, then he

desires the judgment for you, just as a reasonable and kind doctor tries at first with hot applications and soft poultices to reduce a tumor, but, when he sees that the mass is rigidly and obstinately resisting, casting away the olive oil and the gentle method of treatment, he prefers henceforth the use of the knife. Therefore, God loves mercy in the case of those repenting, but he also loves judgment in the case of the unyielding. HOMILIES ON THE PSALMS 15.3 (Ps 33).[23]

TWO REALITIES IN GOD. AUGUSTINE: Make no mistake, brothers and sisters: in God these two realities cannot be separated. We might think that they are mutually exclusive, so that a person who is merciful is not allowing judgment its rights, while someone who insists on judgment is forgetting mercy. But God is almighty, and he neither loses sight of judgment when exercising mercy nor abandons mercy when passing judgment. He looks mercifully on his image, taking our frailty into account, and our mistakes and our blindness; he calls us, and when we turn back to him, he forgives our sins. But he does not forgive those who refuse to turn back. Is he merciful to the unjust? He has lost sight of judgment, has he? Is he not right to judge between the converted and the unconverted? Or does it seem just to you that the converted and unconverted should receive the same treatment, that one who confesses and one who lies, the humble and the proud, should all be welcomed without distinction? Even as he exercises mercy, God has a place for judgment. EXPOSITIONS OF THE PSALMS 33.11.[24]

FULL OF MERCY. CASSIODORUS: He praises the Lord by recounting what he has done or what he does every day. We say that we love the things that we perform regularly; so here it is said of the Lord that he loves mercy . . . because he frequently grants us mercy. . . . So in this world

---

[16]Mt 10:29. [17]Mt 10:29. [18]Cf. Mt 10:30. [19]FC 46:232. [20]WGRW 9:101. [21]WGRW 5:291. [22]PG 93:1188. [23]FC 46:233*. [24]WSA 3 15:403.

"he loves mercy," for he spreads it far and wide, obviously when he is forbearing with sinners, when he patiently waits on blasphemers, when he grants life to the unworthy and performs such actions clearly to be attributed wholly to divine kindness.... What ensues is that "the earth is full of the mercy of the Lord." It is precisely this that supports us in our wretchedness, when we struggle under the devil's attack, when through weakness of the flesh we abandon the divine commands.... So let us seek here the mercy of which the whole world is full. EXPLANATION OF THE PSALMS 33.5.[25]

THE TIME FOR MERCY. AUGUSTINE: This present time is the season for mercy, but the season for judgment will come later. Why do we say that this is the season for mercy? Because at this present time God calls those who have turned away from him and forgives their sins when they return; he is patient with sinners until they are converted, and when they are converted at last he forgets everything in their past and promises them a future, encouraging the sluggish, comforting the troubled, guiding the eager and helping the embattled. He deserts no one who struggles and calls out to him; he bestows on us the wherewithal to offer him sacrifice; and he himself gives us the means of winning his favor. Let us not allow this time of mercy to pass away, my brothers and sisters, let it not pass us by. Judgment is coming. EXPOSITIONS OF THE PSALMS 33.10.[26]

33:6 By the Word of the Lord

IMMEDIATE CREATION. THEODORET OF CYR: Effort and time on the part of workers was not required: a word was sufficient for creating on his part. He said, Let a firmament be made, and so it was. Let lights be made in the firmament of heaven, and it was.[27] Such is the surface meaning of the text. True theology, however, gives a glimpse of God the Word with the all-holy Spirit making the heavens and the heavenly powers. The inspired composition of the Old Testament anticipates the Gospel teaching: as the divinely inspired John, the son of thunder, taught the whole world, "In the beginning was the Word, and the Word was with God, and the Word was God; all things were made through him, and without him was made not one thing that was made."[28] COMMENTARY ON THE PSALMS 33.4.[29]

THE BREATH OF DIVINE COMMAND. HILARY OF POITIERS: Is the preparation of the heavens a matter of time for God, so that a sudden movement of thought crept into his understanding, as if it had been previously inactive and dull, and in a human way he searched for material and instruments for the building of the world? The prophet, however, has a different explanation for the operations of God. The heavens were in need of a command from God in order to be established, for their splendor and power in this stability of their unshakable nature did not arise from the proper blending and mixture of any material but by the breath of the divine mouth. ON THE TRINITY 12.39.[30]

METAPHOR. THEODORE OF MOPSUESTIA: You see, when it says "mouth" in these cases, it intends to indicate an operation affecting visible creation, as when it also says "hand" and "feet" and the like. Elsewhere, too, Scripture says, "The mouth of the Lord said this," in the sense that God revealed what had been determined in our regard; nowhere does the divine Scripture by such corporeal expression describe the Lord's nature or the creation of invisible nature, such as angels and the like, as in our case it is in the habit of saying, "Your hands made me." So by "breath of his mouth" he means "by his decision." COMMENTARY ON PSALMS 33.6B.[31]

THE TRINITY. JEROME: The Trinity is clearly declared here: Lord, Word, Spirit of the Lord. BRIEF COMMENTARY ON PSALMS 33.[32]

---

[25]ACW 51:317*. [26]WSA 3 15:402. [27]Gen 1:6-7, 14-15. [28]Jn 1:1, 3. [29]FC 101:203-4*. [30]FC 25:527. [31]WGRW 5:95. [32]CCL 72:204.

THE TRINITY'S WORK OF CREATION. JEROME: There is clear demonstration in this verse that the Father, the Son and the Holy Spirit are the creators of all things. HOMILY 87, ON JOHN 1:1-14.[33]

THE TRINITY MADE MANIFEST. CASSIODORUS: If we examine the passage more carefully, we see that it signifies here the holy Trinity. By speaking of "the word" he announces the Son, by adding "of the Lord" he mentions the Father, and "by the spirit of his mouth" he wishes to be interpreted as nothing other than the Holy Spirit, who came forth from the Father before time began. And so that you might grasp the manifest unity in three persons, he spoke of his mouth, not of their mouths. EXPLANATION OF THE PSALMS 33.6.[34]

THE WORD IS THE SON. NICETAS OF REMESIANA: By the "word" we must here understand the Son, through whom, as St. John declares, "all things were made." And what is "the spirit of his mouth" if not the Spirit whom we believe to be holy? Thus, in one text, you have the Lord, the Word of the Lord and the Holy Spirit making the full mystery of the Trinity. THE POWER OF THE HOLY SPIRIT 7.[35]

RULE OF TRUTH. IRENAEUS: The rule of the truth that we hold is this: There is one God almighty, who created all things through his Word; he both prepared and made all things out of nothing. . . . From this "all" nothing is exempt. Now, it is the Father who made all things through him, whether visible or invisible, whether sensible or intelligible, whether temporal for the sake of some dispensation or eternal. These he did not make through angels or some powers that were separated from his thought. For the God of all things needs nothing. No, he made all things by his Word and Spirit, disposing and governing them and giving all of them existence. This is the one who made the world, which indeed is made up of all things. This is

the one who fashioned humankind. This is the God of Abraham and Isaac and Jacob, above whom there is no other God, or a Beginning, or a Power or a Fullness. This is the Father of our Lord Jesus Christ. AGAINST HERESIES 1.22.1.[36]

THE DIVINE SPIRIT. BASIL THE GREAT: Where are those who set at naught the Spirit? Where are those who separate it from the creative power? Where are those who dissever it from union with the Father and Son? Let them hear the psalm that says, "By the word of the Lord the heavens were established; and all the power of them by the spirit of his mouth." The term "Word" will not be considered as this common form of diction that consists of names and expressions; nor will the Spirit be considered as vapor poured out in the air but as the Word, which was in the beginning with God,[37] and as the Holy Spirit, which has obtained appellation as its own. As, then, the Creator, the Word, firmly established the heavens, so the Spirit, which is from God, which proceeds from the Father, that is, which is from his mouth (that you may not judge that it is some external object or some creature but may glorify it as having its substance from God) brings with it all the powers in him. . . . Since, then, the Savior is the Word of the Lord and the Holy Spirit is the Spirit from his mouth, both joined with him in the creation of the heavens and the powers in them, and for this reason the statement was made: "By the word of the Lord the heavens were established; and all the power of them by the spirit of his mouth." For nothing is made holy except by the presence of the Spirit. HOMILIES ON THE PSALMS 15.4 (Ps 33).[38]

SPIRIT IS GOD. JOHN OF DAMASCUS: Now a spirit that is sent, and acts, and strengthens and maintains is not breath that is dissipated any more than the mouth of God is a bodily member.

---

[33]FC 57:214. [34]ACW 51:317-18. [35]FC 7:30. [36]ANF 1:347**. [37]Jn 1:1. [38]FC 46:234-35*.

Both in fact are to be understood as appropriately referring to God. ORTHODOX FAITH 1.7.[39]

NOTHING SUBORDINATE IN THE TRINITY.
ORIGEN: Nothing in the Trinity can be called greater or less, for there is but one fount of deity, who upholds the universe by his word and reason and sanctifies "by the spirit of his mouth" all that is worthy of sanctification. ON FIRST PRINCIPLES 1.3.7.[40]

THE ERROR OF IDOLATRY. CLEMENT OF ALEXANDRIA: Some, however, who have fallen into error, I know not how, worship God's work instead of God himself—the sun and moon, and the rest of the starry choir—absurdly imagining these, which are but instruments for measuring time, to be gods; "for by his word they were established, and all their host by the breath of his mouth." EXHORTATION TO THE GREEKS 4.[41]

33:7 God Gathered the Waters

THE DEPTHS OF GOD. BASIL THE GREAT: The reasons according to which he dispenses all things individually are stored up only in the knowledge of God. In fact, we learned in another psalm, which said, "Thy judgments are a great deep,"[42] that the judgments made about each one are called a deep. Therefore, if you seek to know why the life of a sinner is continued but the days of sojourning of the just are cut short; why the unjust thrive but a just person is afflicted; why the young child is snatched away before coming to maturity; whence are wars; why there are shipwrecks, earthquakes, droughts, heavy rains; why things destructive of people are created; why one person is a slave, another free, one is rich, another poor (and the difference in sins and in virtuous actions is great; she who was sold to a brothel keeper is in sin by force, but she who immediately obtained a good master grows up with virginity); why this one is treated with kindness and that one condemned; and what is the reward in the case of each of these

from the Judge; taking all these questions into your mind, consider that the judgments of God are the depths and, because they are enclosed in the divine storehouses, are not easily grasped by those encountering them. To one who believes, a promise is given by God: "I will give you hidden treasures, unseen ones."[43] When we have been deemed worthy of knowledge face to face, we shall see also the depths in the storehouses of God. HOMILIES ON THE PSALMS 15.5 (Ps 33).[44]

THE MOVEMENT OF THE SPIRIT. EVAGRIUS OF PONTUS: Praise is the movement of the spirit translated from ignorance to virtue and knowledge. NOTES ON THE PSALMS 32[33].8.[45]

33:8 Fear the Lord

HUMANITY. CASSIODORUS: The prophet rightly asks that all things be moved by the Lord, because all that is arranged by his dispensation is always applied to useful ends. But though he had spoken first of all things in general, he passes now to people, for though all things need to be administered by his command, the human race in particular is known to be subject to sins because it has degenerated from its nature through the vices that creep into it. EXPLANATION OF THE PSALMS 33.8.[46]

33:9 For God Spoke

THE ONE WHO CAME FROM HEAVEN. GREGORY OF NYSSA: The psalm bids us to exult in the one who has come to earth from heaven, as in one who is set over the entirety, and who has brought the entirety into being from not being and who maintains all things in being, whose command becomes reality. For this is the meaning of the divine words, "He spoke, and they were made; he commanded, and they were created." ON THE INSCRIPTIONS OF THE PSALMS 2.8.79.[47]

---

[39]FC 37:176. [40]OFP 37. [41]ANF 2:189. [42]Ps 36:6 (35:7 LXX). [43]Is 45:3. [44]FC 46:236-37*. [45]PG 12.:1305. [46]ACW 51:318*. [47]GNTIP 145.

33:10 *The Counsel of the Nations*

CONTRARY TO GOD'S WILL. EVAGRIUS OF PONTUS: The plans of the nations and the councils of the leaders and the understanding of the peoples are tested by the Lord as contrary to his will—who desires all people to come to salvation and truth.[48] NOTES ON THE PSALMS 32[33].10.[49]

LOOK TO THE LORD. BASIL THE GREAT: It is possible to refer these things to the time of Jesus' passion when they thought that they were crucifying the King of glory, but he through the economy of the cross was renewing humanity. For in the resurrection the counsel of nations, of Pilate and his soldiers, and of whoever was active in the matter of the cross was brought to nought; the counsels of the princes were rejected, and also those of the high priests and scribes and kings of the people. In fact, the resurrection destroyed their every device. . . . Therefore, when you hear someone making great threats and announcing that he will bring on you all sorts of ill treatment, losses, blows or death, look up to the Lord, who brings to nothing the counsels of nations and rejects the devices of the people. HOMILIES ON THE PSALMS 15.6 (Ps 33).[50]

33:11 *The Counsel of the Lord*

THE MYSTERY OF CHRIST. CASSIODORUS: We do well to understand his counsel as the secret of the incarnation, known to have been granted in the interests of the human race. It is dissolved by no period of time but stands forever, because the Lord's triumphant death has blotted out forever the destruction imposed by the devil. EXPLANATION OF THE PSALMS 33.11.[51]

THE LORD PREVAILS. THEODORE OF MOPSUESTIA: Even if a vast number were scheming, while God wanted the opposite, the vast number would be of no significance to the schemes. Even if rulers planned something, the object of their concern would come to nothing, and they would get no benefit from the government or the vast number of the subjects. Then the more important consideration. . . . Not only can [God] render the schemes of others ineffectual, but also he can bring great reliability to his own. Now, "thoughts of his heart" is a bodily expression by which he refers to God's determined limit and authoritative decree, as if to say, Such a decision of the Lord is irrevocable. COMMENTARY ON PSALMS 33.10B, C-11.[52]

THE LORD'S UNCHANGING PLAN. AUGUSTINE: The Lord's plan, according to which he grants happiness only to those who submit to him, abides forever. . . . The thoughts of his wisdom are not subject to change but abide forever and ever. . . . Before the world came into being, he saw us, made us, corrected us, sent to us, redeemed us. This is his plan, the plan that abides forever; this is the thought of his heart that endures from age to age. EXPOSITIONS OF THE PSALMS 33.11, 14.[53]

THE ENDURING COUNSEL OF THE LORD. FULGENTIUS OF RUSPE: There is no thought in him that varies with the passing of time nor, like human beings, did he think one way before he made the world, nor does he think another way after he made the world, nor will he think still another way after the appearance of this world has passed away; for the "counsel of the Lord stands forever." BOOK TO VICTOR AGAINST THE SERMON OF FASTIDIOSUS THE ARIAN 6.1.[54]

33:12 *The Nation Whose God Is the Lord*

THE BLESSED PEOPLE. THEODORET OF CYR: One should declare blessed, he is saying, not those priding themselves on their wealth but those trusting in God and enjoying aid from him. COMMENTARY ON THE PSALMS 33.6.[55]

---

[48]1 Tim 2:4. [49]PG 12:1305. [50]FC 46:239-40*. [51]ACW 51:319*. [52]WGRW 5:303. [53]WSA 3 15:389, 415. [54]FC 95:401. [55]FC 101:205.

UNCHANGING KINDNESS. THEODORE OF MOPSUESTIA: You the people chosen by him are fortunate for the reason that the Lord's kindness to you is unchanging. COMMENTARY ON PSALMS 33.12.[56]

TRUE HAPPINESS. AUGUSTINE: Whatever people do, good or bad, their motive is always to get rid of their misery and win happiness; invariably they want to be happy. People who lead good lives and people who lead bad lives, they all want to be happy; but what they all want does not come the way of all. They all want happiness, but the only ones who will get it are those who want to be just. It may even happen that someone wants to be happy in order to do wrong. And where do people look for happiness? To money, silver and gold, estates, farms, houses, slaves, worldly pomp, the prestige that will swiftly slip away and be lost. They want to be happy by possessing things. . . . He who poured all your gifts on you, who brought you into existence, who bestows on you his sun and his rain in common with all your neighbors even if they are wicked, who gives you crops, springs of water, life, health and immense consolations, he is keeping for you something that he will give to no one else but you. What is this that he is keeping for you? Himself. Ask for something else, if you can think of anything better. God is reserving himself for you. . . . Our happiness, then, will consist in possessing God. How should we understand this? We shall possess him, yes; but will he not also possess us? . . . God both possesses and is possessed, and all this is for our benefit; for although we possess him in order that we may be happy, the converse is not true: he does not possess us in order that he may be happy. He possesses us, and he is possessed by us, to no end other than our happiness. EXPOSITIONS OF THE PSALMS 33.15, 16, 18.[57]

33:13 The Lord Looks Down

THE LOFTY SPECTATOR. BASIL THE GREAT:

Consider the lofty spectator; consider him who is bending down regarding the affairs of humankind. Wherever you may go, whatever you may do, whether in the darkness or in the daytime, you have the eye of God watching. "From his habitation that he has prepared." The gates are not being opened, the curtains are not being drawn together, the habitation of God is ready for viewing. He looks on all people. No one escapes his sight; no darkness, no concealing walls, nothing is a hindrance to the eyes of God. He is so far from failing to look on each individually that he even looks into the hearts, which he himself formed without any admixture of evil. God, the Creator of humankind, made the heart simple according to his saving image; but later we made it, by union with passions of the flesh, a complicated and manifold heart, destroying its likeness to God, its simplicity and its integrity. Since he is the Maker of hearts, therefore, he understands all our works. But we call both words and thoughts and, in general, every movement of a person, his works. With what feelings or for what purpose they are, whether to please people or to perform the duties of the commands given us by God, he alone knows, who understands all our works. Therefore, for every idle word we give an account.[58] Even for a cup of cold water, we do not lose our reward,[59] because the Lord understands all our works. HOMILIES ON THE PSALMS 15.8 (Ps 33).[60]

THE GRACE OF THE LORD. CASSIODORUS: People did not look to the Lord, but the Lord looked to people. . . . The words "and has looked on" denote the grace of the pitying Lord, for we say that we look on those to whom we claim something has been granted. Notice that he does not mention the sins that he looked on, but the people. When he looks on faults, he punishes, but when he gazes on people, he pardons. EXPLANATION OF THE PSALMS 33.13.[61]

---

[56]WGRW 5:305. [57]WSA 3 15:415, 417, 418*. [58]Mt 12:36. [59]Mt 10:42. [60]FC 46:242*. [61]ACW 51:320*.

33:14 *God Looks Forth*

HIS HUMAN VANTAGE POINT. AUGUSTINE:
From that abode where he took on human nature, the dwelling he made ready for himself. . . .
He has looked in mercy on all who dwell in the
flesh, willing to be their leader and rule them.
EXPOSITIONS OF THE PSALMS 33.14.[62]

33:15 *Who Fashions and Observes*

GOD IS NOT IGNORANT. THEODORET OF CYR:
The God of all looks down . . . not as ignorant
and anxious to learn but as judging and sentencing. How could the one who made the soul be
ignorant of its movements? COMMENTARY ON
THE PSALMS 33.7.[63]

FORMED INDIVIDUALLY. THEODORE OF MOPSUESTIA: Some commentators thought that
here blessed David means that he individually
formed people's souls apart from their body, as
though "hearts" meant "souls." Whether this
is so or not (it is a topic requiring fuller treatment), here it does not have that sense. Rather,
"their hearts" means "them," referring to the
whole from the part. So "he forms them individually" means that none of humankind was in
existence, as if to say, when they did not exist,
he produced them. COMMENTARY ON PSALMS
33.15.[64]

ACCORDING TO GOD'S PURPOSE. CASSIODORUS: God has "fashioned the hearts" of those on
whom he has bestowed the gifts of his understanding. We say that modelers fashion, for they
create certain shapes to achieve the purposes
of their work. In the same way the Lord forms
and arranges the minds of the just to lead them
to the gifts of his mercy. EXPLANATION OF THE
PSALMS 33.15.[65]

INTENTIONS. AUGUSTINE: One human being sees the actions of another by observing
that person's bodily movements, but God sees
within the heart. And because he sees inwardly,
the psalm says, "He has understood all their
actions." Suppose two people give alms to the
poor: one is seeking a heavenly reward in doing
so, the other seeks human approval. You see the
same action in both cases, but God understands
the two as different, for he understands what
is within and appraises what is within; he sees
their purposes, he sees their intentions. EXPOSITIONS OF THE PSALMS 33.22.[66]

THE CREATOR KNOWS YOUR THOUGHTS.
THEODORE OF MOPSUESTIA: Nothing done by
human beings can escape [God's] attention,
since he is the creator of the thoughts' inner
chamber, namely, the heart. In fact, this was the
meaning, completely consistent with what went
before: Blessed are you who are devoted to him
who conducts an examination of everything that
is done; instead of anything escaping his notice,
he has a precise knowledge of everything. COMMENTARY ON PSALMS 33.15.[67]

DEMON KNOWLEDGE. EVAGRIUS OF PONTUS:
The demons do not know our hearts, as some
people think, for the Lord alone is "knower of
hearts,"[68] "who knows the mind of human beings"[69] and "who alone fashioned their hearts."[70]
Rather, [demons] recognize the many mental
representations that are in the heart on the basis
of a word that is expressed and movements of the
body. ON THOUGHTS 37.[71]

ONLY GOD CAN HELP US. ORIGEN: When we
fail to remember the one who formed each one
of us in the womb, and formed all our hearts
individually and understands all our works, we
do not perceive that God is a helper of those who
are lowly and inferior, a protector of the weak,
a shelterer of those who have been given up in
despair and Savior of those who have been given

---

[62]*WSA* 3 15:389. [63]FC 101:206. [64]WGRW 5:308. [65]ACW 51:321.
[66]*WSA* 3 15:420. [67]WGRW 5:309. [68]Cf. Acts 1:24; 15:8. [69]Job
7:20. [70]Ps 32:15 (LXX). [71]GAC 179.

up as hopeless. COMMENTARY ON THE GOSPEL OF JOHN 13.168.[72]

THE CREATOR OF HEARTS CURES THEM.
CHRYSOSTOM: Only [God] can cure our hearts, he who alone created our hearts and perceives all our deeds. He alone has the power to enter into our conscience, touch our thoughts and comfort our soul. And if he does not console our hearts, all that people may do is superfluous and unprofitable. Just as when God comforts and pacifies us again, even if people greatly disturb us with myriad troubles, they will be unable to injure us in anything, for when he strengthens our heart, no one is able to shake it. HOMILIES ON REPENTANCE AND ALMSGIVING 4.3.17.[73]

33:16 A King Is Not Saved

ONLY HELP FROM HEAVEN. HESYCHIUS OF JERUSALEM: The king is not saved through much strength. In vain we care for the strength of the body, and we rashly judge our power from the ones near us, friends and money: for nothing except help sent from heaven is able to save us. Take the example from Goliath or Pharaoh. He, a giant, although he was the strongest, was overcome easily by the simple boy David. The other [Pharaoh] pursued Israel with large chariots and a multitude of horses; he has the sea for a grave. LARGE COMMENTARY ON PSALMS 33.16.[74]

HUMAN THINGS ARE WEAK. BASIL THE GREAT: All things that are at once human, when compared with the true power, are weakness and infirmity. HOMILIES ON THE PSALMS 15.9 (Ps 33).[75]

RECOGNIZE GOD AS GOD. AUGUSTINE: All of us should be looking to the Lord, all of us should be grounded in God. Let God be your life, let God be your strength, let God be your constancy, let him be the focus of your most earnest entreaty, let him be the object of your praise, let him be the end in which you find rest, let him

be your helper when you are tackling hard work. EXPOSITIONS OF THE PSALMS 33.23.[76]

33:17 The War Horse

NOT SAFE FROM GOD. ARNOBIUS THE YOUNGER: You will not be safe any more than the man who trusted in his own horse, of whom it was sung, "He cast the horse and its rider into the sea."[77] The horse failed to save him. And so even if you are a giant in courage you are not safe in your own strength. COMMENTARY ON THE PSALMS 33.[78]

33:18 The Eye of the Lord

HOPE IN GOD'S MERCY. ARNOBIUS THE YOUNGER: For the eyes of the Lord are not looking on those trusting in their own strength but those hoping in his mercy. He will snatch their spirits from death and shelter them. COMMENTARY ON THE PSALMS 33.[79]

DO NOT TRUST YOUR OWN GOOD DEEDS.
BASIL THE GREAT: He who does not trust in his own good deeds or expect to be justified by his works has, as his only hope of salvation, the mercies of God. For, when he considers that the expression "Behold the Lord and his reward"[80] refers to each according to his work, and when he ponders his own evil deeds, he fears the punishment and cowers beneath the threats. There is good hope that gazes steadfastly at the mercies and kindness of God lest it be swallowed up by grief. He hopes that his soul will be delivered from death and will be fed by him in famine.[81] HOMILIES ON THE PSALMS 15.10 (Ps 33).[82]

SEEKING SALVATION. AUGUSTINE: If it is salvation that you seek, be aware that the elective love

---

[72]FC 89:104*. [73]FC 96:51.* [74]PG 93:1188. [75]FC 46:243. [76]WSA 3 15:420. [77]Ex 15:1. [78]CCL 25:43. [79]CCL 25:43. [80]Is 40:10. [81]Ps 33:19 (32:19 LXX). [82]FC 46:244-45.

of the Lord rests on those who fear him "and trust in his mercy," rather than putting their hope in their own strength. EXPOSITIONS OF THE PSALMS 33.18.[83]

WATCHFULNESS. SALVIAN THE PRESBYTER: God is said to watch over the just, that he may maintain and protect them. Watchfulness by his gracious divinity is the function of his relationship with people. THE GOVERNANCE OF GOD 2.1.[84]

33:19 God Delivers Their Souls

SALVATION, PRESENT AND FUTURE. PSEUDO-ATHANASIUS: Those who fear him, those who hope for his mercy, he saves from spiritual death and nourishes in a spiritual way, that they may also say, "Let your mercy be on us, Lord, as we have hoped in you." EXPOSITION ON PSALMS 33.[85]

THE TWO PRAYERS OF THE FAITHFUL. CASSIODORUS: These are the two prayers of the most faithful Christian, that at the future judgment he may be rescued from perpetual death, and that on earth he may live his life with spiritual nourishment. The Lord rescues the souls of the just from death when he removes them from the power of the devil, when by his kindness he sets free those whom the domination of sin had held captive. He feeds them in hunger when in this world, where there is a shortage of good things; he does not cease to nourish with spiritual food those whom he has redeemed. EXPLANATION OF THE PSALMS 33.19.[86]

33:20 A Soul Waiting for the Lord

PATIENCE. CASSIODORUS: The psalmist's word *waits* reflects the patience of the Christian. . . . Patience is what makes glorious martyrs, what guards the blessings of our faith, what conquers all adversity not by wrestling but by enduring, not by grumbling but by giving thanks. Patience represses the extravagance that beguiles us. It overcomes hot anger, it removes the envy

that ravages the human race, it makes people gentle, it smiles becomingly on the kind, and it orders people who are cleansed to attain the rewards that are to come. Patience wipes away the dregs of all pleasure; patience makes souls pure. Through patience we soldier for Christ, through it we conquer the devil, through it we blessedly attain the kingdom of heaven. As Scripture says, "In your patience you shall possess your souls."[87] EXPLANATION OF THE PSALMS 33.20.[88]

PROTECTIVE SHIELD. THEODORE OF MOPSUESTIA: [God] is always helping and providing us with salvation. The term "protector," you see, is a metaphor from those thrusting their own shields among the enemy and by protection from these often sheltering others and freeing them from every disaster. COMMENTARY ON PSALMS 33.20A.[89]

33:21 Glad in the Lord

THE LORD SUSTAINS US. ARNOBIUS THE YOUNGER: Even in this hour, we are hungry and thirsty and naked, yet our spirits act patiently and are not disturbed, for the Lord sustains us. He is our helper and protector, and, as it says in the heading of the psalm, we are commanded to "rejoice in the Lord, righteous ones, let your heart be joyful in him, and hope in his holy name." He brings his mercy over us as we hope in him. COMMENTARY ON THE PSALMS 33.[90]

HIGHER DELIGHTS. EVAGRIUS OF PONTUS: The heart of the righteous does not delight in food and drink but in justice, knowledge and wisdom. NOTES ON THE PSALMS 32[33].20.[91]

REJOICE IN GOD. AUGUSTINE: Not in ourselves,

---

[83]WSA 3 15:390. [84]FC 3:56*. [85]CSCO 387:22. [86]ACW 51:322. [87]Lk 21:19. [88]ACW 51:323*. [89]WGRW 5:313. [90]CCL 25:43. [91]PG 12:1305.

where there is nothing but vast penury without him, but in him will our heart rejoice. . . . This is why we have hoped that we shall reach the Lord: while we are still at a distance he has put his own name on us through our faith. EXPOSITIONS OF THE PSALMS 33.21.[92]

---

[92]WSA 3 15:390*.

34:1-22 PRAISE FOR DELIVERANCE

If you have chanced upon enemies and yet have prudently fled from them
and their schemes, call together people of gentle disposition
and give thanks in the words of Psalm 34.

ATHANASIUS ON THE INTERPRETATION OF THE PSALMS 18 [OIP 68]

A Psalm of David, when he feigned madness before Abimelech, so that he drove him out, and he went away.

¹*I will bless the LORD at all times;*
his praise shall continually be in my mouth.
²*My soul makes its boast in the LORD;*
let the afflicted hear and be glad.
³*O magnify the LORD with me,*
and let us exalt his name together!

⁴*I sought the LORD, and he answered me,*
and delivered me from all my fears.
⁵*Look to him, and be radiant;*
so your[r] faces shall never be ashamed.
⁶*This poor man cried, and the LORD heard him,*
and saved him out of all his troubles.
⁷*The angel of the LORD encamps*
around those who fear him, and delivers them.
⁸*O taste and see that the LORD is good!*
Happy is the man who takes refuge in him!
⁹*O fear the LORD, you his saints,*

for those who fear him have no want!
¹⁰*The young lions suffer want and hunger;*
but those who seek the LORD lack no good thing.

¹¹*Come, O sons, listen to me,*
I will teach you the fear of the LORD.
¹²*What man is there who desires life,*
and covets many days, that he may enjoy good?
¹³*Keep your tongue from evil,*
and your lips from speaking deceit.
¹⁴*Depart from evil, and do good;*
seek peace, and pursue it.

¹⁵*The eyes of the LORD are toward the righteous,*
and his ears toward their cry.
¹⁶*The face of the LORD is against evildoers,*
to cut off the remembrance of them from the earth.
¹⁷*When the righteous cry for help, the LORD hears,*
and delivers them out of all their troubles.

¹⁸*The Lord is near to the brokenhearted,*
   and saves the crushed in spirit.

¹⁹*Many are the afflictions of the righteous;*
   but the Lord delivers him out of them all.
²⁰*He keeps all his bones;*
   not one of them is broken.

²¹*Evil shall slay the wicked;*
   and those who hate the righteous will be
      condemned.
²²*The Lord redeems the life of his servants;*
   none of those who take refuge in him will
      be condemned.

r Gk Syr Jerome: Heb *their*

Overview: The thirty-fourth psalm exhorts us to bless the Lord at all times, no matter what our circumstances (ATHANASIUS, AUGUSTINE). Such is the mind (BASIL) of a person of peace (CAESARIUS). Such is the sign of humility (AUGUSTINE). We are to seek the Lord in our hearts (CASSIODORUS), seeking not just favors from him but seeking the Lord himself (AUGUSTINE), for God delivers his saints (BASIL). He delivers them from all fears (CASSIODORUS). We approach him in faith and receive in turn his radiance (THEODORET). The inaccessible light becomes accessible to us (CASSIODORUS) without our being ashamed (AUGUSTINE). Gazing on him, we are made into his likeness (SAHDONA).

David was heard when he cried out to the Lord (THEODORET), as also was Christ (ARNOBIUS THE YOUNGER). We need to approach God like a poor person (AUGUSTINE), poor in spirit (BASIL), poor in vice (CASSIODORUS), like one in need of everything (DIODORE). The Lord provides his servants with superior strength (MAXIMUS OF TURIN). He invites us to a feast beyond comparison (LEO). He himself is the life-giving food to be tasted in faith and enjoyed in knowledge (EVAGRIUS). How sweet is the Lord (ARNOBIUS THE YOUNGER)! Let us trust only in God (AUGUSTINE), let us know him by personal experience (BASIL), and let us feed on his Word (JEROME), for in Christ we have everything (AMBROSE). The one who fears God lacks nothing (ARNOBIUS THE YOUNGER). We need to understand and practice the faith of fear (AUGUSTINE) and the discipline of fear (BASIL). Then we will know the success of fear (DIODORE). We will re-

ceive riches from God that do not fail (ARNOBIUS THE YOUNGER)—the true wealth, which is God himself (BASIL). The right fear induces us to love and opens up heaven (CASSIODORUS). Let us hasten to salvation (CLEMENT OF ALEXANDRIA). Let us look for good days in God (AUGUSTINE).

We need to check our tongues (BEDE, AMBROSE) lest our tongue be an assistant to sin (BASIL). Rather, we should train it for the good (CHRYSOSTOM). We need to be peaceful people (THEODORET, CYPRIAN), which entails not mere abstinence from evil (BASIL) but the pursuit of good works (CASSIODORUS). Those who seek it here will know it there (AUGUSTINE). God sees all, but he looks with favor on the righteous (THEODORE OF MOPSUESTIA) and hears them for their own good (AUGUSTINE). On the wicked, he casts a different gaze (CASSIODORUS). The righteous render to God a spiritual cry (BASIL) and continue to trust and obey God (AUGUSTINE). They are heard for eternity (CASSIODORUS). Intentional lowliness (THEODORE OF MOPSUESTIA) constitutes a contrite heart (BASIL) and is the way to reach God (AUGUSTINE). Like athletes (BASIL), the righteous will suffer trials (JEROME). They may in fact appear to have greater afflictions than the wicked (CASSIODORUS). But God's help is always with them (THEODORET, THEODORE OF MOPSUESTIA).

The statement about keeping "his bones" was a prophecy about Christ (AUGUSTINE). But we also see endurance and constancy as the bones of faith (AUGUSTINE). People who have strong spiritual bones are the bones of the church (BASIL). Those who hate the righteous one

(Augustine) will meet with failure (Theodore of Mopsuestia). Their true end is in complete contrast to their funeral eulogies (Augustine). But the hope of the righteous lasts forever (Cassiodorus).

34:1 Bless the Lord at All Times

In Whatever Circumstances. Athanasius: The Lord loves thankful people. They never cease to praise him, and they regularly thank him. In both good times and bad times they offer praise and thanksgiving to God. They worship the Lord, the God of times, without regard to what the times are like. Festal Letters 3.5.[1]

Always Bless the Lord. Augustine: When are you to "bless the Lord?" When he showers blessings on you? When earthly goods are plentiful? When you have a plethora of grain, oil, wine, gold, silver, slaves, livestock; while your mortal body remains healthy, uninjured and free from disease; while everything that is born on your estate is growing well, and nothing is snatched away by untimely death; while every kind of happiness floods your home and you have all you want in profusion? Is it only then that you are to bless the Lord? No, but "at all times." So you are to bless him equally when from time to time, or because the Lord God wishes to discipline you, these good things let you down or are taken from you, when there are fewer births or the already-born slip away. These things happen, and their consequence is poverty, need, hardship, disappointment and temptation. But you sang, "I will bless the Lord at all times; his praise shall be in my mouth always," so when the Lord gives you these good things, bless him, and when he takes them away, bless him. He it is who gives, and he it is who takes away, but he does not take himself away from anyone who blesses him. Expositions of the Psalms 34.3.[2]

A Person of Peace. Caesarius of Arles: Who is there who blesses the Lord at all times?

The person whom good fortune does not corrupt or adversity frighten. This, then, is the first and real peace, to be at peace with God. When this has been accomplished, then we can also possess peace within ourselves. However, if a person is unwilling to have peace with God, he will not be able to possess peace with himself. Sermon 166.4.[3]

In My Thoughts. Basil the Great: The prophet seems to promise something impossible. For how can the praise of God be always in a person's mouth? When he engages in the ordinary conversations pertaining to daily life, he does not have the praise of God in his mouth. When he sleeps, he will keep absolute silence. And how will the mouth of one who is eating and drinking produce praise? We answer to this that there is a certain spiritual mouth of the inner person by which he is fed when he partakes of the word of life, which is the bread that comes down from heaven.[4] Concerning that mouth the prophet also says, "I opened my mouth and panted."[5] The Lord even urges us to have it open wide so as to receive plentifully the food of truth. "Open your mouth wide," he says, "and I will fill it."[6] The thought of God, therefore, having been once for all molded and, as it were, sealed in the authoritative part of the soul, can be called praise of God, since it is always present in the soul. Moreover, according to the counsel of the apostle, the zealous person can do all things for the glory of God, so that every act and every word and every work has in it power of praise. Whether the just person eats or drinks, he does all for the glory of God.[7] Homilies on the Psalms 16.1 (Ps 34).[8]

34:2 Boast in the Lord

Humility. Augustine: What prompts a person to bless the Lord at all times? Being humble.

---

[1]ARL 74-75*. [2]WSA 3 16:25. [3]FC 47:400*. [4]Jn 6:33. [5]Ps 119:131 (118:131 LXX). [6]Ps 81:10 (80:11 LXX). [7]1 Cor 10:31. [8]FC 46:250*.

What does being humble consist in? Being unwilling to be praised in yourself. Any of us who want to be praised in ourselves are proud, but whoever is not proud is humble. Expositions of the Psalms 34.5.[9]

34:4 Seeking the Lord

Seek God in the Heart. Cassiodorus: "I sought the Lord," not over massive tracts of lands or broad and far-flung regions but in the heart, for if we ponder his majesty there, we find it present in every way. Explanation of the Psalms 34.5.[10]

Seek the Lord. Augustine: It is one thing to seek some favor from the Lord, quite another to seek the Lord himself. . . . Do not seek any extraneous thing from the Lord, but seek the Lord himself. He will hearken to you, and even while you are still speaking he will say, "Here I am."[11] Expositions of the Psalms 34.9.[12]

God Delivers His Saints. Basil the Great: The whole life of the just person is filled with affliction. . . . But God delivers his saints from their afflictions. Though he does not leave them without trial, yet he bestows on them patient endurance. For if "tribulation works out endurance, and endurance tries virtue,"[13] he who excludes tribulation from himself deprives himself of his tried virtue. As no one is crowned without an adversary, so also he cannot be declared tried except through tribulations. Homilies on the Psalms 16.4 (Ps 34).[14]

Delivered from All Fears. Cassiodorus: By saying "from all," he leaves no possible remaining obstacle still surviving. Explanation of the Psalms 34.5.[15]

34:5 Radiant and Unashamed

Faith Receives Radiance. Theodoret of Cyr: Whoever approaches him in faith receives rays of intellectual light. Commentary on the Psalms 34.4.[16]

Accessible Light. Cassiodorus: His light is said to be inaccessible when the unique and almighty nature of its substance is described; but when the grace of the sacred Godhead pours forth, we both approach him and obtain blessed enlightenment. Explanation of the Psalms 34.6.[17]

No Shame. Augustine: The only red faces are those of the proud. Why is that? Because proud persons aspire to be high and mighty, and when they encounter insults, or ignominy, or make some *faux pas* or suffer some affliction, they are ashamed. But you need not be afraid; simply draw near to God, and there will be no shamefacedness for you. Your enemy may score off you, and in the eyes of the world he will seem to have demonstrated his superiority; but in God's eyes you are superior to him. . . . As that Light cannot be extinguished, so he does not allow anyone whom he has illumined to be extinguished either. Expositions of the Psalms 34.10.[18]

In His Likeness. Sahdona: Let us therefore also gaze on God, raising up and exalting his holy name in praise. Let us take refuge with his purity by continual recollection of his name; let us sculpt out the beauty of our souls by gazing on the likeness of his glory, so that we may be seen to be glorious statues of his divinity within creation. Book of Perfection 2.62.[19]

34:6 The Lord Heard

David Was Heard. Theodoret of Cyr: Learn from my experience, he is saying, to trust in the God of all: though lowly and a mere shepherd, he accorded me his personal providence

---

[9]WSA 3 16:26. [10]ACW 51:327. [11]Is 65:24; 52:6. [12]WSA 3 16:30. [13]Rom 5:3. [14]FC 46:254*. [15]ACW 51:327. [16]FC 101:208. [17]ACW 51:327. [18]WSA 3 16:31-32*. [19]CS 101:228*.

and rendered me superior to my enemies. COMMENTARY ON THE PSALMS 34.4.[20]

CHRIST WAS HEARD. ARNOBIUS THE YOUNGER: Draw near to him who is pure of heart, draw near and be enlightened. Let your faces not be ashamed in their poverty. If you remember the wealth of the Lord of heaven and earth was made poor for the sake of your poverty, tried for the sake of our tribulation, you will not be ashamed, nor will you fail. For that poor one cries from the cross. Who is this poor one? He who, although rich, was made poor: "Made obedient even to the cross"[21] so that he could free you from crosses. He shouted, and the Lord heard. He sent his angels to guard his body and removed the stone and snatched him from the tomb. COMMENTARY ON PSALMS 34.[22]

BE LIKE THE ONE WHO IS POOR. AUGUSTINE: Perhaps someone may object, "How can I draw near to him? I am laden with grave offenses, burdened with serious sins. The foulest crimes raise their clamor from my conscience. How can I dare to approach God?" How? Quite easily, if you have first humbled yourself in repentance. "But I am ashamed to repent," you answer. . . . Think it through. If the fear of being put to shame deters you from repentance but repentance causes you to draw near to God, do you not see that you are wearing your punishment on your face? Your face has gone red because it has not drawn near to God, and the reason it has not drawn near to him is that it is unwilling to repent! The prophet bears witness that "this poor man cried out, and the Lord heard." He is teaching you how to win a hearing. You see why you are not listened to: you are too rich. . . . Cry out in poverty, cry as a poor person, and the Lord will listen. "But how am I to cry out as a poor person?" Cry to him in such a way that even if you have possessions, you do not trust in your own resources, cry to him in a frame of mind that understands your need, cry to him in the knowledge that you will always be a pauper as long as you do not possess him who makes you rich. How did the Lord hear this poor person? "He saved him from all his troubles." EXPOSITIONS OF THE PSALMS 34.11.[23]

POOR IN SPIRIT. BASIL THE GREAT: Poverty is not always praiseworthy, but only that which is practiced intentionally according to the evangelical aim. Many are poor in their resources but very grasping in their intention; poverty does not save these; on the contrary, their intention condemns them. Accordingly, not he who is poor is by all means blessed, but he who has considered the command of Christ better than the treasures of the world. HOMILIES ON THE PSALMS 16.5 (Ps 34).[24]

POOR IN VICE. CASSIODORUS: "This" denotes the poor in spirit who is empty not only of worldly wealth but also of abundance of vices. This is the poor person who comes to God and is enlightened, whose face does not blush, whose cry to the Lord gets a salutary and appropriate hearing; and then he emerges to be freed not from a single affliction but from all worldly difficulties. This often happens to the just when they devote their souls to a holy manner of life and pass from the anarchic disaster of this world to enduring freedom from care. EXPLANATION OF THE PSALMS 34.7.[25]

ONE IN NEED OF EVERYTHING. DIODORE OF TARSUS: The one who was in need of everything and given up as lost by people implored God in a moment of tribulation, and the Lord heard him and saved him against the odds. COMMENTARY ON PSALMS 34.[26]

34:7 The Angel of the Lord

SUPERIOR STRENGTH. MAXIMUS OF TURIN: Christ is more powerful to protect his servants

---

[20]FC 101:209. [21]Phil 2:8. [22]CCL 25:44. [23]WSA 3 16:32*. [24]FC 46:255-56. [25]ACW 51:328. [26]WGRW 9:105*.

than the devil is to provoke our enemies. For although this same devil collects mobs for himself and arms them with cruel rage, nonetheless they are easily destroyed because the Savior surrounds his people with superior auxiliaries, as the prophet says: "The angel of the Lord comes round about those who fear him, and he will save them." If the angel of the Lord snatches those who fear him from dangers, then one who fears the Savior cannot fear the barbarians, nor can one who observes the precepts of Christ be afraid of the onslaught of the foe. These are our weapons, with which the Savior has outfitted us: prayer, mercy and fasting. For fasting is a surer protection than a rampart, mercy saves more easily than pillage, and prayer wounds from a greater distance than an arrow, for an arrow only strikes the person of the adversary at close range, while a prayer even wounds an enemy who is far away. SERMON 83.1.[27]

34:8 Taste and See

A FEAST BEYOND COMPARISON. LEO THE GREAT: God's people have spiritual feasts and pure delicacies that it is healthy for them to look for and laudable for them to desire, for the prophet says in praise of them, "Taste and see that the Lord is sweet." Whoever have touched with the taste of their hearts the sweetness of the justice and mercy of God, by which all his ordinances are carried out, and have drunk from the experiences of supernal joys never to be diminished by any pride, they will despise the corruptible and temporal good in their admiration of the eternal, and they will glow in that fire that the love of God kindles. As when cold is changed to warmth and night is changed to daylight, the Holy Spirit by one stroke in the hearts of the faithful takes away darkness and destroys sin. SERMON 50.2.[28]

FAITH AND KNOWLEDGE. EVAGRIUS OF PONTUS: If we taste the Lord, we taste through faith. If he is good, it is through the knowledge of his

goodness that we taste. NOTES ON THE PSALMS 33[34].9.[29]

HOW SWEET IS THE LORD. ARNOBIUS THE YOUNGER: Taste the body of life and see how sweet is the Lord. He has life in himself who eats his flesh and drinks his blood, and then he will be blessed. COMMENTARY ON THE PSALMS 34.[30]

TRUST ONLY IN GOD. AUGUSTINE: Whoever does not trust in the Lord is in a wretched state. But who are they who do not trust in the Lord? Those who trust in themselves. Sometimes, brothers and sisters, there is an even worse condition: think now. There are some who do not even trust in themselves but put their trust in other people . . . . "I'm all right, I'm under the protection of So-and-So." . . . How ready people are to talk like this, but not to say, "I trust in God, and he will not let you hurt me." Nor do they say, "I trust in my God, because even if he does give you some license to harm my property, he will give you no power over my soul." EXPOSITIONS OF THE PSALMS 34.13.[31]

PERSONAL EXPERIENCE. BASIL THE GREAT: As the nature of honey can be described to the inexperienced not so much by speech as by the perception of it through taste, so the goodness of the heavenly Word cannot be clearly taught by doctrines, unless, examining to a greater extent the dogmas of truth, we are able to comprehend by our own experience the goodness of the Lord. HOMILIES ON THE PSALMS 16.6 (Ps 34).[32]

FEED ON HIS WORD. JEROME: Just as the body dies unless it is given proper food, even so does the soul if it is not given spiritual food. Why am I making such a point of this? Because there are some who insist on saying, I have no need for sacred Scripture; the fear of God is enough for me.

---

[27]ACW 50:198. [28]FC 93:216. [29]PG 12:1308. [30]CCL 25:44. [31]WSA 3 16:33. [32]FC 46:258.

That is, therefore, precisely why we affirm that just as there are foods for the body, so there are, likewise, foods for the soul, namely, the sacred Scripture. HOMILY ON PSALM 127[128].[33]

EVERYTHING IN CHRIST. AMBROSE: In Christ we possess everything. Let every soul approach him, whether it is sick with the sins of the flesh, infixed by the nails of worldly desires, admittedly still imperfect, progressing by intense medication or already perfect in its many virtues. Everyone is in the Lord's power, and Christ is all things to us. If you desire to heal your wounds, he is your doctor; if you are on fire with fever, he is your fountain; if you are burdened with iniquity, he is your justification; if you need help, he is your strength; if you fear death, he is your life; if you desire heaven, he is your way; if you are fleeing from darkness, he is your light; if you are seeking food, he is your nourishment. Taste and see that the Lord is good. Happy is the one who takes refuge in him. ON VIRGINITY 16.99.[34]

34:9 Fear the Lord

LACKING NOTHING. ARNOBIUS THE YOUNGER: Fear the Lord, all his saints, because the ones fearing him lack nothing—nothing of excellence in the present, nothing of perfection, nothing of future joy. COMMENTARY ON THE PSALMS 34.[35]

THE FAITH OF FEAR. AUGUSTINE: There are plenty of people who hesitate to fear the Lord, because they think they may go hungry if they do. They are told, "Do not cheat." And they protest, "How am I to eat, then? Handicrafts need a little dishonesty to succeed, and business cannot flourish without fraud . . . if I fear God, I will not have enough to live on." . . . If we entertain thoughts like these we are in danger of being throttled by the noose of scandal. We are seeking on earth food that will perish, and not seeking the true recompense in heaven. We are putting our head into the devil's noose; it tightens round our throat, and the devil holds us enslaved to wrongdoing.

EXPOSITIONS OF THE PSALMS 34.14.[36]

THE DISCIPLINE OF FEAR. BASIL THE GREAT: Unless fear disciplines our life, it is impossible successfully to attain holiness in body. . . . In him who fears there is not want, that is, he is failing with regard to no virtue who is prevented by fear from every absurd act, since he falls short of nothing good that belongs to human nature. As he is not perfect in body who is lacking in any necessary part but is imperfect because of what he lacks, so also he who is disposed contemptuously about one of the commands, because he is wanting in it, is imperfect in that in which he lacks. But he who has assumed perfect fear and through piety shrinks beneath all things will commit no sin because he despises nothing; he will not experience any want because he will possess fear sufficiently in all things. HOMILIES ON THE PSALMS 16.6 (Ps 34).[37]

SUCCESS OF FEAR. DIODORE OF TARSUS: It is not possible for the one who fears God and hopes in him to fail. COMMENTARY ON PSALMS 34.[38]

34:10 Lacking No Good Thing

THE RICHES GOD GIVES. ARNOBIUS THE YOUNGER: The rich dwell in uncertainty concerning the things the world gives. The riches that God gives do not fail, but they remain because these riches arise in the fear of the Lord. COMMENTARY ON THE PSALMS 34.[39]

TRUE WEALTH. BASIL THE GREAT: Wealth is unstable and like a wave accustomed to change hither and thither by the violence of the wind. . . . God himself is absolute Good, and they who seek him will not be without him. HOMILIES ON THE PSALMS 16.7 (Ps 34).[40]

34:11 The Fear of the Lord

---

[33]FC 48:319-20. [34]AOV 44-45*. [35]CCL 25:44-45. [36]WSA 3 16:34. [37]FC 46:259. [38]WGRW 9:105. [39]CCL 25:45. [40]FC 46:260.

THE RIGHT FEAR. CASSIODORUS: This is not fear that induces dread but that which induces love. Human fear contains bitterness, but this contains sweetness. The first forces us to slavery; the second draws us toward freedom. Finally, the first fears the bars that exclude us; the second opens up the kingdom of heaven. So he rightly claimed that this fear is useful, so that we should learn of it with eager mind. EXPLANATION OF THE PSALMS 34.12.[41]

34:12 Who Desires Life?

HASTEN TO SALVATION. CLEMENT OF ALEXANDRIA: But are you so devoid of fear, or rather of faith, as not to believe the Lord himself, or Paul, who in Christ's stead thus entreats, "Taste and see that Christ is God"? Faith will lead you in; experience will teach you; Scripture will train you, for it says, "Come hither, O children; listen to me, and I will teach you the fear of the Lord." Then, as to those who already believe, it briefly adds, "Who is he who desires life, who loves to see good days?" It is we, we shall say—we who are the devotees of good, we who eagerly desire good things. Hear, then, you who are far off, hear you who are near: the word has not been hidden from any; light is common, it shines "on all people." No one is a Cimmerian[42] in respect to the word. Let us haste to salvation, to regeneration; let us who are many haste that we may be brought together into one love, according to the union of the essential unity; and let us, by being made good, conformably follow after union, seeking after the One who is good. EXHORTATION TO THE GREEKS 9.[43]

GOOD DAYS. AUGUSTINE: Do you not grumble every day, "How long do we have to put up with this? Things get worse and worse by the day. Our parents had happier days, things were better in their time." Oh, come on! If you questioned those parents of yours, they would moan to you about their days in just the same way. . . . So you are looking for good days. Let us all

look for them together, but not here. . . . There are always evil days in this world, but always good days in God. Abraham enjoyed good days, but only within his own heart; he had bad days when a famine forced him to migrate in search of food. But everyone else had to search, too. What about Paul: did he have good days, he who had "often gone without food, and endured cold and exposure"?[44] But the servants have no right to be discontented; even the Lord did not have good days in this world. He endured insults, injuries, the cross and many a hardship. EXPOSITIONS OF THE PSALMS 34.17.[45]

34:13 Guard Your Tongue

CHECK YOUR TONGUE. BEDE: Let us restrain our tongues from evil, since they have been sanctified by our confession of faith. Let us fear to use that [same tongue] with which we bless our God and Father to curse human beings, who have been made according to God's likeness. HOMILIES ON THE GOSPELS 2.6.[46]

ANGER AND THE TONGUE. AMBROSE: If . . . anger has got the start, and has already taken possession of your mind and mounted into your heart, forsake not your ground. Your ground is patience, it is wisdom, it is reason, it is the allaying of indignation. And if the stubbornness of your opponent rouses you and his perverseness drives you to indignation: if you cannot calm your mind, check at least your tongue. For so it is written: "Keep your tongue from evil, and your lips that they speak no guile. Seek peace and pursue it." . . . First, then, calm your mind. If you cannot do this, put a restraint on your tongue. Last, do not neglect to seek for reconciliation. These ideas the speakers of the world have borrowed from us and have set down in their writings. But he who said it first has the credit

---

[41]ACW 51:330. [42]Cimmerian refers to the mythical people described by Homer as inhabiting a land of perpetual fog and darkness (*Odyssey*, Bk. 11). [43]ANF 2:196-97*. [44]2 Cor 11:27. [45]WSA 3 16:36-37. [46]CS 111:55*.

of understanding its meaning. DUTIES OF THE CLERGY 1.21.92.[47]

ASSISTANT TO SIN. BASIL THE GREAT: The most common and varied sin is that committed through the tongue. Were you provoked to anger? The tongue is already running on. Are you possessed by concupiscence? Before all things you have a tongue, a sort of pimp and promoter, as it were, assistant to the sin, subduing your neighbors by histrionic arts. Your tongue is also a weapon for your injustice, not uttering the words from the heart but bringing forth those inspired by deceit. But what need is there to put in words all the sins committed through the tongue? Our life is filled with faults due to the tongue. Obscenity, scurrility, foolish talk, unbecoming words, slanders, idle conversation, perjuries, false testimony, all these evils, and even more than these, are the work of the tongue. HOMILIES ON THE PSALMS 16.9 (Ps 34).[48]

TRAIN YOUR TONGUE. CHRYSOSTOM: Let us train therefore our tongue to speak good words. For "refrain," it is said, "your tongue from evil." For God gave it not that we should speak evil, that we should revile, that we should calumniate one another, but to sing hymns to God, to speak those things that "give grace to the hearers,"[49] things for edification, things for profit. ON THE EPISTLE TO THE HEBREWS 1.4.[50]

34:14 Depart from Evil, and Do Good

THE PEACEFUL PERSON. THEODORET OF CYR: The peaceable person entertains peace toward everyone, not purloining the neighbor's property furtively, not committing homicide, not undermining marriages, not speaking evil, not doing evil, doing favors, showing respect, sharing, lending support, sharing dangers and struggles—such is unalloyed love and genuine friendship. COMMENTARY ON THE PSALMS 34.8.[51]

THE PERSON OF PEACE SEEKS PEACE. CY-

PRIAN: The person of peace ought to seek and follow peace; he who knows and loves the bond of charity ought to restrain his tongue from the evil of dissension. Among his divine commands and salutary instructions the Lord now very near his passion added the following: "Peace I leave you, my peace I give you." This inheritance he gave us, all the gifts and rewards of his promise he assured us in the conservation of peace. If we are heirs of Christ, let us remain in the peace of Christ; if we are children of God, we ought to be peacemakers. "Blessed," he said, "are the peacemakers, for they shall be called the children of God." The children of God should be peacemakers, gentle in heart, simple in speech, harmonious in affection, clinging to one another faithfully in the bonds of unanimity. THE UNITY OF THE CHURCH 24.[52]

NOT MERE ABSTINENCE FROM EVIL. BASIL THE GREAT: Mere abstinence from evil is not a characteristic of a perfect person, but for one recently instructed in basic principles it is fitting to turn aside from the impulse to evil and, being delivered from the habits of a depraved life as from a bad road, to pursue the performance of good. In fact, it is impossible to cling to the good unless one has withdrawn entirely and turned away from the evil, just as it is impossible to repair one's health unless one rids himself of the disease, or for one who has not completely checked a chill to be in a state of warmth; for, these are inadmissible to each other. So also, it is proper for one who intends to live a good life to depart from all connection with evil. . . . Yet, as long as we were bound to the flesh, we were yoked to many things that also troubled us. Seek, then, after peace, a release from the troubles of this world; possess a calm mind, a tranquil and unconfused state of soul that is neither agitated by the passions nor drawn aside by false doctrines that challenge by their

---

[47]NPNF 2 10:16*. [48]FC 46:265. [49]Eph 4:29. [50]NPNF 1 14:368*. [51]FC 101:210. [52]FC 36:119*.

persuasiveness to an assent, in order that you may obtain "the peace of God that surpasses all understanding and guards your heart."[53] HOMILIES ON THE PSALMS 16.10 (Ps 34).[54]

Good Works. Cassiodorus: To see good days, it is not enough merely to refrain from evil deeds; we must also be induced by devoted love to carry out good works. The first step to virtue is not to see other people's possessions, but the second and higher step is not to refuse one's own to those in need. By this action we avoid blame; by it we win the palm of brotherly love. EXPLANATION OF THE PSALMS 34.15.[55]

Seek It Here. Augustine: In this life there is no true peace, no tranquility. We are promised the joy of immortality and fellowship with the angels. But anyone who has not sought it here will not find it on arriving there. EXPOSITIONS OF THE PSALMS 34.19.[56]

34:15 Eyes and Ears

A Favorable Look. Theodore of Mopsuestia: God takes care of the righteous (by "eyes" referring not simply to sight but also to what is done by God in beneficence and providence). . . . He also accepts their requests. . . . But he has an eye also for the wicked, though not in the same way as for the good. To what effect? "To destroy remembrance of them from the land": . . . God gives evidence of great care for the righteous, accepting their supplication while completely disregarding those guilty of wrong actions and inflicting destruction on them. COMMENTARY ON PSALMS 34.16A-17B.[57]

For Our Good. Augustine: "But if he heard me, he would take my trouble away; I appeal to him, but I still have the trouble." Just hold steady and keep to his ways, and when you are in trouble he hears you. But he is a physician, and there is still some diseased tissue in you. You cry out, but he goes on cutting, and he does not

stay his hand until he has done all the cutting he knows to be necessary. In fact, it is a cruel doctor who listens to the patient's cries and leaves the festering wound untouched. And think how mothers rub their children down vigorously in the bath, for their own good. The little ones cry out in their mothers' hands, don't they? Does that mean the mothers are cruel in not sparing them, in ignoring their tears? Are they not really full of tender love? All the same, the children cry, and they are not let off. So too our God is full of charity, but he seems to be deaf to our entreaty because he means to heal us and spare us for all eternity. EXPOSITIONS OF THE PSALMS 34.20.[58]

34:16 Against Evildoers

A Different Gaze. Cassiodorus: Having explained the favor granted to the just, he now turns to punishment of the wicked. . . . Be aware that he sees both groups, but the outcome of his gaze is different; he hears the just but destroys sinners. When he says "from the earth," he means from the native land to come, which only those pleasing to God will possess. Their "remembrance" will die because there will be no recollection of them among the just. . . . Those who pass from the Lord's remembrance undoubtedly go to eternal punishment. EXPLANATION OF THE PSALMS 34.17.[59]

34:17 The Righteous Cry

A Spiritual Cry. Basil the Great: The cry of the just is a spiritual one, having its loudness in the secret recess of the heart, able to reach even to the ears of God. . . . They sought after nothing petty, nothing earthly, nothing lowly. For this reason the Lord received their voice, and he delivered them from all their tribulations, not so much freeing them from their troubles as

---

[53]Phil 4:7. [54]FC 46:266*. [55]ACW 51:331. [56]WSA 3 16:39. [57]WGRW 5:333. [58]WSA 3 16:39. [59]ACW 51:332.

making them victorious over the circumstances. Homilies on the Psalms 16.12 (Ps 34).[60]

Trust and Obey. Augustine: But what about me? I cried to him, and he did not rescue me; so either I am not righteous, or I am not following his instructions or perhaps he cannot see me. Do not be afraid, just do what he orders; and if he does not rescue you in bodily fashion he will rescue you spiritually. . . . God rescued Peter when the angel came to him as he lay in fetters and said to him, "Get up and leave";[61] the fetters were suddenly loosened, Peter followed the angel, and so God delivered him. But he did not rescue Peter from the cross. . . . But did God really not deliver him from the cross? . . . Perhaps God heard him at that later time even more surely, because this time he truly did deliver him from all his pains. When Peter was rescued the first time, what a lot of suffering still lay ahead of him! But at this later time God sent him to a place where he would never suffer again. Expositions of the Psalms 34.22.[62]

Heard for Eternity. Cassiodorus: What are we to say, then, of martyrs who cannot be shown to have been delivered from the execution of tyrants? They were indeed delivered when they were escorted to the kingdom of heaven; they were clearly rid of all their troubles. The cry of the just is always heard above all for their profit in eternity, not merely for their passing benefit. Explanation of the Psalms 34.18.[63]

34:18 Near to the Brokenhearted

Intentional Lowliness. Theodore of Mopsuestia: He did not apply the terms "lowly" and "contrite of heart" simply to those reduced to this condition from the disasters but to those in this condition by intent and resolve. Even if tested by disasters, on the basis of their lowliness of intent they thought that they received their just deserts, asked God with due reverence for help and received it by gift. So it is clear from this that even by saying above "let the gentle hear and be glad" he refers neither to those humbled of necessity by disasters nor to those in this condition by nature, whom the general run of good people like to think gentle, but to those in this condition in heart and purpose, who emerge by their zeal in bearing nobly the wrongs done them since they look to God for help. This, in fact, is gentleness, not being insensitive or keeping complete silence while ignoring sensation even in situations that are often unavoidable, when it is possible to effect a greater good. Commentary on Psalms 34.19b.[64]

A Contrite Heart. Basil the Great: He who has despised present things, and has given himself to the word of God and is using his mind for thoughts that are above and are more divine, he would be the one who has a contrite heart and has made it a sacrifice that is not despised by the Lord. For "a contrite and humbled heart, O God, you will not despise."[65] . . . He who has no vanity and is not proud of anything human, he is the one who is contrite in heart and humble of spirit. Homilies on the Psalms 16.12 (Ps 34).[66]

How to Reach God. Augustine: These are the great mysteries, brothers and sisters. God is above all things; if you lift yourself up, you do not touch him, but if you humble yourself, he comes down to you. Expositions of the Psalms 34.23.[67]

34:19 Many Afflictions

Like Athletes. Basil the Great: He who says that affliction is not proper to the just says nothing else than that an adversary is not proper for the athlete. But what occasions for crowns will the athlete have who does not struggle? Homilies on the Psalms 16.12 (Ps 34).[68]

---

[60]FC 46:268. [61]Acts 12:7. [62]WSA 3 16:40. [63]ACW 51:332. [64]WGRW 5:335. [65]Ps 50:19. [66]FC 46:269*. [67]WSA 3 16:41. [68]FC 46:270*.

The Righteous Suffer. Jerome: One who does not suffer trial, therefore, is not just. Brief Commentary on Psalms 34.[69]

Greater Afflictions. Cassiodorus: Truly the afflictions of the just are many, because on the one hand the devil attacks them more powerfully, and on the other people often oppress them through jealousy. Then too the wicked person, if he suffers a reverse in solitude, can be troubled, but the just person is both afflicted by his own sufferings and through charity shares the sufferings of others. Explanation of the Psalms 34.20.[70]

God's Help. Theodoret of Cyr: While God allows them to descend into the arena of tribulations, he comes to their assistance and renders them superior to the calamities besetting them, confirming their resolve and making it strong. Commentary on the Psalms 34.10.[71]

Testing. Theodore of Mopsuestia: It often happens that the righteous are put to the test in extreme troubles and severe tribulations. . . . Even if they are tested by many troubles and many tribulations, God allowing this to their advantage, he nevertheless definitely frees them from the troubles, not allowing them to be overcome by the disasters in the end. . . . He rescues them after allowing the tribulations for a while to their advantage, keeps those in the midst of tribulations free from harm and preserves their strength completely. Commentary on Psalms 34.20-21.[72]

34:20 Not One Bone Broken

Prophecy of Christ. Augustine: The prophecy was fulfilled in our Lord, because as he hung on the cross he expired before the soldiers arrived; they found his body already lifeless, so they had no wish to break his legs; thus the Scripture was fulfilled. But the promise was made to all Christians. Expositions of the Psalms 34.24.[73]

Bones of Faith. Augustine: The "bones" are the firm supports of the faithful. In our bodies the bones provide strong support, and in the same way faith provides firm support in the heart of a Christian; and endurance born of faith is like a spiritual skeleton. These are the bones that cannot be broken. Expositions of the Psalms 34.24.[74]

Bones of the Church. Basil the Great: There should also be certain bones of the inner person in which the bond of union and harmony of spiritual powers is collected. Just as the bones by their own firmness protect the tenderness of the flesh, so also in the church there are some who through their own constancy are able to carry the infirmities of the weak. And as the bones are joined to each other through articulations by sinews and fastenings that have grown on them, so also would be the bond of charity and peace, which achieves a certain natural junction and union of the spiritual bones in the church of God. Homilies on the Psalms 16.13 (Ps 34).[75]

34:21 The Wicked Condemned

The Righteous One. Augustine: Who else is this just one, but our Lord Jesus Christ, who is also the propitiatory offering for our sins? Those who hate him therefore do meet that most wretched death, because all who are not reconciled to our God through him die in their sins. Expositions of the Psalms 34.26.[76]

Failure. Theodore of Mopsuestia: Not only do sinners meet such a fate, but also those hostile to the righteous will fall foul of troubles. Now, he says this to bring out the extent of the providence that God shows for the righteous. "Will come to grief" means that they will stumble, will trip up, will fail in their hostile

---

[69]CCL 72:204. [70]ACW 51:333*. [71]FC 101:211. [72]WGRW 5:335. [73]WSA 3 16:41. [74]WSA 3 16:41. [75]FC 46:272. [76]WSA 3 16:43.

intent against the righteous by being punished by God; "come to grief" meaning "missing the mark," which means failing to achieve a purpose and intent at odds with that prescribed—hence our calling a wrong action a sin as being at odds with the proper intention. COMMENTARY ON PSALMS 34.22B.[77]

BEYOND THE FUNERAL. AUGUSTINE: What looks like a good death to you would seem very dreadful if you could see the inner side of it. Outwardly you see him lying in bed, but do you see the inner reality, as he is dragged off to hell? . . . Do not put your questions to beds draped with costly coverings, or flesh muffled up in rich clothes, or mourners with their extravagant laments, or a weeping family, or a crowd of flunkeys before and behind when the corpse is taken out for burial or monuments marble and gilded. If you put your questions to these, they tell you lies, for many people there are who have not merely sinned in small mat-

ters but have been thoroughly wicked, who yet have had a plush death like this, who have been judged worthy of being mourned, embalmed, clothed, carried in procession to the grave and buried in no other fashion than this. Put your questions rather to the gospel, and it will reveal to your faith the soul of the rich man burning in torments, helped not a whit by the honors and obsequies that the vanity of the living has lavished on his dead body. EXPOSITIONS OF THE PSALMS 34.25.[78]

34:22 Refuge in God

THE HOPE OF THE RIGHTEOUS. CASSIODORUS: How appropriately this psalm ends with the hope of the good, so that they may abandon the gatherings of the wicked and may instead be directed towards future blessings! EXPLANATION OF THE PSALMS 34.23.[79]

---

[77]WGRW 5:337.　[78]WSA 3 16:42-43.　[79]ACW 51:334.

35:1-28 PLEA FOR DIVINE ASSISTANCE

If [enemies] persist, and, with hands red with blood,
try to drag you down and kill you, remember that God is the proper judge
(for he alone is righteous while that which is human is limited)
and so say the words of [Psalm] 35.
ATHANASIUS *ON THE INTERPRETATION OF THE PSALMS* 17 [OIP 67]

A Psalm of David

[1]*Contend, O LORD, with those who contend with me;*
fight against those who fight against me!

[2]*Take hold of shield and buckler,*
and rise for my help!
[3]*Draw the spear and javelin*
against my pursuers!
Say to my soul,

"I am your deliverance!"

⁴Let them be put to shame and dishonor
  who seek after my life!
Let them be turned back and confounded
  who devise evil against me!
⁵Let them be like chaff before the wind,
  with the angel of the LORD driving them on!
⁶Let their way be dark and slippery,
  with the angel of the LORD pursuing them!

⁷For without cause they hid their net for me;
  without cause they dug a pitˢ for my life.
⁸Let ruin come upon them unawares!
And let the net which they hid ensnare them;
  let them fall therein to ruin!

⁹Then my soul shall rejoice in the LORD,
  exulting in his deliverance.
¹⁰All my bones shall say,
  "O LORD, who is like thee,
thou who deliverest the weak
  from him who is too strong for him,
  the weak and needy from him who
    despoils him?"

¹¹Malicious witnesses rise up;
  they ask me of things that I know not.
¹²They requite me evil for good;
  my soul is forlorn.
¹³But I, when they were sick—
  I wore sackcloth,
  I afflicted myself with fasting.
I prayed with head bowedᵗ on my bosom,
  ¹⁴as though I grieved for my friend or my
    brother;
I went about as one who laments his mother,
  bowed down and in mourning.

¹⁵But at my stumbling they gathered in glee,
  they gathered together against me;
cripples whom I knew not
  slandered me without ceasing;
¹⁶they impiously mocked more and more,ᵘ
  gnashing at me with their teeth.

¹⁷How long, O LORD, wilt thou look on?
  Rescue me from their ravages,
  my life from the lions!
¹⁸Then I will thank thee in the great
    congregation;
  in the mighty throng I will praise thee.

¹⁹Let not those rejoice over me
  who are wrongfully my foes,
and let not those wink the eye
  who hate me without cause.
²⁰For they do not speak peace,
  but against those who are quiet in the land
  they conceive words of deceit.
²¹They open wide their mouths against me;
  they say, "Aha, Aha!
  our eyes have seen it!"

²²Thou hast seen, O LORD; be not silent!
  O Lord, be not far from me!
²³Bestir thyself, and awake for my right,
  for my cause, my God and my Lord!
²⁴Vindicate me, O LORD, my God, according
    to thy righteousness;
  and let them not rejoice over me!
²⁵Let them not say to themselves,
  "Aha, we have our heart's desire!"
Let them not say, "We have swallowed him
    up."

²⁶Let them be put to shame and confusion
    altogether
  who rejoice at my calamity!
Let them be clothed with shame and dishonor
  who magnify themselves against me!

²⁷Let those who desire my vindication
  shout for joy and be glad,
  and say evermore,
"Great is the LORD,
  who delights in the welfare of his servant!"
²⁸Then my tongue shall tell of thy
    righteousness
  and of thy praise all the day long.

s The word *pit* is transposed from the preceding line   t Or *My prayer turned back*   u Cn Compare Gk: Heb *like the profanest of mockers of a cake*

OVERVIEW: The thirty-fifth psalm presents a challenge for interpreters. It can be related to David's situation (THEODORET) and to the experience of later prophets, such as Jeremiah (THEODORE OF MOPSUESTIA). One way to view it is Christ praying for us (HESYCHIUS, AUGUSTINE). If we pray it ourselves, we should do so against spiritual enemies (ARNOBIUS THE YOUNGER).

The psalm begins with an appeal to God to fight against our enemies. The enemies may be understood as the devil and his angels (CASSIODORUS), or if they are human, the hope is that they be defeated and be made slaves of Christ (EVAGRIUS). The psalmist prays that God extend his will (CASSIODORUS) and send forth his chastening powers (PSEUDO-ATHANASIUS). There is no other savior, and we need to hear this with spiritual ears (AUGUSTINE). May the desires of the wicked be blown heavenward (CASSIODORUS), for they are now on the path of ignorance and sensuality (AUGUSTINE). May they be pursued as in times past (THEODORET). The devil mistook the cross for his victory (EVAGRIUS). All evildoers harm themselves (AUGUSTINE). But God blesses us with the gift of himself (AUGUSTINE).

Our spiritual bones (CASSIODORUS) are strengthened by recognizing that there is no one like our God (THEODORE). We read of how David was slandered (THEODORET), as was also Christ (PSEUDO-ATHANASIUS). Let us not have a fruitless soul (EVAGRIUS). Let us be obedient in all circumstances (DIODORE). Even though his opponents were defeated by reason (CASSIODORUS), Christ was the object of blasphemy (HESYCHIUS). The words of the psalm especially apply to the Lord's passion at this point (ARNOBIUS THE YOUNGER) as he expresses a longing for help (THEODORET). The enemies speak deceptively, under pretense (THEODORE OF MOPSUESTIA), offering words of peace like meat on a hook (ARNOBIUS THE YOUNGER). In all this, we see the patience of Christ (CASSIODORUS).

The psalmist addresses the Lord in human fashion (CASSIODORUS), the Lord who is always alert but also long-suffering (DIODORE). He gives us an example for prayer (CASSIODORUS). Mockery is shameful (THEODORET). And the psalmist prays that the mockers be self-condemned (CASSIODORUS), baptized into confusion (EVAGRIUS). We, however, find our joy in his praises (CASSIODORUS). Finally, we are reminded to distinguish the interpretation of the psalm from the standpoint of the law from that interpretation that accords with the gospel (THEODORET).

Superscription: *A Psalm of David*

DAVID'S SITUATION. THEODORET OF CYR: Blessed David uttered this psalm likewise when pursued by Saul. He mentions also Doeg's wickedness, who personally reported to Saul what happened with Ahimelech the priest and was responsible for that awfully great slaughter. He mentions also the Ziphites and the others who betrayed David to Saul, as the verses themselves will teach. COMMENTARY ON THE PSALMS 35.1.[1]

THE EXPERIENCE OF JEREMIAH. THEODORE OF MOPSUESTIA: It is possible for someone reading the actual book of blessed Jeremiah to find in many places agreement between what is said by him or done to him and what is forecast by blessed David in this psalm. The result is that it is also possible to learn from there that the prophet's accuracy is such that he often states with great precision both the events and the words. In the text, for example, he says "let their way be darkness and sliding," while in the prophet Jeremiah it says, "Hence let their way be for them sliding in gloom."[2] In our text he says "because they hid their destructive snare for me without cause," whereas there the prophet says on behalf of the people, "Observe his intentions to see if he will be led astray and we shall prevail over him."[3] Again, in our text blessed David says, "Unjust witnesses rose up against me and asked me of matters of which I had no knowledge,"

---

[1]FC 101:212. [2]Jer 23:12. [3]Jer 20:10.

whereas there it explains that at the time when the Chaldean force went up to Jerusalem the prophet Jeremiah left and traveled to the land of Benjamin to buy bread there, but a certain Irijah detained him . . . and claiming that he was trying to flee to the Chaldeans. And the words said by blessed David, "They repaid me evil for good," you will find in similar terms also in the prophet Jeremiah, such as when he prays to God against them, "Is evil a recompense for good?"[4] And one who reads closely can find in the book much, both of what happened to him and of what was said by him, that resembles the psalm. In this way, in fact, both the truth and the precision of inspired composition is proven from the harmony of the words and from the similarity of the events. COMMENTARY ON PSALMS 35, PROLOGUE.[5]

CHRIST PRAYING FOR US. HESYCHIUS OF JERUSALEM: The inscription of this psalm is clear. But it must refer to spiritual David, who forms the prayer not by reason of divinity but by the humility of assumed flesh, when he humbled himself taking the form of a servant. He does not pray about his suffering but for those beset by afflictions. LARGE COMMENTARY ON PSALMS 35, PROLOGUE.[6]

THE STRONG-HANDED AND DESIRABLE ONE. AUGUSTINE: The title need not delay us, because it is short and not difficult to understand. . . . This . . . is for David, and the name "David" means "strong of hand" or "desirable." The psalm is for him who is both strong-handed and desirable, who conquered our death and promised us life. . . . In view of this we are right to listen to his voice, knowing that it is sometimes the voice of his body, sometimes that of the Head. This psalm in particular invokes God's help against enemies amid the tribulations of this world; and it is undoubtedly Christ who is praying, for once the Head was beset by tribulation, and now it is his body. Nonetheless through these tribulations he gives eternal life to all his members, and in promising it he has made himself desirable to us.

EXPOSITIONS OF THE PSALMS 35.1.[7]

HOW TO PRAY THIS PSALM. ARNOBIUS THE YOUNGER: What are we to do with this psalm? If we curse our enemies, we disregard the gospel, in which we are ordered not to curse them but to bless them. If we wish to keep the gospel commands, we would leave behind the psalms in which frequently enemies are cursed. . . . He says, Judge those who harm. . . . Beware lest you think bad things against those who oppose you, but, fixed in faith, pray for your enemies, and pray this prayer of the present psalm, not against flesh and blood but against the spirits of the air who daily harm us, who daily commit wars. Put on sackcloth and humble your spirit through fasting, because they are not conquered unless through prayer and fasting. What do you pray, having put on sackcloth? That the Lord will war and fight those who are against you as you grasp the arms of his own help against invisible enemies. COMMENTARY ON THE PSALMS 35.[8]

35:1 Contend, O Lord

THE DEVIL AND HIS ANGELS. CASSIODORUS: This has reference to the devil and his followers, through whom sprouted the evil of the Jews' willfulness. Since he himself commands us, "Pray for your enemies," this statement cannot aptly be referred to people. So he begs that they be damned who by the power of his prescience he knows cannot attain the remedies of repentance; for in what follows when he turns to people, he begs that they be converted rather than perish. EXPLANATION OF THE PSALMS 35.1.[9]

MAKE THEM YOUR SLAVES. EVAGRIUS OF PONTUS: He who conquers in war reduces the enemies to slavery: Christ has overcome the world. Hence, . . . all become his servants. NOTES ON THE PSALMS 34[35].2.[10]

---

[4]Jer 18:20. [5]WGRW 5:349-51. [6]PG 93:1188. [7]WSA 3 16:45. [8]CCL 25:46. [9]ACW 51:336-37*. [10]PG 12:1312.

35:2 Shield and Buckler

THE LORD'S WILL. CASSIODORUS: Armor and shield are nothing other than the Lord's will, by which he protects one in danger and takes the enemy by storm. EXPLANATION OF THE PSALMS 35.2.[11]

CHASTENING. PSEUDO-ATHANASIUS: He indicates through the arms and shield and sword the chastising powers sent by God to help those who fear him. EXPOSITION ON PSALMS 35.[12]

35:3 The Lord Brings Deliverance

NO OTHER SAVIOR. AUGUSTINE: I will seek no salvation other than the Lord my God. . . . Even in your temporal problems it is God who helps you through human agency, for he is your salvation. . . . All things are subject to him, and he undoubtedly supports our temporal life, differently in the case of each person; but eternal life he gives only from himself. . . . Let us all call on him, brothers and sisters . . . and to open our spiritual ears so that we may hear him saying, "I am your salvation." He says it, but some of us are getting deaf, so that when we find ourselves in trouble we prefer to listen to the enemies that harry us. EXPOSITIONS OF THE PSALMS 35.6.[13]

35:5 Like Chaff

BLOWN HEAVENWARD. CASSIODORUS: Dust is an earthy but exceedingly dry and thin substance that when the wind blows is not permitted to remain in its place but is raised into the bright air. So the desires of sinners, once admonished by inspiration of the truth, are raised from earthly vices and through the Lord's help led to heavenly virtues. So here the wish is expressed for wicked people that by blessed self-improvement they may attain heavenly life. . . . The angel afflicts the converted so that by the gift of humility they may be brought to the blessed homeland. This affliction is a kindness, for the prayer that it may come to pass is expressed as if it were a great gift. EXPLANATION OF THE PSALMS 35.5.[14]

35:6 A Dark and Slippery Way

IGNORANCE AND SENSUALITY. AUGUSTINE: Darkness alone is enough to frighten anyone. And everyone is anxious on a slippery surface. But with both together, in darkness and on slippery ground, how can you walk at all? Where will you find firm footing? These two evils are the great scourges of humankind: the darkness of ignorance and the slipperiness of sensuality. . . . The psalmist has not been praying for these calamities to occur but foretelling that they will. And even though, speaking by God's Spirit, he has cast them in the form of a petition, he does so in the same way that God fulfills the prophecy; for God acts with unerring judgment, a judgment good, just, holy and calm; he is not discomposed by anger, or by bitter jealousy or by any urge to vent his animosity. His intention is solely justice, in the due punishment of vices. EXPOSITIONS OF THE PSALMS 35.9.[15]

AS IN TIMES PAST. THEODORET OF CYR: Put them to flight, entrusting the pursuit to the unseen angels. This is the way we also find the Assyrians exterminated by an angel and the way the exterminator destroyed the firstborn of the Egyptians. COMMENTARY ON THE PSALMS 35.3.[16]

35:8 Ensnared and Ruined

THE DEVIL'S MISTAKE. EVAGRIUS OF PONTUS: I think this speaks about the cross on which the devil falls unknowingly. For if he had known never would he have affixed the Lord of glory to the cross. NOTES ON THE PSALMS 34[35].8.[17]

THEY HARM THEMSELVES. AUGUSTINE: There is no one who does evil without first of all doing

---

[11]ACW 51:337. [12]CSCO 387:23. [13]WSA 3 16:49**. [14]ACW 51:338-39*. [15]WSA 3 16:52. [16]FC 101:213. [17]PG 12:1312.

mischief to himself. EXPOSITION I OF PSALM 35.11.[18]

35:9 Rejoice in the Lord

THE GIFT OF GOD. AUGUSTINE: What better thing than God shall be given to me? God loves me; God loves you. Look, he has made you an offer: ask whatever you will. If the emperor were to say to you, "Ask whatever you will," you would be blurting out a mouthful of requests for the office of tribune or lordly rank. What splendid possibilities you would pass in review, things you could ask for yourself and distribute to others! But when God invites you, "Ask what you will," what request will you make? Cudgel your brains, out with your greed, stretch it as far as you possibly can, widen your desire. It is not just any ordinary person but almighty God who has said to you, "Ask what you will." . . . Nothing more precious will you find, though, nothing better, than him who made them all. Ask for him who made them; in him and from him you will have everything he has made. They are all precious because they are all beautiful, but what is more beautiful than he? They are strong, but what is stronger than he? And what he wants most of all to give you is himself. If you have discovered anything better, ask for it. But if you do ask for anything else, you will be insulting him and inflicting loss on yourself, because you will be esteeming something he has made more highly than its Maker, even though the Maker wants to give you himself. EXPOSITIONS OF THE PSALMS 35.12.[19]

35:10 All My Bones

SPIRITUAL BONES. CASSIODORUS: Bones must be interpreted as strength of spirit and constancy of mind. These are rightly compared with bones, for just as bones hold the body together, so these qualities strengthen pious intentions. So the bones, that is, firmness, not the flesh, which is slackness, must utter this mystery, for only courage of mind can speak such praise.

EXPLANATION OF THE PSALMS 35.10.[20]

NO ONE LIKE YOU. THEODORE OF MOPSUESTIA: I shall say no one is like you, he means, and shall confess you to be more powerful than everyone, even those considered strong and powerful; you are capable of rescuing the poor and insignificant and delivering them from their scheming against the odds. . . . You see, both the insignificance by comparison with him of the one who suffers and is rescued and also the might of the schemers brought out his greatness: the more effective the release from the schemers was shown to be, the more powerful did the one who effected it appear. COMMENTARY ON PSALMS 35.10B, C.[21]

35:11 Malicious Witness

DAVID, AN OBJECT OF SLANDER. THEODORET OF CYR: When Saul under the influence of envy, remember, suspected him of plotting a coup and for that reason maintained a state of war, the slanderers (whom he calls false "witnesses") took occasion not to desist from spreading calumny against him. Some of these were Doeg, the Ziphites, and many others in addition to them. COMMENTARY ON THE PSALMS 35.6.[22]

THE EXPERIENCE OF CHRIST. PSEUDO-ATHANASIUS: The person of Christ is introduced here, denounced and falsely accused at the tribunal of the chief priests when there rose up evil witnesses against him, and they repaid evil things for good and bereavement for his soul. They were called sons of God but acted wickedly against him. EXPOSITION ON PSALMS 35.[23]

35:12 A Forlorn Soul

A FRUITLESS SOUL. EVAGRIUS OF PONTUS: Fruitless is the soul that births nothing good and

---

[18]*WSA* 3 16:5. [19]*WSA* 3 16:54-55. [20]ACW 51:340. [21]WGRW 5:361. [22]FC 101:213-14. [23]CSCO 387:23.

does good for no one. NOTES ON THE PSALMS 34[35].12.[24]

35:13 A Bowed Head

OBEDIENT. DIODORE OF TARSUS: Even if my prayer proved unacceptable to God and was sent back to me on account of the unworthiness of what I prayed for, I nevertheless did everything on my part with the purpose of obeying God. COMMENTARY ON PSALMS 35.[25]

35:16 Gnashing Their Teeth

DEFEATED BY REASON. CASSIODORUS: This is what savages do when defeated by reason. When words fail them because of the truth of an issue, they lose patience and gnash their teeth, revealing their wishes by silent threats. All this is aimed at the great pride of the human race, so that his members may not think it burdensome to suffer what they realize their Head suffered. EXPLANATION OF THE PSALMS 35.16.[26]

BLASPHEMY. HESYCHIUS OF JERUSALEM: Certain ones say the power of the teeth is the evil of speech. He wanted his Father to be a witness against those who blasphemed him. LARGE COMMENTARY ON PSALMS 35.16.[27]

35:17 How Long, O Lord?

APPLY TO THE LORD'S PASSION. ARNOBIUS THE YOUNGER: So you will apply this to the suffering of the Lord so that then you may draw out the logic of the explanation having begun, because the passion of the Lord happens so that we may be built up. The more you cling to God, the more the demons beset you with floggings. They tempt you, mock you and gnash their teeth. You call out: Lord, look down and restore my spirit from their evil deeds, my very self from the lions. Our spirit is one in number and disposition. When, therefore, you restore it in good will and you free me from their evil deeds,

then I will confess you in the great assembly and the great throng of people, not by summoning solemn processions or by playing roles, but by guarding your respect amongst serious people; in this there will be constant attention by me, and I will praise you before those same people. Therefore, let them not triumph, the evil ones who turn against me, who hate me and wink with indulgent eyes. As I have said, apply these things to the suffering of the Lord so that you do not thoroughly overlook the message of your edification. COMMENTARY ON THE PSALMS 35.[28]

A LONGING FOR HELP. THEODORET OF CYR: Now, he says this not by way of accusation but out of a longing for help. When will you appear, he is saying, and assist the wronged? . . . Render my soul proof against their machinations. COMMENTARY ON THE PSALMS 35.9.[29]

35:20 Words of Deceit

LIKE FOOD ON A HOOK. ARNOBIUS THE YOUNGER: Daily the demons speak peacefully to us. This peace is the fruit of lust, but through anger they devise deceits, just like sweet food on a hook in our sight—it is deadly to eat. They open wide their mouths against me, and lovers of this age daily commit unspeakable crimes, and nothing is thoroughly denounced by anyone. COMMENTARY ON THE PSALMS 35.[30]

PRETENSE. THEODORE OF MOPSUESTIA: They make a pretense by uttering words under the guise of peace, but in reality their words are com-pletely full of anger and evil. All the words, in fact, were not of peace, though they seemed to give that impression; rather, they were spoken with complete viciousness under pretense, for they continued hatching plots and schemes against me, planning such things and turn-

---

[24]PG 12:1312. [25]WGRW 9:109. [26]ACW 51:344. [27]PG 93:1189. [28]CCL 25:47. [29]FC 101:215. [30]CCL 25:47-48.

ing them over in their soul. COMMENTARY ON PSALMS 35.20.[31]

35:22 Be Not Far from Me!

PATIENCE OF CHRIST. CASSIODORUS: What wonderful patience in One whose majesty was the greatest! Could he not have descended living from . . . the cross to confound his enemies, since after dying he could rise again from the tomb on the third day? But it was not appropriate for God's power to react to the words of abusive people, for they were to blush all the more when all that was foretold came to pass. EXPLANATION OF THE PSALMS 35.21.[32]

35:23 Take Up My Cause

HUMAN FASHION. CASSIODORUS: We often in our human fashion say "Arise" to him who in fact is always awake and always attentive, and since he continually supervises all things, he is considered to have paid attention when he punishes. EXPLANATION OF THE PSALMS 35.23.[33]

LONG-SUFFERING. DIODORE OF TARSUS: Since by his long-suffering he gives the impression of sleeping, as it were, he urges him to arise and deliver a verdict in his favor. COMMENTARY ON PSALMS 35.[34]

35:24 Vindicate Me

AN EXAMPLE OF PRAYER. CASSIODORUS: Though he who had committed no sins had an excellent cause, he nonetheless asks to be judged according to the Lord's mercy, to show an example of prayer to us who could not undertake a like activity. EXPLANATION OF THE PSALMS 35.24.[35]

35:26 Shame and Confusion

MOCKERY IS SHAMEFUL. THEODORET OF CYR: Shame is fitting for those who mock their neighbor; thus the inspired author calls it down on

their arrogance and boasting. COMMENTARY ON THE PSALMS 35.12.[36]

SELF-CONDEMNED. CASSIODORUS: One who blushes at his own deeds is condemned on his own assessment; one who is enchained with the bonds of embarrassment is tortured by the vengeance that he exacts from himself. EXPLANATION OF THE PSALMS 35.26.[37]

BAPTIZED INTO CONFUSION. EVAGRIUS OF PONTUS: Those who are baptized into Christ put on Christ; this is justice and wisdom. Those who are baptized into Satan are clothed in confusion and shame. NOTES ON THE PSALMS 34[35].26.[38]

35:27 Great Is the Lord

THE JOY OF THE FAITHFUL. CASSIODORUS: Persecutors bestow worldly pleasures on their own souls, but the faithful turn their prayers to the Lord and place their joy not in themselves but in his praises. EXPLANATION OF THE PSALMS 35.27.[39]

35:28 Telling of God's Righteousness

LAW AND GOSPEL. THEODORET OF CYR: While the psalm had this ending, therefore, I beseech those reading it not to incur even the slightest harm from the prayer of the righteous person or make it the occasion for curses against one's enemies. Instead, realize that the inspired author was adopting the way of life sanctioned by the Law, not by the Gospels. Now, the Law speaks plainly of loving the neighbor and hating the enemy. By contrast, Christ the Lord, to show virtue in its perfection, said, "It was said to those of old, you shall love your neighbor and hate your enemy, but I say to you. Love your enemies and bless those who persecute you."[40] The divine apostle also said something in harmony with this, "Bless and do not

---

[31]WGRW 5:379. [32]ACW 51:346*. [33]ACW 51:347. [34]WGRW 9:111. [35]ACW 51:347. [36]FC 101:216. [37]ACW 51:348*. [38]PG 12:1313. [39]ACW 51:349. [40]Mt 5:43-44.

curse."[41] Looking at this difference, therefore, realize what is in keeping with the Law and what with grace. In particular, it was not to deliver a curse that David said this; rather, in inspired fashion he foretold what would clearly come to be. Now, for proof that in keeping with the gospel requirements even he did not take vengeance on those who wronged him, listen to him saying, "If I repaid in like fashion those rendering me evil, let me then end up empty-handed before my foes. Let my foe then hunt my soul down, apprehend it, trample my life in the ground and bury my glory in the dust."[42] And he did not say this without doing it: he put

his words into practice, and the actions are clearer than the words. Twice when he had his enemy in his hands, remember, he not only did not do away with him; . . . when he fell in battle, he wept bitterly over him, and the one who brought word of his death he dispatched for exulting and boasting of the execution. Now, I was obliged to recount these events because of those who boast and quote the case of the divine David so that they may have the best values of David as a beneficial model. COMMENTARY ON THE PSALMS 35.13.[43]

---

[41]Rom 12:14. [42]Ps 7:4-5 (7:5-6 LXX). [43]FC 101:216-17*.

36:1-12 THE WICKED AND THE RIGHTEOUS

When you see transgressors of the law being so zealous in their evildoing,

do not attribute this evil to nature—this is what the heretics teach—

but in saying Psalm 36 know that

they are the cause of their own sinful behavior.

ATHANASIUS *On the Interpretation of the Psalms* 18 [OIP 68]

To the choirmaster. A Psalm of David, the servant of the LORD.

¹*Transgression speaks to the wicked deep in his heart;
there is no fear of God before his eyes.*
²*For he flatters himself in his own eyes that his iniquity cannot be found out and hated.*
³*The words of his mouth are mischief and deceit;
he has ceased to act wisely and do good.*
⁴*He plots mischief while on his bed;
he sets himself in a way that is not good;
he spurns not evil.*

⁵*Thy steadfast love, O LORD, extends to the heavens,
thy faithfulness to the clouds.*
⁶*Thy righteousness is like the mountains of God,
thy judgments are like the great deep;
man and beast thou savest, O LORD.*

⁷*How precious is thy steadfast love, O God!
The children of men take refuge in the shadow of thy wings.*
⁸*They feast on the abundance of thy house,
and thou givest them drink from the river of thy delights.*
⁹*For with thee is the fountain of life;
in thy light do we see light.*

> ¹⁰*O continue thy steadfast love to those who know thee,*
> *and thy salvation to the upright of heart!*
> ¹¹*Let not the foot of arrogance come upon me,*
> *nor the hand of the wicked drive me away.*
> ¹²*There the evildoers lie prostrate,*
> *they are thrust down, unable to rise.*

Overview: There are two types of sinners (Cassiodorus). The thirty-sixth psalm deals with the bold sinner who thinks his or her deceit is hidden (Theodore of Mopsuestia). In reality, this person inflicts punishment on himself (Ambrose). There is no room in his or her heart for the fear of God (Augustine) and consequently, no hatred of sin (Arnobius the Younger). Although his sin is obvious to everyone (Theodoret), he is self-deceived (Augustine) and self-condemned (Theodore). He practices the wrong kind of meditation (Ambrose) in the inner bedroom of his heart (Augustine). Instead of being on the road to freedom (Augustine), he or she lingers in sin (Cassiodorus). Mercy must be sought from heaven (Ambrose, Caesarius). The Lord has sent his preachers (Augustine) like clouds to shower his truth throughout the earth. God's truth is deep, beyond our grasp (Theodoret, Cassiodorus), but given to us in the person of Christ (Arnobius the Younger). His judgments are inscrutable (Theodore of Mopsuestia), but nevertheless they are wise (Origen).

True refreshment is found in Christ (Pseudo-Athanasius). In him we find a joy beyond telling (Augustine), a divine inebriation (Ambrose, Cassiodorus, Chrysostom), the hope of the thirsty (Augustine). From God came the abundance of life and discernment (Theodore), a fountain that refreshes the heart (Caesarius). By the light of the Scripture, we come to understand God, who is light (Sahdona). But the water and light here have a special reference to Christ, in whom the imagery comes together (Cassiodorus). In him, we see God (Origen, Evagrius). The language of the psalm presents to us the revelation of the holy Trinity (Theodoret, Jerome, Gregory of Nazianzus, Ambrose), which was a basis for the orthodox confession that the Son is of one substance with the Father (Athanasius). It also teaches us the proper relations of Father and Son (Augustine). We were made to know God (Theodore) but come to know him through his mercy (Augustine). Humility is the way of advance (Augustine). Pride is the dark path (Ambrose), the way of departure from God (Augustine), an unsound vehicle for our pilgrimage (Evagrius). Let us beware lest the hand of sinners pluck us from the root of virtue (Ambrose).

Superscription: *A Psalm of David*

36:1 *The Wicked Do Not Fear God*

Two Types of Sinners. Cassiodorus: There are two types of sinners. The first believes Scripture but cannot fulfill its commands because of the weakness of the flesh. . . . The other type is bold, irremediable, blasphemous and plans to commit evil of its own free will. It despises everything and whispers to itself, believing that God does not tend mortal affairs. Explanation of the Psalms 36.2.[1]

Hidden Within. Theodore of Mopsuestia: The lawbreaker thinks his sinning is [hidden] within—that is, he believes that he is escaping notice in sinning. . . . Now, it is typical of the person employing deceit to think that schemers escape notice, because they are always under that impression when they use flattering language; after all, unless they expected to escape notice, they would not have persisted in their deceitful pretense. Commentary on Psalms 36.2a.[2]

---

[1]ACW 51:350. [2]WGRW 5:389-91.

SELF-INFLICTED PUNISHMENT. AMBROSE: The wicked person speaks, and the inner conscience is mangled. Every word he utters is laden with malice and trickery. Who undergoes punishment greater than that which he inflicts on himself, when every word he says is piercing him through and through? The serpent pours out his poison into others; the unjust pours it into himself. Whatever he spills forth, he is spilling into his own self. COMMENTARY ON TWELVE PSALMS 36.6.[3]

NO ROOM FOR THE FEAR OF GOD. AUGUSTINE: All the sinner has in his sights is fear of other people; he does not dare to make a public declaration of his iniquity, lest he be rebuked or condemned by others. He withdraws from human observation, but where to? Into himself! He ushers himself within, where no one can see him. There within himself no one watches him as he plans his trickery, his ruses and his crimes. He would not be able to plot, even there within himself, if he considered that God is scrutinizing him; but because there is no fear of God before his eyes, he thinks he has no one to fear once he has withdrawn from human view into his own heart. But God is present there, isn't he? Assuredly, but in the sinner's outlook there is no room for the fear of God. EXPOSITIONS OF THE PSALMS 36.2.[4]

CONSEQUENTLY, NO HATRED OF SIN. ARNOBIUS THE YOUNGER: There is no fear of God in the sight of one who sins against himself that he may find his own iniquity and hate it. He praises injustice as the unjust one is praised. He does not wish to understand good actions by which he will be made worthy in the recesses of his own heart. He meditates on evil as he draws near to the way that is not good, and he does not abhor evil. COMMENARY ON THE PSALMS 36.[5]

36:2 The Wicked Flatter Themselves

OBVIOUS TO EVERYONE. THEODORET OF

CYR: He so distracts himself, he is saying, and banishes the fear of God from his own sight that his lawlessness, which in fact is obvious, is seen and discovered by everyone and thus attracts loathing. He has given himself unswervingly to lawlessness. Now, he adopts this ignorance so willingly that he is not prepared to assess what he has done or loathe his evil exploits. COMMENTARY ON THE PSALMS 36.2.[6]

SELF-DECEIVED. AUGUSTINE: Many are dishonest in the way they look for their iniquity; they go about it without sincerely wanting to find it and hate it. Consequently, because there is dishonesty in their search, there will be an attempt to defend the iniquity when it comes to light. Once it is found, its true character will be out in the open, and the sinner will not be able to deny that it is iniquity indeed. "Don't do it," you say. And what do they reply, these people who faked the search and now that they have found the sin do not hate it? "Oh, but everybody does it," they say. "You won't find anyone who doesn't do that. Do you imagine that God is going to send the whole lot of us to hell?" Or at any rate they protest, "If God really did not want these things to be done, would the people who do them have been left alive?" Don't you see that you were being dishonest when you pretended to look for your iniquity? If you had not been dishonest, but had acted with sincerity, you would have found it by now and found it hateful; but as things are, you have found it, and you defend it. This proves that you were acting deceitfully when you were searching. EXPOSITIONS OF THE PSALMS 36.3.[7]

SELF-CONDEMNED. THEODORE OF MOPSUESTIA: If he had "the fear of God before his eyes," he would not have employed deceit in the belief that he was escaping our notice (realizing that it was not possible to escape God, everything being known to him, who knows and understands

---

[3]ACTP 40. [4]WSA 3 16:73. [5]CCL 25:48. [6]FC 101:219. [7]WSA 3 16:74.

everything clearly). If he really had dread of the Lord, he would have shown much zeal in guarding against sin. COMMENTARY ON PSALMS 36.3A.[8]

36:4 Plotting Evil

THE WRONG MEDITATION. AMBROSE: [This is] the very place where one should meditate on the truth. For in bed we should weep bitterly for our sins—lament sin rather than commit it. As the prophet says, "The things you say in your hearts, be sorry for them on your own beds."[9] COMMENTARY ON TWELVE PSALMS 35.16.[10]

OUR INNER BEDROOM. AUGUSTINE: Our bedroom is our heart, for there we toss and turn if we have a bad conscience, but there, if our conscience is easy, we find rest. . . . But the person of whom our psalm is speaking retired there to hatch his evil plots, where no one would see him. And because such wickedness was the subject of his meditation, he could find no rest, even in his heart. EXPOSITIONS OF THE PSALMS 36.5.[11]

THE ROAD TO FREEDOM. AUGUSTINE: If we cannot be free from wickedness, at least let us hate it. When you have begun to hate it, you are unlikely to be tricked into committing a wicked act by any stealthy temptation. . . . Hate sin and iniquity, so that you may unite yourself to God, who will hate it with you. Already you are at one with God's law in your mind, for in your mind you are servant of God's law. If in your carnal nature you are still enslaved to the law of sin because the pleasures of the flesh are still powerful in you, remember that they will be there no longer when your fight is over. To be free from the need to fight, to enjoy true and everlasting peace—this is something quite different from fighting and winning, different from fighting and being vanquished, different yet again from declining even to fight and being carried off as a prisoner. For there certainly are some people who do not put up a fight, like this one of whom the psalm says, "He did not

hate wickedness"; for how could he have been fighting against something for which he felt no hatred? Such a person is dragged away by wickedness without even resisting. There are others who do begin to fight, but because they rashly rely on their own strength, and God wants to prove to them that is he who wins the victory if we enlist under his leadership, they are worsted in the battle. They have apparently begun to hold fast to righteousness, but they become proud, and consequently they are knocked out. People like this fight but are overcome. Who is it who fights and is not overcome? The one who says, "I am aware of a different law in my members that opposes the law of my mind." Look at this fighter. He does not presume on his own strength, and that is why he will be the victor. What does the next line say? "Who will deliver me from this death-ridden body, wretch that I am? Only the grace of God, through Jesus Christ our Lord."[12] He relies on the One who has commanded him to fight, and he defeats the enemy because he is helped by his Commander. But the other person we heard about "did not hate wickedness." EXPOSITIONS OF THE PSALMS 36.6.[13]

LINGERING IN SIN. CASSIODORUS: He did not traverse [the life of this world] like those who proclaim that they are leaving it behind but lingered in it and was absorbed by it. EXPLANATION OF THE PSALMS 36.5.[14]

36:5 The Extent of God's Love

HEAVENLY MERCY. AMBROSE: It is from heaven that mercy must be sought; it is from the oracle of the prophets that truth must be gathered—for they like clouds veil the mysteries of divine knowledge. God made darkness his covering,[15] so that you would first receive the downpour of

---

[8]WGRW 5:393. [9]Ps 4:4 (4:5 LXX). [10]ACTP 45. [11]WSA 3 16:74, 76. [12]Rom 7:23-25. [13]WSA 3 16:76-77. [14]ACW 51:352. [15]Ps 18:11 (17:12 LXX).

mystical fruitfulness, and then, refreshed with heavenly dew, have strength to gaze on the splendor of heavenly light. COMMENTARY ON TWELVE PSALMS 36.18.[16]

MERCY IS TO BE EXERCISED. CAESARIUS OF ARLES: Mercy abides in heaven, but it is reached by the exercise of it on earth. SERMON 25.1.[17]

PREACHERS OF GOD'S WORD. AUGUSTINE: Who could have any idea of the heavenly mercy of God, unless God had announced it to human beings? How did he announce it? By sending his truth to the clouds. And what are these clouds? The preachers of God's word. . . . Truly, brothers and sisters, these clouds are the preachers of the word of truth. When God utters threats through his preachers, he is thundering through his clouds. When he works miracles through his preachers, he is sending brilliant flashes of lightning through his clouds. He terrifies us through his clouds, and through them waters the earth with rain. These preachers, through whom the gospel of God is proclaimed, are God's clouds. Let us hope for mercy, then, but let it be the mercy that is in heaven. EXPOSITIONS OF THE PSALMS 36.8.[18]

36:6 Righteousness and Judgments

BEYOND OUR GRASP. THEODORET OF CYR: While those people turn their hand to such things as though no one were watching, you, Lord, possess immeasurable mercy, incalculable truth and righteousness comparable to the highest mountains. Now, your truth comes to human beings through the inspired authors as though through some clouds, regaling them with saving rain. "Your judgments are like the great deep": possessing such wonderful truth and righteousness, why you show long-suffering I do not know; your judgments resemble the impenetrable depths. That is to say, just as the bottom of the sea is beyond human vision, so an understanding of your judgments is beyond our grasp.

COMMENTARY ON THE PSALMS 36.4.[19]

THE DEPTHS OF DIVINE JUDGMENT. CASSIODORUS: A deep is a depth of waters that we can neither measure nor wholly plumb with our eyes. Who could either descry the depths of the great ocean or embrace its huge extent? In the same way we can neither embrace in mind the divine judgments nor define them by any rational explanation. EXPLANATION OF THE PSALMS 36.7.[20]

CHRIST HIMSELF. ARNOBIUS THE YOUNGER: The truth is Christ, whose justice is just like the mountains of God, whose judgments are an abyss, who saves people and beasts by his advent, that is, both Jews and Gentiles. For people who, being without hope, standing in the sin of Adam, hope in the protection of his wings, that is, in the expanse of his hands fixed on the cross. COMMENTARY ON THE PSALMS 36.[21]

INSCRUTABLE JUDGMENT. THEODORE OF MOPSUESTIA: His decisions and decrees, which he applies in judging and examining human beings, are immeasurable, like the deep. Thus, it is impossible to find out why he allows righteous people often to suffer at the hands of the unrighteous, as I find happening in my own case. While the fact that his care and providence for us is wonderful is clear from his never allowing our sufferings to be unbearable, I am unable to discover precisely why he does not leave us in perfect peace but permits us for a time to be pursued unjustly by them. Hence, "your judgments" strike me as more inaccessible than any "deep." COMMENTARY ON PSALMS 36.7B.[22]

WISE JUDGMENT. ORIGEN: Human beings, being ignorant of the judgments of God, which are "a great abyss," are accustomed to complain against God and to say, Why do unjust people and unjust robbers and impious and wicked ones

[16]ACTP 46. [17]FC 31:127. [18]WSA 3 16:78-79. [19]FC 101:219. [20]ACW 51:353. [21]CCL 25:49. [22]WGRW 5:399.

suffer nothing adverse in this life but everything yields prosperity to them, honors, riches, power, health, and the health and strength of the body even serves them. On the contrary, innumerable tribulations come on the innocent and pious worshipers of God; they live rejected, humble, contemptible, under the blows of the powerful. Sometimes even more severe diseases dominate them in their body. But as I said, the ignorant complain about what order there is in the divine judgments. For however much more severely they want those to be punished whose power and iniquities they lament, there is that much greater necessity that the penalties be differed, that if they are not differed, . . . it is certain that they will be eternal and last forever. On the contrary, therefore, if they wanted good things to be given to the just and innocent in the present age, the good things themselves would also be temporal and would have to come to a quick end; but the more they are deferred into the future, by so much the more will they be perpetual and not know an end. HOMILIES ON LEVITICUS 14.4.5.[23]

36:7 In the Shadows of God's Wings

REFRESHED BY CHRIST. PSEUDO-ATHANASIUS: But people will hope in the shadow of your wings; that is, they have you as helper and protector, and they will be illuminated and spiritually refreshed by Christ—the true light and spring of life [who is] with you. EXPOSITION ON PSALMS 36.[24]

36:8 A River of Delights

A JOY BEYOND TELLING. AUGUSTINE: We have been given a joy beyond all telling. The human mind almost vanishes, becoming in some sense divinized, and is inebriated by the rich abundance of God's house. EXPOSITIONS OF THE PSALMS 36.14.[25]

DIVINE INEBRIATION. AMBROSE: It is good to be inebriated on the cup of salvation. There is

also the intoxication arising from the riches of Scripture. There is, too, the inebriation that follows on the infusion of the Holy Spirit. We read in the Acts of the Apostles[26] of those who spoke in foreign tongues and appeared, to those who heard them, to be drunk on new wine. In brief, the house is the church; the riches of the house is the abundance of grace; the torrent of delight is the Holy Spirit. COMMENTARY ON TWELVE PSALMS 36.19.[27]

A PRAISEWORTHY INEBRIATION. CASSIODORUS: "Inebriated" is adopted from the sinful habit of people afloat with too much wine, who become sluggish, when their minds are afflicted; but here it describes the role of good people. This heavenly inebriation cuts off recollection of worldly matters and thus makes the things of the flesh depart from the mind, just as intoxication from wine divorces people's actions from their senses. . . . How very praiseworthy is that inebriation! That drunkenness should be sought in every prayer, for moderation springs from it, and integrity of mind is fully attained from it. It does not cause staggering confusion, mental delirium or blackouts; the soul is made healthier, according as it is filled with that drunkenness. So let us drink this draught eagerly, not with our bodily lips but with the heart's purest devotion. From it we do not obtain temporal happiness but seek the joys of eternal life. EXPLANATION OF THE PSALMS 36.9, 13.[28]

DRUNKENNESS CAN MEAN TO BE SATISFIED. CHRYSOSTOM: The word for drunkenness, dearly beloved, is not always used in sacred Scripture for that failing only, but also for satiety. . . . Listen, after all, to David's words: "They will become intoxicated from the richness of your house," that is, they will be filled. [By contrast], those who give themselves up to drunkenness never have their fill; the more wine they imbibe,

---

[23]FC 83:253-54*. [24]CSCO 387:24. [25]WSA 3 16:85. [26]Acts 2:4, 13. [27]ACTP 47. [28]ACW 51:354, 356-57*.

the more they burn with thirst, and indulgence proves to be a constant fueling of their thirst; by the time all that remains of the pleasure has disappeared, the thirst proves to be unquenchable and leads the victims of drunkenness to the very precipice. HOMILIES ON GENESIS 29.12.[29]

THE HOPE OF THE THIRSTY. AUGUSTINE: Water rushing with a mighty force is called a torrent. God's mercy will flow with a mighty force to water and inebriate those who in this present life fix their hope beneath the shadow of his wings. What is that delight? It is like a torrent that inebriates the thirsty. Let any who are thirsty now fix their hopes there; let the thirsty have hope, because one day, inebriated, they will have the reality. Until they have the reality, let them thirstily hope. EXPOSITIONS OF THE PSALMS 36.14.[30]

36:9 The Fountain of Life

ABUNDANT LIFE AND DISCERNMENT. THEODORE OF MOPSUESTIA: You flood us with life, abundantly supplying us with it from the great number and variety of what is given us by you for sustenance and life. . . . Without light we can see nothing that exists, for when we are deprived of light and plunged into darkness, we have no recognition of what is at hand; whereas when light is available, we see and discern by recognition. So for discerning other things we need light, whereas light itself requires nothing else any longer for our being able to see; instead, with the aid of light itself we succeed in seeing everything through light and discern everything, including even light itself. . . . His meaning was to present the utter generosity and abundance of God's gift—thus his mention of these two things in particular: the light (he made clear that from it he provided us both with existence itself and with sustenance) and enjoyment of the light, through which he conveyed the pleasure of life. COMMENTARY ON PSALMS 36.10A, B.[31]

HEART REFRESHMENT. CAESARIUS OF ARLES: It is a good fountain that cools us after the heat of this life and with its flood tempers the aridity of our heart. SERMON 170.3.[32]

BY THE LIGHT OF SCRIPTURE. SAHDONA: Without the light of the Scriptures we are unable to see God, who is Light, or his justice, which is filled with light. The effort involved in reading the Scriptures is thus greatly beneficial to us, all the more so since it causes us to become illumined in prayer. For anyone whose soul, after having labored in reading and been purified by spiritual meditation, is fervent with love for God will pray in a luminous manner when he turns to prayer. . . . His mind has labored in mediating on divine providence and so is filled with joy. In his soul he carries the model for virtue that he has received from training through the agency of the Spirit; he has depicted before his eyes, as though in a picture, the lovely beauty of the saints' way of life: wrapped up in reading about these things, he will exult over them and become fervent in spirit, so that the words of his Office and the incense of his prayer become illumined and pure, seeking that they flow out from the pure spring of his heart. BOOK OF PERFECTION 2.50-51.[33]

WATER AND LIGHT. CASSIODORUS: In human usage light and fountains are different things; in fact, they are antithetical, because a fountain of water extinguishes the light of flames. But with God they are one, for whatever term you employ is true but still inadequate. We say that God is the Light, because "he enlightens every person who comes into the world";[34] a Fountain, because he fills the thirsty and empty; . . . The verse rightly says of the Savior, "In your light we shall see light"; that is, the light of the Father and of the Holy Spirit, because through his preaching it happened that the whole Trin-

---

[29]FC 82:206-7. [30]WSA 3 16:86. [31]WGRW 5:405-7. [32]FC 47:421. [33]CS 101:223. [34]Jn 1:9.

ity became clear to us. EXPLANATION OF THE PSALMS 36.10.[35]

IN CHRIST WE SEE GOD. ORIGEN: What other light of God can we speak of, in which a person sees light, except God's spiritual power, which when it lightens a person causes him either to see clearly the truth of all things or to know God, who is called the truth? Such then is the meaning of the saying, "In your light shall we see light"; that is, in your word and your wisdom, which is your Son, in him shall we see you, the Father. ON FIRST PRINCIPLES 1.1.1.[36]

THE WINDOW OF CREATION. EVAGRIUS OF PONTUS: Since the fount is life and life is Christ, the fount is Christ. . . . By meditating on what is made we will see Christ, and in understanding Christ, we will see God. NOTES ON THE PSALMS 35[36].10.[37]

THE HOLY TRINITY. THEODORET OF CYR: Here he clearly reveals to us the mystery of the holy Trinity: he called the Only-begotten Word of God a "fountain of life." This is the name, too, remember, God personally gave himself through the prophet Jeremiah: "They have forsaken me, a fountain of living water, taken their leave and dug for themselves cracked cisterns incapable of holding water."[38] So he says this fountain is in the presence of the Father, according to the following Gospel teaching: "I in the Father and the Father in me." "In your light we shall see light": Illumined by the all-holy Spirit we shall perceive the rays of your Only-begotten; Scripture says, "No one can say Jesus is Lord except by the Holy Spirit,"[39] and "God revealed to us through his Spirit."[40] We have consequently come to a precise knowledge of the three persons in the one divinity through the inspired words. COMMENTARY ON THE PSALMS 36.6.[41]

CHRIST IS LIGHT OF THE FATHER. JEROME: The Light of the Father is Christ. In Christ we will see the light of the Holy Spirit in the light of the Father. BRIEF COMMENTARY ON PSALMS 36.[42]

THE LIGHT OF THE TRINITY. GREGORY OF NAZIANZUS: And now we have both seen and proclaim concisely and simply the doctrine of God the Trinity, comprehending out of light [the Father], light [the Son], in light [the Spirit]. ON THE HOLY SPIRIT, THEOLOGICAL ORATION 5(31).3.[43]

THE WORD OF LIFE. AMBROSE: Our psalm prophesies the coming into the world of the Lord and Savior, who would say, "The Father and I are one."[44] This means: We are one light even as we are one name; one in light, and one in name, we two are one. Truly, in substance the Trinity is one; in distinction of persons it is three. A trinity signifies distinction of persons; unity signifies power. It can be said to the Father: "With you is the fountain of life."[45] From him proceeded the life that was the Word, that ever was and always was the Word, so it can be said, "With you was the Word." Through him and in him all things were made,[46] and he himself is the life of all people. He has shown you, Father, to us. He has enlightened the hearts of people that they might know your majesty. COMMENTARY ON TWELVE PSALMS 36.22.[47]

ONE SUBSTANCE. ATHANASIUS (VIA THEODORET OF CYR): The bishops [at the Council of Nicea], having detected the Arians' deceitfulness in this matter, collected from Scripture those passages that say of Christ that he is the glory, the fountain, the stream and the express image of the person; and they quoted the following words: "In your light we shall see light"; and likewise, "I and the Father are one." They, then, with still greater clearness, briefly declared that the Son is of one substance [*homoousios*] with the Father; for this, indeed, is the signification of the passages that have been quoted. ECCLESIASTICAL HISTORY 1.7.[48]

---

[35]ACW 51:354-55*. [36]OFP 7*. [37]PG 12:1316. [38]Jer 2:13. [39]1 Cor 12:3 [40]1 Cor 2:10. [41]FC 101:220-21. [42]CCL 72:205. [43]LCC 3:195. [44]Jn 10:30. [45]Ps 36:9 (35:10 LXX). [46]Cf. Jn 1:3. [47]ACTP 49*. [48]NPNF 2 3:45*.

PROPER RELATIONS. AUGUSTINE: Christ . . . is man and God. He prays as man and gives what he prays for as God. Now what you have to grasp is that he assigns everything to the Father for the simple reason that the Father is not from him, but he is from the Father. He gives everything to the fount from which he is derived. But he too is the fount born of the Father; he is himself the "fountain of life." So the Father as fount begot the fountain; fountain indeed begot fountain; but begetting fountain and begotten fountain are one fountain. Just as God begetting and God begotten, namely, the Son born of the Father, are one God. The Father is not the Son, the Son is not the Father; the Father is not from the Son, the Son is from the Father; but still Father and Son are one thing . . . because of their inseparable divinity. SERMON 217.1.[49]

36:10 God's Continuing Love

MADE TO KNOW GOD. THEODORE OF MOPSUESTIA: They were formed by you so as to be able, if they wished, both to know you and to hope in you, and to enjoy the good things stemming from this. COMMENTARY ON PSALMS 36.11A.[50]

MERCY LEADS TO KNOWLEDGE. AUGUSTINE: He extends his mercy, not because they know him but in order that they may know him: he extends his righteousness whereby he justifies the ungodly, not because they are upright in heart but that they may become upright in heart. This consideration does not lead astray into pride—the fault that arises from trust in self and making the self the spring of its own life. To go that way is to draw back from the fountain of life, whose draught alone gives the righteousness that is good life, and from that changeless light by whose participation the reasonable soul is as it were set burning so as to be itself a light made and created. ON THE SPIRIT AND THE LETTER 11.[51]

36:11 The Foot of Arrogance

THROUGH HUMILITY. AUGUSTINE: Advance on the road to sublimity by the footstep of humility. He himself exalts those who follow him humbly, who was not ashamed to descend to the fallen. HOLY VIRGINITY 52(53).[52]

THE DARK PATH. AMBROSE: Oh, beware of pride, for it plants its foot when all is going well and prosperously. Adam fell in paradise far more ruinously that if he had fallen on earth. To fall from great heights is precipitous; to fall on level ground is simply a case of losing one's footing. The foot of the proud person strays, because he has lost his head.[53] As Scripture says, "The eyes of a wise person are in his head."[54] Is it any wonder that feet go astray if a person has no eyes in his head? The eye leads, and the foot follows. You, who are on a journey, how can you make your way in the dark? We stumble easily by night, unless perhaps the moon, like a sort of eye of the world, should lend its beams and light the way. You are in the night of this world; let the church shed its light on your journey; let the sun of justice[55] illumine you from on high. In that way, you need have no fear of falling. COMMENTARY ON TWELVE PSALMS 36.26.[56]

DEPARTURE FROM GOD. AUGUSTINE: The foot of pride approached him, and the hand of the sinner dislodged him, the proud hand of the devil. . . . So it was that we fell by pride and were reduced to this mortal condition. And so too, as it was pride that wounded us, humility makes us whole. Our humble God came to heal humankind of its grievous wound of pride. . . . Why did he call it the foot? Because by growing proud, humankind abandoned God and walked away. EXPOSITIONS OF THE PSALMS 36.17-18.[57]

---

[49]WSA 3 6:177. [50]WGRW 5:409. [51]LCC 8:201. [52]FC 27:208. [53]Cf. Col 2:19. [54]Eccles 2:14. [55]Cf. Mt 4:2. [56]ACTP 51*. [57]WSA 3 16:87-88.

AN UNSOUND VEHICLE. EVAGRIUS OF PONTUS: Pride is an unsound vehicle, and one who gets into it is quickly thrown. The humble person always stands firm, and the foot of pride will never trip him. ON THE EIGHT THOUGHTS 8.13.[58]

PLUCKED FROM THE ROOT OF VIRTUE. AMBROSE: Let not the actions of sinful people make me stir from the way of justice. For very often when we see sinners abounding in prosperity and enjoying great success, we waver in our allegiance; a sort of hand steals out from these sinners, and we are plucked from the root of virtue. Beware, beware, do not let the hand of the enemy uproot those whom the hand of God has planted in his house. COMMENTARY ON TWELVE PSALMS 36.27.[59]

---

[58]GAC 88*. [59]ACTP 51.

37:1-40 TRUST IN THE LORD

If, when evil and lawless people are opposing the lowly,

and you wish to admonish the latter not to pay attention or to be provoked

to envy—since such evildoers will speedily be destroyed—

say to yourself and to the others Psalm 37.

ATHANASIUS *ON THE INTERPRETATION OF THE PSALMS* 18 [OIP 68]

A Psalm of David.

¹*Fret not yourself because of the wicked,*
be not envious of wrongdoers!
²*For they will soon fade like the grass,*
and wither like the green herb.

³*Trust in the* LORD, *and do good;*
so you will dwell in the land, and enjoy
security.
⁴*Take delight in the* LORD,
and he will give you the desires of your heart.

⁵*Commit your way to the* LORD;
trust in him, and he will act.
⁶*He will bring forth your vindication as the*
light,

and your right as the noonday.

⁷*Be still before the* LORD, *and wait patiently*
for him;
fret not yourself over him who prospers in
his way,
over the man who carries out evil devices!

⁸*Refrain from anger, and forsake wrath!*
Fret not yourself; it tends only to evil.
⁹*For the wicked shall be cut off;*
but those who wait for the LORD *shall*
possess the land.

¹⁰*Yet a little while, and the wicked will be no*
more;
though you look well at his place, he

will not be there.
¹¹But the meek shall possess the land,
and delight themselves in abundant
prosperity.

¹²The wicked plots against the righteous,
and gnashes his teeth at him;
¹³but the LORD laughs at the wicked,
for he sees that his day is coming.

¹⁴The wicked draw the sword and bend their
bows,
to bring down the poor and needy,
to slay those who walk uprightly;
¹⁵their sword shall enter their own heart,
and their bows shall be broken.

¹⁶Better is a little that the righteous has
than the abundance of many wicked.
¹⁷For the arms of the wicked shall be broken;
but the LORD upholds the righteous.

¹⁸The LORD knows the days of the blameless,
and their heritage will abide for ever;
¹⁹they are not put to shame in evil times,
in the days of famine they have abundance.

²⁰But the wicked perish;
the enemies of the LORD are like the glory
of the pastures,
they vanish—like smoke they vanish away.

²¹The wicked borrows, and cannot pay back,
but the righteous is generous and gives;
²²for those blessed by the LORD shall possess
the land,
but those cursed by him shall be cut off.

²³The steps of a man are from the LORD,
and he establishes him in whose way he
delights;
²⁴though he fall, he shall not be cast headlong,
for the LORD is the stay of his hand.

²⁵I have been young, and now am old;

yet I have not seen the righteous forsaken
or his children begging bread.
²⁶He is ever giving liberally and lending,
and his children become a blessing.

²⁷Depart from evil, and do good;
so shall you abide for ever.
²⁸For the LORD loves justice;
he will not forsake his saints.

The righteous shall be preserved for ever,
but the children of the wicked shall be cut
off.
²⁹The righteous shall possess the land,
and dwell upon it for ever.

³⁰The mouth of the righteous utters wisdom,
and his tongue speaks justice.
³¹The law of his God is in his heart;
his steps do not slip.

³²The wicked watches the righteous,
and seeks to slay him.
³³The LORD will not abandon him to his
power,
or let him be condemned when he is brought
to trial.

³⁴Wait for the LORD, and keep to his way,
and he will exalt you to possess the land;
you will look on the destruction of the
wicked.

³⁵I have seen a wicked man overbearing,
and towering like a cedar of Lebanon.^v
³⁶Again I^w passed by, and lo, he was no more;
though I sought him, he could not be
found.

³⁷Mark the blameless man, and behold the
upright,
for there is posterity for the man of peace.
³⁸But transgressors shall be altogether
destroyed;
the posterity of the wicked shall be cut off.

³⁹*The salvation of the righteous is from the*
    LORD;
  he is their refuge in the time of trouble.
⁴⁰*The LORD helps them and delivers them;*

he delivers them from the wicked, and
    saves them,
because they take refuge in him.

v Gk: Heb obscure   w Gk Syr Jerome: Heb *he*

OVERVIEW: The thirty-seventh psalm is an exhortation on proper conduct that David learned by experience (THEODORET). We all share the typical weakness of being tempted by the prosperity of the wicked (DIODORE). However, we must avoid the temptation to imitate them (AMBROSE). The wicked are like seasonal plants, but the righteous have deep roots in Christ (AUGUSTINE). Let us cultivate our hearts (ORIGEN) and maintain constant communion with the Lord (THEODORET). Let us seek a divine luxury (ORIGEN). Be good openly (DIODORE), and offer yourself to God (THEODORET). Your faith will be revealed as righteousness (AUGUSTINE). There will be no hidden judgment (AMBROSE). God is in control (THEODORET). He is able and trustworthy (AUGUSTINE).

Anger is the source of many vices (BASIL). When you feel it coming on, drop it (AMBROSE) and remember what it is God has promised you (AUGUSTINE). The wicked face a sure punishment (THEODORE OF MOPSUESTIA), for destruction by God is total and complete (EVAGRIUS). We need to refocus (THEODORET) and pursue compassion and sweetness (CLEMENT OF ROME). The prosperity as well as the punishment of the wicked happens according to divine foreknowledge (DIODORE). They fulfill a function in the divine plan—a function that shall cease (AUGUSTINE). We, however, are exhorted to be meek (TEACHING OF THE TWELVE APOSTLES). God rests in the meek (AMBROSE), and he will be their peace (AUGUSTINE). The meek inherit the world to come (CASSIODORUS).

The wicked attack the righteous by whom they are convicted (CASSIODORUS). Attacks come every day (ARNOBIUS THE YOUNGER). But God gives us the means of consolation (CASSIODO-

RUS). The sword of the wicked is the opposite of the sword of the Spirit (AMBROSE). However, we need not fear them. They will not succeed (THEODORE). They, in fact, hurt only themselves (AUGUSTINE). Tempting thoughts may be turned back by analytical reflection (EVAGRIUS). By his knowledge, the Lord makes us his possession (DIODORE), and his eyes illumine our days (AMBROSE). The righteous find joy in divine providence (THEODORET). Those who hope in God are not disconcerted (AUGUSTINE). The wicked, however, pass swiftly (AMBROSE). Their life is tenuous (AUGUSTINE).

The righteous are generous with the currency of kindness (THEODORET), paying back gratitude for what they receive (AUGUSTINE). By virtue of God's enablement (FULGENTIUS), we must walk in the way of Christ (AUGUSTINE). God grants assistance (THEODORET) and does not abandon his own (AMBROSE), ever supplying him with the bread from heaven (ORIGEN). We are to be lenders of the gospel (AMBROSE). We should not just refrain from evil but go on to good deeds (AUGUSTINE).

All that destroys a person perishes (CASSIODORUS). The righteous have the Word of God in their hearts (AUGUSTINE) and possess a mouth of wisdom (AMBROSE), which speaks the Lord Jesus (AMBROSE). Thereby, they learn how to behave (THEODORET). This is what attracts the hostility of the wicked, but God watches over us (AMBROSE). We live a life of expectancy by obeying his commands (THEODORE OF MOPSUESTIA), and so, we wait for him with the Word (ARNOBIUS THE YOUNGER). Consequently, the righteous have perspective on life (AMBROSE). In one way or another, all will pass by this world (CASSIODORUS). When the just are saved, the wicked perish (ARNOBIUS THE YOUNGER). Salvation comes from God alone (AMBROSE) and is granted to those who hope in him (THEODORET, CASSIODORUS).

Superscription: *A Psalm of David*

AN EXHORTATION FROM EXPERIENCE. THEODORET OF CYR: The divine David learned from experience the vast number of goods gentleness brings, and the fact that a grievous end befitting their life awaits those addicted to injustice and practiced in arrogance. This he learned from his dealings with Saul and Absalom, and with the others who perpetrated similar things to them. So he offers all people an exhortation, urging them to take in good spirit the troubles that come their way and not to consider as blessings wicked people's prosperity and success, but rather to call them wretched. COMMENTARY ON THE PSALMS 37.1.[1]

37:1 Do Not Fret

A TYPICAL WEAKNESS. DIODORE OF TARSUS: Being human, we are all irked by the prosperity of the affluent, especially when they are dishonest. So from the outset he immediately gives this exhortation: Do not imitate evildoers, even if they are rich, nor lawbreakers, even if from their wickedness they amass wealth. Why not? Because . . . though flourishing for a time, such people have a rapid end. He did well to compare them with flowers: they also delight the eye for a time but are unable to bear the heat and dry up at once. COMMENTARY ON PSALMS 37.[2]

THE TEMPTATION TO IMITATE. AMBROSE: Not infrequently good people, seeing others arrive at riches and honors by fraud and trickery, become green with jealousy and want to imitate them. They, too, are tempted to attain riches and fame by similar tricks and malpractices. . . . Do not be an imitator of wrongdoing and fraud. Rather, be an imitator of apostolic doctrine, of prophetic

grace and of the virtue of the saints. Then you will bear fruit and reap the harvest of your good deeds. COMMENTARY ON TWELVE PSALMS 37.11.[3]

37:2 Withering Like Grass

THE DEEP ROOT. AUGUSTINE: What seems slow to you is swift to God; submit yourself to God, and it will seem swift to you as well. The word *grass* we take to mean the same as "plants in the meadow." They are inconsiderable things that cling to the surface of the soil and have no deep roots. They thrive through the winter, but in summer when the sun begins to grow hot they wilt. This present time is your winter. Your glory does not show yet. But like the winter trees you have the deep root of charity, and so when the cold weather passes and summer comes (judgment day, I mean) the green grass will dry up and your glory burst forth, like the foliage of the trees. "You are dead," says the apostle: you look as dead as the trees do in winter, parched and apparently lifeless. What hope have we, then, if we are dead? We have the root within us, and where our root is fixed, there is our life, for there is our charity. "Your life is hidden with Christ in God," the apostle continues. How can anyone with such a root ever wilt? But when will spring arrive for us? Or our summer? When shall we be arrayed in fair foliage or laden with luscious fruit? When will that be? Listen to Paul's next line: "When Christ appears, Christ who is your life, then you too will appear with him in glory."[4] EXPOSITIONS OF THE PSALMS 37.3.[5]

37:3 Do Good and Inhabit the Land

CULTIVATE YOUR HEART. ORIGEN: The "land" here indicates the heart of the listener and his soul. We are ordered, therefore, to indwell this land, that is, not to stray far from it, not to run to and fro, far and near, but to dwell and to

---

[1]FC 101:222. [2]WGRW 9:115-16. [3]ACTP 58. [4]Col 3:3-4. [5]WSA 3 16:94.

stand firm within the bounds of our spirits and to consider the land very carefully and to become its tiller just as Noah was and to plant in it the vine and till the land that is within us, "to renew the fallowed ground of our spirits and sow not among the thorns."[6] Namely, let us purge our spirit from faults, and let us refine rough and harsh ways with the gentleness and the imitation of Christ, and thus finally we may feed from its wealth. Homily 1 on Psalm 37.3.[7]

37:4 Delight in the Lord

Constant Communion. Theodoret of Cyr: In everything he taught the benefit of hope in God: the person hoping in God, he says, and fed by him will enjoy the goods supplied by him while those who find delightful constant converse with him will most of all attain them. Commentary on the Psalms 37.2.[8]

Divine Luxury. Origen: The expression "we have need" is applied to those things that are necessary for life. Consequently, applied to material things, it means that one does not need most things but only those of which Paul says, "but having food and clothing, we shall be satisfied with these things." Those things, [by contrast], that are accumulated in wealth and luxury are the result of abundance among those who live luxuriously. They are not considered to be necessary and absolutely essential but to be superfluous. So, therefore, there are also things that are necessary for us in the realm of divine matters, which bring us into life and cause us to be in the one who says, "I am the life." But what supersedes these things would be said to supersede need. It is said of such things, "Delight in the Lord, and he will give you the requests of your heart." These include all the things that are considered in relation to the paradise of luxury and in relation to wealth and glory, the things in the left hand of wisdom according to him who said, "For length of life and years of life are in her right hand, but in her left hand are wealth and glory."[9] One would say that these go

beyond necessity. Commentary on the Gospel of John 32.106.[10]

37:5 Trust the Lord

Be Good Openly. Diodore of Tarsus: Be sincere in pursuing good, not pretending to be honest while being evil; instead, be good openly and as it were without disguise so that God may openly repay you with good. Commentary on Psalms 37.[11]

Offer Yourself to God. Theodoret of Cyr: Offer up to God, he is saying, both yourself and your actions, and expect grace from him; for his part he will bring forth a just verdict like a judge, will extol you and make you famous to the extent of being known to everyone, like the light at midday. Commentary on the Psalms 37.2.[12]

37:6 The Noonday Light

Faith Will Be Revealed as Righteousness. Augustine: Your righteousness is hidden at present; it is a reality, but in faith, not something that can be seen. You believe in something that prompts you to action, but you do not yet see what you believe in. When you begin to see the object of your faith, your righteousness will be led out into the light. Your faith itself was all along your righteousness, for the one who lives by faith is just. Expositions of the Psalms 37.6.[13]

No Hidden Judgment. Ambrose: God brings [justice] out into the light. He does not permit judgment to lie hidden. He reveals the good that you have chosen to do and the evil that you have refused to do. Not only does he make your judgment shine, but also he makes it shine like the sun at midday. Commentary on Twelve Psalms 37.15.[14]

---

[6]Jer 4:3. [7]SC 411:72. [8]FC 101:222-23. [9]Prov 3:16. [10]FC 89:362. [11]WGRW 9:116. [12]FC 101:223. [13]WSA 3 16:96. [14]ACTP 61.

37:7 Wait Patiently for the Lord

GOD IS IN CONTROL. THEODORET OF CYR: Even if you see one choosing wickedness and not deviating from his purpose but being borne downstream, do not be worried and concerned that no one is in control of the world. COMMENTARY ON THE PSALMS 37.3.[15]

GOD IS ABLE AND TRUSTWORTHY. AUGUSTINE: How do you show yourself subject to [God]? By doing what he commanded. You do not receive your reward yet, but that may be because you are not yet capable of it. He is already able to give it, but you are not able to receive it. Exert yourself in your tasks, labor in the vineyard, and when evening comes ask for your wages, for he who brought you into the vineyard is trustworthy. EXPOSITIONS OF THE PSALMS 37.8.[16]

37:8 Refrain from Anger

THE SOURCE OF MANY VICES. BASIL THE GREAT: If, by the prudent use of reason, you could cut away the bitter root of indignation, you would remove many other vices along with this, their source. Deceit, suspicion, faithlessness, malice, treachery, rashness, and a whole thicket of evils like these are offshoots of this vice. . . . It is a malady on the soul, a dark mist over the reason. It brings estrangement from God, forgetfulness of the ties of kindred, cause for a strife, a full measure of disaster. It is a wicked demon coming to birth in our very souls, taking prior possession of our interior, like a shameless tenant, and barring entrance to the Holy Spirit. HOMILY AGAINST THOSE WHO ARE PRONE TO ANGER.[17]

DROP IT. AMBROSE: Anger destroys not just the ordinary run of people, but even the wise. David warns the wise, saying to them, "Cease from anger," for once that fire is set alight it will not cease until its flames have consumed you. "Leave aside," he says, "your rage." Here is his

meaning: nature catches hold of you, it stirs up your feelings, you get excited about some fault, some slight that has offended you, you begin to rage but not to the point where you cannot stop. Drop it. Put an end to it, or it will drag you into sin. COMMENTARY ON TWELVE PSALMS 37.18.[18]

REMEMBER GOD'S PROMISE. AUGUSTINE: Did you believe in Christ? Yes? Then why did you believe? What did he promise you? If Christ promised you happiness in this world, then go ahead and complain against him; complain when you see the unbeliever happy. But what sort of happiness did he, in fact, promise you? Nothing else but happiness when the dead rise again. And what did he promise you in this life? Only what he went through himself; yes, I tell you, he promised you a share in his own experience. Do you disdain it, you, a servant and a disciple? Do you disdain what your master and teacher went through? Do you not recall his own words: "A servant is not greater than his master, nor a disciple above his teacher"?[19] For your sake he bore painful scourging, insults, the cross and death itself. And how much of this did he deserve, he, a just man? And what did you, a sinner, not deserve? Keep a steady eye, and do not let it be deflected by wrath. EXPOSITIONS OF THE PSALMS 37.9.[20]

37:9 The Wicked Cut Off

A SURE PUNISHMENT. THEODORE OF MOPSUESTIA: Do not consider blessed those people for being in a position even to do whatever they wish, nor with your eyes on their suffering no harsh fate decide to attempt at any time in your own case to do some wrong. "Because the evildoers will be wiped out": those guilty of wickedness will some day pay the full penalty and perish. COMMENTARY ON PSALMS 37.8B-9A.[21]

---

[15]FC 101:223. [16]WSA 3 16:97. [17]FC 9:460-61. [18]ACTP 64*. [19]Mt 10:24; Jn 13:16. [20]WSA 3 16:98. [21]WGRW 5:421.

TRUE DESTRUCTION. EVAGRIUS OF PONTUS: Nothing else is destroyed but that which is cut off from God. NOTES ON THE PSALMS 36[37].9.[22]

REFOCUS. THEODORET OF CYR: Instead of considering their prosperity, await their end, and you will see their ruin. COMMENTARY ON THE PSALMS 37.3.[23]

COMPASSION AND SWEETNESS. CLEMENT OF ROME: Therefore it is right and proper, brothers, that we should be obedient to God rather than follow those who in arrogance and unruliness have set themselves up as leaders in abominable jealousy. For we shall bring on us no common harm, but rather great peril, if we surrender ourselves recklessly to the purposes of people who launch out into strife and seditions, so as to estrange us from that which is right. Let us be good one toward another according to the compassion and sweetness of him that made us. 1 CLEMENT 14.[24]

37:10 The Wicked Will Disappear

DIVINE FOREKNOWLEDGE. DIODORE OF TARSUS: The wicked not only grows rich but even plots against the righteous, God's permission causing both developments to go ahead; but let it not alarm you. God in his foreknowledge [is] aware of the fate of the wicked and [sees] the righteous person's endurance. . . . God looks ahead to [the wicked person's] fate and mocks his threats and his frenzy, aware as he is of the future. Thus in many cases when the wicked think they have gotten the better of the righteous, then it is that sudden ruin overtakes them when unexpected punishment is inflicted on them by God. COMMENTARY ON PSALM 37.[25]

HIS FUNCTION WILL CEASE. AUGUSTINE: What does "his place" mean? His function. Does the sinner have a function? Yes, he does. God uses sinners in the present world to test the just, as he used the devil to test Job and used Judas to betray Christ. So the sinner does have a certain role in this life. This role is his "place." EXPOSITIONS OF THE PSALMS 37.11.[26]

37:11 The Meek Possess the Land

BE MEEK. DIDACHE: But be meek, for "the meek shall inherit the land." Be patient, merciful, guileless, and mild and gentle, and in every regard "fearful of the words" that you have heard. Do not exalt yourself or allow impudence in your soul. Your soul shall not cling to the proud but associate with good and humble people. Accept the troubles that come to you as good, knowing that nothing happens without God. DIDACHE 3.7-10.[27]

GOD RESTS IN THE MEEK. AMBROSE: It is their right to possess the land, for in them God finds rest. We see this from the words of divine prophecy spoken by Isaiah: "On whom shall I rest, if not on those who are poor and little and who tremble at my word?"[28] Who are the meek? They are those not easily roused to wrath, not quick to quarrel. Anger does not trouble them, fierceness does not drive them mad, raging cruelty does not enflame them. While still in the body they loved the peace of the Lord better than wine, banquets and riches. They thought to give up bodily pleasures and delights to gain instead eternal grace; these are the people who "shall delight in abundance of peace." COMMENTARY ON TWELVE PSALMS 37.22.[29]

GOD WILL BE YOUR PEACE. AUGUSTINE: Peace will be your gold, peace will be your silver, peace will be your broad estates, peace your very life. Your God will be your peace. Peace will be for you whatever you long for. In this world gold cannot also be silver for you, wine cannot be bread for you, what gives you light cannot provide you with drink; but your God will be every-

---

[22]PG 12:1317 [23]FC 101:223. [24]ANF 1:8**. [25]WGRW 9:117. [26]WSA 3 16:100. [27]FC 1:173-74*. [28]Is 66:2. [29]ACTP 67-68*.

thing to you. You will feed on him, and hunger will never come near you; you will drink him, never to thirst again; you will be illumined by him that you may suffer no blindness; you will be supported by him and saved from weakness. He will possess you whole and undivided, as he, your possessor, is whole and undivided himself. You will lack nothing with him, for with him you possess all that is; you will have it all, and he will have all there is of you, because you and he will be one, and he who possesses you will have this one thing and have it wholly. EXPOSITIONS OF THE PSALMS 37.12.[30]

THE WORLD TO COME. CASSIODORUS: The meek will possess the Jerusalem to come, a city always filled with sweet blessings, in which its inhabitants do not live by trade but feed on delight in God. None there toils to live but in tranquility receives all that his blessed spirit desires. There the inner eye is fattened by blessed hunger, there the soul is renewed by sight alone, for all that it desires is granted by contemplation of the Lord's face. EXPLANATION OF THE PSALMS 37.11.[31]

37:12 The Wicked Plot

CONVICTION. CASSIODORUS: When the wicked person sees the just person cultivating good manners, he believes that he himself is being particularly indicted. He gnashes his teeth and rages in mind. He at once tries to take the very life of him whose manners he cannot corrupt. EXPLANATION OF THE PSALMS 37.12.[32]

EVERY DAY. ARNOBIUS THE YOUNGER: Be careful, for daily the devil considers you and gnashes his teeth over you; but [as it says in the next verse] the Lord mocks him because he knows his day will come. COMMENTARY ON THE PSALMS 37.[33]

CONSOLATION. CASSIODORUS: Wonderful is the nature of the consolation revealed to us, for who

should feel delight at the luxury of one whose recklessness he knows is soon to perish? If we do not wish to be confounded by any jealousy, let us follow what the Lord does. Let us laugh at him whose fall we foresee; let us account as unhappy the possessions that we realize are soon to fade. Let us believe most securely in such an outcome, for it has been promised us by the truth. It will come to pass that the sinner will depart as an object of derision, though he earlier waxes proud with a happiness that is fleeting. EXPLANATION OF THE PSALMS 37.13.[34]

37:14 The Wicked Draw the Sword

A DIFFERENT SWORD. AMBROSE: What is the sword of the wicked? It is the absolute opposite to the sword of the Holy Spirit. . . . God's Word is the sword of the Holy Spirit. But the sword of the wicked is the evil word. . . . Stupid and petulant speech issues from their mouths as from a scabbard, and would it not have been better to restrain it and bury it? In like manner the Word of the Lord is brought forth as a sword; so, too, the speech of the sinner, and the bow that they bend is their mind. The arrow that they shoot is the venomous word. Our arrow is Christ, the Word of God. COMMENTARY ON TWELVE PSALMS 37.24.[35]

37:15 Their Bows Broken

THEY WILL NOT SUCCEED. THEODORE OF MOPSUESTIA: Even if the sinner tries to plot against the righteous person and is bent on carrying it through in every way, do not then grind your teeth at his going unpunished. God will spit on his plot, knowing that he will suffer sometime and that it is he who will sustain harm from his plot against the righteous. COMMENTARY ON PSALMS 37.15.[36]

---

[30]WSA 3 16:101. [31]ACW 51:362. [32]ACW 51:363*. [33]CCL 25:50 [34]ACW 51:363*. [35]ACTP 69. [36]WGRW 5:425.

THEY HURT THEMSELVES. AUGUSTINE: What do you think: does the scoundrel's wickedness harm you without harming himself? Of course not. How is it possible that the malice that springs from his ill will and hatred and lashes out to do you harm should not devastate him within before making its attempt outwardly on you? Hostility rides roughshod over your body; iniquity rots his soul. Whatever he launches against you recoils on him. His persecution purifies you but leaves him guilty. Who comes off worse, then? . . . Clearly, then, all who persecute the just are more severely damaged and more gravely wounded themselves, because in their case it is the soul itself that is laid waste. EXPOSITIONS OF THE PSALMS 37.3.[37]

TURN THEM BACK. EVAGRIUS OF PONTUS: When one of the enemies approaches to wound you and you want to "turn his own sword back against his heart," according to the Scripture text, then do as we tell you. Distinguish within yourself the thought he has launched against you, as to what it is, how many elements it consists of and among these what sort of thing it is that most afflicts the mind. . . . As you engage in this careful examination, the thought will be destroyed and dissipate in its own consideration, and the demon will flee from you when your intellect has been raised to the heights by this knowledge. ON THOUGHTS 19.[38]

37:16 Better Is a Little

BETTER OUTCOME. AMBROSE: A person might be rich in disputation, as are certain irreligious philosophers of this world. They can discourse on the movement of the heavenly bodies, of the stars, of Jupiter and Saturn, on the generation of humankind, on the cult of idols, on geometry and dialectics. Those philosophers are therefore rich in eloquence, but in faith they are poor, and in truth they are needy. On the other hand, very often the Lord's priests are simple people. They are poor in eloquence but sublime in abstinence

and virtue. Those philosophers utter falsehood to the multitude; these priests preach the faith to the few. Those others lose priests every day; but this poor priest adds whole peoples to the number of believers and to the church. Anyone who hears and sees the quality of their works will say, "Better is a little to the just than the great riches of the wicked." COMMENTARY ON TWELVE PSALMS 37.28.[39]

37:18 The Lord Knows

POSSESSION. DIODORE OF TARSUS: "Knows" means makes his own, as in the first psalm, "Because the Lord knows the ways of the righteous,"[40] that is, makes them his own. COMMENTARY ON PSALMS 37.[41]

GOD'S EYES. AMBROSE: His eyes are light; those on whom he looks he illumines; and therefore his eyes are the days of the just. COMMENTARY ON TWELVE PSALMS 37.33.[42]

37:19 Not Put to Shame

JOY IN DIVINE PROVIDENCE. THEODORET OF CYR: Those choosing a blameless life enjoy providence completely; even if they encounter disasters, they will emerge superior to them; and when need becomes endemic, they will receive sufficiency from God, and in addition will enjoy everlasting goods. COMMENTARY ON THE PSALMS 37.6.[43]

DISCONCERTED. AUGUSTINE: Who is disconcerted? The person who says, "I have not found what I was hoping for." . . . You are disconcerted because your hope has proved illusory; hope founded on a lie is always an illusion, and every mortal is a liar. If you rest your hope on your God, you will not be disconcerted, because you have rested it on one who cannot be deceived.

---

[37]WSA 3 16:105. [38]GAC 166. [39]ACTP 72*. [40]Ps 1:6. [41]WGRW 9:118. [42]ACTP 75. [43]FC 101:224.

. . . For sinners there is no place to rest in anything outside themselves, because there they endure afflictions; nor does their conscience offer them any consolation, because they are not comfortable with themselves. It is not comfortable to live with someone bad. But those who are bad live unpleasantly with themselves; inevitably such persons are tormented and are their own tormentor. Those with a torturing conscience are their own punishment. They can flee wherever they like from an enemy, but where will they flee from themselves? EXPOSITIONS OF THE PSALMS 37.9-10.[44]

37:20 The Wicked Vanish

THEY PASS SWIFTLY. AMBROSE: The Greek puts it more forcibly, showing that where a person appears honored and exalted, there, by his very own failure, he is brought to a halt. It is rather like the current of a river: you think that it flows past you more swiftly than it came and that, while you are waiting for the waters to flow toward you, they have already rushed past you even as you waited. COMMENTARY ON TWELVE PSALMS 37.39.[45]

TENUOUS. AUGUSTINE: Smoke bursts from the place where the fire is and wafts upward; and as it rises it billows into a great round cloud. But the bigger this cloud grows, the more tenuous it becomes; its very size means that it cannot be something durable and solid. It hangs loose and inflated, and it is carried away into the air and disperses; you can see that its very size was its undoing. The higher it rises, and the wider it spreads, and the more it extends itself over an increasing area, the weaker it is and the wispier, until it vanishes. EXPOSITIONS OF THE PSALMS 37.12.[46]

37:21 The Righteous Are Generous

THE CURRENCY OF KINDNESS. THEODORET OF CYR: Saul was like that, ever the object of kindness at the hands of the divine David but reluctant to repay kindness with kindness; blessed David . . . , in imitation of his Lord, who makes his sun rise on wicked and good, continued showing kindness. COMMENTARY ON THE PSALMS 37.7.[47]

GRATITUDE. AUGUSTINE: He or she receives but will not give back. Give back what? Gratitude. What does God want of you, what does God demand of you, except what it profits you to give? What great benefits has a sinner received! Yet he makes no return. EXPOSITIONS OF THE PSALMS 37.13.[48]

37:23 Walk in God's Ways

ENABLEMENT. FULGENTIUS OF RUSPE: God gives a new heart so that we may walk in his justifications that pertain to the beginning of a good will. He also gives that we may observe and do his judgments that pertain to the doing of good works. Thus we know both the will to do good and the ability to do good from God. David agrees completely with this, showing that by the command of divine generosity the grace of a good will is granted. LETTER TO MONIMUS 1.8.3-9.1.[49]

CHRIST'S WAY. AUGUSTINE: Once you have set out to follow Christ's way, do not promise yourself worldly prosperity. He walked through hard things but promised great things. Follow him. Do not think too much about the way but more about the goal ahead of you. You will have to put up with tough conditions on your journey through time, but you will attain joys that last forever. . . . But God has willed not only that our toil shall be temporary but also that it be brief. An entire human life lasts but a few days, even if no joyful ones are interspersed among the hard ones; and in fact joyful periods certainly occur more often and last longer than the difficult

---

[44]WSA 3 16:110-11. [45]ACTP 78. [46]WSA 3 16:112. [47]FC 101:225. [48]WSA 3 16:113. [49]FC 95:198.

times. The hard ones are designedly briefer and fewer, so that we may hold out. So even if a person spent his or her whole life amid hard work and bitter experiences, in pain and agony, in prison, amid pestilence; if he or she were hungry and thirsty every day, every hour, throughout life, even to old age, it would still be true that human life is an affair of a few days only. Once all this toil is over, the eternal kingdom will come, happiness without end will come, equality with the angels will come, Christ's inheritance will come, and Christ, our fellow heir, will come. What did the toil amount to, if we receive so great a reward? . . . If you choose Christ's way and are a true Christian (for a Christian is one who does not reject Christ's path but wills to walk that way through Christ's own sufferings), do not seek to travel by any route other than that by which he went. It seems a hard road, but it is a safe one. Any other may offer attractions but is beset by brigands. Expositions of the Psalms 37.16.[50]

37:24 The Stay of the Lord's Hand

Divine Assistance. Theodoret of Cyr: It is impossible for anyone to travel blamelessly the way of virtue without God's grace. He works in association with those who have this intent: for the acquisition of virtue there is need of human zeal and divine assistance at one and the same time. Thus, you see, even if the one traveling this path should slip, he will gain divine support. Likewise, when blessed David stumbled and ran the risk of coming to grief, he was borne up by divine grace. Commentary on the Psalms 37.8.[51]

37:25 The Righteous Forsaken

Not Abandoned by God. Ambrose: If you take it at face value, the meaning is obvious: in his own lifetime, David never saw the just forsaken. But a lifespan is brief, and the statement is moreover incredible. We have seen plenty of just people in this world who have been forsaken

by people as soon as those just ones are persecuted by people in power. No one dares to go near them so long as they are subject to fear and injury. Remember what Job said: "My brothers have departed far from me, they recognize strangers more than they recognize me; my friends have become merciless and those who knew me once have forgotten even my name."[52] As for David, not only was he deserted, but also he was even attacked by his friends and those closest to him by family ties: "My friends," he says, "and my neighbors have advanced against me."[53] How, I ask, can David state that which is the exact opposite of this? We can only understand it in this sense: the just person, even if forsaken by the world, is not abandoned by the Lord. Even Job on his dunghill[54] was not deserted by the Lord. In the council of the angels, the Lord had praised Job with his own voice; and he allowed him to be tempted only so that he might win the crown. He allowed Job's body to undergo severe testing, but he spared his life. Commentary on Twelve Psalms 37.58.[55]

The Bread of the Righteous. Origen: They can never be oppressed by the fasting of famine whose bread is that "they should do the will of the Father who is in heaven" and whose soul that "bread that comes down from heaven" nourishes. Homilies on Genesis 16.3.[56]

37:26 Ever Giving

Lenders of the Gospel. Ambrose: There is money lent out at interest, and there is money lent in kindness. But the Lord expects a return. Money gets interest paid in cash. The grace of kindness wins an increase of faith. Lend out your faith generously to the Gentiles, and your grace will be multiplied. Do not go about borrowing like a pauper. Act like someone really rich and lend out so as to make great profit. Pe-

---

[50]WSA 3 16:115-16. [51]FC 101:225-26*. [52]Job 19:13-14. [53]Ps 38:12 (137:12 lxx). [54]Cf. Job 2:8. [55]ACTP 89*. [56]FC 71:218.

ter lent; Paul lent; John the Evangelist lent; and certainly they were not in want. What they lent was Christ's money; they were not charging high rates of interest. So lend and do not grow weary. COMMENTARY ON TWELVE PSALMS 37.62.[57]

GIVING THE EARTH, RECEIVING HEAVEN. AUGUSTINE: Study the moneylender's methods. He wants to give modestly and get back with profit; you do the same. Give a little, and receive on a grand scale. Look how your interest is mounting up! Give temporal wealth and claim eternal interest; give the earth and gain heaven. EXPOSITIONS OF THE PSALMS 37.6.[58]

37:27 Depart from Evil, and Do Good

GO ON TO GOOD DEEDS. AUGUSTINE: Do not imagine that you have done enough if you have refrained from stealing anyone's clothes. By not stripping someone, you have turned away from evil, but be careful not to dry up at that point and remain barren. You must take care not to strip someone of his clothes, certainly, but you must also clothe another who is naked; this is what turning away from evil and doing good implies. "What will I get out of it?" did you say? He to whom you are lending has already told you what recompense he will make to you: he will give you eternal life, so be easy in your mind and give to him. EXPOSITIONS OF THE PSALMS 37.8.[59]

37:28 Children of the Wicked

THAT WHICH PERISHES. CASSIODORUS: All that destroys a person perishes; the only things surviving are those that make him abide in the kingdom of the Lord. EXPLANATION OF THE PSALMS 37.28.[60]

37:30 Speaking Wisdom and Justice

THE WORD OF GOD. AUGUSTINE: The Word of God in his heart frees one from the snare, the Word of God in his heart steers one clear of the crooked path, the Word of God in his heart keeps one steady in a slippery place. If God's Word never leaves your heart, God is with you. EXPOSITIONS OF THE PSALMS 37.12.[61]

THE MOUTH OF WISDOM. AMBROSE: The just, when he speaks God's judgment or when he himself utters opinions that are just and full of wisdom, never speaks in an angry, passionate way. He does not speak in bitterness of soul; he does not speak from anguish, grievance or any passion. He simply speaks out the truth and states what is honest, just and fair. He weighs things not according to personal feelings but according to truth. He carefully considers what things should be said and what should not be said. He is like the one of whom it is said, "The lips of the wise shall be bound by good sense."[62] All that the wise say will be seen to accord with sound common sense; and such people, guided by their own prudence, understand well when they ought to remain silent. Matters that ought to be kept silent they keep confined to their own bosom and imprisoned, so to speak, by tightly closed lips. But when something ought to be said, then they loosen the bonds of their lips and come out with what they must say. Therefore the prophet aptly said, "The mouth of the just shall meditate wisdom." COMMENTARY ON TWELVE PSALMS 37.68.[63]

SPEAK THE LORD JESUS. AMBROSE: Let us speak the Lord Jesus, for he is wisdom. He is the Word, the very Word of God. Does not Scripture say, "Open your mouth to the word of God"?[64] Echo his speech, meditate his words, and you will breathe Jesus. When we speak of wisdom, it is he. . . . When we speak of truth and life and redemption, it is he. COMMENTARY ON TWELVE PSALMS 37.65.[65]

---

[57]ACTP 93. [58]WSA 3 16:133. [59]WSA 3 16:135. [60]ACW 51:370*. [61]WSA 3 16:138. [62]Prov 15:7. [63]ACTP 98-99. [64]Prov 31:8. [65]ACTP 96.

37:31 God's Law in the Heart

Learning How to Behave. Theodoret of Cyr: It is fitting, the psalmist says, to carry around the divine sayings both on one's tongue and in one's mind and constantly give attention to them; learning in this way how to behave, the lover of virtue remains intrepid and unmoved, proof against efforts at overthrow. Commentary on the Psalms 37.11.[66]

37:32 The Wicked Seek to Kill the Righteous

God Watches Over Us. Ambrose: The sinner cannot stand the just person who speaks wisdom with his mouth and meditates on it in his heart. He sees this one keeping the law of the Lord in his heart, and he does all in his power to make him sin mortally. But the Lord watches over the just. We need not fear the snares laid for us by the sinner, because God is for us. Commentary on Twelve Psalms 37.70.[67]

37:34 Wait for the Lord

A Life of Expectancy. Theodore of Mopsuestia: Since, then, God does not allow the righteous, even if vulnerable to sinners, to be subject completely to their verdict, do not be despondent if ever you fall foul of disaster; instead, expect help from God by observing his decrees and commands, being attentive to his good pleasure and not withdrawing from virtue on account of the hardships besetting you. "And he will exalt you to inherit the land": if you do this, he will shelter you, even if vulnerable to the sinner, and make you exalted by ensuring you secure occupancy of the land. "In the destruction of sinners you will see": not only will you be freed from their scheming, but also you will see them destroyed. Commentary on Psalms 37.34a-c.[68]

Waiting with the Word. Arnobius the Younger: The law of God is in the heart [of the righteous person], and his step is not supplanted.

The devil considers him and desires to humiliate him, but God does not abandon him or curse him when he is judged. Await the Lord and guard his ways so you may inherit the land; in time you will see sinners perish. Commentary on the Psalms 37.[69]

37:35 Towering Like a Cedar

Perspective. Ambrose: You see a cedar raised to a great height on the loftiest peak, yet it can be shattered by the wind; it can be burned down by fire; it can grow old and decay. Such are the rich in this world. They make a grand display and shine, with a worldly sort of splendor, like Mount Lebanon. They are propped up by the powers of this world and positively exult in their money and their riches. To you the rich person seems to be something, that is, until you are able to say, "Passing over, I shall see."[70] For just as Moses passed over, in mind and soul, material things and saw God; you, too, if you will only pass over from this place and lift up the footsteps of your mind to God's grace, will see that the rich person is nothing. Yes, nothing, even though in this world he appeared so high and mighty. Commentary on Twelve Psalms 37.77.[71]

37:36 The Wicked Person Was No More

Pass by the World. Cassiodorus: The world is passed by in two ways. Either it is abandoned by seeking better company, or it will be quitted in the end by the dead. So the person who passes to God by a most holy life does not now behold the sinner wielding power, because he sees everything in which humans boast weakened. . . . The place of sinners is known to be in this world, in which they both commit crimes and are enriched with transitory happiness. But this place is destroyed together with their success when the glory of the entire world, doomed to corruption,

---

[66]FC 101:227. [67]ACTP 100*. [68]WGRW 5:435-37. [69]CCL 25:51. [70]Ex 3:3. [71]ACTP 103*.

is ended. EXPLANATION OF THE PSALMS 37.36.[72]

37:38 *Transgressors Destroyed*

WHEN THE JUST ARE SAVED. ARNOBIUS THE YOUNGER: The wicked will perish when salvation comes to the just from God, their protector in time of tribulation. The Lord helps and frees them and snatches them from sinners and saves them since they hope in our Lord Jesus Christ. COMMENTARY ON THE PSALMS 37.[73]

37:39 *Salvation from the Lord*

GOD ALONE. AMBROSE: To God alone, who remains forever, I entrust; to God alone who can forgive sins,[74] I entrust my salvation. He will be my protector in time of trouble and will help and deliver me. He will snatch me away from sinful people when the hour comes for him to give judgment. He will save me because in him I have hoped. Only in him have I hoped. For he does not wish that we should serve both him and another. The one who serves God alone is set free; for God's is

the praise and the glory. He alone is eternal. To him all honor and power from the beginning of the ages, and now, and always, and to all ages of ages. Amen. COMMENTARY ON TWELVE PSALMS 37.83.[75]

37:40 *The Lord Helps the Righteous*

BECAUSE THEY HOPE IN HIM. THEODORET OF CYR: Those who practice righteousness . . . will enjoy divine aid and attain salvation, and by reason of placing complete hope in him, they will prevail over those endeavoring to wrong them. COMMENTARY ON THE PSALMS 37.14.[76]

FREE TO HOPE. CASSIODORUS: The reason for this liberation [is that] "they have hoped in him"; not because they have not sinned, but because they have put their hope in the Lord's devoted love. This can be applied also to the judgment, when he will deign to bestow eternal rewards on his saints. EXPLANATION OF THE PSALMS 37.40.[77]

---

[72]ACW 51:374*. [73]CCL 25:51-52. [74]Mk 2:7. [75]ACTP 106*. [76]FC 101:228. [77]ACW 51:376.

38:1-22 PRAYER IN SICKNESS

When you feel the Lord's displeasure,
if you see that you are troubled by this, you can say Psalm 38.
ATHANASIUS *ON THE INTERPRETATION OF THE PSALMS* 15 [OIP 66]

A Psalm of David, for the memorial offering.

[1]*O* LORD, *rebuke me not in thy anger,*
nor chasten me in thy wrath!
[2]*For thy arrows have sunk into me,*

and thy hand has come down on me.

[3]*There is no soundness in my flesh*
because of thy indignation;
there is no health in my bones

because of my sin.
⁴*For my iniquities have gone over my head;*
  they weigh like a burden too heavy for me.

⁵*My wounds grow foul and fester*
  because of my foolishness,
⁶*I am utterly bowed down and prostrate;*
  all the day I go about mourning.
⁷*For my loins are filled with burning,*
  and there is no soundness in my flesh.
⁸*I am utterly spent and crushed;*
  I groan because of the tumult of my
    heart.

⁹*Lord, all my longing is known to thee,*
  my sighing is not hidden from thee.
¹⁰*My heart throbs, my strength fails me;*
  and the light of my eyes—it also has gone
    from me.
¹¹*My friends and companions stand aloof*
  from my plague,
  and my kinsmen stand afar off.

¹²*Those who seek my life lay their snares,*
  those who seek my hurt speak of ruin,
  and meditate treachery all the day long.

¹³*But I am like a deaf man, I do not hear,*

Like a dumb man who does not open his
  mouth.
¹⁴*Yea, I am like a man who does not hear,*
  and in whose mouth are no rebukes.

¹⁵*But for thee, O Lord, do I wait;*
  it is thou, O Lord my God, who wilt
    answer.
¹⁶*For I pray, "Only let them not rejoice over*
  me,
  who boast against me when my foot slips!"

¹⁷*For I am ready to fall,*
  and my pain is ever with me.
¹⁸*I confess my iniquity,*
  I am sorry for my sin.
¹⁹*Those who are my foes without cause^x are*
  mighty,
  and many are those who hate me
    wrongfully.
²⁰*Those who render me evil for good*
  are my adversaries because I follow after
    good.

²¹*Do not forsake me, O Lord!*
  O my God, be not far from me!
²²*Make haste to help me,*
  O Lord, my salvation!

x Cn: Heb *living*

Overview: The thirty-eighth psalm is a penitential psalm divided into four parts (Cassiodorus) resembling the sixth psalm in its theme (Diodore). In the first verse, the psalmist asks God to be to him a surgeon, not a judge (Theodoret), to discipline him by the Word, not in the indignation of wrath (Ambrose) as the Lord's hand is on him (Ambrose). The Lord has given us a weight to suppress our sins (Augustine), even our head, who is Christ (Arnobius the Younger). Sin is better understood after the fact (Chrysostom). We need eyes that see the true nature of sin (Ambrose). Only God can cure the wounds of sin (Fulgentius). His Word is the cleansing agent (Methodius of Olympus). From hope we receive a fragrance in our souls (Augustine).

It is best to begin and end words and deeds with God (Gregory of Nazianzus) and better to humble ourselves than to be forced down by sin (Augustine). A change of desire is needed (Theodoret). Truth came incarnate to drive fantasy away (Augustine). The lack of love silences the heart (Augustine). Depression closes the eyes (Theodoret). Evil thoughts lead to a life of falsehood (Athanasius). It is better to remain silent like the Lord than to strike back at evil (Ambrose). We need to be patient like

David (THEODORET). We need to be deaf, dumb and blind to sin (JOHN CASSIAN).

David was unwavering in his trust in God (CASSIODORUS), confident to be tried in the court of God (AUGUSTINE). Enemies rejoice in the downfall of the righteous (AUGUSTINE). But we receive the discipline of the Father for our good (AUGUSTINE, THEODORET). We have a God who saves (AMBROSE), and beyond our present trials we have a sure future salvation (AUGUSTINE).

Superscription: *A Psalm of David*

A PENITENTIAL PSALM. CASSIODORUS: This psalm of the penitent is divided into four sections. First there is an exordium in which the penitential life moves the pity of the kindly Judge. Next comes the narration in two parts, in which he relates the affliction to his body by different punishments and the harsh wounding of his spirit by the accusations of friends. Since no consolation remains in either respect, he prays to the Lord with all his strength. Appended as the third part is the consolation of the saving remedy: this he says is the hope that he has placed in the Lord in the midst of his manifold disasters. Like a wholly devoted servant, he further says that he is ready to endure a whipping, for he thinks that he deserves still more than he is seen to have suffered. After this emerges the joyful conclusion always granted to penitents, in which he is now delivered from all disasters and proclaims God as the Author of his salvation. EXPLANATION OF THE PSALMS 38.1.[1]

SIMILAR TO PSALM 6. DIODORE OF TARSUS: The thirty-eighth psalm resembles in its theme the sixth: just as that one is a confession of sin with Bathsheba and a plea to God, so here too [David] begs to be freed from the misfortunes arising from Absalom's rebellion, which brought a range of tribulations on him, at the same time confessing the sin and giving evidence at every point of the sincerity of repentance. COMMENTARY ON PSALMS 38.[2]

38:1 *Not in Anger*

A SURGEON, NOT A JUDGE. THEODORET OF CYR: David made this beginning to the sixth psalm as well, asking to be disciplined in the manner of a surgeon, not a judge, and to be treated not with harsh remedies but with mild ones. COMMENTARY ON THE PSALMS 38.2.[3]

THE WORD, NOT WRATH. AMBROSE: The prophet . . . acknowledges his fault, recognizes his wounds and asks to be cured. One who wants to be cured does not shrink from correction. Still, he does not want to be chastised in the fury of indignation but in the word of God. God's word is healing. As we read, "He sent his word and healed them."[4] David does not want to be corrected in wrath but to be disciplined in doctrine. It is as though you were to ask the surgeon not to apply his knife to your wound but to pour in ointment. He begs for the remedy but not for the knife. There is pain but not beyond measure. The remedy stings, but the patient's blood does not flow. COMMENTARY ON TWELVE PSALMS 38.19.[5]

38:2 *The Hand of the Lord*

THE LORD'S HAND. AMBROSE: We observe . . . that when Scripture speaks of "the Lord's hand," it refers to temptation that a person undergoes from the attacks of Satan. . . . When the devil wounds him, the arrows are the Lord's, and it is the Lord who has given Satan the power of hurting him. . . . There is, too, that . . . reason why the Lord gives power to the tempter; it is so that one's love might be tested by temptations. That is why there are persecutions, so that faith may shine out and virtue excel and the inner thoughts of one's heart may be made manifest to all. COMMENTARY ON TWELVE PSALMS 38.21.[6]

---

[1]ACW 51:377. [2]WGRW 9:121*. [3]FC 101:229. [4]Ps 107:20 (106:20 LXX). [5]ACTP 117. [6]ACTP 119*.

38:4 *The Weight of Sin*

The Sinner's Weight. Augustine: Lifting up one's head is an act of levity; anyone who does so feels there is no burden to bear. But because the sinner finds it such a light matter to lift himself up, he is given a weight to squash him down. His enterprise will rebound onto his own head, and his iniquities will descend to crown him.[7] Expositions of the Psalms 38.8.[8]

Our Head Is Christ. Arnobius the Younger: "Our head is Christ." When we do something against his precepts, our iniquities go over our head, and we are pressed as a heavy burden on us. Commentary on the Psalms 38.[9]

38:5 *Festering Wounds*

After the Fact. Chrysostom: If you wish to learn the foulness of sin, think of it after it has been committed, when you are rid of the evil desire, when its fires no longer cause disturbance, and then you will perceive what sin is. Homilies on the Gospel of John 52.[10]

The Foulness of Sin. Chrysostom: Sin is more foul than putrefaction itself. What, for instance, is more offensive than fornication? And if this is not perceived at the time of its commission, yet, after it is committed, its offensive nature, the impurity contracted in it, and the curse and the abomination of it is perceived. So it is with all sin. Before it is committed, it has something of pleasure, but after its commission, the pleasure ceases and fades away, and pain and shame succeed. But with righteousness it is the reverse. At the beginning it is attended with toil but in the end with pleasure and repose. Homilies on 1 Timothy 2.11.[11]

Eyes That See. Ambrose: Now look at some lascivious youth openly displaying his debauchery; his life is spent in love affairs; he lounges around like that rich man who was clothed in fine linen and purple; daily he enjoys the most sumptuous dinners; his pavements swim in wine; the ground is covered with flowers and strewn with fish bones; and the dining room is filled with the perfume of sweet-smelling incense. He is perfectly delighted with himself and flatters himself that he smells sweetly. . . . He does not know that his soul is bleeding and festering, and he will not accept that his wounds are foul-smelling. . . . But the holy prophet David found for himself a remedy of everlasting salvation. For he freely spoke of his own wounds and confessed that his sores were foul and festering because of his foolishness. . . . This world covers up its wounds and does not show them to the Lord. Better the foolishness that has eyes to see its sores than wisdom that has not. Commentary on Twelve Psalms 38.30-31.[12]

Only God Can Help. Fulgentius of Ruspe: Let not earth and ashes glory because in its life it has abandoned its inmost thoughts; wounded, let it not exult as if healthy concerning that which it thinks healthy in itself. But with the humility of an afflicted heart, let it meditate on the rottenness of its wounds in order that, crying out with the prophet, "My wounds grow foul and fester because of my foolishness," it can receive healing from the divine piety, not of its own merits but by a free gift. For what does a person have that he has not received? But if he has received, why is he glorying as if he had not received? Therefore, God alone can give to all to whom he wishes the means by which true salvation can be acquired. He alone is able to safeguard what he has given in the one receiving. Letter 4.4.[13]

The Cleansing of the Word. Methodius: For as the putrid humors and matter of flesh, and all those things that corrupt it, are driven out by salt, in the same manner all the irrational appetites . . . are banished from the body by

---

[7]Ps 7:16 (7:17 LXX). [8]WSA 3 16:152. [9]CCL 25:52. [10]FC 41:54. [11]NPNF 1 13:415. [12]ACTP 123-24. [13]FC 95:335.

divine teaching. For it must . . . be that the soul that is not sprinkled with the words of Christ, as with salt, should stink and breed worms, as King David, openly confessing with tears in the mountains, cried out, "My wounds stink and are corrupt," because he had not salted himself with the exercises of self-control and so subdued his carnal appetites, but [he] self-indulgently had yielded to them and became corrupted in adultery. BANQUET OF THE TEN VIRGINS 1.1.[14]

A FUTURE FRAGRANCE. AUGUSTINE: You only need a healthy sense of smell in spiritual matters to be aware how sins fester. The opposite to this reek of sin is the fragrance of which the apostle says, "We are the fragrance of Christ offered to God in every place, for those who are on the way to salvation."[15] But where does the fragrance come from? From hope. . . . We bewail the bad smell in this life, but already we catch the scent of the life to come. We bewail our stinking sins but breathe the fragrance of what awaits us. EXPOSITIONS OF THE PSALMS 38.9.[16]

38:6 Bowed Down

BEGINNING AND END. GREGORY OF NAZIANZUS: The very best order of beginning every speech and action is to begin from God and to end in God. IN DEFENSE OF HIS FLIGHT TO PONTUS, ORATION 2.1.[17]

BETTER TO HUMBLE YOURSELF. AUGUSTINE: If you humble yourself, you will be raised up; if you are proud and lofty, you will be bent down, for God will certainly find a weight to bend you down with. The weight he will use is the burden of your sins. It will be tied onto your head, and you will be bent over. EXPOSITIONS OF THE PSALMS 38.10.[18]

38:7 Filled with Burning

A CHANGE OF DESIRE. THEODORET OF CYR: So, he means, my handling of desire not fit-

tingly but wastefully proved the cause of these troubles. . . . From that desire [as he says in the next verse] I garnered the fruit, which was my stooping to earth, he is saying, and constant bewailing on account of my heart's bitter pangs. For this reason I changed the force of desire and made it a minister to the divine will. . . . Since once I used it wrongly, I shall always apply it to the benefit of your commands. COMMENTARY ON THE PSALMS 38.3-4.[19]

TRUTH AND FANTASY. AUGUSTINE: The soul is brimful of deceitful fantasies. . . . So insistent are they that we are scarcely permitted to pray. If we think about material things, we have no way of doing so except through images, and often intrusive images rush in on us, ones we are not seeking. We are tempted to pass from one to another, to flit here and there. Then you want to go back to your starting point and rid yourself of what you are currently thinking about, but something else occurs to you. You try to remember something you have forgotten, but it does not present itself to your mind; something else that you did not want comes instead. Where had that thing you had forgotten gone to? Why did it slip into your mind later, when you were no longer looking for it? While you were looking for it, innumerable other things occurred to you instead, things that were not required. . . . These illusions came in as a penalty, and the soul lost the truth, for just as the deceitful fantasies are the soul's punishment, so is truth the soul's reward. But when we were locked fast in those illusions, Truth came to us. He found us immersed in them, so he took our flesh, or rather took flesh from us, from the human race. He made himself visible to eyes of flesh in order to heal by faith those to whom he meant to manifest the truth, so that once those eyes were healed, truth might begin to dawn on them. He himself is the truth, and this truth he promised

---

[14]ANF 6:311.　[15]2 Cor 2:15.　[16]WSA 3 16:153.　[17]NPNF 2 7:205.
[18]WSA 3 16:153.　[19]FC 101:230.

us when his flesh was made visible, so that there might be implanted in us the beginnings of that faith whose reward is truth. Expositions of the Psalms 38.11.[20]

38:9 Sighing

Silence of the Heart. Augustine: The chilling of charity is the silence of the heart; the blazing of charity is the heart's clamor. Expositions of the Psalms 38.14.[21]

38:10 Light Gone

Depression and Deprivation. Theodoret of Cyr: By these statements he implies two things: both the extraordinary degree of depression, by which the light does not even seem to be light, and the deprivation of divine care, which he rightly called "light of my eyes." Commentary on the Psalms 38.4.[22]

38:12 Those Who Seek My Life

Evil Thoughts. Athanasius: People who cling to evil thoughts do not stand for truth but for falsehood. They do not stand for righteousness but for iniquity, because their tongue learns to speak lies. They have done evil, never pausing so that they could repent. Persevering with delight in wicked actions, they run to them without even looking back. They even tread underfoot the commandment about neighbors, and instead of loving them, they plot evil against them. As the ancient saint testifies, "Those who plot evil against me have spoken lies and plan treachery all day long." Festal Letters 9.4.[23]

38:13 Like One Who Does Not Speak

Silent Like the Lord. Ambrose: The just person will want to conform his life to the image and likeness of Jesus, and though accused, he will be silent; if he is hurt, he will forgive. Wrongs done to him he will cover up, not opening his mouth. In this way he will be imitating him who like a lamb was led to the slaughter, never opening his mouth.[24] Though he could have made an answer, he preferred silence to speech. For the Lord Jesus was silent when they accused him, and when they struck him he did not strike back. . . . You too, my friend, if you are given cause to answer back with a sharp rebuke, be silent. It will be better so. If you answer back in the same tone as your aggressor, it could lead to uproar and loud wrangling. Better to hide the injury done to you than, by arguing back, to gain some point or other. Good is the dumb person who knows not how to speak evil and from whose lips no injurious words can pass. Truly blessed is this dumb person, for inwardly he is saying, "Lord, give me a learned tongue when it is my duty to break into speech."[25] Commentary on Twelve Psalms 38.45.[26]

38:14 No Rebukes

The Patience of David. Theodoret of Cyr: History teaches this more clearly. Even when Absalom mounted a case against his father and drew to his side those who had lost cases in judgment, blessed David was long-suffering. When Shimei berated him with voice and hand upraised, he took the abuse in silence; and he forbade Abishai to try to exact justice against the culprit in the words, "Let him curse me because the Lord bade him curse David."[27] Commentary on the Psalms 38.6.[28]

Deaf, Dumb and Blind. John Cassian: You should walk as one that is deaf and dumb and blind, so that, putting aside the contemplation of him who has been rightly chosen by you as your model of perfection, you should be like one who is blind and not see any of those things that you find to be unedifying. Nor should you be

---

[20]WSA 3 16:154*. [21]WSA 3 16:157. [22]FC 101:230. [23]ARL 151. [24]Cf. Jer 11:19. [25]Cf. Is 50:4. [26]ACTP 133-34. [27]2 Sam 16:9-11. [28]FC 101:231.

influenced by the authority or fashion of those who do these things and give yourself up to what is worse and what you formerly condemned. If you hear anyone disobedient or insubordinate or disparaging another or doing anything different from what was taught to you, you should not go wrong and be led astray by such an example to imitate him, but, "like one who is deaf," as if you had never heard it, you should pass it all by. INSTITUTES 4.41.[29]

38:15 Waiting for the Lord

UNWAVERING. CASSIODORUS: In the course of his harsh disasters his trust never failed. He continually hoped in the Lord, who can transform sadness into joy. EXPLANATION OF THE PSALMS 38.16.[30]

THE COURT OF GOD. AUGUSTINE: In this saying he has advised you what to do, if you find yourself in trouble. . . . Guard your innocence within yourself, where no one seeks to undermine your case. Perhaps false evidence has swayed the verdict against you, but this is so only in the human court; will it have any weight with God, before whom your case is to be heard? When God is judge, there will be no other witness than your own conscience. Between the just judge and your own conscience you will have nothing to fear except the state of your case itself. If your case is not a bad one, you need be terrified of no plaintiff, and you need neither rebut a lying witness nor call a truthful one. Simply arm yourself with a good conscience, so that you may say, "You will hear me, O Lord my God, because in you, Lord, I have trusted." EXPOSITIONS OF THE PSALMS 38.21.[31]

38:16 Let Them Not Rejoice

WHY ENEMIES REJOICE. AUGUSTINE: In the conditions of this life it sometimes happens that our feet slip, and we slide into some sin. Then the wicked tongues of our enemies get busy, and

from their reaction we understand what their objective has been all along, even though they did not admit it. They comment harshly, with no hint of gentleness, delighted to have found what they ought to have deplored. "I said, Let my enemies never gloat over me"; yes, I prayed so, yet perhaps for my correction you have made them speak unrestrainedly against me "when my feet slip." EXPOSITIONS OF THE PSALMS 38.22.[32]

38:17 Ready to Fall

THE FATHER'S DISCIPLINE. AUGUSTINE: Every son or daughter must be whipped. So universal is this rule that even he who was without sin was not exempt. EXPOSITIONS OF THE PSALMS 38.23.[33]

I LONG FOR TREATMENT. THEODORET OF CYR: Sin made me deserve whipping, he is saying; thus I submit myself to punishment. I long for treatment at your hands, pricked as I am by the pangs of sin. COMMENTARY ON THE PSALMS 38.7.[34]

38:21 Do Not Forsake Me

A GOD WHO SAVES. AMBROSE: Lord, you heal and are not polluted; you help and are not contaminated; for you are a God who saves. Your hands, O Lord, do not lose those that are your own but heal them. COMMENTARY ON TWELVE PSALMS 38.57.[35]

38:22 O Lord, My Salvation

A FUTURE SALVATION. AUGUSTINE: This is the salvation the prophets sought to discover, as the apostle Peter says. They did not receive what they sought, but they inquired about it and foretold it, and now we have come along and found what they sought. Yet we have not received it either, and others will be born after us who

---

[29]NPNF 2 11:232-33*. [30]ACW 51:384. [31]WSA 3 16:162. [32]WSA 3 16:162. [33]WSA 3 16:163. [34]FC 101:231. [35]ACTP 141.

will also find yet not receive, and they too will pass away, so that at the day's end we may all receive together, along with the patriarchs and prophets and apostles, . . . everlasting salvation. Contemplating God's glory and seeing him face to face we shall be enabled to praise him forever, without wearying, without any of the pain of iniquity, without any of the perversion of sin. We shall praise God, no longer sighing for him but united with him for whom we have sighed even to the end, albeit joyful in our hope. For we shall be in that city where God is our good, God is our light, God is our bread, God is our life. Whatever is good for us, whatever we miss as we trudge along our pilgrim way, we shall find in him. EXPOSITIONS OF THE PSALMS 38.28.[36]

[36]WSA 3 16:166-67.

39:1-13 INTIMATIONS OF MORTALITY

If . . . you wish to pray on your own behalf as the enemy prepares the attacks,
there is all the more reason, in arming yourself for the battle,
to sing the words of Psalm 39.

ATHANASIUS ON THE INTERPRETATION OF THE PSALMS 19 [OIP 68]

To the choirmaster: to Jeduthun.
A Psalm of David.

[1]I said, "I will guard my ways,
that I may not sin with my tongue;
I will bridle[y] my mouth,
 so long as the wicked are in my presence."
[2]I was dumb and silent,
 I held my peace to no avail;
my distress grew worse,
 [3]my heart became hot within me.
As I mused, the fire burned;
 then I spoke with my tongue:

[4]"LORD, let me know my end,
 and what is the measure of my days;
 let me know how fleeting my life is!
[5]Behold, thou hast made my days a few
 handbreadths,

and my lifetime is as nothing in thy sight.
Surely every man stands as a mere breath!
Selah

[6]Surely man goes about as a shadow!
Surely for nought are they in turmoil;
 man heaps up, and knows not who will
 gather!

[7]"And now, Lord, for what do I wait?
 My hope is in thee.
[8]Deliver me from all my transgressions.
 Make me not the scorn of the fool!
[9]I am dumb, I do not open my mouth;
 for it is thou who hast done it.
[10]Remove thy stroke from me;
 I am spent by the blows[z] of thy hand.
[11]When thou dost chasten man
 with rebukes for sin,
thou dost consume like a moth what is dear

306

to him;*
surely every man is a mere breath!
Selah

[12] "Hear my prayer, O LORD,
and give ear to my cry;

hold not thy peace at my tears!
For I am thy passing guest,
a sojourner, like all my fathers.
[13]Look away from me, that I may know
gladness,
before I depart and be no more!"

y Heb *muzzle* z Heb *hostility* * LXX *you make his life consume away like a spider's web*

OVERVIEW: The thirty-ninth psalm instructs us on how to endure hardship (THEODORE OF MOPSUESTIA). David determined in his heart not to sin and put a guard on his mouth (DIODORE). Here we see the just person's cloister (AMBROSE), a response contrary to most (THEODORE OF MOPSUESTIA). It behooves us to be deaf, dumb and blind to sin (JOHN CASSIAN), and there is a great advantage to silence (AMBROSE). But there is also a problematic silence (HESYCHIUS) and a silence brought on by temptation (EVAGRIUS). David's heart grew hot, which leads to the question, What sets you on fire (ORIGEN)? David placed his focus on the true end of all (AMBROSE), true being (AUGUSTINE), the greatest measure (DIODORE), the knowledge of God (EVAGRIUS). We make a humbling comparison of our life with his (AUGUSTINE, THEODORE OF MOPSUESTIA). Our life is transitory (GREGORY OF NAZIANZUS), measured by his heavenly hand (AMBROSE). Our condition is made harsh on account of our fallenness (AUGUSTINE). But we are undergoing a great transition (AUGUSTINE).

The Lord is our hope (AMBROSE), our endurance (ORIGEN). We have a sin problem (AMBROSE) for which mercy is needed (CASSIODORUS). The one who permits suffering is the one from whom help comes (DIODORE). The one who wounds is the one who heals (AMBROSE), for his correction is for our good (DIODORE). Our condition is extremely fragile (AUGUSTINE). Our one concern should be our salvation (THEODORE OF MOPSUESTIA). Forgiveness of sins brings a different perspective on death (JEROME). So let us petition the Lord for forgiveness (AMBROSE), for now is the time for repentance (JEROME).

Superscription: *To Jeduthun, of David*

HOW TO ENDURE. THEODORE OF MOPSUESTIA: This psalm . . . is instructive beyond any other, capable of giving more than adequate instruction in how to give evidence of endurance in the midst of hardships. COMMENTARY ON PSALMS 39.1.[1]

39:1 Guarding One's Ways

DETERMINED NOT TO SIN. DIODORE OF TARSUS: "I said" [has] the sense, "I determined," his meaning being, I determined within myself not to sin against my oppressor simply in action but also not to say anything against him by word of mouth, especially since what is initially verbal abuse turns to physical abuse, and the person who is determined not to do physical harm ought not have recourse to verbal abuse. COMMENTARY ON PSALMS 39.[2]

THE JUST PERSON'S CLOISTER. AMBROSE: Have no doubt about it, when people annoy and torment you when you are doing the right thing, those people are the lackeys of the wickedest sinner of all. They are slaves of the author of every evil deed. David saw this with prophetic eyes and recognized the face of the evil one. So he kept quiet. He had no wish whatever to do the will of the evil one. So he kept quiet. He had no wish whatever to do the will of him who ruins one's peace of mind. He simply said nothing. He closed his doors in silence; patience lay before him, and silence kept a sleepless vigil. No enemy

---

[1]WGRW 5:463. [2]WGRW 9:125.

could creep in, and from his cloistered lips no ambivalent speech, no heedless talk, could issue forth. Mightier far is the patient person who can govern himself than the valiant one who captures citadels.[3] The just person is his own cloister; he is his own eternal guard. COMMENTARY ON TWELVE PSALMS 39.6.[4]

CONTRARY TO MOST. THEODORE OF MOPSUESTIA: It is a universal custom to be upset when you see your plans at the mercy of sinners, and to be upset also at your own misfortunes, especially when you are badly treated by wrongdoers while conscious of your own virtuous behavior. The general run of people react to such developments by turning to criticism and displeasure with the God of all. Hence, blessed David says, "I shall guard my ways so as not to sin with my tongue": I kept my words to myself, that is, I made a decision and judgment to guard myself against any sin. COMMENTARY ON PSALMS 39.2.[5]

39:2 Silent

BE SILENT. JOHN CASSIAN: If insults are offered to you or to anyone else, or wrongs done, be immovable, and as far as an answer in retaliation is concerned, be silent "as one that is dumb," always singing in your heart this verse of the psalmist. INSTITUTES 4.41.[6]

THE ADVANTAGE OF SILENCE. AMBROSE: If you know there is sin, be silent. Do not add to your guilt by denying it. If you are not aware of sin, be silent. You are secure in your innocence. The reports of other people cannot nail any sin to a conscience that knows itself to be innocent. COMMENTARY ON TWELVE PSALMS 39.13.[7]

A PROBLEMATIC SILENCE. HESYCHIUS OF JERUSALEM: When he was silent he ceased from good, that is, from the meditation of the Law, which is the teacher of good. When the grief of the sin renewed, the wound from sin became more serious, as when we lead others from meditation on the

Law. It becomes a festering sore, having applied no medicine from divine precepts. And so he has not stood in silence, but when he had returned to his senses, he cast out that very thing bringing such harm to his spirit. He shows this by "my heart grew hot." LARGE COMMENTARY ON PSALMS 39.3.[8]

THE SILENCE OF TEMPTATION. EVAGRIUS OF PONTUS: In temptation, good words flee from us and the spirit is silent. The soul speaks about those temptations that it recognizes and is silent about those it does not. In this place "good" indicates the virtues and knowledge that flee in the time of temptation. NOTES ON THE PSALMS 38[39].3.[9]

39:3 A Heart Grown Hot

WHAT SETS YOU ON FIRE? ORIGEN: In the Gospel it was written, after the Lord spoke to Cleopas, "Was not our heart burning within us when he opened the Scriptures to us?"[10] Where will you burn? Where will "the coals of fire" be found in you who are never set on fire by the declaration of the Lord, never inflamed by the words of the Holy Spirit? Hear also . . . David . . . saying, "My heart burned within me, and in my meditation fire became inflamed." From where do you glow? Where is the fire kindled in you? HOMILIES ON LEVITICUS 9.9.7.[11]

39:4 The Measure of Days

THE TRUE END. AMBROSE: It is not that he was enquiring about his own death—death is not the end of one who will rise again—but rather his enquiry concerned that end of which the apostle speaks: "Afterwards there will be the end, when he shall have delivered up the kingdom to God and the Father"[12] . . . Evil will fade to nothingness, and eternal good will take its place. . . .

---

[3]Cf. Prov 16:32. [4]ACTP 145-46*. [5]WGRW 5:465. [6]NPNF 2 11:233. [7]ACTP 149-150. [8]PG 93:1192. [9]PG 12:1388. [10]Lk 24:18, 32. [11]FC 83:198*. [12]1 Cor 15:24.

That, surely, is the true end. It is not the end of one person alone, but the end of all. Why then does David say "my end"? But consider a moment who it is that is speaking. He speaks as humankind or as one representing men and sharing the same substance as they; he is one who stands for all, is in the likeness of all and is truly versed in that perfection that belongs to the consummate man. COMMENTARY ON TWELVE PSALMS 39.16.[13]

THE TRUE BEING OF MY DAYS. AUGUSTINE: But here the prayer is not simply, "Make me know the number of my days," but "Make me know the number of them that 'is.'" What does that mean? . . . These days of ours do not have being; they depart almost before they arrive, and when they do arrive they cannot stand still. They join onto each other; they follow one another and cannot hold themselves together. Nothing of the past can be called back, and the future that we await will pass away; as long as it has not come, we do not possess it, and when it has come, we cannot keep hold of it. . . . What I am seeking is the simple "is." I seek the true "is," . . . which is the bride of my Lord, where there will be no death, no deficiency, where the day passes not but abides, the day that is preceded by no yesterday and hustled on by no tomorrow. "Make known to me the number of my days," this number, "the number that is." EXPOSITIONS OF THE PSALMS 39.7.[14]

THE GREATEST MEASURE. DIODORE OF TARSUS: Not even all the possessions amassed nor all humankind, if measured by their lifetime, from Adam to the last human being—not even this measure is anything in comparison with the measure of your life, Lord. COMMENTARY ON PSALMS 39.[15]

THE KNOWLEDGE OF GOD. EVAGRIUS OF PONTUS: The end of the rational nature is the understanding of the holy Trinity. NOTES ON THE PSALMS 38[39].5.[16]

A HUMBLING COMPARISON. AUGUSTINE: With

my eyes on him who is, and comparing with him these present things that have no being in that sense, I shall see that what I lack is greater than what I have, and so I shall be more humbled about what is missing than elated about what is at hand. EXPOSITIONS OF THE PSALMS 39.8.[17]

39:5 A Few Handbreadths

MEASUREMENT OF A HANDBREADTH. THEODORE OF MOPSUESTIA: By handbreadths he means not, as many commentators believed, that he made us for fighting, certain commentators of this mind being swept away to the extremes of fairy tales. Instead, since handbreadth refers to the hand measurements made by women in weaving garments, he meant here, you wove my life as with a kind of measurement, not making it indeterminate and without conditions but subjecting it to time limits. "And my being is as nothing before you": you measured my life in such a way that my existence and constitution are counted as nothing in comparison with you. COMMENTARY ON PSALMS 39.6A-B.[18]

TRANSITORY LIFE. GREGORY OF NAZIANZUS: Such, brothers, is our life, we whose existence is so transitory. Such is the game we play on earth: we do not exist, and we are born, and being born we are dissolved. We are a fleeting dream, an apparition without substance, the flight of a bird that passes, a ship that leaves no trace on the sea. We are dust, a vapor, the morning dew, a flower growing but a moment and withering in a moment. "A person's days are as grass: as the flower of the field, so shall he flourish."[19] Beautifully has holy David meditated on our weakness . . . and he defines the days of a person as the measure of a span. ON HIS BROTHER ST. CAESARIUS, ORATION 7.19.[20]

HIS HEAVENLY HAND. AMBROSE: God, who knows precisely the allotted days of each one

---

[13]ACTP 152*. [14]WSA 3 16:176-78. [15]WGRW 9:126. [16]PG 12:1389. [17]WSA 3 16:178*. [18]WGRW 5:477-79. [19]Ps 103:15 (102:15 LXX). [20]FC 22:19*.

of us, regards nothing as immeasurable. His knowledge embraces the measure of all things. To him nothing is beyond his understanding, nothing is unweighed, nothing is unmeasured, nothing is unnumbered. He says, "The very hairs of your head have been numbered."[21] . . . We know that God is said to have measured the heavens with the palm of his hand[22]— the palm, from thumb to little finger, being the span by which a thing is measured and its length ascertained. Those who accept this reading understand that our days are measured or numbered, and in that sense they are short. However, the all-knowing God has measured, as we said above, and fully comprehends the very heavens. . . . The prophet's days are not short but great, for God has measured them with the same palm as that with which he measured the heavens. Commentary on Twelve Psalms 39.20-21.[23]

Fallen Image. Augustine: Mortal life is a harsh condition. What else is its birth but an entry into a life of toil? Even the infant's cry bears witness to the toil that awaits it. From this burdensome banquet no one is excused. We must drink of the chalice that Adam has filled for us. We have been fashioned by the hands of Truth; yet, on account of sin, we were cast out in the day of vanity. We have been fashioned to the image of God, but we have marred that image by sinful transgression. Thus the psalm reminds us how we have been made and to what state we have fallen. Sermon 60.2.[24]

A Great Transition. Augustine: As we regard our sin, our mortality, our fleeting seasons, our groaning and toil and sweat, the stages of our life that succeed one another and will not stand still but slip by imperceptibly from infancy to old age, as we regard all these, let us see in them the old self, the old day, the old song, the Old Covenant. But when we turn to our inner being, to all that is destined to be renewed in us and replace the things subject to change, let

us find there the new self, the new day, the new song, the New Covenant, and let us love this newness so dearly that the oldness we meet there does not frighten us. As we run our race, we are passing from the old things to the new. This transition is effected as the old things decay and the inner are made new, until our outer decaying self pays its debt to nature and meets its death, though it too will be renewed at the resurrection. Then all things that at the present are new only in hope will be made new in very truth. Expositions of the Psalms 39.9.[25]

39:7 Hope in God

God Is My Hope. Ambrose: Our hope and our patience is Christ; he is our redemption;[26] he is our expectation. . . . Look on us, Lord, when you come in judgment; let your mercy look on us. . . . In the power of your mercy lies the substance of our soul and life. We must not fear physical death; rather, we should fear him who can save or destroy our soul.[27] Our soul's substance is that virtue that God has poured into hearts made in the image of himself. Commentary on Twelve Psalms 39.28.[28]

Our Endurance. Origen: We will have to say that if we give in to troubles, we do not believe in him insofar as he is endurance; and if we are weak, we have not believed in him insofar as he is strength. Commentary on the Gospel of John 19.157.[29]

39:8 Deliverance from Transgressions

Our Sin Problem. Ambrose: It is not merely one lapse that he is confessing, for he prays to be forgiven all his iniquities. He knows that without God's forgiveness no one can be saved. For we were born in sin. We have inherited a stain. Our

---

[21]Lk 12:7. [22]Cf. Is 40:12. [23]ACTP 154*. [24]FC 11:260*. [25]WSA 3 16:179. [26]Cf. Eph 1:7. [27]Cf. Mt 10:28. [28]ACTP 158. [29]FC 89:203.

human condition has a congenital tendency to sin. COMMENTARY ON TWELVE PSALMS 39.29.[30]

MERCY IS NEEDED. CASSIODORUS: Although this holy man applied himself with edifying devotion, he nonetheless asks to be freed by the Lord's pity from all his iniquities. EXPLANATION OF THE PSALMS 39.9.[31]

39:9 God Has Done It

DIVINE PERMISSION AND HELP. DIODORE OF TARSUS: For my part, I realized that this happens to me with your permission, and I waited longer in the knowledge that I would receive help from the same quarter from which comes also the allowance of my suffering. COMMENTARY ON PSALMS 39.[32]

39:10 The Blows of God's Hand

HE WOUNDS AND HEALS. AMBROSE: The strong hand strikes as though harshly, but it is swift to heal. If it is powerful to wound, it is also powerful when it comes to applying a remedy. As the Lord says, "I will strike, and I will heal."[33] ... This hand of the Lord took from Job all that he had and gave it all back again. In fact, he greatly added to Job's store of good things, even doubling what he had before. Do not be troubled because David says he has fainted. A person can faint and rise up stronger than before. "The Lord lifts up all that fall and sets up all that are cast down."[34] Whoever is corrected will rise up with virtue. COMMENTARY ON TWELVE PSALMS 39.33.[35]

39:11 Like a Moth

FOR OUR GOOD. DIODORE OF TARSUS: I realize that all your scourging proves to be for a person's correction and betterment; it is not as though you were indifferent to human beings in allowing them to suffer, instead preferring to improve their souls. COMMENTARY ON PSALMS 39.[36]

POINTLESS ANXIETY. AUGUSTINE: The psalmist returns now to the truth of which he reminded us earlier. However much progress a person has made here, "all human anxiety in this life is pointless," for we live in uncertainty. Which of us can be secure even about the good in ourselves? We fret in vain. Each of us must cast our anxiety on the Lord, cast on him whatever worries us, believing that he will sustain and protect us. What is certain on this earth? Only death. . . . You have made some progress, have you? You know what you are today, but you do not know what you will be tomorrow. . . . You hope to get money, but whether it will come your way is uncertain. You hope to find a wife, but it is uncertain whether you will find one, or what she will be like if you do. You hope to have children, but you cannot be certain that any will be born. If they are born, it is not certain that they will survive. If they do live, you cannot know whether they will grow up well or prove to be weaklings. Whichever way you turn, everything is uncertain, except for one sole certainty: death. If you are poor, there is no certainty that you will ever be rich; if you are uneducated, you cannot be certain of being taught; if you are in poor health, it is uncertain whether you can recover your strength. You have been born, and so you can at least be certain that you will die, but even in this certainty of death uncertainty lurks, because you do not know the day of your death. We live beset with uncertainties, holding one thing only as certain, that we shall die, but without even the certainty of when that will be. The only thing we ultimately fear is the one thing that we cannot possibly avoid. "All human anxiety in this life is pointless." EXPOSITIONS OF THE PSALMS 39.19.[37]

OUR ONE CONCERN. THEODORE OF MOPSUESTIA: So this is what should concern us, being rescued from sins and attaining reconciliation

---

[30]ACTP 159. [31]ACW 51:393. [32]WGRW 9:127. [33]Deut 32:39. [34]Ps 145:14 (144:14 LXX). [35]ACTP 161. [36]WGRW 9:127. [37]WSA 3 16:190.

with you, which results in complete resolution of problems, and not taking pains over other things, which are futile and useless for the painstaker, never bringing one an outcome for the pains or providing one with lasting benefit from the pains. COMMENTARY ON PSALMS 39.12C.[38]

39:12 A Sojourner

A DIFFERENT PERSPECTIVE. JEROME: What the psalmist means is: As long as I am in this body, I am unhappy. Who of us could say that? If we are octogenarians, we are afraid to die; if we are centenarians and sick besides, still we cling to life and beg for respite. Why do we do that? Because sin gnaws at our conscience. We know that if we leave our body, we are going not to Christ but to hell. On the contrary, what does the apostle say? "I desire to depart and to be with Christ."[39] Give me freedom from anxiety, for after death I am going to be with Christ; even now I long to die. So our psalmist, because he is one who loves the Lord, cries: Unhappy man that I am, because my sojourn is prolonged! HOMILY ON PSALM 119[120].[40]

39:13 To Know Gladness

FORGIVE ME. AMBROSE: Forgive me, so that I need no longer be a pilgrim and a wayfarer. Forgive me so that I may be called home from exile. If you forgive me, before I go from this place, I shall no longer be an exile and a pilgrim. Once you will have forgiven me, I will no longer be in foreign parts. I shall be a fellow citizen of your saints; I shall be with my ancestors, who were pilgrims before me and are now truly citizens. I shall be a member of God's household. I shall not dread punishment but shall merit grace through our Lord Jesus; with whom, Lord God, be praise to you, and honor and glory forever; now and always and for ages of ages. Amen. COMMENTARY ON TWELVE PSALMS 39.39.[41]

NOW IS THE TIME. JEROME: Grant me a little time that I may repent for my sins, for in hell no one has the power to confess his sins. HOMILY ON PSALM 103[104].[42]

---

[38]WGRW 5:487. [39]Phil 1:23. [40]FC 48:311. [41]ACTP 165. [42]FC 48:229.

40:1-17 WAITING PATIENTLY

During the attack, as you suffer the afflictions
and wish to learn the advantage of steadfast patience, sing [Psalm] 40.

ATHANASIUS ON THE INTERPRETATION OF THE PSALMS 19 [OIP 68]

To the choirmaster. A Psalm of David.

¹*I waited patiently for the LORD;*
he inclined to me and heard my cry.
²*He drew me up from the desolate pit,ᵃ*

out of the miry bog,
and set my feet upon a rock,
making my steps secure.
³*He put a new song in my mouth,*
a song of praise to our God.

Many will see and fear,
and put their trust in the LORD.

⁴Blessed is the man who makes
the LORD his trust,
who does not turn to the proud,
to those who go astray after false gods!
⁵Thou hast multiplied, O LORD my God,
thy wondrous deeds and thy thoughts
toward us;
none can compare with thee!
Were I to proclaim and tell of them,
they would be more than can be numbered.

⁶Sacrifice and offering thou dost not desire;
but thou hast given me an open ear.ᵇ
Burnt offering and sin offering
thou hast not required.
⁷Then I said, "Lo, I come;
in the roll of the book it is written of me;
⁸I delight to do thy will, O my God;
thy law is within my heart."

⁹I have told the glad news of deliverance
in the great congregation;
lo, I have not restrained my lips,
as thou knowest, O LORD.
¹⁰I have not hid thy saving help within my
heart,
I have spoken of thy faithfulness and thy
salvation;
I have not concealed thy steadfast love and
thy faithfulness

from the great congregation.

¹¹Do not thou, O LORD, withhold
thy mercy from me,
let thy steadfast love and thy faithfulness
ever preserve me!
¹²For evils have encompassed me
without number;
my iniquities have overtaken me,
till I cannot see;
they are more than the hairs of my head;
my heart fails me.

¹³Be pleased, O LORD, to deliver me!
O LORD, make haste to help me!
¹⁴Let them be put to shame and confusion
altogether
who seek to snatch away my life;
let them be turned back and brought to
dishonor
who desire my hurt!
¹⁵Let them be appalled because of their
shame
who say to me, "Aha, Aha!"

¹⁶But may all who seek thee
rejoice and be glad in thee;
may those who love thy salvation
say continually, "Great is the LORD!"
¹⁷As for me, I am poor and needy;
but the Lord takes thought for me.
Thou art my help and my deliverer;
do not tarry, O my God!

a Cn: Heb *pit of tumult*   b Heb *ears thou hast dug for me*

OVERVIEW: The fortieth psalm follows the thirty-ninth as an answer to a prayer (ARNOBIUS THE YOUNGER). David functions as a type (THEODORET) of the new people in Christ (PSEUDO-ATHANASIUS). The pit is evil, and the rock is Christ (EVAGRIUS, CASSIODORUS). He is the One who has come to save us (AMBROSE). We sing the song of those renewed (EVAGRIUS), a song of God's favor (THEODORET), not to manipulate God but to praise him (AUGUSTINE). Righteousness is granted by him as a gift of grace to the one who believes (AUGUSTINE, CASSIODORUS). Great are the wonders of divine providence (THEODORET).

Christ offered himself as a voluntary sacrifice (HILARY OF POITIERS). He came in fulfillment of Old Testament types (CASSIODORUS). The book prophesying Christ refers to the Psalms (ARNObius the Younger) or the law and the prophets (Pseudo-Athanasius), which is the entire Scripture (Didymus). Our sacrifice is prefigured in him. He is the true sacrifice (Theodoret), offered according to his own will and the Father's (Jerome) for our sake (Ambrose). The message of grace (Chrysostom) has been declared, and the church throughout the world responds in worship (Theodoret). We must maintain a true and bold witness in the world (Augustine) of righteousness imputed by grace (Ambrose).

The great congregation includes those who have believed from Israel, past and present (Pseudo-Athanasius). In Christ, mercy and truth meet (Cassiodorus), and we are guided by love and fear (Augustine). We are not yet perfect (Theodoret). We have nothing of our own (Augustine) but are totally dependant on Christ (John Cassian). We are totally in his care (Augustine).

Superscription: *A Psalm of David*

An Answer to Prayer. Arnobius the Younger: The speaker in the previous psalm said, "What is my expectation? Is it not the Lord?"[1] Now, in this psalm, he says, Patiently, I awaited the Lord and he attended to me. He who said, "Hear my prayer," now says, "He heard my prayer." What have you prayed? I prayed that you may lead my thinking from the pit of misery and mud of desire, which is called clay, and set my feet on the rock so that I not be moved beyond by blowing winds, that is, from unclean spirits giving aid. He directs my steps; then he will give my mouth a new song. He sings not reckoning himself, or to Pharaoh, for there is no deliverance without God, but he sings a hymn to God, in whom we will have strength, and he himself will reduce our enemies to nothing. Commentary on the Psalms 40.[2]

David, a Type. Theodoret of Cyr: Some people applied this psalm to blessed Jeremiah, others to the remarkable Daniel, since the one

and the other were thrown into a pit and the psalm's opening mentions a pit; they were led to that interpretation by attending to the one verse. Some, [by contrast], claimed the psalm fits the situation of the captives dwelling in Babylon. For my part, however, I believe it was written to address the events affecting David as a type and refers to the whole human race, who receive the hope of resurrection from our God and Savior. Now, it is the divinely inspired Paul who guides us to this understanding, quoting individual verses in the epistle to the Hebrews. Commentary on the Psalms 40.1.[3]

A New People. Pseudo-Athanasius: He sings this psalm in the person of the new people, who waited for the Lord and were lifted up from the deep pit of sin, which like mud fouls those who are held in it. And he raised their feet onto a rock—Christ—and put into their mouth a new hymn—of the gospel of God who worked many miracles without number. He inclined to me and heard my cry. Exposition on Psalms 40.[4]

40:2 *From a Bog to a Rock*

The Pit and the Rock. Evagrius of Pontus: The pit of misery is evil and ignorance.... The rock is faith in Christ. "And he directs my steps" by actions and true teachings. Notes on the Psalms 39[40].3.[5]

Our Spiritual Rock. Cassiodorus: Just as mud in a lake is foul-smelling and oppressive, so the sins of people are slimy, for they smell foul and drown us with their weight. Then he sets our feet on a rock when we walk in the commands of the Lord Christ, for he is our spiritual Rock that does not allow the feet planted on it to sink. Explanation of the Psalms 40.3.[6]

Christ, the Savior. Ambrose: Christ has

---

[1]Ps 39:7 (38:8 lxx). [2]CCL 25:55-56. [3]FC 101:237. [4]CSCO 387:25-26. [5]PG 12:1409. [6]ACW 51:398*.

heard the prayer of his own servants and has brought us out from the pit of misery and from the mire of dregs. We were drowning there; our whole flesh was clinging to the mire, trapped in the whirlpool of our sins. Our soul was powerless to save itself; fallen and ruined as it was by the multiplicity and dreadfulness of our offenses. Thanks be to the Lord Jesus, God's only Son, who came down from heaven to forgive us our sins.[7] He came to save us from the pit and slime of this world, from the mud and mire of this earth, from this body doomed to death.[8] In his own flesh he has restored our soul and steadied our tottering footsteps. Strengthened by God's Word and absolved through the cross of our Lord's body, we walk no longer in the shame and disfigurement of vice but in the forgiveness of sin. Rooted and built in Christ,[9] David declares that the Lord has set his feet on a rock. As the apostle says, "They drank of the spiritual rock that followed them, and the rock was Christ."[10] May that rock, which follows those who thirst, confirm the weak and unsteady; may that water never be lacking to those who long for it; and may that firm foundation never be wanting to those in danger of falling. COMMENTARY ON TWELVE PSALMS 40.2.[11]

40:3 A New Song

THE SONG OF THOSE RENEWED. EVAGRIUS OF PONTUS: After we are made free from all unbridled emotion, we sing a new song, having been renewed in our home. NOTES ON THE PSALMS 39[40].4.[12]

A SONG OF GOD'S FAVOR. THEODORET OF CYR: In place of the impious worship of the idols I was taught to sing the praises of the true God and offer a song—not an old one but a new one, suited to the new favors. I no longer make supplication in dirges, you see; instead, I sing of the favors. So this is related, as I said, to the sufferings of David as a type and to the favors done to him. And it is related in particular to the human race sunken to the very depths of sin and consigned

to death but retrieved through the incarnation of our Savior and given the hope of resurrection. COMMENTARY ON THE PSALMS 40.3.[13]

PRAISE, NOT MANIPULATION. AUGUSTINE: A hymn is a song of praise. Make sure when you call on God that you do so in praise and not in an attempt to coerce him. If you invoke God, begging him to suppress your enemy, or if you invoke God as your ally when you are minded to make merry over someone else's misfortune, you are making him collude with your malice. And if you do that, you are not calling on him with praise but trying to manipulate him. EXPOSITIONS OF THE PSALMS 40.4.[14]

40:4 Making the Lord His Trust

RIGHTEOUS BY FAITH. AUGUSTINE: Who are these righteous people? Believers, clearly, because it is the one who lives by faith who is just. EXPOSITIONS OF THE PSALMS 40.6.[15]

THE ETERNAL SAVIOR. CASSIODORUS: The name of the Lord is the eternal Savior, and trust is put in his name by one who believes that he is to be saved not by his own merits but by the Lord through grace. EXPLANATION OF THE PSALMS 40.5.[16]

40:5 God's Wondrous Deeds

WONDERS OF DIVINE PROVIDENCE. THEODORET OF CYR: The wonders performed by your power, he is saying, defy counting and all description: there is no one who can do the like. While your creation is great and beautiful, what you arrange time after time in your providence surpasses human praise—in Egypt, in the wilderness, in the case of Moses, in the case of Joshua, in the case of Samuel, and

---

[7]Cf. Col 1:12-14. [8]Cf. Rom 7:24. [9]Cf. Col 2:7. [10]1 Cor 10:4. [11]ACTP 166-67. [12]PG 12:1409. [13]FC 101:238. [14]WSA 3 16:199. [15]WSA 3 16:201. [16]ACW 51:399.

earlier instances than those, having to do with Abraham, Isaac, Jacob, the royalty Joseph gained through slavery, not to mention all the other cases individually. COMMENTARY ON THE PSALMS 40.4.[17]

40:6 Sacrifice and Offering

A VOLUNTARY SACRIFICE. HILARY OF POITIERS: [Christ] offered himself to the death of the accursed that he might break the curse of the Law, offering himself voluntarily a victim to God the Father, in order that by means of a voluntary victim the curse that attended the discontinuance of the regular victim might be removed. Now of this sacrifice mention is made in another passage of the psalms: "Sacrifice and offering you did not desire, but a body have you prepared for me"; that is, by offering to God the Father, who refused the legal sacrifices, the acceptable offering of the body that he received. Of this offering the holy apostle thus speaks: "For this he did once for all when he offered himself up,"[18] securing complete salvation for the human race by the offering of this holy, perfect victim. HOMILY ON PSALM 53(54).13.[19]

40:7 In the Roll of the Book

FULFILLMENT OF THE TYPE. CASSIODORUS: This verse embraces the mysteries of the Old and New Testaments. It says that God later spurned the sacrifice and oblation earlier made to honor the Lord by immolation of cattle; from this source the priests obtained food. Earlier he deigned to accept such sacrifices, since through them a kind of prefiguration of Christ's body seemed to exist. But after the Messiah, the Lord Christ who had been foretold, came and revealed himself as Victim of devoted love for us all, it was unnecessary, now that the truth was fulfilled, for that forerunning type to continue. . . . The body previously promised by the images of sacrifices . . . was fulfilled by his coming. EXPLANATION OF THE PSALMS 40.7.[20]

IN THE PSALMS. ARNOBIUS THE YOUNGER: That is, it is written about me in the beginning of the Psalter: "Blessed is the man," so I may do your will. COMMENTARY ON THE PSALMS 40.[21]

THE LAW AND THE PROPHETS. PSEUDO-ATHANASIUS: Here the psalmist introduces the person of Christ, who says, By the will of the Father he came and completed the things that are written concerning him in the law and the prophets. And he declared his righteousness in a great church, which is in all peoples and is more excellent than that of the law. EXPOSITION ON PSALMS 40.[22]

ALL SCRIPTURE. DIDYMUS THE BLIND: He calls the "roll of the book" every divinely inspired Scripture, both the legal and the prophetic. In these Scriptures things are written concerning the memory of the Savior among us. The psalmist calls it a roll because everything is summed up into one. FRAGMENTS ON THE PSALMS 40.8.[23]

OUR SACRIFICE PREFIGURED IN CHRIST. THEODORET OF CYR: The apostolic exhortation sings a similar note to this, "I urge you, brothers, by the mercies of God, to present your bodies as a living sacrifice, holy, pleasing to God, the worship according to reason."[24] In place of the rites of the Law, the Lord required us to consecrate our limbs. Now, seeing your grace, he says, I offered myself to you in the words "Here I am." This statement, of course, blessed Paul applies to Christ the Lord, and rightly so: he is our nature's first fruits, and it is fitting for him in the first place to speak for us and in himself to prefigure in type what is appropriate in our case. COMMENTARY ON THE PSALMS 40.5.[25]

40:8 Delighting to Do God's Will

CHRIST'S WILL AND THE FATHER'S. JEROME:

---

[17]FC 101:239. [18]Heb 7:27. [19]NPNF 2 9:246-47*. [20]ACW 51:401*. [21]CCL 25:56. [22]CSCO 387:26. [23]PG 39:1354. [24]Rom 12:1. [25]FC 101:239-40.

Let the Jews perceive that they have not prevailed against me, but that it is your will that I suffer. Besides, I desired to suffer; that is why I say in my human nature: "To do your will, O my God, is my delight." It was your will and mine that I suffer; not their plottings and power did it, but you and I desired it. You, in truth, struck your Shepherd, and the sheep have been scattered. . . . That I suffer was your will and mine also. What you desired, I also desired. Homily on Psalm 108[109].[26]

For Our Sake. Ambrose: Because there is one will, there is one substance, there is inseparable majesty and the power of the Trinity. But there is another voice, that of the flesh; and yet, it too consents to God's will. . . . Christ accepted death and crucifixion so as to crucify the flesh. For my sake he took on himself the combat, so that he might conquer me. Though Christ's flesh was strong and not liable to sin, he nevertheless took on my sins. He took on my weaknesses and infirmities, though he himself was without infirmity. . . . He who is all pure took on our flesh to make it all pure. He, the immortal one, took on our flesh to make us immortal. Commentary on Twelve Psalms 40.18-19.[27]

40:9 The Great Congregation

The Message of Grace. Chrysostom: What does he mean when he says, "I have declared your justice"? He did not simply say, "I have given," but "I have declared." What does this mean? That he has justified our race not by right actions, not by toils, not by barter and exchange but by grace alone. Paul, too, made this clear when he said, "But now the justice of God has been made manifest independently of the Law."[28] But the justice of God comes through faith in Jesus Christ and not through any labor and suffering. Discourses Against Judaizing Christians 7.3.2.[29]

The Church's Response. Theodoret of

Cyr: Blessed David promises to preach God's righteousness, the truth of inspired composition, the admirable salvation and immeasurable mercy in a great assembly gathered by divine grace throughout the whole world. And redeemed nature itself promises to give this response to its salvation by flocking to church, moving its lips in hymn singing, proclaiming God's righteous judgment, recounting his ineffable care and giving a glimpse of the truth of the inspired promises. Commentary on the Psalms 40.7.[30]

A Bold and True Witness. Augustine: This is said to warn us that we must not out of fear restrain our lips from proclaiming what we have believed. There are Christians who live among ill-disposed pagans, among people who are sophisticated in an unwholesome way, squalid, unfaithful people without good sense, mockers. These Christians nonetheless have faith in their hearts, but once they begin to find themselves hounded for being Christians they are afraid to confess with their lips the faith they have in their hearts, and they restrain their lips from giving expression to what they know, what they have within. The Lord rebukes them: "If anyone is embarrassed about me in the presence of men and women, I will be embarrassed about that person in my Father's presence";[31] that is to say, "I will not recognize anyone who has been ashamed of confessing me before other people; I will not confess that person before my Father." The lips must proclaim what is in the heart: this is an injunction against fear. But the heart must have in it what the lips say: this is an injunction against insincerity. Sometimes you are afraid and dare not say what you know to be true, what you believe; but at other times you are tempted to be insincere and say something that is not in your heart. Your lips and your heart must be in agreement. If you seek peace from God, be reconciled with yourself; let there be no harmful conflict

---

[26]FC 48:266. [27]ACTP 173-74. [28]Rom 3:21. [29]FC 68:186. [30]FC 101:241. [31]Mk 8:38.

between your mouth and your heart. EXPOSITIONS OF THE PSALMS 40.16.[32]

40:10 Saving Help

IMPUTED JUSTICE. AMBROSE: A person can speak of his own justice without arrogance, . . . if he has faith in God and believes that on account of his faith he will be reckoned as just.[33] . . . It was for this reason that Christ came, to establish faith and to grant us forgiveness of sin. COMMENTARY ON TWELVE PSALMS 40.25.[34]

ISRAEL INCLUDED. PSEUDO-ATHANASIUS: [At this point in the psalm] he introduces the persons of those who believed from Israel; for he confesses to God that he did not remove his mercy from it but then and now saved and supported them. EXPOSITION ON PSALMS 40.[35]

40:11 Steadfast Love and Faithfulness

MERCY AND TRUTH. CASSIODORUS: The "mercy" lay in rescuing human nature, which was wounded through the sin of transgression, by means of the holy incarnation; the "truth" lies in his sitting at the Father's right hand through the blessing of the promised resurrection, and from there he will come to judge the living and the dead. EXPLANATION OF THE PSALM 40.12.[36]

LOVE AND FEAR. AUGUSTINE: I would not dare to turn back to you if I were not confident of your forgiveness; I would not go on persevering were I not confident of your promise. . . . I see you to be good, and I see you to be just; I love you because you are good and fear you because you are just. Love and fear jointly are my guides. EXPOSITIONS OF THE PSALMS 40.20.[37]

40:12 Evils, Iniquities

NOT YET PERFECT. THEODORET OF CYR: The church of God, buffeted by billows from the godless, in its struggles is not carried away but

attributes developments to sins and failings and begs to enjoy assistance from the Savior. In a particular way, the church of God is not composed completely of perfect people; instead, it numbers also those addicted to sloth and inclined to the careless life, who choose to serve pleasure. Since it is one body, both features are displayed as in the case of one person. COMMENTARY ON THE PSALMS 40.8.[38]

40:17 Poor and Needy

NOTHING OF MY OWN. AUGUSTINE: There is nothing of my own in me that deserves praise. May he tear off my sackcloth and clothe me in his own robe, for it is not I who live now, but Christ lives in me. If Christ lives in you, and all the good you have belongs to Christ, and all the good you ever will have belongs to Christ, what are you of yourself? "I am needy and poor." EXPOSITIONS OF THE PSALMS 40.27.[39]

DEPENDANT ON CHRIST. JOHN CASSIAN: Truly, what higher or holier poverty can there be than this, that a person knowing he is defenseless of his own, asks help for daily life from another's generosity and realizes his life and being to depend every moment on God's help. Such a one truly confesses himself "the beggar of the Lord," like the psalmist, who said, "I am a beggar and a poor man, and God helps me." CONFERENCES 10.11.[40]

IN GOD'S CARE. AUGUSTINE: Since God cared for you before you even existed, how can he fail to care for you now that you are what he willed you to be? You are a believer now; you are already walking the path of righteousness. Is it likely that he will not care for you, he who makes his sun rise over good and bad people and sends his rain on just and unjust alike? Now that

---

[32]WSA 3 16:211. [33]Cf. Rom 4:5. [34]ACTP 178*. [35]CSCO 387:26. [36]ACW 51:403. [37]WSA 3 16:214. [38]FC 101:241-42. [39]WSA 3 16:220. [40]LCC 12:243*.

you are righteous by living through faith, will he neglect you, abandon you, send you away? Of course not. In your present life he cherishes you, and helps you, and provides all you need here and cuts away all that could harm you. By giving you all these things he comforts you so that you can hold out, and by taking them away he corrects you so that you may not perish. The Lord has you in his care, so do not worry. EXPOSITIONS OF THE PSALMS 40.27.[41]

---

[41]WSA 3 16:220*.

41:1-13 PRAYER FOR HEALING

When many are poor and needy and you wish to show pity for them,
on the one hand acknowledging the generosity of some people,
and urging others on to similar deeds of mercy, say Psalm 41.
ATHANASIUS ON THE INTERPRETATION OF THE PSALMS 19 [OIP 68]

To the choirmaster.* A Psalm of David.

¹*Blessed is he who considers the poor!ᶜ*
The LORD *delivers him in the day of trouble;*
²*the* LORD *protects him and keeps him alive;*
he is called blessed in the land;
thou dost not give him up to the will of his enemies.
³*The* LORD *sustains him on his sickbed;*
in his illness thou healest all his infirmities.ᵈ

⁴*As for me, I said, "O* LORD, *be gracious to me;*
heal me, for I have sinned against thee!"
⁵*My enemies say of me in malice:*
"When will he die, and his name perish?"
⁶*And when one comes to see me, he utters empty words,*
while his heart gathers mischief;
when he goes out, he tells it abroad.

⁷*All who hate me whisper together about me;*
they imagine the worst for me.

⁸*They say, "A deadly thing has fastened upon him;*
he will not rise again from where he lies."
⁹*Even my bosom friend in whom I trusted,*
who ate of my bread, has lifted his heel against me.
¹⁰*But do thou, O* LORD, *be gracious to me,*
and raise me up, that I may requite them!

¹¹*By this I know that thou art pleased with me,*
in that my enemy has not triumphed over me.
¹²*But thou hast upheld me because of my integrity,*
and set me in thy presence for ever.

¹³*Blessed be the* LORD, *the God of Israel,*
from everlasting to everlasting!
Amen and Amen.

c Or *weak*   d Heb *thou changest all his bed*   * LXX *To the end*

OVERVIEW: The forty-first psalm speaks of a future David, who is none other than Christ, the end and object of hope (AMBROSE, THEODORET). The first verse speaks of the principle of mercy to the merciful (CYPRIAN). The one who gives to the poor profits himself (VALERIAN). The Christian should recognize Christ in the poor (LEO). In fact, we need to consider the poor man Jesus and understand his poverty (AMBROSE, THEODORET, GREGORY OF NYSSA). The evil day is the day of our trouble in which God is ready to help (DIODORE). But it also reminds us of the bitter day of judgment (AMBROSE).

The psalmist is blessed by the many favors of God (THEODORE OF MOPSUESTIA), but we are blessed in Christ by faith (AUGUSTINE). Our bed, in this psalm, may refer to our body (MAXIMUS OF TURIN), or it may refer to earthly circumstances that the Lord, from time to time, overturns (AUGUSTINE). But, with the Lord, there is healing now and in the future (HESYCHIUS). We need to have a healthy awareness of our sickness (CASSIODORUS) and personally acknowledge our sin (AUGUSTINE), which is the most we can do. It takes God to save (AUGUSTINE). This prayer may apply to Christ if translated, "Even if I sinned" (THEODORET). We need to let the physician do his work (CAESARIUS). There is no comfort in a crowd of the damned (CAESARIUS). The name of Christ did not perish with his death, and neither will the names of those who belong to him (AUGUSTINE).

The psalm prophesies the plot against Christ (THEODORET). Judas went out (AMBROSE), but those who truly belong come in and hold fast to Christ (AUGUSTINE). It would not be expected that an apostle would turn (AMBROSE). An inside traitor poses a greater threat than an outside foe (DIODORE). We pray that the Lord will sustain us as he sustained Christ (ARNOBIUS THE YOUNGER). He truly rose and so will we. Judgment fell on the Jews, but it was not a final condemnation (AUGUSTINE). We see, in the Christ who speaks, a stable unity (THEODORET). There was no joyous victory for his opponents (DIODORE). We marvel at his holy innocence and simplicity (CASSIODORUS). We find him to be completely reliable (AUGUSTINE), and we are upheld through repentance (ARNOBIUS THE YOUNGER). With the "amen" pronounced at the end of this psalm, we reach the end of the first book of the psalter (AMBROSE).

Superscription: *A Psalm of David*

CHRIST, THE END AND OBJECT OF HOPE. AMBROSE: He who had perished in Adam had to be restored in Christ. That is why we have, at the head of the psalm, "To the end," because Christ is the end to which all our hope is directed. He is our consuming interest, the object of all our wishes and desires. He is the fullness, the consummation, of all the universe. He is the very sum and pinnacle of every virtue. . . . He, and he alone of all the world, took our sins on himself in his own flesh. He is the one and only Lamb of God who took away the sins of the world.[1] Only he wiped out our bond by the shedding of his blood. He took that bond and fastened it to his own cross. He who is all wisdom knew how to undo the ancient sin that held fast the world. He who is our redemption[2] knew how to renew our race and free it from guilt. He who is holiness knew how to sanctify and make us holy, leading us back to grace. COMMENTARY ON TWELVE PSALMS 41.1.[3]

THE PSALM APPLIES TO CHRIST. THEODORET OF CYR: Since the Lord says, "for the Scripture to be fulfilled," and shows the present psalm applies to him and no one else, I consider it rash and presumptuous to develop another explanation not applicable to him. COMMENTARY ON THE PSALMS 41.1.[4]

41:1 *One Who Considers the Poor*

MERCY TO THE MERCIFUL. CYPRIAN: [One] will not be able to merit the mercy of God who

---

[1]Cf. Jn 1:29. [2]Cf. 1 Cor 1:30. [3]ACTP 180. [4]FC 101:243.

himself has not been merciful, nor will [one] gain any request from the divine love by his prayers who has not been humane toward the prayer of the poor. WORKS AND ALMSGIVING 5.[5]

PROFIT TO THE GIVER. VALERIAN OF CIMIEZ: Clearly, as often as we succor the wretched, we give to ourselves. The dispensing of our resources is our gain. For if you consider again the hope of future reward, whatever is given to the poor is reckoned as a profit. That is what the prophet states: "Blessed is he who understands concerning the needy and the poor: the Lord will deliver him in the evil day." HOMILY 8.2.[6]

RECOGNIZE CHRIST IN THE POOR. LEO THE GREAT: You should "recognize" Christ "in the needy" to the extent that your resources "allow." Christ our Lord gives testimony to the fact that he is the one whom we clothe, support and feed in them. That is how strongly he has recommended the poor to us. SERMON 6.2.[7]

UNDERSTAND CHRIST'S POVERTY. AMBROSE: Faith comes first, and mercy comes second. . . . Happy, therefore, is the one who understands the poverty of Christ, his utter destitution. Christ, though he was very rich, became poor for us.[8] In his kingdom, he was rich; in his flesh, he was poor, for he took on himself the flesh of the poor. We had indeed become very poor, because, by fraud practiced on us by the serpent, we lost the rich robes of virtue and were put out of paradise. We were thrown out of our native land and banished into exile. We were even stripped of clothing. Our lovely vesture of virtue that once covered our body was snatched from us by sin. . . . Have understanding as regards the poverty of Christ, so that you may be rich; understand his weakness and suffering, so that you may become strong and whole; understand his cross, so that you will never blush for it; understand his wound, so that your wounds may be cured; understand his death, so that you may gain eternal life; understand his tomb, so that you

may discover the resurrection. COMMENTARY ON TWELVE PSALMS 41.4.[9]

THE LORD IS LAID IN A MANGER. THEODORET OF CYR: Though having lordship of visible and invisible things, he had nowhere to lay his head, was born of a virgin and through lack of bed was laid in a manger. Consequently, the inspired Word declares blessed the one able to understand this poverty and filled with zeal to sing the praises as far as possible of the one who accepted it. COMMENTARY ON THE PSALMS 41.2.[10]

THE NATURE OF GOODNESS. GREGORY OF NYSSA: The Word defines blessedness for us in another way than at the beginning. For in the first psalms, to depart from evil was blessed, but here to know the good more fully is pronounced blessed. Now the nature of the good . . . is the "only-begotten God," "who, though he was rich, for our sake became poor."[11] The Word here predicts his "poverty" in the flesh, which is pointed out to us through the Gospel account, pronouncing the one who has recognized that "poverty" with understanding blessed. He was "poor" in relation to the "form of a servant"[12] but blessed in relation to the nature of deity. For in the opening words of the psalm the Word calls him "needy and poor"; at the end of the section he says, "Blessed be the Lord God of Israel from eternity to eternity. So be it. So be it."[13] ON THE INSCRIPTIONS OF THE PSALMS 2.12.157-58.[14]

THE DAY OF OUR TROUBLE. DIODORE OF TARSUS: By "evil day" he refers not to it as naturally evil—a day not being evil by nature, since if it were, the day would transfer the responsibility to its creator. Instead, by "evil day" he refers to the one on which a person is enveloped in distress, affliction and pain or falls victim to illness or some other hazard. So he means, when such

---

[5]FC 36:231. [6]FC 17:352*. [7]FC 93:35-36. [8]Cf. 2 Cor 8:9. [9]ACTP 181-82. [10]FC 101:244. [11]2 Cor 8:9. [12]Phil 2:7. [13]Ps 41:13. [14]GNTIP 170-71.

a day comes, God, who lends help, is not asleep. Commentary on Psalms 41.[15]

A Bitter Day. Ambrose: The day of judgment is bitter, and we dread it. There is no one to whom it does not appear evil, because it is fraught with terror. It is the day on which the Lord will judge not only what we did in public but even our most secret actions.[16] On that day each of us will have to show clearly what we have done and what we have thought. Therefore many will be condemned, and few will win the crown. Commentary on Twelve Psalms 41.7.[17]

41:2 Blessed in the Land

Many Favors. Theodore of Mopsuestia: He comments on God's favors to him in different ways: he will give freedom from perils, he says, will closely guard him so that he will suffer nothing, provide him with life and make him appear as blessed by the vast number of favors in the sight of everyone. Commentary on Psalms 41.3A.[18]

Blessed through Faith. Augustine: All believers live in Christ's name, and all in their different walks of life fulfill Christ's commandments, whether as married people or as celibates and virgins; they live the best and fullest lives the Lord's gift enables them to live, and they do not rely on their own powers to do so but know that they may boast only in him.[19] . . . So do not say to me, "Who is able to keep such a law?" He keeps it in me, he who was rich but came to the poor, indeed came as a poor man to the poor but as fullness to those who were empty. Anyone who bears all this in mind . . . does not disdain Christ's poverty but rather understands Christ's riches. Such a person is blessed on earth and is not delivered into the hands of that enemy who tries to persuade us that we should worship God with an eye to heavenly benefits but the devil for our earthly needs. Expositions of the Psalms 41.4.[20]

41:3 God Heals Infirmities

Our Body, Our Bed. Maximus of Turin: We can call our bodies themselves our beds, in which our souls linger very comfortably as if in a bed. I think that this is what the holy prophet means when he says, "You have turned his whole bed in his sickness." Blessed is the one whose bed the Lord turns in his sickness, so that the person who a little before was prone to anger, adulterous, wanton and full of the infirmities of every crime becomes chaste, humble and modest when the Lord turns his body that had been accustomed to evil. Sermon 19.3.[21]

God Overturns Our Bedding. Augustine: Bedding suggests something to do with the earth. Every weakly soul looks for something earthly to rest on in this life, because it is too great an effort to keep the mind stretched toward God uninterruptedly. It looks for something on earth on which it can rest, where it can take time off from its efforts and lie down. This could be an attraction for innocent people just as much. We need not speak of the desires of bad people. . . . Yet because God wants us to be in love only with eternal life, he mingles bitter elements even with these innocent pleasures, so that even in them we experience distress. He overturns all our bedding. . . . We are being taught to love better things by the pain we endure in those that are inferior; the wayfarer traveling toward his homeland must not fall in love with a stable instead of home. Expositions of the Psalms 41.5.[22]

Healing Now and in the Future. Hesychius of Jerusalem: May the Lord help him. That even in the present time the truth of these prophetic promises may be found. Many, laboring in sickness and disease, when they leave

---

[15]WGRW 9:131-32. [16]Cf. Rom 2:16. [17]ACTP 183. [18]WGRW 5:511. [19]1 Cor 1:31. [20]WSA 3 16:229-30. [21]ACW 50:48. [22]WSA 3 16:230-31.

behind their own poor and needy works, are changed for the better. For if even on a future day judgment triumphs over mercy, what a marvel it would be, if also he would turn away by his rich mercy the death which we await, and he would restore strength? Surely this is the frailty of spirit, which is received in the inner man, wherein he has determined hands or the strength to do things. Even crippled knees are healed that were not strong before to walk on the way to life. Then the mercy bequeathed to the poor heals and revives the spirit held back by its grave disease of folly and brought to death from its sin. He, therefore, immediately added: "I said: Lord, have mercy on me, heal my soul, because I have sinned against you." LARGE COMMENTARY ON PSALMS 41.4.[23]

41:4 Heal Me, for I Have Sinned

A HEALTHY AWARENESS OF SICKNESS. CASSIODORUS: Every sin is a disease of the soul, and when it spreads, the inner person's health is impaired. He who cried out to the Physician realized his sickness, but he was healthy in understanding when he was aware of his infirmity. So he longs for his soul to be healed, that is, by remission of sins. EXPLANATION OF THE PSALMS 41.5.[24]

ACKNOWLEDGE SIN YOURSELF. AUGUSTINE: Your accuser goes on scoring points off you, as long as you insist on making your own excuses. So do you want to ensure that your accuser—the devil, that is—suffers and groans? Do what you have heard, do what you have learned, and say to your God, "I myself have said it, Lord. Have mercy on me, heal my soul, since I have sinned against you." "I myself," he says, "I myself have said it; not the devil, not luck, not fate. I myself have said it. I'm not making excuses, on the contrary, I accuse myself. I have said it. Have mercy on me, heal my soul." SERMON 29.3.[25]

IT TAKES GOD TO SAVE. AUGUSTINE: The reason he says, "I myself have said it, Lord," is to

thrust before our eyes the fact that the will and decision to sin arises from the soul and that we are fully capable of destroying ourselves, while it takes God to seek that which was lost and to save that which had wounded itself. SERMON 20.1.[26]

EVEN IF I SINNED. THEODORET OF CYR: I am the one who is poor, he is saying, who embraced voluntary poverty, the Lamb of God who takes away the sin of the world, who makes my own the sufferings of human beings, who though having committed no sin offers the prayer for human nature as nature's firstfruits. It should be noted, however, that Symmachus said not "because I sinned against you" but "even if I sinned against you." COMMENTARY ON THE PSALMS 41.4.[27]

LET THE PHYSICIAN WORK. CAESARIUS OF ARLES: God will heal you if only you admit your wound. You lie under the physician's hands; patiently implore his aid. If he bathes or burns or cuts it, bear it calmly; do not even pay any attention to it, provided you are cured. Moreover, you will be cured if you present yourself to the doctor. Not that he does not see you hide, but confession is the very beginning of restoration to health. SERMON 59.5.[28]

NO COMFORT IN A CROWD. CAESARIUS OF ARLES: When sinners are rebuked for their crimes . . . they do not all accept it with humility and obedience. Many do not blush to reply with most insolent boldness, saying, Am I the only one who did this? Have not those people, and those, done similar things or worse? Do not even the clergy with major orders commit such sins? Unhappy soul! A crowd of miserable people is a comfort to you. Can the individual sinner be tormented any less if immense crowds of sinners begin to be tortured in eternal punishment with

---

[23]PG 93:1193. [24]ACW 51:410-11*. [25]WSA 3 2:117. [26]WSA 3 2:15. [27]FC 101:244-45. [28]FC 31:293.

him? How much better it would be for each one to flee the evil of his sins and exclaim in humble confession, "I said, O Lord, be merciful to me. Heal my soul, for I have sinned against you," and, "I know my iniquity, and my sin is always before me." For the good of his soul he should follow the examples of those who were honestly converted after many sins, rather than propose for imitation those who will suffer endless punishment after brief joy. SERMON 5.2.[29]

41:5 When Will His Name Perish?

HIS NAME DOES NOT DISAPPEAR. AUGUSTINE: He died, but his name did not disappear; far from it. Rather was his name sown like seed. . . . As the grain was dead, the harvest sprang up. No sooner had our Lord Jesus Christ been glorified than people came to believe in him far more strongly and in much greater numbers; and then his members began to hear the same mutterings that their Head had heard. Our Lord Jesus Christ is enthroned in heaven, but in us his members he is still struggling on earth. . . . For the devil stirred up persecutions against the church to destroy the name of Christ. . . . The martyrs were killed so that Christ might suffer anew, not in himself but in his body. The holy blood was shed because it was powerful for the growth of the church, and the death of the martyrs was added to Christ's sowing. . . . The Christians multiplied and multiplied again, and the expectations of their enemies who asked, "When will he die and his name disappear?" were not fulfilled. But the same thing is still being said today. . . . Still they are asking, "When will he die and his name disappear?" You have been proved wrong twice; at least have some sense this third time. . . . Christ foretold his own death and resurrection; he foretold the deaths of his martyrs and their crowning; he also foretold the future fortunes of his church. If he spoke truly in the first two instances, did he lie in the third? EXPOSITIONS OF THE PSALMS 41.1.[30]

41:6 Empty Words and Mischief

THE PLOT AGAINST CHRIST. THEODORET OF CYR: Now, the outcome of events testifies to these things: furtively they conversed together and looked for the way to implement the plot. Then they made a charge of overthrow, saying to Pilate, "He makes himself king and forbids us paying tribute to Caesar,"[31] which is what the prophecy says: "They set up a lawless plan against me." That is, they leveled a charge of lawlessness against me. COMMENTARY ON THE PSALMS 41.5.[32]

JUDAS WENT OUT. AMBROSE: Judas went out, and he spoke. He went out from the faith, he went out from the council and number of the apostles. He went out from Christ's banquet to the villainy of Satan; he went out from the grace that sanctifies to the noose that strangles. He went to speak vain things to infidels. He went outside, leaving behind the mysteries of life that lay within. He went out, for he had never known the mysteries that are contained in Scripture. COMMENTARY ON TWELVE PSALMS 41.17.[33]

COME INSIDE. AUGUSTINE: Judas was close to our Head; he was accustomed to come in and see: to spy on him, I mean, not looking for something in which he might believe but hoping to find grounds for betrayal. . . . The same one who came in to see used to go outside and talk. If only he were inside and spoke the truth! Then he would not go outside, where he tells lies. He is a traitor and a persecutor, and after going outside, he talks. If you belong among Christ's members, come inside and hold fast to the Head. EXPOSITIONS OF THE PSALMS 41.8.[34]

41:9 A Dear Friend

NOT TO BE EXPECTED. AMBROSE: We need not

---

[29]FC 31:34*. [30]WSA 3 16:225-26. [31]Lk 23:2. [32]FC 101:245. [33]ACTP 189. [34]WSA 3 16:232-33.

imagine that Jesus did not know that Judas was going to betray him. . . . Of course Jesus knew it. But in order to emphasize how damnable was the deed, Jesus speaks of the hopes he had held regarding Judas' loyalty. . . . We come down more heavily on one in whom we say we had high hopes or great trust, if afterwards that person robs us of our hope and high opinion. . . . This is why Jesus says that he had hoped, it was as though he had a right to hope. For surely one would expect an apostle to lay aside his old ways and follow new and better ways. COMMENTARY ON TWELVE PSALMS 41.21-22.[35]

INSIDE, A GREATER THREAT. DIODORE OF TARSUS: The one who shared the same table with me and the same food proved to be a foe the more threatening the more he concealed his malice under his close relationship. The Lord also suffered this in the case of Judas: in that case, too, it was not someone from the outer group of disciples who concocted plots but one who gave the impression of being closely related and sharing with him table and food. COMMENTARY ON PSALMS 41.[36]

41:10 Be Gracious to Me

SUSTAIN ME, AS YOU DID YOUR SON. ARNOBIUS THE YOUNGER: O Lord, as you have raised your Son from death, so lift me from sin. Lift me, and I will repay them. In this I know that you suffered for me so that my enemies may not rejoice over me. You have not refused even to die for me. I feared you lying in the tomb, but since you have arisen my enemy will not rejoice over me. You have sustained me on account of my innocence. The church speaks in the apostles and prophets because the farmers and fishermen raised up by God, not the philosophers and teachers, have built the church that God has confirmed in his sight forever. COMMENTARY ON THE PSALMS 41.[37]

NOT THE FINAL CONDEMNATION. AUGUSTINE: Notice when this prayer was made, and how

it has been answered. The Jews killed Christ in order not to forfeit their national place. But after killing him they lost it; they were uprooted from their territory and dispersed. When Christ was raised from the dead he requited them with tribulation, but the recompense was dealt out as a warning, not a final condemnation. EXPOSITIONS OF THE PSALMS 41.12.[38]

41:11 By This I Know

A STABLE UNITY. THEODORET OF CYR: All this was said on the part of the nature assumed, which was involved also in the passion. . . . Since, then, the assumed nature remained free of all wickedness, it was right for him to say, "But you supported me for my innocence and confirmed me in your presence forever": I received a stable unity, the combining was indivisible, the glory everlasting. COMMENTARY ON THE PSALMS 41.7.[39]

NO JOYOUS VICTORY FOR THEM. DIODORE OF TARSUS: You notice that he hints more clearly at the repayment here in his mentioning, not vengeance by the wronged but personal disappointment by the frustrated, which resulted in their punishing themselves on seeing the one they envied held in high esteem. His meaning here is, in fact, Show, Lord, how you care for me by their not rejoicing in the vile hopes they have for me. COMMENTARY ON PSALMS 41.[40]

41:12 You Have Upheld Me

HOLY INNOCENCE AND SIMPLICITY. CASSIODORUS: His holy innocence, simplicity and blessed humility are truly in evidence. . . . He did not defend himself by any struggling. He went to the cross with a calm spirit, to die with untroubled mind. With truth unspotted he fulfilled every word foretold through the prophets. He grieved at the misfortunes of those who persecuted him,

---

[35]ACTP 192. [36]WGRW 9:133*. [37]CCL 25:58. [38]WSA 3 16:236. [39]FC 101:246-47. [40]WGRW 9:134.

and when nailed to the cross he prayed with all compassion for his enemies, for he had decreed that this should be done by all the faithful too. . . . Having laid aside the weakness of a mortal body, the God-man of and in two distinct and perfect natures abides in eternal glory. His name is above every name; his power governs heaven and earth. EXPLANATION OF THE PSALMS 41.13.[41]

HE IS RELIABLE. AUGUSTINE: God has disposed all things and ordered all things for our salvation. He foretold it before we existed, he has fulfilled it in our time, and what he has not fulfilled yet, he will. We hold fast to him as one who keeps his promises, and therefore we can believe him to be our debtor still; for as he has already given what had not been given when it was prophesied, so will he give what has not been given yet. EXPOSITIONS OF THE PSALMS 41.14.[42]

UPHELD THROUGH REPENTANCE. ARNOBIUS THE YOUNGER: Be not offended, careful reader, that we draw a mystical matter from a moral explanation. For just as the Pharisees beset Judas to betray the Lord by offering him his own safety to turn him over, so also unclean spirits beset my outer man which eats my bread and offer to it now money through greed, now luxury through desire, by which, if it accepts, it fails, and when it fails they drive him "to hang himself in a noose,"[43] that is, so that he despairs that he is able to be freed by repentance. But he says to them: He who sleeps, will he not arise? . . . Let us cease to harm ourselves, and let us be made innocent so that each one may say rightly to God: On account of my innocence you have sustained me, and you who had cast me away from your countenance because of sin, now through repentance strengthen me in your sight forever. COMMENTARY ON THE PSALMS 41.[44]

41:13 Amen and Amen

THE END OF BOOK 1. AMBROSE: "So be it, so be it" is also an indication that you have reached the end of a book. The psalter appears to be divided into five books, and the first book ends with this psalm, namely, the forty-first. The forty-first psalm concludes very fittingly with the passion, just as the forty-day period of Lent concludes with the Lord's passion. This allows the second book to begin with the mysteries of regeneration. COMMENTARY ON TWELVE PSALMS 41.37.[45]

---

[41]ACW 51:413-14. [42]WSA 3 16:238. [43]See Mt 27:5. [44]CCL 25:59. [45]ACTP 201*.

42:1-11 THIRST FOR GOD

If in your intense longing for God, you hear the reviling of your enemies,

do not give way to fear but know that such a longing

bears an immortal fruit, and comfort your soul with hope in God.

When you are uplifted by this, and earthly sorrow

has been assuaged a little, say Psalm 42.

ATHANASIUS ON THE INTERPRETATION OF THE PSALMS 19 [OIP 68-69]

To the choirmaster.
A Maskil of the Sons of Korah.

¹As a hart longs
 for flowing streams,
so longs my soul
 for thee, O God.
²My soul thirsts for God,
 for the living God.
When shall I come and behold
 the face of God?
³My tears have been my food
 day and night,
while men say to me continually,
 "Where is your God?"

⁴These things I remember,
 as I pour out my soul:
how I went with the throng,
 and led them in procession to the house of
 God,
with glad shouts and songs of thanksgiving,
 a multitude keeping festival.
⁵Why are you cast down, O my soul,
 and why are you disquieted within me?
Hope in God; for I shall again praise him,
 my help and my God.

My soul is cast down within me,
 therefore I remember thee
from the land of Jordan and of Hermon,
 from Mount Mizar.
⁷Deep calls to deep
 at the thunder of thy cataracts;
all thy waves and thy billows
 have gone over me.
⁸By day the LORD commands his steadfast
 love;
 and at night his song is with me,
 a prayer to the God of my life.

⁹I say to God, my rock:
 "Why hast thou forgotten me?
Why go I mourning
 because of the oppression of the enemy?"
¹⁰As with a deadly wound in my body,
 my adversaries taunt me,
while they say to me continually,
 "Where is your God?"

¹¹Why are you cast down, O my soul,
 and why are you disquieted within me?
Hope in God; for I shall again praise him,
 my help and my God.

OVERVIEW: The forty-second psalm speaks of a holy longing for God (AUGUSTINE). The psalmist longs to worship him (THEODORET). Christ is the fountain that always refreshes us (CASSIODORUS) and transforms us (GREGORY OF NYSSA). Tears for God nourish the spirit (EVAGRIUS), tears of longing for future light (JOHN CASSIAN). A Christian cannot point to an idol in answer to the question, Where is your God (AUGUSTINE)? As the Creator, by his power, our God is in everything made (EVAGRIUS). However, his substance is not there; he transcends all things (AUGUSTINE).

Israel looks forward to a return by God's grace (THEODORET), and we look forward to an everlasting celebration in the house of God (AUGUSTINE). In our praise of God, lamentation meets with joy (CASSIODORUS). God is the restorer of his own image (ARNOBIUS THE YOUNGER). So, let hope strengthen you (AMBROSE). Anxiety is sometimes a problem of reference (AUGUSTINE). Seeking God in humility (CASSIODORUS) brings an internal consolation (EVAGRIUS). The figure of deep calling to deep brings to mind the Son calling to the Father (ARNOBIUS THE YOUNGER), the Old Testament predicting the New Testament (AMBROSE) and one person witnessing the faith to another (AUGUSTINE). Apart from God's salvation, suffering and judgment threaten to overwhelm us (AUGUSTINE). But God's help comes rapidly (THEODORE OF MOPSUESTIA). Let us learn God's Word in repose so that we may utter it in tribulation (CASSIODORUS). God, indeed, is our helper. He is not limited; he is free (EVAGRIUS). Conflicted thoughts are typical of people who are suffering (DIODORE). But we must not let temptations grow (JEROME). Quench your discouragement (THEODORET). Remember your reward (ORIGEN). Let God be your personal savior (THEODORE OF MOPSUESTIA).

42:1 A Soul Longing for God

LONGING FOR GOD. AUGUSTINE: Let us burn together with this thirst; let us run together to the fountain of understanding. Let us . . . long rather for it as a hart yearns for a spring . . . let us long for the wellspring of which Scripture says, "With you is the fountain of life." . . . Long for the fountains of water. With God is the fountain of life, a fountain that can never dry up. . . . God has everything that will refresh you. He is able to fill anyone who comes to him. . . . This is what I am thirsting for, to reach him and to appear before him. I am thirsty on my pilgrimage, parched in my running, but I will be totally satisfied when I arrive. EXPOSITIONS OF THE PSALMS 42.2, 3, 5.[1]

TO WORSHIP GOD. THEODORET OF CYR: I am longing and thirsting for the worship of my living God, he is saying. "To see the face of God" means worshiping him according to the Law, and such worship was confined to Jerusalem. . . . very appropriately do they name God "strong and living" as they take note of the lifeless and immobile idols of the Babylonians. COMMENTARY ON THE PSALMS 42.2.[2]

42:2 Thirsting for God

CHRIST, THE FOUNTAIN. CASSIODORUS: Christ the Lord is the fount of water from which flows all that refreshes us. Flowing water can often dry up, but a fountain of water always irrigates. So we are rightly told to hasten to the waters of the sacred spring, where our longing could never experience thirst. EXPLANATION OF THE PSALMS 42.2.[3]

A TRANSFORMING FOUNTAIN. GREGORY OF NYSSA: The person, however, who has once tasted virtue and has come to understand its nature by his own experience of the good is no longer the kind of person who must be dragged away from his passionate attachment to evil by necessity and warning and compelled to look to virtue. On the contrary, he has an excessive thirst for what is superior. . . . [He] "thirsts" for participation in God more than "the hart" longs for "the fountains of water." And it follows that the person who finds the fountain after this excessive thirst draws in as much water as the

---

[1]WSA 3 16:240-43. [2]FC 101:248-49. [3]ACW 51:416.

abundance of his desire draws off. But he who has received what he desired in himself is full of what he desired. For that which has become full is not again emptied on the model of physical satiety, nor does that which was drunk remain inactive in itself. In whomever the divine fountain has come into existence, it transforms the one who has embraced it to itself and imparts to this person a portion of its own power.[4] ON THE INSCRIPTIONS OF THE PSALMS 1.5.40-41.[5]

42:3 Where Is Your God?

SPIRIT NOURISHMENT. EVAGRIUS OF PONTUS: Nothing nourishes like that which nourishes the spirit. Blessed are those who weep, for they will laugh. NOTES ON THE PSALMS.[6]

LONGING FOR FUTURE LIGHT. JOHN CASSIAN: There is a weeping that springs from contemplating eternal good and longing for future light, and tears of joy and desire cannot help but break out as the soul is athirst for the mighty living God. CONFERENCES 9.29.[7]

NOT LIKE IDOLS. AUGUSTINE: "Where is your God?" If a pagan says this to me, I cannot retort, "What about you? Where is *your* God?" because the pagan can point to his god. He indicates some stone with his finger and says, "Look, there's my god! *Where is yours?*" If I laugh at the stone, and the pagan who pointed it out is embarrassed, he looks away from the stone toward the sky; then perhaps he points to the sun and says again, "Look, there's my god! *Where is yours?*" He has found something he can demonstrate to my bodily eyes. For me it is different, not because I have nothing to demonstrate but because he lacks the kind of eyes to which I could demonstrate it. He was able to point the sun out to my bodily eyes as his god, but how can I point out to any eyes he has the sun's Creator? EXPOSITIONS OF THE PSALMS 42.6.[8]

IN EVERYTHING MADE. EVAGRIUS OF PONTUS:

Seeing that God is Creator, he is in everything made; seeing that he is excellence and wisdom, he is in all holy powers. . . . God is even in people sometimes in excellence, sometimes in accomplishment: it is of angels to behave always according to God; of demons, never; of people to behave sometimes rightly, sometimes not. NOTES ON THE PSALMS 41[42].4.[9]

42:4 Pouring Out One's Soul

TRANSCENDS ALL THINGS. AUGUSTINE: I look for my God in every bodily creature, whether on earth or in the sky, but I do not find him. I look for his substance in my own soul but do not find him there. Yet still I have pondered on this search for my God and, longing to gaze on the invisible realities of God by understanding them through created things, "I poured out my soul above myself," and now there is nothing left for me to touch, except my God. For there, above my soul, is the home of my God; there he dwells, from there he looks down on me, from there he created me, from there he governs me and takes thought for me, from there he arouses me, calls me, guides me and leads me on, and from there he will lead me to journey's end. EXPOSITIONS OF THE PSALMS 42.8.[10]

ISRAEL'S RETURN. THEODORET OF CYR: After the sad events, therefore, he proclaims pleasant ones and ahead of time teaches that they will quickly secure their recall, and with the guidance of God's grace, they will return to the land of their desire and will rebuild God's house, will celebrate the customary festivals and welcome into their ears the festive sound and spiritual melody. COMMENTARY ON THE PSALMS 42.3.[11]

AN EVERLASTING CELEBRATION. AUGUSTINE: In God's home there is an everlasting party.

---

[4]Jn 4:13-14; 7:37-38. [5]GNTIP 97-98*. [6]PG 12:1416. [7]LCC 12:228. [8]WSA 3 16:243-44. [9]PG 12:1415. [10]WSA 3 16:246. [11]FC 101:249.

What is celebrated there is not some occasion that passes; the choirs of angels keep eternal festival, for the eternally present face of God is joy never diminished. This is a feast day that does not open at dawn or close at sundown. EXPOSITIONS OF THE PSALMS 42.9.[12]

LAMENTATION MEETS JOY. CASSIODORUS: Joy implies psalm singing, confession laments for sins; the combination of the two molds the wholly perfect Christian. . . . What is sweeter or more wholesome than praise of God and constant self-condemnation? EXPLANATION OF THE PSALMS 42.5.[13]

42:5 My God and My Help

RESTORER OF HIS IMAGE. ARNOBIUS THE YOUNGER: Do not be sad, spirit, but hope in the Lord because I confess to him. He is the Savior of my countenance, that is, my God is the restorer of his own image. COMMENTARY ON THE PSALMS 42.[14]

LET HOPE STRENGTHEN YOU. AMBROSE: Troubled by the hazardous turnings of this world, David says, "Why are you sad, O soul, why do you trouble me? Hope in God, for I will give praise to him, the salvation of my countenance and my God." Therefore, when we are distressed and apprehensive, let hope strengthen us with the expectation of things that are to come. Look to each phrase individually. "Hope, for I will give praise," he says; not "I give praise," but "I will give praise." This means: I will give praise better at that time when I shall behold the glory of God with face unveiled and be transformed into the same image. As he was consoling himself, suddenly turning to himself, he says, "My soul is troubled within myself"; that is, I, who ought to strengthen others, am myself disturbed, and because I do not have strength of myself, let us receive it from the Creator. THE PRAYER OF JOB AND DAVID 4.3.12-13.[15]

42:6 A Soul Cast Down

A PROBLEM OF REFERENCE. AUGUSTINE: "My soul was troubled as it turned to me." It would not be, would it, if it turned to God? It is troubled when it turns to myself. When turned toward the unchangeable, it received new strength, but when turned to what is prone to change it was disturbed. . . . Since there is in me no stability, neither is there any hope for me in myself. "My soul was troubled as is turned to me." Would you like to free your soul from its anxiety? Then do not let it linger in yourself. . . . Put no trust in yourself but only in your God. If you trust in yourself, your soul will be turned toward yourself and gravely troubled, because it cannot yet find any grounds for security in you. So then, if my soul turned toward myself and found itself disturbed, what is left to me but humility, the humble refusal of the soul to place any reliance on itself? What course is open to it, except to make itself very small indeed, and to humble itself so that it may be raised up? Let it attribute nothing to itself, and then what is profitable may be granted to it by God. EXPOSITIONS OF THE PSALMS 42.12.[16]

SEEK GOD IN HUMILITY. CASSIODORUS: God is not sought from the height of arrogance but is recollected in modest lowliness. EXPLANATION OF THE PSALMS 42.7.[17]

INTERNAL CONSOLATION. EVAGRIUS OF PONTUS: When we come up against the demon of acedia, then with tears let us divide the soul and have one part offer consolation and the other receive consolation. And sowing within ourselves goodly hopes, let us chant with holy David this [verse]. PRAKTIKOS 27.[18]

42:7 Deep Calls to Deep

---

[12]WSA 3 16:247. [13]ACW 51:418. [14]CCL 25:60. [15]FC 65:398. [16]WSA 3 16:249-50. [17]ACW 51:420. [18]GAC 102*.

THE SON TO THE FATHER. ARNOBIUS THE YOUNGER: When deep calls deep, the Son calls the Father from the depth of land and river, and you have opened the cataracts of heaven. As the Holy Spirit descends, the Father addresses the Son from the height of the heavens. When he calls from the deep to deep, the glory of the Lord comes to me. COMMENTARY ON THE PSALMS 42.[19]

OLD TESTAMENT TO NEW TESTAMENT. AMBROSE: Listen to this: "Deep calls on deep at the voice of your floodgates." Scripture of the Old Testament calls on Scripture of the New Testament for the consummation of holiness and the fullness of grace; it calls with the voice of grace and the outflowing of spiritual abundance. COMMENTARY ON TWELVE PSALMS 36.18.[20]

PERSON TO PERSON WITNESSING. AUGUSTINE: Any human being, even a holy, good-living person, even one who has made great progress, is a deep place, and such a person calls on another depth when he proclaims to another some part of the faith, some part of the truth, with a view to eternal life. But the deep that preaches is profitable to the deep he calls to if he calls in the sound of God's cataracts. "Deep calls to deep," one person wins over another, but not with his own voice only: he calls in "the sound of your cataracts." EXPOSITIONS OF THE PSALMS 42.13.[21]

SUFFERING AND JUDGMENT. AUGUSTINE: The waves wash over me in the sufferings I undergo now, but your threats are judgments poised above me. All my present hardships are your waves, but all your menaces hang over me, ready to break on my head. In the waves this abyss that I am calls out, but behind your impeding threats is that other abyss to which this one calls. Already I flounder amid your waves, but your threats are far more serious and they hang over me, for a threat is something not yet pressing down but poised overhead. Yet you set me free, and therefore I have said to my soul, "Hope in God, because I will confess to him, the salvation

of my countenance, my God." The more my woes are multiplied, the gentler will be your mercy. EXPOSITIONS OF THE PSALMS 42.15.[22]

42:8 The Lord Is with Me

RAPID HELP. THEODORE OF MOPSUESTIA: I considered further that though the impending troubles are so numerous, it is very easy for you to provide a solution; if by day you bid lovingkindness to be shown us—in other words, relief from the troubles to occur—it happens so quickly that immediately those in receipt of good things set about singing through the night and offering hymns of praise to you for what has happened. When God enjoins mercy by day, then, immediately by night "his song is with me," as if to say, So prompt will be the discharge of his command that, with his command given by day, it is possible for me to sing by night of the good things done to me. COMMENTARY ON PSALMS 42.9A.[23]

LEARN THE WORD IN REPOSE. CASSIODORUS: It is precisely what we learn in repose that we utter in tribulation. The words of the Law are learned in leisure, but their fruit is demonstrated in affliction. EXPLANATION OF THE PSALMS 42.9.[24]

42:10 A Taunt from Enemies

GOD IS FREE. EVAGRIUS OF PONTUS: It is of the greatest ignorance to think that God is in a place. God does not stand in a place. He is free. NOTES ON THE PSALMS 41[42].11.[25]

42:11 Hope in God

TYPICAL SUFFERING. DIODORE OF TARSUS: Pondering all this within myself, then, I was again encouraged not to be alarmed but to hope

---

[19]CCL 25:60 [20]ACTP 46-47. [21]WSA 3 16:252*. [22]WSA 3 16:253. [23]WGRW 5:529-31. [24]ACW 51:421. [25]PG 12:1419.

in God, who readily provides me with salvation and again makes me esteemed. Turning their thoughts over and over, sometimes in despair, sometimes in hope, is typical of people suffering. Commentary on Psalms 42.[26]

Do Not Let Temptation Grow. Jerome: When the inner person shows signs for a time of wavering between vice and virtue, say, "Why are you cast down, O my soul, and why are you disquieted within me? Hope thou in God, for I shall yet praise him who is the health of my countenance and my God." You must never let suggestions of evil grow on you or a babel of disorder win strength in your breast. Kill the enemy while he is small, and, that you may not have a crop of tares, nip the evil in the bud. Letter 22.6.[27]

Quench Your Discouragement. Theodoret of Cyr: Do not despair of salvation, O soul, he is saying: you have God as Savior; in him you gain sound hope. Quench your discouragement and receive consolation. Commentary on the Psalms 42.7.[28]

Remember the Reward. Origen: I beseech you to remember in all your present contest the great reward laid up in heaven for those who are persecuted and reviled for righteousness' sake, and to be glad and leap for joy on account of the Son of man,[29] just as the apostles once rejoiced when they were counted worthy to suf-fer dishonor for his name.[30] And if you should ever perceive your soul drawing back, let the mind of Christ, which is in us,[31] say to it, when it wishes to trouble that mind as much as it can, "Why are you sorrowful, my soul, and why do you disquiet me? Hope in God, for I shall yet give him thanks." I pray that our souls may never be disquieted, and even more that in the presence of the tribunals and of the naked swords drawn against our necks they may be guarded by the peace of God, which passes all understanding,[32] and may be quieted when they consider that those who are foreigners from the body are at home with the Lord of all.[33] But if we are not so strong as always to preserve calm, at least let not the disquiet of the soul be poured forth or appear to strangers, so that we may have the opportunity of giving an apology to God, when we say to him, "My God, my soul is disquieted within me." Exhortation to Martyrdom 4.[34]

A Personal Savior. Theodore of Mopsuestia: "My personal savior is my God": I trusted that you would doubtless meet my request, since you personally are my salvation and my Lord (the term "personal savior" meaning "my support, my glory"—in other words, It is you yourself who provides me with this). Commentary on Psalms 42.12c.[35]

---

[26]WGRW 9:136-37*. [27]NPNF 2 6:24*. [28]FC 101:251. [29]Mt 5:10-12; Lk 6:23. [30]Acts 5:41. [31]Phil 2:5. [32]Phil 4:7. [33]2 Cor 5:8. [34]OSW 43. [35]WGRW 5:533.

43:1-5 HOPE IN GOD

If [enemies] persist, and, with hands red with blood,

try to drag you down and kill you, remember that God

is the proper judge (for he alone is righteous

while that which is human is limited),

and so say the words of . . . [Psalm] 43.

ATHANASIUS *ON THE INTERPRETATION OF THE PSALMS* 17 [OIP 67]

---

[1]*Vindicate me, O God, and defend my cause*
  against an ungodly people;
from deceitful and unjust men
  deliver me!
[2]*For thou art the God in whom I take refuge;*
  why hast thou cast me off?
Why go I mourning
  because of the oppression of the enemy?

[3]*Oh send out thy light and thy truth;*
  let them lead me,

let them bring me to thy holy hill
  and to thy dwelling!
[4]*Then I will go to the altar of God,*
  to God my exceeding joy;
and I will praise thee with the lyre,
  O God, my God.

[5]*Why are you cast down, O my soul,*
  and why are you disquieted within me?
Hope in God; for I shall again praise him,
  my help and my God.

OVERVIEW: The forty-third psalm is similar to the preceding one in meaning (THEODORET). The first verse asks God to distinguish the psalmist's cause from that of the unrighteous (AUGUSTINE). The psalm shows us how the desires of the believer and the desires of the unbeliever are different (AUGUSTINE). Light and truth refer to God's reliable assistance (DIODORE) that brings us renewal (ARNOBIUS THE YOUNGER). The two are one reality in Christ (AUGUSTINE), who is prefigured in the assistance given to the psalmist (LEO). God dwells in the righteous (EVAGRIUS), who praise him in joy and in suffering (AUGUSTINE). The psalm ends by reminding us to hope in God, not in ourselves (DIODORE, THEODORET).

43:1 *Vindicate Me, O God*

SIMILAR TO THE PRECEDING PSALM. THEODORET OF CYR: The psalm is without a title in the Hebrew for the reason of having a similar meaning to the preceding one. COMMENTARY ON THE PSALMS 43.1.[1]

DISTINGUISH MY CAUSE. AUGUSTINE: Some one, perchance, hears a person saying, "Judge me, O God," and he is amazed. For one usually says, "May God pardon me; spare me, O God." Who is there who says, "Judge me, O God"? And sometimes in the psalm this very verse is

---

[1]FC 101:252.

placed at a pause point, that it may be proffered by the reader and answered by the people. Is there perhaps anyone whose heart is not deeply affected and who is not afraid to sing to God and say, "Judge me, O God"? And yet the people sing it, believing, and do not think that they wrongly desire what they have learned from the divinely inspired text; and if they little understand. . . . For it continued and showed in the words coming next what kind of judgment it meant, that it is not [the judgment] of damnation but of discerning. For the psalm says, "Judge me, O God." What does it mean, "Judge me, O God"? "And discern my cause from an unholy nation." . . . According to that mode whereby judgment is called distinction, "All of us must be revealed before the judgment seat of Christ so that there" a person "may receive what he has done through the body, whether good or evil"; for it is distinction that good things be distributed to the good, evil things to the evil. For if judgment were received always in regard to evilness, the psalm would not say, "Judge me, O God." Tractates on the Gospel of John 22.5.1-2.[2]

Different Desires. Augustine: Let a distinction be drawn between one who believes in you and one who does not. In weakness they are equal but in conscience far apart; there is parity of travail, disparity of desire. The desire of the ungodly will be extinguished, but what of the desire of the just? We should certainly be apprehensive about that, if the one who makes the promise were not totally reliable. The goal of our desire is the one who has promised; he will give us himself because he has already given us himself. He will give his immortal self when we are immortal, as he has already given himself to us as mortal in our mortality. Expositions of the Psalms 43.2.[3]

43:3 God's Light and Truth

Reliable Assistance. Diodore of Tarsus: Dispatch your reliable assistance (by "light"

referring to the support, and by "truth" to its reliability) . . . so that your reliable help may conduct me to the holy places and your holy temple. Commentary on Psalms 43.[4]

Renewal. Arnobius the Younger: Send your light and overcome my shadows. Send your truth and conquer my lying. Your light and truth lead me to your holy mountain and into your tabernacle. When I draw near, you lead me to the altar of God, where, although old, I become as a youth. Commentary on the Psalms 43.[5]

One Christ. Augustine: "Your light" and "your truth": we have two names here but one single reality, for what else is God's light, if not God's truth? And what is God's truth, if not God's light? But both of these are the one Christ, who says, "I am the light of the world. Whoever believes in me will not walk in darkness. I am the way, the truth and the life."[6] He is light, and he is truth. May he come, then, and deliver us, distinguishing our cause from that of an unholy people even now; may he deliver us from the wicked and deceitful. May he separate wheat from weeds, for he will send in his angels at harvest time to collect from his kingdom all the things that make people stumble and throw them into a blazing fire, but his wheat they will gather into the barn. Expositions of the Psalms 43.4.[7]

Prefiguration. Leo the Great: The beam that emanates from light does not come after the light. True light never lacks a beam, having it as part of its substance to shine, just as it always has it as part of its substance to exist. But the manifestation of this beam has been called a "sending," by which Christ appeared to the world. Although he filled all things with his invisible majesty, he came, nevertheless, to those who had not known him, as if from a very

---

[2]FC 79:200-201*. [3]WSA 3 16:257. [4]WGRW 9:137. [5]CCL 25:61. [6]Jn 8:12; 14:6. [7]WSA 3 16:258-59.

remote and deep seclusion. At that time, he took away the blindness of ignorance, as it has been written: "For those sitting in darkness and in the shadow of death, a light has risen."[8] Of course the light of truth has been sent out in prior ages to enlighten the holy fathers and prophets, as when David said, "Send out your light and your truth." Of course the divinity of the Son has made clear the works of his presence "in various ways and by many signs."[9] Yet all these prefigurations and all these miracles bore testimony about that "sending" of which the apostle speaks: "When the fullness of time came, God sent his Son, made from a woman, made under the Law."[10] SERMON 25.3.2–4.1.[11]

THE RIGHTEOUS. EVAGRIUS OF PONTUS: The holy mount of God is Christ. His tabernacle indwells the virtues of the righteous. NOTES ON THE PSALMS 42[43].3.[12]

43:4 Praise with the Lyre

JOY AND SUFFERING. AUGUSTINE: What is the difference between confessing to him on the lyre and confessing to him on the psaltery? . . . Each of them is carried in the hands and plucked manually. . . . Each of them is good, provided that the player is skilled. . . . But here is the difference: the psaltery has its vaulted part at the top: that wooden, concave, sounding chamber, its drumlike piece, I mean, on which the strings are stretched and that gives them their resonance. The lyre has its hollow sounding chamber at the bottom. Accordingly our activities can be distinguished into those that are played on the psaltery and those played on the lyre, but both are pleasing to God and melodious in his ears.

When we do something in harmony with God's commandments, obeying his orders and careful to comply with his precepts, and when we feel no pain in the doing, that is the music of the psaltery. The angels do this all the time, and they never feel pain. But sometimes we do suffer from troubles, temptations and obstacles on earth. Our pain is only in our lower part, because it is due to our mortal condition and the debt of tribulation we contract from our primitive origins. Moreover, the things that give us pain are not above us. In these cases we are playing the lyre. The sweet sounds proceed from the lower part; we suffer as we sing our psalms; or rather, we sing and play the lyre. . . . All patient endurance is melody to God's ears. But if you give way under tribulations like that, you have broken your lyre. EXPOSITIONS OF THE PSALMS 43.5.[13]

43:5 Why Are You Cast Down?

HOPE IN GOD. DIODORE OF TARSUS: I shall console myself and . . . not allow myself to be alarmed by my thoughts but to hope in you, my God, to whom I should also give thanks, for from you it is also possible to hope for salvation. COMMENTARY ON PSALMS 43.[14]

ENCOURAGEMENT. THEODORET OF CYR: From this it is clear that both psalms have the same meaning. Those using them encourage themselves to have stronger hope, overcome the feeling of discouragement and await the salvation from God that will doubtless be given them. COMMENTARY ON THE PSALMS 43.5.[15]

---

[8]Is 9:2. [9]Heb 1:1. [10]Gal 4:4. [11]FC 93:101. [12]PG 12:1421. [13]WSA 3 16:260-61*. [14]WGRW 9:138. [15]FC 101:253.

44:1-26 PRAYER FOR VICTORY

If you wish to call to mind constantly the benefits of God
to the patriarchs, the exodus out of Egypt,
the passage through the desert, and how, while God is so good,
human beings are ungrateful, you have Psalm 44.

ATHANASIUS ON THE INTERPRETATION OF THE PSALMS 19 [OIP 69]

To the choirmaster.
A Maskil of the Sons of Korah.

¹We have heard with our ears, O God,
 our fathers have told us,
what deeds thou didst perform in their days,
 in the days of old:
²thou with thy own hand didst drive out the
 nations,
 but them thou didst plant;
thou didst afflict the peoples,
 but them thou didst set free;
³for not by their own sword did they win the
 land,
 nor did their own arm give them victory;
but thy right hand, and thy arm,
 and the light of thy countenance;
 for thou didst delight in them.

⁴Thou art my King and my God,
 who ordainest*e* victories for Jacob.
⁵Through thee we push down our foes;
 through thy name we tread down our
 assailants.
⁶For not in my bow do I trust,
 nor can my sword save me.
⁷But thou hast saved us from our foes,
 and hast put to confusion those who hate us.
⁸In God we have boasted continually,
 and we will give thanks to thy name for
 ever.   Selah

⁹Yet thou hast cast us off and abased us,
 and hast not gone out with our armies.
¹⁰Thou hast made us turn back from the foe;
 and our enemies have gotten spoil.
¹¹Thou hast made us like sheep for slaughter,
 and hast scattered us among the nations.
¹²Thou hast sold thy people for a trifle,
 demanding no high price for them.

¹³Thou hast made us the taunt of our
 neighbors,
 the derision and scorn of those about us.
¹⁴Thou hast made us a byword among the
 nations,
 a laughingstock*f* among the peoples.
¹⁵All day long my disgrace is before me,
 and shame has covered my face,
¹⁶at the words of the taunters and revilers,
 at the sight of the enemy and the avenger.

¹⁷All this has come upon us,
 though we have not forgotten thee,
 or been false to thy covenant.
¹⁸Our heart has not turned back,
 nor have our steps departed from thy way,
¹⁹that thou shouldst have broken us in the
 place of jackals,
 and covered us with deep darkness.

²⁰If we had forgotten the name of our God,
 or spread forth our hands to a strange god,

²¹*would not God discover this?*
  For he knows the secrets of the heart.
²²*Nay, for thy sake we are slain all the day*
      long,
  and accounted as sheep for the slaughter.

²³*Rouse thyself! Why sleepest thou, O Lord?*
  Awake! Do not cast us off for ever!

²⁴*Why dost thou hide thy face?*
  Why dost thou forget our affliction and
      oppression?
²⁵*For our soul is bowed down to the dust;*
  our body cleaves to the ground.
²⁶*Rise up, come to our help!*
  Deliver us for the sake of thy steadfast love!

e Gk Syr: Heb *Thou art my King, O God; ordain*   **f** Heb *a shaking of the head*

OVERVIEW: The forty-fourth psalm begins with the recollection of stories of God's deeds passed down by the psalmist's ancestors (CHRYSOSTOM). We are reminded that the will of God is declared by the Word of God (PRUDENTIUS). God's exploits on behalf of the people were a marvelous and extraordinary sight (CHRYSOSTOM). This happened on the basis of the special relationships the people had with God (THEODORET). They did not succeed by their merits but by God's grace (AMBROSE), given in utter kindness (AMBROSE).

We recognize, as did the psalmist, that we have the same God (THEODORET). We proceed by faith (BEDE), not by our own strength (MARTIN). Praise is a blessing for us (EVAGRIUS). The Lord is the glory of the righteous (AMBROSE). The faith of the remnant was not conquered (AMBROSE). Those cut off were like sheep (CHRYSOSTOM), like things having no value (CHRYSOSTOM). From these things we learn to worship God for his sake only (AUGUSTINE) and to develop perseverance (CHRYSOSTOM). God alone (ZEPHYRINUS) knows the secrets of each heart (AUGUSTINE), for he occupies our minds (DIODORE). His face may be hidden, but we see it by faith (AMBROSE). We are saved by his mercy alone (CHRYSOSTOM), for his sake (AUGUSTINE) and on account of his name (DIODORE). From all of this, we resolve to wait on the Lord (THEODORET).

44:1 We Have Heard

DIVINE STORIES. CHRYSOSTOM: Listen to this,

all you who are heedless of your children, who ignore their singing diabolical songs, while you pay no attention to the divine stories. Those people were not like that; on the contrary, they passed their life without interruption in stories of God's great deeds and achieved a double advantage. On the one hand, it was a good experience for them to keep in mind the divine favors, and they were the better for it; on the other, their offspring gained no little grounding in the knowledge of God from these stories, and were moved to imitation of virtue. For them, you see, books were the mouths of their forebears, and these stories were a feature of every study and every employment, nothing being more agreeable or more profitable. After all, if mere adventure stories, fables and fictions generally divert the listeners, much more do these stories reveal his beneficence, power, wisdom and care, stimulate the listener with enjoyment and make them more observant. You see, those who were present during the events and eyewitnesses passed them on for our hearing, and hearing is equally effective for faith development as sight. COMMENTARY ON THE PSALMS 44.2.[1]

DECLARATION BY THE WORD. PRUDENTIUS:
  The majesty that with the Father dwelled,
  His spirit and thought, the way of his
      designs,
  Which made not by his hand or spoken
      word,

---

[1] CCOP 1:233-34*.

Breathed from the Father's heart, declared
his will.
THE DIVINITY OF CHRIST 90-93.[2]

44:2 With God's Own Hand

A MARVELOUS AND EXTRAORDINARY SIGHT.
CHRYSOSTOM: So which triumphs is he recalling?
Which successes? Some in Egypt, some in the
desert, some in the land of promise, but especially those in the promised land. . . . They had
no need of weapons; instead, they captured cities
by a mere shout, and crossing the Jordan they
overran the first city that stood in their way, Jer-
icho, as though by dancing rather than fighting.[3]
I mean, they went out fitted with weapons not as
if for battles but for a festival and dance, bearing
arms for appearance's sake rather than security;
wearing sacred robes and having the Levites preceding the army, they encircled the wall. It was
a marvelous and extraordinary sight to see, so
many thousands of soldiers marching in step and
order, in silence and utter regularity, as though
no one was about, with that daunting harmony
of trumpets keeping everything in time. COM-
MENTARY ON THE PSALMS 44.3.[4]

A SPECIAL RELATIONSHIP. THEODORET OF
CYR: You, O Lord, he is saying, drove out from
here the Canaanites along with the other nations, settling our ancestors in their place: it
was not by trusting in strength or depending
on armor that they emerged stronger that such
people, but led by your grace they felled some
and took others into slavery, since you accorded
them a special relationship with you—the meaning of "you took delight in them." COMMENTARY
ON THE PSALMS 44.2.[5]

44:3 God's Delight in Israel

NOT BY THEIR MERITS. AMBROSE: Our ancestors, as heirs and next of kin of the patriarchs,
were planted in the promised land. They did
not gain this by any merits of their own. It was

not Moses who led them in, for fear they should
attribute it to the Law and not to grace. For the
Law examines our merits; but grace looks to
faith. How excellently the apostle has followed
the faith of his ancestors when he says, "he that
plants is nothing, he that waters is nothing. It is
God who gives the increase."[6] It was not Joshua,
son of Nun, even though he led the people in and
planted them—but God who gave the increase.
To him first be the glory. COMMENTARY ON
TWELVE PSALMS 44.12.[7]

UTTER KINDNESS. AMBROSE: When God is
pleased with us, it is because he has given us the
grace to be pleasing to him. Scripture teaches us
that this is a gift specially bestowed on people in
pure and utter kindness and not to be arrogantly
usurped. COMMENTARY ON TWELVE PSALMS
44.13.[8]

44:4 My King and My God

THE SAME GOD. THEODORET OF CYR: You are
the same even now, Lord, he is saying, ruling
in similar fashion, overpowering in a similar
fashion, exercising the same force, your nature undergoing no change. For you simply a
word suffices for salvation: give the nod, and
the people will enjoy it. COMMENTARY ON THE
PSALMS 44.3.[9]

44:5 Pushing Down Foes

BY FAITH. BEDE: In the Scriptures it is often the
custom for horns to designate the eminence of
faith and of the virtues with which we ought to
strike out against and overcome the hostile advances of our ancient enemy, joining the prophet
in saying to the Lord, "Through you we will
fight against our enemies with the horn." ON
THE TABERNACLE 3.11.[10]

---

[2]FC 52:8*. [3]Cf. Josh 6. [4]CCOP 1:237. [5]FC 101:255. [6]1 Cor 3:7.
[7]ACTP 213*. [8]ACTP 213*. [9]FC 101:255. [10]TTH 18:147.

44:6 Not Trusting in Weapons

Not Our Own Strength. Martin of Braga: Behold, this is the true and the Christian humility. In this you will best govern both yourself and those in your charge. In this you will be able to achieve victory over every vice, by attributing to God rather than to yourself the fact that you have won. The reason why our vices recover their strength at the very moment when they have almost been subdued is, in my opinion, only because we do not say to God what his warrior David said when fighting the wars of the Lord: "Through you," he said, "we have struck down our foes; and through your name we trample down our adversaries." And again: "No one prevails by his own strength. The Lord makes his adversary weak." But perhaps I shall receive the answer: "Are we then not to offer thanks to God, not to render praises?" I think so, but the trouble is that when we do it, we do it in words only, and inwardly: to God we offer thanks in private, to ourselves in public. We render praise to God on our lips, but to ourselves both on our lips and in our heart. This is what often raises up the enemy when he is already humbled, for the sin of our vanity is his strength. Exhortation to Humility 6.[11]

44:8 Boasting in God

A Blessing for Us. Evagrius of Pontus: Blessed is the one engaged in praise the whole day, namely, through his life, which lacks the uproar of emotions and is filled with an understanding of God. Notes on the Psalms 43[44].9.[12]

The Glory of the Righteous. Ambrose: The rich glory in their wealth; the luxurious in their dinner parties; the impure glory in night and darkness; the powerful glory in this life that has nights. But the just does not glory in this life but in the Lord God whom he strives to please in all that he does. Commentary on Twelve Psalms 44.23.[13]

44:10 Enemies Have Gotten Spoil

Our Faith Not Conquered. Ambrose: One who is carried off by people is not necessarily conquered. Take, for example, Paul. He rejoices in his sufferings.[14] He glories in being let out through a window and lowered in a basket.[15] Look at holy Jeremiah, holy Ezekiel, holy Daniel. These were led into captivity and plundered by the Assyrians. But their own personal faith was never taken captive. They never sinned against the Lord's covenant. Commentary on Twelve Psalms 44.35.[16]

44:11 Like Sheep for Slaughter

Like Sheep. Chrysostom: What is the meaning of "like sheep for slaughter"? Making us vulnerable to attack, presenting us as insignificant. Some sheep, you see, those suited to breeding are for purchase; others, . . . whether from age or sterility, are useful only for eating. And what was actually worse, their being scattered even among the nations, which was hardest of all for them, their not being able to observe the Law in all precision there and being divorced from their ancestral way of life. And not in one race, he is saying, but in all parts; we are on the verge of only one thing, and that is being abused, whereas we do not have the strength for taking vengeance or lifting a hand in resistance. This fate, you see, illustrates the likeness of sheep. Commentary on the Psalms 44.7.[17]

44:12 Sold for a Trifle

No Value. Chrysostom: It is our custom, remember, to give away even without cost things that are worthless and insignificant, whereas what we put great store by we sell at a high price, should we sell at all, but make available even gratis what we put little store by. . . . Now, if

---

[11]FC 62:55-56*. [12]PG 12:1424. [13]ACTP 220. [14]Cf. Col 1:24. [15]2 Cor 11:33. [16]ACTP 226*. [17]CCOP 1:245**.

disposing of something below cost demonstrates its lack of value, much more so to take nothing for it, no charge. So this is what he is saying: just as if someone were to let their possessions go without charge, so you too allowed us to be of no value, you spurned us completely. COMMENTARY ON THE PSALMS 44.7.[18]

44:15 Disgrace and Shame

WHAT WE LEARN FROM THIS. AUGUSTINE: Our faith . . . may be made ready for the contemplation of what is invisible. . . . All those disasters befell them so that as God's holy ones were stripped of their possessions, and even of temporal life itself, they might learn not to worship the eternal God for the sake of temporal advantages but in pure love for him to endure all the trials that they had to undergo for a time. EXPOSITIONS OF THE PSALMS 44.16.[19]

44:20 If We Had Forgotten

PERSEVERANCE. CHRYSOSTOM: This is the mark of loyal servants, to persevere in serving their master despite their ill treatment. . . . This verse, too, teaches the listeners not to pretend but to serve God with their whole heart. COMMENTARY ON THE PSALMS 44.8.[20]

44:21 God Knows the Secrets

GOD ALONE. ZEPHYRINUS [DUB.]: To judge rashly of the secrets of another's heart is sin; and it is unjust to reprove him on suspicion whose works seem not other than good, since God alone is Judge of those things that are unknown to people. He alone "knows the secrets of the heart," and not another. EPISTLES OF ZEPHYRINUS I.[21]

GOD KNOWS. AUGUSTINE: He knows, and he inquires? If he knows the secrets of the heart, why does he bother to inquire about them there? "Will God not inquire about these things?" He

knows them in himself, but he inquires about them for our instruction. Sometimes God inquires and seems to be finding out about some matter because he is making it known to you. He is telling you about his work, not making some new discovery on his own behalf. EXPOSITIONS OF THE PSALMS 44.19-20.[22]

HE OCCUPIES OUR MINDS. DIODORE OF TARSUS: It is impossible for anyone transgressing the laws or planning to do so to escape your notice, Lord, because you so carefully occupy our minds. COMMENTARY ON PSALMS 44.[23]

44:24 Why Hide Your Face?

WE SEE IT BY FAITH. AMBROSE: We cannot see God's face. But there is a place where, by faith, God shows himself to us. The place is with God; and if we were to stand on the rock—that is, in awareness of this flesh and in firmness of faith—we will see as much as can be allowed to us to see. We cannot see the fullness, but we can, in a certain sense, drink in some remnant of his light. Moses did not see the full and entire divinity that dwells in Christ corporeally.[24] But he saw the back of Christ. As man he saw his splendor, he saw the glory of his passion, he saw him draw back for us the bolts of the heavenly kingdom. COMMENTARY ON TWELVE PSALMS 44.91.[25]

44:26 For the Sake of Your Love

GOD'S MERCY ALONE. CHRYSOSTOM: See how they concluded the discourse: despite their countless good deeds, on what grounds did they appeal to be saved? On the mercy, the lovingkindness, the name of God. Do you see the humility and contrite heart? On what grounds do they appeal to be saved? Lovingkindness, mercy: as though bereft of good deeds, as though not having any

---

[18]CCOP 1:245-46. [19]WSA 3 16:274*. [20]CCOP 1:248*. [21]ANF 8:610*. [22]WSA 3 16:275. [23]WGRW 9:141. [24]Cf. Col 2:9. [25]ACTP 255.

claim on salvation, despite being in a position to take pride in so many troubles and dangers, they referred everything to God. Let us, too, living in the age of grace, imitate them and offer up glory to God, to whom be the glory for ages of ages. COMMENTARY ON THE PSALMS 44.9.[26]

FOR HIS SAKE. AUGUSTINE: That means "gratis." Not for any deserving on my part but because of your name; because it is worthy of you to do this and not because I am worthy to receive your help. Even the fact that we did not forget you, that our heart did not turn back, that we did not stretch out our hands to any other god—even this would have been beyond our power had you not been helping us. How could we have found the strength for it had you not been speaking to us within, encouraging us and never deserting us? Whether we are enduring amid troubles or rejoicing amid prosperity, redeem us, not for any merit of ours but for your own name's sake.

EXPOSITIONS OF THE PSALMS 44.26.[27]

ON ACCOUNT OF GOD'S NAME. DIODORE OF TARSUS: If we are judged unworthy of gaining mercy for all these things mentioned, he is saying, nevertheless be faithful to yourself; Lord, on account of your name conferred on us, free us from the enemy. COMMENTARY ON PSALMS 44.[28]

WAIT ON THE LORD. THEODORET OF CYR: Now, all this the grace of the Spirit foretold, teaching those who would experience those troubles to bear nobly what befell them and request relief from them from the God of all. Those remarkable people did exactly that: with their words they appeased God, led by him they routed the enemy, and they recovered their former freedom for their fellow citizens. COMMENTARY ON THE PSALMS 44.10.[29]

---

[26]CCOP 1:251. [27]WSA 3 16:279. [28]WGRW 9:142. [29]FC 101:258*.

45:1-17 A WEDDING HYMN

Well aware that the Word is the Son of God, the psalmist sings in 45 in the voice of the Father, "My heart has uttered a good Word."

ATHANASIUS *ON THE INTERPRETATION OF THE PSALMS* 5 [OIP 58]

To the choirmaster: according to Lilies.
A Maskil of the Sons of Korah; a love song.

[1]*My heart overflows with a goodly theme;*
    I address my verses to the king;
    my tongue is like the pen of a ready scribe.

[2]*You are the fairest of the sons of men;*

    grace is poured upon your lips;
    therefore God has blessed you for ever.
[3]*Gird your sword upon your thigh, O mighty*
        one,
    in your glory and majesty!

[4]*In your majesty ride forth victoriously*
    for the cause of truth and to defend[g] the right;

let your right hand teach you dread deeds!
⁵Your arrows are sharp
  in the heart of the king's enemies;
  the peoples fall under you.

⁶Your divine throne^h endures for ever and
  ever.
  Your royal scepter is a scepter of equity;
  ⁷you love righteousness and hate
  wickedness.
Therefore God, your God, has anointed you
  with the oil of gladness above your fellows;
  ⁸your robes are all fragrant with myrrh and
  aloes and cassia.
From ivory palaces stringed instruments make
  you glad;
  ⁹daughters of kings are among your ladies
  of honor;
  at your right hand stands the queen in gold
  of Ophir.

¹⁰Hear, O daughter, consider, and incline your
  ear;

forget your people and your father's house;
  ¹¹and the king will desire your beauty.
Since he is your lord, bow to him;
  ¹²the peopleⁱ of Tyre will sue your favor
  with gifts,
  the richest of the people ¹³with all kinds of
  wealth.

The princess is decked in her chamber with
  gold-woven robes;^j
  ¹⁴in many-colored robes she is led to the
  king,
  with her virgin companions, her escort,^k in
  her train.
¹⁵With joy and gladness they are led along
  as they enter the palace of the king.

¹⁶Instead of your fathers shall be your sons;
  you will make them princes in all the earth.
¹⁷I will cause your name to be celebrated in
  all generations;
  therefore the peoples will praise you for
  ever and ever.

g Cn: Heb and the meekness of   h Or Your throne is a throne of God, or Thy throne, O God   i Heb daughter   j Or people. All glorious is the princess within, gold embroidery is her clothing   k Heb those brought to you

OVERVIEW: The forty-fifth psalm is properly ascribed to Christ (DIODORE), prophesying his accomplishments (THEODORE OF MOPSUESTIA). The psalm begins by presenting the reader with a spiritual metaphor (EUSEBIUS). He speaks of the Word, begotten by the Father (AMBROSE), not created (ALEXANDER OF ALEXANDRIA). The psalmist writes under divine inspiration (CHRYSOSTOM) without any obstacle or error (CHRYSOSTOM) about the eternal Word (AUGUSTINE). His form, while scorned on the one hand, exceeded all others (AUGUSTINE). He was therefore fairer than all to David, as he is to us (GREGORY OF NAZIANZUS). He came to us with grace (AUGUSTINE) and powerful persuasion (DIODORE), quickly filling the world with the grace of his lips (ORIGEN).

The psalm next gives us a glimpse of his power (THEODORET) through a metaphorical description of his operations (CHRYSOSTOM). We see in these descriptions the sword of the cross (HESYCHIUS), the destroyer of evil (EVAGRIUS). We see here not an earthly king (THEODORE OF MOPSUESTIA) but God winning a victory different in nature from those of earthly battles (CHRYSOSTOM). He displays fearful and marvelous deeds (CHRYSOSTOM) manifesting a character different from human beings (THEODORE OF MOPSUESTIA). He directs well-aimed words (BASIL) at all peoples (DIODORE) so that they fall into submission (CHRYSOSTOM) before Christ (AUGUSTINE).

The psalm proceeds to describe his throne and rule, that it is without beginning or end (THEODORET). His kingship (CHRYSOSTOM) entails no temporary THRONE (AUGUSTINE). It is in fact much older than some thought (BASIL), being from everlasting (ATHANASIUS). His scepter is the rod of God (THEODORE OF MOPSUESTIA), a straight rule of righteousness (AUGUSTINE). The psalmist presents to us God, anointed by God (JUSTIN MARTYR, IRENAEUS, AUGUSTINE) by means of an uncommon ointment (EUSEBIUS, CYRIL OF JERUSALEM, BASIL) so that there is none like him (CHRYSOSTOM, JEROME, ARNOBIUS THE YOUNGER). He, being one person, two natures (THEODORE), was anointed as man (THEODORET) by the Spirit at conception (GREGORY THE GREAT), for our sake (ATHANASIUS, BEDE).

The description of his garments should be given a nonmaterial interpretation (CHRYSOSTOM), as a symbol of the gospel (BASIL, DIODORE, THEODORE OF MOPSUESTIA). The queen may be understood as the soul (BASIL, JEROME), the daughters of kings as offspring of the gospel (AUGUSTINE), the church (THEODORE OF MOPSUESTIA), which must forget its former life (DIODORE). The beauty of the queen is the beauty of a soul (CHRYSOSTOM) beautified by God (AUGUSTINE), which reminds us that we need to be pleasing to God (FULGENTIUS), becoming more and more beautiful (HIPPOLYTUS). The husband of the church is its maker (IRENAEUS), who has come to be worshiped by Gentiles (CHRYSOSTOM, AUGUSTINE). The church is robed with gifts of the Spirit (THEODORET), displaying an inward glory (GREGORY OF NAZIANZUS, THEODORE OF MOPSUESTIA) and a spiritual garment interwoven with doctrine and practice (BASIL), a golden ornament of virtue (METHODIUS OF OLYMPUS). The Lord has regenerated for himself sons and daughters (IRENAEUS) and has sent apostolic princes throughout the earth (CHRYSOSTOM). The psalm ends with thanksgiving to him. Let us, too, join in and give praise to Christ (CHRYSOSTOM).

Superscription: *A Love Song*

CHRIST, NOT SOLOMON. DIODORE OF TARSUS: This psalm seems to refer to the Lord Jesus, not to Solomon, as Jews claim: even if under pressure they transfer most of the content to Solomon for being expressed in human fashion, yet the verse "Your throne, O God, is forever and ever, the rod of your kingship a rod of equity" completely shuts their mouth, since Solomon was not called God and did not reign forever. Instead, Christ alone as God also adopted the human condition for our sake and, being God and king forever, also retained his own status by nature. If, however, most of the things it mentions are human, that is no surprise, since in becoming human he accepted also commendation for his humanity. After all, if he accepted suffering as a human being, much more also commendation as a human being, no harm transferring to his divine nature. COMMENTARY ON PSALMS 45.[1]

THE ACCOMPLISHMENTS OF CHRIST. THEODORE OF MOPSUESTIA: In this psalm he prophesies events concerning Christ, foretelling how he will attract many people on the basis of his teaching and, as well, all that he will accomplish by his coming, including the establishment of the church by achieving the assembly of the faithful. He mentions also the spiritual graces, the gift provided by him to the saints and the virtue of those in the church. COMMENTARY ON PSALMS 45.1.[2]

45:1 *A Goodly Theme*

A SPIRITUAL METAPHOR. EUSEBIUS OF CAESAREA: It seems right for me to add what I am accustomed to quote in every question that is debated about his Godhead, that reverent saying: "Who shall declare his generation?" . . . For such expressions are connected with mental imagery alone and are accordingly subject to the laws of metaphor. And so the words "My heart has produced a good word" may be explained as referring to the constitution and coming into being of the primal Word, since it would not

---

[1]WGRW 9:142-43. [2]WGRW 5:555.

be right to suppose any heart, save one that we can understand to be spiritual, to exist in the case of the supreme God. PROOF OF THE GOSPEL 4.15.180.[3]

BY THE FATHER. AMBROSE: The Son lives by the Father, because he is the Son begotten of the Father; by the Father, because he is of one substance with the Father; by the Father, because he is the Word given forth from the heart of the Father, because he came forth from the Father, because he is begotten of the "bowels of the Father," because the Father is the fountain and root of the Son's being. ON THE CHRISTIAN FAITH 4.10.133.[4]

NOT CREATED. ALEXANDER OF ALEXANDRIA: And how can he be made of things that are not, when the Father says, "My heart belched forth a good Word." EPISTLES ON THE ARIAN HERESY 2.3.[5]

DIVINE INSPIRATION. CHRYSOSTOM: The inspired authors were not like the seers. In their case, after all, when the demon takes possession of their soul, it cripples their mind and clouds their reasoning, and so they utter everything without their mind understanding anything of what is said; rather, it is like a flute sounding without a musician to play a tune. This was said also by a philosopher of theirs in these words, "Just like the soothsayers and seers saying many things without knowing anything of what they say."[6] The Holy Spirit, [by contrast], does not act like that; instead, he allows the heart to know what is said. I mean, if the psalmist did not know, how could he have said "good news"? The demon, you see, being enemy and foe, commits an assault on human nature; the Holy Spirit, by contrast, being caring and beneficent, renders those who receive him sharers in his purposes, and with them understanding him he reveals what he has to tell. COMMENTARY ON THE PSALMS 45.1.[7]

NO OBSTACLE, NO ERROR. CHRYSOSTOM: The one who speaks from his own resources, you see, hesitates and thinks twice about the efforts he makes, handicapped in his composition by ignorance, error and uncertainty, and there are many things that undermine the speed of his utterance. When on the contrary it is the Spirit who moves the mind, there is no obstacle. COMMENTARY ON THE PSALMS 45.2.[8]

THE ETERNAL WORD. AUGUSTINE: Any word you speak yourself you bring forth from your heart; there is no other source for the word that sounds audibly and then fades away. Are you surprised that the same should be true for God? But there is this difference: God's speaking is eternal. . . . God's speaking has no beginning and no end, yet he speaks one Word only. He could speak another only if what he had spoken could pass away; but as he by whom the Word is spoken abides eternally, so too does the Word he speaks abide. This Word is spoken once and never ceases to be spoken; nor had the speaking of it any beginning; nor is it spoken twice. . . . But still, why does it say, "I tell my works"? Because in this uttered Word are all the works of God. Whatever God was to create was already present in the Word. Nothing could have existed in the created order that was not present in the Word, just as nothing can be in your own handiwork that was not present in your plan. The gospel makes this plain by saying, "What was made was alive in his life."[9] Created beings existed, but only in the Word; they were there in the Word, though they had as yet no existence in themselves. . . . Let anyone who understands about this Word listen to the Speaker and contemplate both the Father and his everlasting Word, in whom are present all things that will come to be in the future, as are present still all those that have passed away. These are the works of God: works in his Word, in his only-begotten Son, in the Word of God.

---

[3]POG 1:201. [4]NPNF 2 10:279. [5]ANF 6:297. [6]Plato *Apology* 22C; *Meno* 99D. [7]CCOP 1:258-59. [8]CCOP 1:260. [9]Jn 1:3-4.

EXPOSITIONS OF THE PSALMS 45.5.[10]

45:2 *The Fairest of Humankind*

HIS FORM. CHRYSOSTOM: How, then, does another inspired author say, "We saw him: he had no form or beauty; instead, his form was dishonorable, of no importance beside human beings."[11] He is not speaking about deformity—God forbid—but about an object of scorn. You see, once having deigned to become human, he went through every demeaning experience, not choosing a queen for his mother, not placed in a bed of gold at the time of swaddling clothes but in a manger, not reared in an affluent home but in an artisan's humble dwelling. Again, when he picked disciples, he did not pick orators and philosophers and kings but fishermen and tax collectors. He shared this simple life, not owning a house, or clad in rich clothing or enjoying similar fare, but nourished at others' expense, insulted, scorned, driven out, pursued. Now, he did this to trample underfoot human conceit in fine style. So, since he did not fit himself out in any pomp or circumstance or attach to himself hangers on or bodyguards, but went about at times alone, like any ordinary person, thus that author said, "We saw him, and he had no form or beauty," whereas the psalmist says, "Comely to behold beyond all human beings," suggesting grace, wisdom, teaching, miracles. Then to underline the comeliness he says, "Grace streamed out on your lips." COMMENTARY ON THE PSALMS 45.2.[12]

CHRIST EXCEEDS ALL OTHERS. AUGUSTINE: But to ensure that you do not put the man Christ on a par with any other human, it says that he is "fair beyond all humankind." He is human indeed but beyond all humans; he is among humans but beyond them; he takes his human birth from humankind, but he is beyond all humankind. EXPOSITIONS OF THE PSALMS 45.7.[13]

TO DAVID AND TO US. GREGORY OF NAZIANZUS: He had no form or comeliness in the eyes of the Jews, but to David he is fairer than the children of people. And on the mountain he was bright as the lightning and became more luminous than the sun, initiating us into the mystery of the future. ON THE SON, THEOLOGICAL ORATION 3(29).19.[14]

CHRIST CAME WITH GRACE. AUGUSTINE: He came to us with the word of grace on his lips, with the kiss of grace. . . . If he had come as a strict judge, without this grace bedewing his lips, who would have had any hope of salvation? Would anyone have been unafraid of what was owing to a sinner? But he came bringing grace, and so far from demanding what was owed to God, he paid a debt he did not owe. Did one who was sinless owe a debt to death: but you, what was owing to you? Punishment. He canceled your debts and paid off debts that were none of his. This is mighty grace. Grace—why "grace"? Because it is given gratis. It is up to you to give thanks, then, but not to repay him, for that you cannot do . . . because when you look for something to render to him that you did not first receive from him . . . all you will find is your sin. . . . This is the grace of God, bedewing Christ's lips. He made you, and made you gratis, for he could not give anything to you before you were there to receive it. Then when you had gone to ruin, he sought you; he found you and called you back again. He did not hold your past sins against you, and he promised you good things for the future. Truly, O Christ, "grace bedews your lips." EXPOSITIONS OF THE PSALMS 45.7.[15]

POWERFUL PERSUASION. DIODORE OF TARSUS: After mentioning the glory, here he mentions its effect, namely, that you were invested with such persuasion as even to attract disciples merely by your lips: the extraordinary degree of wisdom required no great number of words for persuading. COMMENTARY ON PSALMS 45.[16]

---

[10]WSA 3 16:285-86. [11]Is 53:2-3. [12]CCOP 1:260-61*. [13]WSA 3 16:287. [14]LCC 3:174*. [15]WSA 3 16:287-88. [16]WGRW 9:143.

The World Quickly Filled. Origen: Now a proof that "grace was poured on his lips" is the fact that although the time he spent in teaching was short, . . . the world has been filled with this teaching and with the religion that came through him. For there has arisen "in his days" "righteousness and an abundance of peace" lasting until the consummation. On First Principles 4.1.5.[17]

45:3 Glory and Majesty

A Glimpse of His Power. Theodoret of Cyr: After describing his charm and wisdom, he gives us a glimpse of both his power and his accouterments, which he used to wipe out his adversaries, teaching us the baffling character of it all. Commentary on the Psalms 45.4.[18]

Metaphorical Description of His Operations. Chrysostom: These terms, you see, signify his operations. . . . I mean, just as Scripture says God gets angry, not to attribute passion to him but to indicate through this expression his action of punishing and thus make an impression on more materialistic people, so too by mentioning weapons it suggests this. After all, since we are punished not through ourselves but by other instruments, in his wish to demonstrate God's power to punish he indicates it in terms familiar to us . . . so that we may gain a more vivid impression of his punishing. . . . Why, then, does he say this here? In these rather materialistic terms he shows his operation, through which he set the world on its course, through which he brought the war to an end and set up the trophy. It was a harsh war, after all, more bitter than all wars, not against savages in battle but against the demons exercising their wiles and destroying the whole world. Commentary on the Psalms 45.5.[19]

The Sword of the Cross. Hesychius of Jerusalem: By "sword" he means the cross, using it just like a sword. He hangs amid two enemies,

namely, the devil and death. By "thigh" he means the flesh, using the part for the whole. . . . He says the cross girds itself with the flesh, being powerful in appearance and beauty, so that by this (i.e., his humanity) he takes up our suffering; and by that (i.e., his divinity) he overcomes suffering, as if to have no part in it. We may be able to understand appearance and beauty as mercy. For there is nothing so fitting of God than to deliver his special creation. And "bend the bow" against the enemies, and "prosper" the faithful, and "rule" everywhere, so you may subdue the enemies; you may crown the faithful, because this is fitting of a judge and king. Large Commentary on Psalms 45.5.[20]

Destroyer of Evil. Evagrius of Pontus: The sword separates the spirit from evil and the mind from ignorance, destroying the old man and making him new in Christ. Notes on the Psalms 44[45].4.[21]

45:4 For the Cause of Truth

Not an Earthly King. Theodore of Mopsuestia: It is therefore clear from this that he is not speaking of a human being as king: no human being exercises such zeal for bringing about the kingdom in himself and uses weapons and all such things so as to teach gentleness to his own; on the contrary, he is concerned to gain power, and wipe out the opposition and in every way make his own people fearsome to the enemy. Commentary on Psalms 45.5b.[22]

The Nature of the Victory. Chrysostom: All other people, you see, exercise royal power by making war so as to gain cities or wealth, or because of enmities or vainglory. God, by contrast, acts not for any of these things but for the sake of truth, to plant it on earth; and for the sake of gentleness, to make those who are more

---

[17]OFP 262**. [18]FC 101:261. [19]CCOP 1:266-67. [20]PG 93:1196. [21]PG 12:1429. [22]WGRW 5:571.

savage than wild beasts become gentle; and for the sake of righteousness, to make those who are in thrall to lawlessness become righteous, first from grace, and second from good deeds. COMMENTARY ON THE PSALMS 45.6.[23]

FEARFUL AND MARVELOUS DEEDS. CHRYSOSTOM: What was being achieved was in fact fearful and productive of terror: death was destroyed, hell was broken asunder, paradise was opened, heaven was thrown open, demons were shackled, the lower regions were mingled with the upper, God became human, a human being is seated on the kingly throne, hope in resurrection dawned, expectation reached beyond death, ineffable good things were enjoyed, and all other good things he achieved by his coming. . . . The Septuagint, [by contrast], reads, "Your right hand will guide you in marvelous fashion," that is to say, we should marvel not only at what is achieved but at the fact that it is achieved in surprising fashion: through death is death destroyed, through a curse is a curse lifted and blessing bestowed, through eating were we lately expelled, through eating we have once again been admitted. A maiden expelled us from paradise, through a maiden we find eternal life. What was the means of our being condemned becomes the means of our being crowned. COMMENTARY ON THE PSALMS 45.7.[24]

A DIFFERENT CHARACTER. THEODORE OF MOPSUESTIA: To what human being would he apply this achievement or the magnitude of what is described? To whom would he apply the verse "Your right hand will guide you in marvelous fashion" when the divine Scripture consistently says of all the righteous that it is with God's help that they acquire strength? COMMENTARY ON PSALMS 45.7A.[25]

45:5 Sharp Arrows

WELL-AIMED WORDS. BASIL THE GREAT: The sharp arrows of the Mighty One are the well-aimed words that touch the hearts of the hearers, striking and wounding their keenly perceptive souls. HOMILIES ON THE PSALMS 17.6 (Ps 45).[26]

ALL PEOPLES. DIODORE OF TARSUS: His meaning is, direct well-aimed words, like arrows, at the hearts of the listeners, and as a result all peoples will be subjected to you as well (using a metaphor of people wounding with arrows and subjecting the wounded). He means, your arrows are so effective that not only will they subject disciples but also fall on enemies and bring them into subjection. COMMENTARY ON PSALMS 45.[27]

FALLING INTO SUBMISSION. CHRYSOSTOM: Do you see the successful outcome of the war? The submission of those previously rebellious? The instruction? The catechesis? Their very fall and submission to him, you see, are for everyone the basis and foundation of their exaltation. In fact, having delivered them from their folly and empty conceit and from the demons' error, he subjected them to himself. COMMENTARY ON THE PSALMS 45.7.[28]

FALLING BEFORE CHRIST. AUGUSTINE: The psalm goes on to explain where this falling occurs: "in the heart." There they exalted themselves against Christ, and there they fall before Christ. . . . They were your enemies, they were wounded by your arrows, and they fell before you. So from enemies they were transformed into friends; your enemies died, and your friends live. EXPOSITIONS OF THE PSALMS 45.16.[29]

45:6 The Divine Throne and Scepter

WITHOUT BEGINNING OR END. THEODORET OF CYR: The prophetic word afterwards teaches the nature of God the Word incarnate himself . . . that he is God and eternal king, not having had

---

[23]CCOP 1:270*. [24]CCOP 1:270-71*. [25]WGRW 5:575. [26]FC 46:287. [27]WGRW 9:144*. [28]CCOP 1:272. [29]WSA 3 16:293.

a beginning and not due to have an end. This is what "forever" suggests. COMMENTARY ON THE PSALMS 45.5.[30]

HIS KINGSHIP. CHRYSOSTOM: By "throne" here he means not simply throne but kingship. He calls it eternal here, but elsewhere elevated: "I saw the Lord seated on an elevated throne,"[31] Scripture says. And again: "Because your throne is elevated." Another author . . . contemplates him seated on a throne of glory,[32] whereas David presents also a throne of lovingkindness: "Mercy and judgment the foundation of his throne."[33] Now, all of these references are to his kingship, that it is everlasting (this is the meaning of "for ages of ages"), that it is in high esteem, that it is elevated, that it is powerful and mighty. Also that it has no beginning, when he says, "Your kingdom a kingdom of all ages."[34] COMMENTARY ON THE PSALMS 45.8.[35]

NO TEMPORARY THRONE. AUGUSTINE: How is it that this throne will stand forever and ever? Because it is God's. . . . O eternal Godhead! God could not possibly have a temporary throne. EXPOSITIONS OF THE PSALMS 45.17.[36]

MUCH OLDER. BASIL THE GREAT: That is to say, your kingdom is beyond the ages and older than all thought. HOMILIES ON THE PSALMS 17.7 (Ps 45).[37]

FROM EVERLASTING. ATHANASIUS: Even before he became man, he was King and Lord everlasting, being image and word of the Father. DISCOURSES AGAINST THE ARIANS 2.13.[38]

THE ROD OF GOD. THEODORE OF MOPSUESTIA: Immediately he proceeded to say also "a rod of equity," which suggests correctness and justice in prosecution. Such an expression, however, seems not applicable to a human being—at least such an expression occurs nowhere in reference to a human being—whereas it is applicable to God, of whom he says also in another place, "He will

judge the world in righteousness; he will judge peoples in rectitude," and elsewhere, "Good and upright is the Lord," and "Because the word of the Lord is upright."[39] COMMENTARY ON PSALMS 45.7B.[40]

A STRAIGHT RULE. AUGUSTINE: It is a scepter of righteous rule because it guides us aright. People were bent, distorted, they wanted regal power for themselves, they were in love with themselves, they cherished their own evil ways. They did not submit their wills to God but sought to bend the will of God to their own lusts. . . . You must straighten yourself to fit his will, not attempt to bend his to suit you. You cannot anyway. Your effort is futile, because his will is always perfectly straight. Do you want to be united with him? Then allow yourself to be corrected. Then it will be his rod or scepter that rules you, his scepter of righteous rules. . . . Draw near to this scepter and let Christ be your king, allow this scepter to rule you, because otherwise it may break you; it is an iron rod, and inflexible. . . . Some it rules, others it breaks; it rules the spiritual but breaks the carnal. Come near to this scepter, then. EXPOSITIONS OF THE PSALMS 45.17-18.[41]

45:7 God Has Anointed You

GOD ANOINTED BY GOD. JUSTIN MARTYR: These words also show clearly that he who did all things [God the Father] testified that he [Jesus] is to be worshiped both as God and Christ. DIALOGUE WITH TRYPHO 63.[42]

SON AND FATHER BOTH GOD. IRENAEUS: The Spirit designates both [of them] by the name of God—both him who is anointed as Son and him who does anoint, that is, the Father. AGAINST HERESIES 3.6.1.[43]

[30]FC 101:262. [31]Is 6:1. [32]Dan 7:9. [33]Ps 97:2 (96:2 LXX). [34]Ps 145:13 (144:13 LXX). [35]CCOP 1:274. [36]WSA 3 16:294. [37]FC 46:288*. [38]NPNF 2 4:355. [39]Ps 9:8; 25:8; 33:4. [40]WGRW 5:579. [41]WSA 3 16:294-95. [42]FC 6:248. [43]ANF 1:419.

GOD IS ANOINTED BY GOD. AUGUSTINE: God is anointed by God. In Latin it looks as though the word *God* is just repeated in the nominative case, but in Greek the distinction is perfectly clear: one name belongs to the person addressed, the second to the person who addresses him. . . . You have to accept this and understand the verse in this way, because it is quite clear in the Greek. . . . God was anointed by God, and when you hear the word *anointed*, understand that it means Christ, for "Christ" is derived from "chrism," and the name "Christ" means "Anointed one." EXPOSITIONS OF THE PSALMS 45.19.[44]

UNCOMMON OINTMENT. EUSEBIUS OF CAESAREA: This ointment mentioned was nothing common or earthly, nothing resembling that ordained by the Mosaic law, fashioned of corruptible matter, with which it was the custom to anoint Hebrew priests and kings. PROOF OF THE GOSPEL 5.2.217.[45]

ANOINTED WITH THE SPIRIT. CYRIL OF JERUSALEM: Christ was not anointed by people with oil or material ointment, but the Father, having before appointed him to be the Savior of the whole world, anointed him with the Holy Spirit. . . . As he was anointed with an ideal oil of gladness, that is, with the Holy Spirit, called oil of gladness, because he is the author of spiritual gladness, so you were anointed with ointment, having been made partakers and "fellows of Christ." CATECHETICAL LECTURES 21.2.[46]

A PARTIAL SHARING OF THE SPIRIT. BASIL THE GREAT: The flesh of the Lord was anointed with the true anointing, by the coming of the Holy Spirit into it, which was called "the oil of gladness." And he was anointed above his fellows; that is to say, all people who are members of Christ. Therefore, a certain partial sharing of the Spirit was given to them, but the Holy Spirit descending on the Son of God, as John says, "abode on him."[47] HOMILIES ON THE PSALMS 17.8 (Ps 45).[48]

NONE LIKE HIM. CHRYSOSTOM: Christ, to be sure, was nowhere anointed with oil but with the Holy Spirit. For this reason he added "beyond your companions" to indicate this very fact, that no one was like him. COMMENTARY ON THE PSALMS 45.9.[49]

THE FONT AND THE DROPS. JEROME: You have been anointed with the oil of gladness above your fellow people, above your apostles. You possess the font of unction; they, the drops. HOMILY ON PSALM 132[133].[50]

ANOINTED WITH THE OIL OF JOY. ARNOBIUS THE YOUNGER: God anoints him before his own people with the oil of joy. Just as he appeared before humankind incarnate and perfect, Christ appeared anointed with oil before all Christians. There were many righteous people from Abel to Christ, but none born of a virgin, none of this appearance, this form. Who is like our God among the children of God? Let us, children pleasing to him, listen to this one, anointed with oil of anointing, as angels worshiped, the stars sang out and the prophets prophesied. As John was fearing, the skies opened, the Father called from heaven, and the Spirit descended from the heavens and remained on him. It is Christ, the first before the partakers who share this name. COMMENTARY ON THE PSALMS 45.[51]

ONE PERSON, TWO NATURES. THEODORE OF MOPSUESTIA: On the one hand, he separated the natures by uttering definite statements of different ideas (there being a great difference between "Your throne, O God, is forever and ever" and "Hence, God your God anointed you"), and on the other hand, he gave a glimpse of the union by saying this of one person. COMMENTARY ON PSALMS 45.8B.[52]

---

[44]WSA 3 16:296-97. [45]POG 1:236. [46]NPNF 2 7:149*. [47]Jn 1:32. [48]FC 46:289*. [49]CCOP 1:276. [50]FC 48:335*. [51]CCL 25:63-64. [52]WGRW 5:579-81.

ANOINTED AS MAN. THEODORET OF CYR: He was also anointed in the all-holy Spirit, not as God but as a human being: as God he was of one being with the Spirit, whereas as a human being he receives the gifts of the Spirit like a kind of anointing. Thus he "loved righteousness and hated lawlessness": this is a matter of intentional choice, not of natural power, whereas as God he has "a rod of equity as the rod of his kingship." COMMENTARY ON THE PSALMS 45.6.[53]

ANOINTED AT CONCEPTION. GREGORY THE GREAT: He was anointed above his fellows, because all we people first exist as sinners and afterwards are sanctified through the unction of the Holy Spirit. But he who, existing as God before the ages, was conceived as man through the Holy Spirit in the Virgin's womb at the end of the ages was there anointed by the same Spirit, even where he was conceived. Nor was he first conceived and afterwards anointed; but to be conceived by the Holy Spirit of the flesh of the Virgin was itself to be anointed by the Holy Spirit. LETTER 67.[54]

ANOINTED FOR OUR SAKE. ATHANASIUS: He is here "anointed," not that he may become God, for he was so even before, or that he may become King, for he had the kingdom eternally, existing as God's image, as the sacred Oracle shows; but for our sake is this written. DISCOURSES AGAINST THE ARIANS 1.46.[55]

THE SPIRIT'S ANOINTING. ATHANASIUS: The word *therefore* does not imply the reward of virtue or conduct in the Word but the reason why he came down to us. It indicates that the Spirit's anointing took place in him for our sakes. For he does not say, "Therefore he anointed you so that you will be God or King or Son or Word," for he was already such before and is forever . . . ; but rather, "Since you are God and King, therefore you were anointed, since none but you could unite humanity to the Holy Spirit, you the image of the Father, in which we were made in the beginning; for even the Spirit is yours." For the nature of things originate could give no warranty for this, angels having transgressed and people disobeyed. Therefore there was need of God; and the Word is God, that he himself might set free those who had come under a curse. If then he was of nothing, he would not have been the Christ or Anointed, being one among others and having fellowship as the rest. But, since he is God, being the Son of God, and is everlasting King and exists as radiance and expression of the Father, therefore he is rightly the expected Christ, whom the Father announces to humankind, by revelation to his holy prophets; that as through him we have come to be, so also in him all people might be redeemed from their sins and by him all things might be ruled. And this is the reason for the anointing that took place in him, and of the incarnate presence of the Word, which the psalmist foreseeing, celebrates, first his Godhead and kingdom, which is the Father's, in these tones, "Your throne, O God, is forever and ever; a scepter of righteousness is the scepter of your kingdom"; then announces his descent to us thus, "Wherefore God, even your God, has anointed you with the oil of gladness above your fellows." DISCOURSES AGAINST THE ARIANS 1.49.[56]

SHARERS OF SPIRITUAL GRACE. BEDE: God, his God, has anointed him with the oil of gladness above his companions in order that he may deign to make us also companions of that anointing of his, that is, sharers of spiritual grace. HOMILIES ON THE GOSPELS 1.25.[57]

THE FAVOR OF ANOINTING. BEDE: He himself promised the favor of the same holy anointing to his companions,[58] . . . that is, to the faithful; and he sent what he had promised, as we know, not long after. HOMILIES ON THE GOSPELS 2.15.[59]

---

[53]FC 101:263. [54]NPNF 2 13:83-84*. [55]NPNF 2 4:333*. [56]NPNF 2 4:335**. [57]CS 110:252. [58]Acts 1:8. [59]CS 111:140.

45:8 Robes Fragrant with Myrrh

A NON-MATERIAL INTERPRETATION. CHRYSOSTOM: Just as on hearing reference to bow and sword and all those similar things you do not take them in a material way, so on hearing mention of myrrh and cassia you would not think of them in a material way but at an intellectual level. COMMENTARY ON THE PSALMS 45.10.[60]

THE GOSPEL SYMBOLIZED. BASIL THE GREAT: The sweet odor of Christ gives forth the fragrance of myrrh because of his passion, and of aloes because he did not remain motionless and inactive for three days and three nights but descended to the lower world to distribute the graces of the resurrection. . . . And it breathes forth the fragrance of cassia, a very delicate and fragrant bark, . . . because of the suffering of the cross undertaken in kindness to every creature. Therefore, you have myrrh because of burial; aloes, because of the passage down to the lower world (since every drop is borne downward); and cassia, because of the dispensation of the flesh on the wood. . . . And these aromatic herbs, he says, are not sparingly present in the garments of Christ (that is to say, the parable of the sermons and the preparation of the doctrines) but are brought from all the buildings. He says that the largest of the dwellings are houses and that these are constructed of ivory, because the prophet is teaching, I think, the wealth of the love of Christ for the world. HOMILIES ON THE PSALMS 17.9 (Ps 45).[61]

THE FRAGRANCE OF CHRIST. THEODORE OF MOPSUESTIA: In his wish to imply both the passion and the glory of the passion he says "myrrh, resin, and cassia from your garments," suggesting by "myrrh" the passion, and by mention of "resin and cassia" implying the fragrance and splendor of the passion, as if to say, Even the passion itself, which affects your temple, will be accompanied by great fragrance and glory, with the result that the fragrance from it will spread to the whole world, as the apostle also says: "We are the fragrance of Christ among those who are being saved and among those who are perishing."[62] Now, he did well to mention "myrrh" and associate it with the phrase "from your garments" for us to understand the divinity to be free of suffering. COMMENTARY ON PSALMS 45.9A.[63]

FUTURE CHURCHES. DIODORE OF TARSUS: By "buildings" he means houses, and by "ivory" the splendor of the houses, by this implying the churches. So his intention is to say that after the death of Christ splendid and beautiful temples will be erected to him, like the churches to be seen in our day. COMMENTARY ON PSALMS 45.[64]

45:9 Daughters of Kings, a Queen in Gold

THE QUEEN IS THE SOUL. BASIL THE GREAT: The queen . . . is the soul that is joined with the Word, its Bridegroom; not subjected by sin but sharing the kingdom of Christ, it stands on the right hand of the Savior in gilded clothing, that is to say, adorning itself charmingly and religiously with spiritual doctrines, interwoven and varied. HOMILIES ON THE PSALMS 17.9 (Ps 45).[65]

THE DAUGHTER OF GOD. JEROME: What can be fairer than a soul that is called the daughter of God and that seeks for itself no outward adorning. She believes in Christ, and dowered with this hope of greatness, makes her way to her spouse, for Christ is at once her bridegroom and her Lord. LETTER 54.3.[66]

OFFSPRING OF THE GOSPEL. AUGUSTINE: When these kings preach and spread the gospel, many souls are born to them, and all these souls are "the daughters of kings.". . . The daughters of kings can also be taken to represent the cities that have believed in Christ and were founded by kings. . . . They are no longer seeking to promote

---

[60]CCOP 1:277. [61]FC 46:290-91. [62]2 Cor 2:15. [63]WGRW 5:581-83. [64]WGRW 9:145. [65]FC 46:291*. [66]NPNF 2 6:103*.

the reputation of their city fathers but are concerned to honor you . . . they have found favor with their true King and come to do him honor. And from all of them is formed one single queen. EXPOSITIONS OF THE PSALMS 45.23.[67]

THE CHURCH. THEODORE OF MOPSUESTIA: The church is in attendance on you, he is saying, on your right; that is, it will always be assembled for you. The church is always assembled in union with him both in purpose and in the grace of rebirth, just as members and body are with the head, as the apostle says in one place, "You are the body of Christ and individually members of it."[68] . . . For this reason, "at your right hand" was well put, as if to say by way of underlining the honor stemming from the more important member. [The church] is in attendance on you, enjoying the greatest honor from you. . . . clothed in much adornment. So while it was vouchsafed the dignity of sonship and called and made body of Christ, it was clothed in the greatest adornment, the beauty of the spiritual graces: the marvels performed through the saints were like a kind of golden and marvelous adornment, bringing splendor to the believers in Christ, who composed the church. COMMENTARY ON PSALMS 45.10A-C.[69]

45:10 Forget Your People

FORGET YOUR FORMER LIFE. DIODORE OF TARSUS: The church was formed from pagans and Jews, so he does well to say "Forget your people and your father's house," meaning idolatry and observance of the law, practicing instead a new life by grace. COMMENTARY ON PSALMS 45.[70]

45:11 Beauty

BEAUTY OF SOUL. CHRYSOSTOM: The reference is not to beauty of body, since he says it arises from obedience to him. Obedience, however, gives rise not to beauty of body but to beauty of soul. If you do this, he says, note, then you will

be beautiful, then you will be desirable to the groom. COMMENTARY ON THE PSALMS 45.11.[71]

BEAUTIFIED BY GOD. AUGUSTINE: What beauty is this, if not what he himself created in her? He has desired beauty, but whose? The beauty of a sinner, a wicked, ungodly woman, as she was in the house of her father the devil, and among her own people? No, no; but the beauty of the bride described in the Song of Songs: "Who is this who comes up washed in white?"[72] She was not white before, but now she has been washed pure white, as the Lord promises through a prophet: "Even if your sins are brilliant red, I will wash you white as snow."[73] . . . The King you are marrying is God; he provides you with your portion, by him you are adorned, by him redeemed, by him healed. Whatever you have in you that can please him, you have as his gift. EXPOSITIONS OF THE PSALMS 45.26.[74]

BE PLEASING TO CHRIST. FULGENTIUS OF RUSPE: Do not seek to please the eyes of human beings but seek not to offend the eyes of Christ. Let him see in you what he loves; let him find what he gave; let him recognize that by which he is delighted. "The king will desire your beauty," but "all the glory of the king's daughter is within." LETTER 2.25.[75]

BECOMING MORE BEAUTIFUL. CYRIL OF ALEXANDRIA: By progressing in virtue and attaining to better things, "reaching forth to those things that are before,"[76] according to the word of the blessed Paul, we rise ever to . . . spiritual beauty, so that to us too it may be said hereafter, "The king greatly desired your beauty." GLAPHYRA ON THE PENTATEUCH 49.21-26.[77]

YOUR MAKER. IRENAEUS: You do not make

---

[67]WSA 3 16:300-302. [68]1 Cor 12:27; cf. Col 2:19. [69]WGRW 5:585*. [70]WGRW 9:146. [71]CCOP 1:280. [72]Cf. Song 6:10. [73]Is 1:18. [74]WSA 3 16:304. [75]FC 95:302. [76]Phil 3:13. [77]PG 69:376.

God, but God makes you. If, then, you are God's workmanship, await the hand of your Maker that creates everything in due time; in due time as far as you are concerned, whose creation is being carried out. Offer to him your heart in a soft and tractable state, and preserve the form in which the Creator has fashioned you, having moisture in yourself, lest, by becoming hardened, you lose the impressions of his fingers. But by preserving the framework you shall ascend to that which is perfect, for the moist clay that is in you is hidden [there] by the workmanship of God. His hand fashioned your substance; he will cover you over [too] within and without with pure gold and silver, and he will adorn you to such a degree that even "the king himself shall have pleasure in beauty." . . . For creation is an attribute of the goodness of God; but to be created is that of human nature. If, then, you shall deliver up to him what is yours, that is, faith toward him and subjection, you shall receive his handiwork and shall be a perfect work of God. AGAINST HERESIES 4.39.2.[78]

45:12 The People of Tyre

THE GENTILES. CHRYSOSTOM: The inspired author, forebearing to mention the whole world, refers to the neighboring city, which at that time was in the grip of impiety, the devil's stronghold, with an awful reputation for extravagance, and he thus implies the whole from the part. COMMENTARY ON THE PSALMS 45.11.[79]

TYRE SYMBOLIZES GENTILES. AUGUSTINE: Tyre was a neighbor to the land where prophecy flourished, so Tyre symbolized the Gentiles who were to believe in Christ. EXPOSITIONS OF THE PSALMS 45.27.[80]

45:13 Golden Robes

GIFTS OF THE SPIRIT. THEODORET OF CYR: Within, he is saying, she has the comeliness of virtue and is resplendent with the manifold gifts of the Holy Spirit. COMMENTARY ON THE PSALMS 45.10.[81]

AN INWARD GLORY. GREGORY OF NAZIANZUS: The visible beauty is not hidden, but that which is unseen is visible to God. All the glory of the king's daughter is within, clothed with golden fringes, embroidered whether by actions or by contemplation. ON THE WORDS OF THE GOSPEL, "WHEN JESUS HAD FINISHED THESE SAYINGS," ORATION 37.10.[82]

PURITY OF CONSCIENCE. THEODORE OF MOPSUESTIA: By "within" he refers to the mind, and the words can refer only to not bodily beauty but virtue of soul. This, in fact, is the true glory of the devout, purity of conscience, for which they will be utterly conspicuous in the judge's sight. COMMENTARY ON PSALMS 45.14A.[83]

DOCTRINE AND PRACTICE. BASIL THE GREAT: The spiritual garment is woven when the attendant action is interwoven with the word of doctrine. In fact, just as a bodily garment is woven when the woof is interwoven with the warp, so when the word is antecedent, if actions in accordance with the word should be produced, there would be made a certain most magnificent garment for the soul that possesses a life of virtue attained by word and action. HOMILIES ON THE PSALMS 17.11 (Ps 45).[84]

THE GOLDEN ORNAMENT OF VIRTUE. METHODIUS: The queen who, chosen out of many, stands at the right hand of God, clothed in the golden ornament of virtue, whose beauty the King desired, is, as I said, the undefiled and blessed flesh, which the Word himself carried into the heavens and presented at the right hand of God, "wrought about with many colors," that is, in the pursuits of immortality, which he calls symbolically golden fringes. This garment

---

[78]ANF 1:523**. [79]CCOP 1:281. [80]WSA 3 16:304. [81]FC 101:265. [82]NPNF 2 7:341. [83]WGRW 5:591. [84]FC 46:293-34.

is variegated and woven of various virtues, as chastity, prudence, faith, love, patience, and other good things, which, covering as they do the unseemliness of the flesh, adorn humankind with a golden ornament. BANQUET OF THE TEN VIRGINS 7.8.[85]

45:16 *Princes in the Earth*

REGENERATE SONS AND DAUGHTERS. IRENAEUS: The Lord, having been born "the First-begotten of the dead" and receiving into his bosom the ancient ancestors, has regenerated them into the life of God, he having been made himself the beginning of those that live, as Adam became the beginning of those who die. AGAINST HERESIES 3.22.4.[86]

APOSTOLIC PRINCES. CHRYSOSTOM: The apostles, you recall, traversed the whole world and became rulers more masterful than all other rulers, more powerful than emperors. Emperors, after all, are in power while alive but on their death are no more, whereas the apostles exercise power at their death. And while emperors' laws are in force within their own boundaries, the fishermen's commands extend to every part of the world. The Roman emperor cannot legislate for the Persians, nor the Persian for the Romans, whereas these Palestinians passed laws for Persians, Romans, Thracians, Scythians, Indians, Moors and the whole world. The laws remained in force not only while they were alive but also after their death; and those subject to them would prefer to lose their life rather than abjure those laws. COMMENTARY ON THE PSALMS 45.13.[87]

45:17 *The Peoples Will Praise You*

GIVE PRAISE TO CHRIST. CHRYSOSTOM: Where he began, there he concluded—in Christ. . . . Because you have achieved so much, you have appointed such rulers, you have driven out evil, you have planted virtue, you have plighted your troth to our nature, you have performed these wonderful good things. All the world will offer you hymns of praise, not for a short time, not for ten, not twenty, not a hundred years, or in one part of the world, but earth and sea, both inhabited and uninhabited, will sing praise for all time, giving thanks for all the good things accomplished. For all these good things let us too give thanks to the loving Christ, through whom and with whom be the glory to the Father, together with Holy Spirit, now and forever, for ages of ages. COMMENTARY ON THE PSALMS 45.13.[88]

---

[85]ANF 6:334*. [86]ANF 1:455*. [87]CCOP 1:283. [88]CCOP 1:284.

46:1-11 GOD IS OUR REFUGE

When you have fled to God for refuge and are delivered
from the afflictions round about you, if you wish
to give thanks to God and to recount his kindness toward you,
you have Psalm 46.

ATHANASIUS *ON THE INTERPRETATION OF THE PSALMS* 19 [OIP 69]

*To the choirmaster. A Psalm of the Sons of
Korah. According to Alamoth. A Song.*

*¹God is our refuge and strength,
a very present¹ help in trouble.
²Therefore we will not fear though the earth
should change,
though the mountains shake in the heart of
the sea;
³though its waters roar and foam,
though the mountains tremble with its
tumult.* Selah

*⁴There is a river whose streams make glad
the city of God,
the holy habitation of the Most High.
⁵God is in the midst of her, she shall not be
moved;*

*God will help her right early.
⁶The nations rage, the kingdoms totter;
he utters his voice, the earth melts.
⁷The LORD of hosts is with us;
the God of Jacob is our refuge.ᵐ* Selah

*⁸Come, behold the works of the LORD,
how he has wrought desolations in the
earth.
⁹He makes wars cease to the end of the earth;
he breaks the bow, and shatters the spear,
he burns the chariots with fire!
¹⁰ "Be still, and know that I am God.
I am exalted among the nations,
I am exalted in the earth!"
¹¹The LORD of hosts is with us;
the God of Jacob is our refuge.ᵐ* Selah

l Or *well proved* m Or *fortress*

OVERVIEW: The forty-sixth psalm follows the forty-fifth thematically by speaking of the protection of those who are blessed with Christ (THEODORET). There is one struggle that ultimately concerns us, and one refuge in the fight (BASIL). God helps us with his own presence (CHRYSOSTOM). Our refuge is strength itself (AUGUSTINE), which avails in every tribulation (AUGUSTINE). God can become our refuge when we call to him (ARNOBIUS THE YOUNGER). Christ dwells in our hearts by faith (AUGUSTINE). Every

difficulty is easy for him (CHRYSOSTOM). The river of God's providence extends to all things (CHRYSOSTOM). The river of his spirit gives joy to the city of God (AUGUSTINE), the city administered according to heavenly law (BASIL), according to the gifts of the Spirit (EVAGRIUS), to the point of fruitfulness (THEODORET). God is present throughout the city (THEODORE OF MOPSUESTIA) to provide support on all sides (CHRYSOSTOM).

At the time of darkness (ARNOBIUS THE

YOUNGER), God causes his light to rise and illumines his city by everlasting light (BASIL), just as the Lord's resurrection brought the dawning of spiritual grace (AMBROSE). The kingdom of sin (AMBROSE) is not conquered by any creature (AUGUSTINE) or any other god than the God of Jacob (BASIL). So, let us draw near to him (BASIL) and behold the marvels of the Lord (CHRYSOSTOM). God is sovereign over the enemies of peace (DIODORE), even using their own weapons against them, the weapons of their hearts (EVAGRIUS). He equips us with new weapons, weapons of grace (AUGUSTINE). The Lord alone is God (AUGUSTINE), and he is known in the quiet of a purified mind (ORIGEN), both now and forever (BEDE). This, then, is God (CHRYSOSTOM), who has extended his church throughout the earth and will bring to pass the future he promised for his people Israel (AUGUSTINE).

46:1 God Is Our Refuge

PROTECTION OF BELIEVERS. THEODORET OF CYR: After the previous psalm prophesied about the church's being composed from godless nations and becoming a queen, and showed her sons to be made princes of the whole earth, here it gives a glimpse of the disturbances that occurred in the beginning of the preaching, with uprisings developing and opposing the believers. Then it foreshadows in word how the ranks of the persecuted would be protected by hope in God and scorn the waves crashing around them: with the God of all as strong rampart, he is saying, we shall not notice the tribulations of all kinds. COMMENTARY ON THE PSALMS 46.2.[1]

ONE FLIGHT, ONE REFUGE. BASIL THE GREAT: Do not flee what you do not need to flee, and do not have recourse to him to whom it is unnecessary. But one thing you must flee: sin; and one refuge from evil must be sought: God. Do not trust in princes; do not be exalted in the uncertainty of wealth; do not be proud of bodily strength; do not pursue the splendor of human

glory. None of these things saves you; all are transient, all are deceptive. There is one refuge, God. . . . God is the true aid for the righteous. Just as a certain general, equipped with a noble, heavy-armed force, is always ready to give help to an oppressed district, so God is our helper and an ally to everyone who is waging war against the wiliness of the devil, and he sends out ministering spirits for the safety of those who are in need. HOMILIES ON THE PSALMS 18.1-2 (Ps 46).[2]

GOD'S PRESENCE IN TRIBULATION. CHRYSOSTOM: He does not prevent tribulations coming, but he is at hand when they come, making us tried and tested . . . providing greater encouragement from the assistance than the pain from the tribulations. The assistance he provides us with, you see, is not simply as much as the nature of the troubles requires but much more. COMMENTARY ON THE PSALMS 46.1.[3]

OUR REFUGE IS STRENGTH. AUGUSTINE: Some refuges are anything but strong, so that anyone who flees to them is weakened rather than securely established. . . . But our refuge is quite different; our refuge is "strength." When we flee to it, we shall be secure and unshakable. EXPOSITIONS OF THE PSALMS 46.2.[4]

IN EVERY TRIBULATION. AUGUSTINE: There are many kinds of tribulation, and in all of them we must seek refuge in God, whether the trouble concerns our income, our bodily health, some danger threatening those we love or something we need to support our life. Whatever it is, there should be no refuge for a Christian other than our Savior. He is God, and when we flee to him, we are strong. No Christian will be strong in himself or herself; but God, who has become our refuge, will supply the strength. EXPOSITIONS OF THE PSALMS 46.3.[5]

---

[1]FC 101:268. [2]FC 46:299-300*. [3]CCOP 1:291-92. [4]WSA 3 16:311. [5]WSA 3 16:311.

HE CAN BECOME YOUR REFUGE. ARNOBIUS THE YOUNGER: When in tears and tribulation you pour out a prayer to God, be secure, for God becomes a refuge to you and becomes your strength. COMMENTARY ON THE PSALMS 46.[6]

46:2 We Will Not Fear

CHRIST IN OUR HEARTS. AUGUSTINE: Christ dwells in the heart of each one of us through our faith. . . . If we forget our faith, our heart is like a boat battered and tossed about in this stormy world, because Christ seems to be asleep. But when he awakes, there is calm. EXPOSITIONS OF THE PSALMS 46.5.[7]

EVERYTHING IS EASY FOR GOD. CHRYSOSTOM: Everything he shakes, he rocks, he moves when he wishes, so easy and trouble-free is everything for him. . . . So great is his power, you see, that he simply nods and all this happens. So how can we be afraid when we have such a Lord? COMMENTARY ON PSALM 46.1.[8]

46:4 A River in the City of God

THE RIVER OF GOD'S PROVIDENCE. CHRYSOSTOM: As a river divided into countless tributaries waters the surrounding land, so God's providence flows everywhere, spreading copiously, advancing in a rush and covering everything. COMMENTARY ON THE PSALMS 46.1.[9]

THE RIVER OF THE SPIRIT. AUGUSTINE: Mountains quiver, the sea rages, but God stays faithful to his city by means of this impetuous river. What is it, and what are its impulses? They are the inundation of the Spirit. . . . When Jesus had been glorified after his resurrection and ascension, the Holy Spirit came on the day of Pentecost and filled the believers. They spoke in tongues and began to preach the good news to the Gentiles. At this the city of God was overjoyed, though the sea was heaving with its noisy waves and the mountains were quaking and

asking themselves what they should do, and how they could get rid of this new teaching and how they might uproot the Christian race from the earth. But against whom was all this agitation directed? Against the irresistible impulses of the river that were giving joy to God's city. EXPOSITIONS OF THE PSALMS 46.8.[10]

ADMINISTERED ACCORDINGLY TO HEAVENLY LAW. BASIL THE GREAT: Some give the definition that a city is an established community, administered according to law. And the definition that has been handed down of the city is in harmony with the celestial city, Jerusalem above. For there it is a community of the first-born who have been enrolled in heaven,[11] and this is established because of the unchanging manner of life of the saints, and it is administered according to the heavenly law. Therefore, it is not the privilege of human nature to learn the arrangement of that city and all its adornment. Those are the things "eye has not seen nor ear heard, nor has it entered into the human heart, what things God has prepared for those who love him,"[12] but there are myriads of angels there, and an assembly of saints and a church of the firstborn that are enrolled in heaven. Concerning that David said, "Glorious things are said of you, O city of God."[13] To that city through Isaiah God has promised, "I will make you to be an everlasting glory, a joy unto generation and generation, and there shall not be wasting nor destruction in your borders, and salvation shall possess your walls."[14] Therefore, having raised the eyes of your soul, seek, in a manner worthy of things above, what pertains to the city of God. HOMILIES ON THE PSALMS 18.4 (Ps 46).[15]

GIFTS OF THE SPIRIT. EVAGRIUS OF PONTUS: The city of God, or the church, is the reasonable spirit. The flowing of the river is the gifts of the

---

[6]CCL 25:65. [7]WSA 3 16:314. [8]CCOP 1:292. [9]CCOP 1:293. [10]WSA 3 16:316. [11]Heb 12:23. [12]1 Cor 2:9. [13]Ps 87:3 (86:3 LXX). [14]Is 60:15, 18. [15]FC 46:302-3*.

Spirit. Notes on the Psalms 45[46].5.[16]

Fruitfulness. Theodoret of Cyr: He gave the name "river" here to the preaching of the gospel and "city" to the way of life of God-fearing people, watered by the streams of the river to the point of fruitfulness. Commentary on the Psalms 46.5.[17]

46:5 God in the Midst

Throughout the City. Theodore of Mopsuestia: He was not in one part of the city and cut off from another but "in its midst," surrounding it all, protecting it all equally from the foe. Commentary on Psalms 46.6a.[18]

Support on All Sides. Chrysostom: He who is in fact so exalted, uncircumscribed by place, the ineffable being, deigned to call our city his dwelling and sustains it from every quarter. This, you see, is the meaning of "in her midst," as elsewhere also he says, "Behold, I am with you."[19] He supports it on all sides; thus not only will the city come to no harm, but it will not even be shaken. The reason is that it enjoys the most prompt assistance, which is ever ready and prepared; this, you see, is the meaning of "as day dawns," not pending or delayed but ever fresh and abounding, and at the appropriate time. Commentary on the Psalms 46.2.[20]

At the Time of Darkness. Arnobius the Younger: The Hebrew says God will help the city at early dawn, that is, when the shadows of sinners pass across the flowings of the river, God, who is light, gives the beginning of light to its heart, and he helps the spirit that says, Lord, be our strength, our helper, God of Jacob. Commentary on the Psalms 46.[21]

Illumined by Everlasting Light. Basil the Great: Since God is in the midst of the city, he will give it stability, providing assistance for it at the first break of dawn . . . sending out

equal rays of his providence from all sides to the limits of the world. Preserving the justice of God, he apportions the same measure of goodness to all. . . . Now, the perceptible sun produces among us the early morning when it rises above the horizon opposite us, and the Sun of justice[22] produces the early morning in our soul by the rising of the spiritual light, making day in him who admits it. "At night" means we are in this time of ignorance. Therefore, having opened wide our mind, let us receive "the brightness of his glory," and let us be brightly illumined by the everlasting Light, "God will help it in the morning early." . . . For those on whom the spiritual light will rise, when the darkness that comes from ignorance and wickedness is destroyed, early morning will be at hand. Since, then, light has come into the world in order that he who walks about in it may not stumble, his help is able to cause the early morning . . . who on the third day, early on the morning of the resurrection, gained the victory through death. Homilies on the Psalms 18.5 (Ps 46).[23]

By Christ's Resurrection. Ambrose: By his resurrection at dawn, the Lord confers on us wonderful and heavenly helps. His resurrection dispelled the night and poured on us the light of day. As Scripture says, "Rise, O sleeper; arise from the dead, and Christ shall enlighten you."[24] Consider here a mystery. Christ suffered in the evening, and according to the Old Law, the lamb is slain at evening.[25] . . . In the evening of this world, when the light is failing, he is killed.[26] All this world would have been shrouded by even greater and more horrid darkness only that Christ came to us from heaven. He, the eternal light, came to us from heaven to restore to the human race the age of innocence. The Lord Jesus suffered, and by his blood forgave us our sins. The light of a pure conscience shone out and

---

[16]PG 12:1433. [17]FC 101:270. [18]WGRW 5:609. [19]Mt 28:20. [20]CCOP 1:293*. [21]CCL 25:65. [22]Mal 4:2. [23]FC 46:303-04*. [24]Eph 5:14. [25]Cf. Deut 16:6. [26]Cf. Mt 27:45.

a day of spiritual grace dawned with splendor. COMMENTARY ON TWELVE PSALMS 46.14.[27]

46:6 Kingdoms Totter

THE KINGDOM OF SIN. AMBROSE: Sin is a heavy kingdom, and it subjects to a heavy servitude the souls of all sinners. "Whoever commits sin is the slave of sin."[28] The kingdom of sin is the kingdom of death, and for a long time it held sway over all the earth. . . . The truth came, the figure ceased. Life came, the kingdom of death vanished. Forgiveness of sin came, and the chains of sin were undone. . . . The cult of idols and the enticement of sin began to diminish with the preaching and doctrine of the gospel. Perfidy bowed its head, and faith began to reign in the hearts of the nations. COMMENTARY ON TWELVE PSALMS 46.16.[29]

46:7 The God of Jacob

NOT ANY CREATURE. AUGUSTINE: Not on any human whatsoever, not on any potentate, not even on any angel, not on any creature earthly or heavenly do we rely. But "the Lord of hosts is with us; our supporter is the God of Jacob." He sent angels to us, and after the angels came himself; he came to receive service from the angels and to make us mortals the angels' equals. This was tremendous grace. If God is for us, who stands against us? . . . Let us be secure, then, and in tranquility of heart nourish a good conscience on the bread of the Lord. EXPOSITIONS OF THE PSALMS 46.11.[30]

NOT ANY OTHER GOD. BASIL THE GREAT: Our protector, he says, is not another God besides him who was handed down by the prophets. But [he is] the God of Jacob, who spoke in an oracle to his servant, "I am the God of Abraham, the God of Isaac and the God of Jacob."[31] HOMILIES ON THE PSALMS 18.6 (Ps 46).[32]

46:8 See the Works of the Lord

FIRST, DRAW NEAR. BASIL THE GREAT: Just as . . . great distances make the perception of visible objects dim, but a nearer approach offers a clear knowledge of the objects seen, so also in the case of objects of contemplation in the mind, he who has not drawn near to God is not able to see his works with the pure eyes of his mind. Therefore, "Come," first approach, then see the works of the Lord, which are prodigious and admirable. . . . He who has heard the call and has approached and cleaves to the One commanding will see him who through the cross made all things peaceful "whether on the earth or in the heavens."[33] HOMILIES ON THE PSALMS 18.7 (Ps 46).[34]

THE MARVELS OF THE LORD. CHRYSOSTOM: Since the weak prevailed over the strong, the few over the many, the powerless over the powerful, and the outcome defied expectations, rightly does he call them "marvels" for happening to everyone's surprise and being spread everywhere on earth. COMMENTARY ON THE PSALMS 46.2.[35]

46:9 Wars Cease

GOD IS SOVEREIGN. DIODORE OF TARSUS: He it is who routs all the enemy when he wishes and brings peace to the earth to the degree he wants. . . . He is the God who does away with the enemy with their own weapons when he wishes. COMMENTARY ON PSALMS 46.[36]

THE WEAPONS OF THE HEART. EVAGRIUS OF PONTUS: In this place the writer understands the worst habits and wicked thoughts in the words of bow, weapons and bucklers. NOTES ON THE PSALMS 45[46].10.[37]

NEW EQUIPMENT. AUGUSTINE: When anyone realizes that we are nothing in ourselves and cannot look to ourselves for any help at all, that

[27]ACTP 265. [28]Jn 8:34. [29]ACTP 266. [30]WSA 3 16:319. [31]Ex 3:6. [32]FC 46:305. [33]Col 1:20. [34]FC 46:306. [35]CCOP 1:295. [36]WGRW 9:149*. [37]PG 12:1436.

person's weapons have all been broken, and the wars that raged within him or her are quelled. ... If God takes up our cause, will he abandon us in our unarmed condition? By no means. He equips us, but with weapons of a different order, the evangelical weapons of truth, self-control, salvation, hope, faith and charity. We shall wield these weapons, but they will not come from ourselves. The arms we did have as from ourselves will have been burned, provided that we are enkindled by that fire of the Holy Spirit of which the psalm declares, "The shields he will burn with fire." You aspired to be powerful in yourself, but God has made you weak in order to make you strong with his strength, for your own was nothing but weakness. EXPOSITIONS OF THE PSALMS 46.13.[38]

46:10 God Exalted in the Earth

He Alone Is God. AUGUSTINE: "See, you are not God, but I am. I created you, and I recreate you; I formed you, and I form you anew; I made you, and I remake you. If you had no power to make yourself, how do you propose to remake yourself?" EXPOSITIONS OF THE PSALMS 46.14.[39]

The Quiet of a Pure Mind. ORIGEN: It is not possible to know him if one has not become still and purified one's mind. COMMENTARY ON THE GOSPEL OF JOHN 19.17.[40]

Known Forever. BEDE: When the labors and hardships of this age come to an end, and our debts, [that is] all our faults, have been forgiven, the entire people of the elect will rejoice eternally in the sole contemplation of the divine vision, and that most longed-for command of our Lord and Savior will be fulfilled: "Be still and see that I am God." HOMILIES ON THE GOSPELS 2.17.[41]

46:11 The Lord a Refuge

This Is God. CHRYSOSTOM: This, then, is God, everywhere mighty, everywhere exalted; this is God who takes his place with us always. Have no fear, then, be not disturbed, having an invincible Master as we do, to whom all honor and glory is fitting, together with the peerless Father and his vivifying Spirit, now and forever, and for ages of ages. COMMENTARY ON THE PSALMS 46.3.[42]

A Future for Israel. AUGUSTINE: But now that he is so glorified, will he abandon the Jewish people? Of that race the apostle said, "This I must say to you, to save you from conceit about your wisdom, that blindness has fallen on part of Israel, until the full tally of the Gentiles comes in."[43] Until, that is, the mountains have passed over to us, and the clouds have sent rain here, and the Lord has humbled our kingdoms by his thunder—"until the full tally of the Gentles comes in." And then what? "So that all Israel may be saved."[44] This is why the psalm in its last verse preserves the same order: "I will be exalted among the Gentiles," it says, "and exalted on earth." In the sea, and then on the land. Thus may all of us together sing the refrain, "The Lord of hosts is with us; our supporter is the God of Jacob." EXPOSITIONS OF THE PSALMS 46.15.[45]

---

[38]*WSA* 3 16:321-22. [39]*WSA* 3 16:322*. [40]FC 89:170. [41]CS 111:174. [42]CCOP 1:296. [43]Rom 11:25. [44]Rom 11:26. [45]*WSA* 3 16:323.

47:1-9 GOD IS EXALTED

Psalm 47 announces the Savior's ascension into heaven . . .
and the calling of the gentiles.

ATHANASIUS ON THE INTERPRETATION OF THE PSALMS 26, 8 [OIP 72, 60]**

To the choirmaster.
A Psalm of the Sons of Korah.

¹Clap your hands, all peoples!
    Shout to God with loud songs of joy!
²For the LORD, the Most High, is terrible,
    a great king over all the earth.
³He subdued peoples under us,
    and nations under our feet.
⁴He chose our heritage for us,
    the pride of Jacob whom he loves.   Selah

⁵God has gone up with a shout,

the LORD with the sound of a trumpet.
⁶Sing praises to God, sing praises!
    Sing praises to our King, sing praises!
⁷For God is the king of all the earth;
    sing praises with a psalm!ⁿ

⁸God reigns over the nations;
    God sits on his holy throne.
⁹The princes of the peoples gather
    as the people of the God of Abraham.
For the shields of the earth belong to God;
    he is highly exalted!

n Heb *Maskil*

OVERVIEW: The forty-seventh psalm presents us with a hymn of victory (THEODORET). In contrast to the devil, Christ is welcomed by the nations with a joyful reception (ARNOBIUS THE YOUNGER) because of the joy of the redeemed (CHRYSOSTOM). The Lord is exalted, even in the lowliness of the cross (CHRYSOSTOM). He is unlike any other (CHRYSOSTOM, DIODORE). He has subdued peoples of the earth to his will by means of his incarnation (ARNOBIUS THE YOUNGER) and the gospel message spread abroad by his apostles (CHRYSOSTOM). He has gathered believers from among the Jews (CHRYSOSTOM, THEODORET) as well as from the Gentiles. And let him possess my soul as well (ORIGEN). The Lord ascended joyfully into heaven (BEDE). The one who was once jeered now receives praises from all (AUGUSTINE). Let us, then, rise in our understanding (EVAGRIUS) and sing with understanding (AUGUSTINE, CAESARIUS, NICETAS) to the one confessed as king of all (DIODORE). Christ takes his throne in our minds (EVAGRIUS) and hearts (AUGUSTINE). He reigns over people of all nationalities (THEODORET) in all walks of life (CHRYSOSTOM).

Superscription: *To the Choirmaster. A Psalm of the Sons of Korah*

A HYMN OF VICTORY. THEODORET OF CYR: This psalm foretells the salvation of all the nations and predicts victory over enemies. It also gave a glimpse of the apostolic choir urging all the nations to hymn singing. Now, clapping is typical of victory, and shouting is the sound of victors. So the meaning of this psalm concurs with the previous one: that one foretold the victory indicated after turmoil and disturbances, and this one likewise recommends those who gained the victory to offer the hymn to the provider of the victory. He is revealed to you all, he says, as king most high and fearsome. While in ancient times this was known to Jews alone, in the present time it has been made clear also to the whole human race. COMMENTARY ON THE PSALMS 47.1.[1]

47:1 Clapping Hands

A JOYFUL RECEPTION. ARNOBIUS THE YOUNGER: Just as there is wailing by all the nations in the coming of the devil as we have heard the voice calling from heaven, "woe to land and sea, for the devil has been cast on you,"[2] so in the coming of our Jesus, there is joy: "all nations, clap your hands." COMMENTARY ON THE PSALMS 47.[3]

JOY OF THE REDEEMED. CHRYSOSTOM: With hands that were previously defiled, accursed, daily stained with blood in the impure sacrifices in which you took the lives of your children, performed shameful rites and went beyond the limits of nature itself, with these hands now clap. "Shout to God in a voice of happiness." With that tongue by which you tasted accursed things, by which you uttered blasphemous words, with that tongue shout a victory ode. . . . You have mounted above heavens and the heavens of heavens and have taken your place at the royal throne itself. Accordingly, "Shout to God," that is, offer thanksgiving to him, the victory to him, the trophy to him. The conflict is not human or the battle physical, nor is the contest over any earthly concern but over the heavens and those in the heavens. He personally conducted this war and gave us a share in the victory. COMMENTARY ON THE PSALMS 47.1-2.[4]

47:2 The Lord, a Great King

EXALTED IN LOWLINESS. CHRYSOSTOM: When you hear that your Lord was impaled, that he was hanged on the cross, that he was buried, that he descended to the lower parts of the earth, do not be discouraged or troubled: he is most high, and by nature most high. What is most high by nature would never change its exaltation, nor would it become lowly; rather, even in his lowliness his exaltation remains and is revealed. For even in his dying he then most of all demonstrated his power over death. "The light shines in the darkness," Scripture says, "and the darkness did not overcome it."[5] That was the way his elevation appeared in his lowliness. . . . At that time the sun diverted its rays, rocks were split, the veil torn, the earth disturbed, Judas expired, Pilate and his wife scared, the judge himself on the defensive. So when you hear that he was bound and scourged, do not be disturbed; rather, see him giving evidence of his might even in bondage. He said, "Whom do you seek?"[6] and hurled them on their back. Do you see how he is fearsome, working such marvels by voice and nod alone? COMMENTARY ON THE PSALMS 47.2.[7]

UNLIKE ANY OTHER. CHRYSOSTOM: This is really a great king, one who rids the world of error, and in a short space of time installs truth and abolishes the devil's tyranny, who was a great king even before there were subjects, having the might of his rule not in slaves, nor in pomp and circumstance but in nature itself. . . . This is a great king, the one whose dignity is not from without, who depends on no one for his kingship, who does all he wishes. . . . He chose his subjects in such a way as to persuade them to surrender their spirit rather than disregard what was commanded. Whereas the king enjoys the esteem of his subjects themselves, he by contrast provides the subjects with esteem; thus one is only a name, the other is reality. A great king is the one who made the whole world heaven,

---

[1]FC 101:273**. [2]Rev 12:12. [3]CCL 25:66. [4]CCOP 1:300-301*. [5]Jn 1:5. [6]Jn 18:4. [7]CCOP 1:301.

caused savages to have sound values and persuaded them to imitate angels. COMMENTARY ON THE PSALMS 47.3.[8]

LORD OF ALL. DIODORE OF TARSUS: He became manifest in the events themselves, by which he routed those harassing the godly and proved superior to their scheme, fearsome to the enemy and, in short, king like no other on earth, since he is also Lord of all. COMMENTARY ON PSALMS 47.[9]

47:3 Peoples and Nations Subdued

THROUGH INCARNATION. ARNOBIUS THE YOUNGER: When did he subject people under our feet? When he chose his inheritance for us from the person of Mary, whom the Holy Spirit chose. Then, he ascended with a shout and voice of trumpet. . . . Glory to God on high, angels tell the shepherds. Behold, the Lord rules over every nation. The Lord sits on his holy seat. COMMENTARY ON THE PSALMS 47.[10]

HE WORKED THROUGH THE APOSTLES. CHRYSOSTOM: What a marvel! He convinced those who crucified him to bow down in worship; those who mocked and blasphemed, those addicted to idol worship he taught to let their souls yield to his will. This transformation, you see, was not of the apostles' doing but done by him who led the way before them and moved their spirit. I mean, how could a fisherman or a builder have so changed the world had not the words of this person cleared all these obstacles? Sorcerers and tyrants and demagogues and philosophers and all their opponents they scared away like grains of dust and dissipated like smoke. In this way they spread the light of truth, employing not weapons or abundance of wealth but simple speech—or, rather, the speech was not simple but more potent than any action. So how? They called on the name of the crucified, and death skulked away, demons were put to flight, diseases were cured, bodily disfigurement

righted, wickedness dispelled, dangers dissipated and the elements transformed. . . . He it was who removed the obstacles as he went before them; he himself smoothed out problems and made difficult things easy. And yet everything was beset by conflicts, everything with snares and hazards, no foothold or places to stand firm, all havens obstructed, every house shut, the ears of all stopped. Nevertheless, as soon as they entered and spoke, all strongholds of the enemy fell, with the result that they even surrendered their souls and then withstood countless dangers for the sake of what they had been told. COMMENTARY ON THE PSALMS 47.3-4.[11]

47:4 A Heritage Chosen

BELIEVING JEWS. CHRYSOSTOM: Someone may be bewildered and uncertain, and say, "So how is it that the Jews do not believe today?" . . . Listen to what follows; he added, "the beauty of Jacob, which he loved." Here in fact he seems to me to be referring to the believers, as Paul indicated in saying, "It is not, however, as though the word of God had failed: not all of Israel belong to Israel; . . . it is not the children of the flesh who are children of God, but the children of the promise who are counted as descendants."[12] Now, the believers are rightly spoken of as the people's beauty; what could be more appealing, after all, than those who have come to faith? COMMENTARY ON THE PSALMS 47.5.[13]

THE BEAUTY OF JACOB. THEODORET OF CYR: The God of all, who subjected kings to us and gave us control of all the nations, and in addition to that entrusts the beauty and excellence of Jacob to us—not all the Jewish people, who are named for Jacob, in fact, but "the beauty of Jacob," the excellence and the elite of Jacob, those adorned with faith, who accepted the message without delay, who submitted to the

---

[8]CCOP 1:303*. [9]WGRW 9:150. [10]CCL 25:66. [11]CCOP 1:303-5. [12]Gen 21:12; Rom 9:6-8. [13]CCOP 1:305.

sweet yoke of the Savior. These, you see, he both "chose" and "loved," and to them he entrusted the apostolic governance. COMMENTARY ON THE PSALMS 47.2.[14]

MY SOUL. ORIGEN: But what does it profit me, if the seed of Abraham, "which is Christ,"[15] should possess "the cities of his enemies for an inheritance"[16] and should not possess my city? If in my city, that is, in my soul, which is "the city of the great king,"[17] neither his laws nor his ordinances should be observed? What does it profit me that he has subjected the whole world and possesses the cities of his enemies if he should not also conquer his enemies in me, if he should not destroy "the law that is in my members fighting against the law of my mind and that leads me captive in the law of sin"?[18] So, therefore, let each one of us do what is necessary that Christ may also conquer the enemies in his soul and in his body, and, subjecting and triumphing over them, may possess the city even of his soul. HOMILIES ON GENESIS 9.3.[19]

47:5 God Has Come Up

A JOYOUS ASCENSION. BEDE: He ascended with a shout of jubilation, since he sought heaven as the disciples rejoiced in the glory of his being lifted up. He ascended with the sound of the trumpet, since he went up to the throne of his heavenly kingdom as the angels heralded his return to judge the living and the dead. HOMILIES ON THE GOSPELS 2.15.[20]

47:6 Sing Praises to God

THE ONE THEY ONCE JEERED. AUGUSTINE: Those who were estranged from God jeered at Christ in his manhood, but you "sing psalms to him as our God," for he is not only man; he is God. He is man from the seed of David, but as God he is David's Lord. He took flesh from the Jews, "to whom belong the patriarchs, and from whom Christ was born according to the flesh," as

the apostle reminds us.[21] So Christ is truly sprung from the Jews, but only according to the flesh; for who is this Christ, who took fleshly nature from the Jews? "He is sovereign over all, God, blessed forever."[22] He was God before being made flesh: God in the flesh, God with flesh. Not only was he God before he took flesh: he was God before the earth, from which flesh was made, and not only God before the earth where flesh was made, but God before the sky, which was made earlier, and God before the first day was created, and God before all the angels came to be. Christ is God, because "in the beginning was the Word, and the Word was with God; he was God. Everything was made through him; no part of created being was made without him."[23] He through whom all things were made exists before all things. "Sing psalms to him as our God," then, "sing him psalms." EXPOSITIONS OF THE PSALMS 47.8.[24]

47:7 Sing with a Psalm

RISE WITH UNDERSTANDING. EVAGRIUS OF PONTUS: Pray as is fitting and without trouble, practice psalmody with understanding and harmony, and you will be like a young eagle soaring in the heights. CHAPTERS ON PRAYER 82.[25]

SING WITH UNDERSTANDING. AUGUSTINE: You were called from Gentile races to be Christians, and those Gentile pagans used to worship gods made by human hands and sing psalms to them, but not with understanding. If they had been singing with understanding, they would not have worshiped stones. When a human person endowed with reason sang to a stone devoid of reason, was that singing with understanding? It is different for us, brothers and sisters: we do not see with our eyes what we are worshiping, yet we have been put right in the matter of worship. Not seeing God with our eyes, we have

---

[14]FC 101:273. [15]Gal 3:16. [16]Gen 22:17. [17]Mt 5:35. [18]Rom 7:23. [19]FC 71:156. [20]CS 111:142. [21]Rom 9:5. [22]Rom 9:5. [23]Jn 1:1-3. [24]WSA 3 16:330*. [25]GAC 202.

a far higher notion of him. EXPOSITIONS OF THE PSALMS 47.9.[26]

SING TO FRUSTRATE SATAN. CAESARIUS OF ARLES: Let us, too, lift up our voices by singing or praying in church, so that our adversary, the devil, may depart in confusion at the holy sound. If not in deed, then surely in thought or word the devil usually creeps up to those who are silent or speak of idle, useless matters. When they are singing or praying he can in no way take advantage by his cunning of those whom he sees engaged mentally or vocally in God's praises. SERMON 80.2.[27]

SING IN HARMONY. NICETAS OF REMESIANA: We must sing with our intelligences; not only with the spirit (in the sense of sound of our voice) but also with our mind. We must think about what we are singing, lest we lose by distracting talk and extraneous thoughts the fruit of our effort. The sound and melody of our singing must be suitably religious. It must not be melodramatic but a revelation of the true Christianity within. It must have nothing theatrical about it but should move us to sorrow for our sins. Of course, you must all sing in harmony, without discordant notes. One of you should not linger unreasonably on the notes while his neighbor is going too fast; nor should one of you sing too low while another is raising his voice. Each one should be asked to contribute his part in humility to the volume of the choir as a whole. No one should sing unbecomingly louder or slower than the rest, as though for vain ostentation or out of human respect. The whole service must be carried out in the presence of God, not with a view to pleasing people. LITURGICAL SINGING 13.[28]

CONFESSED AS KING OF ALL. DIODORE OF TARSUS: Since he had said "king," he went on to say, not only ours but of "all the earth": the one responsible for some people conquering and others being conquered, as he wishes, no matter from what quarter they mount their charge, how could he not be confessed as king of all? The phrase "sing with understanding" means with a sense of what has been done and keeping in mind the achievements. COMMENTARY ON PSALMS 47.[29]

47:8 God Sits on His Holy Throne

THE THRONE OF CHRIST. EVAGRIUS OF PONTUS: The throne of God is Christ. The throne of Christ is the reasonable nature. NOTES ON THE PSALMS 46[47].9.[30]

PREPARE HIS THRONE IN YOUR HEART. AUGUSTINE: What is this holy throne? The heavens perhaps? . . . Yes, but do you want to be his throne too? Do not think such a thing beyond you; if you prepare a place for him in your heart, he comes and is pleased to set his throne there. EXPOSITIONS OF THE PSALMS 47.10.[31]

47:9 Shields of the Earth

ALL PEOPLES. THEODORET OF CYR: The promises to the patriarch Abraham, he is saying, took effect. Now the Lord of all promised to bless all the nations in his progeny. Accordingly, both these nations and their rulers abandoned their ancestral gods and are assembled with the God of Abraham, and they call this God theirs. COMMENTARY ON THE PSALMS 47.5.[32]

ALL WALKS OF LIFE. CHRYSOSTOM: Here he shows the extent of the gospel's influence, reaching not only simple people but even the very wearers of the crown and those seated on a royal throne. COMMENTARY ON THE PSALMS 47.6.[33]

---

[26]WSA 3 16:330-31. [27]FC 31:367. [28]FC 7:74*. [29]WGRW 9:151. [30]PG 12:1437. [31]WSA 3 16:331. [32]FC 101:275. [33]CCOP 1:308.

48:1-14 THE BEAUTY OF ZION

If [you wish to give thanks] on the second day of the week,
then [you have] Psalm 48.

ATHANASIUS ON THE INTERPRETATION OF THE PSALMS 23 [OIP 70]

A Song. A Psalm of the Sons of Korah.

¹Great is the LORD and greatly to be praised
in the city of our God!
His holy mountain, ²beautiful in elevation,
is the joy of all the earth,
Mount Zion, in the far north,
the city of the great King.
³Within her citadels God
has shown himself a sure defense.

⁴For lo, the kings assembled,
they came on together.
⁵As soon as they saw it, they were astounded,
they were in panic, they took to flight;
⁶trembling took hold of them there,
anguish as of a woman in travail.
⁷By the east wind thou didst shatter
the ships of Tarshish.
⁸As we have heard, so have we seen
in the city of the LORD of hosts,
in the city of our God,

which God establishes for ever. Selah

⁹We have thought on thy steadfast love,
O God,
in the midst of thy temple.
¹⁰As thy name, O God,
so thy praise reaches to the ends of the
earth.
Thy right hand is filled with victory;
¹¹let Mount Zion be glad!
Let the daughters of Judah rejoice
because of thy judgments!

¹²Walk about Zion, go round about her,
number her towers,
¹³consider well her ramparts,
go through her citadels;
that you may tell the next generation
¹⁴that this is God,
our God for ever and ever.
He will be our guide for ever.

OVERVIEW: The forty-eighth psalm declares the Lord to be great—a greatness without limits (CHRYSOSTOM), which becomes more and more wonderful to us (AMBROSE). Those who declare his greatness form his city, set on a hill (AUGUSTINE). He has made us a work of joy (AMBROSE), a joy rooted in the very being of God (EVAGRIUS), and has extended his peace, even to those places that were formerly sources of trouble (CHRYSOSTOM). We found help in no one else (AUGUSTINE), and God sustains his church in all its parts (THEODORET). We remember God's help (CHRYSOSTOM). When his kingship is recognized, it disturbs even the highest of the earth (ARNOBIUS THE YOUNGER), in light of a judgment newly revealed (ARNOBIUS OF SICCA). We trust God, not the winds of fortune (AUGUSTINE). Our strength is in his grace (CHRYSOSTOM). The promises that we have heard, we now see (AMBROSE) being fulfilled (AUGUSTINE).

Christ is the temple in which we contemplate the grace of God (AMBROSE). He is the right hand of God (EVAGRIUS). Righteousness is proper to his being (CHRYSOSTOM). To find the grains of his wheat in the world of straw, you must be wheat yourself (AUGUSTINE). Let us rejoice in his strength (ARNOBIUS THE YOUNGER), for he makes no mistakes in his judgment (AUGUSTINE). Let us stand firm in faith (CLEMENT OF ALEXANDRIA), let us keep preaching, keep singing (AMBROSE) and go about strengthening the church (THEODORET). Let us keep learning about our God (CHRYSOSTOM) and pass on what we learn to the next generation (THEODORET). Let us proclaim of the one incarnate that this is our God (AUGUSTINE).

48:1 Great Is the Lord

NO LIMITS. CHRYSOSTOM: While they say "great," they do not go so far as to say how great; no one knows that, after all, so he added as well, "and highly to be praised." There is no limit, you see, to his greatness. What it means, however, is something like this: It is necessary to praise him and sing to him alone, and this to an extraordinary degree; but the need is to sing his praises both for this infinite and incomprehensible greatness of his being and for the excess of his beneficence to us. COMMENTARY ON THE PSALMS 48.1.[1]

MORE AND MORE WONDERFUL. AMBROSE: He is everywhere great and powerful, but our narrow mind cannot take in the greatness of his divine power and grace. The closer our knowledge gets to God, the more wonderful his majesty appears to be. COMMENTARY ON TWELVE PSALMS 48.3.[2]

IN OUR LIVES. THEODORET OF CYR: Often the divine Scripture gives the name "city" not to the building but to the way of life. Accordingly, here too he says the Lord of all was shown to be great through the things done by him in connection with his city, which the elevation of its teachings rendered illustrious as though located on a lofty and mighty hill. COMMENTARY ON THE PSALMS 48.1.[3]

CITY ON A HILL. AUGUSTINE: This is the city set on a mountain that cannot be hidden, the lantern that is not concealed under a meal tub but known to all and universally renowned. Not every one is a citizen of it, but only those for whom the Lord is "great and exceedingly worthy of praise." EXPOSITIONS OF THE PSALMS 48.2.[4]

48:2 Joy of All the Earth

A WORK OF JOY. AMBROSE: Truly the Lord is called great. For consider, he has poured exaltation and joy over all the orb of this earth where previously the land produced the most dreadful growth of sin; he has made joyful the earth that once abounded in sorrow, tears and groans.[5] Now our conscience is set free from sin and can rejoice. Before this it was unhappy, it was drowned in the whirlpool of its own sin; but now, through the goodness and kindness of Christ, it is absolved from all error. COMMENTARY ON TWELVE PSALMS 48.4.[6]

DIVINE JOY. EVAGRIUS OF PONTUS: Joy is rooted in Christ. . . . His root is God the Word, which is in himself. NOTES ON THE PSALMS 47[48].3.[7]

SOURCE OF TROUBLE. CHRYSOSTOM: For what reason, tell me, does he now mention the north and describe to us the location of the place? Because from that quarter war generally broke out with the invasion of savages, and generally the inspired authors mention it, calling it "from the north," and speak in terms of a cauldron boiling from that direction. . . . This city generally vulnerable from that quarter you made impregnable. In other words, just as if someone were

---

[1]CCOP 1:312. [2]ACTP 272. [3]FC 101:276. [4]WSA 3 16:336. [5]Cf. Is 35:10. [6]ACTP 273. [7]PG 12:1440.

to say about the body, "That weak part I made stronger," he too is suggesting the same in this verse in the words, "The quarters from which come wailing and weeping," the basis of disasters, these parts run over with satisfaction, with tranquility; [the place from which] come threats and fears and dangers, [from them come] delight and happiness. No one any longer fears that northern part of creation, no one is anguished, no one is suspicious. All enjoy happiness, for you root it in satisfaction. COMMENTARY ON THE PSALMS 48.1.[8]

48:3 God, a Sure Defense

NO OTHER HELP. AUGUSTINE: To emphasize that this is the effect of grace, it adds, "When he upholds her," for what would that city have been, if God had not upheld it? It would collapse immediately if it had no such foundation, wouldn't it? No one can lay any foundation other than that which is laid already, Christ Jesus. That city is truly great, and the Lord is acknowledged in it, only when he upholds it. EXPOSITIONS OF THE PSALMS 48.4.[9]

THE UNITY OF THE CHURCH. THEODORET OF CYR: On the one hand, there is one church throughout all land and sea; thus we say in prayer, For the holy, single, universal and apostolic church, from one end of the world to the other. On the other hand, it is also divided into cities, towns and villages, which the inspired Word called "buildings." As each city is composed of different houses and yet is called one city, so there are countless churches that defy numbering, both on islands and on continents, but all constitute one by being united in the common harmony of the true teachings. In these the God of all became apparent. COMMENTARY ON THE PSALMS 48.3.[10]

48:4 The Kings Assembled

REMEMBERING GOD'S HELP. CHRYSOSTOM: At

this point he is describing a harsh war concerted from every direction and a famous victory. You see, after he said that God comes to [the city's] aid and gives evidence of great care, he then shows also how he came to its aid. When countless nations made an attack (this he suggests, note, in mentioning the great number of kings), and not simply an attack but concerted and combined, such extraordinary developments occurred that they departed, marveling at the surprising turn of events. . . . Thus it is clear that instead of the war being conducted in terms of human logic, it was God whose tactics directed the fighting, who not only depressed the enemies' spirits but also shook their resolve by causing distress in their ranks and prompting an unspeakable fear in them. It was the same as if a great fleet had assembled and an unfavorable wind came on them and smashed the ships, sank the triremes and instilled instant disorder. COMMENTARY ON THE PSALMS 48.2.[11]

48:5 Astounded and Panicked

WHEN GOD IS RECOGNIZED. ARNOBIUS THE YOUNGER: As he is recognized, the kings of the earth are disturbed. COMMENTARY ON THE PSALMS 48.[12]

A JUDGMENT NEWLY REVEALED. ARNOBIUS OF SICCA: This, I say, is man's real death, when souls that know not God shall be consumed in long-protracted torment with raging fire, into which certain fiercely cruel beings shall cast them, who were unknown before Christ and brought to light only by his wisdom. AGAINST THE HEATHEN 2.14.[13]

48:7 The East Wind

TRUST NOT THE WINDS OF FORTUNE. AUGUSTINE: We should no longer put our trust

---

[8]CCOP 1:314*. [9]WSA 3 16:339*. [10]FC 101:277. [11]CCOP 1:315*. [12]CCL 25:67. [13]ANF 6:440.

in setting our sails or in the favorable tide of worldly prosperity; our foundation must be in Zion. There we must find our stability, and not be tossed about by every gust of teaching. Those whose sails are swollen with the uncertain fortunes of this life are liable to be capsized, and all the pride of the Gentiles must be subjected to Christ, who "smashes the ships of Tarshish with a violent wind." EXPOSITIONS OF THE PSALMS 48.6.[14]

48:8 We Have Heard and Seen

GOD'S GRACE. CHRYSOSTOM: So what did he hear, and what did he see? That the grace of God renders the city stronger and intact. This, in fact, is its foundation, this its strength, this makes it impregnable—not human aid and help, or the power of weapons or towers and ramparts. What instead? God rules it as his own. This most of all it was, in fact, that they should have been taught, and towards this the inspired author constantly urges them. COMMENTARY ON THE PSALMS 48.3.[15]

FROM HEARING TO SIGHT. AMBROSE: Outside the city, we have heard. Inside the city, we have seen. God is the eternal light of this city.[16] The light of day shines there without the sun we know in this world, and of the moon there is no need. The foundation of this city belongs not to time but to eternity. COMMENTARY ON TWELVE PSALMS 48.15.[17]

PROMISES FULFILLED. AUGUSTINE: O blessed church, at one time you heard, and at another time you saw. The church heard the promises and now sees the promises fulfilled; it heard in prophecy what it now sees made manifest in the gospel. Everything that is now being realized was prophesied beforehand. Lift up your eyes; let your gaze sweep around the world, look at the inheritance that stretches to the ends of the earth; see how the promise is being made good. EXPOSITIONS OF THE PSALMS 48.7.[18]

48:9 The Temple of God

CHRIST, THE TEMPLE. AMBROSE: God's true temple is the body of Christ, and in that body lies the purification of all our sins. Truly, that flesh is God's temple, and in it there is no contagion of sin. On the contrary, it was itself the sacrifice that takes away the sin of all the world. That flesh is indeed God's temple, and in it shone God's image. In it there dwelled the fullness of divinity in a bodily manner,[19] for Christ is himself that fullness. . . . In that temple, the psalmist tells us, "we have received your mercy." . . . Just as Christ is redemption, so too he is mercy. No greater mercy can there be than that he should offer himself as a victim for our crimes. He sacrificed himself to wash the world clean in his blood, for in no other way could our sin be abolished. COMMENTARY ON TWELVE PSALMS 48.16-17.[20]

48:10 To the Ends of the Earth

CHRIST THE RIGHT HAND. EVAGRIUS OF PONTUS: The right hand of God is Christ, who is filled with righteousness and from his fullness we receive everything. NOTES ON THE PSALMS 47[48].11.[21]

PROPER TO HIS BEING. CHRYSOSTOM: As it belongs to fire to heat, to the sun to give light, just so as well the role of benefactor belongs to him—not in the same manner, however, but even much more. Thus he spoke also this way, "Your right hand is filled with righteousness," suggesting abundance, relation to his being. COMMENTARY ON THE PSALMS 48.3.[22]

WHEAT AMONG THE STRAW. AUGUSTINE: To be sure, we cannot deny that there are very many bad people, so many that the good can scarcely

---

[14]WSA 3 16:341-42. [15]CCOP 1:316*. [16]Rev 21:23. [17]ACTP 279. [18]WSA 3 16:342*. [19]Col 2:9. [20]ACTP 280. [21]PG 12:1440. [22]CCOP 1:317.

be seen among them, just as the grains of wheat are almost invisible on the threshing floor. Anyone who glances at the threshing floor will think there is nothing there but straw. An inexperienced onlooker regards it as a waste of time to send in oxen and have workers sweating away in the heat threshing the straw. But hidden within it is a mass of grain that will be winnowed out. Then the bulky yield of grain, which was hidden by the bulk of the straw, will be evident. Do you want to find the good people? Be one yourself, and you will find them. EXPOSITIONS OF THE PSALMS 48.9.[23]

48:11 Let Zion Be Glad

REJOICE. ARNOBIUS THE YOUNGER: Let Mount Zion rejoice; let the church rejoice; the daughters of Judah rejoice. You have judged all the spirits from the womb of the church, so that you may yoke the devil and may free the souls of people. Now, O freed spirits, encompass your mother Zion, whom you have followed; tell his mercy to the towers. In the towers they defend the city and resist the enemies. Place your hearts in his strength. Consider with what strength he fights for you . . . , so you may tell later generations. COMMENTARY ON THE PSALMS 48.[24]

GOD MAKES NO MISTAKES. AUGUSTINE: God makes no mistakes when he judges. Let your life stand out in contrast, though by birth you blend in with them, for the plea that went up from your lips and your heart has not gone unheard: "Do not destroy my soul with the ungodly, nor my life with those who shed blood."[25] God is a highly skilled winnower. He will bring his winnowing shovel with him and will not let a single grain of wheat fall into the heap of chaff for burning or a single wisp of straw get into the barn to be stored. Dance for joy, daughters of Judea, over the judgments of a God who makes no mistakes, and do not arrogate to yourselves the right to make judgments in advance. It is your job to garner, his to sift

what has been garnered. EXPOSITIONS OF THE PSALMS 48.11.[26]

48:12 Walk Around Zion

STAND FIRM IN FAITH. CLEMENT OF ALEXANDRIA: [This] it intimates, I think, those who have sublimely embraced the Word, so as to become lofty towers and to stand firmly in faith and knowledge. STROMATEIS 7.13.[27]

KEEP PREACHING, KEEP SINGING. AMBROSE: Those who have wisely surrounded Zion and embraced it spiritually climb up onto its towers. There they tell of it to those not able to ascend its turrets. . . . Always the insidious foe has his eye on it, to see if he can approach and capture it. For Satan has his armies, and with them he lays siege to souls. He has siege engines that he moves up close to the walls so as to take its towers by force. But you, says the psalm, must preach from the towers. . . . Preach, proclaim, without intermission, without end. Your enemy does not sleep; he goes round like a raging animal seeking someone to devour.[28] Keep singing the praises of the Lord, for he can smash the lion's teeth and break his jaw to pieces.[29] COMMENTARY ON TWELVE PSALMS 48.22.[30]

STRENGTHEN THE CHURCH. THEODORET OF CYR: He calls the godly form of government "Zion," that is, the church throughout the world, and "its towers" those devoted to virtue and imitating on earth the way of life of the angels, encircling and protecting it like towers. "Buildings" likewise, as we have said before, the churches divided among the cities, towns and villages: he speaks of them as one and many. So the inspired word, the grace of the all-holy Spirit, urges those to whom the saving message was entrusted to go around and move about, both to strengthen

---

[23]WSA 3 16:345. [24]CCL 25:68. [25]Ps 26:9 (25:9 LXX). [26]WSA 3 16:346. [27]ANF 2:547. [28]Cf. 1 Pet 5:8. [29]Cf. Ps 58:6 (57:7 LXX).\ [30]ACTP 283.

the towers with teaching and confirm its other force, and in addition to this to apportion care of the churches, as we have already remarked on the forty-fifth psalm. He urges it here, too: "take its buildings one by one," so that one may care for this church and another for that, and be in charge of each by way of cultivating and exercising due care. COMMENTARY ON THE PSALMS 48.6.[31]

48:13 Consider the Defenses

LEARN ABOUT GOD. CHRYSOSTOM: The psalmist exhorts the people, "Behold this city." . . . Understand something from . . . its structure, its beauty, its fame, so as to learn from this God's power, how he made the lost city more mighty, and recount to your progeny God's power and the enduring course of his providence; his care of us, his leadership and shepherding last forever. Stories of this to those who come after will, in fact, prove an occasion for great advance in wisdom, a basis for more precise knowledge of God and a study of virtue. COMMENTARY ON THE PSALMS 48.3.[32]

PASS IT ON. THEODORET OF CYR: Each generation has to pass on to the next what we have received from the former so that the saving message may pass to all generations, and all people know that he is our God and Lord, good shepherd, everlasting. Since he said, "take its buildings one by one," and entrusted to them the task of shepherding, of necessity he taught that there is one good shepherd, who laid down his life for the sheep, shepherding forever, and shepherding not only the sheep but also those called pastors of the sheep. COMMENTARY ON THE PSALMS 48.7.[33]

48:14 This Is Our God

OUR GOD INCARNATE. AUGUSTINE: The earth was visible, but the Creator of the earth was not. Christ's flesh could be touched, but God in the flesh was not so readily recognized. They from whom his flesh was taken (for the Virgin Mary was from Abraham's stock) held onto his flesh, but they stayed at the level of the flesh and did not perceive his godhead. O you, apostles, O you, great city, preach from your towers and tell them, "This is our God." . . . If he is our God, he is our King as well. He protects us, because he is our God, and saves us from death; he rules us, because he is our King and saves us from falling. . . . For our part, let us choose to be ruled and liberated by him, for "this is our God forever and for ages unending; he it is who will guide us forever." EXPOSITIONS OF THE PSALMS 48.15.[34]

---

[31]FC 101:279. [32]CCOP 1:318. [33]FC 101:279-80. [34]WSA 3 16:348-49.

49:1-20 WHY FEAR DEATH?

If anyone is concerned for the suffering,
let him use these words [of the psalms], and he will help
the sufferers more and at the same time show his
own faith to be firm and true.

ATHANASIUS *ON THE INTERPRETATION OF THE PSALMS* 33 [OIP 77]

*To the choirmaster.**
A Psalm of the Sons of Korah.

1 *Hear this, all peoples!*
Give ear, all inhabitants of the world,
2 *both low and high,*
rich and poor together!
3 *My mouth shall speak wisdom;*
the meditation of my heart shall be understanding.
4 *I will incline my ear to a proverb;*
I will solve my riddle to the music of the lyre.

5 *Why should I fear in times of trouble,*
when the iniquity of my persecutors surrounds me,
6 *men who trust in their wealth*
and boast of the abundance of their riches?
7 *Truly no man can ransom himself,*[o]
or give to God the price of his life,
8 *for the ransom of his*[p] *life is costly,*
and can never suffice,
9 *that he should continue to live on for ever,*
and never see the Pit.

10 *Yea, he shall see that even the wise die,*
the fool and the stupid alike must perish
and leave their wealth to others.
11 *Their graves*[q] *are their homes for ever,*
their dwelling places to all generations,
though they named lands their own.
12 *Man cannot abide in his pomp,*
he is like the beasts that perish.

13 *This is the fate of those who have foolish confidence,*
the end of those[r] *who are pleased with their portion.* Selah
14 *Like sheep they are appointed for Sheol;*
Death shall be their shepherd;
straight to the grave they descend,[s]
and their form shall waste away;
Sheol shall be their home.[t]
15 *But God will ransom my soul from the power of Sheol,*
for he will receive me Selah

16 *Be not afraid when one becomes rich,*
when the glory[u] *of his house increases.*
17 *For when he dies he will carry nothing away;*
his glory[u] *will not go down after him.*
18 *Though, while he lives, he counts himself happy,*
and though a man gets praise when he does well for himself,
19 *he will go to the generation of his fathers,*
who will never more see the light.
20 *Man cannot abide in his pomp,*
he is like the beasts that perish.

o Another reading is *no man can ransom his brother* **p** Gk: Heb *their* **q** Gk Syr Compare Tg: Heb *their inward* (thought) **r** Tg: Heb *after them* **s** Cn: Heb *the upright shall have dominion over them in the morning* **t** Heb uncertain **u** Or *wealth* ***** LXX *To the end.*

OVERVIEW: The forty-ninth psalm causes us to think of the world to come (BASIL). It begins with a call to all people (AMBROSE) of the voice of Christ (ARNOBIUS THE YOUNGER) summoning them by the Spirit (BASIL) to the one grace provided for all (AMBROSE), rich and poor alike (THEODORET). We, also, need to hear that call (CHRYSOSTOM). Meditation has great value (ORIGEN) and is the source of wisdom (DIODORE). The psalmist announces a proverb (CHRYSOSTOM), a harmonious proclamation (BASIL) given by inspiration (THEODORET), through a chosen instrument (AMBROSE), to be received by a spirit of understanding (EVAGRIUS).

There is only one thing to fear in life (CHRYSOSTOM): the day of God's judgment (THEODORET) and the fearful sentence that is evaded only in Christ (AUGUSTINE). The reliance of most people in anticipation of that day is mere presumption (AUGUSTINE). There is no basis for self-confidence (BASIL), no help from ancestors (THEODORET), no help from others (DIODORE). There is only one mediator (AMBROSE) who is no more mere man (BASIL). Sin is worse than anything (THEODORE), and the price of ransom was high (CHRYSOSTOM). Let us, then, not delay to obtain an everlasting life (AUGUSTINE). Let us not entertain foolish thoughts (AMBROSE) but understand what death is (AUGUSTINE) and the fact that all will die (ARNOBIUS THE YOUNGER). The one dead in sins is already a tomb dweller (BASIL). All their wealth and influence will be traded for a tomb (THEODORET). But we should consider where their spirit will be (AUGUSTINE). The honor of being God's image was granted to human beings, but they fell into disgrace (AUGUSTINE) and became ignorant of true dignity (BASIL), like animals (EPHREM), like mindless cattle (ISAAC OF NINEVEH, THEODORE OF MOPSUESTIA). We desperately need to heed these words (AUGUSTINE). Exclusive concern for present wealth is misdirected (AUGUSTINE) and the source of trouble (THEODORE OF MOPSUESTIA). Even those who eschew it can fall to pride (FULGENTIUS).

There are two kinds of death (AUGUSTINE), the second being worse than the first (CHRYSOSTOM), a corruption of the soul in hell (ISAAC OF NINEVEH). But our salvation is in Christ (AUGUSTINE). In him we hope for the resurrection of the body as well as the soul (CHRYSOSTOM), being snatched from death by God (THEODORE OF MOPSUESTIA). And so, our psalmist gives advice to the poor (THEODORET). Trust the providence of God (BASIL) and maintain perspective (AUGUSTINE). THE rich will be naked at the judgment (DIODORE). The glory of their house will disappear (CHRYSOSTOM). Without faith, they will be completely empty (AMBROSE). Even their lavish funerals mislead people about what is really happening with their souls (AUGUSTINE). Their praise is limited to this life (CHRYSOSTOM). They go from the darkness of ignorance to the darkness of hell (AUGUSTINE).

Superscription: *To the Choirmaster*

THE WORLD TO COME. BASIL THE GREAT: Even among the Gentiles certain ones have formed ideas concerning the end of humankind and have arrived at various opinions about the end. Some declared that the end was knowledge; others, practical activity; others, a different use of life and body; but the sensual people declared that the end was pleasure. For us, however, the end for which we do all things and toward which we hasten is the blessed life in the world to come. And this will be attained when we are ruled by God. Up to this time nothing better than the latter idea has been found in rational nature, and to it the apostle stirs us when he says, "Then comes the end, when he delivers the kingdom to God the Father."[1]. . . . To this end, therefore, I think the advantages from the psalms refer. HOMILIES ON THE PSALMS 19.1 (Ps 49).[2]

49:1 *Hear, All Peoples*

---

[1]1 Cor 15:24. [2]FC 46:311*.

UNIVERSAL CALL. AMBROSE: In the very beginning of this psalm we hear the voice of the Lord of salvation inviting the Gentiles into his church. He calls on them to renounce error, to follow truth, to fulfill the duties of love and adoration. The hearts of these people were infected by the Serpent's venom, passed down from generation to generation, and their inclination was toward sin. So long as they despair of pardon, they cannot be called back. But the Lord promises a remedy, and out of the greatness and kindness of his heart he freely assures them of forgiveness. . . . All, without exception, are invited to grace. Without having to pay any ransom money they are redeemed from sin, and they grasp the fruit of eternal life. COMMENTARY ON TWELVE PSALMS 49.1-2.[3]

THE VOICE OF CHRIST. ARNOBIUS THE YOUNGER: The voice of Christ alone, "without exception" calls all as one, rich and poor, noble and base. He invites all living on the earth, equally, as the opening of the psalm says, showing that he is to be feared by us on the evil day. COMMENTARY ON THE PSALMS 49.[4]

SUMMONED BY THE SPIRIT. BASIL THE GREAT: He who is assembling and summoning all by the proclamation is the Paraclete, the Spirit of truth, who brings together through prophets and apostles those who are saved. . . . The sharing of the summons is a uniting in peace, so that those who were, up to this time, opposed to each other because of customs might, through gathering together, become habituated to each other in love. HOMILIES ON THE PSALMS 19.1 (Ps 49).[5]

49:2 Rich and Poor

ONE GRACE FOR ALL. AMBROSE: Both rich and poor together are called to a single vocation and invited to a certain humility and equality. The rich are not to turn up their noses at the poor, and the poor are not to be jealous of the rich. One grace joins both together. The Lord, though

he was rich, became poor,[6] so as to be Savior of poor and rich alike. COMMENTARY ON TWELVE PSALMS 49.57[7]

RICH AND POOR ALIKE. THEODORET OF CYR: All people, listen to my words, city dwellers and country people, more refined and more rustic, all in common and also individuals. . . . Let nature in general hear my words, and each one reap the benefit for themselves. . . . Let those abounding in wealth and those caught up in poverty accept the exhortation alike, the word of instruction respecting no difference between wealth and poverty. COMMENTARY ON THE PSALMS 49.3.[8]

LET US HEAR ALSO. CHRYSOSTOM: The inspired author is now on the point of telling us some great and ineffable truths. I mean, he would not have summoned those in all parts of the earth to listen, nor would he have set up the gallery of the world, were he not about to utter something great and famous and worthy of a gathering of such magnitude. . . . So since he called together the whole race to a hearing, let us too assuredly attend, and see what the psalmist wishes to say, this champion of the whole human race. COMMENTARY ON THE PSALMS 49.1.[9]

49:3 Wisdom and Understanding

VALUE OF MEDITATION. ORIGEN: If the meditation is wisdom, what will the message be? When the meditation of the heart is wisdom, wicked thoughts will not come within it, nor is a place given to the devil or those things that defile people. SELECTIONS FROM THE PSALMS 49.4-5.[10]

SOURCE OF WISDOM. DIODORE OF TARSUS: All wisdom comes to be known by reflection and dissemination. So his meaning is, I deliberate on some wise ideas, and with the intention of disseminating them I want you all to be hearers of what

---

[3]ACTP 285-86. [4]CCL 25:68. [5]FC 46:312-13. [6]Cf. 2 Cor 8:9. [7]ACTP 287. [8]FC 101:282. [9]CCOP 1:321. [10]PG 12:1442, 1444.

is said by me. Hence his reference to "pondering," for each person to realize that far from coming to instruction by accident, they are brought to learn by deep pondering and much practical experience. Commentary on Psalms 49.[11]

49:4 A Proverb

Meaning of Proverb or Parable. Chrysostom: The term "parable" or "proverb" has many meanings. A parable is a saying, an example, a reproach, as when he says, "You have made us a parable among the nations, a shaking of the head among the peoples."[12] A parable is also a riddle, which many call a question, suggesting something not immediately clear from the words but containing a meaning hidden within. . . . A parable also means a comparison: "He proposed another parable to them, saying, 'The kingdom of heaven is like a man sowing good seed.' "[13] A parable also means a figure of speech: "Son of man, tell them this proverb: The great eagle, the one with big wings,"[14] meaning by eagle the king. A parable also means a type, or likeness, as Paul also shows in the words "By faith he sacrificed Isaac . . . whence also in figure he received him back,"[15] that is, in type and in likeness. What then, does the "parable" mean to him here? It seems to me to refer to the narration. . . . The parable, you see, sorts out the worthy listener from the unworthy: whereas the worthy takes steps to find the meaning, the unworthy bypasses it. . . . Do you see the introduction he fashioned? He summoned the world, he abrogated inequality in lifestyle, called their attention to their nature, repressed their arrogance, promised to say something great and noble, denied he was saying anything of his own but what he had heard from him, hinted there was deep obscurity in the message, thus making them more attentive. He promised to teach us spiritual wisdom, on which he had meditated unceasingly. So let us pay attention and not pass it by. If in fact the message is wise, a parable, a riddle, there is need of a mind on the alert. Commentary on the Psalms 49.2-3.[16]

A Harmonious Proclamation. Basil the Great: The things that I teach, he says, from the Spirit, these I proclaim to you, saying nothing of my own, nothing human; but, since I have been listening to the propositions of the Spirit, who hands down in mystery to us the wisdom of God, I am opening for you and am making manifest the proposition; moreover, I am opening not otherwise than through psaltery. The psaltery is a musical instrument that gives out its sounds harmoniously with the melody of the voice. Accordingly, the rational psaltery is opened especially at that time when actions in harmony with the words are displayed. And he is a spiritual psaltery who has acted and has taught. He it is who opens the proposition in the psalms, setting forth the possibility of the teaching from his own example. . . . There is nothing incongruous or out of tune in his life. Homilies on the Psalms 19.2 (Ps 49).[17]

By Inspiration. Theodoret of Cyr: The words put forward by me are full of wisdom, he is saying, but I learned them by submitting my hearing to the words hidden in the depths. And what I learned through hearing I put forward through the organ of the tongue. Now, he means to say, I utter nothing of my own; rather, I am an instrument of divine grace. Commentary on the Psalms 49.4.[18]

A Chosen Instrument. Ambrose: The Lord opens up a theme or problem that has been closed when he finds an apt organ and a chosen instrument.[19] Call it a harp. Such as this was Paul. He rang out the sweet canticle of grace, awaking all the strings of his harp in harmonious sound; plucking the inner chords by grace of the Holy Spirit and playing in ringing tones

[11]WGRW 9:155. [12]Ps 44:14 (43:15 LXX). [13]Mt 13:24. [14]Ezek 17:1-3. [15]Heb 11:17, 19. [16]CCOP 1:325-26*. [17]FC 46:314-15. [18]FC 101:282. [19]Cf. Acts 9:15.

both interiorly and exteriorly. . . . Excellent harp, where a person's life is in tune with his faith, and his flesh with his soul. Sweet harp, where discipline of lifestyle sings a canticle. COMMENTARY ON TWELVE PSALMS 49.7.[20]

THE SPIRIT OF UNDERSTANDING. EVAGRIUS OF PONTUS: One who is in a calm spirit sings psalms. Through psalms he opens teaching. Through tranquility of spirit he understands teaching. NOTES ON THE PSALMS 48[49].4, 5.[21]

49:5 Why Fear?

ONLY ONE FEAR. CHRYSOSTOM: It strikes many people, in fact, as extremely strange and intriguing to say there is nothing to fear in the troubles of life. What, therefore, should I fear, he asks, in the evil day? One thing only, the risk of the lawlessness of my way and my life surrounding me. . . . Those who fear it will never fear anything else; instead, they will mock the goods of this life and scorn its troubles, that fear alone making their mind tremble. Nothing, you see, nothing else is fearsome for the person possessed of this fear, not even death, the very acme of fearsome things apart from this alone. . . . The person afraid only of that, and of nothing else, will be like an angel; there is, in fact, nothing else to be afraid of, if one fears that, as one should fear it—just as the one not fearing it is exposed to many fearsome things. COMMENTARY ON THE PSALMS 49.3-4.[22]

A FEARFUL DAY. THEODORET OF CYR: I fear and dread the day of retribution, on which the righteous Judge will repay everyone according to their works. Now, aware of this, keep such fear before your eyes in your own case. . . . But if you were to inquire why I am afraid, listen closely: it is an evil day, about which countless declamations are made in the inspired Scriptures. The cause of my fear is the life of lawlessness, through which I strayed from the straight and narrow. COMMENTARY ON THE PSALMS 49.5.[23]

A FEARFUL SENTENCE. AUGUSTINE: If a person fears death, what is he or she going to do to avoid dying? How is anyone descended from Adam going to escape paying the debt Adam incurred: Tell me that. But let such a person reflect that though he was born from Adam, he has followed Christ, and that though he is liable for Adam's debt, he is also due to win what Christ has promised. So anyone who fears death has no way of evading it; but anyone who fears damnation fears to hear the sentence that the godless will hear, "Depart from me into eternal fire,"[24] certainly does have a way to evade it. EXPOSITIONS OF THE PSALMS 49.6.[25]

49:6 Those Who Trust in Wealth

PRESUMPTION. AUGUSTINE: Let us not trust in our own strength or boast of our abundant wealth but boast only of him who has promised us that the humble will be exalted and has threatened the arrogant with damnation. . . . Some people rely on their friends, others on their own strength, others on riches. These things are the presumptuous reliance of a human race that does not rely on God. EXPOSITIONS OF THE PSALMS 49.7-8.[26]

NO BASIS FOR SELF-CONFIDENCE. BASIL THE GREAT: Even if he seems to be one of the very powerful people in this life, even if he is surrounded with a great number of possessions, these words teach him to descend from such a notion and to humble himself under the mighty hand of God.[27] . . . Not even the soul is complete in itself for salvation. . . . Every human soul has bowed down under the evil yoke of slavery imposed by the common enemy of all and, being deprived of the very freedom that it received from the Creator, has been led captive through sin. Every captive has need of ransoms for his freedom. Now, neither a brother can ransom his

---

[20]ACTP 288-89. [21]PG 12:1444. [22]CCOP 1:327-28. [23]FC 101:283. [24]Mt 25:41. [25]WSA 3 16:356*. [26]WSA 3 16:357. [27]1 Pet 5:6.

brother, nor can anyone ransom himself, because he who is ransoming must be much better than he who has been overcome and is now a slave. But, actually, no one has the power with respect to God to make atonement for a sinner, since he himself is liable for sin. "All have sinned and have need of the glory of God. They are justified freely by his grace through the redemption that is in Christ Jesus"[28] our Lord. HOMILIES ON THE PSALMS 19.3 (Ps 49).[29]

49:7 No One Can Ransom Himself

NO HELP FROM ANCESTORS. THEODORET OF CYR: Now, you need to understand that virtue and godliness neither of forebears nor brothers is of benefit to those lacking them, nor is it possible after departure from here to buy salvation with money. It is in the present life, you see, as a sage says, "one's own wealth is his ransom."[30] COMMENTARY ON THE PSALMS 49.6.[31]

NO HELP FROM OTHERS. DIODORE OF TARSUS: This alone—namely, sin—is not up for sale, nor does it get help from family connections, as elsewhere also the Lord says that even if Noah, Daniel and Job were to rise up, they would not save their children from their crimes. COMMENTARY ON PSALMS 49.[32]

ONE MEDIATOR. AMBROSE: Just as there is one God, "so too there is only one mediator between God and men, the man Christ Jesus."[33] He is unique. He alone redeems humankind. He goes far beyond brotherly love, for he sheds his own blood for strangers. None other could offer him for his brother. To redeem us from sin, he did not spare his own body "but gave himself as redemption for all."[34] . . . Why, you might ask, is Christ the only one who redeems? I reply that no one has love equal to his; no one but he can lay down his life for his little servants; no one can equal him in innocence and integrity. For we are all under sin;[35] in Adam's fall we all had fallen. No one could be chosen as our redeemer

except the One who was in no way subject to the ancient sin. It follows that by "the man" we must understand the Lord Jesus. He took on himself the human condition, to crucify in his own flesh our sin and so blot out in his blood the handwriting of the charge that had been made against our whole race. COMMENTARY ON TWELVE PSALMS 49.13.[36]

NOT A MERE MAN. BASIL THE GREAT: In fact, what can one find great enough that he may give it for the ransom of his soul? But one thing was found worth as much as all people together. This was given for the price of ransom for our souls, the holy and highly honored blood of our Lord Jesus Christ, which he poured out for all of us; therefore, we were bought at a great price.[37] If, then, a brother does not redeem, will a man redeem? But if man cannot redeem us, he who redeems us is not a man. Now, do not assume, because he sojourned with us "in the likeness of sinful flesh,"[38] that our Lord is only man, failing to discern the power of the divinity, who had no need to give God a ransom for himself or to redeem his own soul because "he did no sin, neither was deceit found in his mouth."[39] No one is sufficient to redeem himself, unless he comes who turns away the captivity of the people, not with ransoms or with gifts, as it is written in Isaiah,[40] but in his own blood. . . . He does not need a ransom, but he himself is the propitiation. HOMILY ON PSALM 19.4 (Ps 49).[41]

49:8 A Costly Ransom

SIN WORSE THAN ANYTHING. THEODORE OF MOPSUESTIA: Sin is worse than everything; it is this that must be feared, not the possibility of being in need of money, since a person who is rich and in the grip of a multitude of sins is in real difficulty and does not find release from the

---

[28]Rom 3:23-24. [29]FC 46:316-17*. [30]Prov 13:8. [31]FC 101:284*. [32]WGRW 9:156. [33]1 Tim 2:5. [34]1 Tim 2:6. [35]Cf. Rom 3:9. [36]ACTP 291*. [37]1 Cor 6:20. [38]Rom 8:3. [39]1 Pet 2:22. [40]Is 52:3. [41]FC 46:318-19*.

troubles. . . . Nor can he then himself by paying money to God prevail on him to desist from punishment; nor does he succeed in redeeming his soul, weighed down as it is with sin. And so sin is worse than anything, since no one who is weighed down by it and is consequently the object of punishment by God can be freed from danger. COMMENTARY ON PSALMS 49.6B-9.[42]

A HIGH PRICE. CHRYSOSTOM: Just as a parent would not choose a house in preference to his child, just so God would not choose the world in preference to the soul. . . . Do you want to learn how great the price for our souls? The Only-begotten, intending to redeem us, gave not the world, not a human being, not land, not sea, but his precious blood. Thus Paul too said, "A price has been paid for you; do not become people's slaves."[43] Do you see the greatness of the price? . . . Do you see how elevated the soul's dignity? Consequently, never despise the soul nor make it captive. COMMENTARY ON PSALMS 49.5.[44]

GET AN EVERLASTING LIFE. AUGUSTINE: People like this reckon that life consists in daily pleasures. And so lacking in firm faith are many of our poor and needy folk, who do not keep their eye on what God promises them for their present labors, that when they see the rich at their daily banquets, glittering and gleaming amid their gold and silver, they say—what do they say? "These are the only people worth talking about, they really live!". . . Do you really think that a rich person is the only one who lives? Let him live; his life will come to an end. Because he does not hand over the price of his soul's redemption, his life will end but his labor will be endless. . . . We who may have to labor and struggle here do not have our life here; but afterwards we shall not be in this state, for Christ will be our life for all eternity, whereas those who want to have their life here will labor forever and have life here only until the end comes. EXPOSITIONS OF THE PSALMS 49.10.[45]

49:10 *Even the Wise Die*

FOOLISH THOUGHTS. AMBROSE: A fool has no discernment, and his thoughts are stupid. The unwise person can think, but what he thinks is bad: "The unwise person has said that there is no God."[46] He is culpably wicked because he knows what goodness is. Yet, though he knows it, he commits iniquity in the evil of his own heart. He is also dishonest. Again, not because he does not know what honesty is but because he is so twisted that he would wish to destroy honesty. COMMENTARY ON TWELVE PSALMS 49.17.[47]

UNDERSTAND WHAT DEATH IS. AUGUSTINE: What does this mean? It means that he will not understand what death is when he sees the wise dying. He says to himself, "That fellow was wise, one who lived in accord with wisdom and devoutly worshiped God. But it didn't save him from death, did it? So I will make the most of all good things as long as I am alive, since people who take a different view are powerless. They must be, otherwise they would not die." The speaker sees a wise person die but does not see what death is. EXPOSITIONS OF THE PSALMS 49.11.[48]

ALL WILL DIE. ARNOBIUS THE YOUNGER: All those great, wise and outspoken will die, not only the foolish and those who gather riches. They are unwilling to have mercy on the ones in need, and they leave their riches behind for others. Although they have many houses, their tombs are their house for eternity. Wretched person. He does not understand that while he is in this body he begins to die. COMMENTARY ON THE PSALMS 49.[49]

49:11 *Their Graves, Their Homes*

---

[42]WGRW 5:637. [43]See 1 Cor 6:20. [44]CCOP 1:330*. [45]WSA 3 16:359-60. [46]Ps 14:1 (13:1 LXX). [47]ACTP 293. [48]WSA 3 16:360*. [49]CCL 25:69.

TOMB DWELLERS. BASIL THE GREAT: One who is dead through sins does not dwell in a house but a sepulcher, since his soul is dead. . . . The thoroughly depraved person dwells in a sepulcher and does not even lay down a foundation of penance because of his dead works, but he is "like a whited sepulcher, which outwardly is very conspicuous but inwardly is full of dead men's bones and of all uncleanness."[50] Therefore, when such a one speaks, he does not open his mouth in the word of God, but he has an open sepulcher as his throat. HOMILIES ON THE PSALMS 19.6 (Ps 49).[51]

TRADED FOR A TOMB. THEODORET OF CYR: Bereft not only of wisdom but also of influence and all affluence, they will meet their end, dispatched from their lavish homes to graves and forced to occupy them forever. COMMENTARY ON THE PSALMS 49.8.[52]

WHERE IS THE SPIRIT? AUGUSTINE: What we need to keep in mind is where the spirit of an ill-living person remains, not where his or her mortal body is laid. EXPOSITIONS OF THE PSALMS 49.15.[53]

49:12 Pomp Fades

DISGRACE. AUGUSTINE: The true honor of humankind is to be the image and the likeness of God that is preserved only in relation to him by whom it is impressed. Thus, he clings to God so much the more, the less he loves what is his own. But through the desire of proving his own power, a person by his own will falls down into himself, as into a sort of center. Since he, therefore, wishes to be like God under no one, then as a punishment he is also driven from the center, which he himself is, into the depths, that is, into those things in which the beasts delight; and thus, since the likeness to God is his honor, the likeness to the beasts is his disgrace. ON THE TRINITY 12.11.16.[54]

IGNORANT OF TRUE DIGNITY. BASIL THE GREAT: Humankind, then, having been advanced above other created things in honor, did not understand and neglected to follow God and to become like the Creator. Becoming a slave of the passions of the flesh, "he is compared with senseless beasts and is become like them": now he is like an amorous horse that neighs after his neighbor's wife,[55] now like a ravenous wolf,[56] lying in wait for strangers, but at another time, because of his deceit toward his brother, he makes himself like the villainous fox.[57] Truly, there is excessive folly and beast-like lack of reason, that he, made according to the image of the Creator, neither perceives his own constitution from the beginning, nor even wishes to understand such great dispensations that were made for his sake, at least, to learn his own dignity from them, but that he is unmindful of the fact that, throwing aside the image of the heavenly, he has taken up the image of the earthly. In order that he might not remain in sin, for his sake "The Word was made flesh and dwelled among us,"[58] and he humbled himself to such an extent as to become "obedient to death, even to death on a cross."[59] HOMILIES ON THE PSALMS 19.8 (Ps 49).[60]

LIKE AN ANIMAL. EPHREM THE SYRIAN:
> David wept for Adam,
> at how he fell
> from that royal abode
> to the abode of wild animals.
> Because he went astray through a beast
> he became like the beasts.
> He ate, together with them
> as a result of the curse,
> grass and roots,
> and he died, becoming their peer.
> Blessed is he who set him apart
> from the wild animals again.

HYMNS ON PARADISE 13.5.[61]

---

[50]Mt 23:27. [51]FC 46:322-23*. [52]FC 101:285. [53]WSA 3 16:364. [54]FC 45:358*. [55]Jer 5:8. [56]Ezek 22:27. [57]Ezek 13:4. [58]Jn 1:14. [59]Phil 2:8. [60]FC 46:325-26*. [61]HOP 170.

MINDLESS CATTLE. ISAAC OF NINEVEH: The honour belonging to rational nature is the discernment that tells good from evil, and those who have destroyed it are justly compared to "mindless cattle," which have no rational and discerning faculty. ASCETICAL HOMILIES 47.[62]

MISUNDERSTANDING THE HONOR GRANTED. THEODORE OF MOPSUESTIA: Despite having so much enjoyment in the present life, possessing many natural advantages by comparison with other living creatures and enjoying a great number of gifts, they did not understand the greatness of the honor conferred on them by God; instead, by their insensitivity to the possession of their attributes they are no different from cattle, which possess no intelligence. . . . While giving little heed to thanking the giver, they live a heedless life and grow old in their sins. Thus, they also are the objects of a rigorous verdict from God. COMMENTARY ON PSALMS 49.13.[63]

HEED THESE WORDS. AUGUSTINE: Read and understand these words, that you may rather with a humble spirit guard against the reproach yourself, than arrogantly throw it out against another person. ON THE SOUL AND ITS ORIGIN 4.15.[64]

49:13 Foolish Confidence

MISDIRECTED. AUGUSTINE: The Spirit of God is describing people who have no concern except for worldly, earthly, present-day affairs and give no thought to what comes after this life. In their estimation there is no happiness other than riches and rank in this world, and transitory strength; they make no provision for what is to come after their death, except for making sure they get a grandiose funeral, and are buried in wonderfully elaborate tombs and have their names invoked on their home ground by members of their households. But they make no arrangements for themselves as to where the spirit will be after this life ends, and they are foolish enough to ignore Christ's warning, "You fool: your life will be take from you this very night; and then who will own what you have prepared?"[65] They do not notice that after lavish daily banquets, after the purple and the fine linen, the rich man in the gospel was condemned to hell and its torments; nor do they remember how the poor man found repose in Abraham's embrace after his toil and ulcers and hunger. They care nothing for these things and focus only on what is present, neglecting to make any provision for their fate after death, apart from ensuring that their names, which are rejected by heaven, shall be lauded on earth. EXPOSITIONS OF THE PSALMS 49.1.[66]

THE SOURCE OF TROUBLE. THEODORE OF MOPSUESTIA: He uses "this" as a demonstrative, meaning, Such behavior is responsible for their troubles, and their heedless enjoyment of God's good things inevitably brings down on them God's punishment. . . . Even when those forebears who were in receipt of riches suffer retribution and just punishment from God, people after them do not come to their senses; on the contrary, they are pleased with the words and actions of the others and hasten to imitate them, acting in similar fashion regarding wealth and the good things of this life, giving too little heed to virtue to be brought around by the punishment of their predecessors. COMMENTARY ON PSALMS 49.14A-B.[67]

THE DANGER OF PRIDE. FULGENTIUS OF RUSPE: Those boast of the abundance of their riches who love their riches in such a way that they place their ultimate happiness in them. They trust in their own strength who scorn riches in such a way that they attribute this contempt to their own strength. Both types are proud; the former, because they trust in their wealth, not in God; the latter, because they wish

---

[62]*AHSIS* 226. [63]*WGRW* 5:641. [64]*NPNF* 1 5:360-61*. [65]Lk 12:20. [66]*WSA* 3 16:367*. [67]*WGRW* 5:643.

to attribute the fact that they spurn riches to themselves, not to God; the former, because they love badly that which cannot be loved well; the latter because they do not spurn well that which can be spurned well; and for this reason, the former do evil badly, the latter do good badly. LETTER 6.7.[68]

49:14 Like Sheep Led to Slaughter

TWO KINDS OF DEATH. AUGUSTINE: But what is meant by that—having death for their shepherd? . . . We can say with certainty that death is either the separation of the soul from body, which is what people fear especially, or the separation of the soul from God, which people do not fear, although this is true death. In fact it often happens that by shunning the death that severs soul from body, people fall prey to that other death by which the soul is severed from God. EXPOSITIONS OF THE PSALMS 49.2.[69]

A FATE WORSE THAN DEATH. CHRYSOSTOM: The manner in which they will be cut down, in which they will perish suddenly and betake themselves to hell with ease, with facility, unexpectedly, effortlessly, is the manner in which sheep are cut down. This is death, or, rather, their fate is much worse than death: after such an end undying death will take possession of them, and thus it will not be into Abraham's bosom they will be seen to repair nor to any place other than hell, the name for retribution, for punishment, for utter destruction. Their end here is vile and despicable, and their sojourn there nothing but punishment. This is the way we, too, customarily speak of those easily lost: Led like sheep to the slaughter. After all, since they lived like brutes, they also die like brutes, with no optimism for the future—and not only that, but that they have come to a bad end . . . completely under the control of ruin. COMMENTARY ON THE PSALMS 49.9.[70]

CORRUPTION. ISAAC OF NINEVEH: They will

be withdrawn from the comely glory of their nature and their bodies will become a desolate place. Recollect at all times that lamentable sight of corruption, that formless dispersion of your senses, that ruin of the edifice of your body, and how your wholesome constitution will become mud in Sheol. Blessed is the man who greets the recollection of this destruction with joy! Blessed is he who with good hope awaits that deed so replete with mystery wherein is concealed the wonder of the Creator's power! ASCETICAL HOMILIES 64.[71]

49:15 God Will Ransom My Soul

IN CHRIST. AUGUSTINE: The psalmist has in mind the salvation that Christ has already demonstrated in himself. He descended into hell and ascended into heaven. What we have seen in the Head, we find also in the body. EXPOSITIONS OF THE PSALMS 49.5.[72]

FACE TO FACE. CHRYSOSTOM: Now we walk through faith, not through sight, but then face to face. With the soul ransomed, the body too will share the good things. COMMENTARY ON THE PSALMS 49.10.[73]

SNATCHED FROM DEATH. THEODORE OF MOPSUESTIA: God is able to pluck one from the midst of death even if it seems already to have taken hold (the phrase "from the hand of hades" meaning, Even if it has one in its grasp, it is possible and very easy for God to snatch one away). COMMENTARY ON PSALMS 49.16.[74]

49:16 Do Not Fear

ADVICE TO THE POOR. THEODORET OF CYR: After this he provides explanation and advice for those condemned to a life of poverty and worn out through the arrogance of the rich. . . . Do not

[68]FC 95:351. [69]WSA 3 16:368*. [70]CCOP 1:338-39. [71]AHSIS 315-16. [72]WSA 3 16:372. [73]CCOP 1:342. [74]WGRW 5:645.

consider present prosperity any great thing, he is saying: wealth that catches all eyes is not lasting; those who raise their eyebrows and are puffed up at it will shortly after leave it all behind and be dispatched to death. Commentary on the Psalms 49.11.[75]

Trust Providence. Basil the Great: When you see the unjust becoming rich and the just poor, do not fear for yourself; do not be dismayed in mind, as if the providence of God is nowhere looking on human affairs, or perhaps, somewhere there is a divine watchfulness, but it does not reach to places near the earth, so as to watch over our affairs; for, if there were a providence, it would be apportioning to each person what is proper to him, so that the just, who understand how to use wealth, would be rich, but the wicked, who have wealth as the instrument of their wickedness, would be poor. . . . Now, since there are many who have such notions and who, because of the apparent inconsistency of the distribution of the fortunes of life, assume that the world is not the work of providence, the Scripture addresses these to calm their uninstructed emotion. . . . Do not be faint about present affairs, but await that blessed and everlasting life. Then you will see that poverty and contempt and the lack of luxuries befall the just person for his good. And do not be troubled now about imagined good things, as though they were unjustly divided. You will hear how it will be said to a certain rich man, "You in your lifetime have received good things,"[76] but to the poor person that he receives evils in his life. As a consequence, therefore, the latter is consoled, but the former suffers pain. Homilies on the Psalms 19.10 (Ps 49).[77]

Maintain Perspective. Augustine: Why did you begin to lose your nerve, when some fellow grew rich? You began to be afraid that you had made a wrong decision when you became a believer, that all your struggle for faith was wasted and that the hope in which you turned to God was futile. Perhaps you could by fraud have made the same fortune as the other person and been rich and not needed to work, but you heeded God's threats, and held back from fraud and turned your back on the fortune. Yet you see how the other fellow did commit fraud and made his pile, and nothing bad has happened to him. So you lose your nerve about being good. But the Spirit of God says to you, "Do not be alarmed: a person may have become rich." . . . Do you really want to have eyes only for present things, and no more? He who rose from the dead gave us promises about the future, but he did not promise us peace on this earth or rest in this life. Every one of us seeks rest, and what we seek is good, but not in our own country do we seek it. There is no peace in this life. What we seek on earth has been promised us in heaven; what we seek in this world has been promised us for the next. Expositions of the Psalms 49.6.[78]

49:17 Carrying Nothing Away

Naked at the Judgment. Diodore of Tarsus: Even if rich in this life, he will not for this reason prove to be blessed after death as well. On the contrary, then, he will leave it all behind and thus present himself naked at the judge's tribunal. Commentary on Psalms 49.[79]

House Glory. Chrysostom: He did not say, note, "when their glory is increased," but "the glory of their house." All these things that I enumerated, after all—fountains, walkways and baths, gold and silver, horses and mules, carpets and clothes—are the glory of the house, not of the person living in the house. A person's glory, in fact, is virtue, which takes the journey from here with its possessor. A house's glory, by contrast, itself remains here, or rather, far even from remaining, it disappears along with the house, doing no good to the one who lived in it. It did

---

[75]FC 101:286. [76]Lk 16:25. [77]FC 46:328-29*. [78]WSA 3 16:373-74*. [79]WGRW 9:159.

not belong to him, after all. COMMENTARY ON THE PSALMS 49.11.[80]

EMPTY WITHOUT FAITH. AMBROSE: Do not be troubled when you hear that the glory of someone's house has increased. Think deeply about it, and you will see that a house is empty if it is not filled with faith. . . . Adam, by his ruin, left us void and empty, but Christ's grace has filled the void. Christ emptied himself[81] so that the fullness of virtue might live in human flesh.[82] COMMENTARY ON TWELVE PSALMS 49.23.[83]

BODILY GLORY. AUGUSTINE: You see a rich person living, yes; but now imagine him dying. You observe what he possesses here, but now consider what he can take with him. What does he take with him? He has plenty of gold, plenty of silver, plenty of land and slaves. Then he dies, and all these things are left behind—for whom, he does not know. Even if he bequeaths them to persons of his own choosing, he cannot ensure that they will remain with persons of his own choosing. Many people have acquired goods that were not left to them, and many others have lost what they did inherit. All these things are left behind, then, and he takes with him . . . what? Someone may say, perhaps, "Well, he does take with him the clothes they wrap him in, and the money they lavish on an expensive marble tomb and on setting up a memorial to him. Those at any rate he does take." But I tell you, no not even those; . . . a person cannot hold onto any of it; nor does the dead person take with him what the burial takes. Only the erstwhile container of the person lies there, the house in which he used to dwell. We call the body a house, and its inhabitant is the spirit. When the spirit is being tormented in hell, what advantage accrues to it if the body is lying amid cinnamon sticks and aromatic herbs, wrapped in precious linen? You might as well decorate the walls of a house whose owner has been sent into exile. He is languishing in a foreign land, subject to penury and hunger, scarcely finding any poky little place to sleep in, and you say, "What a lucky fellow, to have his house decorated like this!" Anyone who heard you would conclude that you were either joking or crazy. But it is the same when you embellish the body while the soul is in torment. If you give the spirit some help, you will have given the dead person something worthwhile; but what will you give, when that rich man begged for even a single drop of water and did not get it? The fact is, he had disdained to send any goods on ahead of him. Why did he disdain to do so? Because "the path they tread is an occasion of stumbling for them." He thought there was no life except the present life, and he had no concern except that he should be wrapped in exquisite clothes when he was buried. His soul was snatched away from him, as the Lord warned: "You fool: your life will be taken from you this very night; and then who will own what you have prepared?"[84] So in him the prediction our psalm makes is verified: "do not be alarmed: a person may have become rich, and the splendor of his household may have increased, but when he dies he will take nothing with him, nor will his glory follow him below." EXPOSITIONS OF THE PSALMS 49.7.[85]

49:18 Receiving Praise

ONLY IN THIS LIFE. CHRYSOSTOM: Since, you see, this is a particular object of interest for the rich—flattery in the marketplace, attention from the populace, public commendation, tributes teeming with hypocrisy, cutting a fine figure at spectacles, applauded at banquets and in the courts, being on everybody's lips, thought to be conscientious—note how this in turn he prunes away in time. "In their lifetime," he says, note; that is, this publicity and being spoken well of lasts for this life, but it disappears along with everything else, being impermanent and perishable. Even when it comes from a display put on

---

[80]CCOP 1:343-44. [81]Cf. Phil 2:7. [82]Cf. Col 2:9. [83]ACTP 297-98. [84]Lk 12:20. [85]WSA 3 16:374-75*.

by the flatterers, after his death it is reversed when the mask of fear is stripped away. COMMENTARY ON PSALMS 49.11.[86]

49:19 Never More Seeing Light

DARKNESS TO DARKNESS. AUGUSTINE: While he was here on earth, he lived in darkness, gloat-ing over false goods and not valuing those that are real, and he will depart from this world in the black infernal regions; those dark torments will summon him from his dark slumbers on earth, and "he will not see the light forever." EXPOSITIONS OF THE PSALMS. 49.11.[87]

---

[86]CCOP 1:344. [87]WSA 3 16:378.

50:1-23 DIVINE JUDGMENT

Psalm 50 speaks of the coming of the Savior,
and that through God, he will come among us.

ATHANASIUS ON THE INTERPRETATION OF THE PSALMS 5 [OIP 58]

A Psalm of Asaph.

¹*The Mighty One, God the* LORD,
  speaks and summons the earth
  from the rising of the sun to its setting.
²*Out of Zion, the perfection of beauty,*
  God shines forth.

³*Our God comes, he does not keep silence,*
  before him is a devouring fire,
  round about him a mighty tempest.
⁴*He calls to the heavens above*
  and to the earth, that he may judge his
    people:
⁵ *"Gather to me my faithful ones,*
  who made a covenant with me by sacrifice!"
⁶*The heavens declare his righteousness,*
  for God himself is judge!   Selah

⁷ *"Hear, O my people, and I will speak,*
  O Israel, I will testify against you.
  I am God, your God.

⁸*I do not reprove you for your sacrifices;*
  your burnt offerings are continually before
    me.
⁹*I will accept no bull from your house,*
  nor he-goat from your folds.
¹⁰*For every beast of the forest is mine,*
  the cattle on a thousand hills.
¹¹*I know all the birds of the air,*ᵛ
  and all that moves in the field is mine.

¹²*"If I were hungry, I would not tell you;*
  for the world and all that is in it is mine.
¹³*Do I eat the flesh of bulls,*
  or drink the blood of goats?
¹⁴*Offer to God a sacrifice of thanksgiving,*ʷ
  and pay your vows to the Most High;
¹⁵*and call upon me in the day of trouble;*
  I will deliver you, and you shall glorify me."

¹⁶*But to the wicked God says:*
  "What right have you to recite my statutes,
  or take my covenant on your lips?

^{17}*For you hate discipline,*
and you cast my words behind you.
^{18}*If you see a thief, you are a friend of his;*
and you keep company with adulterers.

^{19}*"You give your mouth free rein for evil,*
and your tongue frames deceit.
^{20}*You sit and speak against your brother;*
you slander your own mother's son.
^{21}*These things you have done and I have been*
silent;

you thought that I was one like yourself.
But now I rebuke you, and lay the charge
before you.

^{22}*"Mark this, then, you who forget God,*
lest I rend, and there be none to deliver!
^{23}*He who brings thanksgiving as his sacrifice*
honors me;
to him who orders his way aright
I will show the salvation of God!"

v Gk Syr Tg: Heb *mountains*   w Or *make thanksgiving your sacrifice to God*

OVERVIEW: The fiftieth psalm extends the theme of the forty-ninth and predicts the dispensation of the New Testament (THEODORET). The psalm begins with the Word of God calling the whole earth to judgment (EUSEBIUS). The beauty of God has shone forth from Zion (CHRYSOSTOM), culminating in his open manifestation in the flesh (EVAGRIUS). God will personally come in judgment (DIODORE) with a winnowing storm (AUGUSTINE) and a cloud of witnesses (ARNOBIUS THE YOUNGER). The Lord has come visibly (IRENAEUS). His glory was hidden but will be seen when he comes again (THEODORET). He summons all to his judgment (DIODORE). God allowed sacrifices but directed his people to a higher understanding (CHRYSOSTOM). Righteousness was not confined to sacrificial rites (THEODORET) but pointed to an all-consuming love (AUGUSTINE). The words of the psalm would eventually be fulfilled in the destruction of the temple (HESYCHIUS), and we see here the foretelling of the New Covenant (AUGUSTINE). His providence extends over all (EVAGRIUS), and the property of his servants belongs to him (AUGUSTINE). He possesses it all by his knowledge (AUGUSTINE). What God wanted in their sacrifices was their hearts (TERTULLIAN), their love (CHRYSOSTOM).

God invites us to be like angels (HESYCHIUS) and live a life that praises God (CHRYSOSTOM). God has need of nothing, but he desires our praise (CLEMENT OF ROME, PSEUDO-AUGUSTINE) for our sake (DIODORE). This sacrifice is granted to us by grace (AUGUSTINE) but consumes our lives (THEODORE OF MOPSUESTIA). Knowing the law is not enough (THEODORE OF MOPSUESTIA), for a deceiver gets no credit if he happens to speak the truth (ATHANASIUS). Rejection of the law and discipline (EVAGRIUS) also entails the rejection of reason (CHRYSOSTOM). It is spiritual robbery and adultery (CYPRIAN). In these matters, tolerance is no virtue (CHRYSOSTOM). Those who sin against others with their tongues will suffer from verbal recoil (CHRYSOSTOM). Beware the babbling tongue of others lest you be led astray (JEROME). God's silence shows his patience, not his approval (THEODORET). Do not make his silence grounds for sin, for the Lord will come again and will not be silent (CYRIL OF JERUSALEM). Forgetfulness of God is a source of sin (THEODORET). But God's blessing is shown to the one who brings the sacrifice of thanksgiving in words and deeds (ORIGEN), walking the way of truth by faith (CLEMENT OF ROME).

Superscription: *A Psalm of Asaph*

THE JUDGMENT TO COME. THEODORET OF CYR: The present psalm, attributed to Asaph, is in keeping with the previous psalm: it also forecasts the judgment to come and the manifestation of our God and Savior. But it forecasts as well the

New Testament, showing worship according to the Law to be unacceptable to God. Commentary on the Psalms 50.1.[1]

50:1 The Mighty One Speaks

The Coming of the Word. Eusebius of Caesaria: Here the divine prediction clearly prophesies that God will come manifestly, meaning none other but the Word of God. And it shows the reason of his coming, again emphasizing the calling of all nations of the world. For it says, "he has called the earth from the rising of the sun to the setting"; and it teaches that the rejection of the outward worship according to the Mosaic law will follow hard after his manifestation and the calling of the Gentiles, a worship that actually ceased after the manifestation of the Word of God to all people. For from that day to this all people throughout all the world have been called, and all the nations of the east and west. And the former worship has ceased and been abolished, all people being called to worship according to the new covenant of the preaching of the gospel, and not according to the law of Moses. We might also apply these prophecies to our Savior's second and glorious coming. Proof of the Gospel 6.3.261-62.[2]

50:2 God Shines Forth

God's Beauty. Chrysostom: His charm, in fact, was evident from [Zion] even in the Old Testament. I mean, the temple, the Holy of Holies, all the worship and the living of the old legislation, the multitude of priests, sacrifices, whole burnt offerings, sacred hymns and psalmody and everything stemming from it—the type of things to come from this was sketched out ahead of time. But when the reality arrived, it took its beginning from there as well. From there shone out the cross. . . . There occurred the resurrection, there the ascension, there the prelude and commencement of our salvation, there the ineffable teachings began to be pro-

claimed. There the Father was first revealed, the Only-begotten known and the wonderful grace of the Spirit given. And there the apostles took the first steps of preaching about spiritual matters, about the gifts, the powers, the promise of good things to come. Considering all this, the inspired author calls it his maturity. God's beautiful maturity, you see, is his goodness and lovingkindness and his beneficence to all people. Commentary on the Psalms 50.1.[3]

Openly, in the Flesh. Evagrius of Pontus: Our God will come openly. Our God is Christ. Christ will come openly in the flesh. We, therefore, understand that openly means "in the flesh." And this flesh is perceived by the senses. Notes on the Psalms 49[50].3.[4]

50:3 Our God Comes

God Comes Personally. Diodore of Tarsus: He presents his whole discourse as if God personally were present and judging, thus his addition of "he will not keep silence," that is, he will choose to judge the judges in no other way than by personal inspection and as though by his very presence. Then, to bring out that he arrives in retribution and as a cause of deep fear, attended by sanctions like bodyguards, he goes on, "A fire will burn in his presence, with a severe storm around him": just as the rulers of the earth have heralds going ahead to inspire submission with their shouting, so too God comes in person with fire going ahead and a severe storm to inspire fear in those due to be judged. By "storm" he refers to a power capable of drawing down to hades. Commentary on Psalms 50.[5]

A Storm of Judgment. Augustine: This storm will effect the winnowing that will separate every trace of impurity from the saints, all pretense from the faithful and every dismissive

---

[1]FC 101:288. [2]POG 2:5*. [3]CCOP 1:350-51*. [4]PG 12:1449. [5]WGRW 9:160-61.

or proud person from the devout who tremble at God's word. EXPOSITIONS OF THE PSALMS 50.8.[6]

CLOUDS OF WITNESSES. ARNOBIUS THE YOUNGER: He will surely come openly to judge the age through fire. Fire will burn in his countenance, and around him will be strong storms. Then apostles, martyrs and teachers will be gathered, those who have ordained his covenant over sacrifices. These will become the apostles, teachers and advisors in the present. These are the "heavens" who proclaim the glory of God. Then when God begins to judge they announce his righteousness and his mercy. COMMENTARY ON THE PSALMS 50.[7]

HE CAME VISIBLY. IRENAEUS: God came in a visible manner, and was made flesh and hung on the tree, that he might sum up all things in himself.... He is the Word of God, and very man, communicating with invisible beings after the manner of the intellect and appointing a law observable to the outward senses, that all things should continue each in its own order; and he reigns manifestly over things visible and pertaining to people; and he brings in just judgment and worth on all; as David also, clearly pointing to this, says, "Our God shall openly come and will not keep silence." Then he shows also the judgment that is brought in by him, saying, "A fire shall burn in his sight, and a strong tempest shall rage round about him. He shall call on the heaven from above, and the earth, to judge his people." AGAINST HERESIES 5.18.3.[8]

GOD COMES OPENLY. THEODORET OF CYR: Do not think the second coming will be like his first: at that time he concealed his characteristic magnificence in lowliness and poverty, whereas in this case he will reveal plainly to everyone his lordship and kingship, no longer employing long-suffering but judging justly. As he said, "he will not keep silence. A fire will burn in his presence, with a severe storm around him." Blessed Daniel had a vision of this: "A river of fire," he says, "was flowing in front of him, his throne a fiery flame, its wheels flaming fire." COMMENTARY ON THE PSALMS 50.2.[9]

50:4 Calling to Heavens and Earth

GOD SUMMONS ALL. DIODORE OF TARSUS: On arriving in an obvious manner, then, with fire and storm as his bodyguards, God will summon everyone from all quarters as if to appoint those present as witnesses of the judgment. So whom does he summon? The heavenly powers from on high (the sense of "above") and the whole "earth" from below, and he will hold court on them. COMMENTARY ON PSALMS 50.[10]

50:8 Your Sacrifices

WHY GOD ALLOWED SACRIFICES. CHRYSOSTOM: On this score the other inspired authors leveled their accusations, remember, that they had bypassed the more important element of virtue and were resting their hope of salvation in these things.... Yet many are the words spoken about sacrifices, whereas the law about them was passed not because his wish was preeminently for such things but because he was showing considerateness for their limitations.... God should be worshiped, after all, not with fumes and smells but with an impeccable lifestyle, not bodily but of the mind. The demons of the foreigners were not inclined this way, however; rather, they even looked for these things. A poet of the Greeks even seems to be suggesting as much in saying, "It is by the will of the gods, you see, we obtain this portion."[11] But our God is not like that: whereas those gods thirsted for human blood and in their desire to lead them into this bloodguiltiness constantly made such demands, our God by contrast wanted to remove them gradually even from the slaughter of brute beasts and so employed this considerateness in allowing

---

[6]*WSA* 3 16:388. [7]CCL 25:70. [8]ANF 1:547*. [9]FC 101:289. [10]WGRW 9:161. [11]Homer *Iliad*.

sacrifices so as to abolish sacrifices. COMMEN-
TARY ON THE PSALMS 50.4.[12]

UNCONFINED RIGHTEOUSNESS. THEODORET
OF CYR: I do not accuse you of neglect of sacrifices, he is saying: you offer them continually;
rather, I urge you not to confine righteousness to
them. COMMENTARY ON THE PSALMS 50.4.[13]

ALL-CONSUMING LOVE. AUGUSTINE: Now
what is a holocaust? A sacrifice entirely consumed by fire. This is what the word means.
. . . So a holocaust is a sacrifice completely
burned up. But there is another kind of fire: the
fire of intense, ardent charity. May our minds be
inflamed with charity, and may charity take possession of all our members for its own purposes,
not allowing them to fight in the service of our
wayward desires. Anyone who wants to offer
a whole burnt offering to God must be wholly
on fire with divine love. These are the kinds
of whole burnt offerings that are "before me
always." EXPOSITIONS OF THE PSALMS 50.15.[14]

50:9 Sacrifices Cease

THE WORD FULFILLED. HESYCHIUS OF JERUSA-
LEM: The Jews, hearing these things, did not believe, and they doubted they were able to happen.
Now the word is proven. They no longer have the
place of their sacrifice, since the temple has been
destroyed, the altar collapsed and all their administration carried away, even the city overturned,
in which it was necessary to sacrifice according to
law. LARGE COMMENTARY ON PSALMS 50.8.[15]

THE NEW COVENANT FORETOLD. AUGUS-
TINE: He is foretelling the New Covenant,
under which all those old sacrifices have ceased.
They had a part to play in prefiguring a special
sacrifice that was to come, by the blood of which
we would be cleansed. EXPLANATIONS OF THE
PSALMS 50.16.[16]

50:10-11 Every Beast Belongs to God

GOD'S PROVIDENCE OVER ALL. EVAGRIUS OF
PONTUS: All created things are under the providence of God. Does not even one sparrow fall
without the Father who is in heaven knowing?
NOTES ON THE PSALMS 49[50].10.[17]

HIS PROPERTY. AUGUSTINE: If you are my servant, all your personal property belongs to me. If
even the property a slave has gained for himself
belongs to his master, it cannot be the case that
the property the Master has created for the servant does not belong to its Creator. EXPOSITIONS
OF THE PSALMS 50.17.[18]

SUPREME KNOWLEDGE. AUGUSTINE: God's
knowledge is one thing, human knowledge
another, just as God's manner of possessing is
one thing and a human being's way of possessing
quite different. You do not own anything in the
same way that God owns it. What you possess
is not entirely in your power: as long as your ox
is alive it is not in your power to decide that he
will not die or will not graze. But in God there is
supreme power, and there is supreme and secret
knowledge. We must attribute this to God,
and praise God for it. . . . So profound is God's
knowledge that created things were in some
indescribable manner present to him before they
had been created; and do you think he is waiting
to receive anything from you, when he possessed
it even before he had created it? . . . All things
that would come to be in the future were with
him, and all things that have been in the past are
with him; but the future things are with him in
such a way that they do not push the past things
out of his sight. All things are established with
him through a mode of knowing proper to God's
ineffable wisdom in the Word, and all of them
are created for the Word. . . . Everything is with
him, the whole of creation is with him, but not
with him in such a way that he is contaminated
by anything he has made or suffers any need for

---

[12]CCOP 1:357. [13]FC 101:290. [14]WSA 3 16:396*. [15]PG 93:1197.
[16]WSA 3 16:396. [17]PG 12:1452. [18]WSA 3 16:397*.

his creatures. You may have a pillar beside you as you stand there, and when you feel tired you lean against it. You need that thing you have with you, but God does not need the field that is with him. With him is the field, with him the loveliness of the earth, with him the fair heavens and with him all the birds, because he is present everywhere. And why are they all present to him? Because before ever they came to be, before they were created, all of them were known to him. Expositions of the Psalms 50.18.[19]

50:12 The World Belongs to God

God Wanted Their Hearts. Tertullian: Although he had respect to the offerings of Abel and smelled a sweet savor from the whole burnt offering of Noah, yet what pleasure could he receive from the flesh of sheep or the odor of burning victims? And yet the simple and God-fearing mind of those who offered what they were receiving from God, both in the way of food and of a sweet smell, was favorably accepted before God, in the sense of respectful homage to God, who did not so much want what was offered as that which prompted the offering. Against Marcion 2.22.[20]

The Means to Win You Over. Chrysostom: Though I am Lord and Master of everything, I am ready to accept from you what is mine so as to win you over to love of me. Commentary on Psalms 50.4.[21]

50:14 A Sacrifice of Thanksgiving

Be Like Angels. Hesychius of Jerusalem: Be as companions of angels. Imitate the seraphim in glory. Tell the glory of God to the heavens; offer the burnt offering while one praises God continuously. Perhaps "sacrifice of praise" means "virtues" through which God is praised, that is, blessed and glorified, especially when he said to the apostles, "Let your light shine before all people."[22] Large Commentary on Psalms 50.14.[23]

A Life That Praises God. Chrysostom: Praise, in fact, is nothing other than commendation, glory and blessing. So let your life be of such a kind as to bless your Master, and you have performed the perfect sacrifice. Commentary on the Psalms 50.5.[24]

Needless, but Desiring. Clement of Rome: The Master, brothers, has need of nothing at all. He desires not anything of anyone, save to confess to him. 1 Clement 52.[25]

That God's Name Is Magnified. Pseudo-Augustine: God desires and seeks nothing more from us than that, through our actions, his name is magnified by all, as it is written: "Offer to God the sacrifice of praise." This is the sacrifice that God seeks and loves in preference to all victims, namely, that through the works of our justice, his name may be glorified everywhere and that, by the actions and works of his servants, he may be proved to be the true God. They love God in truth who perform only actions by which his name may be glorified. On the Christian Life 9.[26]

Thanksgiving, for Your Sake. Diodore of Tarsus: This is what I need, for you to be grateful, offering thanks and praise for what you receive from me—not because I need this, but out of longing for you to be appreciative, so that I may have occasion to give you further favors. Commentary on Psalms 50.[27]

A Free Sacrifice. Augustine: This is a sacrifice that cost us nothing, given to us gratis! I did not buy what I must offer; you gave it to me, for I could never have found it for myself. "Offer to God a sacrifice of praise." The offering of this sacrifice of praise consists in giving thanks to him from whom you have every good thing you have, to him by whose mercy whatever evil you

[19]WSA 3 16:397-98. [20]ANF 3:314. [21]CCOP 1:358**. [22]Mt 5:16. [23]PG 93:1197. [24]CCOP 1:359. [25]AF 35*. [26]FC 16:26. [27]WGRW 9:163.

have from yourself is forgiven you. . . . The Lord delights in this sweet fragrance. Expositions of the Psalms 50.21.[28]

Offer Yourself. Theodore of Mopsuestia: Offer me this sacrifice of praise. That is, offer yourself as a victim to me, taking pains to live in thanksgiving to me and devoting yourself totally to me. . . . Pray always to me about everything; render me this and perform it. The phrase "pray to me about everything" means, consider me responsible for all your good things, and receive from me all that is at any time good, no one being able to pray unless persuaded of this. . . . It will be no idle conjecture for you, since with this attitude you will, even if calling in the midst of afflictions, be heard and will attain what you aspire to, and so will take occasion from the beneficence to give even greater glory. Commentary on Psalms 50.14a-15.[29]

50:16 What Right Have You to Recite My Statues?

Knowing the Law Is Not Enough. Theodore of Mopsuestia: The fact, he is saying, that you take pains to read the law, mouth the words of its stipulations, and listen carefully to its being read is no excuse. It only sets me more against you, your knowing the law, listening to the commandments and putting them on your lips while in practice pursuing the opposite, the result being that the reading is useless for you. Instead, listening to me when I speak and give commands in the law is an insult to me when there is utter neglect of me in practice. Commentary on Psalms 50.16.[30]

No Credit. Athanasius: For even though he speaks the truth, the deceiver is not worthy of credit. Letter to the Bishops of Egypt 3.[31]

50:17 You Hate Discipline

What Discipline Is. Evagrius of Pontus:

Discipline is the moderation of the emotions. Notes on the Psalms 49[50].17.[32]

Rejection of Law and Reason. Chrysostom: Not only do you not show any benefit from the teaching of the law, but even what you have by nature you have mutilated. The reasoning for what should be done and should not be done is set within us by nature, but you rejected it and had no recollection of it. Commentary on the Psalms 50.7.[33]

50:18 Friend of a Thief

Spiritual Robbery and Adultery. Cyprian: To declare the justices and the covenant of the Lord and not to do the same thing that the Lord did, what else is that but to cast aside his words and to despise the discipline of the Lord and to commit not earthly but spiritual robberies and adulteries? For one who steals from evangelical truth the words and deeds of our Lord both corrupts and adulterates the divine teaching. Letter 63.18.[34]

The Problem with Tolerance. Chrysostom: Most people, after all, do not simply give a verdict on their behavior from their own judgment but are also corrupted by the support of others. If sinners see everyone opposed, they believe they have committed some great crime; but if they see them not only showing no anger or irritation but exhibiting tolerance and joining forces with them, the tribunal of their conscience is then corrupted because the verdict of the majority supports their corrupt attitude. So what crime will they not attempt? When, on the contrary, will they condemn themselves and give up sinning unscrupulously? Thus it is essential that, in the case of people committing sin, they condemn themselves (this, you see, being the path to refraining from wickedness),

---

[28]WSA 3 16:400*. [29]WGRW 5:659-61. [30]WGRW 5:661.
[31]NPNF 2 4:224. [32]PG 12:1452. [33]CCOP 1:363. [34]FC 51:214.

and even if not practicing good, commend the good. The path to performance, after all, is willingness. Yet in this case, since there have been accomplices in crime, it is appropriate to apply the goad with great severity. After all, if evil flourishes to this extent even when reproved, and virtue, even when commended, has difficulty summoning its practitioners to the effort required, what would happen if these conditions did not apply? COMMENTARY ON THE PSALMS 50.7.[35]

50:20 Slandering a Brother

VERBAL RECOIL. CHRYSOSTOM: But you suffered wrong at his hands: why, then, do wrong to yourself? Those who take revenge, after all, strike themselves with a sword. I mean, if you want to do yourself a favor and have revenge on him, speak well of the wrongdoer; in this way you will turn many people into accusers in your place and earn yourself a great reward, whereas if you speak ill of him, you will not be believed, being suspected of bias. And so the results of your exertion go in the opposite direction: whereas you are anxious to undermine his reputation, the opposite happens; it is by commendation, not accusation, that this happens, you see. You bring yourself into disrepute, while your shafts in his direction are wide of the mark. Bias in fact is the impression on the mind of the listeners, not allowing your words to gain entry to their ears. The same thing happens as in judicial objections: when someone raises an objection to evidence in court, the whole process is put on hold. Exactly so, in this instance, suspicion of bias prevents the case becoming admissible. Do not speak ill, accordingly, in case the black mark attaches to you, and instead of preparing mud with clay and bricks, you weave for him wreaths from roses, violets and other flowers. And do not bear dung in your mouth, like beetles (this is what slanderers do, you know: they are the first to be affected by the stench), but bear flowers,

like the bees, and make honeycombs like them, and be gentle to everybody. Everyone feels revulsion for slanderers like a bad smell, as if they were some bloodsucker, fed on others' problems like a beetle on dung; with the person bearing a word of commendation, on the other hand, everyone associates like a member of their own body, their own brother, their son, their father. COMMENTARY ON THE PSALMS 50.10.[36]

50:21 Keeping Silence

BEWARE THE BABBLING TONGUE. JEROME: Beware also of a blabbing tongue and of itching ears. Neither detract from others nor listen to detractors. . . . Keep your tongue from caviling, and watch over your words. Know that in judging others you are passing sentence on yourself and that you are yourself guilty of the faults that you blame in them. It is no excuse to say, "If others tell me things, I cannot be rude to them." No one cares to speak to an unwilling listener. An arrow never lodges in a stone: often it recoils on the shooter of it. Let the detractor learn from your unwillingness to listen not to be so ready to detract. LETTER 52.14.[37]

GOD'S SILENCE. THEODORET OF CYR: I saw these crimes committed by you, I practiced long-suffering, I waited for your repentance. But you took even my long-suffering as an excuse for impiety, guessing that I was pleased with your lawlessness and would not inflict punishment. . . . Since you were not cured by the mild remedy of long-suffering, I shall prepare more painful ones for you and apply burning by censure. Now, this is in keeping with those words of the apostle, "Do you not realize that the goodness of God leads you in the direction of repentance, but by your obduracy and unrepentant heart you store up for yourself wrath on the day of wrath, revelation and just judgment of God, who will repay everyone

---

[35]CCOP 1:364-65. [36]CCOP 1:369-70. [37]NPNF 2 6:95*.

according to their works."[38] COMMENTARY ON THE PSALMS 50.7.[39]

GOD WILL COME AGAIN. CYRIL OF JERUSALEM: The Savior comes again, but not to be judged again, for he will pass judgment on those who passed judgment on him, and he who aforetime kept silence as they judged him now reminds those lawless people who did their outrageous deeds to him on the cross and says, "These things have you done, and I kept silence." He adapted himself when he came then and taught people by persuasion, but this time it is they who will be forced to bow to his rule, whether they will or no. CATECHETICAL LECTURES 15.1.[40]

50:22 Those Who Forget God

FORGETFULNESS OF GOD. THEODORET OF CYR: Give careful thought, he is saying, to each of my words; and you who suffer forgetfulness of God—forgetfulness of God being a source of sin—cure your wounds with the remedies of repentance before you are carried off by death, which like a lion falls on human beings, no one capable of checking its fierce assault. COMMENTARY ON THE PSALMS 50.8.[41]

50:23 Correctly Ordering One's Way

HOLISTIC PRAISE. ORIGEN: Who among us is of such measure and kind to offer to God "salutary sacrifices" and a "sacrifice of praise"? I believe that one to be a person who praises God in all his actions and fulfills through him what our Lord and Savior says: "That people may see your good works and praise your Father who is in heaven."[42] Therefore, this one offered "a sacrifice of praise" for whose deeds, doctrine, word, habits and discipline, God is praised and blessed. Just as, on the contrary, there are those of whom it is said, "Through you my name is blasphemed among the Gentiles."[43] HOMILIES ON LEVITICUS 5.7.2.[44]

WORKING BY FAITH. CLEMENT OF ROME: Let us . . . earnestly strive to be found in the number of those that wait for him, in order that we may share in his promised gifts. But how, beloved, shall this be done? If our understanding is fixed by faith toward God; if we earnestly seek the things that are pleasing and acceptable to him; if we do the things that are in harmony with his blameless will; and if we follow the way of truth, casting away from us all unrighteousness and iniquity, along with all covetousness, strife, evil practices, deceit, whispering and evil speaking, all hatred of God, pride and haughtiness, vainglory and ambition. For they that do such things are hateful to God; and not only they that do them, but also those that take pleasure in them that do them. 1 CLEMENT 35.[45]

---

[38]Rom 2:4-6. [39]FC 101:292-93. [40]LCC 4:148*. [41]FC 101:293. [42]Mt 5:16. [43]Rom 2:24. [44]FC 83:102*. [45]ANF 1:14*.

Appendix

Early Christian Writers and the Documents Cited

The following table lists all the early Christian documents cited in this volume by author, if known, or by the title of the work. The English title used in this commentary is followed in parentheses with the Latin designation and, where available, the Thesaurus Linguae Graecae (=TLG) digital references or Cetedoc Clavis numbers. Printed sources of original language versions may be found in the bibliography of works in original languages.

Alexander of Alexandria
Epistles on the Arian Heresy

Ambrose

Commentary on Twelve Psalms (*Explanatio psalmorum xii*)	Cetedoc 0140
Concerning Repentance (*De paenitentia*)	Cetedoc 0156
Duties of the Clergy (*De officiis ministrorum*)	Cetedoc 0144
Isaac, or the Soul (*De Isaac vel anima*)	Cetedoc 0128
Jacob and the Happy Life (*De Jacob et vita beata*)	Cetedoc 0130
Joseph (*De Joseph*)	Cetedoc 0131
Letters (*Epistulae*)	Cetedoc 0160
On His Brother Satyrus (*De excessu fratris Satyri*)	Cetedoc 0157
On the Christian Faith (*De fide*)	Cetedoc 0150
On the Death of Theodosius (*De obitu Theodosii*)	Cetedoc 0159
On the Patriarchs (*De patriarchis*)	Cetedoc 0132
On the Sacraments (*De sacramentis* [dub.])	Cetedoc 0154
On Virginity (*De virginitate*)	Cetedoc 0147
Six Days of Creation (*Exameron*)	Cetedoc 0123
The Prayer of Job and David (*De interpellatione Job et David*)	Cetedoc 0134

Ammonius of Alexandria

Fragments on Psalms (*Fragmenta in Psalmos*)	TLG 2724.001

Aphrahat
Demonstrations (*Demonstrationes*)

Arnobius of Sicca

Against the Heathen (*Adversus nationes*)	Cetedoc 0093

Arnobius the Younger

Commentary on the Psalms (*Commentarii in Psalmos*)	Cetedoc 0242

Asterius the Homilist

Homilies on the Psalms (*Commentarii in Psalmos*)	TLG 2061.001

Athanasius

Against the Heathen (*Contra gentes*)	TLG 2035.001
Discourses Against the Arians (*Orationes tres contra Arianos*)	TLG 2035.042
Festal Letters (*Epistulae festalis*)	
Letter to the Bishops of Egypt	
(*Epistula ad episcopos Aegypti et Libyae*)	TLG 2035.041
Life of St. Anthony (*Vita sancti Antonii*)	TLG 2035.047
On the Incarnation (*De incarnatione verbi*)	TLG 2035.002
On the Interpretation of the Psalms	
(*Epistula ad Marcellinum de interpretatione Psalmorum*)	TLG 2035.059

Augustine

Against Julian (*Contra Julianum*)	Cetedoc 0351
Against Two Letters of the Pelagians (*Contra duas epistulas Pelagianorum*)	Cetedoc 0346
City of God (*De civitate Dei*)	Cetedoc 0313
Confessions (*Confessionum libri tredecim*)	Cetedoc 0251
Enchiridion (*Enchiridion de fide, spe et caritate*)	Cetedoc 0295
Expositions of the Psalms (*Enarrationes in Psalmos*)	Cetedoc 0283
Faith and Works (*De fide et operibus*)	Cetedoc 0294
Holy Virginity (*De sancta virginitate*)	Cetedoc 0300
Homilies on 1 John (*In Johannis epistulam ad Parthos tractatus*)	Cetedoc 0279
Letters (*Epistulae*)	Cetedoc 0262
On the Christian Life (*De vita Christiana [dub.]*)	Cetedoc 0730
On the Perfection of Human Righteousness (*De perfectione justitiae hominis*)	Cetedoc 0347
On the Soul and its Origin (*De natura et origine animae*)	Cetedoc 0345
On the Spirit and the Letter (*De spiritu et littera*)	Cetedoc 0343
On the Trinity (*De trinitate*)	Cetedoc 0329
On Various Questions to Simplician (*De diversis quaestionibus ad Simplicianum*)	Cetedoc 0290
Sermons (*Sermones*)	Cetedoc 0284
Tractates on the Gospel of John (*In Johannis evangelium tractatus*)	Cetedoc 0278

Babai

Letter to Cyriacus (*Martyanuta d-abahata qadise d-`Idta*)	

Basil the Great

Homilies on the Psalms (*Homiliae super Psalmos*)	TLG 2040.018
Homily Against Those Who Are Prone to Anger	
(*Homilia adversus eos qui irascuntur*)	TLG 2040.026
The Long Rules, Preface (*Prologus 4 [prooemium in asceticum magnum]*)	TLG 2040.047

Bede

Homilies on the Gospels (*Homiliarum evangelii libri ii*)	Cetedoc 1367
On the Tabernacle (*De tabernaculo et vasis eius ac vestibus sacerdotum libri iii*)	Cetedoc 1345

Benedict
Rule of St. Benedict (*Regula*)   Cetedoc 1852

Caesarius of Arles
Sermons (*Sermones*)   Cetedoc 1008

Callistus of Rome
Epistles (*Epistola Papae Calixti ad omnes Galliae episcopos [dub.]*)

Cassian, John
Conferences (*Collationes*)   Cetedoc 0512
Institutes (*De institutis coenobiorum et de octo principalium vitiorum remediis*)   Cetedoc 0513

Cassiodorus
Explanation of the Psalms (*Expositio psalmorum*)   Cetedoc 0900

Clement of Alexandria
Christ the Educator (*Paedagogus*)   TLG 0555.002
Exhortation to the Greeks (*Protrepticus*)   TLG 0555.001
Stromateis (*Stromata*)   TLG 0555.004

Clement of Rome
1 Clement (*Epistula i ad Corinthios*)   TLG 1271.001

Constitutions of the Holy Apostles (*Constitutiones apostolorum*)   TLG 2894.001

Cyprian
The Unity of the Church (*De ecclesiae catholicae unitate*)   Cetedoc 0041
Works and Almsgiving (*De opera et eleemosynis*)   Cetedoc 0047

Cyril of Alexandria
Exposition of the Psalms (*Expositio in Psalmos*)   TLG 4090.100
Glaphyra on the Pentateuch (*Glaphyra in Pentateuchum*)   TLG 4090.097
Letters (*Epistulae in Concilium universale Ephesenum anno 431*)   TLG 5000.001
On the Unity of Christ (*Quod unus sit Christus*)   TLG 4090.027

Cyril of Jerusalem
Catechetical Lectures (*Catecheses ad illuminandos*)   TLG 2110.003
Catechetical Lectures, Procatechesis (*Procatechesis*)   TLG 2110.001
Mystagogical Lectures (*Mystagogiae [sp.]*)   TLG 2110.002

Didache (*Didache xii apostolorum*)   TLG 1311.001

Didymus the Blind
Fragments on the Psalms (*Fragmenta in Psalmos [e commentario altero]*)   TLG 2102.021

Diodore of Tarsus
Commentary on Psalms (*Commentarius in Psalmos I-L*)

Ephrem the Syrian
Homily on Our Lord (*Sermo de Domino nostro*)
Hymns on Paradise (*Hymni de Paradiso*)
Hymns on the Nativity (*Hymni de nativitate*)

Eusebius of Caesarea
Commentary on the Psalms (*Commentaria in Psalmos*)	TLG 2018.034
Ecclesiastical History (*Historia ecclesiastica*)	TLG 2018.002
Proof of the Gospel (*Demonstratio evangelica*)	TLG 2018.005

Evagrius of Pontus
Chapters on Prayer (*De oratione*)	TLG 4110.024
Notes on Psalms (*Selecta in Psalmos*)	TLG 2042.058
On the Eight Thoughts (*De octo spiritibus malitiae*)	TLG 4110.023
On Thoughts (*De diversis malignis cogitationibus*)	TLG 4110.022
Praktikos (*Practicus*)	TLG 4110.001

Fulgentius of Ruspe
Book to Victor Against the Sermon of Fastidiosus the Arian (*Liber ad Victorem contra sermonem Fastidiosi Ariani*)	Cetedoc 0820
Letters (*Epistulae*)	Cetedoc 0817
Letter to Monimus (*Ad Monimum libri III*)	Cetedoc 0814
On the Forgiveness of Sins (*Ad Euthymium de remissione peccatorum libri II*)	Cetedoc 0821

Gregory of Nazianzus
In Defense of His Flight to Pontus, Oration 2 (*Apologetica*)	TLG 2022.016
On His Brother St. Caesarius, Oration 7 (*Funebris in laudem Caesarii fratris oratio*)	TLG 2022.005
On His Father's Silence, Oration 16 (*In patrem tacentem*)	TLG 2022.029
On Holy Baptism, Oration 40 (*In sanctum baptisma*)	TLG 2022.048
On Holy Easter, Oration 45 (*In sanctum pascha*)	TLG 2022.052
On the Words of the Gospel, "When Jesus Had Finished These Sayings," Oration 37 (*In dictum evangelii: Cum consummasset Jesus hos sermones*)	TLG 2022.045
On the Holy Spirit, Theological Oration 5(31) (*De spiritu sancto*)	TLG 2022.011
On the Son, Theological Oration 3(29) (*De filio*)	TLG 2022.009
On the Son, Theological Oration 4(30) (*De filio*)	TLG 2022.010
On Theology, Theological Oration 2(28) (*De theologia*)	TLG 2022.008

Gregory of Nyssa
Address on Religious Instruction (*Oratio catechetica magna*)	TLG 2017.046
Against Eunomius (*Contra Eunomium*)	TLG 2017.030
Answer to Eunomius' Second Book (*Contra Eunomium*)	TLG 2017.030

On the Christian Mode of Life (*De instituto Christiano*)   TLG 2017.024
On the Inscriptions of the Psalms (*In inscriptiones Psalmorum*)   TLG 2017.027
On Virginity (*De virginitate*)   TLG 2017.043

Gregory Thaumaturgus
Homilies (*In annuntiationem sanctae virginis Mariaei [dub.]*)   TLG 2063.009

Gregory the Great
Letters (*Registrum epistularum*)   Cetedoc 1714

Hesychius of Jerusalem
Large Commentary on the Psalms (*Fragmenta in Psalmos*)

Hilary of Poitiers
Homilies on the Psalms (*Tractatus super psalmos I-XCI*)   Cetedoc 0428
On the Trinity (*De trinitate*)   Cetedoc 0433

Hippolytus
Commentary on Genesis (*Fragmenta in Genesim*)   TLG 2115.004
Fragments on the Psalms (*Fragmenta in Psalmos [Sp.]*)   TLG 2115.012

Irenaeus
Against Heresies (*Adversus haereses*)   Cetedoc 1154 f-g

Isaac of Nineveh
Ascetical Homilies

Jerome
Against the Pelagians (*Dialogi contra Pelagianos libri iii*)   Cetedoc 0615
Brief Commentary on Psalms (*Commentarioli in psalmos*)   Cetedoc 0582
Homilies on the Psalms (*Tractatus lix in psalmos*)   Cetedoc 0592
Letters (*Epistulae*)   Cetedoc 0620
Homily 87, On John (*Homilia in Johannem evangelistam [1:1-14]*)   Cetedoc 0597
Homily 89, On the Epiphany and Psalm 28
    (*Sermo de die epiphaniorum et de psalmo xxviii*)   Cetedoc 0599
Homily 94, On Easter Sunday (*In die dominica Pascha, II*)   Cetedoc 0604

John Chrysostom
Against the Anomoeans (*Contra Anomoeos, homilia 8*)   TLG 2062.016
Commentary on the Psalms (*Expositiones in Psalmos*)   TLG 2062.143
Discourses Against Judaizing Christians (*Adversus Judaeos [orationes 1-8]*) TLG 2062.021
Homilies Concerning the Statues (*Ad populam Antiochenum homiliae [de statuis]*) TLG 2062.024
Homilies on 1 Timothy (*In epistulam i ad Timotheum*)   TLG 2062.164
Homilies on Genesis (*In Genesim [homiliae 1-67]*)   TLG 2062.112
Homilies on 2 Corinthians

(*In epistulam ii ad Corinthios [homiliae 1-30]*)   TLG 2062.157
Homilies on the Gospel of John (*In Joannem [homiliae 1-88]*)   TLG 2062.153
On Providence (*Ad eos qui scandalizati sunt*)   TLG 2062.087
On the Epistle to the Hebrews (*In epistulam ad Hebraeos*)   TLG 2062.168

John of Damascus
Barlaam and Joseph (*Vita Barlaam et Joasaph [sp.]*)   TLG 2934.066
Orthodox Faith (*Expositio fidei*)   TLG 2934.004

Justin Martyr
Dialogue with Trypho (*Dialogus cum Tryphone*)   TLG 0645.003

Lactantius
Treatise on the Anger of God (*De ira Dei*)   Cetedoc 0088

Leander of Seville
The Training of Nuns (*De institutione virginum et contemptu mundi*)

Leo the Great
Sermons (*Tractatus septem et nonaginta*)   Cetedoc 1657

Martin of Braga
Driving Away Vanity (*Pro repellenda jactantia*)
Exhortation to Humility (*Exhortatio humilitatis*)

Maximus of Turin
Sermons (*Collectio sermonum antiqua*)   Cetedoc 0219a

Methodius
Banquet of the Ten Virgins (*Symposium* sive *Convivium decem virginum*)   TLG 2959.001

Nicetas of Remesiana
Liturgical Singing (*De utilitate hymnorum*)
The Power of the Holy Spirit (*De spiritus sancti potentia*)
Vigils of the Saints (*De Vigiliis servorum Dei*)

Novatian
On the Trinity (*De Trinitate*)   Cetedoc 0071

Origen
Against Celsus (*Contra Celsum*)   TLG 2042.001
Commentary on the Gospel of John
  (*Commentarii in evangelium Joannis [lib. 1, 2, 4, 5, 6, 10, 13]*)   TLG 2042.005
  (*Commentarii in evangelium Joannis [lib. 19, 20, 28, 32]*)   TLG 2042.079
Commentary on the Gospel of Matthew

(*Commentarium in evangelium Matthaei [lib. 10-11]*)   TLG 2042.029
(*Commentarium in evangelium Matthaei [lib. 10-17]*)   TLG 2042.030
Fragments on Psalms (*Fragmenta in Psalmos [Dub.]*)   TLG 2042.044
Exhortation to Martyrdom (*Exhortatio ad martyrium*)   TLG 2042.007
Homilies on Exodus (*Homiliae in Exodum*)   TLG 2042.023
Homilies on Genesis (*Homiliae in Genesim*)   TLG 2042.022
Homilies on Leviticus (*Homiliae in Leviticum*)   TLG 2042.024
Homilies on Psalms 36, 37, 38 (*Homiliae in Psalmos XXXVI-XXXVII-XXXVIII*)
Homilies on the Gospel of Luke (*Homiliae in Lucam*)   TLG 2042.016
On First Principles (*De principiis*)   TLG 2042.002
On Prayer (*De oratione*)   TLG 2042.008
Selections from the Psalms (*Selecta in Psalmos [dub.]*)   TLG 2042.058

Pachomius
Instructions (*Catecheses*)

Paulinus of Nola
Poems (*Carmina*)   Cetedoc 0203

Peter Chrysologus
Sermons (*Collectio sermonum*)   Cetedoc 0227+

Poemen
Sayings of the Fathers (*Sententiae Patrum*)

Prudentius
The Divinity of Christ (*Liber apotheosis*)   Cetedoc 1439
Hymns for Every Day (*Liber cathemerinon*)   Cetedoc 1438

Pseudo-Athanasius
Exposition on Psalms (*Expositio in Psalmos*)   TLG 2035.061

Sahdona (Martyrius)
Book of Perfection
Salvian the Presbyter
The Governance of God (*De gubernatione Dei*)   Cetedoc 0485

Tertullian
Against Marcion (*Adversus Marcionem*)   Cetedoc 0014
An Answer to the Jews (*Adversus Judaeos*)   Cetedoc 0033
On Flight in Time of Persecution (*De fuga in persecutione*)   Cetedoc 0025

Theodore of Mopsuestia
Commentary on Psalms (*Expositio in Psalmos*)

Theodore of Tabennesi
Instructions (*Catecheses*)

Theodoret of Cyr
Commentary on the Psalms (*Interpretatio in Psalmos*)   TLG 4089.024

Theophilus of Alexandria
Sermon on the Mystical Supper (*In mysticam coenum*)

Valerian of Cimiez
Homilies (*Homiliae*)

Zephyrinus
Epistles of Zephyrinus (*Epistola Zephirini papae [sp.]*)

Bibliography of Works
in Original Languages

This bibliography refers readers to original language sources and supplies Thesaurus Linguae Graecae (=TLG) or Cetedoc Clavis (=Cl.) numbers where available. The edition listed in this bibliography may in some cases differ from the edition found in TLG or Cetedoc databases.

Alexander of Alexandria. "Epistola Alexandri de Ariana haeresi et de Arii depositione." In *Opera omnia*. Edited by J.-P. Migne. PG 18, cols. 547-82. Paris: Migne, 1857-1886. TLG 2035.003.

Ambrose. *Explanatio psalmorum xii*. In *Sancti Ambrosii opera*. Edited by Michael Petschenig. CSEL 64. Vienna, Austria: Tempsky; Leipzig, Germany: Freytag, 1919. Cl. 0140.

———. "De excessu fratris Satyri." In *Sancti Ambrosii opera*. Edited by Otto Faller. CSEL 73, pp. 207-325. Vienna, Austria: Hoelder-Pichler-Tempsky, 1895. Cl. 0157.

———. "De fide libri v." In *Sancti Ambrosii opera*. Edited by Otto Faller. CSEL 78. Vienna, Austria: Hoelder-Pichler-Tempsky, 1962. Cl. 0150.

———. "De interpellatione Job et David." In *Sancti Ambrosii opera*. Edited by Karl Schenkl. CSEL 32, pt. 2, pp. 211-96. Vienna, Austria: F. Tempsky; Leipzig, Germany: G. Freytag, 1897. Cl. 0134.

———. "De Isaac vel anima." In *Sancti Ambrosii opera*. Edited by Karl Schenkl. CSEL 32, pt. 1, pp. 639-700. Vienna, Austria: F. Tempsky; Leipzig, Germany: G. Freytag, 1897. Cl. 0128.

———. "De Jacob et vita beata." In *Sancti Ambrosii opera*. Edited by Karl Schenkl. CSEL 32, pt. 2, pp. 1-70. Vienna, Austria: F. Tempsky; Leipzig, Germany: G. Freytag, 1897. Cl. 0130.

———. "De Joseph." In *Sancti Ambrosii opera*. Edited by Karl Schenkl. CSEL 32, pt. 2, pp. 71-122. Vienna, Austria: F. Tempsky; Leipzig, Germany: G. Freytag, 1897. Cl. 0131.

———. "De obitu Theodosii." In *Sancti Ambrosii opera*. Edited by Otto Faller. CSEL 73, pp. 371-401. Vienna, Austria: Hoelder-Pichler-Tempsky, 1955. Cl. 0159.

———. *De officiis*. Edited by Maurice Testard. CCL 15. Turnhout, Belgium: Brepols, 2000. Cl. 0144.

———. "De patriarchis." In *Sancti Ambrosii opera*. Edited by Karl Schenkl. CSEL 32, pt. 2, pp. 123-60. Vienna, Austria: F. Tempsky; Leipzig, Germany: G. Freytag, 1897. Cl. 0132.

———. *De paenitentia*. Edited by Roger Gryson. SC 179. Paris: Éditions du Cerf, 1971. Cl. 0156.

———. "De sacramentis [dub.]." In *Sancti Ambrosii opera*. Edited by Otto Faller. CSEL 73, pp. 13-85. Vienna, Austria: Hoelder-Pichler-Tempsky, 1955. Cl. 0154.

———. "De virginitate." In *Opere II/2: Verginità e vedovanza*. Edited by F. Gori. Opera omnia di Sant'Ambrogio 14.2, pp. 16-106. Milan: Biblioteca Ambrosiana; Rome: Città nuova, 1989. Cl. 0147.

———. "Epistulae; Epistulae extra collectionem traditae." In *Sancti Ambrosii opera*. Edited by Otto

Faller and Michaela Zelzer. CSEL 82. 4 vols. Vienna, Austria: F. Tempsky; Leipzig, Germany: G. Freytag, 1968-1990. Cl. 0160.

———. "Exameron." In *Sancti Ambrosii opera*. Edited by Karl Schenkl. CSEL 32, pt. 1, pp. 1-261. Vienna, Austria: F. Tempsky; Leipzig, Germany: G. Freytag, 1897. Cl. 0123.

Ammonius of Alexandria. "Fragmenta in psalmos." In *Opera quae exstant omnia*. Edited by J.-P. Migne. PG 85, cols. 1361-64. Paris: Migne, 1864. TLG 2724.001.

Aphrahat. "Demonstrationes (IV)." In *Opera omnia*. Edited by R. Graffin. PS 1, cols. 137-82. Paris: Firmin-Didor, 1910.

Arnobius of Sicca. *Adversus nationes*. Edited by Concetto Marchesi. Corpus scriptorum Latinorum Paravianum. Aug. Taurinorum: In Aedibus I.B. Paraviae, 1953. Cl. 0093.

Arnobius the Younger. *Commentarii in psalmos*. Edited by K.-D. Daur. CCL 25. Turnhout, Belgium: Brepols, 1990. Cl. 0242.

Asterius the Homilist. *Asterii Sophistae commentariorum in psalmos quae supersunt*. Symbolae Osloenses, fasc. suppl. 16. Edited by M. Richard. Oslo: Brøgger, 1956. TLG 2061.001.

Athanasius. "Contra gentes." In *Athanasius. Contra gentes and de incarnatione*. Edited by R. W. Thomson. Pp. 2-132. Oxford: Clarendon Press, 1971. TLG 2035.001.

———. "De incarnatione verbi." In *Sur l'incarnation du verbe*. Edited by C. Kannengiesser. SC 199, pp. 258-468. Paris: Éditions du Cerf, 1973. TLG 2035.002.

———. "Epistula ad episcopos Aegypti et Libyae." In *Opera omnia*. Edited by J.-P. Migne. PG 25, cols. 537-93. Paris: Migne, 1884. TLG 2035.014.

———. "Epistula ad Marcellinum de interpretatione Psalmorum." In *Opera omnia*. Edited by J.-P. Migne. PG 27, cols. 12-45. Paris: Migne, 1857. TLG 2035.059.

———. "Epistulae festales." In *Opera omnia*. Edited by J.-P. Migne. PG 26, cols. 1351-1444. Paris: Migne, 1887. TLG 2035.014.

———. "Expositiones in Psalmos [dub.]." In *Opera omnia*. Edited by J.-P. Migne. PG 27, cols. 60-589. Paris: Migne, 1857. TLG 2035.061.

———. "Orationes tres contra Arianos." In *Opera omnia*. Edited by J.-P. Migne. PG 26, cols. 813-920. Paris: Migne, 1887. TLG 2035.042.

———. "Vita sancti Antonii." In *Opera omnia*. Edited by J.-P. Migne. PG 26, cols. 835-976. Paris: Migne, 1887. TLG 2035.047.

Augustine. "Confessionum libri tredecim." In *Sancti Augustini opera*. Edited by Lucas Verheijen. CCL 27. Turnhout, Belgium: Brepols, 1981. Cl. 0251.

———. "Contra duas epistulas pelagianorum." In *Sancti Aurelii Augustini*. Edited by Karl Franz Urba and Joseph Zycha. CSEL 60, pp. 423-570. Vienna, Austria: F. Tempsky; Leipzig, Germany: G. Freytag, 1913. Cl. 0346.

———. "Contra Julianum." In *Augustini opera omnia*. Edited by J.-P. Migne. PL 44, cols. 641-874. Paris: Migne, 1845. Cl. 0351.

———. *De civitate Dei*. In *Aurelii Augustini opera*. Edited by Bernhard Dombart and Alphons Kalb. CCL 47 and CCL 48. Turnhout, Belgium: Brepols, 1955. Cl. 0313.

———. "De diversis quaestionibus ad Simplicianum." In *Sancti Aurelii Augustini*. Edited by Almut Mutzenbecher. CCL 44. Turnhout, Belgium: Brepols, 1975. Cl. 0290.

———. "De fide et operibus." In *Sancti Aureli Augustini opera*. Edited by Joseph Zycha. CSEL 41, pp. 35-97. Vienna, Austria: Hoelder-Pichler-Tempsky, 1900. Cl. 0294.

———. "De natura et origene animae." In *Sancti Aureli Augustini*. Edited by Karl Franz Urba and Joseph Zycha. CSEL 60, pp. 303-419. Vienna, Austria: F. Tempsky; Leipzig, Germany: G.

Freytag, 1913. Cl. 0345.

———. "De perfectione justitiae hominis." In *Sancti Aureli Augustini opera*. Edited by Karl Franz Urba and Joseph Zycha. CSEL 42, pp. 3-48. Vienna, Austria: F. Tempsky, 1902. Cl. 0347.

———. "De sancta virginitate." In *Sancti Augustii opera*. Edited by Joseph Zycha. CSEL 41, pp. 235-301. Vienna, Austria: F. Tempsky, 1900. Cl. 0300.

———. "De spiritu et littera." In *Sancti Aurelii Augustini*. Edited by Karl Franz Urba and Joseph Zycha. CSEL 60, pp. 155-229. Vienna, Austria: F. Tempsky; Leipzig, Germany: G. Freytag, 1913. Cl. 0343.

———. "De Trinitate." In *Aurelii Augustini opera*. Edited by William John Mountain. CCL 50 and CCL 50A. Turnhout, Belgium: Brepols, 1968. Cl. 0329.

———. "De vita Christiana [dub.]." In *Augustini opera omnia*. Edited by J.-P. Migne. PL 40, cols. 1031-46. Paris: Migne, 1861.

———. *Enarrationes in Psalmos*. In *Aurelii Augustini opera*. Edited by Eligius Dekkers and John Fraipont. CCL 38, CCL 39 and CCL 40. Turnhout, Belgium: Brepols, 1956. Cl. 0283.

———. "Enchiridion de fide, spe et caritate." In *Aurelii Augustini opera*. Edited by E. Evans. CCL 46, pp. 49-114. Turnhout, Belgium: Brepols, 1969. Cl. 0295.

———. *Epistulae 31-123*. In *Sancti Aurelii Augustini*. Edited by A. Goldbacher. CSEL 34. Vienna, Austria: F. Tempsky; Leipzig, Germany: G. Freytag, 1898. Cl. 0262.

———. *Epistulae 185-270*. In *Sancti Aurelii Augustini*. Edited by A. Goldbacher. CSEL 57. Vienna, Austria: F. Tempsky; Leipzig, Germany: G. Freytag, 1911. Cl. 0262.

———. "In Johannis epistulam ad Parthos tractatus." In *Augustini opera omnia*. Edited by J.-P. Migne. PL 35, cols. 1977-2062. Paris: Migne, 1861. Cl. 0279.

———. "In Johannis evangelium tractatus." In *Aurelii Augustini opera*. Edited by R. Willems. CCL 36. Turnhout, Belgium: Brepols, 1954. Cl. 0278.

———. *Sermones*. In *Augustini opera omnia*. Edited by J.-P. Migne. PL 38 and PL 39. Paris: Migne, 1845. Cl. 0284.

Babai. *Martyanuta d-abahata qadise d-`Idta*. Edited by Metro. Mar Yulios Çiçek. Holland: St. Ephrem the Syrian Monastery, 1985.

Basil the Great. "Homilia adversus eos qui irascuntur." In *Opera omnia*. Edited by J.-P. Migne. PG 31, cols. 353-72. Paris: Migne, 1857. TLG 2040.026.

———. "Homiliae super Psalmos." In *Opera omnia*. Edited by J.-P. Migne. PG 29, cols. 209-494. Paris: Migne, 1857. TLG 2040.018.

———. "Prologus 4 [prooemium in asceticum magnum]." In *Opera omnia*. Edited by J.-P. Migne. PG 31, cols. 889-901. Paris: Migne, 1885. TLG 2040.047.

Bede. "De tabernaculo et vasis eius ac vestibus sacerdotum libri iii." In *Bedae opera*. Edited by David Hurst. CCL 119A, pp. 5-139. Turnhout, Belgium: Brepols, 1969. Cl. 1345.

———. "Homiliarum evangelii libri ii." In *Bedae opera*. Edited by David Hurst. CCL 122, pp. 1-378. Turnhout, Belgium: Brepols, 1956. Cl. 1367.

Benedict. "Regula." In *La règle de Saint Benoît*. Edited by A. de Vogüé. SC 181, pp. 412-90, and SC 182, pp. 508-674. Paris: Éditions du Cerf, 1971-1972. Cl. 1852.

Caesarius of Arles. *Sermones Caesarii Arelatensis*. Edited by Germain Morin. CCL 103 and CCL 104. Turnhout, Belgium: Brepols, 1953. Cl. 1008.

Callistus of Rome. "Epistola Papae Calixti ad omnes Galliae episcopos [dub.]." In *Decretalium collectio*. Edited by J.-P. Migne. PL 130, cols. 131-38. Paris: Migne, 1853.

Cassian, John. *Collationes xxiv*. Edited by Michael Petschenig. CSEL 13. Vienna, Austria: F. Tempsky; Leipzig, Germany: G. Freytag, 1886. Cl. 0512.

———. "De institutis coenobiorum et de octo principalium vitiorum remediis." In *Johannis Cassiani.* Edited by Michael Petschenig. CSEL 17, pp. 1-231. Vienna, Austria: F. Tempsky; Leipzig, Germany: G. Freytag, 1888. Cl. 0513.

Cassiodorus. *Expositio psalmorum.* Edited by Mark Adriaen. CCL 97 and CCL 98. Turnhout, Belgium: Brepols, 1958. Cl. 0900.

Clement of Alexandria. "Paedagogus." In *Clement d'Alexandrie: Le pédagogue.* Edited by Marguerite Harl, Chantel Matray and Claude Mondésert. Introduction and notes by Henri-Irénée Marrou. SC 70, pp. 108-294, SC 108, pp. 10-242, and SC 158, pp. 12-190. Paris: Éditions du Cerf, 1960-1970. TLG 0555.002.

———. "Protrepticus." In *Clément d'Alexandrie. Le protreptique.* 2nd ed. Edited by Claude Mondésert. SC 2, pp. 52-193. Paris: Éditions du Cerf, 1949. TLG 0555.001.

———. "Stromata." In *Clemens Alexandrinus.* Vol. 2, 3rd ed., and vol. 3, 2nd ed. Edited by Otto Stählin, Ludwig Früchtel and Ursula Treu. GCS 52, pp. 3-518, and GCS 17, pp. 1-102. Berlin: Akademie-Verlag, 1960-1970. TLG 0555.004.

Clement of Rome. "Epistula i ad Corinthios." In *Clément de Rome: Épître aux Corinthiens.* Edited by Annie Jaubert. SC 167. Paris: Éditions du Cerf, 1971. TLG 1271.001.

Constitutiones apostolorum. See *Les constitutions apostoliques.* Edited by Marcel Metzger. SC 320, SC 329 and SC 336. Paris: Éditions du Cerf, 1985-1987. TLG 2894.001.

Cyprian. "De ecclesiae catholicae unitate." In *Sancti Cypriani episcopi opera.* Edited by Maurice Bévenot. CCL 3, pp. 249-68. Turnhout, Belgium: Brepols, 1972. Cl. 0041.

———. "De opera et eleemosynis." In *Sancti Cypriani episcopi opera.* Edited by Manlio Simonetti. CCL 3A, pp. 53-72. Turnhout, Belgium: Brepols, 1976. Cl. 0047.

Cyril of Alexandria. "Epistulae." In *Concilium Universale Ephesenum.* Edited by E. Schwartz. Berlin: Walter De Gruyter, 1927. TLG 5000.001.

———. "Expositio in Psalmos." In *Opera omnia.* PG 69, cols. 717-1273. Edited by J.-P. Migne. Paris: Migne, 1864. TLG 4090.100.

———. "Glaphyra in Pentateuchum" In *Opera omnia.* PG 69, cols. 9-678. Edited by J.-P. Migne. Paris: Migne, 1864. TLG 4090.097.

———. "Quod unus sit Christus." In *Cyrille d'Alexandrie: Deux dialogues christologiques.* SC 97. Paris: Éditions du Cerf, 1964. TLG 4090.027.

Cyril of Jerusalem. "Catecheses ad illuminandos 1-18." In *Cyrilli Hierosolymorum archiepiscopi opera quae supersunt omnia.* Edited by W. C. Reischl and J. Rupp. Vol. 1, pp. 28-320, and vol. 2, pp. 2-342. Munich: Lentner, 1848 and 1860. Reprint, Hildesheim: Olms, 1967. TLG 2110.003.

———. "Mystagogiae 1-5 [Sp.]." In *Cyrille de Jérusalem: Catéchèses, mystagogigues.* 2nd Ed. SC 126, pp. 82-174. Edited by Auguste Piédagnel. Paris: Éditions du Cerf, 1988. TLG 2110.002.

———. "Procatechesis." In *Cyrilli Hierosolymorum archiepiscopi opera quae supersunt omnia.* Vol. 1. Edited by W. C. Reischl and J. Rupp. Munich: Lentner, 1860. Reprint, Hildesheim: Olms, 1967. TLG 2110.001.

Didache xii apostolorum. In *La Didachè. Instructions des Apôtres,* pp. 226-42. Edited by J. P. Audet. Paris: Lecoffre, 1958. TLG 1311.001.

Didymus the Blind. *Didymus der Blinde: Psalmenkommentar.* Bonn: Rudolf Habelt Verlage, 1969.

———. "Fragmenta in psalmos [e commentario altero]." In *Psalmendommentare aus der Katenenüberlieferung, vol. 1,* pp. 119-375. Translated by Ekkehard Mühlenberg. Berlin: Walter de

Gruyter, 1975. TLG 2102.021.

———. "Fragmenta alia in psalmos." In *Opera omnia*. PG 39, cols. 1617-22. Edited by J.-P. Migne. Paris: Migne, 1858.

Diodore of Tarsus. *Diodori Tarsensis commentarii in Psalmos*, vol. I: *Commentarius in Psalmos I-L*. Edited by Jean-Marie Oliver. CCG 6. Turnhout: Belgium: Brepols, 1980.

Ephrem the Syrian. *Hymni de nativitate*. Edited by Edmund Beck. 2 vols. CSCO 186 and CSCO 187 (Scriptores Syri 82 and 83). Louvain: Secrétariat du Corpus, 1959.

———. "Hymni de Paradiso." In *Des Heiligen Ephraem des Syrers Hymnen de Paradiso und Contra Julianum*. Edited by Edmund Beck. CSCO 174 (Scriptores Syri 78), pp. 1-66. Louvain: Imprimerie Orientaliste L. Durbecq, 1957.

———. "Sermo de Domino nostro." In *Des Heilig Ephraem Sermo de Domino Nostro*. Edited by Edmund Beck. CSCO 270 (Scriptores Syri 116). Louvain: Imprimerie Orientaliste L. Durbecq, 1966.

Eusebius of Caesarea. *Commentaria in Psalmos*. In *Opera omnia*. PG 23-24, cols. 66-1396 and 9-76. Edited by J.-P. Migne. Paris: Migne, 1857. TLG 2018.034.

———. "Commentarii in psalmos." In *Analecta sacra et classica spicilegio solesmensi*. Vol. 3. pp. 365-520. Edited by Jean Baptiste Pitra. Paris: Roger et Chernowitz, 1883.

———. "Demonstratio evangelica." In *Eusebius Werke, Band 6: Die Demonstratio evangelica*. Edited by Ivar A. Heikel. GCS 23. Leipzig: Hinrichs, 1913. TLG 2018.005.

———. "Historia ecclesiastica." In *Eusèbe de Césarée. Histoire ecclésiastique*. Edited by G. Bardy. SC 31, pp. 3-215, SC 41, pp. 4-231, and SC 55, pp. 3-120. Paris: Éditions du Cerf, 1952-1958. TLG 2018.002.

Evagrius of Pontus. "De diversis malignis cogitationibus" (under the name of Nilus of Ancyra). In *Opera omnia*. PG 79, cols. 1199-1235. Edited by J.-P. Migne. Paris: Migne, 1865. TLG 4110.022.

———. "De octo spiritibus malitiae" (under the name of Nilus of Ancyra). In *Opera omnia*. PG 79, cols. 1146-65. Edited by J.-P. Migne. Paris: Migne, 1865. TLG 4110.023.

———. "De oratione" (under the name of Nilus of Ancyra). In *Opera omnia*. PG 79, cols. 1165-2000. Edited by J.-P. Migne. Paris: Migne, 1865. TLG 4110.024.

———. "Practicus (capita centum)." In *Évagre le Pontique. Traité pratique ou le moine*, vol. 2. SC 171. Edited by A. Guillaumont and C. Guillaumont. Paris: Éditions du Cerf, 1971. TLG 4110.001.

———. "Selecta in Psalmos." (Under the name of Origen) In *Opera omnia*. PG 12, cols. 1053-1685. Edited by J.-P. Migne. Paris: Migne, 1862. TLG 2042.058.

———. "Selecta in Psalmos." In *Analecta sacra et classica spicilegio solesmensi*. Edited by Jean Baptiste Pitra. Paris: Roger et Chernowitz; Rome: P. Cuggiani, 1888-1891. Reprint, Farnsborough, England: Gregg Press, 1966.

Fulgentius of Ruspe. "Ad Euthymium de remissione peccatorum libri II." In *Opera*. Edited by John Fraipont. CCL 91A, pp. 649-707. Turnhout, Belgium: Brepols, 1968. Cl. 0821.

———. "Ad Monimum libri III." In *Opera*. Edited by John Fraipont. CCL 91, pp. 1-64. Turnhout, Belgium: Brepols, 1968. Cl. 0814.

———. *Epistulae XVIII*. In *Opera*. Edited by John Fraipont. CCL 91, pp. 189-280, 311-12, 359-44; and CCL 91A, pp. 447-57, 551-629. Turnhout, Belgium: Brepols, 1968. Cl. 0817.

———. "Liber ad Victorem contra sermonem Fastidiosi Ariani." In *Opera*. Edited by John Fraipont. CCL 91, pp. 283-308. Turnhout, Belgium: Brepols, 1968. Cl. 0820.

Gregory of Nazianzus. "Apologetica (orat. 2)." In *Opera omnia*. Edited by J.-P. Migne. PG 35, cols. 408-513. Paris: Migne, 1857. TLG 2022.016.

———. "De filio (orat. 29)." In *Gregor von Nazianz. Die fünf theologischen Reden*, pp. 128-68. Edited by Joseph Barbel. Düsseldorf, Germany: Patmos-Verlag, 1963. TLG 2022.009.

———. "De filio (orat. 30)." In *Gregor von Nazianz. Die fünf theologischen Reden*, pp. 170-216. Edited by Joseph Barbel. Düsseldorf, Germany: Patmos-Verlag, 1963. TLG 2022.010.

———. "De spiritu sancto (orat. 31)." In *Gregor von Nazianz. Die fünf theologischen Reden*, pp. 218-76. Edited by Joseph Barbel. Düsseldorf, Germany: Patmos-Verlag, 1963. TLG 2022.011.

———. "De theologia (orat. 28)." In *Gregor von Nazianz: Die fünf theologischen Reden*, pp. 62-126. Edited by Joseph Barbel. Düsseldorf: Patmos-Verlag, 1963. TLG 2022.008.

———. "Funebris in laudem Caesarii fratris oratio (orat. 7)." In *Grégoire de Nazianze. Discours funèbres en l'honneur de son frére Césaire et de Basile de Césarée*, pp. 2-56. Edited by F. Boulenger. Paris: Picard, 1908. TLG 2022.005.

———. "In dictum evangelii: Cum consummasset Jesus hos sermones (orat. 37)." In *Opera omnia*. Edited by J.-P. Migne. PG 36, cols. 281-308. Paris: Migne, 1886. TLG 2022.045.

———. "In patrem tacentem (orat. 16)." In *Opera omnia*. Edited by J.-P. Migne. PG 35, cols. 933-64. Paris: Migne, 1857. TLG 2022.029.

———. "In sanctum baptisma (orat. 40)." In *Opera omnia*. PG 36, cols. 360-425. Edited by J.-P. Migne. Paris: Migne, 1858. TLG 2022.048.

———. "In sanctum pascha (orat. 45)." In *Opera omnia*. PG 36, cols. 624-64. Edited by J.-P. Migne. Paris: Migne, 1858. TLG 2022.052.

Gregory of Nyssa. "Contra Eunomium." In *Gregorii Nysseni opera*, 2 vols. Vol. 1.1, pp. 3-409, and vol. 2.2, pp. 3-311. Edited by Werner William Jaeger. Leiden: Brill, 1960. TLG 2017.030.

———. "De instituto Christiano." In *Gregorii Nysseni opera*. Vol. 8.1, pp. 40-89. Edited by Werner William Jaeger. Leiden: Brill, 1963. TLG 2017.024.

———. "De virginitate." In *Grégoire de Nysse. Traité de la virginité*. SC 119, pp. 246-560. Edited by Michel Aubineau. Paris: Éditions du Cerf, 1966. TLG 2017.043.

———. *In Inscriptiones psalmorum. Gregorii Nysseni opera*. Vol. 5. Edited by J. McDonough and Paul Alexander. Leiden: Brill, 1962.

———. "Oratio catechetica magna." In *Gregorii Nysseni opera*. Vol. 3.4, pp. 1-106. Edited by Ekkehard Mühlenberg. Leiden: Brill, 1996. TLG 2017.046.

Gregory Thaumaturgus. *Homiliae 1-2 (In annuntiationem sanctae virginis Mariaei [dub.])*. In *Opera omnia*. Edited by J.-P. Migne. PG 10, cols. 1145-1169. Paris: Migne, 1857. TLG 2063.009.

Gregory the Great. *Registrum epistularum*. 2 vols. Edited by Dag Norberg. CCL 140 and CCL 140A. Turnhout, Belgium: Brepols, 1982. Cl. 1714.

Hesychius of Jerusalem. "Fragmenta in Psalmos." In *Opera omnia*. PG 93, cols. 1179-1340. Edited by J.-P. Migne. Paris: Migne, 1860.

Hilary of Poitiers. *De trinitate*. Edited by P. Smulders. CCL 62 and CCL 62A. Turnhout, Belgium: Brepols, 1979-1980. Cl. 0433.

———. *Tractatus super psalmos I-XCI*. Edited by Jean Doignon. CCL 61. Turnhout, Belgium: Brepols, 1997. Cl. 0428.

Hippolytus. "Fragmenta in Genesim." In *Hippolyt's kleinere exegetische und homiletische Schriften*. Edited by Hans Achelis. GCS 1.2, pp. 51-53, 55-71. Leipzig: Hinrichs, 1897. TLG 2115.004.

———. "Fragmenta in Psalmos. [Sp.]" In *Hippolyt's kleinere exegestische und homiletische Schriften*. Edited by H. Achelis. GCS 1.2, pp. 131-53. Leipzig, Germany: Hinrichs, 1897. TLG 2115.012.

———. "L'homilie d'Hippolyte sur les psaumes." In *Le dossier d'Hippolyte et de Méliton dans les florileges dogmatiques et chez les historiens moderns*, pp. 161-183. Translated by Pierre Nautin. Paris: Éditions du Cerf, 1953.

Irenaeus. "Adversus haereses, livres 1-5." In *Contre les hérésies*. Edited by Adelin Rousseau, Louis Doutreleau and Charles A. Mercier. SC 34, 100, 152-53, 210-11, 263-64 and 293-94. Paris: Éditions du Cerf, 1952-1982. Cl. 1154 f-g.

Isaac of Nineveh. *The Ascetical Homilies of Mar Isaac of Nineveh*. A facsimile reprint of the original Syriac edition published by W. Drugulin, Leipzig, 1908. Piscataway, N.J.: Gorgias Press, 2007.

Jerome. *Commentarioli in psalmos*. In *S. Hieronymi Presbyteri opera, Part 1.1*. Edited by G. Morin. CCL 72, pp. 177-245. Turnhout, Belgium: Brepols, 1959. Cl. 0582.

———. *Dialogus adversus Pelagianos*. Edited by Claudio Moreschini. CCL 80. Turnhout, Belgium: Brepols, 1990. Cl. 0615.

———. *Epistulae*. Edited by I. Hilberg. CSEL 54, CSEL 55 and CSEL 56. Vienna, Austria: F. Tempsky; Leipzig, Germany: G. F. Freytag, 1910-1918. Cl. 0620.

———. "Homilia in Johannem evangelistam (1:1-14)." In *S. Hieronymi Presbyteri opera, Part 2*. Edited by Germain Morin. CCL 78, pp. 517-23. Turnhout, Belgium: Brepols, 1958. Cl. 0597.

———. "In die dominica Paschae, II." In *S. Hieronymi Presbyteri opera, Part 2*. Edited by Germain Morin. CCL 78, pp. 548-51. Turnhout, Belgium: Brepols, 1958. Cl. 0604.

———. "Sermo de die epiphaniorum et de psalmo xxviii" In *S. Hieronymi Presbyteri opera, Part 2*. Edited by B. Capelle. CCL 78, pp. 530-32. Turnhout, Belgium: Brepols, 1958. Cl. 0599.

———. "Tractatus lix in psalmos." In *S. Hieronymi Presbyteri opera*. Edited by Germain Morin. CCL 78, pp. 3-352. Turnhout, Belgium: Brepols, 1958. Cl. 0592.

John Chrysostom. "Ad eos qui scandalizati sunt." In *Jean Chrysostome. Sur la providence de Dieu*. Ed. A.-M. Malingrey. SC 79, pp. 52-276. Paris: Éditions du Cerf, 1961. TLG 2062.087.

———. "Ad populam Antiochenum homiliae (de statuis)." In *Opera omnia*. Edited by J.-P. Migne. PG 49, cols. 15-222. Paris: Migne, 1862. TLG 2062.024.

———. "Adversus Judaeos (orationes 1-8)." In *Opera omnia*. Edited by J.-P. Migne. PG 48, cols. 843-942. Paris: Migne, 1862. TLG 2062.021.

———. "Contra Anomoeos (homilia 8): De petitione matris filiorum Zebedaei." In *Opera omnia*. Edited by J.-P. Migne. PG 48, cols. 767-78. Paris: Migne, 1862. TLG 2062.016.

———. "Expositiones in Psalmos." In *Opera omnia*. Edited by J.-P. Migne. PG 55, cols. 39-498. Paris: Migne, 1862. TLG 2062.143.

———. "In epistulam ad Hebraeos (homilae 1-34)." In *Opera omnia*. Edited by J.-P. Migne. PG 63, cols. 9-236. Paris: Migne, 1862. TLG 2062.168.

———. "In epistulam i ad Timotheum (homiliae 1-18)." In *Opera omnia*. Edited by J.-P. Migne. PG 62, cols. 501-600. Paris: Migne, 1862. TLG 2062.164.

———. "In epistulam ii ad Corinthios (homiliae 1-30)." In *Opera omnia*. Edited by J.-P. Migne. PG 61, cols. 381-610. Paris: Migne, 1862. TLG 2062.157.

———. "In Genesim (homiliae 1-67)." In *Opera omnia*. Edited by J.-P. Migne. PG 53 and PG 54, cols. 385-580. Paris: Migne, 1862. TLG 2062.112.

———. "In Joannem (homiliae 1-88)." In *Opera omnia*. Edited by J.-P. Migne. PG 59, cols. 23-482. Paris: Migne, 1862. TLG 2062.153.

John of Damascus. "Expositio fidei." In *Die Schriften des Johannes von Damaskos*. Vol. 2, pp. 3-239. Edited by Bonifatius Kotter. Patristische Texte und Studien 12. Berlin: De Gruyter, 1973.

TLG 2934.004.

———. *Vita Barlaam et Joasaph* [Sp.]. Edited by G. R. Woodward and H. Mattingly. Cambridge, Mass.: Harvard University Press, 1914. Reprint, 1983. TLG 2934.066.

Justin Martyr. "Dialogus cum Tryphone." In *Die ältesten Apologeten*, pp. 90-265. Edited by E. J. Goodspeed. Göttingen: Vandenhoeck & Ruprecht, 1915. TLG 0645.003.

Lactantius. "De ira Dei." In *La colère de Dieu*. Translated and edited by Christiane Ingremeau. SC 289. Paris: Éditions du Cerf, 1982. Cl. 0088.

Leander of Seville. "De institutione virginum et contemptu mundi." In *El "De institutione virginum" de San Leandro de Sevilla, con diez capítulos y medio inéditos*. Edited by Angelus C. Vega. Madrid: El Escorial, 1948.

Leo the Great. *Tractatus septem et nonaginta*. Edited by Antonio Chavasse. CCL 138 and CCL 138A. Turnhout, Belgium: Brepols, 1973. Cl. 1657.

Martin of Braga. "Exhortatio humilitatis." In *Martini Episcopi Bracarensis Opera omnia*, pp. 74-79. Edited by Claude W. Barlow. New Haven, Conn.: Yale University Press, 1950.

———. "Pro repellenda iactania." In *Martini Episcopi Bracarensis Opera omnia*, pp. 65-69. Edited by Claude W. Barlow. New Haven, Conn.: Yale University Press, 1950.

Maximus of Turin. *Collectio sermonum antiqua*. Edited by Almut Mutzenbecher. CCL 23. Turnhout, Belgium: Brepols, 1962. Cl. 0219a.

Methodius. "Symposium *sive* Convivium decem virginum." In *Opera omnia*. Edited by J.-P. Migne. PG 18, cols. 27-220. Paris: Migne, 1857. TLG 2959.001.

Nicetas of Remesiana. "De psalmodiae bono (de utilitate hymnorum)." Edited by C. Turner. *Journal of Theological Studies* 24 (1923): 225-52.

———. "De Spiritus sancti potentia." In *Niceta of Remesiana: His Life and Works*, pp. 18-38. Edited by A. E. Burn. Cambridge: Cambridge University Press, 1905.

———. "De Vigiliis servorum Dei." In *Niceta of Remesiana: His Life and Works*, pp. 55-67. Edited by A. E. Burn. Cambridge: Cambridge University Press, 1905.

Novatian. "De Trinitate." In *Opera*. Edited by Gerardus Frederik Diercks. CCL 4, pp. 11-78. Turnhout, Belgium: Brepols, 1972. Cl. 0071.

Origen. "Contra Celsum." In *Origène Contre Celse*. 4 Vols. Edited by M. Borret. SC 132, 136, 147 and 150. Paris: Éditions du Cerf, 1967-1969. TLG 2042.001.

———. "Commentarii in evangelium Joannis (lib. 1, 2, 4, 5, 6, 10, 13)." In *Origene. Commentaire sur saint Jean*, 3 vols. Edited by Cécil Blanc. SC 120, 157 and 222. Paris: Éditions du Cerf, 1966-1975. TLG 2042.005.

———. "Commentarii in evangelium Joannis (lib. 19, 20, 28, 32)." In *Origenes Werke*, vol. 4. Edited by Erwin Preuschen. GCS 10, pp. 298-480. Leipzig, Germany: Hinrichs, 1903. TLG 2042.079.

———. "Commentarium in evangelium Matthaei (lib. 10-17)." In *Origenes Werke*. Vol. 11. Edited by E. Klostermann. GCS 38.2, pp. 196-200. Leipzig, Germany: Teubner, 1933. TLG 2042.029 (lib. 10-11). TLG 2042.030 (lib. 12-17).

———. "De oratione." In *Origenes Werke*. Vol. 2. Edited by Paul Koetschau. GCS 3, pp. 297-403. Leipzig, Germany: Hinrichs, 1899. TLG 2042.008.

———. "De principiis." In *Origenes Werke*. Vol. 5. Edited by Paul Koetschau. GCS 22. Leipzig, Germany: Hinrichs, 1913. Cl. 0198 E (A). TLG 2042.002.

———. "Exhortatio ad martyrium." In *Origenes Werke*. Vol. 1. Edited by Paul Koetschau. GCS 2, pp. 3-47. Leipzig, Germany: Hinrichs, 1899. TLG 2042.007.

———. "Fragmenta in Psalmos [dub.]." In *Anelecta sacra spicilegio Solesmensi parata*. Edited by Jean Baptiste Pitra. Vol. 2, pp. 444-83, and Vol. 3, pp. 1-364. Venice: St. Lazarus Monastery, 1883. TLG 2042.044.

———. "Homiliae in Exodum." In *Origenes Werke*. Vol. 6. Edited by Willem A. Baehrens. GCS 29, pp. 217-30. Leipzig, Germany: Hinrichs, 1920. Cl. 0198. TLG 2042.023.

———. "Homiliae in Genesim." In *Origenes Werke*. Vol. 6. Edited by W. A. Baehrens. GCS (CB) 29, pp. 23-30. Leipzig, Germany: Teubner, 1920. Cl. 0198 6 (A). TLG 2042.022.

———. "Homiliae in Leviticum." In *Origenes Werke*. Vol. 6. Edited by W. A. Baehrens. GCS (CB) 29, pp. 280-507. Leipzig, Germany: Teubner, 1920. Cl. 0198 3 (A). TLG 2042.024.

———. "Homiliae in Lucam." In *Opera omnia*. Edited by J.-P. Migne. PG 13, cols. 1799-1902. Paris: Migne, 1862. TLG 2042.016.

———. *Homélies sur les Psaumes 36 à 38*. Critical text established by Emanuela Prinzivalli. Introduced, translated and edited by Henri Crouzel and Luc Bresard. SC 411. Paris: Éditions du Cerf, 1995.

———. "Selecta in Psalmos [dub.]." In *Opera omnia*. Edited by J.-P. Migne. PG 12, cols. 1053-1685. Paris: Migne, 1862. TLG 2042.058.

Pachomius. "Catecheses." In *Oeuvres de s. Pachôme et de ses disciples*. Edited by L.-Th. Lefort. CSCO 159 (Scriptores Coptica 23), pp. 1-26. Louvain: Imprimerie Orientaliste, 1956.

Paulinus of Nola. "Carmina." In *Sancti pontii meropii Paulini Nolani carmina*. Edited by W. Hartel. CSEL 30, pp. 1-3, 7-329. Vienna, Austria: F. Tempsky, 1894. Cl. 0203.

Peter Chrysologus. "Collectio sermonum." In *Opera omnia*. Edited by J.-P. Migne. PL 52, cols. 183-680. Paris: Migne, 1859. Cl. 0227+.

Poemen. "Vitae Patrum *(Sententiae Patrum)*." In *Opera omnia*. Edited by J.-P. Migne. PL 73, cols. 855-1022. Paris: Migne, 1849.

Prudentius. "Liber Apotheosis." In *Opera*. Edited by M. P. Cunningham. CCL 126, pp. 73-115. Turnholt, Belgium: Brepols, 1966. Cl. 1439.

———. "Liber cathemerinon." In *Clementis carmina*. Edited by Johan Bergman. CSEL 61, pp. 5-76. Vienna, Austria: Hoelder-Pichler-Tempsky, 1926. Cl. 1438.

Pseudo-Athanasius. *Athanasiana Syriaca*, pt. 4, *Expositio in Psalmos*. Edited by R. W. Thomson. CSCO 386-87. Louvain: Secrétariat du Corpus, 1977.

Sahdona. "Book of Perfection." In *Martyrius (Sahdona): Oeuvres spirituelles*, part 2. Edited by André de Halleux. CSCO 252 (Scriptores Syri 110). Leuven, Belgium: Secrétariat du Corpus, 1965.

Salvian the Presbyter. "De gubernatione Dei." In *Ouvres*. Vol. 2. Edited by G. Lagarrigue. SC 220, pp. 95-527. Paris: Éditions du Cerf, 1975. Cl. 0485.

Tertullian. "Adversus Judaeos." In *Tertulliani opera*. Edited by E. Kroymann. CCL 2, pp. 1339-96. Turnhout, Belgium: Brepols, 1954. Cl. 0033.

———. "Adversus Marcionem." In *Tertulliani opera*. Edited by E. Kroymann. CCL 1, pp. 437-726. Turnhout, Belgium: Brepols, 1954. Cl. 0014.

———. "De fuga in persecutione." In *Opera*. Edited by J. J. Thierry. CCL 2, pp. 1135-55. Turnhout, Belgium: Brepols, 1954. Cl. 0025.

Theodore of Mopsuestia. *Expositionis in Psalmos*. Edited by Lucas de Coninck and Maria Josepha d' Hont. CCL 88A. Turnhout, Belgium: Brepols, 1977.

Theodore of Tabennesi. "Catecheses." In *Oeuvres de s. Pachôme et de ses disciples*. Edited by L.-Th. Lefort. CSCO 159 (Scriptores Coptica 23), pp. 37-60. Louvain: Imprimerie Orientaliste, 1956.

Theodoret of Cyr. "Interpretatio in Psalmos." In *Opera omnia*. Edited by J.-P. Migne. PG 80, cols. 857-1997. Paris: Migne, 1860. TLG 4089.024.

Theophilus of Alexandria. "In mysticam coenum." In *Opera omnia*. Edited by J.-P. Migne. PG 77, cols. 1016-29. Paris: Migne, 1864.

Valerian of Cimiez. "Homiliae." In *Opera omnia*. Edited by J.-P. Migne. PL 52, cols. 691-758. Paris: Migne, 1845.

Zephyrinus. "Epistola Zephirini papae [dub.]." In *Opera omnia*. Edited by J.-P. Migne. PL 130, cols. 127-30. Paris: Migne, 1853.

Bibliography of Works
in English Translation

Alexander of Alexandria. "Epistles on the Arian Heresy." In *Fathers of the Third Century*, pp. 291-302. Translated by James B. H. Hawkins. ANF 6. Edited by Alexander Roberts and James Donaldson. 10 vols. 1885-1887. Reprint, Peabody, Mass.: Hendrickson, 1994.

Ambrose. *Commentary on Twelve Psalms*. Translated by Íde M. Ní Riain. Dublin: Halcyon Press, 2000.

———. "Concerning Repentence." In *Select Works and Letters*, pp. 329-59. Translated by H. De Romestin. NPNF 10. Series 2. Edited by Philip Schaff and Henry Wace. 14 vols. 1886-1900. Reprint, Peabody, Mass.: Hendrickson, 1994.

———. "Duties of the Clergy." In *Select Works and Letters*, pp. 1-89. Translated by H. De Romestin. NPNF 10. Series 2. Edited by Philip Schaff and Henry Wace. 14 vols. 1886-1900. Reprint, Peabody, Mass.: Hendrickson, 1994.

———. "Isaac, or the Soul." In *Seven Exegetical Works*, pp. 10-65. Translated by Michael P. McHugh. FC 65. Washington, D.C.: The Catholic University of America Press, 1972.

———. "Jacob and the Happy Life." In *Seven Exegetical Works*, pp. 119-84. Translated by Michael P. McHugh. FC 65. Washington, D.C.: The Catholic University of America Press, 1972.

———. "Joseph." In *Seven Exegetical Works*, pp. 189-237. Translated by Michael P. McHugh. FC 65. Washington, D.C.: The Catholic University of America Press, 1972.

———. "Letters." In *Early Latin Theolology*, pp. 182-278. Translated by S. L. Greenslade. LCC 5. Philadelphia: The Westminster Press, 1956.

———. *Letters*. Translated by Mary Melchior Beyenka. FC 26. Washington, D.C.: The Catholic University of America Press, 1954.

———. "On His Brother Satyrus." In *Funeral Orations by Saint Gregory Nanzianzen and Saint Ambrose*, pp. 161-259. Translated by John J. Sullivan and Martin R. P. McGuire. FC 22. Washington, D.C.: The Catholic University of America Press, 1953.

———. "On the Christian Faith." In *Select Works and Letters*, pp. 201-314. Translated by H. De Romestin. NPNF 10. Series 2. Edited by Philip Schaff and Henry Wace. 14 vols. 1886-1900. Reprint, Peabody, Mass.: Hendrickson, 1994.

———. "On the Death of Theodosius." See "On Emperor Theodosius." In *Funeral Orations by Saint Gregory Nanzianzen and Saint Ambrose*, pp. 307-32. Translated by Roy J. Deferrari. FC 22. Washington, D.C.: The Catholic University of America Press, 1953.

———. "On the Patriarchs." In *Seven Exegetical Works*, pp. 243-75. Translated by Michael P. McHugh. FC 65. Washington, D.C.: The Catholic University of America Press, 1972.

———. "On the Sacraments." In *Theological and Dogmatic Works*, pp. 269-328. Translated by Roy J. Deferrari. FC 44. Washington, D.C.: The Catholic University of America Press, 1963.

———. *On Virginity.* Translated by Daniel Callam. Toronto: Peregrina Publishing, 1996.

———. "The Prayer of Job and David." In *Seven Exegetical Works*, pp. 329-420. Translated by Michael P. McHugh. FC 65. Washington, D.C.: The Catholic University of America Press, 1972.

———. "Six Days of Creation." In *Hexamaeron, Paradise, and Cain and Abel*, pp. 3-283. Translated by John J. Savage. FC 42. Washington, D.C.: The Catholic University of America Press, 1961.

Aphrahat. "Demonstrations." In *Gregory the Great, Ephraim Syrus, Aphrahat*, pp. 345-412. Translated by James Barmby. NPNF 13. Series 2. Edited by Philip Schaff and Henry Wace. 14 vols. 1886-1900. Reprint, Peabody, Mass.: Hendrickson, 1994.

Arnobius of Sicca. "Against the Heathen." In *Gregory Thaumaturgus, Dionysius the Great, Julius Africanus, Anatolius and Minor Writers, Methodius, Arnobius*, pp. 413-539. Translated by Hamilton Bryce and Hugh Campbell. ANF 6. Edited by Alexander Roberts and James Donaldson. 10 vols. 1885-1887. Reprint, Peabody, Mass.: Hendrickson, 1994.

Athanasius. "Against the Heathen." In *Selected Works and Letters*, pp. 4-30. Translated by Archibald Robertson. NPNF 4. Series 2. Edited by Philip Schaff and Henry Wace. 14 vols. 1886-1900. Reprint, Peabody, Mass.: Hendrickson, 1994.

———. "Discourses Against the Arians." In *Select Works and Letters*, pp. 306-447 [Fourth Oration Considered Spurious]. Translated by John Henry Newman. Revised by Archibald Robertson. NPNF 4. Series 2. Edited by Philip Schaff and Henry Wace. 14 vols. 1886-1900. Reprint, Peabody, Mass.: Hendrickson, 1994.

———. "Festal Letters." In *Selected Works and Letters*, pp. 506-53. Translated by Payne Smith. Edited by Archibald Robertson. NPNF 4. Series 2. Edited by Philip Schaff and Henry Wace. 14 vols. 1886-1900. Reprint, Peabody, Mass.: Hendrickson, 1994.

———. "Festal Letters." See *The Resurrection Letters.* Translated by Henry Burgess. Revised by Payne Smith. Paraphrased and introduced by Jack N. Sparks. Nashville: Thomas Nelson, 1979.

———. "Letter to the Bishops of Egypt." In *Selected Works and Letters*, pp. 223-35. Translated by M. Atkinson. Revised by Archibald Robertson. NPNF 4. Series 2. Edited by Philip Schaff and Henry Wace. 14 vols. 1886-1900. Reprint, Peabody, Mass.: Hendrickson, 1994.

———. "Life of St. Anthony." In *The Life of Antony and the Letter to Marcellinus*, pp. 29-99. Translated by Robert C. Gregg. Classics of Western Spirituality. New York: Paulist Press, 1980.

———. "On the Incarnation." In *Christology of the Later Fathers*, pp. 55-110. Translated by Archibald Robertson. Edited by Edward Rochie Hardy. LCC 3. Philadelphia: The Westminster Press, 1954.

———. "On the Interpretation of the Psalms." In *Early Christian Spirituality*, pp. 56-77. Translated by Pamela Bright. Sources of Early Christian Thought. Philadelphia: Fortress, 1986.

Augustine. *Against Julian.* Translated by Matthew A. Schumacher. FC 35. Washington, D.C.: The Catholic University of America Press, 1957.

———. "Against Two Letters of the Pelagians." In *Anti-Pelagian Writings*, pp. 377-434. Translated by Robert Ernest Wallis. NPNF 5. Series 1. Edited by Philip Schaff. 14 vols. 1886-1889. Reprint, Peabody, Mass.: Hendrickson, 1994.

———. *City of God: Books 8-16* and *Books 17-22.* Translated by Gerald G. Walsh, Daniel J. Honan and Grace Monahan. FC 14 and FC 24. Washington, D.C.: The Catholic University of

America Press, 1952-1954.

———. "Confessions." In *Confessions and Enchiridion*, pp. 31-333. LCC 7. Translated by Albert C. Outler. Philadelphia: The Westminster Press, 1955.

———. "Enchridion." In *Confessions and Enchiridion*, pp. 337-412. LCC 7. Translated by Albert C. Outler. Philadelphia: The Westminster Press, 1955.

———. *Expositions of the Psalms*. Translated by Maria Boulding. WSA 15-19. Part 3. Edited by John E. Rotelle. New York: New City Press, 2000-2003.

———. "Faith and Works." In *Treatises on Marriage and Other Subjects*, pp. 215-82. Translated by Marie Liguori. FC 27. Washington, D.C.: The Catholic University of America Press, 1955.

———. "Holy Virginity." In *Treatises on Marriage and Other Subjects*, pp. 135-212. Translated by John McQuade. FC 27. Washington, D.C.: The Catholic University of America Press, 1955.

———. "Homilies on 1 John." In *Augustine: Later Works*, pp. 251-348. Translated by John Burnaby. LCC 8. Philadelphia: The Westminster Press, 1955.

———. "Homilies on 1 John." In *Tractates on the Gospel of John 112-124, Tractates on the First Epistle of John*, pp. 119-277. Translated by John W. Rettig. FC 92. Washington, D.C.: The Catholic University of America Press, 1995.

———. *Letters*. Translated by Wilfrid Parsons. FC 18, FC 30 and FC 32. Washington, D.C.: The Catholic University of America Press, 1953-1956.

———. "The Christian Life [dub.]." In *Treatises on Various Subjects*, pp. 3-43. Translated by Mary Sarah Muldowney. FC 16. Washington, D.C.: The Catholic University of America Press, 1952.

———. "On the Perfection of Human Righteousness." In *Anti-Pelagian Writings*, pp. 159-76. Translated by Peter Holmes. NPNF 5. Series 1. Edited by Philip Schaff. 14 vols. 1886-1889. Reprint, Peabody, Mass.: Hendrickson, 1994.

———. "On the Soul and Its Origin." In *Anti-Pelagian Writings*, pp. 315-71. Translated by Peter Holmes. NPNF 5. Series 1. Edited by Philip Schaff. 14 vols. 1886-1889. Reprint, Peabody, Mass.: Hendrickson, 1994.

———. "On the Spirit and the Letter." In *Anti-Pelagian Writings*, pp. 83-114. Translated by Peter Holmes. NPNF 5. Series 1. Edited by Philip Schaff. 14 vols. 1886-1889. Reprint, Peabody, Mass.: Hendrickson, 1994.

———. "On the Spirit and the Letter." In *Augustine: Later Works*, pp. 182-250. Translated by John Burnaby. LCC 8. Philadelphia: The Westminster Press, 1955.

———. "On the Trinity." See *The Trinity*. Translated by Stephen McKenna. FC 45. Washington, D.C.: The Catholic University of America Press, 1963.

———. "On Various Questions to Simplician." See "To Simplician." In *Augustine: Earlier Writings*, pp. 370-406. Translated by J. H. S. Burleigh. LCC 6. Philadelphia: The Westminster Press, 1953.

———. "Sermons." In *Commentary on the Lord's Sermon on the Mount with Seventeen Related Sermons*. Translated by Denis J. Kavenaugh. FC 11. Washington, D.C.: The Catholic University of America Press, 1951.

———. "Sermons." In *Sermons on the Liturgical Seasons*. Translated by Mary Sarah Muldowney. FC 38. Washington, D.C.: The Catholic University of America Press, 1959.

———. *Sermons*. Translated by Edmund Hill. WSA 1-11. Part 3. Edited by John E. Rotelle. New

York: New City Press, 1990-1997.

———. *Tractates on the Gospel of John 11-27.* Translated by John W. Rettig. FC 79. Washington, D.C.: The Catholic University of America Press, 1988.

Babai. "Letter to Cyriacus." In *The Syriac Fathers on Prayer and the Spiritual Life*, pp. 138-63. Translated by Sebastian Brock. CS 101. Kalamazoo, Mich.: Cistercian Publications, 1987.

Basil the Great. "Homilies on the Psalms." In *Exegetic Homilies*, pp. 151-359. Translated by Agnes Clare Way. FC 46. Washington, D.C.: The Catholic University of America Press, 1963.

———. "Homily Against Those Who Are Prone to Anger." See "Homily 10: Against Those Who Are Prone to Anger." In *Ascetical Works*, pp. 223-337. Translated by M. Monica Wagner. FC 9. New York: Fathers of the Church, 1950.

———. "The Long Rules." In *Ascetical Works*, pp. 447-461. Translated by M. Monica Wagner. FC 9. New York: Fathers of the Church, 1950.

Bede. *Homilies on the Gospels.* Translated by Lawrence T. Martin and David Hurst. CS 110 and CS 111. Kalamazoo, Mich.: Cistercian Publications, 1991.

———. *On the Tabernacle.* Translated by Arthur G. Holder. TTH 18. Liverpool: Liverpool University Press, 1994.

Benedict. "Rule of St. Benedict." In *Western Asceticism*, pp. 290-337. Translated by Owen Chadwick. LCC 12. Philadelphia: The Westminster Press, 1958.

Caesarius of Arles. *Sermons.* Translated by Mary Magdeleine Mueller. FC 31, FC 47 and FC 66. Washington, D.C.: The Catholic University of America Press, 1956-1973.

Callistus. "The Epistles [dub.]." In *Fathers of the Third and Fourth Centuries*, pp. 613-18. Translated by S. D. F. Salmond. ANF 8. Edited by Alexander Roberts and James Donaldson. 10 vols. 1885-1887. Reprint, Peabody, Mass.: Hendrickson, 1994.

Cassian, John. "Conferences." In *Western Asceticism*, pp. 190-289. Translated by Owen Chadwick. LCC 12. Philadelphia: Westminster Press, 1958.

———. *Conferences.* Translated by Colm Luibheid. The Classics of Western Spirituality. Mahwah, N.J.: Paulist Press, 1985.

———. "Institutes." In *Sulpitius Severus, Vincent of Lerins, John Cassian*, pp. 201-90. Translated by Edgar C. S. Gibson. NPNF 11. Series 2. Edited by Philip Schaff and Henry Wace. 14 vols. 1886-1900. Reprint, Peabody, Mass.: Hendrickson, 1994.

Cassiodorus. *Explanation of the Psalms.* Translated by P. G. Walsh. ACW 51, ACW 52 and ACW 53. Mahwah, N.J.: Paulist Press, 1990-91.

Clement of Alexandria. *Christ the Educator.* Translated by Simon P. Wood. FC 23. Washington, D.C.: The Catholic University of America Press, 1954.

———. "Exhortation to the Greeks." See "Exhortation to the Heathen." In *Fathers of the Second Century: Hermas, Tatian, Athenagoras, Theophilus, and Clement of Alexandria (Entire)*, pp. 171-206. Translated by William Wilson et al. ANF 2. Edited by Alexander Roberts and James Donaldson. 10 vols. 1885-1887. Reprint, Peabody, Mass.: Hendrickson, 1994.

———. "Stromateis." In *Fathers of the Second Century: Hermas, Tatian, Athenagoras, Theophilus, and Clement of Alexandria (Entire)*, pp. 299-556. Translated by William Wilson et al. ANF 2. Edited by Alexander Roberts and James Donaldson. 10 vols. 1885-1887. Reprint, Peabody, Mass.: Hendrickson, 1994.

Clement of Rome. "1 Clement." See "The Epistle to the Corinthians." In *The Apostolic Fathers, Justin Martyr, Irenaeus*, pp. 1-21. Translated by Alexander Roberts and James Donaldson. ANF 1. Edited by Alexander Roberts and James Donaldson. 10 vols. 1885-1887. Reprint,

Peabody, Mass.: Hendrickson, 1994.

———. "1 Clement." See "The Letter of the Church of Rome to the Church of Corinth, Commonly Called Clement's First Letter." In *Early Christian Fathers*, pp. 43-73. Translated by Cyril C. Richardson. LCC 1. Philadelphia: Westminster Press, 1953.

———. "1 Clement." See "The Letter of St. Clement of Rome to the Corinthians." In *The Apostolic Fathers*, pp. 9-58. Translated by Francis X. Glimm. FC 1. New York: Christian Heritage, 1947.

———. "1 Clement." See "The Epistle of S. Clement to the Corinthians." In *The Apostolic Fathers*, pp. 13-41. Translated by J. B. Lightfoot. 1891. Reprint, Grand Rapids, Mich.: Baker Book House, 1956.

"Constitutions of the Holy Apostles." In *Lactantius, Venantius, Asterius, Victorinus, Dionysius, Apostolic Teaching and Constitutions, 2 Clement, Early Liturgies*, pp. 385-508. Translated by W. Whiston. Revised by Irah Chase. ANF 7. Edited by Alexander Roberts and James Donaldson. 10 vols. 1885-1887. Reprint, Peabody, Mass.: Hendrickson, 1994.

Cyprian. *Letters 1-81*. Translated by Rose Bernard Donna. FC 51. Washington, D.C.: The Catholic University of America Press, 1964.

———. "The Unity of the Church." In *Treatises*, pp. 91-121. Translated by Roy J. Defarrari. FC 36. Washington, D.C.: The Catholic University of America Press, 1958.

———. "Works and Almsgiving." In *Treatises*, pp. 225-53. Translated by Roy J. Defarrari. FC 36. Washington, D.C.: The Catholic University of America Press, 1958.

Cyril of Alexandria. *Letters 1-50*, and *51-110*. Translated by John I. McEnerney. FC 76 and FC 77. Washington, D.C.: The Catholic University of America Press, 1987.

———. *On the Unity of Christ*. Translated by John A. McGuckin. Crestwood, N. Y.: St. Vladimir's Seminary Press, 1995.

Cyril of Jerusalem. "Catechetical Lectures." In *Cyril of Jerusalem and Nemesius of Emesa*, pp. 64-199. Translated by William Telfer. LCC 4. Philadelphia: Westminster Press, 1955.

———. "Catechetical Lectures." In *St. Cyril of Jerusalem and St. Gregory Nazianzen*, pp. 1-157. Translated by Edwin Hamilton Gifford. NPNF 7. Series 2. Edited by Philip Schaff and Henry Wace. 14 vols. 1886-1900. Reprint, Peabody, Mass.: Hendrickson, 1994.

———. "Catechetical Lectures." In *The Works of Saint Cyril of Jerusalem*. Translated by Leo P. McCauley and Anthony A. Stephenson. FC 61 and FC 64. Washington, D.C.: The Catholic University of America Press, 1969-70.

———. "Mystagogical Lectures." In *The Works of Saint Cyril of Jerusalem*, pp. 153-203. Translated by Leo P. McCauley and Anthony A. Stephenson. FC 64. Washington, D.C.: The Catholic University of America Press, 1970.

"Didache." See "Didache or Teaching of the Apostles." In *The Apostolic Fathers*, pp. 171-84. Translated by Francis X. Glimm. FC 1. New York: Christian Heritage, 1947.

Diodore of Tarsus. *Commentary on Psalms 1-51*. Translated by Robert C. Hill. WGRW 9. Atlanta: Society of Biblical Literature, 2005.

Ephrem the Syrian. "Homily on Our Lord." In *Selected Prose Works*, pp. 269-332. Translated by Edward G. Mathews and Joseph P. Amar. FC 91. Washington, D.C.: The Catholic University of America Press, 1994.

———. "Hymns on the Nativity." See "Nineteen Hymns on the Nativity of Christ in the Flesh." In *Gregory the Great, Ephraim Syrus, Aphrahat*, pp. 223-262. Translated by J. B. Morris and A. Edward Johnston. NPNF 13. Series 2. Edited by Philip Schaff and Henry Wace. 14 vols.

1886-1900. Reprint, Peabody, Mass.: Hendrickson, 1994.

————. *Hymns on Paradise*. Translated by Sebastian Brock. Crestwood, N.Y.: St. Vladimir's Seminary Press, 1998.

Eusebius of Caesarea. *Ecclesiastical History*. Translated by Roy J. Defarrari. FC 19. Washington, D.C.: The Catholic University of America Press, 1953.

————. "Ecclesiastical History." See *Eusebius, the Church History: A New Translation with Commentary*. Translated by Paul L. Maier. Grand Rapids, Mich.: Kregel Publications, 1999.

————. *The Proof of the Gospel*. Translated by W. J. Ferrar. London: SPCK, 1920. Reprint, Grand Rapids: Baker, 1981.

Evagrius of Pontus. "Chapters on Prayer." In *Evagrius of Pontus: The Greek Ascetic Corpus*, pp. 191-209. Translated by Robert E. Sinkewicz. Oxford Early Christian Studies. Oxford: Oxford University Press, 2003.

————. "Chapters on Prayer." In *Evagrius Ponticus: The Praktikos, Chapters on Prayer*, pp. 52-80. Translated by John Eudes Bamberger. CS 4. Spencer, Mass.: Cistercian Publications, 1970.

————. "On the Eight Thoughts." In *Evagrius of Pontus: The Greek Ascetic Corpus*, pp. 73-90. Translated by Robert E. Sinkewicz. Oxford Early Christian Studies. Oxford: Oxford University Press, 2003.

————. "On Thoughts." In *Evagrius of Pontus: The Greek Ascetic Corpus*, pp. 153-82. Translated by Robert E. Sinkewicz. Oxford Early Christian Studies. Oxford: Oxford University Press, 2003.

————. "Praktikos." In *Evagrius of Pontus: The Greek Ascetic Corpus*, pp. 95-114. Translated by Robert E. Sinkewicz. Oxford Early Christian Studies. Oxford: Oxford University Press, 2003.

————. "Praktikos." In *Evagrius Ponticus: The Praktikos, Chapters on Prayer*, pp. 12-42. Translated by John Eudes Bamberger. CS 4. Spencer, Mass.: Cistercian Publications, 1970.

Fulgentius of Ruspe. "Letter to Monimus." In *Selected Works*, pp. 185-275. Translated by Robert B. Eno. FC 95. Washington, D.C.: The Catholic University of America Press, 1997.

————. "Letters." In *Selected Works*, pp. 277-565. Translated by Robert B. Eno. FC 95. Washington, D.C.: The Catholic University of America Press, 1997.

————. "On the Forgiveness of Sins." In *Selected Works*, pp. 109-83. Translated by Robert B. Eno. FC 95. Washington, D.C.: The Catholic University of America Press, 1997.

————. "Book to Victor Against the Sermon of Fastidiosus the Arian." In *Selected Works*, pp. 392-423. Translated by Robert B. Eno. FC 95. Washington, D.C.: The Catholic University of America Press, 1997.

Gregory of Nazianzus. "In Defense of His Flight to Pontus, Oration 2." In *Cyril of Jerusalem and Gregory Nazianzen*, pp. 204-27. Translated by Charles Gordon Browne and James Edward Swallow. NPNF 7. Series 2. Edited by Philip Schaff and Henry Wace. 14 vols. 1886-1900. Reprint, Peabody, Mass.: Hendrickson, 1994.

————. "On His Brother St. Caesarius, Oration 7." In *Funeral Orations*, pp. 5-25. Translated by Leo P. McCauley. FC 22. Washington, D.C.: The Catholic University of America Press, 1953.

————. "On His Father's Silence, Oration 16." See "On His Father's Silence, Because of the Plague of Hail." In *Cyril of Jerusalem, Gregory Nazianzen*, pp. 247-54. Translated by Charles Gordon Browne and James Edward Swallow. NPNF 7. Series 2. Edited by Philip Schaff and Henry Wace. 14 vols. 1886-1900. Reprint, Peabody, Mass.: Hendrickson, 1994.

————. "On Holy Baptism, Oration 40." See "The Oration on Holy Baptism." In *Cyril of Jerusalem,*

Gregory Nazianzen, pp. 360-77. Translated by Charles Gordon Browne and James Edward Swallow. NPNF 7. Series 2. Edited by Philip Schaff and Henry Wace. 14 vols. 1886-1900. Reprint, Peabody, Mass.: Hendrickson, 1994.

———. "On Holy Easter, Oration 45." See "The Second Oration on Easter." In *Cyril of Jerusalem, Gregory Nazianzen*, pp. 422-34. Translated by Charles Gordon Browne and James Edward Swallow. NPNF 7. Series 2. Edited by Philip Schaff and Henry Wace. 14 vols. 1886-1900. Reprint, Peabody, Mass.: Hendrickson, 1994.

———. "On the Holy Spirit, Theological Oration 5[31]." See "The Fifth Theological Oration—On the Spirit." In *Christology of the Later Fathers*, pp. 194-214. Translated by Edward R. Hardy. LCC 3. Philadelphia: Westminster Press, 1954.

———. "On the Son, Theological Oration 4[30]." See "The Fourth Theological Oration, Which is the Second Concerning the Son." In *Cyril of Jerusalem, Gregory Nazianzen*, pp. 309-18. Translated by Charles Gordon Browne and James Edward Swallow. NPNF 7. Series 2. Edited by Philip Schaff and Henry Wace. 14 vols. 1886-1900. Reprint, Peabody, Mass.: Hendrickson, 1994.

———. "On the Son, Theological Oration 3[29]." See "The Third Theological Oration—On the Son." In *Christology of the Later Fathers*, pp. 160-76. Translated by Edward R. Hardy. LCC 3. Philadelphia: Westminster Press, 1954.

———. "On the Words of the Gospel, 'When Jesus Had Finished These Sayings,' Oration 37." In *Cyril of Jerusalem, Gregory Nazianzen*, pp. 338-44. Translated by Charles Gordon Browne and James Edward Swallow. NPNF 7. Series 2. Edited by Philip Schaff and Henry Wace. 14 vols. 1886-1900. Reprint, Peabody, Mass.: Hendrickson, 1994.

———. "On Theology, Theological Oration 2[28]." See "The Second Theological Oration." In *Cyril of Jerusalem, Gregory Nazianzen*, pp. 288-301. Translated by Charles Gordon Browne and James Edward Swallow. NPNF 7. Series 2. Edited by Philip Schaff and Henry Wace. 14 vols. 1886-1900. Reprint, Peabody, Mass.: Hendrickson, 1994.

———. "On Theology, Theological Oration 2[28]." See "The Second Theological Oration—On God." In *Christology of the Later Fathers*, pp. 136-59. Translated by Edward R. Hardy. LCC 3. Philadelphia: Westminster Press, 1954.

Gregory of Nyssa. "Address on Religious Instruction." In *Christology of the Later Fathers*, pp. 268-325. Translated by Edward R. Hardy. LCC 3. Philadelphia: The Westminster Press, 1954.

———. "Against Eunomius." In *Select Writings and Letters*, pp. 33-248. Translated by H. C. Ogle. Revised by Henry Austine Wilson. NPNF 5. Series 2. Edited by Philip Schaff and Henry Wace. 14 vols. 1886-1900. Reprint, Peabody, Mass.: Hendrickson, 1994.

———. "Answer to Eunomius' Second Book." In *Select Writings and Letters*, pp. 250-314. Translated by M. Day. NPNF 5. Series 2. Edited by Philip Schaff and Henry Wace. 14 vols. 1886-1900. Reprint, Peabody, Mass.: Hendrickson, 1994.

———. "On the Christian Mode of Life." In *Ascetical Works*, pp. 127-58. Translated by Virginia Woods Callahan. FC 58. Washington, D.C.: The Catholic University of America Press, 1967.

———. *On the Inscriptions of the Psalms*. Translated by Ronald E. Heine. Oxford Early Christian Studies. Oxford: Clarendon Press, 1995.

———. "On Virginity." In *Select Writings and Letters*, pp. 343-371. Translated by William Moore and Henry Austine Wilson. NPNF 5. Series 2. Edited by Philip Schaff and Henry Wace.

14 vols. 1886-1900. Reprint, Peabody, Mass.: Hendrickson, 1994.

Gregory Thaumaturgus. "Homilies [dub.]." See "Four Homilies." In *Gregory Thaumaturgus, Dionysius the Great, Julius Africanus, Anatolius and Minor Writers, Methodius, Arnobius*, pp. 58-71. Translated by S. D. F. Salmond. ANF 6. Edited by Alexander Roberts and James Donaldson. 10 vols. 1885-1887. Reprint, Peabody, Mass.: Hendrickson, 1994.

Gregory the Great. "Letters." See "Selected Epistles of St. Gregory the Great." In *Gregory the Great, Ephraim Syrus, and Aphrahat*, pp. 1-111. Translated by James Barmby. NPNF 13. Series 2. Edited by Philip Schaff and Henry Wace. 14 vols. 1886-1900. Reprint, Peabody, Mass.: Hendrickson, 1994.

Hilary of Poitiers. "Homilies on the Psalms." In *St. Hilary of Poitiers, John of Damascus*, pp. 236-248. Translated by E. W. Watson et al. NPNF 9. Series 2. Edited by Philip Schaff and Henry Wace. 14 vols. 1886-1900. Reprint, Peabody, Mass.: Hendrickson, 1994.

———. "On the Trinity." See *The Trinity*. Translated by Stephen McKenna. FC 25. Washington, D.C.: The Catholic University of America Press, 1954.

Hippolytus. "Fragments on the Psalms." See "On the Psalms." In *Hippolytus, Cyprian, Caius, Novatian, Appendix*, pp. 199-203. Translated by S. D. F. Salmond. ANF 5. Edited by Alexander Roberts and James Donaldson. 10 vols. 1885-1887. Reprint, Peabody, Mass.: Hendrickson, 1994.

Irenaeus. "Against Heresies." In *The Apostolic Fathers with Justin Martyr and Irenaeus*, pp. 315-567. Translated by Alexander Roberts and W. H. Rambaut. ANF 1. Edited by Alexander Roberts and James Donaldson. 10 vols. 1885-1887. Reprint, Peabody, Mass.: Hendrickson, 1994.

Isaac of Nineveh. "Ascetical Homilies." In *The Ascetical Homilies of Saint Isaac the Syrian*, pp. 3-385. Translated by the Holy Transfiguration Monastery. Brookline, Mass.: Holy Transfiguration Monastery, 1984.

Jerome. "Against the Pelagians." In *Dogmatic and Polemical Works*, pp. 223-378. Translated by John N. Hritzu. FC 53. Washington, D.C.: The Catholic University of America Press, 1965.

———. "Homilies on the Psalms." In *The Homilies of St. Jerome, Vol. 1; Vol. 2*, pp. 3-117. Translated by Marie Liguori Ewald. FC 48 and FC 57. Washington, D.C.: The Catholic University of America Press, 1964-1966.

———. "Homily 87, On John 1:1-14." In *The Homilies of St. Jerome*, pp. 212-20. Translated by Marie Liguori Ewald. FC 57. Washington, D.C.: The Catholic University of America Press, 1966.

———. "Homily 94, On Easter Sunday." In *The Homilies of St. Jerome*, pp. 251-54. Translated by Marie Liguori Ewald. FC 57. Washington, D.C.: The Catholic University of America Press, 1966.

———. "Homily on the Epiphany and Psalm 28." See "Homily 89, For Epiphany." In *The Homilies of St. Jerome*, pp. 229-32. Translated by Marie Liguori Ewald. FC 57. Washington, D.C.: The Catholic University of America Press, 1966.

———. "Letters." In *Letters and Select Works*, pp. 1-295. Translated by W. H. Fremantle. NPNF 6. Series 2. Edited by Philip Schaff and Henry Wace. 14 vols. 1886-1900. Reprint, Peabody, Mass.: Hendrickson, 1994.

John Chrysostom. "Against the Anomoeans." In *On the Incomprehensible Nature of God*. Translated by Paul W. Harkins. FC 72. Washington, D.C.: The Catholic University of America Press, 1982.

———. *Commentary on the Psalms.* Vol. 1. Translated by Robert Charles Hill. Brookline, Mass: Holy Cross Orthodox Press, 1998.

———. *Discourses Against Judaizing Christians.* Translated by Paul W. Harkins. FC 68. Washington, D.C.: The Catholic University of America Press, 1977.

———. "Homilies Concerning the Statues." In *On the Priesthood, Select Homilies and Letters, and Homilies on the Statues,* pp. 331-489. Translated by W. R. W. Stephens. NPNF 9. Series 1. Edited by Philip Schaff and Henry Wace. 14 vols. 1886-1900. Reprint, Peabody, Mass.: Hendrickson, 1994.

———. "Homilies on 1 Timothy." In *Homilies on Galatians, Ephesians, Philippians, Colossians, Thessalonians, Timothy, Titus, and Philemon,* pp. 407-73. Translated by Philip Schaff. NPNF 13. Series 1. Edited by Philip Schaff and Henry Wace. 14 vols. 1886-1900. Reprint, Peabody, Mass.: Hendrickson, 1994.

———. *Homilies on Genesis 1-17, and 18-45.* Translated by Robert C. Hill. FC 74 and FC 82. Washington, D.C.: The Catholic University of America Press, 1985-1990.

———. "Homilies on the Gospel of John." See *Commentary on Saint John the Apostle and Evangelist.* Translated by Thomas Aquinas Goggin. FC 33 and FC 41. Washington, D.C.: The Catholic University of America Press, 1957-1959.

———. "Homilies on Repentance and Almsgiving." See *On Repentance and Almsgiving.* Translated by Gus George Christo. FC 96. Washington, D.C.: The Catholic University of America Press, 1998.

———. "Homilies on 2 Corinthians." In *Homilies on the Epistles of Paul to the Corinthians,* pp. 271-420. Translated by Talbot W. Chambers. NPNF 12. Series 1. Edited by Philip Schaff and Henry Wace. 14 vols. 1886-1900. Reprint, Peabody, Mass.: Hendrickson, 1994.

———. "On the Epistle to the Hebrews." In *Homilies on the Gospel of Saint John and the Epistle to the Hebrews,* pp. 363-522. Translated by Frederic Gardiner. NPNF 14. Series 1. Edited by Philip Schaff and Henry Wace. 14 vols. 1886-1900. Reprint, Peabody, Mass.: Hendrickson, 1994.

———. "On Providence." In *Divine Providence and Human Suffering,* pp. 49-53, 92-93, 130-31, 172-74. Translated by James Walsh and P. G. Walsh. MFC 17. Wilmington, Del.: Michael Glazier, 1985.

John of Damascus. *Barlaam and Joseph.* Translated by G. R. Woodward and H. Mattingly. LCL 34. Reprint, Cambridge, Mass.: Harvard University Press, 1937.

———. "Orthodox Faith." In *Writings,* pp. 165-406. Translated by Frederic H. Chase. FC 37. Washington, D.C.: The Catholic University of America Press, 1958.

Justin Martyr. "Dialogue with Trypho." In *Writings of Saint Justin Martyr,* pp. 139-366. Translated by Thomas B. Falls. FC 6. New York: Christian Heritage, 1948.

Lactantius. "Treatise on the Anger of God." In *Lactantus, Venantius, Asterius, Victorinus, Dionysius, Apostolic Teaching and Constitutions, Homily, and Liturgies,* pp. 259-80. Translated by William Fletcher. ANF 7. Edited by Alexander Roberts and James Donaldson. 10 vols. 1885-1887. Reprint, Peabody, Mass.: Hendrickson, 1994.

Leander of Seville. "The Training of Nuns." In *Iberian Fathers (Volume 1): Martin of Braga, Paschasius of Dumium, Leander of Seville,* pp. 183-228. Translated by Claude W. Barlow. FC 62. Washington, D.C.: The Catholic University of America Press, 1969.

Leo the Great. *Sermons.* Translated by Jane Patricia Freeland and Agnes Josephine Conway. FC 93. Washington, D.C.: The Catholic University of America Press, 1996.

Martin of Braga. "Driving Away Vanity." In *Iberian Fathers (Volume 1): Martin of Braga, Paschasius of Dumium, Leander of Seville*, pp. 35-41. Translated by Claude W. Barlow. FC 62. Washington, D.C.: The Catholic University of America Press, 1969.

———. "Exhortation to Humility." In *Iberian Fathers (Volume 1): Martin of Braga, Paschasius of Dumium, Leander of Seville*, pp. 51-57. Translated by Claude W. Barlow. FC 62. Washington, D.C.: The Catholic University of America Press, 1969.

Maximus of Turin. "Sermons." See *The Sermons of St. Maximus of Turin*. Translated by Boniface Ramsey. ACW 50. New York: Newman Press, 1989.

Methodius of Olympus. "Banquet of the Ten Virgins." In *Gregory Thaumaturgus, Dionysius the Great, Julius Africanus, Anatolius and Minor Writers, Methodius, Arnobius*, pp. 309-55. Translated by William R. Clark. ANF 6. Edited by Alexander Roberts and James Donaldson. 10 vols. 1885-1887. Reprint, Peabody, Mass.: Hendrickson, 1994.

Niceta of Remesiana. "Liturgical Singing." In *Niceta of Remesiana, Sulpicius Severus, Vincent of Lerins, and Prosper of Aquitaine*, pp. 65-76. Translated by Gerald G. Walsh. FC 7. Washington, D.C.: The Catholic University of America Press, 1949.

———. "The Power of the Holy Spirit." In *Niceta of Remesiana, Sulpicius Severus, Vincent of Lerins, and Prosper of Aquitaine*, pp. 23-41. Translated by Gerald G. Walsh. FC 7. Washington, D.C.: The Catholic University of America Press, 1949.

———. "Vigils of the Saints." In *Niceta of Remesiana, Sulpicius Severus, Vincent of Lerins, and Prosper of Aquitaine*, pp. 55-64. Translated by Gerald G. Walsh. FC 7. Washington, D.C.: The Catholic University of America Press, 1949.

Novation. "The Trinity." In *The Trinity, The Spectacles, Jewish Foods, In Praise of Purity, and Letters*, pp. 11-111. Translated by Russell J. DeSimone. FC 67. Washington, D.C.: The Catholic University of America Press, 1974.

Origen. "Against Celsus." In *Tertullian (IV); Minucius Felix; Commodian; Origen (I and III)*, pp. 395-669. Translated by Frederick Crombie. ANF 4. Edited by Alexander Roberts and James Donaldson. 10 vols. 1885-1887. Reprint, Peabody, Mass.: Hendrickson, 1994.

———. "Against Celsus." In *The Writings of Origen: Volume 2, Origen Contra Celsum Books 2-8*. Translated by Frederick Crombie. ANCL 23. Edinburgh: T & T Clark, 1894.

———. "Against Celsus." See *Contra Celsum*. Translated by Henry Chadwick. Cambridge: Cambridge University Press, 1953.

———. "Exhortation to Martyrdom." In *An Exhortation to Martyrdom, Prayer, and Selected Works*, pp. 41-79. Translated by Rowan A. Greer. The Classics of Western Spirituality. New York: Paulist Press, 1979.

———. "Commentary on the Gospel of Matthew." In *Gospel of Peter, Diatessaron, Testament of Abraham, Epistles of Clement, Origen, Miscellaneous Works*, pp. 413-512. Translated by John Patrick. ANF 9. Edited by Allan Menzies. 10 vols. 1885-1887. Reprint, Peabody, Mass.: Hendrickson, 1994.

———. "Commentary on the Gospel of John." See *Commentary on the Gospel According to John, Books 1-10 and 13-32*. Translated by Ronald E. Heine. FC 80 and FC 89. Washington, D.C.: The Catholic University of America Press, 1989-1993.

———. "Homilies on Exodus." In *Homilies on Genesis and Exodus*, pp. 227-387. Translated by Ronald E. Heine. FC 71. Washington, D.C.: The Catholic University of America Press, 1982.

———. "Homilies on Genesis." In *Homilies on Genesis and Exodus*, pp. 47-224. Translated by Ronald E. Heine. FC 71. Washington, D.C.: The Catholic University of America Press, 1982.

———. *Homilies on Leviticus*. Translated by Gary Wayne Barkley. FC 83. Washington, D.C.: The Catholic University of America Press, 1990.

———. "Homilies on the Gospel of Luke." See *Homilies on Luke*. Translated by Joseph T. Lienhard. FC 94. Washington, D.C.: The Catholic University of America Press, 1996.

———. *On First Principles*. Translated by G. W. Butterworth. Gloucester, Mass.: Peter Smith, 1973.

———. "On Prayer." In *An Exhortation to Martyrdom, Prayer and Selected Works*, pp. 81-170. Translated by Ronald A. Greer. The Classics of Western Spirituality. New York: Paulist Press, 1979.

Pachomius. "Instructions." In *Pachomian Koinonia: Instructions, Letters, and Other Writings of Saint Pachomius and his Disciples*, pp. 13-49. Translated by Armand Veilleux. CS 47. Kalamazoo, Mich.: Cistercian Publications, 1982.

Paulinus of Nola. *Poems*. Translated by P. G. Walsh. ACW 40. New York: Newman Press, 1975.

Peter Chrysologus. *Saint Peter Chrysologus: Selected Sermons and Saint Valerian: Homilies*, pp. 1-282. Translated by George E. Ganss. FC 17. New York: Fathers of the Church, 1953.

Poemen. "Sayings of the Fathers." In *Western Asceticism*, pp. 33-189. Translated by Owen Chadwick. LCC 12. Philadelphia: The Westminster Press, 1958.

Prudentius. "The Divinity of Christ." In *The Poems of Prudentius*, pp. 3-40. Translated by Sister M. Clement Eagan. FC 52. Washington, D.C.: The Catholic University of America Press, 1965.

———. "Hymns for Every Day." In *The Poems of Prudentius*, pp. 3-92. Translated by M. Clement Eagan. FC 43. Washington, D.C.: The Catholic University of America Press, 1962.

Sahdona. "Book of Perfection." In *The Syriac Fathers on Prayer and the Spiritual Life*, pp. 202-37. Translated by Sebastian Brock. CS 101. Kalamazoo, Mich.: Cistercian Publications, 1987.

Salvian the Presbyter. "The Governance of God." In *The Writings of Salvian, the Presbyter*, pp. 27-232. Translated by Jeremiah F. O'Sullivan. FC 3. Reprint, Washington, D.C.: The Catholic University of America Press, 1962.

Tertullian. "Against Marcion." In *Latin Christianity: Its Founder, Tertullian*, pp. 271-475. Translated by Peter Holmes. ANF 3. Edited by Alexander Roberts and James Donaldson. 10 vols. 1885-1887. Reprint, Peabody, Mass.: Hendrickson, 1994.

———. "An Answer to the Jews." In *Latin Christianity: Its Founder, Tertullian*, pp. 151-73. Translated by S. Thelwall. ANF 3. Edited by Alexander Roberts and James Donaldson. 10 vols. 1885-1887. Reprint, Peabody, Mass.: Hendrickson, 1994.

———. "On Flight in Time of Persecution." In *Disciplinary, Moral, and Ascetical Works*, pp. 271-307. Translated by Edwin A. Quain. FC 40. Washington, D.C.: The Catholic University of America Press, 1959.

Theodore of Tabennesi. "Instructions." In *Pachomian Koinonia: Instructions, Letters, and Other Writings of Saint Pachomius and His Disciples*, pp. 91-122. Translated by Armand Veilleux. CS 47. Kalamazoo, Mich.: Cistercian Publications, 1982.

Theodore of Mopsuestia. *Commentary on the Psalms 1-81*. Translated by Robert C. Hill. WGRW 5. Atlanta: Society of Biblical Literature, 2006.

Theodoret of Cyr. *Commentary on the Psalms: Psalms 1-72*. Translated by Robert C. Hill. FC 101. Washington, D.C.: The Catholic University of America Press, 2000.

———. "Ecclesiastical History." In *Theodoret, Jerome, Gennadius, Rufinus: Historical Writings, Etc.*, pp. 33-159. Translated by Blomfield Jackson. NPNF 3. Series 2. Edited by Philip Schaff and Henry Wace. 14 vols. 1886-1900. Reprint, Peabody, Mass.: Hendrickson, 1994.

Theophilus of Alexandria. "Sermon on Mystical Supper." In *The Eucharist*, pp. 148-57. Translated by Daniel J. Sheerin. MFC 7. Wilmington, Del.: Michael Glazier, 1986.

Valerian of Cimiez. "Homilies." In *Saint Peter Chrysologus: Selected Sermons and Saint Valerian: Homilies*, pp. 299-435. Translated by George E. Ganss. FC 17. New York: Fathers of the Church, 1953.

Zephyrinus. "The Epistles of Zephyrinus [dub.]." In *Fathers of the Third and Fourth Centuries*, pp. 609-12. Translated by S. D. F. Salmond. ANF 8. Edited by Alexander Roberts and James Donaldson. 10 vols. 1885-1887. Reprint, Peabody, Mass.: Hendrickson, 1994.

See the volume *Commentary Index and Resources* for a collection of supplemental ACCS material, including a comprehensive Scripture index and authors/writings index.

Subject Index

abandonment
    of Christ, 232
    form of discipline, 105
    of God, our, 392
    no divine, 296
Absalom, 235, 289, 301
absolution, 240
abundance, divine, 369
acrostic psalm, 193
Adam, 4, 6, 379
adultery, spiritual, 390
advent
    of Christ, 20, 109, 111,
        144, 160, 281, 384, 386
    of God, 386
    of the Holy Spirit, 158
affliction, 260, 261, 307, 310,
    355
Ahithophel, 65
altar, mind as, 202
Ambrose of Milan, xxiv-xxv
ancestors, no help from, 377
angels
    acknowledge lordship, 72
    creator of, 71
    help of, 273
    imitations of, 389
    as messengers, 188
    revelation to, 188
anger
    beware of, 231, 232
    controlled, 49
    different kinds of, 32
    divine, 63
    do not sin in, 31
    poison of, 231
    problems with legitimate,
        54
    putting an end to, 33
    refrain from, 291
    and the tongue, 264
anointing
    of Christ, 182, 348, 349,
        350
    divine, 349

second, 205
    of the Spirit, 349, 350
anthropomorphism, 49, 104,
    111, 249, 343, 346
antichrist, 85, 90
anxiety, 105, 231, 311
apostles, 63, 354, 363
ark, 207
Arnobius the Younger, xxvi
ascension
    our, 189
    Christ's, 185, 189, 361, 364
Asterius the Homilist, xxiii
Athanasius, xx-xxi
atheism, 109, 147
athletes, 267
atonement, 377
audacity, 172
Augustine of Hippo, xxv-xxvi
authority, 72
Babylonian captivity, 314
baptism
    and anointing, 213, 349
    of Jesus, 216
    refreshing waters of, 179
    Satan's or Christ's, 276
    spiritual waters of, 216
Basil of Caesarea, xxi, xxv
battle, spiritual, 143
beasts, wild, 90
beauty
    and the blessed nature,
        224
    of God's house, 203
    of Jacob, 363-64
    divinely created, 352
    God's, 386
    soul, 352
    true, 352
beds symbolize earthliness,
    322
beneficiaries, 121
betrayal, 324, 325
birth of Jesus, 15, 321
blameless, 140

blasphemy, 44, 90, 97, 275, 392
blessedness, xxi, 1, 2-3, 4, 6, 45,
    224, 322
blessing
    in Christ, 101
    divine, 45, 46, 88, 121
    of forgiveness, 283
    the Lord, 259
    and mercy, 186-87
    sated with, 182
    true, 29
blessings
    of baptism, 213
    everlasting, 183
    future, 269
    of God, 121, 234
    in the church, 183
blindness, spiritual, 85, 106,
    223, 304
blood
    of the Lord, 181-82
    precious, 378
    ransom, 203
boasting, 61, 107, 157, 160
    in God, 45
body
    as a bed, 322
    of Christ as a temple,
        369
    Christ's, 174, 369
    Christ's resurrected, 123,
        124
    future glory of, 381
    as God's house, 220
    and music, 222
bones
    dead, 379
    rational, 50
    spiritual, 274
bread
    of God, 359
    the living, 181
    of the righteous, 296
brothers of Christ, 174
    call,

of Gentiles, 67, 361
    universal, 374, 387
Calvary, 174
Canaanites, 338
Cassiodorus, xxvi
catenae on the Psalms, xvii-
    xviii
cattle, mindless, 380
chance, 247-48
choices, 194
Christ
    alone, 76, 176
    ascending and descending
        of, 138, 251
    as bridegroom, 122, 152
    cry of dereliction, 169
    firstborn of all creation,
        138
    the foundation, 186
    gaining of, 111
    garment of, 174
    our head, 302, 325
    homoousios, 284
    human and divine, 152,
        162, 210, 285, 325, 326,
        349, 377
    human soul of, 125
    human suffering of, 124,
        169
    humiliation, 123, 230, 231,
        345, 364
    humiliation and exaltation
        of, 120
    in the Psalms, 120, 210,
        320
    the mediator, 210
    mysteries of, 57
    need for, 111
    only begotten, 14, 15
    our representative, 169
    return of, 131, 191
    the righteous, 268
    the way, 5, 19, 194, 201,
        241, 334
    the Word, 124, 341, 351

Christian walk, 45, 115, 179
Chrysostom, John, xxii-xxiii
church
    attendance, 207
    blessings in the, 183
    established after ascension, 9
    fruitful, 218
    of God, 318
    inheritance of the, 39
    perfection of, 215
    replaces idols, 218
    salvation of, 317
    speaks in apostles and prophets, 325
    spiritual forming of, 268
    strengthened, 370
    in union with God, 352
    unity of, 368
    as winepress, 67
circumcision, spiritual, 48
city on a hill, 367
cleansing, , 41, 51
comfort, divine, 327
commandments, 114
commentaries on Psalms, xvii-xxvii
compassion, 292
conceit, self, 380-81
condemnation, self, 279
condescension, divine, 267
confession, 75, 238-39, 240, 243, 246, 323
confidence
    of Christ, 206
    in God's mercy, 200
    self, 376
conscience, 37, 358
consolation, 180, 293, 330
contemplation of God, 131, 187, 340
contrition, 16-17
conversion, 50, 60, 78, 159, 164-65
conviction, 293
correction, 16, 208. See discipline
corruption
    moral, 90,
    of body, 124
counsel, 32, 33, 252
courage, 28, 209
court, the divine, 305

covenant, new, 388
creation, 71, 147, 219, 249, 254, 284, 329, 343, 344, 353
creator, 151, 185
cross,
    horn of, 136
    Lord of glory's, 273
    prayer for forgiveness from the, 325-26
    as weapon, 144, 346
    words from, 230
crucifixion, 170, 173
crying out, 40-41
cup
    of the Lord, 180
    of love, 182
    of wrath, 97-98
Cyril of Alexandria, xxiv
darkness, 41, 167, 358, 384
David
    and Absalom, 31, 235, 289, 301
    and Bathsheba, 301
    blessed life of, 135
    deliverance of, 230
    descendants of, 144
    enemies of, 296
    example of, 211, 213
    flight of, 19
    and Goliath, 31, 136, 255
    honored by Gentiles, 143
    lamp of, 141
    life of, 200, 271
    a mere shepherd, 260
    as object of reproach, 232
    patience of, 304
    praise of, 144
    prophecy of, 228
    and Saul, 289
    sin of, 235
    slander of, 274
    testing of, 128, 272, 315
    as type, 314
day
    evil, 321-22, 376
    judgment, 48
    last, 322
    the Lord's, 185
    of Noah, 240
    resurrection, 48
    of salvation, 170
death, 37, 44, 51, 82, 124, 179, 190, 208, 223, 372, 378, 383

certainty of, 311
    Christ's, 75
    destruction of, 76, 212
    fate worse than, 381
    hope beyond, 269
    no fear of, 310
    saved from, 381
    shadows of, 126
    two kinds of, 381
    universal, 378
deceit, 28, 28, 29, 42, 100, 186
deception
    dangerous, 101
    the enemy's, 230
    of praise, 88
    self, 88, 269, 279, 294-95, 390
defilement, 89
deliverance, 99, 100, 230, 260
demonic delusion, 139
demons, 206, 255, 272
dependence on God, 178
depression, 304
depths of God, 251
desire
    for God, 328
    for God's Word, 155
    transformed, 303
desires
    different, 334
    examined, 61
    sinful, 273
destruction
    of old Adam, 16
    ultimate, 292
devil, the, 5, 58, 64, 89, 106, 202, 213, 272
devotion, xxvi, 17
diapsalma, xxii, 20-21, 84. See Selah
Didymus the Blind, xxi-xxii, xxv
Diodore of Tarsus, xxii
discernment, 173, 283
discipline, divine, 49, 77, 140, 142, 180, 195, 196, 208, 212, 235, 242-43, 263, 266, 273, 276, 301, 305, 311, 390
discouragement, 332, 335
dishonesty, 263, 378
dissipation, 242
doctrine, xxi, xxiv, 353
dominion, heavenly, 71, 72

drunkenness
    a blessed, 182
    a praiseworthy, 282
duplicity, 212
earth and heaven, 70
eighth day, 99, 103
election, 256
encouragement, 335
endurance, 307, 310
"the end, Christ is," 26, 109, 320
enemies
    of Christ, 19-20, 169, 172
    of David, 296
    conversion of, 164
    death as last, 190
    defeated, 60
    everywhere, 197
    of flesh, 206
    laugh of, 193
    persistence of, 333
    plans of, 38
    pray for, 55, 233
    pray against, 233
    pursuit of, 143
    rejoicing of, 305
    spiritual, 58, 68, 78, 83, 106
    spiritual and human, 54
    walls of, 141
    without cause, 19
    of Zion, 370
entertainment, danger of, 17
eternal and temporal, 77
eternity, 186
    rewards of, 266-67
ethics, 116
Eucharist, 181, 262
Eusebius of Caesarea, xix, xx
Evagrius of Pontus, xxii
evangelists, sending of, 139
evil, 42, 65,
    persistence in, 5
    triumph of, 88
exaltation, 165, 361, 362
    human, 70-71, 189-90
    in Christ, 222
    of Christ, 120
example, 171
    of David, 211, 213
    of faith, 193-94
    of prayer, 276
exchange, heavenly, 229

exodus, the, 336
experience
    and knowledge, 110
    personal, 262, 289
    as our teacher, 206
eyes, 302
    God's, 294
    of the heart, 105
    of the mind, 106
    protection of, 130
face
    of God, 104, 233
    of mercy, 207
failure
    of free will, 239
    of materialism, 293
    of sinners, 293
    spiritual, 268
    of wealth, 298
    of wicked, 295
    of the world, 298
faith, xxvi, 23, 24, 27, 60, 95,
    163, 179-80, 194, 200, 338
    blessed through, 322
    in Christ, 314
    as compass, 136
    as confidence, 22
    examples of, 193-94
    experienced, 22
    firm, 370
    first article of, 147
    and humility, 233
    Israel's, 318
    and knowledge, 262
    necessity of, 234, 383
    people of, 144
    prayer of, 137
    radiant, 260
    revealed, 290
    saved by, 198, 201, 315
    sight of, 340
    skeleton of, 268
    stumbling in, 148
    unconquered, 339
    working, 392
    and works, 8, 114
Fall, the, 1, 379
Father
    and Son, 123
God the, 101
faultfinding, 129
favor, divine, 315
fear, 112, 179-80, 196, 197, 372

and discipline, 263
    enduring, 155
    freedom from, 231
    of God, 140, 206, 208
    lack of, 279
    of the Lord, 154, 263
    and love, 264, 318
    only one, 376
feast, divine, 262
fingers, God's, 69
fire
    consuming, 164
    of illumination, 218
    of punishment, 218
    the Word extinguishes,
        218
firmament, 149
firstborn of all creation, 138
flattery, peril of, 89, 115,
    383-84
flesh
    covering of, 138
    crucified, 317
    resurrection of, 123
    and spirit, 70
    weakness of, 249
food
    for the soul, 178
    heavenly, 181
fools, 12, 109
foreknowledge
    Christ's, 22
    divine, 128, 292
forgetting, divine, 104
forgotten, 232
forgiveness, 52, 197, 238, 240,
    302, 304, 310, 312, 318, 358,
    377, 392
fountain
    Christ the, 328
    divine, 328
fragrance of Christ, 303
freedom, 212, 299, 370
    from fear, 231
    road to, 280
free will, 239
friends
    betrayal of, 325
    of God, 235
fruitfulness, 8, 218, 358
future, 174
    blessings, 269
    celebration, 329

glory, 381
    of God's people, 217
    healing, 322
    of Israel, 360
    judgment, 79, 385-86
    kingdom, 92, 308, 312
    life, 383
    light, 329
    reward, 129, 131, 321
    salvation, 256, 305-6
    temples, 351
    world, 293, 373
garments
    blood-stained, 190
    changed, 225
gathering of God's people, 387
gates, 189, 190
Gentiles, 84, 185, 365
    calling of, 67, 361
    conversion of, 159, 353
    evangelization of, 354
    fullness of, 360
gifts, 121
    of God, 274
    of grace, 163, 345
    of Holy Spirit, 357-58
    mercy, 228
    spiritual, 122
    of understanding, 241
glory
    false, 217
    our future, 191, 381, 382,
        383
    of God, 68, 163, 219, 259,
        387
    humble, 71
    inward, 353
    king of, 190-91
    otherworldly, 21, 102
    received, 358
    of the righteous, 339
God
    almighty, 360, 367
    daughters and sons of,
        351, 354
    depths of, 251
    goodness of, 225, 262, 337,
        386, 391
    hiding from, 239
    leading of, 230
    likeness of, 264
    name of, 257, 341, 389, 392
    not dependent on creation,

388-89
    omniscience of, 96, 253,
        254
    paths of, 194
    presence of, 331
    proof of existence of, 109
    right hand of, 123
    security in, 231, 359
    sovereignty of, 359
    timing of, 234
    transcendence of, 329
    unchanging, 252, 338
    unfathomable, 139, 281,
        359
    will of, 223, 246, 273, 348
godless, the, 164
Goliath, 136, 255
goodness, 3, 182
    of God, 225, 262, 337,
        386, 391
    nature of, 321
gospel, 228-29
    being generous with the,
        296-97
    Law and, 243, 248, 276-77
    power of, 78
    proclamation of, 81, 354
    symbolized, 351
    thunder of, 216
    universal influence of, 365
grace, 81, 102, 116, 121, 154,
    157, 207, 229
    abundance of, 27, 282
    Christ giver of, 207
    crown of, 164
    divine, 341, 369
    freed by, 160
    gift of, 163, 345
    of God, 7, 140
    heat of divine, 153
    message of, 317
    need for, 243
    oil of, 141
    partakers of, 350
    present and future, 201
    profit of, 225
    prophesied, 238
    and righteousness, 248
    of understanding, 238
    pursued by, 143
gratitude, 24, 41, 107, 295,
    336, 366
graves, 44

Gregory of Nyssa, xxi
guidance, 180
    divine, 43
    of Spirit, 283
Hades, 52
hand of God, 91, 123, 301, 309-10, 353
    heavy, 239
    right, 123, 369
hands
    of the Lord, 233
    uplifted, 211
happiness, 30, 75, 253
harp
    body as a, 246
    of the Holy Spirit, 375-76
    and Psalter, 246-47
harvest, spiritual, 67
healing, 220, 319, 322
    divine, 301, 305
    prayer for, 319
hearing, 369
heart
    Christ dwells in the, 357
    clean, 159
    contrite, 267
    a cultivated, 289-90
    deceitful, 100
    enlarged, 28
    eyes of the, 105
    humble, 159
    inner, 254, 343
    known by God, 253
    the mourning, 41
    new, 295
    praise from the, 223
    right, 243
    silence of the, 304
    sincere, 389
    the sleeping, 105
    soul as, 175
    strong, 208
    tested, 128
    throne of the, 365
    troubled, 255, 280
    truth in the, 115
    undivided, 75
    weapons of the, 359
heaven,
    earth and, 70
    free access to, 238
hell, 164
help, 171

angelic, 273
divine, 59, 80, 100, 103, 129, 135,136, 142, 206, 208, 229, 254, 255, 256, 261, 268, 272, 275, 296, 299, 302, 311, 318, 331, 334, 356, 368, 372, 377
    hidden, 235
    to the poor, 321
heresy, 42, 125
    downfall of, 44
    lacks Christ, 43-44
heretics, 63, 95
heroism, spiritual, 94
Hesychius of Jerusalem, xxiv
Hezekiah, 144, 205, 210-11, 223
Hilary of Poitiers, xxiv
Hippolytus, xviii-xix
holiness, 17, 140
Holy One, the, 222
Holy Spirit, 8
    breath as, 249
    the Comforter, 209
    destroys sin, 262
    divinity of, 250-51
    empowered by, 216
    gifts of, 122, 357-58
    guidance of, 283
    harp of, 375-76
    indwelling of, 245, 282, 344
    movement of, 251
    participation in, 138
    person of, 144
    power of, 157, 209
    revelation and, 284
    river of, 357
    and the Son, 238
    summoned by, 374
home, eternal, 207
honor bestowed, 70
hope, 94, 95, 107, 162, 197, 198, 290, 303
    beyond death, 269
    in Christ, 232, 233
    in God, 170, 229, 299, 310, 335
    our greatest, 50
    rest in, 37
    of resurrection, 125
    strengthening, 21, 330

house
    beauty of God's, 203
    body as God's, 220
    glory of our, 382
    of the Lord, 207
    soul as God's, 220
human nature, 5
human race, degeneration of, 251
humility, 170, 196, 208, 217, 232, 259-60, 267, 285, 292, 294, 303, 330, 362
    of Christ, 231
    and faith, 233
hymn
    of praise, 174
    of victory, 362
idolatry, 147, 217, 218, 251, 329
ignorance
    bestial, 242
    corrupting, 89
    former, 144
    of God, 10, 60, 88, 91, 111, 112
    as punishment, 223
    and sensuality, 273
    of the wicked, 279
illumination, 7, 105, 141, 153, 205-6, 218, 282
image of God
    Christ as, 284, 384
    fallen, 310
    made according to the, 379
    restored, 34, 35, 330
imitation of Christ, 34, 59, 189-90, 207, 381
immortality, 9, 37, 124, 266
improvement, spiritual, 208
impure thoughts, 130
incarnation, 14, 124, 126, 137, 152, 176, 212, 254, 347, 350, 353, 363, 371, 387
indwelling, divine, 45, 180, 220, 245, 282, 308, 318, 335, 344
inheritance, 34, 39, 40, 122, 131, 296-97, 265
innocence, 325
inspiration, divine, 343, 344, 375
intelligent design, 69, 147
intentions, 186, 254
intercession of Christ, 170,

225, 272
interest, monetary, 117
invasion, spiritual, 367-68
invocation, one God of, 40
Israel
    faith of, 318
    future of, 360
    return of, 329
    salvation of, 112
    sin of, 195
    triumphs of, 338
Jeremiah, 271
Jerome, xix, xxv
Jerusalem, 235
Jesse, root of, 212
Jews, the
    believing, 363
    and the Gentiles, 15-16
    and Jesus' crucifixion, 325
Joshua, 338
Josiah, 17
joy, 82, 125, 159, 276, 294, 330, 335, 370
    divine, 367
    of the heart, 35-36
    inexpressible, 282
    of mourning, 225
    oil of, 349
    of the redeemed, 362
    resurrection, 224
    true, 240
    through the Word, 28
    work of, 367
Judah, captivity of, 144
Judas, 186, 324, 325, 362
judge, righteous, 62
judging others, 340
judgment, 10, 163, 182, 187, 200, 236, 248, 281, 292, 299, 301, 331, 333, 334, 368, 376, 382
    day of, 48, 78
    divine, 55, 61, 62, 63, 71, 76, 84, 85, 96, 97, 98, 299, 384
    future, 256, 385-86
    mercy and, 243, 248
    of nations, 77
    present and future, 77, 79
    revealed, 290
    wise, 281-82
    of words used, 40
justice, 38, 97, 98, 201, 212,

318
justification, xxv, 295
kindness, God's, 134, 135, 137, 174, 187, 253, 295, 338
kingdom
future, 92, 185
of God, 176, 185, 348, 371
of sin, 359
kingship of Christ, 14, 21, 348, 362, 365
knowledge
demonic, 254
divine, 96, 122
and existence, 10
experienced, 110
and faith, 262
God's, 219, 341
of God, 51, 139, 140, 197, 285, 309
mercy and, 285
natural, 95, 109
seeds of, 153
supreme, 388
labor in the Lord, 209
lamb of God, 320
lamentation, 330
lamp, 141, 179
land, distribution of, 123
language, universal, 151
laughter, divine, 13
Law, the
Christ kept, 207
delight in, 6-7
of God, 298
and Gospel, 228-29, 243, 248, 276-77
heavenly, 357
learning of, 331
Mosaic, 154
natural, 154
new, 86
observing the, 390
and prophets, 316
purpose of, 195
transgressors of, 277
laws, divine, 146
leading, God's, 230
Lebanon, cedars of, 217
lending, 117
liars, 42
lies. See deceit
life
abundant, 283

the Christian, 114, 154, 297
eternal, 378, 383
expectant, 298
fountain of, 284
hidden with Christ, 289
length of, 309
perspective on this, 295
spiritual, 256
transitory, 309
of virtue, 353
Word of, 284
light
accessible, 260
of Christ, 153
desirable, 155
in the darkness, 179
divine, 105
do not quench the, 141
everlasting, 358
future, 329
from God, 41
participation in, 35
of Scripture, 283
source of, 205
sun's, 151
true, 334-35
and truth, 334
water and, 283
withdrawn, 224
likeness
of Christ, 155, 260
God's, 264
lion, destructive, 90
lions, 172
liturgy, xxi
Lord of hosts, 190
lost, the, 197
love
cup of, 182
divine, 150
empowered by, 129, 247
fear and, 264, 318
of God, 122, 226
God known by, 138
God's, 107, 226
song, 76
surrounded by, 235
wings of mercy and, 130
lovingkindness, 182
lowly, the, 116

Luther, Martin, xxv
majesty, divine, 68, 148, 150
martyrs, 81
Mary, virgin, 212
materialism, 383
meditation, 6, 7, 280, 374
meekness, 196
memory, God's, 159
mercy, 43, 46, 50-51, 82, 96, 97, 107, 130, 162, 180, 182, 183, 186, 195, 196, 201, 240, 248, 255, 295, 305, 311, 318, 319, 320-21
divine, 55, 200, 208, 222, 223, 243, 253, 280-81, 310, 340
ever present, 194
face of, 207
gifts of, 228
greater than sin, 234
and judgment, 243, 248
and knowledge, 285
and repentance, 226
time for, 249
waiting for, 194
merit, lack of, 28, 107, 179, 194-95, 229, 238, 302, 338, 341
message
divine, 215
of grace, 317
metaphor, 23
mind
eyes of the, 106
purified, 360
spirit as, 230
moderation, 32
money, 117
morning, 41-42
Moses, 35, 102, 224, 340
mourning
blessed, 52
joy of, 225
music, 246
primal, 149
and contemplation, 222
mystery, divine, 69
name
Christ's enduring, 324
divine, 68, 80, 341
gift of God's, 257
of God blasphemed, 392
of God magnified, 389

nations, the
calling of all, 176, 365
judgment of, 77
plans of, 12-13, 252
punishment of, 242
natural order, 149
new
people, 314
song, 315
Noah, 240
nourishment, spiritual, 329
numerology, 48-49, 58
oath, God's, 116
obedience, 6, 135, 144, 267, 275
offering, burnt, 388
old nature, the, 169
Origen, xix-xx, xxii, xxv
orphans, 92
parable, 375
pardon, 253
participation in Christ, 2-3, 27, 35
path
the dark, 285
of righteousness, 123
paths
of God, 194
of Scripture, 129
patience, 63, 85, 88, 92, 194, 256, 276, 304, 312
peace
blessing of, 24
false, 275
with God, 259
God's, 292-93
heavenly, 37, 382
and joy, 36-37
with ourselves, 259
peacemakers, 265
penitential psalm, 301
perfection, 43, 118, 126, 148, 200, 215, 318
permanence, 247
persecution, 18, 222, 233-34, 235
perseverance, 102, 208, 234-35, 340
perspective
different, 266, 312
divine, 382
on this life, 295
perversion, 91

plan
    against Christ, 324
    God's unchanging, 252
Pharaoh, 255
philosophy
    empty, 44
    error of, 69
physician, divine, 49, 50, 110, 263, 301, 311,323
Pilate, 362
pitfalls, 197
pits, 83
    of death, 160
    of misery, 314
    versus wells, 64-65
poor, the
    advice for, 381-82
    blessed, 175
    Christ among, 261
    help for, 321
    nations, 118,
    rich and, 96, 374, 379, 381, 382
    in spirit, 261
    spiritually, 92
    in vice, 261
pot, crushed, 16
poverty of Christ, 261, 321, 323
power
    Christ's, 346
    God's, 76, 92, 274, 357, 371
    limits of, 92
praise, 60, 68, 82, 122, 134, 157-58, 175, 215, 246, 259
    to Christ, 354
    continual, 259
    David's, 144
    deception of, 88
    everyday, 339
    from God, 175
    from the heart, 223
    holistic, 392
    hymn of, 174
    the power of, 136
    right, 315
    Satan hates, 365
    satisfactory, 207
prayer, 15, 27, 30, 33, 53, 82, 94, 101, 102, 104, 175, 197, 229, 240, 256, 272, 283, 359, 364
    answer to, 314

Christ's, 163, 261
    through Christ, 159, 160
    continuous, 128
    during trials, 261
    effective, 26-27, 59
    for enemies, 55
    example of, 276
    of faith, 137
    for healing, 319
    power of, 262
preservation, 62
pride, 59, 60, 85, 88, 101, 107, 157, 175-76, 217, 236, 260, 267, 276, 285, 286, 380
proclamation, 81,176, 215, 281, 283, 346, 370, 374, 375
profit, 117
progress, spiritual, xxi, 180
promises
    fulfilled, 269
    of God, 208, 291, 326
prophecy
    of Christ, 168, 228, 343
    of David, 228
prophets, 168, 316
protection, divine, 45-46, 79, 95, 102, 112, 121, 130, 183, 212, 356, 358
proverb, 375
providence, divine, 27, 36, 65, 85, 101, 103, 105, 121, 137, 138, 142, 150, 171, 174, 194, 247, 253, 281, 291, 294, 298, 310, 315, 318, 357, 382, 388
Pseudo-Athanasius, xx
punishment
    beneficial, 195, 305
    divine, 91, 131
    eternal, 84
    fire of, 218
    of nations, 242
    of pride, 236
    self-inflicted, 279, 294
    of wicked, 243
    wrath and, 223
purification, 114
purity, 102, 128
rational order, 149
reason
    crown of, 163
    those defeated by, 275
    human, 72
    importance of, 242

    lack of, 380
    rejection of, 390
rebellion against God, 89, 111
rebirth, 179, 187
reconciliation, 104, 311
redemption, 188, 198, 203
refuge, divine, 58, 79-80, 94, 229-30, 241, 355, 356, 357, 359
rejection
    of Christ, 84
    by God, 231
    of God, 4, 380
    of reason, 390
rejoice in the Lord, 243, 245
remorse, psalm of, 238
renewal, inner, 310
renunciation, 155
repentance, 13, 51, 52, 53, 75, 92, 217, 240, 242, 248, 276, 294, 323, 326
    divine, 50,
    limited, 240
    mercy and, 226
    reward of, 201
    and tears, 239
    timely, 312
reproof, 142
rescue, 226
    divine, 256
    of Peter, 267
restoration, our, 221
resurrection, 185, 197, 230, 269, 358
    of Christ, 22, 60, 123, 124, 126, 221, 228
    of Christ and us, 160
    day of, 48
    of flesh, 123
    glorious, 9
    hope of, 125
    joy of, 224
    to punishment, 10
revelation
    of Christ, 110, 138
    of heaven, 150
    and the Holy Spirit, 284
    to myself, 201
    natural, 151
    the place of, 211-12
    universal, 150
revenge, 212, 391
reward, future, 129, 131,

266-67, 321, 332
rhetoric, xxi, xxiii
rich and poor, 374, 378, 379, 381, 382
riches, 236. *See also* wealth
righteous, the, 91
righteousness
    divine, 61
    gift of, 229
    grace and, 248
    hills of, 186
    imperfect, 61
    imputed, 98
    mercy and, 46
    path of, 123
    sun of, 151
river of God, 357
robbery, spiritual, 390
rock, spiritual, 314
rule of truth, 250
rulers, warning to, 17
sacraments, 178
sacrifice
    Christ's, 162, 320
    Christ's and ours 316
    free, 389-90
    fulfilled, 388
    holocaust, 388
    in name only, 389
    our, 390
    reasons for, 387-88
    spiritual, 388
    voluntary, 316
saints, 23
salvation, 15, 163, 168, 179, 188, 198, 207, 213, 229, 264, 273, 299, 305, 324, 335
    through Christ, 24
    by grace, 23, 42, 46,
    church's response to, 317
    day of, 170
    future, 162, 305-6
    of Israel, 112
    our, 58, 61, 62, 70, 81, 82, 120, 137
    power of, 159
    present and future, 256
    seeking, 255-56
    sufficiency of, 233
Saul, 128
Savior, 59, 273, 314-15, 332
Scripture
    African interpretation

of, xxvi

Alexandrian interpretation
of, xxiv

alone, 77

Antiochene interpretation
of, xxiii-xxiv

departing from, 43, 110

divine, 67

inspired, 316

interpretation of, xxii, 8,
72, 95, 109, 125, 351

light of, 283

need for, 262-63

Old and New Testament,
331

paths of, 129

trained in, 196

transmission of, 115

second coming, 131, 387, 392

security, 95, 225, 231

Selah, meaning of, 20-21

self control, 264

self esteem, 97

semi-Pelagian, xxvi

shame, 55

sheep, 178, 339

Sheol, 10

shepherd, 178, 371

shield
of Christ, 213
divine help as a 62
of divine protection, 45-46,
256

Shimei, 304

sickness, spiritual, 299, 323

sight, God-given, 106, 369

silence
benefits of, 304
divine, 211, 391-92
of the heart, 304
of the just person, 307-8
lying and, 233
temptation in the midst
of, 308

simplicity, 212

sin
assisted by tongue, 265
bondage of, 65, 83
brings trouble, 19
confession of, 238-39
of David, 235
determined not to, 307
forgiveness of, 195

foulness of, 302
harm of, 65, 83
hidden, 278, 302
Holy Spirit destroys, 262
human, 101
Israel's, 195
kingdom of, 359
lingering, 280
mercy greater than, 234
is more than abstinence,
265
original, 156
saved from, 221
as sickness, 323
snare of, 106
stain of, 310
wall of, 141
washing away of, 219
ways of committing, 4
weight of, 302
worse than anything,
377-78

singing, 223, 244, 247, 365,
370

sinners
crowd of, 323-24
destroyed, 299
failure of, 293
God's use of, 292

sins, 41, 156

snares
set for Christ, 164
set for Jeremiah, 271
set for us, 83, 106, 206,
230, 298, 258
unsuccessful, 293

Solomon, 7, 8, 84, 187, 221,
343

Son of God, 171
begotten, 344
and the Father, 72, 101,
123, 343, 348
forsaken, 169
Holy Spirit and the, 238
speaking as man, 171
witness of, 153
the Word, 250
wounds of, 54

sons and daughters of God,
351, 354

sorrow, 105, 224

soul,
as the heart, 175

beauty of the, 352
Christ's, 174
conquered, 364
disquiet of, 332
flights of the, 95
food for the, 178
fruitless, 274-75
as God's house, 220
God's work in the, 114
hope-filled, 107
in the wilderness, 218
light of, 54
married to the Word, 351
movements of the, 3-4
prosperity of the, 224
renewed, 220
the righteous, 130
secure, 206
sick, 53
structure of the, xxii
trampled, 59

spirit, human, 379

spirits, age of, 239

spiritual direction, 235

spiritual gifts, 122

stewardship, 388

strength
church's, 370
divine, 43, 62, 172, 198,
208, 236, 255, 262, 339,
347, 356, 376
God's Word provides, 213
of Holy Spirit, 209
loss of, 23
and refuge, 229-30
renewed, 212

submission, 289, 347

suffering
of Christ, 19, 124, 168,
169, 173, 228, 275
of David, 315
human, 28, 155, 168, 268,
331, 332, 335, 372
immune to, 126
vicarious, 169

sufficiency
from God, 226
of salvation, 233

suicide, 97

sun
of righteousness, 151
light, 151
creator of, 151

sustenance, divine, 325, 326

sword
God's Word as, 130
punishing, 63

tabernacle
our bodies as, 221
God's, 207, 335

table, spiritual, 179-80

teachers, 176

teaching, xxvi, 195, 196

temple
body of Christ as, 369
Christ as the, 187-88
completion of, 215
dwelling in God's, 207
future raising of, 172
holiness of God's, 114, 219
the Lord's, 96
Solomon's, 221

temples, future, 351

temptation, 9-10, 231, 275,
291, 301, 308, 332

tent of cleansing, 114

testing, 102

thanksgiving, 178, 258, 259,
389

Theodore of Mopsuestia, xxiii

Theodoret of Cyr, xviii, xxiii-
xxiv

thoughts
evil, 156, 304
hidden, 157
impure, 23, 130
revealed, 239

timing, God's, 234

tolerance, problems with,
390-91

tombs, 379

tongue, restraining the, 33,
264, 265, 391

tradition, 371

trap set against Christ, 164. *See
also* snares

trials, 180, 200, 260

tribulation, 24, 27-28, 106,
231, 261, 268, 272, 295, 356,
376, 380

Trinity, 41, 215, 249, 251, 284,
317, 330-31, 337-38, 348

trust
exchange of, 193
futile, 230-31
in God, 21, 34, 91, 105,

106, 107, 130, 135, 193,
200, 212-13, 239, 243,
252, 255, 262, 286, 291
in providence, 382
and obey, 267
objects of, 160
truth
in business, 116
Christ is, 201, 281, 303
and fantasy, 303
God's words of, 102
in the heart, 115
lack of, 100
light and, 334
many expressions of, 100
mercy and, 318
rule of, 250
victory of, 91
type
biblical, 223
David as, 314
fulfillment of, 316
Tyre, 353
uncertainty, 311
understanding
beyond, 31
divine, 122
gift of, 241, 364
spirit of, 376
ungodly, nature of the, 4-5, 9
unity
of the church, 368
of Father and Son, 101
in harmony, 26
unrepentant, 42
usury, 117, 118
Uzziah, 144
values, inverted, 339
vanity, 202
vengeance, divine, 63, 81, 91

vice, 88, 291
victory, 26, 30, 134, 159, 160,
162, 190, 211, 299, 325, 336,
346-47, 362
vindication, 200, 276, 333
virtue
departing from, 285-86
life of, 57, 354
virtues, 68, 115, 229, 298
voice
of Christ, 374
that cries out, 225
of the Lord, invincible, 217
waiting
on God, 194, 208
on the Lord, 305, 341
for mercy, 194
warfare, spiritual, 207, 272,
306, 360
washing
of sin, 219
spiritual, 202
as symbol of purity, 202
watchfulness, divine, 256
water, 219
and light, 283
living, 64
spiritual, 216
way
of Christ, 129, 194, 196,
295
heaven's, 142
of life, 367, 389
ways, God's, 194, 196
weakness, 62, 170, 289
of flesh, 249
human, 129, 255
wealth, 75, 295, 378, 380
failure of, 298
and generosity, 297

true, 263
weeping, 329
wells and pits, 64-65
wicked, the, 1, 10-11, 83, 84,
92, 99, 103, 202, 378
council of, 201-2
downfall of, 293, 295
presumption of, 278
punishment of, 243
warning to, 78-79
wickedness, 88, 96, 97
hidden, 280
vanishing, 10
will
Christ's and the Father's,
22, 316-17
failure of, 239
God's, 223, 246, 273, 348
voluntary and involuntary,
156
wall of the, 141
winds of fortune, 368-69
winepresses, churches as, 67
winnowing, divine, 369-70
wisdom, 8, 33, 115
Christ as, 297
divine, 173
eternal generation of, 14
expressed, 297
source of, 374
tree of, 7-8
witness, bold and true, 317
witnesses, cloud of, 387
witnessing, 331
women, blessed, 3
Word
advent of the, 386
cleansing, 302-3
desire of the, 155
the eternal, 343, 344, 347

ever present, 211
of God, 130, 213, 250, 281,
297. See also Scripture
healing, 301
nourishment of, 262
seeking the, 211
sovereign, 14
strengthening, 213
words
and deeds, 165
importance of, 186
well-aimed, 347
works
faith and, 114
of the Father and Son,
13, 213
good, 266, 290, 297
revealed, 290
world, the, 137
concerns of, 380
divine ordering of, 69
failure of, 298
future, 293, 373
material, 290
overcome, 272
philosophy of, 294
prosperity of, 295
remains in darkness, 41
worm, 170
worship, xxvi, 43, 215, 216, 328
not people-pleasing, 365
pure, 340
wrath, 223, 301
cup of, 97-98
delayed, 63
divine, 13, 96
and punishment, 223
Zion, 21-22, 80, 82, 369, 370